MICROCOMPUTER APPLICATIONS

ABOUT THE AUTHORS

ROBERT GRAUER received a Bachelor's degree in Mechanical Engineering
from Rensselaer Polytechnic Institute and a Ph.D. in Operations
Research from the Polytechnic Institute of Brooklyn (now New York).
He is currently an Associate Professor in the Department of Computer
Information Systems at the University of Miami, where he has
received the School of Business Distinguished Teaching Award.

Dr. Grauer is the author of several leading texts in the areas
of COBOL programming, IBM operating systems, and dBASE programming.
His work has been translated into at least two foreign
languages, and has several times been featured as a Book of the
Month selection by the Library of Computer Science and
Information Systems.

PAUL SUGRUE holds a Bachelor's degree from the U.S. Naval Academy,
a Master's degree from the University of Rhode Island, and a Ph.D.
in Business Administration from the University of Massachusetts
at Amherst. He is a full professor in the Department of
Management Science at the University of Miami, and is a recipient
of the School of Business Distinguished Award. Dr. Sugrue is
currently the Vice Provost for the University of Miami, after
having served as Assistant Dean in the School of Business.

Dr. Sugrue has published in professional journals in the areas of
competitive bidding and motor freight transportation.

To
Charles Babbage and **Augusta Ada Lovelace**
Two people a century ahead of their time

Contents in Brief

CONTENTS

PREFACE

$\mathbf{W}$e wish to thank the hundreds of instructors and tens of thousands of students who used the first edition of *Microcomputer Applications*, and thereby justified this revision. We have, however, retained all of the elements associated with the first edition including a generic text, program-specific Laboratory Manuals, corporate profiles, detailed case studies, and humorous anecdotes and graphics which collectively made our book successful. Nevertheless, we found ample opportunity for improvement as follows:

- *Addition of new material* to reflect continued advances in the microcomputer area, in the form of new chapters on graphics and desktop publishing. Corporate profiles have been added for Aldus Corporation (desktop publishing), Hercules (graphics), and WordPerfect (word processing).

- *A new chapter for the "power user,"* covering advanced features of DOS, as well as popular utility programs such as SideKick and the Norton Utilities.

- *Revision of existing material* to reflect the 1988 to 1989 time frame including: updated corporate profiles, IBM's PS/2 family of computers, Microsoft's OS/2 operating system, today's more powerful generation of word processors, spreadsheet macros, the increased use of local area networks, and so on.

- *Additional exercises* at the end of every chapter, in addition to an all new set of 15 multiple choice questions, also for every chapter.

- *Improved pedagogy* through the addition of two entirely new spreadsheet chapters, emphasizing spreadsheet concepts (in lieu of business cases) and presented via simpler examples. (The original case studies have been moved to an appendix.) A glossary has also been added.

- *Expansion of the Laboratory Manuals* to better reflect available software. As of this writing, two distinct versions of the Laboratory Manuals are available—*WordStar 4.0, Lotus (VP Planner), and dBASE III PLUS* and *WordPerfect 4.2, Lotus (VP Planner), and dBASE III PLUS*. It is anticipated that the Laboratory Manuals will be updated appropriately as new software becomes available.

The greatest change, however, has occurred in the classroom and the way in which computer literacy is defined. Introductory courses that once emphasized the mainframe and BASIC programming now stress the microcomputer and its applications. Students in all disciplines (including business, liberal arts, and the sciences) are learning how to use word processors, spreadsheets, graphics, and database management software.

Microcomputer Applications, both the first edition and this new edition, was written precisely to satisfy this need. It is an introductory text that teaches concepts while simultaneously providing hands-on access to the computer. Indeed, the unique combination of generic text and program-specific Laboratory Manuals enables us to maintain the delicate balance between theory and practical application.

CONTENT OVERVIEW

Microcomputer Applications has 13 chapters (divided into 5 sections) and 3 appendixes. Collectively, this material provides comprehensive coverage of the microcomputer and its major applications.

PART 1:   COMPUTER LITERACY

Part 1 is introductory in nature and assumes no previous background in computers on the part of the reader. Those students already familiar with the fundamentals of personal computers may skip this part entirely or use it as a review. Chapter 1 describes the basic components of any computer system (micro or mainframe) and highlights the major application areas. Chapter 2 presents the rudiments of PC-DOS (the predominent operating system for the IBM PC and its compatibles) and previews OS/2 (a newer and more powerful operating system).

PART 2:   WORD PROCESSING

Since word processing is the most widely used application for students, it is the first to be presented. Chapter 3 introduces features common to all word processors, and describes how these programs are used to create, edit, save, and print documents. Chapter 4 presents supporting features including a dictionary, thesaurus, syntax checker, and mail merge operation for the preparation of form letters. Chapter 5 is devoted entirely to desktop publishing, covering the essentials of typography (type selection) and material on basic principles of graphic design.

PART 3:   SPREADSHEETS

This section has been completely redone from the first edition, and substitutes simpler applications for the more detailed case studies (which now appear in Appendix C). Chapter 6 describes the historical development of the spreadsheet and prepares students for the virtually unlimited number of spreadsheet applications. Chapter 7 presents various concepts needed to achieve basic proficiency in the use of spreadsheets (move, copy, relative versus absolute addresses, ranges, pointing, and formatting). Chapter 8 delves into advanced material including macros, windows, automatic versus manual recalculation, and table lookup functions.

Chapter 9 is devoted exclusively to graphics and begins with the conversion of spreadsheet data to its graphic equivalent. The chapter also includes material on the various IBM graphics standards (CGA, EGA, and VGA).

PART 4:   DATABASE MANAGEMENT

Chapter 10 begins the section with an introduction to database management. The students are shown the fundamentals of creating a database and how database management systems are used to enter and manipulate data. Chapter 11 describes how a menu-driven system can be created to access data, and focuses on the underlying programming concepts.

PART 5: ADVANCED TOPICS

Chapter 12 details how the personal computer may be connected to the outside world and presents the basics of communication theory. It also describes information utilities, computer bulletin boards, local area networks, and IBM's token ring system. Chapter 13 describes in detail the use of subdirectories and generally reflects the increasing sophistication of individuals who use microcomputers today. The chapter contains additional material on advanced DOS concepts such as the file allocation table, filters (SORT, FIND, and MORE), new commands such as ATTRIB and XCOPY, and popular utility programs.

APPENDIXES

The appendixes provide useful information for those students interested in the more technical details of computer software and hardware. Appendix A discusses the binary and hexadecimal number systems. Appendix B covers ASCII and the DEBUG utility.

Appendix C contains four business cases, each of which may be covered at two levels. Students interested in learning how to use spreadsheet features may read the case descriptions and work through the solutions provided in the text (and laboratory manuals). Students with previous business courses who would like to gain experience in the use of spreadsheets in business situations may solve the case studies themselves, and then check their solutions against those provided.

FLEXIBILITY OF APPROACH

Microcomputer Applications is appropriate for virtually any course that employs microcomputer packages. Students without prior computer experience can learn the fundamentals of microcomputer systems by studying Part 1, while students who are already familiar with microcomputers can use Part 1 for review and reference.

The chapters on word processing, spreadsheets, and database management illustrate the virtually unlimited applications of these packages. Students can learn the basics of each type of software by studying the first chapter in each of Parts 2 to 4, and they can improve their skills in the remaining chapters of each part. The material on communications, advanced DOS concepts, and case studies should be included as time permits. The interests and needs of the students can be used to determine the selection of topics.

This flexibility of approach makes *Microcomputer Applications* suitable for introductory courses, more advanced applications courses, and all varieties in between.

FEATURES OF THE TEXT

Microcomputer Applications provides a careful blending of generic concepts, hands-on exercises, corporate profiles, current literature, and detailed case studies.

PEDAGOGY

Each chapter begins with a chapter outline and list of chapter objectives. Concept summaries, set off in color boxes throughout the text, continually reinforce new material. Each chapter ends with a chapter summary, a list of key words and concepts, true/false and multiple choice questions, and chapter exercises.

HANDS-ON EXERCISES

The hands-on exercises provide students with an opportunity to gain practical experience using the computer. However, to avoid having students develop a narrow view of a specific package, the presentation is kept generic with no particular program discussed. At the same time, the documentation in the accompanying Laboratory Manuals enables students to gain practical experience with specific packages.

CORPORATE PROFILES

Every chapter includes an informative corporate profile which helps to convey the growth and vitality of the computer industry. The profiles chronicle the well-known success of early pioneers such as Jobs and Wozniak's Apple Computer, Bill Gates' $1 billion fortune (Microsoft), the flamboyance of Philippe Kahn (Borland International), and the staggering size of IBM with annual sales in the neighborhood of $60 billion.

CASE STUDIES

The detailed case studies are one of the book's strongest features and certainly distinguish *Microcomputer Applications* from other books in the area. Each presentation begins with a case preview and includes a detailed solution. Students gain experience with applications packages in a realistic setting by either solving the cases themselves or working through the solutions provided.

SUPPLEMENTARY MATERIAL

Microcomputer Applications is accompanied by a complete support package of instructional material.

LABORATORY MANUALS AND SUPPORTING SOFTWARE

Microcomputer Applications presents important concepts without focusing on specific packages, because inevitably today's "hot" product will be replaced by something better tomorrow. Nevertheless, students eventually have to interact with the computer; thus, we provide Laboratory Manuals to implement the generic exercises in the text with specific software packages (including WordStar or WordPerfect, Lotus, VP Planner, and dBASE).

Educational versions of related software—WordPerfect or WordStar, VP Planner, and dBASE—are available. Master disks can be supplied to instructors for copying. The software can also be packaged with the text so that schools are freed from the concern of having to supply students with software. The manuals and accompanying software will be updated appropriately as new releases of the programs become available from the vendors.

INSTRUCTOR'S MANUAL

A complete Instructor's Manual is provided that parallels the development of the material in the text. For each chapter, the Instructor's Manual provides: (1) detailed lecture notes and teaching suggestions, (2) answers to all exercises, (3) answers to all true/false and multiple choice questions, and (4) transparency masters of text illustrations.

TEST BANK

The Test Bank contains a battery of test questions for each chapter. Instructors may select from approximately 1300 true/false and multiple choice questions. Answers to all questions are provided with the Test Bank. The Test Bank is also offered in a computerized format for automatic test generation.

OVERHEAD TRANSPARENCIES

A set of color overhead transparencies is available to facilitate classroom presentation.

ACKNOWLEDGMENTS

Publishing tradition has it that only the authors' names go on the title page of a book. This fails, however, to acknowledge the many individuals who by their skill and professionalism help to bring a project to its successful conclusion and without whom there would be no book. Accordingly, we express our gratitude to the following individuals:

- **Karen Jackson,** sponsoring editor, who believed in us, and committed the resources of McGraw-Hill to the project
- **Shelly Langman,** development editor, who read and reread several drafts of the manuscript, helping it along at every stage of the way
- **Sheila Gillams,** editing supervisor, who put manuscript, galleys, and art together to form the finished product
- **Chuck Carson,** designer, who developed the cover and interior design, and whose presence is felt on every page
- **Leroy Young,** production supervisor, who guided the book through a very hectic production cycle
- **Cheryl Mannes,** photo researcher, whose innumerable letters and countless phone calls secured the extras needed to make the text come alive
- **Jim Dodd and Debbie Dennis,** marketing managers, whose innovative campaign helped make our book a commercial success
- **Maryann Barber, Joel Stutz, Vicar Hernandes, Raymond Frost, and Alina Padron,** our colleagues at the University of Miami for their attention to detail, their wise counsel, and continued encouragement
- **Our students** at the University of Miami, especially Nicole Wishart, who make teaching a pleasure and writing a joy
- The many companies, cartoonists, authors, and artists who granted permission to reprint their work

Last, but certainly not least, we thank our reviewers from both editions who through their comments and constructive criticism made this a far better book:

Harvey R. Blessing, Essex Community College

Cathy J. Brotherton, Riverside Community College

John E. Castek, University of Wisconsin, La Crosse

Donald L. Davis, University of Mississippi

Gaye C. Dawson, Virginia Commonwealth University

Ernest Ferguson, Southwest Baptist University

W. Michael Field, National Institutional Food Distributors

George T. Geis, University of California, Los Angeles

Matthew W. Hightower, California State University, Bakersfield

Seth Hock, Columbus Technical Institute

Hilary H. Hosmer, Bentley College

Fred Hulme, Hankamer School of Business, Baylor University

William Kenney, San Diego Mesa College

Michael Lahey, Kent State University

David Mandel, State University of New York at Buffalo

Carol O'Reilly Messer, Tulsa Junior College

Carol Naegele, University of San Francisco

Alan R. Neibauer, Holy Family College

Bill Newman, University of Nevada, Reno

Robert E. Norton, San Diego Mesa College

Leonard Presby, William Paterson State College of New Jersey

Sandra M. Stalker, North Shore Community College

Nicholas Vitalari, University of California, Irvine

Robert T. Grauer
Paul K. Sugrue

MICROCOMPUTER APPLICATIONS

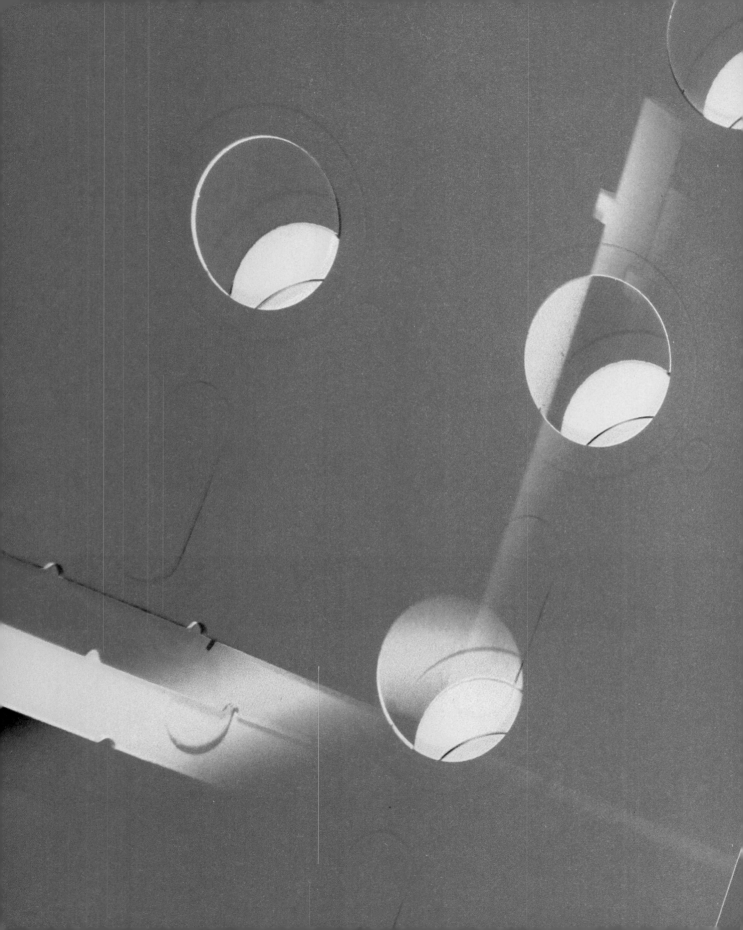

PART 1

*COMPUTER
LITERACY*

1

CHAPTER 1

INTRODUCTION

2

After reading this chapter, you should be able to:

1. Distinguish between hardware and software; describe the components of a computer system.

2. Describe the five major business applications of the microcomputer.

3. Distinguish between RAM and ROM; define the units used to measure computer memory.

4. Distinguish between the IBM PC and the PS/2 series of computers; describe several machines in each family.

5. Identify the special keys on the PC keyboard(s) and state the purpose of each.

6. Describe the various types of floppy disks used with the PC and PS/2 series of computers; list several considerations for the care of floppy disks.

7. Name three types of printers and distinguish between them.

8. Turn on the computer; describe what is meant by booting the system.

Overview

This book is about computers; in particular it is about microcomputers and their applications in business. Our overall objective is to help you achieve a degree of computer literacy, that is, to help you feel comfortable with microcomputers and make them work for you. We assume no prior knowledge of computers, and we encourage "learning by doing" through a series of Hands-On Exercises, the first of which appears at the end of this chapter.

We begin by highlighting the five major business applications for microcomputers: word processing, spreadsheets, data management, graphics, and communications. We distinguish between hardware and software, describe the major components of any computer system, and differentiate between mainframes, minicomputers, and microcomputers.

The second half of the chapter deals specifically with the IBM PC and Personal System/2 (PS/2) series of microcomputers, and by extension the various IBM compatibles. We discuss the different models and show how prices have fallen continually while capabilities have increased. Of special import is the Hands-On Exercise that covers the simple (or not so simple) act of turning on the computer. Inherent in this exercise is a focus on the special keys of the PC keyboard, and the care and handling of floppy disks.

The chapter concludes with a corporate profile of IBM.

You and the Computer Revolution

Today we accept as commonplace things which were once considered highly advanced or simply impossible. Italian noblemen during the middle ages were advised to send their sons to German universities, because those schools taught long division, a subject not covered in Italy. Imagine the noblemen's astonishment if they could see all that has transpired in 500 years. Imagine also the reaction of the early computer pioneers viewing today's desktop marvels after a passage of only 40 years.

The march of technology is relentless and astounding. One eye-catching computer ad of several years ago claimed that "had the aircraft industry evolved as spectacularly as the computer industry over the past 25 years, a Boeing 767 would cost $500 and circle the globe in 20 minutes on five gallons of fuel." Put another way, in 1957 a single transistor cost $10 and a Cadillac limousine $7600; if the limousine had followed the same cost curve as the transistor, it would sell today for about 3 cents instead of $40,000.

Statements like these are mind-boggling to us, yet were utterly unfathomable to our ancestors. An English mathematician named William Shanks actually spent fifteen years calculating the value of pi to 707 places. Today, many college freshmen or even high school students could solve the same problem in a few hours with the aid of a microcomputer.[1]

Two centuries ago we evolved from an agrarian to an industrial society, and now we are changing to an information society. The original computers which filled large rooms and were tended to by armies of white-coated "computer experts" have been replaced by desk-top versions that cost considerably less, are far more powerful, and (most significantly) can be used by everyone. The IBM Personal System/2 Model 80, for example, sells for about $10,000 yet has the same raw processing power as an IBM mainframe 370/Model 168, which commanded a price of $3.4 million in 1972. It is also interesting to note that an early (vintage 1950) survey forecast a maximum demand for 50 computers in the entire country, because at the time computers were so expensive as to be affordable only by the largest organizations.

What's clear from all this is that computers are fast becoming a way of life, and that **computer literacy** is the buzzword for the 1980s. Corporations want their employees to be computer literate, many parents expect their children to become computer literate, and you are probably taking this course in order to fulfill the computer literacy requirement at your school or university. We hope, therefore, that when you finish you will feel comfortable with the microcomputer and be able to make it work for you. You will be aware of its potential

---

[1]Dennie L. Van Tassel, *The Compleat Computer*, SRA Research Assocciates, 1983.

as well as its limitations when applied to businesses (both large and small). You will learn how to enter data into the computer and how to plan for useful output. You will become an intelligent consumer of microcomputers and related products, and you will be able to effectively use computers in a world of rapidly changing technology.

Let's begin at the beginning, by distinguishing hardware from software.

EDUCATIONAL MEGATREND: READIN', WRITIN' AND 'RITHMATIC REPLACED BY COMPUTIN'

Hardware and Software

Sit down in front of a computer and you can see **hardware,** that is, physical equipment such as a monitor, keyboard, disk drive, and so on. The hardware can do nothing by itself; it requires a set of instructions or programs collectively called **software,** without which the desk-top computer becomes an expensive desk-top ornament. The availability of software justifies the purchase of hardware, and it is the software which eventually determines how successful a computer system will be in satisfying your needs.

Software can be broadly divided into two classes: **system software** (referred to as the **operating system**) and **application software**. Perhaps you are already familiar with different kinds of application software, for example, word processing, spreadsheets, graphics, games, and so on. The operating system, on the other hand, links the application software to the hardware and essentially manages the computer. An application program (such as a word processor or spreadsheet) reads or writes data through the operating system, which locates the data on a disk, accepts information from a keyboard, directs output to the printer, and so on.

The wonderful thing about application software is that replacing one application program with another completely changes the personality of the computer. The same computer used for word processing can also be used to communicate with online databases in cities thousands of miles apart, prepare long-range financial forecasts using spreadsheet models, derive graphic analysis of a company's sales figures, or perform hundreds of other chores.

One important aspect of computer literacy is knowing what a computer can and cannot do. This boils down to an appreciation of software, for it is the software which drives the hardware and dictates the uses to which the computer will be put.

Five Major Business Applications

The microcomputer revolution has taken the power of mainframe computers and put it on your desk. Now that it's there, what do you do with it? Essentially there are five major areas where the microcomputer is used in business: word processing (and by extension desktop publishing), spreadsheets, graphics, data management, and communications.

Word processing was the first major business application of microcomputers. A novelty in the 1970s, it is accepted as commonplace in the 1980s. With a word processor you enter a document into the computer using the keyboard; should you make a typographical error, simply backspace and retype the correct entry. You can insert new phrases and/or delete superfluous material. A powerful set of editing commands enables you to move words, sentences, or even paragraphs from one place to another, and/or to alter the appearance of your document by changing margins or line spacing. Additional features will check spelling, provide access to a thesaurus, and prepare form letters.

Spreadsheets are the application most widely used by business managers. A spreadsheet is an accountant's ledger, and as such has been around for centuries. Anything which lends itself to expression in row and column format is a potential spreadsheet (for example, a professor's grade book with student names in rows and test grades in columns, a financial forecast with revenues and expenses in rows and years in columns, and so on). The advantages to the electronic spreadsheet are that changes are far easier to make than with pad and pencil, and that the necessary calculations and recalculations are made instantly, accurately, and automatically.

Graphics have long been recognized as an effective way of communicating statistical information. The availability of the microcomputer in conjunction with graphics software enables you to quickly convert tabular data to graphic form without having to rely on a

WHY IS A COMPUTER LIKE AN ELEPHANT?

A computer is a dynamic elephant, for other than the obvious reason. Sure, computers remember many, many things for a long time. But they're also like the pachyderm in the old story about the blind men and the elephant, because computers represent different things to different people.

To some, a computer is a game machine. To others, it's a writing machine that has obsoleted the typewriter. To the quantitatively oriented, it's a fabulous number cruncher that works at preposterous speeds. To still others, a computer keeps files, draws pie charts, or maintains contact with huge storehouses of information.

Computers are dynamic because their uses change. A microwave oven cooks food, a lawn mower cuts grass, and a stereo plays music. Most appliances always did, and always will, have defined uses. But computers change: today they do lots of different things, at home, in our offices, and in the huge private and governmental organizations with which we deal; by 1990, with voice recognition and other technology I couldn't even begin to predict, computers will be something else entirely.

The very fact that computers are dynamic elephants is what keeps more and more of us totally fascinated, and many of us absolutely addicted.

Source Ken Uston, *Digital Deli,* © 1984, Workman Publishing, New York. Reprinted with permission of the publisher.

Authors' Comments:
Just as the elephant appeared as different creatures to the blind men who touched it in different places, a computer projects different images depending on the software it is running. As you progress through the book, we will take you through its enormously diverse capabilities.

graphics artist to prepare the material. Exploded pie charts, three-dimensional bar charts, and other forms of sophisticated graphs, all in stunning color, are available in minutes with a few simple keystrokes.

Data management allows you to maintain records electronically, be they student records in a university, customer records in a business, or inventory records in a warehouse. Data management software provides for the addition of new records as well as the modification or deletion of existing data. You can retrieve your data in any order that you like, for example, alphabetically or by identification number. You can display all the information or only a selected portion. For example, you could see only those students who are on the dean's list, only those customers with delinquent accounts, or only those inventory items which need reordering.

Communications software connects your microcomputer to the outside world. You can "talk" to your friend in the next dormitory or call a computer across the country. You may access information services, such as *Compuserve* or *The Source*, which provide stock and financial data, flight and hotel information, and just about anything else you can think of. You can shop or bank by computer, send and receive electronic mail, or chat on one of thousands of local computer bulletin boards.

Components of a Computer System

Now that you have some idea of *what* microcomputers can do, we can begin the discussion of *how* they do it. The idea of a general-purpose machine to solve mathematical problems was first proposed over 150 years go by a farsighted individual named **Charles Babbage** (see insert on 11 famous computers). The device Babbage proposed to build consisted of four components that uncannily resemble a modern computer:

- The *store* to hold data and the results of calculations; Babbage designed the store to contain 1000 numbers of 50 digits each

- The *mill* to perform the mathematical operations

- Gears and levers to transfer data back and forth between the store and the mill

- An *input/output* unit to read external data into the store and display results of calculations produced by the mill

Babbage's machine (named the Analytical Engine and subsequently modified into a more ambitious Difference Engine) would, had it been completed, have been the first general-purpose computer. Unfortunately, the technology of the day was incapable of producing the mechanical components to the required precision. Babbage died alone and penniless having lost 17,000 pounds of his own money (and an equal amount of government funding). His critics wrote that "the government received nothing for its money and should at least have gotten a clever toy."

As with so many other geniuses who were ahead of their time, Babbage was proved correct nearly a century after his death, since all modern computers are designed along the lines he laid out. A computer accepts data from an external source (input), stores it temporarily in memory while calculating an answer (processing), and

Charles Babbage and his Difference Engine.

11 INFLUENTIAL COMPUTERS AND/OR THEIR PROGRAMS— PAST TO PRESENT

1. *The Analytical Engine (1835–1869):* Because of lack of government support, English mathematician Charles Babbage (1792–1871) never got to build his invention, whose design presaged the modern electronic computer. Had it seen the light of day, the engine would have used data fed by punched cards, performed arithmetical calculations, and stored information in a memory bank. Lady Lovelace, the mathematically brilliant daughter of Lord Byron, developed some potential problems for the future machine, in effect acting as its first programmer.

2. *Mark I (1944):* Conceived by Howard H. Aiken of Harvard University in 1937, the first automatic digital computer was built by International Business Machines in 1944. An automatic sequence controlled calculator, it was used for computing ballistic data. The computer could do three additions per second, working as fast as 20 people on calculators (incredibly slow compared to the speed of today's machines). Mark I took up a lot of space; it was 51 ft long and 8 ft high, with 750,000 parts.

3. *ENIAC (Electronic Numerical Integrator and Calculator) (1945–1946):* Built only a year or two after Mark I, the first electronic computer was thousands of times faster; it could perform 5,000 additions per second. It, too, was a monster, with 18,000 vacuum tubes, a weight of 30 tons, and a need for 1,500 sq. ft. of floor space. Made at the University of Pennsylvania in Philadelphia, it was designed by physicist John W. Mauchly and electronics engineer J. Presper Eckert, who later started their own computer company. According to legend, when ENIAC was first switched on, lights all over Philadelphia dimmed.

4. *UNIVAC I (Universal Automatic Computer) (1951):* Storing its input digitally, the universal automatic computer was delivered to the U.S. government in 1951 to help with the census. It cut the hours of work by humans from 200,000 to 28,000. On October 3, 1963, the computer was retired with full honors after 73,000 hours of operation and is now on display at the Smithsonian Institution.

5. *The ''Pi'' Computer (1961):* In *Mathematics and the Imagination*, published in 1940, Edward Kasner and James Newman stated: "Even today it would require 10 years of calculation to determine pi to 1,000 places." Twenty-one years later, one of the computers at the IBM Data Center calculated pi to 100,265 places in 8 hours and 43 minutes. In one slightly long working day it performed 100 times (or more) the amount of work a person could do in 10 years.

6. *The Checker-Playing Computers (1962):* Programmed to play checkers, the IBM 704 used by A. L. Samuels in 1955 easily defeated Samuels. In 1962 an IBM Model 7014 electronic computer whipped checkers champion Robert W. Nealey at Yorktown Heights, N.Y. Nealey said, "In the matter of the end game, I have not had such competition from any human being since 1954, when I lost my last game."

7. *Marchack VI (1967):* A computer program devised by MIT student Richard Greenblatt was the first to win a chess match against a human in tournament play. Nicknamed MacHack, the computer's programming was crude compared to later programs, which were able to win against much better players. For example, CHESS 4.5, devised by David Slate and Larry Atkin, won every game at the Paul Masson Tournament in Saratoga, California, in 1976. In

1978 a homemade microcomputer—the result of six months' hard work—won the first all-computer tournament, which required that the computers be physically present.

8. *The Moon-Landing Computer that Failed (1969):* As Eagle approached its landing on the moon, the on-board computer, slated to guide the landing, set off an alarm indicating an overload. Astronauts Neil Armstrong and Edwin Aldrin took charge, telemetering measurements to Mission Control in Houston, Texas. Later it was determined that interference from the radar system had scrambled the computer's circuits.

9. *The Story-Writing Computer (1973):* Programmed by Sheldon Klein, the computer writes detective stories 2,100 words long. Humans can still do much better, as one may judge from this excerpt: "James invited Lady Buxley. James liked Lady Buxley. Lady Buxley liked James. Lady Buxley was with James in a hotel. Lady Buxley was near James. James caressed Lady Buxley with passion. James was Lady Buxley's lover. Marion following them saw the affair. Marion was jealous."

10. *The IBM 2740s that Were ''Killed'' (1976–1977):* Armed terrorists known as Unita Combattenti Communiste planned 10 attacks on computers in Italy, according to E. Drake Lundell, Jr., in an August, 1977, article in *Computerworld.* The first attack occurred in May, 1976, when 15 men burst into a tax office in Rome and destroyed eight IBM 2740 terminals by tossing Molotov cocktails.

11. *The Computer that Helped Steal $10.2 Million (1978):* In one of the biggest bank thefts in history, computer analyst Mark Rifkin used the services of a computer to transfer $10.2 million from the Security Pacific Bank in Los Angeles to an account in Switzerland. Unable to keep the amazing feat to himself, Rifkin made several revealing remarks to a businessman, who called the FBI. He was arrested on November 5, 1978. While out on bail, Rifkin attempted a second illegal wire-transfer of $50 million and was rearrested. In March 1979 he was convicted and sentenced to eight years in prison. The computer was not prosecuted.

Source: The Book of Lists, 2.

And Three More (of the Authors' Choosing)

12. *Altair 8800 (1975):* The January 1975 issue of *Popular Electronics* featured the Altair 8800 on its cover: the first personal computer and a machine that the hobbyist could build from a kit. 2000 adventurous readers sent in their orders (sight unseen) for a kit that cost $439. The Altair had no keyboard or monitor and no available software. It was programmed by flipping switches on the front panel.

13. *Apple II (1977):* The Apple II was a fully assembled home computer in an attractive case, complete with keyboard, connection to a TV screen, color, memory to 64K, and BASIC interpreter. It was to launch the personal computer revolution and vault its founders, Steve Wozniak and Steve Jobs, from garage to glory. Apple made it to the Fortune 500 in seven years, with 1984 sales of almost $2 billion.

14. *IBM PC (1981):* IBM was neither first nor technologically innovative, but their announcement put the personal computer on the desks of America's businesspeople, just as Apple had put the computer in the home. By 1985 IBM had manufactured its three millionth PC, and had spawned an entire industry in the process.

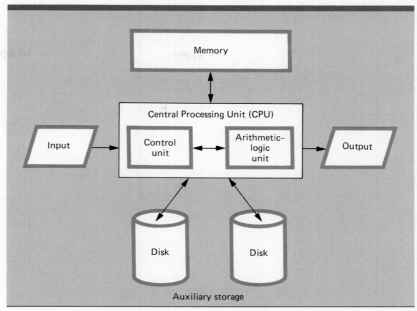

FIGURE 1.1   Components of a microcomputer system.

presents the results (output). Thus the computer itself is only one element of the total picture, as can be seen from Figure 1.1, which depicts the essential hardware components of a **computer system**. These components and their relationship to one another are found in all computer systems, from the tiniest micro to the largest mainframe, from Babbage's dream to the latest technological marvel. Consider:

- *Central processing unit (CPU)* performs the actual calculations and consists of a control unit and an arithmetic-logic unit. The components of the CPU are more fully described in the next section.

- *Main memory* [also known as primary memory or random-access memory (RAM)] temporarily stores any program executed by the computer as well as the data on which the program operates. Main memories are designed for high-speed, short-term (temporary) access to data as opposed to auxiliary storage, which provides permanent (albeit slower) access.

- *Auxiliary storage* (also called secondary storage or external storage) provides a place where data can be permanently stored, and from where it can be transferred to and from main memory. Floppy disks with storage capacities of up to 1.44 million characters and hard (fixed) disks with capacities of 10 to 100 million characters are examples of auxiliary storage used with personal computers.

- *Input devices* accept data from an external source and convert it to electric signals which are sent to the CPU. The keyboard, mouse, and joystick are common input devices used with microcomputers.

- *Output devices* accept electric signals from the CPU and convert them to a form suitable for output. Printers and monitors are the most common type of output devices used with microcomputers. Printers provide a permanent record (hard copy) of computer output.

We continue now with an in-depth explanation of each component.

The Central Processing Unit

The computer or **central processing unit** (CPU) consists of an arithmetic-logic unit and a control unit. The **arithmetic-logic unit** (ALU) performs the arithmetic (addition, subtraction, multiplication, and division) and logical (comparison) operations, whereas the **control unit** functions as a "traffic controller" which decides what will be done and when. The control unit provides instructions to read data from an input or auxiliary storage device, transfer it to main memory, process it in the ALU, and finally move the results back to main memory and then to an output device.

Main Memory

Main memory is divided into a large number of storage locations, with each location having a unique address and holding the same amount of information: one byte, or one character. The size of the computer's memory is equal to the number of locations it contains. Memories are measured in terms of kilobytes (Kb) or megabytes (Mb), where one Kb and one Mb are equal to approximately 1000 and 1 million characters, respectively. (In actuality 1Kb equals 1024, or 2^{10}, the power of 2 closest to 1000. In similar fashion 1Mb is 1,048,576, or 2^{20}, the power of 2 closest to 1 million.) The first IBM personal computer came equipped with only 16Kb RAM, whereas a typical configuration in today's environment is likely to contain 640Kb (640 * 1024, or 655,360) locations.

The amount of memory a system has is important because the larger the memory, the more sophisticated the programs are that the

---

OUR FAVORITE ACRONYM

As you will soon discover, if you haven't already, acronyms abound in the computer field. We are only a few pages into the first chapter and have already encountered several: CPU, RAM, ROM, and ALU, to be specific.

However, our favorite acronym by far is not even related to computers, and can only be considered an element of fate or destiny. Consider IACOCCA, an acronym for I Am Chairman Of Chrysler Corporation of America."

computer is capable of executing. Realize that in order to accomplish any task at all, the program and the data on which it operates are first read into memory, from where all processing is initiated. In other words, main memory must be large enough to hold the instructions of the program (for example, a word processor or a spreadsheet) that the CPU will execute as well as the data.

Strictly speaking, there are two kinds of memory: **read-only memory (ROM)** and **random-access memory (RAM)**. Read-only memory is accessed when the computer is turned on initially; it contains the instructions telling the computer to check itself and then it locates the essential portions of the operating system. The contents of ROM are established at the factory and cannot be altered by application programs; hence the name "read only."

The contents of RAM, however, are changed constantly as different programs are executed, or even every time the same program (for example, a word processor) is executed with different data. Accordingly, most people tend to equate the size of a computer's memory with the amount of RAM available.

Auxiliary Storage

Disks, the most common type of **auxiliary storage** device, fall into two general categories: floppy disks and hard disks. The **floppy disk** gets its name because it is made of a flexible mylar plastic; the **hard disk** uses rigid metal platters. In any event, the characteristic of greatest concern is **capacity**, namely, how much data can be stored. A hard disk holds significantly more data than a floppy, and it accesses that data much faster. Hard disks, as you would expect, are also more expensive but are well worth the money.

The capacity of a hard disk is measured in megabytes, with disks of 20, 30, or even 100 megabytes common in today's environment. Floppy disks come in different sizes and capacities, with the once ubiquitous $5\frac{1}{4}$-inch disk being challenged by the more compact $3\frac{1}{2}$-inch version. (IBM's newest series of computers, for example, uses two different versions of the $3\frac{1}{2}$-inch disk, with capacities of 720Kb and 1.4Mb, respectively. In similar fashion, the $5\frac{1}{4}$-inch disk used in the original PC series held 360Kb, while later versions could hold 1.2Mb).

It is absolutely essential that you handle floppy disks carefully, so that the information you worked so hard to create will be available when you need it. Do not, for example, leave your disks in a car (especially in the summer). Keep them away from all magnetic influences, and store them vertically, in their protective paper sleeves, at least one foot away from electrical appliances and computer components. Beware of fluorescent desk lights and magnetic holders for memos or secretarial stands. (Airport metal detectors are generally not a problem.) Do not leave your disks under heavy objects (for example, textbooks), and never force a disk into a disk drive.

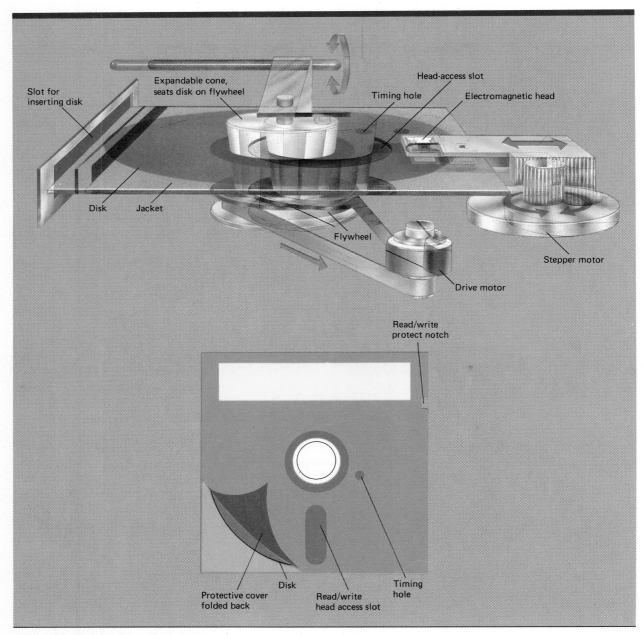

Top: Floppy disk schematic. Bottom:
Cutaway view in protective jacket.

By all means label your disks (preferably with a felt-tip pen), and write on the paper label before putting it on the disk. (Writing on the label afterward, especially with a ballpoint pen, can cause permanent indentations in the disk surface, which will ultimately cause problems.) Note, too, that no matter how well you care for your disks, you should have *backup* (duplicate) copies, a procedure we will discuss in Chapter 2.

Input and Output Devices

The **keyboard** is the most important input device and is described in detail immediately prior to the Hands-On Exercise found later in the chapter. **Monitors** and **printers** are the most common output devices and are both discussed in this section.

The monitor (or video display) provides instant feedback as you are working at the computer. Most monitors are designed to display 24 lines of text of 80 characters each (although there are many monitors which show more or less than these amounts). The characters themselves are formed by an array of tiny blocks called **pixels** (picture elements), with the **resolution** of the monitor proportional to the number of pixels available on the screen. For example, a monitor whose maximum resolution is 320 × 200 (320 pixels across and 200 down) would produce significantly inferior characters to one with a resolution of 640 × 480.

A **color monitor** provides visually stunning graphics, but the resolution of its **text** may not be as clear as that produced by a **monochrome monitor**. Monochrome monitors generally come in one of two colors, amber or green; there is no consensus on which is easier on the eyes. Note, too, that while the output of a color monitor may look perfectly fine in isolation, you should view the same screen on monochrome and color monitors side by side before making any purchase.

Printers vary greatly in terms of design, price, and capability; the dot matrix, daisy wheel, and laser printers are the most common. **Dot matrix printers** are the most versatile type of printer, the kind you are most likely to see in school or to purchase initially. These printers produce an image on paper by driving a series of small pins against a ribbon. They create letters, numbers, symbols, and/or graphics out of a series of dots, and they can print any shape at all according to the accompanying software.

The dot matrix is a rectangle, typically 9 dots high and 5 pins wide, with each character represented as a particular combination of pins. Dot matrix printers operate at a variety of speeds, from 50 to 1000 characters per second (cps). A reasonably priced model of $500 or less will operate in the range of 200 cps. Most models work in a **bidirectional mode;** that is, they print from left to right and (unlike a typewriter) in the reverse direction as well, which increases their speed.

The only disadvantage to a dot matrix printer is a less than perfect print quality (although that quality is constantly improving), since its characters are formed as a pattern of dots. To alleviate this, some dot matrix printers also operate in a **correspondence** (or nearletter-quality) **mode**, in which each character is struck four times.

Monochrome and color monitors.

Dot matrix printhead.

Daisy wheel

IBM Proprinter XL24   Apple Inc. Laserwriter II

Speed is reduced by a factor of 4; for example, a 200-cps dot matrix printer operates at 50 cps in the correspondence mode, but the appearance of the printed document is improved significantly. Recent advances, notably the introduction of a 24-pin printhead in lieu of the conventional 9-pin version used in earlier models, has significantly improved the quality of output.

Daisy wheel (or letter-quality) **printers** produce sharp, solid characters of high quality, making this type of printer suitable for normal business correspondence. The characters exist as petal-like projections on a flat disk resembling a daisy, which are spun into position and hit by a hammer.

Daisy wheel printers produce better-quality output than dot matrix printers because the characters are fully formed as opposed to consisting of a series of dots. The drawbacks to the daisy wheel are the slow speed (typically in the range of 50 cps) and the inability to produce graphic output. However, the improvement in quality of dot matrix printers makes it appear inevitable that the daisy wheel will become obsolete.

Laser printers are the top-of-the-line devices, creating new expectations in terms of print quality, speed, and quietness of operation. They produce consistently dense characters and graphics, suitable for both reports and presentations. Their only drawback is price, but this too is falling (starting prices have dropped from about $4000 to $2000 in a period of two years).

Micros, Minis, and Mainframes

Traditionally, computers have been divided into three broad classes: mainframes, minis, and micros. The criteria for classification were as follows:

1. The speed with which it performs computations (measured in hundreds of thousands or millions of operations per second)

2. Memory capacity

3. Amount of data it can manipulate at one time

4. Cost

The classification of a computer into one of these categories is becoming increasingly difficult as mainframes continue to become smaller, while micros grow more powerful. Indeed, the machine on your desk has more capability than that of the early mainframes such as the ENIAC, which weighed 30 tons and took up 1500 square feet of floor space. Nevertheless, the following definitions may be of interest if only as a historical perspective on the development of computers.

A **mainframe computer** is a large computer costing hundreds of thousands (or millions) of dollars. Mainframes have very large memories, execute several million instructions per second, and first appeared in the late 1940s. They require a specially prepared site and a staff of data processing professionals for operation and management. Mainframe computers in today's environment allow several hundred (thousand) individuals to access the machine simultaneously.

The **minicomputer** was the initial result of minaturization in technology, and it cost anywhere from $20,000 to $300,000. The mini arrived in the late 1960s, with the Digital Equipment and Data General corporations leading the way. Minis were attractive to individuals who needed significant computing power but who could manage the machine themselves, typically engineers and those in university departments.

The **microcomputer** ("computer on a chip") first appeared in the late 1970s and is characterized by the fact that the entire CPU is contained on a single silicon chip known as a **microprocessor**. It is logical, therefore, that the characteristics of any microcomputer depend heavily on the microprocessor on which it is based, and that as microprocessors themselves increase in capability, so too do the computers which use them. The original IBM PC, for example, used a more powerful microprocessor than did the Apple II, and so the IBM machine was more powerful.

IBM 3090 mainframe.

The IBM Personal Computer

Where were you in 1981? President Reagan was celebrating a huge tax cut, Prince Charles and Lady Diana were on their honeymoon, Michael Jackson was three years away from "Thriller," and on August 12, IBM announced its personal computer. To quote one IBM executive, "No one dreamed that we would create a product that would spawn an industry." What was initially a group of a dozen people, working on a machine that was estimated to sell a maximum of 250,000 units, has grown to a division of 10,000 employees producing more than $5 billion in annual revenue.

In rushing its machine to market (the Apple II and Radio Shack TRS-80 were each three years old at the time), IBM broke a long-standing tradition by going to external sources for supporting hardware and software. The 8088 microprocessor inside the PC was produced by Intel Corporation, and the operating system was developed by Microsoft Corporation. In addition, IBM announced its machine would be sold through retail outlets including Sears and Computerland.

In terms of today's prices and capabilities, the initial offering was hardly spectacular. The original PC had a standard memory of only 16Kb, and was expandable to just 256Kb. The system could accommodate two 160Kb floppy drives, and hard disks were unavailable. The dot matrix printer, which accompanied the computer, could print at only 80 cps. Systems for home or school use were sold without a disk drive (a tape cassette was used instead) and without a monitor (a TV was suggested). An expanded 256Kb "business" system, with two drives, monitor, and printer, was priced at $4425.

Software for the PC was practically nonexistent. Lotus 1-2-3 didn't exist, and WordPerfect, WordStar, and dBASE were little-known programs, not yet modified to run on a PC. The world in 1981 was very different from the place it is today.

Yet with little software available, and with limited hardware capability, the PC was an instant success for two reasons. The IBM name and its reputation for quality and service meant that a business could order the machine and be assured that it would perform as promised. Of equal or even greater significance was the fact that the PC was designed as an "open" machine, enabling independent vendors to offer supporting products. IBM deliberately made the technical specifications of its machine known, and it effectively invited the world to make its computer better.

The openness of the machine would, however, eventually come back to haunt IBM. **PC compatibles** (based on the Intel 8088 microprocessor and capable of running the Microsoft operating system) began to appear as early as 1982 and offered superior performance for less money. Companies and individuals who were once willing to pay a premium for the IBM name and reputation began ordering the "same" machine from other vendors (Compaq, Leading Edge, and Tandy, to name just a few). Indeed, IBM's share of the PC market has declined steadily since 1981, to the point where it is now less than 40 percent.

Nevertheless, the PC was an enormous success, selling over 3 million units since its creation and expanding into a family of five additional models, which sold millions more. The various PC models are described below, each with its date of announcement and distinguishing characteristics. Prices (at the time of each announcement) are included for historical interest.

- *PC*   Announced August 12, 1981, the original PC came without a disk and only 16Kb RAM. It was priced at $1565. An upgraded system with 64Kb RAM and a single 160Kb floppy disk was offered for $2880 (monitor not included). (Eventually you could purchase a PC with 640Kb and two 360Kb floppy disks for under $2000.) IBM ceased manufacturing the PC in 1985 in favor of the XT, but not before it sold its 3-millionth unit.

- *PC XT*   Announced March 8, 1983, the XT came equipped with a single 360Kb floppy disk, a 10Mb hard disk (the main attraction), a base memory of 128Kb, and other minor improvements, all for $4995.

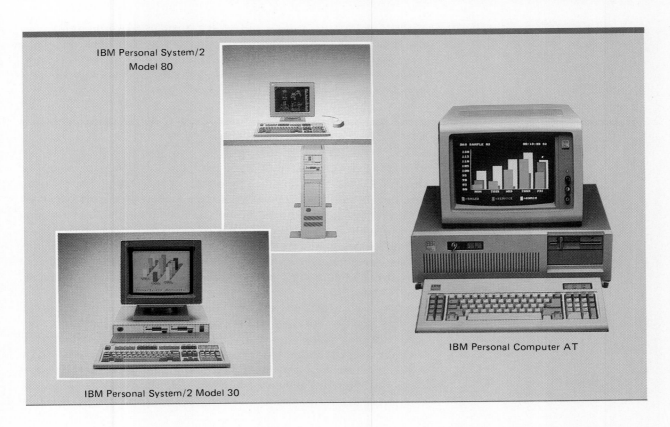

IBM Personal System/2 Model 80

IBM Personal System/2 Model 30

IBM Personal Computer AT

The XT went on to become the second most popular model, with over 2 million units in place by the end of 1987.

- *PC*jr. Announced November 1, 1983, enhanced July 31, 1984, and terminated in March 1985. The arrival of "junior" was eagerly anticipated, but IBM badly misjudged the home computer market and produced a disappointing machine. The "chiclet-like" keyboard and relatively high price tag ($699 for a 64Kb machine without a disk drive, or $1269 for a machine with 128Kb RAM and one 360Kb floppy drive) doomed the machine from the beginning.

- *PC portable* Announced February 16, 1984, the portable offered 256Kb RAM and two 360Kb floppy drives for $2895. Weighing in at a hefty 34 pounds, the machine faired poorly against comparable Compaq machines, which offered superior performance for less money. The portable was discontinued upon the announcement of the smaller convertible model in 1986.

- *PC AT* Announced August 14, 1984, the AT was the first machine to be based on the Intel 80286 microprocessor, and the first to offer a true increase in performance. The basic configuration included only 256Kb RAM and a single 1.2Mb floppy drive. It was priced at $3995. An enhanced configuration offering 512Kb RAM and a 20Mb hard disk was listed at $5795.

- *PC convertible* Announced April 2, 1986, this lap-top model was the first to incorporate the smaller $3\frac{1}{2}$-inch (720Kb) disk drive and weighed just under 13 pounds. It used rechargeable nickel-cadmium batteries to provide 6 to 10 hours of service. It came with 256Kb RAM and two floppy drives, and it was priced at $1995.

The IBM Personal System/2

The IBM Personal System/2 made its debut in a 1-day extravaganza on April 2, 1987. Four distinct models (Models 30, 50, 60, and 80) were announced, the most powerful of which offered up to 16Mb RAM and 230Mb of disk storage. All four models are capable of running the vast majority of existing PC-DOS software (although a new release of the operating system, PC-DOS 3.3, is required). At the same time, a new operating system, OS/2, was introduced to take advantage of the advanced 80286 and 80386 microprocessors used in Models 50, 60, and 80.

The new machines vary considerably in terms of price and capability, yet they contain several common features. First and foremost, the PS/2 does away with the $5\frac{1}{4}$-inch disk, substituting a $3\frac{1}{2}$-inch version with increased capacity and durability. All models share a new (and vastly improved) keyboard, the specifics of which will be discussed shortly. The new systems are easier to assemble than were their predecessors (they eliminate the internal setup, or "dip," switches)

TABLE 1.1

The IBM PS/2*

	Model 30	Model 50	Model 60	Model 80
Microprocessor	8086	80286	80286	80386
Standard memory	640Kb	1Mb	1Mb	Up to 2Mb
(expandable to)	N/A	7Mb	15Mb	16Mb
Diskette size	3.5 inch	3.5 inch	3.5 inch	3.5 inch
(and capacity)	720Kb	1.44Mb	1.44Mb	1.44Mb
Maximum color resolution	320 × 200	640 × 480	640 × 480	640 × 480
Standard disk	N/A	20Mb	44Mb	44Mb
Maximum configuration	20Mb	20Mb	185Mb	230Mb
Expansion slots	3	3	7	7
Operating system(s)	DOS 3.3	DOS 3.3, OS/2	DOS 3.3, OS/2	DOS 3.3, OS/2
Base price	$1695	$3595	$5295	$6995

*Reflects the initial PS/2 announcement on April 2, 1987.

and incorporate as standard many features which previously had to be purchased separately.

Specifications of the various models (at the time of the announcement) are shown in Table 1.1. IBM has subsequently introduced the Model 25 and Model 70 (neither of which is listed in the table). In addition it offers each machine in several configurations, making it difficult to differentiate one model from the next. You can, however, distinguish to some extent by focusing on the microprocessor. The Model 25 and Model 30 are based on the 8086, and are considered "entry-level" machines. The Model 50 (floor standing) and Model 60 (desktop) use the 80286, while the Model 70 (desktop) and Model 80 (floor standing) are "top-of-the-line" 80386 machines.

SOFTENING A STARCHY IMAGE

A mustachioed little clown with an undersize jacket and oversize trousers to symbolize IBM's first computer aimed at the mass market? That hardly fits IBM's stuffy old image, but when the company needed an advertising campaign for its new personal computer 2½ years ago, it turned to one of the 20th century's most enduring and endearing characters: Charlie Chaplin's Tramp. Says Charles Pankenier, director of communications for the PC: "We were dealing with a whole new audience that never thought of IBM as a part of their lives." Industry insiders estimate that the firm has spent $36 million in one of the largest ad campaigns ever mounted for a personal computer.

Manufacturers of personal computers have been using readily recognizable people for some time to make the slightly intimidating machines seem warmer and more empathetic. Apple has Dick Cavett for its commercials, Texas Instruments recruited Bill Cosby, Commodore has William Shatner, and Atari just hired Alan Alda. None of these living celebrities, however, has had the impact of the Tramp. The character has starred in three widely seen television commercials, plus more than 20 print ads. He has won numerous advertising-industry awards.

Chaplin's enduring, endearing Tramp.

Chaplin once explained that he created the character in 1915, after an accidental meeting with a hobo in San Francisco. The Tramp's resurrection was only slightly less serendipitous. IBM's advertising agency, the Madison Avenue firm Lord, Geller, Federico, Einstein, was looking for someone, or something, that would attack the problem of computer fright head on. The agency was talking about using the Muppets or Marcel Marceau, the mime, when, according to Creative Director Thomas Mabley, the idea for the Tramp "sort of walked in and sat down."

Some officials at both the company and the agency were afraid that the floppy character was not in keeping with IBM's starched white-collar image. The question of whether the Tramp represented antitechnology sentiment, as epitomized in the most famous scene from one of Chaplin's best-known movies, *Modern Times*, was also raised. In the scene, Chaplin gets caught in the giant gears of a factory. But both the agency and IBM eventually concluded that the character, in Pankenier's words, "stands fear of technology on its head and would help the PC open up a new technological world for the nontechnician."

The company obtained rights from Bubbles, the Chaplin family company that licenses use of the actor's image, to use the Tramp. To cast the part, the agency interviewed some 40 candidates in New York City and 20 on the West Coast. The winner was 5-ft. 6-in. Billy Scudder, 43, who has been doing Tramp impersonations since 1971. Says he: "Nobody tires of the little Tramp. He creates instant sympathy."

The commercials are elaborate Madison Avenue extravaganzas. In one 60-second spot, which symbolizes the problems of inventory control in a small business, the Tramp stands at the intersection of two assembly lines in a bakery. He comes a cropper when the fast-moving line spews cakes onto the floor after he tries to jam a giant-size one into an economy-size box. Taping the sequence required 30 takes—and 150 layer cakes.

Authors' Comments:
The announcement of the PS/2 series was accompanied with a new advertising campaign featuring the characters of the MASH TV series. Both advertising themes accomplish their objective.

The Tramp campaign has been so successful that it has created a new image for IBM. The firm has always been seen as efficient and reliable, but it has also been regarded as somewhat cold and aloof. The Tramp, with his ever present red rose, has given IBM a human face.

Source: Time Magazine, July 11, 1983.

Authors' Comments:
Philip D. Estridge will be remembered
as a giant in the microcomputer
industry. He founded IBM's Personal
Computing Division and in three short
years saw it grow from zero to $5
billion in revenue. Mr. Estridge
perished with his wife and several other
IBM employees in a tragic airplane
accident in Dallas on August 2, 1985.

Getting Started

We could go on and talk about computers indefinitely only to risk having you lose interest rather quickly. We believe very strongly that learning is best accomplished by doing, and that you will benefit most from working directly with the computer. Accordingly, we set the stage for the many Hands-On Exercises which appear throughout the text by discussing the PC keyboard, a primary means of data entry.

The Keyboard

As you might expect, the keys on the PC keyboard are arranged much like those of a typewriter, in the standard QWERTY pattern (named for the first six characters in the third row). There have been, however, several different keyboards associated with the various PC models, (the original PC keyboard, the PC*jr.*'s chiclet keyboard, the convertible keyboard, and the enhanced keyboard, to name just a few; and this list does not include the various arrangements used by PC compatibles).

Figure 1.2*a* and 1.2*b* contains the two layouts you are most likely to see: the original PC layout and the enhanced computer keyboard (available on later models of the XT and AT as well as the new PS/2 computers). The functions of the individual keys are described below.

Shift keys are located in the normal shift position of a regular typewriter and are represented by large arrows. The shift keys work in the same fashion as on a regular typewriter, producing an uppercase letter or a special character (for example, holding down the shift key while pressing the key containing a zero on the top row produces a closing parenthesis). Touch typists should be aware of an annoying

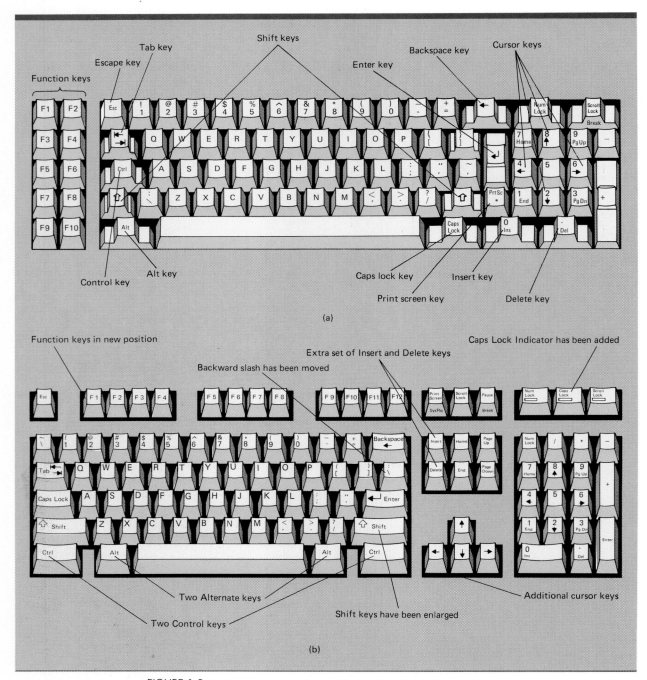

FIGURE 1.2
IBM keyboards. (a) Original
PC keyboard. (b) Enhanced keyboard
(PS/2 series).

feature of the PC keyboard, namely IBM's insertion of an extra key between the Z on the bottom row and the left shift key. (This quirk has been corrected on the enhanced keyboard.)

The **Caps Lock key** eliminates the need to continually press the shift key to enter uppercase letters. The Caps Lock key functions as a **toggle switch;** that is, pressing it once causes all uppercase letters to be entered, pressing it a second time returns to lowercase, pressing it again returns to uppercase, and so on. (There is no visible indicator on the PC keyboard as to whether the machine is in the upper- or lowercase mode, so that you can frequently wind up in the wrong case. This, too, has been corrected on the enhanced keyboard.)

Function keys (F1 through F10) are located on the left side of the PC keyboard; F1 through F12 appear on the top row of the enhanced keyboard. These are special-purpose keys, defined by various application programs (for example, WordPerfect, Lotus 1-2-3, and dBASE) to accomplish specific functions and save keystrokes. The exact purpose of a particular function key varies from program to program.

Cursor keys [the four arrow keys, up (↑), down (↓), right (→), and left (←)] control movement of the **cursor** (the blinking line or box), which shows where on the monitor the data will next be entered.

The **enter** (return) **key** signals the completion of an entry and correspondingly causes the response typed on the keyboard to be transmitted to the CPU. One common mistake is to type a response and forget to press the enter key, in which case the computer waits patiently and does nothing. Note, too, that the shape and position of the enter key has been changed on the enhanced keyboard, making it easier to reach.

Insert (Ins) and Delete (Del) **keys**, located on the lower right side of both keyboards, are used by application programs to insert and/or delete characters, respectively.

The **Escape (Esc) key** is used by many programs to cancel (or escape from) the last command that was issued.

The **Control (Ctrl) key** is always used in conjunction with another key(s) to perform a particular command or function. (An extra Ctrl key as been added on the enhanced keyboard.)

The **Alternate (Alt) key** is similar in concept to the Control key and is used in combination with other key(s) to perform a command or function. (An extra Alt key has been added on the enhanced keyboard.)

The **Print Screen (PrtSc) key**, when pressed simultaneously with a shift key, displays on the printer whatever currently appears on the monitor. This is a valuable aid in reconstructing your lab sessions with the computer.

The **Tab key** functions as a tab key on a typewriter, but it can tab in either direction. A "tab left" is accomplished by pressing a shift key simultaneously with the tab key.

HANDS-ON EXERCISE 1: TURNING ON THE COMPUTER

OBJECTIVE: Turn on the computer, load a DOS system disk, and answer the date and time prompts. Use the PrtSc key to obtain a printed record of your session at the computer.

This exercise will acquaint you with the IBM PC. It is not difficult and requires only that you turn on the computer and follow some simple start-up procedures. Nevertheless, it will provide a feeling of accomplishment and set the stage for the more involved exercises which follow in later chapters.

Step 1: Locate a DOS Disk
You may skip this step if your system has a hard disk; otherwise you will need a disk containing the operating system (described in Chapter 2). The disk you use depends on where you are doing this exercise (for example, in school, at home, or at work). At home or at work, you probably have access to the manuals which came with the computer. If so, locate the original system disk (it's in the binder with the DOS manual) and use that. If you are in the PC lab at school, request a DOS disk.

Remove the disk from its paper sleeve. Do not try to remove it from its permanent envelope, and don't touch the exposed surfaces that show through the envelope. Gently place the DOS disk *with the label side up and the label held toward you* in drive A, the drive on your left as you face the computer. (Some systems will have the drives one on top of another, in which case drive A is usually the drive on top.) Close the door on the disk drive.

Step 2: Turn on the Computer
The number and location of the on/off switches depends on the nature and manufacturer of the devices connected to the computer. (The easiest possible setup is when all components of the system are plugged into a surge protector, in which case only a single switch has to be turned on.) In any event you must:

1. Turn on the printer. (On the standard IBM printer the on/off switch is a rocker switch on the right side, as you face the machine, on the back of the printer.)

2. Turn on the monitor. (The standard IBM monochrome monitor does *not* have its own power switch.)

3. Turn on the power switch of the system unit (a red switch located on the right side of the standard IBM PC, as you face the machine).

Step 3: Wait
At this point you have placed a DOS disk in drive A and turned on the system. Depending on the amount of memory, it can take up to a minute or two for something to happen; the machine goes through a series of self-checking diagnostics each time the power is turned on (known as a **cold start**). Be patient.

Soon you will hear the whirring sound of the disk drive followed by a beep; then you will see a red blinking light on the door of the disk drive. This means that the computer is reading (writing) information from the disk. *Do not open the drive door when the red ''in use'' light is on.*

If all goes well, the system will ask you to enter the current date, at which point you may *skip* step 4.

Step 4: Correct Problems (Which, Ideally, Do Not Occur)
A number of problems can occur when starting up, the most common of which is using the wrong disk in drive A or using the right disk but forgetting to close the door of the disk drive. Should you make either of these mistakes, you are apt to see one of the messages:

```
      Invalid COMMAND.COM in drive A

or    Disk boot failure

or    Nonsystem disk or disk error

or    The IBM Personal Computer Basic
      Version C1.00 Copyright IBM Corp
      61404 Bytes free
      Ok
```

Check that there is a DOS disk in drive A, with the label side up and toward you. Now close the door of drive A and press the Ctrl, Alt, and Del keys *simultaneously*. The screen should clear and the process begin anew.

Step 5: Answer the Date and Time Prompts

After you have accomplished step 3 (or step 4), the monitor will display the message:

```
Current date is Tue 1-01-1980
Enter new date:
```

Supply the current date, using either hyphens or slashes to separate the month, day, and year. 3-16-1988 and 3/16/88 are both valid entries for March 16, 1988 (year may be entered as either a two- or a four-digit number).

The system will then return a message of the form:

```
Current time is: 0:00:20.00
Enter new time:
```

Time is expressed in hours:minutes:seconds. hundredths (on a twenty-four-hour military clock). To enter the time, colons are required between hours, minutes, and seconds, and a period between seconds and hundredths of a second. Any value which is omitted is assumed to be zero. 11:30 a.m. may be entered as 11:30 or 11:30:00 (hundredths are generally omitted). In similar fashion, 11:30 p.m. would be entered as 23:30 or 23:30:00.

If all goes well, you should see the message:

```
The IBM Personal Computer DOS
Version 3.00 (C)Copyright IBM
```

You may see a version other than 3.00 depending on when the operating system was purchased. Failure to enter the date or time in accordance with these rules will result in a message by DOS of the form:

```
Invalid date
Enter new date:
```

or
```
Invalid time
Enter new time:
```

It won't take long for you to realize that it is possible to bypass the date and time requests by pressing the enter key twice in a row. We recommend very strongly, however, that you take the trouble to enter date and time properly so that the operating system will automatically associate this information with every file (for example, a spreadsheet or word processing document) you create.

Step 6: Reboot the System

There may be times when the system is locked, when the cursor refuses to move, and so on. Although this condition does not occur often, and certainly should not be the case now, we will practice the procedure for a **warm start** or **boot**.

Use your left hand to hold down the Ctrl and Alt keys, and *while keeping these keys depressed*, use your right hand to press the Del key. Almost immediately, you will hear the sound of the disk drive, see the red light come on, and view the date (and time) prompts on the monitor.

A warm start causes the computer to start over (it forgets what it what was doing, and anything in RAM is lost). The process is faster than a cold start, as the machine bypasses the self-checking procedure of step 3. As you might have guessed, the placement of the Ctrl, Alt, and Del keys is deliberately awkward to avoid an accidental rebooting of the system, with its associated memory loss.

Step 7: Print the Screen

Be sure the printer is turned on. (Most printers have two indicator lights (one to show the power is on, and one to show it is "on-line" to the computer. Check that both of these are on.)

The contents of the screen may be "dumped" to the printer at any time. Press the shift key, and while holding it down, press the PrtSc key as well, and the contents of the screen will be reproduced on the printer. Obtaining **hard copy** in this fashion is a useful practice to permanently record a session at the computer and will help in solving any problems you may have. It is impossible for an instructor to answer questions unless he or she has an *exact* copy of what happened, as provided by the PrtSc key. You can also use this technique to create your own reference manual.

Step 8: Shut the System Down

You have now completed the first Hands-On Exercise and are ready to begin using the computer effectively. You have turned on the machine and its peripheral devices, loaded a disk, initialized the date and time, and obtained printed copy of your session at the computer.

Turn the power off to shut down the system. (The disk may be removed from the drive either before or after the power is turned off.)

There's Always a Reason

A computer does exactly what you tell it to do, which is not necessarily what you want it to do. It is a source of wonderful satisfaction when everything works, but it also causes unbelievable frustration when results are not what you expect. The point is well illustrated by an article in *PC World* (see "Mystery of the month," *PC World*, April 1983) which relates the story of a manager who purchased a PC and enthusiastically began using it. Unfortunately, the feeling did not rub off on his assistant, who was apprehensive of computers in general but who finally agreed to try the new technology.

As is frequently the case, the assistant's experience with the computer was as frustrating as the manager's was rewarding. Every time the assistant tried to use the computer an error message appeared, yet when the manager tried the same procedure it worked fine. Finally manager and assistant went through a systematic comparison of everything they did: turning the machine on and off, handling disks, using the keyboard, and so on. They could find no difference in their procedures and could not account for the repeated disk errors which plagued the assistant but left the manager alone.

Just as they were about to give up, the manager noticed that his assistant was wearing a charm bracelet. He looked closely, and sure enough one of the charms was a tiny magnet containing just enough force to interfere with reading the disk. The assistant stored the bracelet in a drawer and the machine has been fine ever since.

The point of our story is that there is always a logical reason for everything a computer does or does not do, although that reason may be less than obvious. You are about to embark on a wonderful journey toward computer literacy. Be patient, be inquisitive, and enjoy.

Thomas J. Watson, Sr., first president of IBM.

Year-end statistics for 1987:
Sales: $54.2 billion
Profits: $5.3 billion
CEO: John Akers
Headquarters: Old Orchard Rd.
Armonk, NY 10504
(914) 765-1900

Just how large is IBM? Its 1987 sales of approximately $55 billion placed it fourth on the Fortune 500. Put another way, by the close of business on January 1, 1987, IBM had already grossed nearly $140 million. The company has almost 800,000 shareholders (more people than live in the cities of San Francisco or Washington), and its work force of nearly 400,000 approximates the population of Zurich, Switzerland. And, incidentally, IBM is typically the first or second largest corporate taxpayer in the United States, and among the top 10 in Europe, the Middle East, and Africa.[2]

The corporation that has come to epitomize American business owes its existence, in part, to a requirement of the United States Constitution mandating that a census be taken every ten years. The purpose of the census is to allocate representation within the House of Representatives, and little did the Founding Fathers suspect that this would spur the development of data processing and lead to the eventual founding of IBM.

The rapid growth of the country during the latter part of the nineteenth century made tabulation of the census data an increasingly complex and time-consuming task. The 1880 census took seven and a half years to complete, and it was projected that the 1890 census would not be finished for twelve years, or two years after the census of 1900 began! To alleviate the problem, the Census Bureau held a competition to select a more efficient census-taking system. The contest was won by **Herman Hollerith**, who proposed the use of punched cards. Hollerith's machines completed the census of 1890 in "only" $2\frac{1}{2}$ years, and were later used shortly thereafter in Austria, Canada, and Russia.

In 1896 Hollerith formed the Tabulating Machine Company. The organization was later merged into the Computing Tabulating Recording Company and was eventually renamed **International Business Machines (IBM)**.

Thomas J. Watson, Sr., managed the fledgling company through the depression, World War II, and into the computer age. His dynamic personality left its mark on the company and helped it to prosper. Watson instituted a strict dress code (dark suit and white shirt) in order to lend respectability to the

[2]"Facts, Factoids, Folklore", *Datamation*, January 1986.

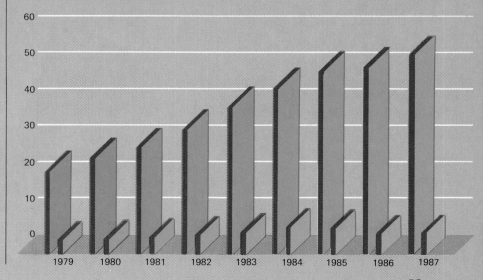

IBM
SALES AND NET INCOME
(billions of dollars)

Herman Hollerith

then lowly position of salesperson. Watson himself never took his jacket off, even on the hottest day (despite his affection for white socks during his earlier career at NCR). He also came up with the slogan THINK as a source of inexpensive publicity, then saw it become the most widely quoted corporate motto in history.

IBM introduced its first computer, the Selective Sequence Electronic Calculator (SSEC), in 1948. But it was not until the mid-1960s that IBM began to assume the dominant role it enjoys today. The System 360 was announced in 1964 in a move that the April 1964 issue of *Fortune Magazine* called "the billion dollar gamble," and which would establish IBM's preeminence in the mainframe area. IBM was led at this time by Thomas J. Watson, Jr., who assumed control of the company in 1956, and who effectively goaded the 360 into production and spurred IBM to take the most substantial risk in its history. Perhaps the most significant aspect of the 360 series was the concept of "upward compatibility," which allowed a customer to upgrade from one machine to another, *without* having to reprogram existing applications.

IBM has essentially maintained this philosphy from one generation of machines to the next (subsequent mainframe systems included the 370, 3030, 4300, 3080, and 3090 series of computers). Today, IBM has approximately 75 percent of the mainframe market and is truly the machine of the Fortune 500.

The years 1985 through 1987 produced cumulative revenues and profits in excess of $150 and $17 billion, respectively, yet they are viewed as disappointing by a company that has historically maintained a compound growth rate of 15 percent. However, the company has undergone considerable cost cutting during this period, and hence future increases in revenues and profits are expected, albeit on a smaller scale than previously.

THE NEW CENSUS OF THE UNITED STATES—THE ELECTRICAL ENUMERATING MECHANISM. [See page 132.]

Summary

A computer is conceptually a very simple device, a machine designed to follow instructions. It receives, stores, and manipulates data by breaking a task into logical operations, then performing hundreds of thousands (or millions) of those operations a second. A computer system consists of input and output devices and primary and secondary storage facilities, in addition to the processing unit itself. All told, however, a computer does not do anything that a human being couldn't do if given sufficient time and memory capabilities; it simply does things much, much faster, and more accurately.

This chapter described the major business applications of microcomputers (word processing, spreadsheets, graphics, data management, and communications). Perhaps of greatest importance, the chapter set the stage for future work through the first Hands-On Exercise, which had you turn on the computer and "boot" the system. Implicit in the exercise was a discussion of the PC's keyboard and the care and handling of floppy disks.

Key Words and Concepts

Alternate (Alt) key
Arithmetic-logic unit (ALU)
Application software
Auxiliary storage
Charles Babbage
Bidirectional mode
Byte
Caps Lock key
Central processing unit (CPU)
Cold start
Color monitor
Communications
Computer literacy
Computer system
Control (Ctrl) key
Control Unit
Correspondence mode
Cursor
Cursor keys
Daisy wheel printers
Data management
Disk operating system (DOS)
Dot matrix printers
Enter key
Escape (Esc) key
Floppy disk

Function keys
Graphics
Hard copy
Hard disk
Hardware
Herman Hollerith
Insert (Ins) and Delete (Del) keys
Intel Corporation
International Business Machines (IBM)
Keyboard
Kilobyte (Kb)
Laser printers
Main memory
Mainframe computer
Megabyte (Mb)
Microcomputer
Microprocessor
Microsoft Corporation
Minicomputer
Monitors
Monochrome monitor
PC compatibles
Pixels
Print Screen (PrtSc) key
Printers

Random-access memory (RAM) Tab key
Read-only memory (ROM)   Text
Resolution   Toggle switch
Shift keys   Warm start
Software   Thomas J. Watson, Sr.
Spreadsheets   Word processing
System software

True/False

1. A computer with 640Kb memory has exactly 640,000 memory locations.

2. The contents of read-only memory (ROM) may be changed by the user.

3. Communications and graphics are the two most widely used applications of microcomputers.

4. A program is a set of instructions.

5. Random-access memory (RAM) refers to the amount of auxiliary storage available on a microcomputer.

6. Computers are capable of original thought.

7. The contents of RAM are erased when the computer is turned off.

8. The contents of a floppy disk are erased when the computer is turned off.

9. A warm start is accomplished by pressing the Ctrl, Alt, and Ins keys simultaneously.

10. Rebooting the system causes the computer to forget what was in RAM.

11. A time value of 22:20 indicates a time of twenty minutes past 10 a.m.

12. A computer's RAM is found within its central processing unit (CPU).

13. All IBM computers are produced with the same keyboard.

14. It is very easy to categorize a computer as a mainframe, mini, or micro.

15. The IBM Personal Computer (PC) was the first microcomputer purchased in large quantities by the public at large.

16. Input and output devices are part of the CPU.

17. A computer does precisely what it is instructed to do.

18. The same computer cannot be used for both word processing and spreadsheets.

19. Every personal computer must be equipped with two floppy drives.

20. A floppy disk is insensitive to magnetic fields and temperature extremes.

21. Turning on the computer automatically turns on the printer and monitor.

22. It is not necessary to answer the requests for date and time information when you boot the system.

23. A $3\frac{1}{2}$-inch floppy disk holds approximately 60 percent of the data as its $5\frac{1}{4}$-inch counterpart.

24. All models in the IBM Personal System/2 (PS/2) family use the same microprocessor.

25. The IBM PC is built entirely of IBM-supplied components.

Multiple Choice

1. The central processing unit of a computer system contains:
   (a) The ALU and control unit
   (b) RAM and ROM
   (c) Primary and secondary storage
   (d) All of the above

2. How many bytes are in 1Kb?
   (a) 1,000
   (b) 1,024
   (c) 1,000,000
   (d) 1,024,000

3. The size of a computer's memory typically refers to:
   (a) The capacity of its hard disk
   (b) The capacity of its floppy disk
   (c) The amount of ROM available
   (d) The amount of RAM available

4. Which number most closely approximates the annual sales of IBM?
   (a) $55 million
   (b) $550 million
   (c) $5 billion
   (d) $55 billion

5. The most popular type of printer in today's environment is the:
   (a) Daisy wheel
   (b) Ink jet
   (c) Dot matrix
   (d) Laser

6. The $3\frac{1}{2}$-inch floppy disk:
   (a) Is not used in the PS/2 series
   (b) Has a capacity approximately three-fifths that of the $5\frac{1}{4}$-inch disk
   (c) Is used exclusively with the PC, XT, and AT computers
   (d) None of the above
   (e) All of the above

7. Hard copy refers to:
   (a) The difficulty of duplicating a copy-protected disk
   (b) Information stored on a hard drive
   (c) Written material that is difficult to read
   (d) None of the above

8. Who designed the difference engine, which, had it been built, would have been the first general-purpose computer?
   (a) Charles Babbage
   (b) Herman Hollerith
   (c) Thomas J. Watson
   (d) Philip D. Estridge

9. Choose the sequence listing the computer in the chronological order in which they were introduced.
   (a) Apple II, IBM PC, IBM XT, IBM AT
   (b) IBM XT, IBM PC, IBM AT, Apple II
   (c) Apple II, IBM AT, IBM PC, IBM XT
   (d) IBM PC, Apple II, IBM XT, IBM AT

10. Which of the following was the first major application of microcomputers?
    (a) Word processing
    (b) Spreadsheets
    (c) Graphics
    (d) Data management

11. The microprocessors in the IBM PC and PS/2 series of computers are manufactured by:
    (a) IBM
    (b) Intel
    (c) Motorola
    (d) Microsoft

12. The contents of ROM:
    (a) Are constantly changed as different programs are executed
    (b) Contain information to start the system initially

(c) Can be easily changed by the user

(d) Can be changed only through the operating system

13. Which combination of keys do you press to reboot (warm start) the computer?
    (a) Ctrl, Alt, Shift
    (b) Tab, Alt, Del
    (c) Ctrl, Ins, Del
    (d) Ctrl, Alt, Del

14. The function keys:
    (a) Are in the same position on every keyboard
    (b) Perform identical functions, regardless of which program is being executed
    (c) Vary in position on different keyboards, but are constant in number
    (d) None of the above

15. A floppy disk can be safely stored:
    (a) In extreme temperatures
    (b) Under a heavy object
    (c) Near a magnetic influence
    (d) None of the above
    (e) All of the above

Exercises

1. Date and time prompts.
   (a) What happens if you fail to answer the date and time prompts and merely press the enter key? Is it a good idea to ignore these prompts?
   (b) Are the following dates acceptable to DOS?
       (i) 11/24/1988
       (ii) 3/16/88
       (iii) 10-31-88
       (iv) 12/88
   (c) How do you enter 2:00 a.m. into the computer? 2:00 p.m.?

2. Use the resources of your school library to locate a PC-oriented magazine (for example, *PC World* or *PC Magazine*), then search the magazine's advertisements to obtain prices for the following:
   (a) An 8086- or 8088-based machine, with two floppy drives (either $3\frac{1}{2}$- or $5\frac{1}{4}$-inch), 640Kb RAM, and monochrome monitor; what is the additional cost of substituting a 20Mb (or larger) hard drive for one of the floppies?
   (b) An 80286-based machine, one floppy drive (either $3\frac{1}{2}$- or $5\frac{1}{4}$-inch), 640Kb RAM, 20Mb (or larger) hard drive, and a monochrome monitor.

(c) An 80386, one floppy drive (either $3\frac{1}{2}$ or $5\frac{1}{4}$), 640Kb RAM, 20Mb (or larger) hard drive, and a monochrome monitor.

(d) Regardless of which configuration you purchase, you will also need a dot matrix printer (at least 160 cps), surge protector, and software. Obtain prices for these components as well as the *current* versions of the following packages: PC-DOS, Lotus 1-2-3, WordStar, WordPerfect, and dBASE.

3. Each of the major application areas has one or more software packages which have become dominant, or at least have their own loyal following. For each area, word processing, spreadsheets, database management, graphics, and communications:

(a) Identify one or two programs which are currently popular for use with the PC.

(b) Find out the name and address of the company which developed the programs you cite in part (a).

(c) Find a "best price" either from a magazine advertisement or computer store for each product in part (a).

4. Visit an IBM branch office, or if distance precludes this possibility, try writing to the company for the information required for this problem.

(a) Obtain a copy of the latest annual report. What additional information (besides financial results) is contained in the report? Is this information of interest to you as a student in this course?

(b) What employment opportunities exist for you within IBM? Does this seem like a company for which you would like to work?

(c) Obtain copies of articles written about the company. (See *Time* magazine, "A Colossus that Works," July 11, 1983; *Business Week*, "IBM: More Worlds to Conquer," February 18, 1985; and the August 1987 issue of *PC World* as examples of articles written for the general public. Can you discern anything about the company which might help to explain its phenomenal success?

CHAPTER 2

PC–DOS

CHAPTER OUTLINE

After reading this chapter, you should be able to:

1. Define an operating system.

2. Discuss the evolution of PC-DOS.

3. Format a disk.

4. Write-protect a disk.

5. Distinguish between internal and external DOS commands; name three commands of each type.

6. Describe the function of DIR, ERASE, RENAME, COPY, DISKCOPY, CHKDSK, DISKCOMP, COMP, DEL, and CLS.

7. Define "wild card" as it pertains to PC-DOS file names; distinguish between the use of an asterisk and a question mark as the wild card character.

8. Describe the hardware requirements for running OS/2.

Overview

DOS stands for disk operating system. *PC-DOS*, or DOS for short, is the operating system most often used with the IBM PC. It was developed for IBM by *Microsoft Corporation* (the subject of the corporate profile in the chapter), which also supplies *MS-DOS* for use with IBM-compatible computers. From the user's view, as well as for all practical purposes, PC-DOS and MS-DOS are really one and the same.

An elementary knowledge of PC-DOS (MS-DOS) is necessary in order for you to run any application (word processing, spreadsheets, database, and so on). Accordingly, we describe the necessary *DOS commands* which will enable you to perform the basic tasks associated with these and other programs. These commands include *FORMAT* (to initialize a disk so that it can store information), *DIR* (to list the files contained on a disk), and *COPY* (to copy a file allowing you to make a *backup*, or duplicate, copy of your work).

You will find that this chapter contains a wealth of information, much of it overwhelming on a first reading. Only the beginning portion (through the first Hands-On Exercise) needs to be covered now, although at some point in the future you will want to know more about DOS. When that time arises you can return to the latter portions of this chapter and/or move to Chapter 13, which contains yet additional material.

Introduction

PC-DOS coordinates activity between you and the computer. It is always available, either to you directly, or to the application you are running. Thus, programs within DOS read and write files on disk, make backup copies of complete disks or individual files, erase and rename files, indicate the amount of space available in memory, and so on.

DOS is divided into three components; the input/output (I/O) handler, the command processor, and utility programs. The I/O handler in turn is made up of two programs, IBMBIO.COM and IBMDOS.COM, both of which are "hidden" from view (that is, they do not appear in a file directory) and are therefore beyond your control and concern. Application programs however (WordPerfect, Lotus, dBASE III Plus, and so on) depend on these programs to perform the basic functions of storing and retrieving data on disk.

The **command processor**, a program known as **COMMAND.COM**, interprets whatever commands are entered on the keyboard and executes them accordingly. Thus COMMAND.COM (as well as the two hidden files) must be on every disk used to boot the system so that it can be loaded into memory and remain there throughout a session.

Included in the COMMAND.COM program are several commands, known as **internal commands**. Among them:

DIR	to list the files contained on a disk
ERASE	to erase a file from a disk
RENAME	to change the name of a file
COPY	to copy one or more files
CLS	to clear the screen

The third component of DOS is a set of **utility programs** that reside on disk and are loaded into memory only when needed. These programs enable the execution of less frequently used commands which are not part of COMMAND.COM (and hence are not resident in memory); these commands are known as **external commands**.

Execution of an external command requires the availability of the corresponding utility program, whereas execution of an internal command has no such requirement. In other words, execution of the external FORMAT command mandates that the utility program FORMAT.COM be read from disk and loaded into memory. However, execution of the internal DIR command takes place immediately because the directory function is included in COMMAND.COM, which itself is always resident in memory.

"This is not compatible with that, and that is not compatible
with those, and those aren't compatible with these,
and the new models aren't compatible with
any of them—however, *I'm* compatible and
I'll take care of you!"

Authors' Comments:
*These are only a few of the literally
hundreds of PC-compatible computers,
each one of which runs the MS-DOS
operating system.*

AT&T 6312 WGS

Tandy 1000, Radio Shack

Zenith Z-150

Compaq Deskpro 386/20

Leading Edge Model D

File Specification

A **file** is a group of related data stored on a disk. It consists of a program or data used by a program; that is, both a word processing program and the documents it creates, are considered files by the operating system.

The number of files that can be stored on a particular disk depends on the capacity of the disk and the size of the file(s). A standard $5\frac{1}{4}$-inch floppy disk contains approximately 360Kb, whereas a $3\frac{1}{2}$-inch disk holds either 720Kb or 1.44Mb. A hard disk, on the other hand, can contain in the neighborhood of 100Mb and emerging CD-ROM technology (see insert) offers storage potential beyond that of a hard disk.

DOS must have a way of distinguishing one file from another and does so through a unique **file specification** which is assigned to every file. The file specification consists of a **file name** and an optional **extension**; for example, the file specification HOMEWORK.ONE, is made up of the file name HOMEWORK and the extension ONE (a period separates the two). The file name may contain from one to

---

OPTICAL STORAGE MEDIA FOR PCs

The same 4.7-inch compact disks that have revolutionized audio recording are beginning to have an impact on the personal-computer market as desktop mass storage devices. Compact disks are an optical storage device that records digital data in the form of microscopic pits etched in a spiral on a plastic surface. A laser beam just 1 μm wide is scattered by the pits and reflected by the flat "lands" between them, enabling the encoded information to be read. Because information recorded on the most common form of compact disks can be read but not erased, this approach to storing data is known as CD-ROM, for Compact Disk/Read-Only Memory. A single CD-ROM disk can store 550 Mb, the equivalent of 1,500 floppy disks or 200,000 pages.

The first applications of CD-ROM will give personal-computer users access to huge databases such as financial databases, patent information, books in print and other library data, medical and drug references, and so on. Previously these large databases have been available to PC users only via on-line information services that link the user's PC to a host mainframe via telephone lines. CD-ROM has the potential to greatly reduce the cost of access to these databases.

Not only can CD-ROM store large databases, it permits them to be manipulated in many useful ways. For example, a disk that contains abstracts of engineering articles could be searched for all abstracts containing the words "optical," "storage," and "data." This is possible because the huge storage capacity of CD-ROM means that the disks have room for a full text inversion—an index showing the location of every word in the entire recorded text.

Further advances are on the horizon. One is the CD-WORM ("write once, read many times"). This technique allows the user to write data on the disk, but not to erase it. Erasable disks are also in the development stage. Researchers are also attempting to overcome one of the present disadvantages of CD-ROM: access times and data transfer rates that are inferior to those of today's magnetic hard disks.

Source: Jeffrey Bairstow, "CD-ROM: Mass Storage for the Mass Market," *High Technology,* October 1986. pp. 44–51.

Authors' Comments: Although widespread applications of CD-ROM technology have yet to appear, the potential is too great to ignore. See, for example, the discussion on Microsoft's Bookshelf *program in the corporate profile.*

eight characters, with valid characters consisting of the letters A through Z, the digits 0 through 9, and the symbols $, &, #, @, !, %, (,), −, {, }, and _. The extension consists of one to three characters which are chosen from the same set as the file name.

You are free to choose file names and extensions within the very general rules just described. However, DOS (as well as many application programs) predefines specific file names and/or extensions. DOS, for example, uses the extensions COM and EXE for program files, and the extension BAT to indicate a file containing a set of DOS commands. In similar fashion, BASIC uses BAS as the extension for BASIC programs, dBASE uses DBF for its data files, and Lotus (version 2) uses WK1 for its spreadsheets.

Drive Specification

DOS uses a **drive specification** to determine where (on which drive) a file is located; for example, *B:*HOMEWORK.ONE indicates that the file HOMEWORK.ONE is contained on the disk mounted in drive B. The drive specification is not a permanent part of the file specification because the disk containing the file may be mounted in different drives.

The absence of a drive specification causes DOS to search the **default drive**. (A default is the action taken by hardware or software unless you specify otherwise.) Drive A is the initial default in a two-drive floppy system (recall that the system disk was placed in drive A in the Hands-On Exercise in Chapter 1), and drive C is the default drive in a system with a hard disk. The default drive may be easily changed once the operating system has been loaded.

To change the default drive from A to B, type B: in response to the **DOS prompt**. The prompt, which consists of the default drive and a greater than (>) sign, is the DOS way of asking (prompting) you for a command. In other words:

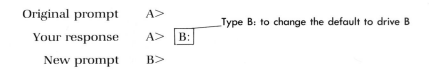

Original prompt	A>	Type B: to change the default to drive B
Your response	A> B:
New prompt	B>

The system now regards drive B as the default drive, that is, the drive it will search for programs and/or data. In similar fashion, you could change the default drive from drive C (the default drive on a system with a hard disk) to drive A as follows:

Original prompt	C>	Type A: to change the default to drive A
Your response	C> A:
New prompt	A>

Getting Started

Thus far we have covered the very basics of DOS, with emphasis on COMMAND.COM and the rules for file and disk specification. We proceed now to cover three basic commands, FORMAT, DIR, and COPY, after which you will be directed to a Hands-On Exercise to implement this material.

FORMAT

A new disk must always be formatted (initialized) before it can hold any data. Thus formatting is the process of making a disk usable, and enables DOS to subsequently read and write files to and from the disk.

The procedure to format a disk on a two-drive floppy system is typically accomplished by placing the DOS system disk (containing the external program FORMAT.COM) in drive A, and the disk to be formatted in drive B. Next you issue the command FORMAT B: to format the disk in drive B, a process which takes about a minute. Be sure to specify the target disk (drive B) in the FORMAT command, otherwise you will format the default drive, that is, drive A, and cause the system disk to be erased.

Users of a system with a hard drive should be especially careful, as inadvertently formatting drive C will erase the entire hard disk! This can happen through the command FORMAT C: or even FORMAT by itself if drive C is the default drive. One precaution (in effect at our office) is to remove the FORMAT.COM program from the hard drive, which in turn requires that a DOS disk be made available when formatting of floppies is required.

The FORMAT command may also include a system option (for example, FORMAT B:/S) to place COMMAND.COM (and the two hidden system files) on the target disk. The advantage of the system option is that the formatted disk becomes bootable, meaning that it can be used to boot the system and that you no longer need a DOS system disk. There is a disadvantage, however, in that the system files require as much as 76Kb (depending on the version of DOS in use) so that the formatted disk has that much less space available for data.

FORMAT is an external command.

DIR

The DIR (directory) command displays all the files contained on a disk. The easiest form of the command is DIR, which produces output as shown in Figure 2.1a. As can be seen, the directory lists the name and extension of every file, followed by the size of the file and the date and time it was last updated. The importance of responding to the date and time prompts should now become apparent, as DOS uses the date and time you supply to date and time stamp its files. Also, observe the indication of the remaining space (186880 bytes free) on the disk. This useful information can prevent you from winding up in a situation where you attempt to save a file, only to have the system respond with an error message of the form "insufficient disk space available."

A disk may occasionally contain more files than can be viewed on a single screen, in which case the command DIR/W (directory/wide) comes in handy. As can be seen from Figure 2.1*b*, only the file names and extensions are shown (date, time, and file size are omitted), and appear in several columns across the screen. Hence many more file names are visible at one time. You may also want to see the directory for a drive other than the default drive, in which case you must include the drive specification in the DIR command, for example, DIR B:, as shown in Figure 2.1*c*. (Note that the files returned by this command are different from those in Figure 2.1*a* and 2.1*b*, because you are viewing a different disk than before.)

DIR is an internal command.

COPY

The **COPY** command copies a file (or files) onto a formatted disk. The syntax of the command is, *COPY source-file destination-file*; for example, the command COPY A:WORK.ONE B:WORK.TWO places a duplicate copy of the file WORK.ONE, as it exists on drive A, onto the disk in drive B, naming the copied version WORK.TWO. It is also possible to give the copied file the same name as the original, for example, COPY A: FORMAT.COM B: FORMAT.COM. Note, however, that in instances where the names of the source and destination file are the same, the latter need not be specified. In other words, the command can be given more simply as: COPY A: FORMAT.COM B:.

DOS will indicate completion of a successful copy operation with a message of the form "1 file copied." In addition you can verify the results of a COPY command by displaying directories of the destination disk before and after the command is executed. Note, too, that execution of a COPY command does not erase what was previously on the destination disk.

COPY is an internal command.

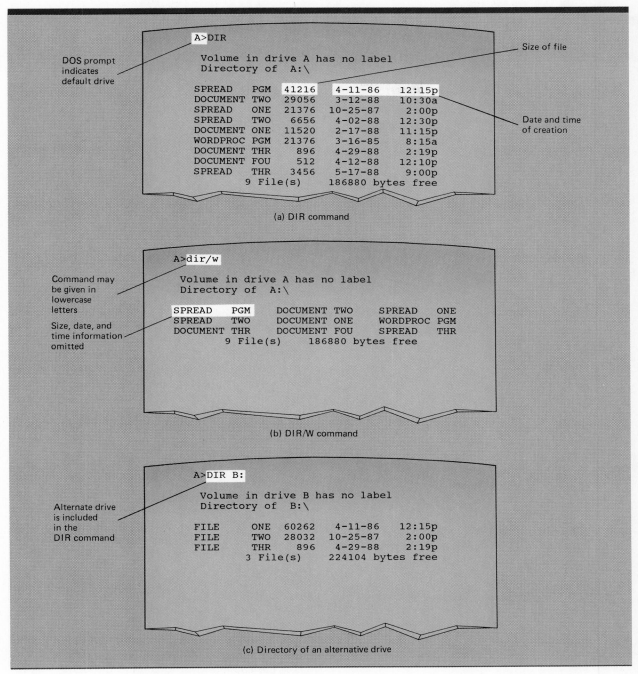

DOS prompt indicates default drive

Size of file

Date and time of creation

(a) DIR command

Command may be given in lowercase letters

Size, date, and time information omitted

(b) DIR/W command

Alternate drive is included in the DIR command

(c) Directory of an alternative drive

FIGURE 2.1

HANDS-ON EXERCISE 1:
INTRODUCTION to PC-DOS

OBJECTIVE: Boot the system, format a disk, and use the DIR and COPY commands.

Step 1: Boot the System
Place a DOS system disk in drive A, and the disk to be formatted in drive B. Boot the system, being sure to answer the prompts for date and time.

Step 2: Format a Disk
Format the disk in drive B by typing the command

```
FORMAT B:/S
```

Remember that the S option places the essentials of DOS onto the formatted disk. The system will respond with the message:

```
Insert new diskette for drive B:
and strike ENTER key when ready
```

Be sure that the disk to be formatted is in the proper drive, that is, in drive B. Strike the enter key (earlier versions of DOS allowed you to press any key), then relax for about one minute. The system will respond:

```
Formatting . . .
Format complete
System transferred

362496 bytes total disk space
 60416 bytes used by system
302080 bytes available on disk

Format another (Y/N)?
```

Respond N, for no, and the formatting operation is complete.

Step 3: View the Directory (DIR Command)
Type DIR B: after which you should see the following directory (the size of COMMAND.COM will depend on the version of DOS you are using):

```
Volume in drive B has no label
Directory of B:\

COMMAND  COM  22042  8/14/84  8:00a
    1 File(s)   302080 bytes free
```

At first this directory may appear slightly puzzling in that the formatting messages in step 2 indicate that 60416 bytes were used by the system (the exact amount will depend on the version of DOS that you are using), yet COMMAND.COM takes only 22042. What happened to the remaining 38,374? The answer is that the portion of the operating system which was transferred to the formatted disk consisted of *three* files, not one. Only COMMAND.COM is visible, but there are also two **hidden files** which aren't listed in the directory. (The presence of these files can be verified by the CHKDSK command, as described in a subsequent section.)

Step 4: The COPY Command
Enter the command, COPY A:FORMAT.COM B: to copy the file FORMAT.COM from the disk in drive A to the disk in drive B. Be sure to specify B: in the COPY command to indicate that the destination of the new file is the disk in drive B. Note, too, that the command could also have been written without specifying drive A (COPY FORMAT.COM B:), in which case the system would look to the default drive for the FORMAT.COM program.

Step 5: Change the Default Drive
Enter the command B: to change the default drive from drive A to drive B, after which the system should return the prompt B> (in lieu of the previous A>.) Now enter the DIR command to obtain the directory of drive B, and observe the following:

```
Volume in drive B has no label
Directory of B:\

COMMAND   COM   22042  8/14/84   8:00a
FORMAT    COM    9015  8/14/84   8:00a
   2 File(s)   292864 bytes free
```

The disk in drive B contains the FORMAT.COM file in addition to COMMAND.COM, reflecting the results of the COPY operation from step 4.

Answering the Date and Time Prompts

```
La fecha actual es Mar  1/01/1980
Introduzca nueva fecha:  (dd/mm/aa):  31/01/88

La hora actual es  0:00:37,21
Introduzca nueva hora:  10:00

IBM Personal Computer, Versión DOS   3.00
```

Copying a File

```
A> copy file.one file.two
        1 Archivo(s) copiado(s)
```

Formatting a Disk

```
A> format b:/s
Inserte un nuevo diskette en la unidad B:
y pulse Intro para continuar

Formateando...Formateo completo
Sistema transferido

362496 bytes es el espacio total en disco
 61440 bytes usados por el Sistema
301056 bytes disponibles en disco

Formatear otro diskette (S/N)?
```

Authors' Comments:
PC-DOS is available in many other languages as indicated by the illustrative session in Spanish. Note in particular the European format for the date (dd/mm/yy) and also the concluding question about formatting another disk; that is, one has to answer "S" (for si) as opposed to "Y" to repeat the operation.

Evolution of PC-DOS

DOS 1.00 made its debut with the introduction of the PC in August 1981. The original operating system supported only single-sided disks with a capacity of 160Kb (then the standard). Version 1.1 brought several significant improvements including support for double-sided (320Kb) disks and date and time stamping of files.

EVERYTHING YOU EVER WANTED TO KNOW ABOUT OS/2 BUT WERE AFRAID TO ASK

Q: What is an operating system?
A: *An operating system is a program that allows other programs to run. At the very least, the operating system is responsible for loading programs into memory and managing the file system of the computer. It also provides access to commands like COPY, SAVE, and DIR.*

Q: What makes OS/2 so much better than DOS?
A: *OS/2 provides facilities that will allow software developers to create better programs for the rest of us to use. These new programs can be multitasked (run at the same time) under OS/2.*

Q: What happened to DOS 5 and ADOS?
A: *OS/2 is DOS 5 and ADOS.*

Q: Can OS/2 also run programs I already have?
A: *Most of them. OS/2 provides a "DOS compatibility mode" for running most existing DOS programs. However, OS/2 provides no advantages over DOS for these programs.*

Q: Do you need a PS/2 to run OS/2?
A: *No. Although they have similar names and IBM announced the PS/2 series and OS/2 at the same time, they have little to do with each other. OS/2 doesn't run on the PS/2 Models 25 and 30 because they do not have 80286 microprocessors. OS/2 also runs on the IBM PC AT and the IBM PC-XT Model 286.*

Q: I currently have DOS 3.x on my hard disk. Do I have to reformat to install OS/2?
A: *No.*

Q: Do I need an IBM machine to run OS/2?
A: *No. What you do need, however, is an AT compatible—a machine that has an 80286 or 80386 microprocessor. Most major manufacturers of AT compatibles will release versions of OS/2 configured for their own machines.*

Q: What's the difference between the IBM version of OS/2 and other manufacturers' versions of OS/2?
A: *Different versions of OS/2 are available from different manufacturers because OS/2 must be specially configured for a particular manufacturer's hardware. Every hardware manufacturer gets OS/2 from Microsoft. The differences in the retail versions will be mostly in device drivers that are specific for a particular manufacturer's products and installation procedures. There should be no differences that will affect application programs.*

Q: Who wrote OS/2, Microsoft or IBM?
A: *The official word is that OS/2 was developed under the IBM/Microsoft Joint Development Agreement. Details about the actual division of work are closely guarded. Some important structural elements of OS/2—such as dynamic linking—have their origin in Microsoft Windows. On the other hand, the Program Selector seems to have been influenced by IBM's TopView.*

Q: I heard that OS/2 is big and slow. Is this true?
A: *It's big, but it's not slow. In some ways it's faster than DOS, in other ways about the same.*

Q: What's the Presentation Manager?
A: *The Presentation Manager is part of OS/2 1.1. It should be available later this year. It's a graphical windowing environment for OS/2 that looks and acts like Microsoft Windows, Version 2.0.*

Q: How does OS/2 use the Micro Channel architecture (MCA) of the PS/2?
A: *OS/2 does not take any special advantage of MCA.*

Q: How long will DOS be around?
A: *Probably longer than any of us would like to believe.*

From *PC Magazine,* April 12, 1988, page 274.

Authors' Comments:
The July 1988 announcement of DOS 4.00, coupled with delays in the Presentation Manager, have slowed widespread acceptance of the new operating system. Indeed most current estimates indicate that OS/2 will not supplant DOS until the early 1990s.

DOS 2.0 (and its subsequent revision 2.1) is still widely used despite the availability of later releases. DOS 2.0 accompanied the announcement of the XT in 1983 and introduced the use of hard disks and tree-structured directories (see Chapter 13). It also increased the capacity of a floppy disk to 360Kb. DOS 2.1 was introduced with the PC*jr.* and supported the half-height disk drive first found on the PC*jr.*

DOS 3.0 was announced with the AT in 1984 and incorporated support for the AT's high-density 1.2Mb floppy disk together with other minor improvements. DOS 3.1 was released in early 1985 and contained features such as file sharing and data locking to enable DOS to support PC networks. Release 3.2 provided support for the $3\frac{1}{2}$-inch drives, which were first used by IBM in the convertible model. DOS 3.3 was announced in April 1987.

DOS 4.0 was announced in July 1988 and included a graphic user interface and built-in file manager. Its most important feature, however, was the lifting of the 32Mb limit associated with a hard disk.

Table 2.1 depicts how the increased capability inherent in each new release of PC-DOS is not without its associated cost, as each successive version required more RAM than its predecessor. DOS 3.3, for example, is six times larger than DOS 1.0, and its retail price of $120 is approximately double that of earlier versions.

The introduction of the PS/2 series coincided with the announcement of **OS/2**, a new operating system designed to take advantage of the Intel 80286 and 80386 microprocessors. OS/2 can access 16Mb of RAM, or more than 25 times the 640Kb allowed under the original PC-DOS. Its most significant feature, however, is the support of **multitasking** (the ability of a CPU to run several programs concurrently), meaning that you no longer have to exit one application in order to run another. The first release of OS/2 appeared in January 1988, required 1.5Mb RAM, and retailed for $325.

TABLE 2.1

The Increasing Size of DOS

DOS Version	COMMAND.COM (Bytes)	IBMBIO.COM (Bytes)	IBMDOS.COM (Bytes)	Total Bytes Used by System
DOS 1.0	3,231	1,920	6,400	13,312
DOS 1.1	4,959	1,920	6,400	14,336
DOS 2.0	17,664	4,608	17,152	40,960
DOS 2.1	17,792	4,736	17,024	40,960
DOS 3.0	22,042	8,964	27,920	60,416
DOS 3.1	23,210	9,564	27,760	62,464
DOS 3.2	23,791	16,369	28,477	69,632
DOS 3.3	25,307	22,100	30,159	78,848
DOS 4.0	37,637	32,810	35,984	108,544

Source: *PC Magazine,* July 1987.

Additional DOS Commands

At this point, you can format a disk, list a directory, and copy a file, and hence can go directly to the application chapters on word processing, spreadsheets, and data management. All these chapters contain Hands-On Exercises which require a formatted disk.

The additional DOS commands in this section are more complex, and are best appreciated as you gain experience with the computer. You may want to skim the material at the present time, but there is no need to master it now. You will learn how to make backup copies of important disks (DISKCOPY), indicate the amount of space available on a disk or in main memory (CHKDSK), determine whether two files or disks are identical (COMP and DISKCOMP), erase files (ERASE), clear the screen (CLS), and rename (RENAME) files. We also discuss the use of a wild card designation.

Remember, too, the difference between **internal commands** and **external commands**. The former are contained in COMMAND.COM, which means they are resident in memory and so can be executed at any time. The latter are utility programs which require the availability of a DOS system disk for their execution.

Use of Wild Cards

There are occasions when it is convenient to work with several files at once, for example, when copying all files with a given extension from one disk to another. Rather than copying the files one at a time through repeated use of the COPY command, DOS provides a **wild card** designation that enables several files to be processed in a single command.

A wild card is a character that stands for one or more other characters, just as a wild card may substitute for any other card in a poker game. The question mark (?) and asterisk (*) are both recognized as wild cards in DOS. The question mark stands for a single character, with one question mark per designated character; for example, D??K could be used to represent both DISK and DARK, but not DARKER. The asterisk is more powerful, as it represents any number of characters; that is, D* could stand for DISK, DARK, and DARKER.

Either wild card may be applied to the file name and/or the extension, as illustrated through the examples in Table 2.2.

CLS

The **CLS** command *cl*ears the *s*creen and is useful any time the screen becomes cluttered or confusing. CLS affects only the screen display and does not disturb the contents of memory or a disk. CLS is an internal command.

TABLE 2.2

DOS Wild Card Designation

Wild Card Designation	Explanation
*.ONE	All files with extension of ONE, regardless of file name; returns ASSIGN.ONE, WORK.ONE, and WORKER.ONE
ASSIGN.*	All files with file name ASSIGN, regardless of extension; returns ASSIGN.ONE, ASSIGN.TWO, ASSIGN.10, and ASSIGN.20
WOR?.ONE	All four-character file names, whose first three characters are WOR, and whose extension is ONE; returns WORK.ONE
ASSIGN.?	All files with file name ASSIGN and a one-character extension; does not return any files

Note: The examples in the table are based on the existence of the files: ASSIGN.ONE, ASSIGN.TWO, ASSIGN.10, ASSIGN.20, and WORK.ONE, WORK.TWO, WORKER.ONE, WORKER.TWO.

ERASE or DEL

ERASE and DEL are equivalent commands which *permanently* remove a file(s) from disk. The command, ERASE HOMEWORK.ONE, deletes HOMEWORK.ONE from the default drive, whereas ERASE B: HOMEWORK.ONE removes the file from the disk in drive B. The asterisk (wild card) designation can be used to delete groups of files with similar names or extensions. For example, ERASE HOMEWORK.* erases every file named HOMEWORK regardless of its extension; ERASE *.ONE erases every file with an extension of ONE regardless of its name; and ERASE *.* erases *every* file! (In the latter case, the system at least attempts to save you from disaster by asking "Are you sure?", but once you reply in the affirmative, all your files are gone.)

Needless to say, you should be extremely careful with ERASE and DEL, because once a file is erased, it is effectively gone from your disk and *cannot* be retrieved with normal DOS commands. Note, too, that the effects of the ERASE and/or DEL commands can be confirmed by viewing directories before and after the command was issued.

The **write-protect notch** on a disk protects against accidental erasure. A disk is write-protected when the notch is covered, and it is write-enabled when the notch is open. The older $5\frac{1}{4}$-inch disks are made write-protected by covering the notch with a piece of *opaque* tape (Scotch or transparent tape will *not* do), whereas the newer $3\frac{1}{2}$-inch disks have a built-in cover which slides easily into place. A write-protected disk cannot be written on, meaning that existing files cannot be erased and new files cannot be stored. All valuable disks, especially those containing original copies of purchased programs, should be write-protected.

ERASE and DEL are internal commands.

(a) Disk is write-protected (notch is covered). (b) Disk is write-enabled (notch is not covered).

RENAME

The **RENAME** command changes a file name and/or its extension. The syntax is *RENAME oldname newname*, meaning that you first supply the existing (old) name, after which you indicate the new name. Thus the command RENAME HOMEWORK.ONE HOME-WORK.TWO changes the name of the file HOMEWORK.ONE (located on the disk in the default drive) to HOMEWORK.TWO. You can verify the results of the RENAME command by viewing directories, before and after, which should include HOMEWORK.ONE and HOME-WORK.TWO, respectively.

RENAME is an internal command.

DISKCOPY

The **DISKCOPY** command duplicates an entire disk (as opposed to the COPY command, which copies only the designated file(s)). The command, DISKCOPY A: B: copies the source disk (in drive A) to the target disk in drive B, *first formatting the target disk, and erasing its contents*. The system directs you to put the **source disk** (the disk you are copying from) in drive A and the **destination disk** (the disk you are copying to) in drive B. After the copy operation is complete, DOS will ask if you want to copy another disk (respond Y or N).

The DISKCOPY command can still be used to duplicate a disk even if only a single floppy drive is available. In this instance you would issue the command DISKCOPY A:, after which the system will direct you to continually insert and remove the source and destination disks, a tedious chore.

The two commands, COPY A:*.* B: and DISKCOPY A: B: appear at first to be equivalent, but there are two important differences. The first is that COPY requires the target disk to be previously formatted, whereas DISKCOPY formats the target disk (erasing whatever was there).

The second difference is more subtle and has to do with the fact that as a file is constantly saved (and resaved) to a disk, the file eventually becomes **fragmented**; that is, pieces of it are scattered all over the disk. Although the fragmentation is transparent to you, accessing the file is much less efficient than with a nonfragmented file. The DISKCOPY command maintains existing fragmentation because it makes an exact copy of the source disk, fragmentation and all. COPY *.*, on the other hand, duplicates files one at a time as opposed to copying the disk as a whole.

DISKCOPY is an external command.

CHKDSK

The CHKDSK (check disk) command checks the contents of a disk and reports in more detail than a DIRectory command how much space is available. To check the disk in drive B, for example, enter the command CHKDSK B:. The CHKDSK command indicates the amount of RAM in the system, the number of user files and hidden files, the space available on the specified disk, and the existence of any bad sectors.

CHKDSK is an external command.

DISKCOMP and COMP

The result of a copy operation (COPY or DISKCOPY) is most often error-free; but if you are working with a critical file or disk, "most often" may not be good enough. Accordingly, the DISKCOMP and COMP commands are used to compare two disks or two files, to determine whether they are exact copies of one another. For example, DISKCOMP A: B: or COMP A: FILEONE B: FILEONE compare the disks in drives A and B, or FILEONE and FILETWO, respectively.

DISKCOMP and COMP are both external commands.

HANDS-ON EXERCISE 2: PRACTICING DOS COMMANDS

OBJECTIVE: Illustrate the use of various DOS commands and demonstrate how to write-protect a disk.

This nine-step exercise illustrates the DOS commands just discussed and helps demonstrate their capabilities. Pay particular attention to the portions which discuss how to create backup copies of individual files and entire disks, as well as the section on write-protecting a disk. These are precautions well worth taking.

Step 1: Boot the System

Continue where you left off in Hands-On Exercise 1, with a DOS disk in drive A and a formatted disk in drive B. Reboot the system (Ctrl, Alt, and Del), being sure to answer the prompts for date and time.

Step 2: The CHKDSK Command

Type the command:

```
CHKDSK B:
```

You should see a message similar to the following appear on the monitor (with the size of the various files dependent on the version of DOS you are using):

```
362496 bytes total disk space
 37888 bytes in 2 hidden files
 22528 bytes in 1 user file
302080 bytes available on disk
655360 bytes total memory
618336 bytes free
```

Now we see the approximately 38,000 bytes which were missing from the directory in the first Hands-On Exercise. Note, also, that the sum of 37888 and 22528 is 60416, which matches the number of bytes used by the system from step 2 in the previous exercise.

The indication of 655360 bytes is the total amount of RAM in the system of which 618336 are still available. Note, too, that although 640Kb (655360/1024) is a common configuration, your system may register a different amount, for example, 262,144 or 256Kb, depending on how much memory was purchased with your computer.

Step 3: The COPY Command

Making duplicate (backup) copies of individual files is critical. Type the command:

```
COPY A:*.* B:
```

to copy every file from drive A to drive B. (Specification of a wild card for both file name and extension, that is, *.*, is the equivalent of listing every file individually.)

Step 4: Review the DIR Command

When the COPY program is complete, list the directory of drive B. Type the commands:

```
        DIR B:
```

and   `DIR/W B:`

Compare the two directories. The first command shows the size, date, and time of creation for each file, whereas the W option omits this information but fits more files on the screen at one time.

At the bottom of either screen is an indication of the amount of space remaining on the disk, which is less than the 302,080 bytes that were available after the initial formatting. The additional space was taken by the files that were just copied onto the disk.

Step 5: The RENAME Command

The name of an existing file can be changed through the RENAME command. Type the command:

```
RENAME B:CHKDSK.COM CHECKDSK.COM
```

to change the name of CHKDSK.COM to CHECKDSK.COM. Verify the results of this operation by taking a directory of drive B before and after issuing the RENAME command.

Step 6: The ERASE Command

Enter the command DIR B:FOR*.* to list all the files on drive B that have FOR as the first three characters of the file name. Erase those files with the command ERASE B:FOR*.*, then obtain a second directory to verify that the files have in fact been deleted.

Step 7: The DISKCOPY Command

DISKCOPY copies every file from one disk to another while simultaneously formatting the target disk. Place a blank disk in drive B (or leave the current disk in). Type the command:

```
DISKCOPY A: B:
```

The system will tell you to place the source disk in drive A and the target disk in drive B, and to strike any key when ready. When the copy operation is finished, it will ask you whether you wish to copy another. Respond N for no.

The disk in drive B now contains a duplicate copy of the original DOS system disk.

Step 8: The DISKCOMP Command

The DISKCOMP command checks whether two disks are identical to one another. Type the command:

```
DISKCOMP A: B:
```

and follow instructions. The messages provided by DOS are clear and you should have no difficulty.

Step 9: Write-Protecting a Disk

Step 6 illustrated the ERASE command and showed how files can be made to disappear provided the disk was write enabled. To illustrate the concept of write protection, cover the write-protect notch of the disk in drive B (according to the procedure for a 5¼- or 3½-inch disk described earlier). Return the disk to the drive, close the door, and issue the command: ERASE B:*.*.

The system asks if you are sure (type Y), and then prints the message:

```
Write protect error writing drive B
Abort, Retry, Ignore?
```

In effect, DOS is telling you that you are trying to erase information from a disk which has been write-protected. Answer A to abort the command.

Authors' Comments:
Several companies offer a keyboard template that provides a handy reference to DOS commands. Templates such as the one pictured are offered not only for DOS, but for many other programs as well.

CONCEPT SUMMARY

Common DOS Commands

Internal Commands
Internal commands are part of COMMAND.COM and do not require a system disk for their execution. The following are all internal commands:

DIR	Lists directory of a disk
COPY	Copies individual file(s) to a formatted disk; does not erase existing files on the target disk
ERASE or DEL	Erases (deletes) individual files
CLS	Clears the screen
RENAME or REN	Renames an individual file

External Commands

External commands are not part of COMMAND.COM and require a system disk for their execution. The following are all external commands:

FORMAT	Formats (initializes) a disk for use, erasing what was previously on the target disk
DISKCOPY	Duplicates the contents of an entire disk after first formatting the target disk
COMP	Compares contents of two files
DISKCOMP	Compares contents of two disks
CHKDSK	Checks a disk and displays the total amount of memory and remaining disk space

PROGRAMMING TIP

Read the Manual

The largest publisher in the United States is neither McGraw-Hill nor Prentice-Hall, nor any of the major publishing houses. Nor is it the United States government, which happens to be second. The largest publisher in the country (and, for that matter, the world) is none other than IBM.

IBM's publishing volume is attributable to the virtually unlimited number of reference manuals it produces, which contain a treasure trove of information *if only you take the time to look*. The DIR command, for example, has several additional options that come to light only after consulting the DOS reference manual.

Consider **DIR/P**, which lists complete information for each file but which stops when the screen is full. In other words, if you have more files on a disk that can be seen on one screen, DIR/P stops at the bottom of the screen and allows you to look at the partial directory which is visible. Then when you are ready, you press any key to continue, whereupon the next portion of the directory will be made visible.

You can obtain hard copy of the directory, with the command **DIR** > **LPT1:**, which sends the output of the directory command to the printer (make sure it is turned on).

The point of this discussion is not to supply endless variations on the DIR command, but to indicate the source of this information. The answers to many of your questions regarding DOS as well as word processing, spreadsheet, and data management programs are found in the appropriate reference manual if only you will take the trouble to look.

Guarding against DOS Disaster

One of the more unsettling experiences you will have when working with computers is looking for a file and not finding it. Should you accidentally erase a file (and you will), no amount of pleading will bring it back. Realize, also, that files can be made to disappear with commands other than ERASE or DEL; FORMAT or DISKCOPY can be just as damaging if used incorrectly.

In this section we suggest several precautions to guard against disaster, and in so doing we review many of the commands that were covered earlier. First and foremost *backup* your important files and/or disks by making duplicate copies. Do not succumb to Stephen Manes's "Humpty Dumpty" definition of backup as "the duplicate copy of crucial data that no one bothered to make." Remember to keep your disk and its backup in *separate* places, for example, at home and in your office.

Clearly label your important disks, storing printed copies of the directory together with the disk. Answer the date and time prompts when you boot the system, so that files are stored with the proper date and time of creation. You will be amazed at how important it may become to know which version of a file (that is, when it was created) you have stored on a disk.

Remember to use the write-protect tab to write-protect a disk. That small piece of tape can be a lifesaver, especially if you inadvertently attempt to erase a file. The DOS message "Write protect error" can be very comforting at times.

Be especially careful with the FORMAT command. Should you specify this command without any parameters, for example, FORMAT instead of FORMAT B:, the disk in the default drive (often drive A or drive C) will be formatted, which can become a small catastrophe.

The DISKCOPY command may not be as convenient as appears initially. Remember that, unlike the simpler COPY command, DISKCOPY formats (and consequently erases) the target disk. It is all too easy to confuse source and destination drives, and insert the wrong disk in the wrong drive. Pay attention to what you are doing. Placing a write-protect tab on the source disk will prevent mistakes as well.

ERASE commands are of course necessary, but watch out for the wild card specification. ERASE *.* erases every file on a disk, and even though the system prompts with the message, "Are you sure?," hours of work can be wiped out with a single keystroke. A good procedure is to issue a DIR command first in order to see exactly which files are on your disk. (In actuality the ERASE and DEL commands do not physically erase a file from a disk, but instead erase its directory entry. The **Norton Utilities**, perhaps the best known of the commercially available programs that go beyond the capabilities of DOS, allow you to restore the directory entry and thus "unerase" the file. See Chapter 13 for additional information.)

Many of these precautions take all of an extra minute or so. Yes, it is a pain to type in the date and time, to label each disk, to put on the write-protect tab, and to print the directory. It's also true that making an extra copy of a disk can be annoying when you've had it with the machine and can't wait to leave. However, you have only to resort to using a backup copy one time before the old adage "better safe than sorry" assumes greater significance.

MICR⊕SOFT

Year-end statistics for 1987:
Sales: $345.9 million
Profits: $71.9 million
CEO: William H. Gates III
Headquarters: 16011 NE 26 Way
Redmond, WA 98073
(206) 882-8080

The wonder is that it took so long. Standing pat when its major rivals Lotus and Ashton-Tate went public in 1983, Microsoft waited until March 13, 1986. On that day, 29-year-old **Bill Gates** took his company public and happily watched as Wall Street valued his 45 percent share in the company in excess of $300 million. Within a year the raging bull market had more than tripled the price of Microsoft stock, making Gates America's youngest billionaire.

Microsoft began as a partnership between William Gates and his friend Paul G. Allen in 1975, when they developed the first BASIC interpreter written expressly for microcomputers. (This was two full years before Apple was founded and six years before IBM's announcement of the PC.) Gates and Allen sold their program to Micro Instrumentation Telemetry Systems (MITS), the manufacturer of the Altair microcomputer, and have prospered ever since. Sales have increased substantially every year, while the number of employees has grown from 5 to approximately 1500.

No doubt the biggest break came when IBM decided to make MS-DOS the operating system for its PC. It was the first time the giant corporation had gone outside for an operating system, and it meant that every computer rolling out of the IBM factory would carry the imprint of Microsoft. Today there are approximately 100 companies

licensed to use MS-DOS, making it the standard operating system in the industry. IBM's decision in April 1987 to choose Microsoft Windows as the operating environment for the Personal System/2 means that the dominance will continue into the next generation of machines.

In addition to its well-known Microsoft BASIC, Microsoft sells compilers for FORTRAN, COBOL, C, muLISP, and Pascal, and has ventured into application programs as well. Microsoft Word, for example, has captured

approximately 15 percent of the very competitive market for full-featured word processors. Microsoft Excel, a highly successful spreadsheet written originally for the Macintosh, was converted to run under MS/DOS and is doing well in head to head competition with Lotus. The company has also entered into a joint agreement with Ashton-Tate to develop database technology for the PS/2 series. In addition Microsoft markets educational and recreational software, and its Flight Simulator program is one of the

MICROSOFT CORPORATION
FISCAL YEAR SALES
(millions of dollars)

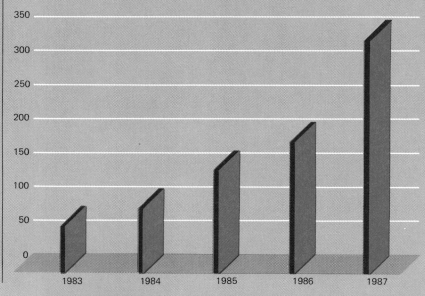

Flight Simulator is one of the most successful "games" ever.

most successful "games" ever written.

Microsoft is actively pursuing CD-ROM technology, as demonstrated by its $295 Bookshelf program. Intended for use by professional journalists, the Bookshelf (in conjunction with a $1000 CD-ROM drive) offers instant access to all of the following: *The American Heritage Dictionary, Roget's II: The New Thesaurus, The World Almanac and Book of Facts, Bartlett's Familiar Quotations*, and *The U.S.A. Zip Code Directory*, to name just a few.

The atmosphere among Microsoft's 1500 employees is decidedly informal. Programmers set their own hours (except for scheduled meetings) and work long hours as well. Gates himself works from 9:30 a.m. to midnight on weekdays, as well as four or five hours on many Sundays. Executives dress casually, even in jeans. Gates will wear a suit when visiting customers but not when he is the host. The median age is 31, and turnover averages less than 10 percent.

William "Bill" Gates

Microsoft OS/2.

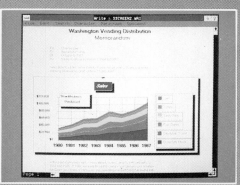

A graph generated by Microsoft Excel.

59

HUMPTY DUMPTY DICTIONARY

"I can explain all the computer terms ever invented," boasted Mr. H. Dumpty in a recent interview," and a good many that haven't been invented just yet.

"When I use a word, it means just what I choose it to mean—neither more nor less," he added from his lofty perch at the pinnacle of the looking-glass world of computer lexicography. "The question is which is to be master—that is all. And the forward-looking (by which I mean devious) computer industry has adopted my philosophy lock, stock, and disk drive.

"Really, some of the commonest usages in the business are too goofy for wo. . . ."

Chortling gleefully at his own research, Mr. Dumpty lost his balance, and a heavy crash abruptly terminated the session. Dumpty Associates, his consulting firm, has kindly permitted us to reprint portions of his work as a fitting epitaph to this farsighted pioneer.

100% IBM-compatible: Compatible with most available hardware and software, but not with the blockbusters IBM always introduces the day after tomorrow.

Portable: Smaller and lighter than the average refrigerator.

Hard disk: A device that allows naive users to delete vast quantities of data with simple mnemonic commands.

Modem: A peripheral used in the unsuccessful attempt to get two computers to communicate with each other.

Network: An electronic means of allowing more than one person at a time to corrupt, trash, or otherwise cause permanent damage to useful information.

Documentation: A perplexing linen-bound accessory resorted to only in situations of dire need when friends and dealers are unavailable, usually employed solely as a decorative bookend.

User-friendly: Supplied with a full-color manual.

Very user-friendly: Supplied with a disk-and-audiotape tutorial so the user needn't bother with the full-color manual.

Extremely user-friendly: Supplied with a mouse so that the computer user needn't bother with the disk-and-audiotape tutorial, the full-color manual, or the program itself.

Easy to learn: Hard to use.

Easy to use: Hard to learn.

Easy to learn and use: Won't do what you want it to.

Powerful: Hard to learn and use.

Copy-protection: (1) A clever method of preventing incompetent pirates from stealing software and legitimate customers from using it; (2) a means of distinguishing honest users from thieves by preventing larceny by the former but not the latter.

Warranty: An unconditional guarantee that the program purchased is actually included on the disk in the box.

Version 2.0: The version originally planned as the first release.

Spreadsheet: A program that gives the user quick and easy access to a wide variety of highly detailed reports based on highly inaccurate assumptions.

Word processor: Software that magically transforms its user into a professional author.

Integrated software: A single product that deftly performs hundreds of functions the user never needs and awkwardly performs the half-dozen he uses constantly.

Windows: A method of dividing a computer screen into two or more unusably tiny portions.

Business graphics: Popular with managers who understand neither decimals, fractions, percentages, Roman numerals, nor pi, but have more than a passing acquaintance with pies and bars.

Standard: Similar to something else on the market.

Backup: The duplicate copy of crucial data that no one bothered to make; used only in an abstract sense.

Computer journalist: (1) A data processing manager who can't write a coherent English sentence; (2) a writer who can produce a definitive opinion on a product after spending an hour with its manual; (3) a person with an insatiable lust for free hardware and software; (4) a harmless drudge.

Source: Stephen Manes, PC Magazine, April 2, 1985.

Authors' Comments:
The appropriateness of these tongue-in-cheek definitions will become more apparent as you progress through the chapter. Take, for example, the definition of a hard disk: "A device that allows naive users to delete vast quantities of data with simple mnemonic commands." Anyone who has unintentionally reformatted drive C will groan with understanding.

Summary

As stated in the chapter opening, we expect that you will continually refer to this chapter as you progress through the text. For the present you need to understand the concept of an operating system, know how to format a disk, and be comfortable with the DIR and COPY commands. This information will enable you to do the Hands-On Exercises in the word processing, spreadsheet, and database management chapters. The tips for obtaining hard copy and reading the manual should be reviewed and taken to heart.

As you gain familiarity with the PC, you will find yourself wanting to know more about DOS in order to take fuller advantage of the computer's capabilities. At that point you should return to this chapter and/or direct your attention to Chapter 13, which contains advanced material.

Key Words and Concepts

Backup	COMP
CD-ROM	COPY
CLS	Default drive
Command processor	DEL
COMMAND.COM	Destination disk

DIR	Internal commands
DIR/P	Microsoft Corporation
DIR/W	MS-DOS
DISKCOMP	Multitasking
DISKCOPY	Norton Utilities
DOS prompt	Operating system
Drive specification	OS/2
ERASE	PC-DOS
Extension	Prompt character
External commands	RENAME
File	Source disk
File name	Utility programs
File specification	Wild card
FORMAT	Write-protect notch
FORMAT/S	*
Bill Gates	?
Hidden files	

True/False

1. DOS requires that you enter current values for its date and time prompts.

2. The operating system for the PC family was developed by IBM.

3. PC-DOS is usually included with the purchase of an IBM PC at no additional cost.

4. Data can be stored on a new floppy disk immediately as it is taken from the box.

5. The capacity of the standard 5¼-in. floppy is 360Kb.

6. The left and right drives are known as drives 1 and 2, respectively.

7. The prompting character of DOS is an asterisk.

8. The DISKCOPY command will format a disk as it is copying files.

9. The COPY command will format a disk as it is copying files.

10. The command COPY A:ALLFILES B: copies every file on drive A to drive B.

11. It is desirable to use a DOS release of 5.00 or higher.

12. PC-DOS (or MS-DOS) can be used on machines other than the IBM PC.

13. DOS requires that commands be entered in uppercase.

14. The PRTSCREEN command prints the screen.

15. The DIR command automatically lists files in alphabetical order.

16. The COPY command requires the target disk to be formatted.

17. The default drive can never be changed.

18. A file specification consists of a file name and an optional extension.

19. The question mark and asterisk are equivalent wild card characters.

Multiple Choice

1. A file specification consists of:
   (a) A file name and optional extension
   (b) The file size and disk specification
   (c) The date and time the file was created
   (d) The file name, extension, size, and disk specification

2. Which command will make an *exact* copy of the disk in drive A?
   (a) DISKCOPY A: B:
   (b) COPY A:*.* B:
   (c) Either (a) or (b) above
   (d) Neither (a) nor (b) above

3. Which keys are used to display the contents of the screen on the printer?
   (a) Shift and PrtSc
   (b) Ctrl, Alt, and Del
   (c) Alt and PrtSc
   (d) Ctrl, Alt, and PrtSc

4. A disk which is write-protected means that:
   (a) New files cannot be written on the disk
   (b) Existing files cannot be erased from the disk
   (c) The write-protect notch is covered
   (d) All of the above
   (e) None of the above

5. The command DIR B: will:
   (a) Make drive B the default drive
   (b) List every file on the disk in drive B
   (c) Make drive B the default drive and then list every file on the disk in drive B
   (d) List every file on the hard drive, regardless of what the default drive may be

6. Which of the following is an external DOS command?
   (a) DIR
   (b) FORMAT
   (c) COPY
   (d) ERASE

7. The command FORMAT B:/S
   (a) Erases every file currently on the disk in drive B
   (b) Formats the disk in drive B, and further makes it possible to boot the system from the formatted disk
   (c) Requires the availability of the FORMAT program
   (d) All of the above

8. MS-DOS and PC-DOS:
   (a) Are entirely different operating systems
   (b) Are used with the PC and PS/2 respectively
   (c) Are written into ROM of every IBM personal computer
   (d) None of the above
   (e) All of the above

9. Which of the following will erase all of the files on the disk in drive B?
   (a) FORMAT B:
   (b) ERASE B:*.*
   (c) DISKCOPY A: B:
   (d) DEL B:*.*
   (e) All of the above

10. Which command indicates the amount of memory in RAM?
    (a) CHECKDSK
    (b) CHECKRAM
    (c) CHKDSK
    (d) CHKRAM

11. Which individual is most closely associated with MS-DOS?
    (a) Bill Gates
    (b) Don Estridge
    (c) Dan Bricklin
    (d) Herman Hollerith
    (e) Mitch Kapor

12. The COPY command:
    (a) Copies the contents of an entire disk
    (b) Does not require previous formatting of the target disk
    (c) Deletes all files previously on the target disk
    (d) None of the above
    (e) All of the above

13. The DISKCOPY command:
    (a) Copies the contents of an entire disk
    (b) Does not require previous formatting of the target disk

(c) Deletes all files previously on the target disk

(d) None of the above

(e) All of the above

14. Which command will erase every file with the extension LED from the default drive?

(a) ERASE ?.LED

(b) ERASE ALL.LED

(c) ERASE *.LED

(d) All of the above

15. Which is the most recent release of DOS?

(a) DOS 1.1

(b) DOS 2.2

(c) DOS 3.3

(d) DOS 4.4

(e) None of the above

Exercises

1. Indicate the DOS command which will:

(a) Copy the contents of an entire disk onto another while also formatting the destination disk.

(b) Copy every file from drive A to a formatted disk in drive B without erasing what was previously on the disk in drive B.

(c) Erase the screen.

(d) Display the name of every file on the disk in drive B.

(e) Indicate the amount of memory in RAM.

(f) Erase every file on the disk in drive A.

(g) Copy the file MY.BK on drive B to drive A, naming the copied version YOUR.BK.

(h) Format a blank disk in drive B, placing the system files on the formatted disk.

(i) Display the names of only those files on drive B which have the extension COM.

(j) Compare the contents of two disks to see whether they are identical.

2. Indicate what each of the following commands will accomplish. (Some of the commands, however, are deliberately invalid and will produce error messages; identify these as invalid.)

(a) DIR

(b) DIR C:

(c) DIR *.INT

(d) DISKCOMP A: B:

(e) FORMAT B:

(f) FORMAT

(g) DISKCOPY B: A:

(h) CHECKDSK C:

(i) COPY A:FILE.ONE B:

(j) COPY B:FILE.ONE A:FILE.TWO

(k) COPY *.* B:

(l) DIR ?.*

3. State the difference between the following:
   (a) Booting a PC with the door on the floppy drive open, and the door on the disk drive closed (and a disk in the drive)
   (b) Typing the command DIR B: versus typing two commands B: followed by DIR
   (c) The commands COPY A:*.* B: and DISKCOPY A: B:
   (d) MS-DOS and PC-DOS
   (e) The commands DIR and DIR/W
   (f) The commands DIR FW.*, DIR *.FW, and DIR FW
   (g) The source and target disk
   (h) The commands FORMAT and FORMAT B:
   (i) The commands FORMAT B: and FORMAT B:/S
   (j) Covering versus uncovering the write-protect notch
   (k) COPY A:FILE1 B: and COPY A:FILE1 B
   (l) COPY A:FILE B: and COPY B:FILE A:
   (m) DISKCOPY A: B: and DISKCOPY A:
   (n) DIR ??ONE and DIR *.ONE

4. Which command, DISKCOPY A: B: or COPY A:*.* B:
   (a) Requires the target disk to be formatted?
   (b) Erases every file originally on the target disk?
   (c) Guarantees that every file on the source disk will be copied to (that is, will fit on) the target disk?
   (d) Results in more efficient organization of the copied files?

5. Consider Figure 2.2, illustrating the results of a DIR command:
   (a) What is the default drive?
   (b) For which drive is the directory given?
   (c) When was the file DOCUMENT.FOU created? How large is it?
   (d) Was the file DOCUMENT.THR really created on 1/1/80? Why is this particular date shown?
   (e) How much space is still available on the disk?
   (f) Which files appear in response to the command DIR *.ONE?
   (g) Which files appear in response to the command DIR SP*.*?

```
A>DIR B:

Volume in drive B has no label
Directory of   B:\

SPREAD     PGM   41216    4-11-86    12:15p
DOCUMENT   TWO   29056    3-12-88     2:00p
SPREAD     ONE   21376   10-25-87     2:19p
SPREAD     TWO    6656    4-11-86    12:15p
DOCUMENT   ONE   11520    3-12-88     2:00p
SPRINT     PGM   21300    4-11-86    12:15p
DOCUMENT   THR     896    1-01-80     2:19p
DOCUMENT   FOU     512    4-12-88    12:15p
SPRINT     ONE    3456    5-17-88     2:00p
         9 File(s)      186880 bytes free
```

FIGURE 2.2   DIR command for Exercise 5.

(h) Which files appear in response to the command DIR A:?
(i) What is the difference between the commands: DIR B: and DIR B:/W?
(j) With respect to this particular disk, is there any difference between the commands DIR B: and DIR B:/P?

6. Variations in the FORMAT command:
   (a) What are the commands to format a disk with, and without, the system files? What is the advantage to each approach?
   (b) What is the difference between specifying (or not) the destination disk in the FORMAT command?
   (c) What is the difference (if any) between formatting a disk with the system files, versus formatting without the system, and subsequently copying COMMAND.COM onto the formatted disk?
   (d) What is the difference between formatting a disk with the system files under DOS 2.1 versus DOS 3.3?

PART 2

WORD PROCESSING

CHAPTER 3

INTRODUCTION TO WORD PROCESSING

CHAPTER OUTLINE

After reading this chapter, you should be able to:

1. Define word processing.

2. Define the following terms: ruler line, status line, insertion mode, replacement (typeover) mode, scrolling, word wrap, justification, and on- and offscreen formatting.

3. Create, save, edit, and print a document on the word processing program available to you.

4. Reformat a document to change margins, line spacing, and/or justification using the word processing program available to you.

5. Describe various types of backup procedures to ensure the protection of your documents.

6. Implement the generic discussion in the text on the word processor available to you.

Overview

The language of business is communicated through the typewritten page, revision of which is often a tedious and time-consuming process. Cutting and pasting, together with the ubiquitous bottle of white-out, have become a way of life. Enter **word processing**, which allows you to change your mind. It can be used for anything that can be put down in writing, from a simple note to your friend to term papers, articles, and books.

This chapter presents elementary concepts in word processing from a *generic* viewpoint; that is, the definitions and other information we convey are applicable to word processors in general and are not tied to a specific program. Nevertheless, there comes a point when learning can be achieved only by doing, and so we suggest three Hands-On Exercises which require your participation at the computer. The objectives of the exercises are also written generically, so that you can use *any* word processor available to you. (You can also find a set of exercises tailored to WordStar and/or WordPerfect in the optional laboratory manuals which accompany this text.)

The chapter highlights what word processing can do for you, the student, and continues with definitions of commonly used word processing terms. These terms include: scrolling, insertion and deletion, reformatting, cursor control, ruler and status lines, word wrap, on- and offscreen formatting, help menus, and justification. A capsule history of word processing is also included.

The corporate profile focuses on MicroPro Corporation, which recently shipped its 3-millionth program in the WordStar family. Although MicroPro and WordStar no longer enjoy their earlier dominance, they do in fact represent a significant milestone in word processing, and were selected for that reason.

Word Processing for the Student

Have you ever produced the "perfect" term paper only to find it was three pages too short or one page too long after final typing? Wouldn't it be nice to be able to automatically change the margins or the line spacing between paragraphs, both at the touch of a button, to conform to the professor's requirements?

How often have you written what you thought was a great paper, then doubted its value when you read it the next day? If you did it on a typewriter, you had two choices: hand in something that was not your best work or retype the entire paper. Short of retyping, the process of revising typewritten text is cumbersome at best. You find yourself using scissors, correction tape, and white-out to make changes, and a copy machine to get a reasonable copy of a polished page. It's almost easier to retype the paper entirely, or for that matter to find the money to pay a typist to do it for you.

Welcome to the world of word processing! You are no longer stuck with having to retype everything. Instead, you retrieve your work from disk and insert additional words or sentences or delete superfluous material. If you make a typographical error, you simply find your mistake and type the correct entry. You can also use a powerful set of editing commands to move text from one place to another or reformat your document by changing margins or line spacing. Then at the touch of a button you print the revised version.

Words are the student's stock in trade. As a student, you do more writing than most people and are in an excellent position to take advantage of a word processor. The availability of this tool makes it possible for you to prepare a perfect term paper with respect to its appearance (the content, of course, is still up to you). No longer can you make excuses for not correcting spelling or grammatical errors.

With a word processor, you enter text into the computer's memory via a keyboard and then save it on a permanent storage medium such as a floppy or hard disk. You can subsequently print the doc-

---

Word processing might be defined as the use of a computer and appropriate software to assist in creating and organizing words to produce written documents. It's the verbal equivalent of "data processing." It also provides one of the most extraordinary sensations I've ever experienced. For a person who has the slightest interest in writing, or simply in organizing thoughts in written form, word processing opens up almost unlimited possibilities.

Source: Richard B. Byrne, "Word on Word Processing," *Personal Computing Magazine,* September 1985.

ument on continuous form paper, a personal letterhead, or any other type of paper. You can also retrieve your document at a later time, change it, and print it again, repeating the entire process as often as you like.

What Word Processing Can Do

Figures 3.1*a* and 3.1*b* show an example of a rough draft and the subsequent edited version produced by a word processor. The draft is entirely fictitious and contains typical changes which are easily incorporated into the final version. Observe, for example, that the draft contains several instances of text insertions and deletions. Note also that the draft is double-spaced with no right **justificiation** (that is, the right margin is not aligned). The final version is single-spaced and right-justified. (Of course, Lincoln produced the Gettysburg Address without benefit of modern technology. He is reputed to have written his draft on the back of an envelope while riding on a train to Gettysburg.)

FIGURE 3.1   Using a word processor. (a) Document in draft form with indicated corrections. (b) Document after editing by a word processor.

(a)

(b)

A comparison of the draft and final versions in Figure 3.1 provides an example of the editing capabilities of a word processor. Although the commands to implement these functions will vary from one program to the next, you may expect to find the following features in any word processing program:

Insertion and deletion of text: These most basic of functions allow you to add text which was initially omitted and/or delete text which doesn't belong. Since most of a writer's time is spent adding or deleting words from sentences and paragraphs, this capability alone makes a word processor worthwhile.

Search and replace: A word processing program can search an entire document for a particular character string, for example, a word or name, and automatically replace the incorrect version with the proper one.

Block move and copy: The block move allows a portion of text (a word, sentence, paragraph, and so on) to be moved from one place in a document to another. A block copy capability is also possible, in which case the text is duplicated in another location and so appears in two places.

Reformatting: This function changes the appearance of the document by altering margins, line spacing, and justification.

Page formatting: Page breaks and page numbers are automatically created and changed as necessary to accommodate other revisions. Many word processors have the capability to print headings and/or footings at the top (bottom) of every page.

Special effects: A word processor, in conjunction with a dot matrix or laser printer, can dress up any document. Blocks of text or single characters can appear in **boldface** or <u>underlined</u>, or be smaller or **larger** than normal.

"IT DOES DATA PROCESSING, WORD PROCESSING AND LIST PROCESSING. GET ME SOME DATA, SOME WORDS AND SOME LISTS."

CONCEPT SUMMARY

Capabilities of a Word Processing Program

All word processing programs perform the following basic functions:

1. *Creating a document:* the original naming and typing of a document. A newly created document appears as a blank screen waiting to accept text.

2. *Editing (revising) a document:* the major function of a word processor, and the one from which it derives most of its power; includes insertion, deletion, block moves and copies, reformatting, and so on.

3. *Saving a document:* the copying of a document from temporary memory (RAM) to a permanent storage medium, for example, a floppy or a hard disk.

4. *Printing a document:* the production of hard copy (that is, a printed document).

President Jimmy Carter using a
word processor.

Online help: Online help means that you can access detailed information screens about any of the commands in your word processor at the touch of a key from anywhere within a document.

SELECTING A WORD PROCESSOR

Which Word Processor Do You Use Now?

The results show that the most popular word processing program on the market today is *WordPerfect*. Twenty-seven percent of those responding named it as the word processing program they currently use. *WordStar* was number 2, with 19 percent, and *Microsoft Word* came in third with 11 percent. Rounding out the top five were *MultiMate* with 7 percent and *PC-Write* with 6 percent. In total, readers named more than 70 other programs as the ones they used, although some received only one vote.

Program	% Users
WordPerfect	27%
WordStar	19
Microsoft Word	11
MultiMate	7
PC-Write	6
DisplayWrite 4	6
PFS: Profesional Write	4
Q&A Write	2
Volkswriter	2
Leading Edge	2
Other	15

If You Were Going To Change Word Processors Now, What Program Would You Change To?

Fifty-eight percent of the respondents said they wouldn't even consider switching programs. Of the rest, 16 percent like *WordPerfect*, and 13 percent would try *Microsoft Word*. Standouts in the write-in crowd included Lotus's *Manuscript*, *PC-Write*, and *Volkswriter*. What features might induce a change? Dozens of suggestions were made, including things like automatic grammar checking, the ability to strike through text, strong mouse support, or greater graphics integration with text.

Program	% Users
WordPerfect	16%
Microsoft Word	13
XyWrite	4
MultiMate	2
Q&A Write	2
WordStar	2
PFS:Professional Write	2
DisplayWrite 4	1
Other	5

Source: PC MAGAZINE, February 29, 1988, pages 100–101.

Authors' Comments:
These percentages reflect the results of a survey conducted by PC Magazine of its readers in which 1271 people responded.

The cumulative effect of these functions is that any document can be written on the screen and revised continually until it is letter perfect. Then, and only then, will it be printed in its final form, without errors. In other words, you are spared the tedium of having to continually retype a document to accommodate change. Word processing is especially useful when a document goes through several drafts or revisions before it is completed.

Vocabulary of Word Processing

Since all word processors are designed to accomplish the same function, namely, to help in the creation of a document, the same fundamental definitions apply regardless of the particular program you are using. Some word processing programs are more elaborate than others, but there are at least as many similarities as differences. This section presents basic concepts of word processing.

Toggle Switches

Sit down at the keyboard and type a message, any message at all, to the computer. We ask only that you refrain from pressing the shift key(s), which means that your message will be all in lowercase. Now press the Caps Lock key *once*, and retype your message, again without pressing the shift key. This time your message is all in uppercase. Repeat the process as often as you like, noting that each time you press the Caps Lock key your message switches from lowercase to uppercase and back again.

The point of this exercise is to introduce the concept of a **toggle switch,** a device which causes the computer to alternate between two states. The Caps Lock key is an example of a toggle switch, as it continually changes from uppercase to lowercase and back again. (The terms "uppercase" and "lowercase" originate from the time when type was set by hand, where the case containing the capital letters was always placed above the case with the smaller letters.)

As we proceed in our discussion of word processing, we will see several other examples of toggle switches.

Screen Display

Word processors vary greatly as to the format of their commands and the amount of associated onscreen information, as shown in Figure 3.2. Word processors such as the hypothetical example in Figure 3.2*a* are **menu driven;** that is, they display the available commands on the screen. The alternative approach is to depend on specific **keystroke combinations** (for example, the function keys, the function keys in combination with the shift keys, and so on) for execution of word processing commands, as depicted in Figure 3.2*b* (in which menus per se do not exist).

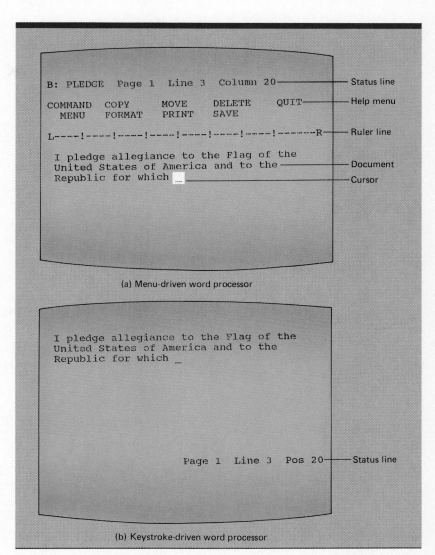

FIGURE 3.2 Screen displays. (a) Menu-driven word processor. (b) Keystroke-driven word processor.

Observe, however, that 3.2*a* and 3.2*b* both contain a **status line** (which is common to virtually every word processor) to indicate the name of the document that is currently being edited and the current location of the cursor within the document (page 1, line 3, column 20). Note, too, that the precise contents and/or the location of the status line on the screen will vary from one word processor to the next. Thus the status line is shown at the top of Figure 3.2*a* and at the bottom of Figure 3.2*b*. Figure 3.2*a* also contains a second line, known as the **ruler line**, which shows the margins and tab stops currently in effect. Both screens contain space for the document itself, but (as you would expect) the more space devoted to the menu and ruler line, the less space available for the actual document.

Cursor Control

The cursor is where the action is; that is, in order to make any change in a document, the cursor is first moved to where the change is to take place. There are many different ways this can be accomplished, and not all word processors have all the indicated features. The most common means of **cursor control** are:

The four arrow keys   to move the cursor left or right one character at a time, or up or down one line at a time.

The Home and End keys   to move the cursor to specific points on the screen; for example, the upper left and bottom left corners, respectively.

The use of commands or function keys   to move to the beginning or end of a document, the beginning or end of a line, or the beginning or end of a paragraph. Some word processors provide additional functions to move to the next word or next sentence.

The PgUp (Page Up) and PgDn (Page Down) keys   to move one screen at a time within a large document that extends over several screens.

Place markers   to move to predetermined places within a document and/or to move directly to a specific page. The keys to establish and/ or access the place markers vary from program to program.

Inserting and Replacing Text

The insertion and/or replacement of text is one of the most common word processing operations. A word processor is always in one of two modes, **insertion** or **replacement (typeover)**, and uses a toggle switch to go from one to the other. In other words, text is entered into a document in one of two ways:

- It can be inserted within existing text.
- It can replace (that is, type over) existing text.

Figure 3.3 clarifies the distinction. Figure 3.3*a* shows the pledge of allegiance before corrections are made. (Note the contents of the status line on the top of Figure 3.3*a*, indicating the position of the cursor.) As the pledge is now written, the word "for" is missing on the last line and has to be inserted between the words "justice" and "all." The correction may be accomplished in one of two ways, in the insertion or replacement modes, as illustrated in Figure 3.3*b* and 3.3*c*.

Figure 3.3*b* illustrates the *insertion* mode, and shows the screen *after* the word "for " (followed by a blank space) has been inserted.

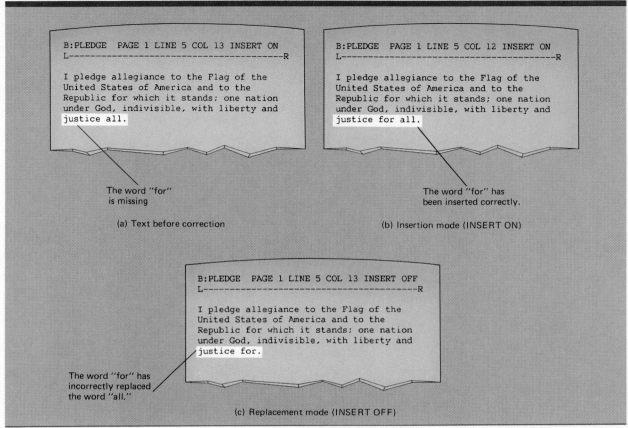

FIGURE 3.3 Insertion and replacement modes. (a) Text before correction. (b) Insertion mode. (c) Replacement (typeover) mode.

In the insertion mode, new text ("for ") is entered into the document, and existing text ("all") is moved to the right. The correction worked as intended. Note, too, that after the insertion is completed, the cursor is positioned under the letter "a" in the word "all," as that is where the insertion ended. Observe, also, that the upper right portion of the screen indicates INSERT ON to signify the insertion mode.

Figure 3.3*c* depicts the effects of *replacement* (INSERT OFF or TYPEOVER) mode. This time the new text ("for ") replaces existing text ("all") and the latter disappears. Thus to complete the correction, it is necessary to retype the word "all," but this is less efficient than using the insertion mode originally.

As stated previously, a word processor alternates between the two modes; it is always in one or the other. Some word processors use the Ins key on the lower right portion of the keyboard to toggle back and forth between the two. For example, pressing the key will change insertion to replacement or vice versa.

Deleting Text

All word processors make provision for **deleting** (erasing) existing text. As with cursor control, deletion can be accomplished at several levels:

- A character at a time
- A word at a time
- A line at a time
- A sentence at a time
- A paragraph at a time
- A block of text at a time
- A document at a time

Unlike a typewriter, the word processor does not leave a blank space in its wake. When a character (word, line, and so on) is deleted, the remaining text shifts to remove all trace of the deleted entry. Many word processors allow backward as well as forward deletion, and provide separate commands to delete the word to the right (forward) or left (backward) of the current cursor position.

The concept of deletion is straightforward and should pose no problem in understanding. Realize, however, that once a portion of text is deleted, it is *permanently* removed unless your word processor has an **undelete** (or **undo**) **function,** in which case the text may be restored.

Word Wrap

Should a typist fail to return the carriage at the end of a line, everything comes to a screeching halt. Just the opposite is true of a word processor. You type continually when entering text in a document, *without* pressing the enter key at the end of a line, because text will be automatically sent to the beginning of the next line. In other words, when the word being typed is too long to fit within the right margin

FIGURE 3.4
Word wrap.

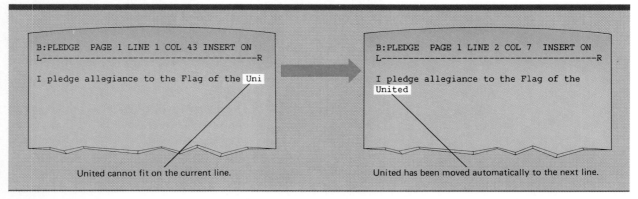

```
B:PLEDGE   PAGE 1 LINE 1 COL 43 INSERT ON
L--------------------------------------R

I pledge allegiance to the Flag of the Uni
```

```
B:PLEDGE   PAGE 1 LINE 2 COL 7  INSERT ON
L--------------------------------------R

I pledge allegiance to the Flag of the
United
```

United cannot fit on the current line.

United has been moved automatically to the next line.

of the current line, the word processor automatically starts a new line. The only time you use the enter key is at the end of a paragraph (or when you want the cursor to move to the next line and the end of the current line doesn't reach the right margin). This feature is known as **word wrap** and increases the rate at which text can be entered.

Word wrap is illustrated in Figure 3.4. As can be seen, the word "United" is too long to fit on the current line, and is automatically shifted to the next line without the operator having to press the return (enter) key.

Scrolling

Most documents are too large to fit on a single screen, meaning that at any instant you are viewing only a portion of an entire document. Figure 3.5 illustrates the concept of **scrolling**, in which new lines of a document are continually brought into view as old lines disappear.

Scrolling comes about automatically as you near the bottom of the screen. Pressing the down arrow key brings another line into

FIGURE 3.5
Scrolling.

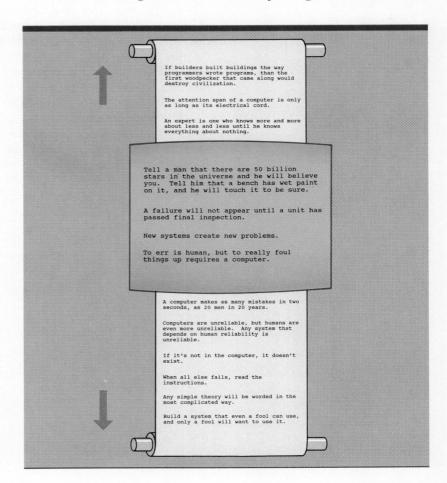

view at the bottom of the screen and simultaneously removes a line near the top. (The process is reversed at the top of the screen.) Depending on the particular word processor, pressing the PgDn and PgUp keys scrolls a screen at a time instead of a line at a time. Other commands will scroll immediately to the beginning or end of the document.

Figure 3.5 implies that you can scroll only up or down. It is also possible, however, to scroll right or left when a document contains more than the 80 characters per line.

On- and Offscreen Formatting

Dot matrix and laser printers make it possible to achieve a variety of effects in the printed document; for example, underlining or **boldface.** The version of the document displayed on the monitor, however, may or may not show these effects, depending on whether on- or offscreen formatting is used by the word processor.

Older word processing programs used **offscreen formatting** (obsolete in today's environment) where the text displayed on the monitor was *not* the same as what finally emerged on the printed piece of paper. Offscreen formatting made use of control characters in the document to indicate that special effects were intended; for example, ^S may indicate the start or end of underlining, as shown in Figure 3.6*a*. The technique was awkward in that it was difficult to visualize how the finished document would appear, but it was used because earlier word processors were limited in capability.

The opposite of offscreen formatting is **onscreen formatting,** or "*what you see is what you get*" (also known as WYSIWYG, pronounced "whizzy-wig"), as shown in Figure 3.6*b*. Onscreen formatting is a virtual standard in today's environment and enables characters that are underlined in the printed document to be underlined on the screen, boldfaced characters to appear in boldface, and so on.

FIGURE 3.6 (a) Offscreen and (b) onscreen formatting.

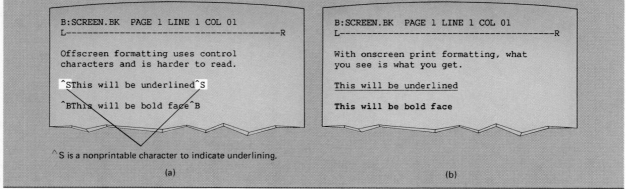

THE McWILLIAMS II WORD PROCESSOR

Features

- Portable.

- Prints characters from every known language.

- Graphics are fully supported.

- Gives off no appreciable degree of radiation.

- Uses no energy.

- Memory is not lost during a power failure.

- Infinitely variable margins.

- Type sizes from 1 to 945,257,256,256 points.

- Easy to learn.

- User-friendly.

- Not likely to be stolen.

- No moving parts.

- Silent operation.

- Occasional maintenance keeps it in top condition.

- Five-year unconditional warranty.

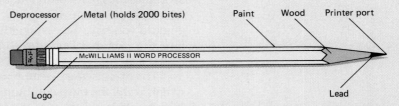

Deprocessor   Metal (holds 2000 bites)   Paint   Wood   Printer port

McWILLIAMS II WORD PROCESSOR

Logo   Lead

Source: Peter A. McWilliams, *The Personal Computer Guide*. The complete *McWilliams II Word Processor Instruction Manual* is available from Prelude Press, Box 69773, Los Angeles, CA 90069.

Authors' Comments:
Peter Mcwilliams's description of a word processor is typical of the humor in his book, The Personal Computer Guide, *suggested reading for all.*

CONCEPT SUMMARY

Word Processing Vocabulary

The following terms are basic to all word processing programs:

Insertion mode: The method of adding text in which new text goes between existing text

Replacement mode: The method of adding text in which new text replaces (types over) existing text (opposite of insertion mode)

Toggle switch: A means of alternating between two modes or states

Word wrap: A feature which automatically shifts text to the beginning of a new line when the word you are typing cannot fit on the current line

Scrolling: A technique in which part of a document is brought into view

> *Offscreen formatting:* The use of control characters in a document to indicate special printing effects such as underlining or boldface
>
> *Onscreen formatting:* The opposite of onscreen formatting in which "what you see is what you get"
>
> *Status line:* A line on a word processing screen that gives information such as the drive, document name, and the page, line, and column of the current cursor position
>
> *Ruler line:* A line on a word processing screen that indicates current margins and tab stops

Learning by Doing

We believe strongly in learning by doing. Hence, while it is fine to talk about word processing in generic terms, there comes a point when you must do something at the computer if the discussion is to have real meaning. Accordingly, we suggest that you sit down in front of the computer and complete the next two exercises.

Our only assumption is that you have a word processing program at your disposal. It doesn't matter which one, because the capabilities we demonstrate are so basic as to be available in any word processor. (Should you have access to either WordStar or WordPerfect, you may find the optional laboratory manuals useful. If not, *any* word processor will do.)

The exercises are written for a system with two floppy disk drives, which is still the most common configuration in school and university PC labs. (If, however, you are using a hard drive, consult Chapter 13 for information on subdirectories and their use with word processing programs.)

HANDS-ON EXERCISE 1: CREATING, SAVING, AND PRINTING A DOCUMENT

OBJECTIVE: Load the word processing program, create a document, save it, and print it.

This exercise consists of six steps which require you to locate the word processing program available to you, create a one-sentence document (file), save it on a separate data disk, and eventually print the document. Each of the steps is described in the ensuing discussion. Use the commands specific to your word processing system.

Step 1: Boot the System
Boot the system as described in the very first Hands-On Exercise in Chapter 1. Be sure to supply the necessary date and time information. You have completed this step successfully when you see the DOS prompt A>.

Step 2: Load the Word Processing Program
Place the disk containing the word processing program in drive A and a *formatted* data disk (see Hands-On Exercise 1 in Chapter 2) in drive B. Issue the command to load your word processing program.

Step 3: Create the Document
The document you create will be kept short for the sake of simplicity. Enter a one-sentence document consisting of the sentence, "The fox jumped over the fence."

Step 4: Save the Document
Save the document you created in step 3 under the name FOX. This procedure is very important, as it stores a copy of the document currently in the computer's memory (RAM) on a floppy disk for permanent storage. (The document now exists in *both* places, that is, in RAM and on disk.)

Step 5: Print the Document
Print your document. Make sure the printer is turned on prior to issuing the print command; also check that the paper is properly aligned in the printer.

Note, also, that the document was saved in step 4 prior to printing it in step 5 to guard against the unexpected.

Step 6: Exit the Word Processor
Congratulations, you're done. It wasn't so difficult after all. Regardless of the simplicity of your document, you have completed three important word processing operations—creating, saving, and printing a document.

Exit the word processor and return to DOS. That's all there is to it.

HANDS-ON EXERCISE 2: RETRIEVING AND EDITING A DOCUMENT

OBJECTIVE: Retrieve an existing document, revise it, save the revision, and print the revised document

Word processing is a repetitive process. Its power comes from creating a document, revising it, reviewing the revision, making additional changes, and so on. This exercise has you retrieve the document created in Hands-On Exercise 1, change it, save the revision, and print the revised document.

Step 1: Load the Word Processing Program
Repeat steps 1 and 2 from the previous exercise, being sure to use the same data disk in drive B as in the other exercise.

Step 2: Retrieve an Existing Document
Retrieve the document just created. Remember that your document is named FOX and that it is stored on the disk in the drive B, as the word processor will need to know the name and location of the document to retrieve. The retrieval operation makes a copy of the document on the disk and places it in the computer's memory. Retrieving a document is the opposite of saving it; that is, the document is still in both places, on disk and in memory.

Step 3: Edit the Document
Once FOX is back in memory, you can use the word processor to change it. Use whatever command is necessary to place your word processor in the insertion mode, and insert the words "quick brown" in front of fox. Your document should now read "The quick brown fox jumped over the fence."

Step 4: Resave the Document
Once again you must save the document, so that the changes you have made will be permanently stored on disk. Accordingly, execute whatever command is necessary to save the revised document.

Step 5: Print the Document and Exit
Repeat steps 5 and 6 from the first exercise. Even though the change itself was trivial, you have accomplished two more significant word processing operations, namely retrieving and editing an existing document.

Backup Procedures

One of Murphy's laws states that "If there is a possibility of several files being lost, the one that will cause the most damage will be the one that will be lost." In other words, no matter how well you plan, something will always go wrong. The only prudent course of action is to anticipate that files will be lost and to take the necessary precautionary action, which in the case of a word processor translates to always having a backup copy of the document in question.

Consider, for example, the sequence of events depicted in Figure 3.7, which is typical of many word processing programs, and which shows the backup procedures associated with the two Hands-On Exercises just completed. Recall that in Hands-On Exercise 1, you created the sentence "The fox jumped over the fence" and saved it on the data disk as the document FOX. Then in Hands-On Exercise 2 you retrieved the document created in the first exercise, changed it to read "The *quick brown* fox jumped over the fence," and again saved the document.

At this point most (not all) word processors will create a backup version by changing the name of the first document from FOX to FOX.BAK. (WordStar, for example, creates the backup version automatically; WordPerfect requires you to request the backup copy.) In other words, the disk now contains two versions of the document: the current version (FOX) and the most recent previous version (FOX.BAK). The document called FOX contains, "The *quick brown* fox jumped over the fence"; FOX.BAK contains the previous version, "The fox jumped over the fence."

It is important to realize that the contents of FOX and FOX.BAK are not the same; however, the existence of the latter allows you to retrieve the previous version of your work if for some reason you inadvertently destroy (or perhaps unintentionally edit beyond repair) the current FOX version. The availability of a backup copy of a document also offers a degree of protection in the event that you accidentally delete the first file. Should this event occur (and it will), you can always retrieve its predecessor and salvage your work prior to the last save operation.

Multiple Copies of a Disk

The old adage "better safe than sorry" pertains to any situation, including word processing. Merely having two versions of a document on the same disk is far from adequate protection, and we cannot overemphasize the importance of establishing additional safeguards. What if you lose your disk? What if you leave it in your car on a hot summer day?

The potential for disaster is aptly illustrated by a friend of ours, a self-employed CPA, who was among the first to purchase an IBM

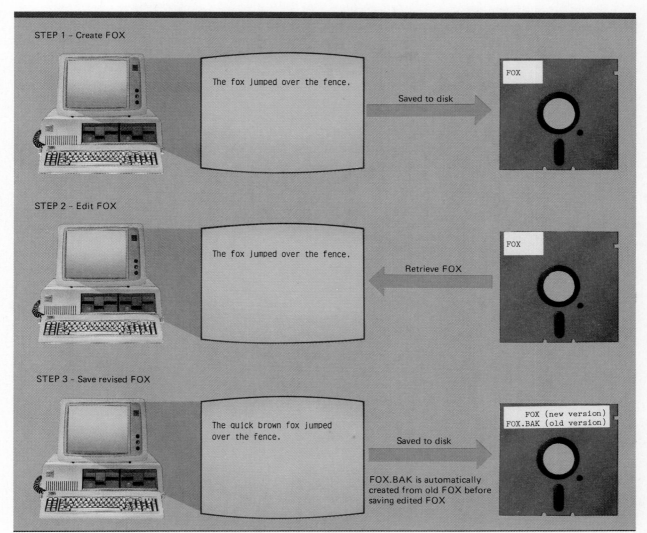

STEP 1 – Create FOX

The fox jumped over the fence.

Saved to disk →

FOX

STEP 2 – Edit FOX

The fox jumped over the fence.

← Retrieve FOX

FOX

STEP 3 – Save revised FOX

The quick brown fox jumped over the fence.

Saved to disk →

FOX.BAK is automatically created from old FOX before saving edited FOX

FOX (new version)
FOX.BAK (old version)

FIGURE 3.7   Backup procedures.

PC. He spent several months entering his manual files on the computer, and in short order he had a first-rate system. Then one bleak December day his machine was stolen, and along with it his data disks. The hardware was insured, but the $5000 he received to buy a replacement system did nothing to compensate for the months of work necessary to reenter his data.

Accordingly, you should always make a *second copy* of important disks (programs as well as data), keeping the extra copies in a different place from your originals, for example, at home and in the office. (Recall that the DOS DISKCOPY command duplicates an entire disk, while the COPY command copies individual files.)

Additional Safeguards

As you gain proficiency in word processing, you will undoubtedly develop your own procedures for protecting your work. Before leaving the subject entirely, however, we offer two additional suggestions which we hope will reduce any frustration you may encounter.

Save your work repeatedly: Some areas of the country are particularly susceptible to power fluctuations, which can erase the contents of RAM. Accordingly, save your work at least once every half hour, so that you lose no more than that amount of work in the event power is lost.

Maintain a printed copy of your work: It is certainly not necessary (or desirable) to print every version of a document, but do print a copy at the end of a session. This provides an additional degree of backup, and in addition gives you the flexibility to review your work away from the computer.

> Perhaps the worst of missed opportunities are the precautions never taken. These are things you could easily have done but didn't because you were too busy, in too much of a hurry, or just forgetful. The unlatched door. The unfastened seat belt. The disk backup you didn't make.
>
> *Source:* Winn L. Rosch, "Downtime," PC Magazine, October 29, 1985

"WELL, THEN, IT'S YOUR WORD PROCESSOR'S WORD AGAINST MY WORD PROCESSOR'S WORD."

Reformatting a Document

One of the most dramatic features of a word processor is the ability to radically change the appearance of a document with a minimum of effort. You can, for example, change the margin settings, go from single spacing to double spacing (or vice versa), justify or unjustify text, and so on. The procedure of changing a document's appearance is known as **reformatting.**

Most word processors work on the paragraph level for reformatting; that is, they operate on one paragraph at a time. This is logical when you recall that in entering text in a document, the only time the enter key is used is at the end of a paragraph. Most word processors reformat automatically (whenever settings are changed); a few, however, require you to explicitly issue reformatting commands.

Right justification and reformatting are illustrated in Figure 3.8. Figure 3.8*a* was entered without right justification, whereas Figure 3.8*b* contains a second paragraph which was entered with right justification in effect. Recall from the chapter opening that "justification" is a synonym for alignment. Text which is right-justified is vertically aligned on the right margin.

Observe that the extreme right-hand column in all lines of Figure 3.8*a* and 3.8*b* are blank with the exception of the last line, which

FIGURE 3.8   Justification of text. (a) Text without right justification. (b) Text with right justification.

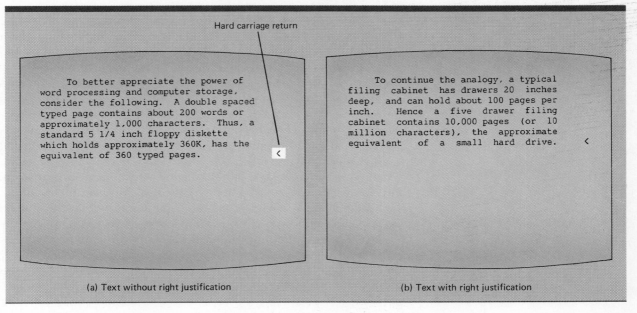

Hard carriage return

To better appreciate the power of word processing and computer storage, consider the following. A double spaced typed page contains about 200 words or approximately 1,000 characters. Thus, a standard 5 1/4 inch floppy diskette which holds approximately 360K, has the equivalent of 360 typed pages.   <

To continue the analogy, a typical filing cabinet has drawers 20 inches deep, and can hold about 100 pages per inch.   Hence a five drawer filing cabinet contains 10,000 pages (or 10 million characters), the approximate equivalent of a small hard drive.   <

(a) Text without right justification

(b) Text with right justification

ends with a less than (<) symbol. The < is the symbol of our word processor to indicate the end of a paragraph and is known as a **hard carriage return.** This is in contrast to an automatic line change (**soft carriage return**) produced by word wrap, in which the word processor automatically goes to a new line at the end of the current line. The reformatting operation is effective from the position of the cursor to the first hard carriage return.

Take a closer look at the right-justified paragraph in Figure 3.8*b*, noting the *uneven* spacing between words. For example, there are two spaces between "cabinet" and "has," but there is only one space between "has" and "drawers." This is because many word processors (and/or the associated monitors or printers) cannot show less than a full character between adjacent words. Contrast Figure 3.8*b* to the text in this book, which is also right-justified but which takes advantage of **proportional spacing,** in which each character is allocated a variable amount of space depending on its size (for example, the letter m requires more space than the letter i). Although right justification has a more professional look, text with **ragged right margins** is generally easier to read when proportional spacing is not available.

Reformatting can be done at any time. In other words, after a paragraph (or document) has been entered, you can change any parameter, or parameters, such as justification, line spacing, margin settings, and so on and then reformat the document according to the new settings. Indeed many of today's word processors *automatically* reformat a document whenever a change is made.

Hyphenation

Reformatting a document often results in the realignment of existing text, especially when margins have been changed. Thus a word which previously fit at the end of a line before reformatting may be moved to a different line after reformatting has taken place. Indeed, moving long words from one line to the next during the reformatting process often leaves a large space at the end of the current line or large gaps between words (when justification is on). Hyphenation provides a solution (albeit, not always a desirable one) if **hyphen-help** is available.

When hyphen-help is on, the word processor pauses during reformatting at the end of any line where awkward spacing will result, whereupon you are asked whether to hyphenate the current word, and if so where to place the hyphen. Realize, however, that hyphen-help is not a panacea. First, it is time-consuming, and for this reason many people choose not to use it. Second, if you are not careful, hyphen-help may result in the insertion of **hard hyphens,** hyphens which remain (inappropriately) even if the document is subsequently reformatted so that the word ultimately fits on one line. Our suggestion, therefore, is not to use this feature.

HANDS-ON EXERCISE 3: REFORMATTING A DOCUMENT

OBJECTIVE: Create a new document, then use the reformatting capabilities of a word processor to alter its appearance.

This exercise is designed to illustrate the reformatting capabilities of a typical word processor. It begins by having you create a new document, then change its appearance by altering margins, line spacing, and justification. The exercise also introduces special effects such as underlining and boldface.

Step 1: Create the Document

Boot the system, then load your word processor and data disk as described in the earlier exercises. Create a document containing the preamble to the United States Constitution, as shown below.

We, the people of the United States, in order to form a more perfect Union, establish justice, insure domestic tranquility, provide for the common defense, promote the general welfare, and secure the blessings of liberty to ourselves and our posterity, do ordain and establish this Constitution for the United States of America.

Type just as you would on a regular typewriter. *Do not press the return (enter) key* when you come to the end of a line, as the word wrap feature will automatically begin new lines as necessary.

Step 2: Correcting Errors

The beauty of any word processor is the ease with which you can make corrections. If you made a mistake in step 1, there are two operations you might require: inserting text you omitted and/or correcting (typing over) existing text. (Recall the earlier discussion on toggling between the two modes.) It may also be necessary to delete superfluous text, so that you should learn the commands to delete a character, a word, and an entire line.

Use these capabilities to correct your preamble for any typing errors. Now the hard part is over, and you can have some fun with the word processor. We

suggest you try a few simple commands, and watch the preamble change radically.

Step 3: Change the Margins

Determine the margins currently in effect in your document, then issue the commands to alter these margins. Reformat the document according to the new settings. Remember, however, that since reformatting is generally done on the paragraph level, you will have to move the cursor to the beginning of the document before issuing the reformatting command (or before changing the margin settings if reformatting is done automatically).

Step 4: Change the Justification

Invoke the command to change the justification, then reformat the document with the new setting.

Step 5: Change the Line Spacing

Invoke the command to change to double (or single) spacing, then reformat the document with the new setting.

Step 6: Use Underlining and Boldface

Most word processors provide for underlining and boldface. Learn the commands for your program, then underline one portion of the preamble and boldface another.

Step 7: Save and Print the Document

When you have finished experimenting, save one version of the preamble and print it. Exit the word processor and return to DOS.

> **COMMAND SUMMARY**
>
> **Word Processing Commands**
>
> Although commands for every word processor are different, it will be helpful for you to review the three Hands-On Exercises and establish the following reference for use with your word processor.
>
> Supply the command(s) to:
> Load the word processor
> Create a document
> Save a document
> Retrieve a document
> Print a document
>
> Supply the commands to:
> Toggle between insertion and replacement (type over) modes
> Delete one character
> Delete one word
> Delete one line
> Reformat the document
> Change the left margin
> Change the right margin
> Turn justification on and off
> Set line spacing
> Begin and end underlining
> Begin and end boldface

A Capsule History of Word Processing

The invention of the typewriter was the single major event which shaped the history of the modern office, leading to the eventual development of word processing. Although a typewriter patent was issued as early as 1714 in England, it wasn't until 1868 that **Christopher Sholes,** a newspaper editor from Milwaukee, developed the first practical typewriter (that is, one that was at least as fast as writing by hand). The standard letter arrangement known as QWERTY (named for the first six letters on the second row) also dates back to Sholes and is anything but arbitrary. The keys were placed in this pattern to deliberately *slow down* typists to keep the early machines from jamming.

Mark Twain was the first author to embrace the new machine, and his *Life on the Mississippi* was the first manuscript prepared on a typewriter. Twain reputedly typed at 19 words a minute, but the typewriter itself was slow to catch on as a business tool, selling only 1200 units in all of 1881. It wasn't until innovations such as the elimination of separate keys for upper- and lowercase and the ability to see the paper as it was being typed that the success of the machine was assured. The basic design remained unchanged until 1961, when IBM introduced the "golfball" element in its Selectric typewriter, which eliminated the moving carriage.

KEYBOARD LAYOUT:

QWERTY versus Dvorak

The QWERTY configuration stood unchallenged until 1930, when **August Dvorak** published the results of a study concluding that the standard keyboard is unbalanced with respect to hand, finger, and row distribution. Dvorak found that the operator types the great majority of words with the left hand, and uses unnecessary finger hurdles and complicated patterns. Consider:

1. More than 2700 commonly used words are typed with the left (or weak) hand, while the right hand is idle.

2. Fifty-seven percent of the work is done with the left hand.

3. Forty-five percent of the work is done with the index fingers.

4. Fifty-two percent of the keystrokes are made on the top (or reach) row versus only 32 percent on the home row.

As a result of his study Dvorak designed his own keyboard, which has the following properties:

1. Only 69 words are typed with the left hand and none with the right hand, while the other hand is idle.

2. Forty-four percent of the work is done with the left hand.

3. Thirty-three percent of the work is done with the index fingers.

4. Twenty-two percent of the keystrokes are made on the top row and 70 percent on the home row.

Subsequent studies have verified that the Dvorak keyboard is faster, less fatiguing, and easier to learn (for beginners) than the standard layout.

*Authors' Comments:
Although the Dvorak arrangement offers several advantages, the tens of millions of entrenched QWERTY keyboards may ultimately relegate Dvorak to the status of an interesting curiosity.*

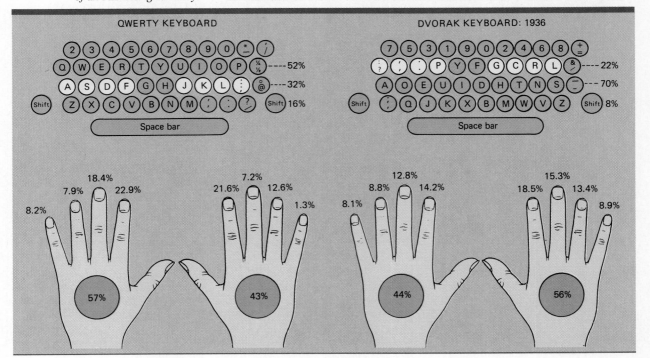

The arrival of the Beatles in the United States in 1964 coincided with the effective beginning of word processing.

It was in 1964, however (almost a century after Sholes and the year the Beatles took America by storm), that IBM revolutionized typing and in essence began word processing, with its introduction of the Magnetic Tape/Selectric Typewriter (MT/ST). The MT/ST was the first true word processor, as it used a tape cartridge (similar to a tape cassette) for storage of repetitive text.

Lexitron and 3M pioneered video display word processors in the early 1970s which let users see and change text on a screen, rather than on paper. In 1973 Vydec introduced a word processor which used the floppy disk and allowed *random* rather than sequential access.

Personal computers, primarily the Apple II and Radio Shack TRS-80, began appearing in the late 1970s, and with them came the first attempts at word processing programs. However, it was the introduction of the IBM PC that led eventually to word processing as we know it, as motivated vendors rushed to develop applications for the new machine.

Today's generation of full-featured word processing programs includes standard capabilities that were not possible just a few years ago. On-line help, complex block operations, undo commands, and 100,000-word dictionary and thesaurus programs are just a few of the many features we take for granted. More and more, word processing programs are encroaching on the low end of desktop publishing (see Chapter 5), extending the word processor well beyond what the imagination once projected.

THE TREK FROM TYPEWRITERS

In the beginning, there were typewriters . . . and then IBM introduced the PC. Word processing would never be the same, evidenced by the forerunners of today's powerful programs that would eventually doom the stand-alone system.

Volkswriter by Lifetree Software: The first word processor announced for the PC was introduced to the public in April, before the PC itself, as capable of running on IBM's soon-to-be-released machine. (Announced in April 1981.)

WordStar by MicroPro International Corp.:   Generally regarded as the first "serious" word processor for the PC, and the program that quickly became the early market leader. (Announced in June 1982.)

WordPerfect by Satellite Software International: The first version included such novel (at the time) features as mail merge, a 30,000-word dictionary, and proportional spacing. The program would eventually prove so successful that the vendor changed the company name to WordPerfect Corporation. (Announced in December 1982.)

Microsoft Word by Microsoft Corp.:   The first word processor to operate in graphics mode; hence, it was able to extend on-screen formatting to include boldface, underlined, or italic characters. (Announced in late 1983.)

Source: Carol Ellison, "The Trek from Typewriters," PC Magazine, February 29, 1988.

CORPORATE PROFILE:
MICROPRO INTERNATIONAL CORPORATION

Year-end statistics for 1987:
Sales:	$41.3 million
Profits:	$ 2.9 million
CEO:	Leon Williams
Headquarters:	33 San Pablo Avenue
	San Rafael, CA 94903
	(415) 499-1200

WordStar—you love it or you hate it, but you've heard about it, because it has been around for so long. It was first introduced when the Apple II was less than a year old, and three years before the announcement of the IBM PC. Indeed the very thought of using a personal computer for word processing was not even commonly accepted at the time of WordStar's introduction.

WordStar is the product of **MicroPro International Corporation**, founded in 1978 by Seymour I. Rubinstein, who sought

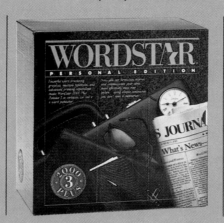

to capitalize on the power of the then new operating system CP/M. Ten months later came WordStar, a revolutionary software package written not for programmers, but for typists. The rest is history: MicroPro and WordStar thrived before the IBM announcement and absolutely took off afterward. It is still one of the most widely used word processing packages, with probably more pirated copies in existence than all other word processing programs combined.

Yet beneath all its success (the company shipped its 3-millionth

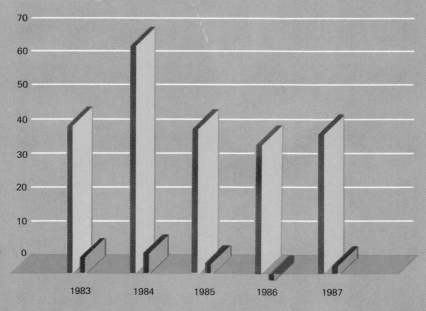

MICROPRO
SALES AND NET INCOME
(millions of dollars)

WORDSTAR®

2000 Plus Release 3 Personal Edition

William F. Buckley expounding on the virtues of WordStar 2000.

product in 1987) lies a tale of what might have been. The early PC version of WordStar was essentially the same as its CP/M predecessor which ran in 64Kb, and so it failed to take advantage of the new machine's greater memory. MicroPro waited nearly seven years, long after competing programs had taken away significant market share, before improving on its original offering, and even then was only marginally successful with WordStar 2000. Sales and earnings have declined steadily since their peak in 1984, culminating in a $1 million loss in 1986.

Fortunately, for the literally millions of WordStar devotees, MicroPro finally turned the corner in 1987 with the long awaited release of WordStar 4.0. Among the 125 new features were "undo" and "go to page" commands, a dictionary and thesaurus, line and box drawing, onscreen formatting, the ability to store margins within a document, and (best of all) improved speed of execution. The announcement was coupled with a stroke of marketing genius, an "amnesty period" allowing existing users to upgrade regardless of how they might have come by the program. For $89 plus $5 shipping, anyone could upgrade merely by supplying a serial number (which appears whenever the program is loaded) of an older copy. 100,000 copies were shipped within the first 100 days after the announcement.

WordStar 5.0 was released in July 1988 and contained an additional 300 user-requested features, including a new user interface with pull down menus and windows for concurrent editing of multiple documents. The new release also offered a Page Preview mode to display font styles and sizes as they appear in a finished document, displayed facing pages (to check page breaks), and a thumbnail display that could show up to 144 pages on high-resolution monitors.

MicroPro also strengthened its commitment to customer support by increasing the number of service staff from 25 to 70, enabling it to field an increase in monthly calls from 10,000 to almost 40,000. Dial the telephone number listed in the profile and the voice on the other end responds with "Good Morning, the new MicroPro." (We did, and we received a helpful answer to our problem within five minutes.) One customer was reported to have been so pleased that she responded, "It's a pleasure to have a problem with your company."

WordStar today is sold in the United States as well as 50 foreign countries, and it is available in nine foreign languages. (International sales account for approximately 34 percent of total revenues.) The company distributes its products through approximately 4000 retail dealer outlets in the United States, four wholly owned subsidiaries in Europe and Japan, and a network of international distributors.

WordStar 5.0 contains 300 additional features.

MICROPRO'S RODENT PROCESSOR

The only thing more difficult than inventing a palindrome is inventing a plausible explanation for it. Regular PC contributor Dean Hannotte came up with an elegant, PC-related sentence that reads the same forwards and backwards. Since it's not the sort of thing you'd find occasion to say most days of the week, I'll suggest a way to justify dropping Hannotte's polished gem into a conversation:

"I'm sure you've heard of debugging software. But did you know that a popular program can dispose of larger pests? Yes, it's true. . .

"RATS DROWN IN WORDSTAR."

Source: PC Magazine, March 19, 1985. © Ziff-Davis Publishing Company.

The Authors Came Upon Another List of Palindromes. Here Are Four:

1. Lewd did I live, & evil I did dwel. (The first palindrome recorded in the English language.)

2. Madam, I'm Adam.

3. A man, a plan, a canal—Panama. (Our favorite.)

4. Able was I ere I saw Elba. (Napoleon's lament.)

Source: The Book of Lists. © 1977 by David Wallechinesky, Irving Wallace, and Amy Wallace. By permission of William Morrow & Company.

Authors' Comments: The piece in PC Magazine spurred our curiosity about palindromes which resulted in our finding the entries from The Book of Lists. We're not sure of their practical value, but we think they make for interesting reading.

Summary

Each of the more than 100 word processing programs currently on the market contains certain basic capabilities. Thus any word processor allows you to *create* a document, *save* it on a permanent storage device such as a floppy or hard disk, *retrieve* the document for subsequent *editing*, and finally *print* the revised document.

In addition, certain vocabulary is common to the operation of all word processors. Accordingly, the chapter began with the definition of basic terms such as status and ruler line, insertion and replacement (typeover) mode, word wrap, and on- and offscreen formatting. We showed that the editing capabilities of any word processor enable you to insert or delete text and to reformat a document by changing line spacing, justification, and/or the margin settings. Another key concept was the automatic backup procedures provided by some programs.

The most important portions of the chapter were the three Hands-On Exercises, which assume only that you have a word processor available. We could have gone on and on about the benefits of word processing, but nothing would have made sense until you actually sat down in front of a computer and did the exercises. Suffice it to say that we cannot overemphasize the importance of learning by doing in this as well as all subsequent chapters.

Key Words and Concepts

Backup procedures
Creating a document
Cursor control
Deleting
August Dvorak
Editing (revising) a document
Hard carriage return
Hard hyphens
Help menus
Hyphen-help
Insertion (or insert) mode
Justification
Keystroke combinations
Menu driven
MicroPro International
  Corporation
Offscreen formatting
Onscreen formatting
Place markers

Printing a document
Proportional spacing
QWERTY
Ragged right margins
Reformatting
Replacement (typeover) mode
Retrieving an exising document
Ruler line
Saving a document
Scrolling
Christopher Sholes
Soft carriage return
Status line
Toggle switch
Undelete (or undo) function
Word processing
Word wrap
WordStar

True/False

1. There are many word processing programs which will run on the IBM PC.

2. All word processing programs allow you to create, edit, save, and print a document.

3. An entire document can usually be seen on the screen at one time.

4. Documents produced by a word processor may be saved onto an unformatted disk.

5. On a two-drive floppy system, the word processing program is typically put into drive A and the document disk into drive B.

6. A Dvorak keyboard may be connected to an IBM PC.

7. Onscreen formatting is available with most word processors in today's environment.

8. The word wrap feature means you do not have to hit the return key at the end of every line.

9. The backup procedure provided by a word processor is all that is needed to adequately protect your data disks.

10. The commands of a word processor must generally be entered in uppercase letters.

11. Ruler line and status line are different names for the same information.

12. The insertion mode of a word processor replaces (that is, types over) existing text.

13. A toggle switch alternates between conditions or commands.

14. QWERTY is the only recognized keyboard layout.

15. Text which is right-justified may have awkward spacing between words.

16. Displaying extensive menu information on the screen decreases the amount of a document which can be displayed at one time.

17. A hard carriage return is generated when the enter key is pressed.

18. Reformatting operations generally work on the paragraph level.

19. The enter key should be pressed only at the end of every paragraph, not the end of every line.

20. Text which is right-justified will have a ragged margin on the right side.

Multiple Choice

1. All word processors should be capable of:
   (a) Printing documents
   (b) Reformatting documents
   (c) Saving and retrieving documents
   (d) All of the above

2. The process of viewing only a portion of a document at one time is called:
   (a) Hyphenation
   (b) Justification
   (c) Scrolling
   (d) None of the above.

3. When entering text with a word processor, the return key is normally pressed at the end of every:
   (a) Line
   (b) Sentence
   (c) Paragraph
   (d) Page
   (e) None of the above

4. The process of vertically aligning the character at the end of every line is called:
   (a) Ragged edging
   (b) Word wrap
   (c) Justification
   (d) Reformatting

5. The input mode of a word processor that adds new text by typing over existing text is known as:
   (a) Insertion mode
   (b) Deletion mode
   (c) Escape mode
   (d) Replacement mode

6. Alternating between insertion and replacement is done via:
   (a) A toggle switch
   (b) Alternation
   (c) Justification
   (d) Reformatting

7. Which of the following are not cursor control keys?
   (a) Home and End keys
   (b) Arrow keys
   (c) PgUp and PgDn keys
   (d) Shift keys

8. The acronym WYSIWYG (what you see is what you get) refers to the ability of a word processor to do:
   (a) Off-screen formatting
   (b) Graphics
   (c) On-screen formatting
   (d) Real time editing

9. Which of the following spacing options would be the most professional looking?
   (a) Left-justified text
   (b) Right-justified text
   (c) Proportional spacing with right justification
   (d) Proportional spacing with no right justification

10. A save operation:
    (a) Copies a document in RAM to disk
    (b) Copies a document on disk to RAM
    (c) Copies a document in ROM to disk
    (d) Copies a document from a floppy disk to a hard disk

11. The procedure by which a word processor automatically moves a word to a new line if it cannot fit on the current line is called:
    (a) A hard carriage return
    (b) Word wrap

(c) Automatic line end

(d) Line wrap

12. The status line in a word processor usually contains:
    (a) The name of the document currently being edited
    (b) The current position of the cursor (page, line, and column)
    (c) Both (a) and (b) above
    (d) Neither (a) nor (b) above

13. Which pair of terms is not synonymous?
    (a) Justification/alignment
    (b) Replacement/typeover
    (c) On-screen formatting/wysiwyg
    (d) QWERTY/DVORAK

14. Backup copies of word processing documents:
    (a) Are automatically created by all word processors
    (b) Can be created only if the disk is write-protected
    (c) Are unnecessary
    (d) None of the above

15. Which word processor was the first to gain popularity on the PC?
    (a) Microsoft Word
    (b) WordStar
    (c) Easy Writer
    (d) WordPerfect

Exercises

1. Figure 3.9 contains a screen display of a typical word processor. Answer the following:
    (a) Is the insertion or replacement (typeover) mode currently active?
    (b) What is the current cursor position?
    (c) What is the name of the document being edited? On which disk drive is it located?
    (d) Which editing commands are available from this screen?
    (e) What is the approximate right margin?
    (f) Does this word processor use onscreen formatting or off-screen formatting?
    (g) For the trivia buff: From which play was this quotation taken? Who said it to whom? What other famous piece of advice preceded this quotation?

FIGURE 3.9
Screen display of a
typical word processor.

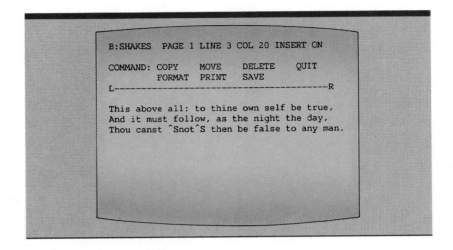

```
B:SHAKES   PAGE 1 LINE 3 COL 20 INSERT ON

COMMAND: COPY    MOVE     DELETE    QUIT
         FORMAT  PRINT    SAVE
L----------------------------------------R

This above all: to thine own self be true,
And it must follow, as the night the day,
Thou canst ^Snot^S then be false to any man.
```

2. Prepare a one-page memo (approximately 250 words) from student to instructor detailing your background; include any previous knowledge of computers you may have, prior computer courses you have taken, your objectives for the course, and so on. Also, indicate whether you own a PC, whether you have access to one at work, and/or whether you are considering purchase. Include any other information about yourself and/or your computer-related background. Your one page of text should consist of at least two paragraphs. After you have created your memo, print it and submit it to your instructor.

3. Use a computer magazine to obtain price information for an IBM or IBM-compatible computer. Decide on a common configuration for the class so that price comparisons will be meaningful (for example, an IBM Personal System/2 Model 30, with one $3\frac{1}{2}$-inch floppy drive and one 20Mb hard drive, 640Kb RAM, correspondence-quality printer, monochrome monitor, required cables and cards, box of ten $3\frac{1}{2}$-inch disks, box of paper, and a surge protector). Decide in class on a common word processing program and obtain price information for that as well. Try to avoid a bundled price so that class comparisons can be made more easily. Present your results in memo form (from student to instructor).

4. Certain capabilities are basic to the operation of any word processor. Accordingly, answer the following with respect to the word processing program available to you:
   (a) How do you toggle between the insertion and replacement modes?
   (b) Is there on- or offscreen formatting?
   (c) How do you position the cursor at the beginning of a document? at the end of a document?

(d) How do you save a document? retrieve a document?

(e) Is a backup copy of a document automatically created with every save operation?

(f) How do you delete a character? A word? A line?

5. Use your word processor to create a document containing either (or both) of the paragraphs below. Use standard defaults, for example, margins of 1 and 65, single spacing, and right justification. When you are finished with the initial version, experiment with reformatting as follows: (a) Change the margins to 20 and 60. (b) Double-space. (c) Eliminate right justification.

> From the Declaration of Independence, "...We hold these truths to be self-evident: That all men are created equal; that they are endowed by their Creator with certain unalienable rights; that among these are life, liberty, and the pursuit of happiness. That, to secure these rights, governments are instituted among men, deriving their just powers from the consent of the governed; that, whenever any form of government becomes destructive of these ends, it is the right of the people to alter or to abolish it, and to institute a new government, laying its foundation on such principles, and organizing its powers in such form, as to them shall seem most likely to effect their safety and happiness..."

> According to one IBM ad, "If technology and productivity in other industries had progressed at the same rate as computer technology, an around-the-world airline flight would take 24 minutes, and a standard size car would get 550 miles per gallon." The ad goes on to say that if the cost of other items had gone down the way computing costs have, you would be able to buy sirloin steak for 9 cents a pound, a good suit for $6.49, a four-bedroom house for $3500, a standard size car for $200, and an around-the-world airline ticket for $3.00.

6. A typical double-spaced typed page holds approximately 200 words or 1000 characters. The standard file cabinet contains 5 drawers, each 20 inches deep. There are approximately 100 typed sheets per linear inch.

(a) How many typed pages can fit on a standard (360Kb) floppy disk?

(b) Approximately how many sheets of typing paper can fit into a filing cabinet? Approximately how many characters? Can an entire filing cabinet be contained on a single hard drive of 20 Mb?

7. What is the difference between:

(a) The insertion and replacement modes?

(b) Deleting a character as opposed to replacing the character with a blank (space)?

(c) Right justification on and off?

(d) Displaying or not displaying help information?

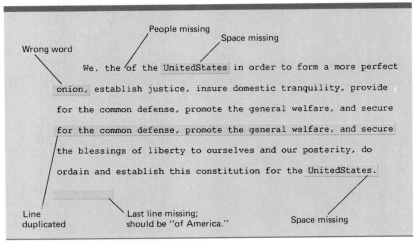

FIGURE 3.10   Screen display for exercise 7.

(e) Reformatting a paragraph with the cursor positioned at the beginning of the paragraph and in the middle of the paragraph?

(f) Deleting a word right or a word left?

(g) Pressing the enter key at the end of every line rather than every paragraph?

8. (a) What problems would you encounter if you pressed the return key at the end of every line when entering a paragraph of text?

(b) What word processing feature makes it unnecessary to enter a return at the end of every line, enabling you to enter it once at the end of the paragraph?

(c) How does your word processor indicate the presence of a carriage return?

(d) How would you go about reformatting a paragraph which had been created with a carriage return at the end of every line?

9. Figure 3.10 shows an initial attempt at re-creating the preamble to the United States Constitution. Enter Figure 3.10 *as is* on your word processor, then use the word processor to obtain a corrected version.

10. Use your word processor to prepare a bibliography (consisting of at least five sources) for a research paper on any subject of interest to you. This assignment will give you the opportunity to experiment with the underlining and indentation features of your word processor, as well as communicate something about yourself to the instructor.

GAINING PROFICIENCY

CHAPTER OBJECTIVES

After reading this chapter, you should be able to:

1. Use block commands to move and/or copy a block of text, and to read from or write to an external file.

2. Use the search-and-replace facility of a word processor; list at least three options associated with this command.

3. Distinguish between the various save operations available with a word processor.

4. Describe the default page layout of your word processor.

5. Describe the use of a dictionary and thesaurus in conjunction with a word processor.

6. Define the following terms: field, record, and file.

7. Describe what is meant by a mail merge operation; list at least three potential applications.

Overview

The previous chapter introduced the concept of word processing and showed how the availability of this tool greatly facilitates the task of writing. This chapter continues the discussion by presenting additional features commonly found in a word processor, namely, the search-and-replace command, as well as various block operations to move or copy text from one place in a document to another. As in the previous chapter, the discussion is generic. However, you are again directed to a Hands-On-Exercise, which calls for you to practice these concepts on the computer using the word processing program available to you.

The chapter also presents some of the more creative aspects associated with word processing. We present the concept of a *mail merge operation*, in which a form letter (prepared with the aid of a word processor) is combined with a set of names and addresses to produce a series of individual letters. We illustrate the dictionary and thesaurus capabilities common in today's generation of word processors, and we discuss the more esoteric concept of a syntax checker or style analyzer program. We also present a list of suggestions to help you use any word processor more effectively.

The Corporate Profile focuses on WordPerfect Corporation, the developer of the WordPerfect word processing program, and an acknowledged leader in today's highly competitive word processing market.

Block Operations

Block operations are the "cut and paste" component of word processing. They allow you to take a block of text from one place in a document, pick it up (cut), and move it somewhere else (paste). The block can be as large as you wish, and may consist of a word (or words), a sentence (or group of sentences), a paragraph (or group of paragraphs), or even an entire document.

Several different types of block operations are possible. The **copy operation** takes the designated block and duplicates it in a second place within the document. When the copy operation has been completed, the block exists in *two* different places within the document. The **move operation** is the true "cut and paste." After a move has been completed the block is no longer in its original location; instead, it occupies a new position in the document. The difference between a move and a copy is shown in Figure 4.1.

Figure 4.1a contains the original document, consisting of Murphy's four laws of project management. Figure 4.1b illustrates the

FIGURE 4.1
Move and copy operations: (a) the original document; (b) the move operation; (c) the copy operation. (*Source: Murphy's Laws on Technology*, Harvey Hunter and Co., Inc.)

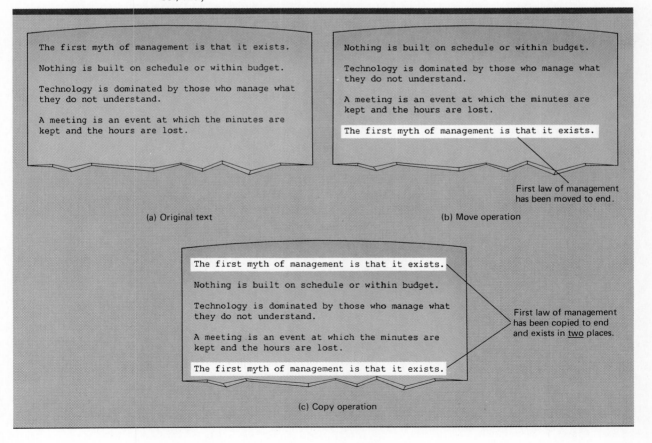

The first myth of management is that it exists.

Nothing is built on schedule or within budget.

Technology is dominated by those who manage what they do not understand.

A meeting is an event at which the minutes are kept and the hours are lost.

(a) Original text

Nothing is built on schedule or within budget.

Technology is dominated by those who manage what they do not understand.

A meeting is an event at which the minutes are kept and the hours are lost.

The first myth of management is that it exists.

First law of management has been moved to end.

(b) Move operation

The first myth of management is that it exists.

Nothing is built on schedule or within budget.

Technology is dominated by those who manage what they do not understand.

A meeting is an event at which the minutes are kept and the hours are lost.

The first myth of management is that it exists.

First law of management has been copied to end and exists in <u>two</u> places.

(c) Copy operation

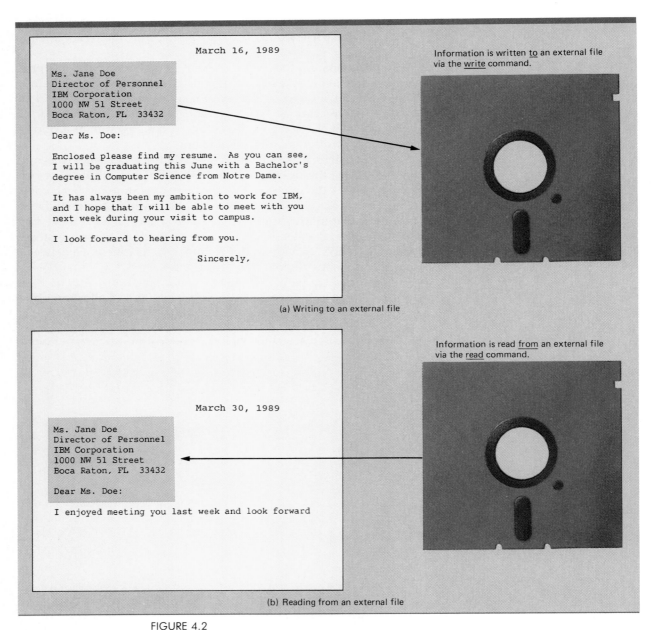

March 16, 1989

Ms. Jane Doe
Director of Personnel
IBM Corporation
1000 NW 51 Street
Boca Raton, FL 33432

Dear Ms. Doe:

Enclosed please find my resume. As you can see,
I will be graduating this June with a Bachelor's
degree in Computer Science from Notre Dame.

It has always been my ambition to work for IBM,
and I hope that I will be able to meet with you
next week during your visit to campus.

I look forward to hearing from you.

Sincerely,

(a) Writing to an external file

Information is written <u>to</u> an external file
via the <u>write</u> command.

March 30, 1989

Ms. Jane Doe
Director of Personnel
IBM Corporation
1000 NW 51 Street
Boca Raton, FL 33432

Dear Ms. Doe:

I enjoyed meeting you last week and look forward

(b) Reading from an external file

Information is read <u>from</u> an external file
via the <u>read</u> command.

FIGURE 4.2
Operations with an external file.
(*a*) Writing to an external file.
(*b*) Reading from an external file.

move operation, in which the first law, "The first myth of management is that it exists," has been moved to the end of the document. Figure 4.1*c* depicts the copy operation in that the first law exists in two places, at the beginning and end of the document.

Block operations may also involve an *external* document. You can *write* the designated block to a new file or *read* an external file into the current document. The **write operation** is analogous to a copy, except that the block of text is copied to a file of its own (that is, a separate file that is created and stored on disk). The **read operation** allows you to take an existing file and incorporate it into the document currently being edited.

Figure 4.2 illustrates how the read and write operations can be extremely useful. A letter is created in Figure 4.2*a*, with the name, address, and salutation saved to an external file using the **write** command. Figure 4.2*b* depicts the start of a second document which is written a week later. The opening information is copied into the second document via a **read** command, which saves time as well as ensures accuracy.

Search and Replace

The **search-and-replace** (or find-and-replace) function lets you scan a document for a particular character string and replace it with another. A **character string** is a combination of letters, numbers, and/or other symbols which are deemed significant. It may be a single word, a group of words, a part of a word, a number, and so on.

The search-and-replace operation normally begins at the current cursor location and proceeds forward in the document until it finds the first occurrence of the designated string. You can, however, specify one or more options to alter the normal operation of this command. Among them:

Global replacement: This option instructs the word processor to find all occurrences of the designated character string throughout the document. If global (or replace all) is not specified, only the first occurrence will be found.

Automatic replacement: All changes are made automatically, that is, without a confirming response from the user. This option can be dangerous, however, because some unintentional changes may result. For example, changing "there" to "their" will also change "therefore" to "theirfore."

Selective replacement: The word processor will prompt you for a confirming response (Y/N) prior to making each change—the opposite of automatic replacement.

Whole word replacement: Makes the change for whole words only. If this option is specified, changing "there" to "their" will *not* change "therefore" to "theirfore."

Ignore case: This option performs the change regardless of whether upper- or lowercase letters are found.

Backward search: The word processor searches toward the top of the document, moving the cursor in that direction rather than moving toward the end of the document.

```
    In 1946 ENIAC was the scientific marvel of the day.  It
weighed 30 tons, stood two stories high, covered 1500 square
feet, and contained 18,000 vacuum tubes.  Its price was a modest
$486,840 in 1946 dollars.  ENIAC consisted of forty panels, each
two feet wide and four feet deep, and had a storage capacity of
700 bits in RAM.
```
Text to be replaced
```
    Unfortunately vacuum tubes, like light bulbs, have the
exasperating tendency to burn out at the wrong time which caused
ENIAC to constantly break down.  The Army finally stationed a
platoon of soldiers manning baskets filled with replacement tubes
around the computer.  This strategy didn't work as intended
because the engineers could never tell which of the 18,000 tubes
burned out.
```

(a) Before replacement

```
    In 1946 ENIAC was the scientific marvel of the day.  It
weighed 30 tons, stood two stories high, covered 1500 square
feet, and contained eighteen thousand vacuum tubes.  Its price was a modest
$486,840 in 1946 dollars.  ENIAC consisted of forty panels, each
two feet wide and four feet deep, and had a storage capacity of
700 bits in RAM.
```
Text has been replaced
```
    Unfortunately vacuum tubes, like light bulbs, have the
exasperating tendency to burn out at the wrong time which caused
ENIAC to constantly break down.  The Army finally stationed a
platoon of soldiers manning baskets filled with replacement tubes
around the computer.  This strategy didn't work as intended
because the engineers could never tell which of the eighteen thousand tubes
burned out.
```

(b) After replacement

FIGURE 4.3
Search-and-replace operation.
(a) Before replacement. (b) After replacement.

The search-and-replace operation is illustrated in Figure 4.3, in which all occurrences of "18,000" in Figure 4.3a have been replaced by "eighteen thousand" in Figure 4.3b. To accomplish this substitution the search-and-replace function requires three pieces of information:

1. The character string to find ("18,000")

2. The replacement string ("eighteen thousand")

3. Additional options to govern the operation (global)

Note, also, that the two character strings need *not* be the same length, although reformatting may be required (depending on the word processor in use) after the replacement has taken place.

Another use for a search-and-replace operation is a consistent change in phraseology. You could, for example, replace all instances of "Information Systems" with "Information Services." You can also use the command to provide a shortcut in data entry for a consistently used phrase, for example, entering "USA" and later changing it to "United States of America."

In addition to the search-and-replace command, all word processors also offer a simple search (or find) operation to position the

ENIAC, an early general-purpose electronic calculator. Its co-inventors, J. Presper Eckert, Jr., and John W. Mauchly, are in the foreground.

cursor at the first occurrence of the designated character string. A find operation is simply the first half of a complete search-and-replace operation, and is a convenient way to move to a particular place in a document.

Save Operations

A **save operation** copies the document currently being edited (the document in RAM) to a permanent storage medium, that is, to disk. Note well that if the document you are editing already exists on disk, the new version replaces the existing version and the latter disappears (or is saved as a backup file with a different extension, depending on the word processor in use). In addition, most word processors provide for three distinct types of save operation, each slightly different, but each with its own rationale. These are:

Save and continue editing: Saves what has been done so far and returns to the editing mode. Normally, you should save a document periodically so that in the event of a power interruption or other problem, only the last increment of your work is lost.

Save and quit: Saves the document and returns to the opening screen of the word processor, to a new document, or to DOS.

"Think back ... which keys did you press?"

Quit without saving: Exits the word processor and returns to the opening screen or operating system *without* saving any changes. This is extremely useful if you made several mistakes and consequently do not wish to save the revised version. [Most current word processors have an **undo (or undelete) command,** which reverses the effects of the last command given, and which is less extreme than quitting a document altogether.]

HANDS-ON EXERCISE 1: ADDITIONAL CAPABILITIES

OBJECTIVE: Experiment with different block operations, the search-and-replace function, and various save commands. Use the following text from the Ideas and Trends section of *Lotus Magazine*, July 1987, page 10.

Microprocessors are often misleadingly described with a single parameter, such as 8-bit, 16-bit, or 32-bit. In fact, you need at least four measurements to characterize a microprocessor: (1) external data-bus width, (2) arithmetic/logical unit width, (3) register width, and (4) address-bus width.

For each parameter, the general rule is "the bigger, the better." Increase any one of these numbers, and throughput, measured in mips (million instructions per second), increases, often with non-linear bonuses. An inevitable corollary is "the bigger, the more expensive."

Step 1: Boot the System and Load Your Word Processor

Boot the system and load your word processor as was done in the previous chapter. Remember to place your program disk in drive A and a formatted data disk in drive B.

Step 2: Create the Document

Enter the paragraphs shown at the top of the exercise, which discuss characteristics of microprocessors. At the end of each paragraph, execute the save and resume editing command.

Step 3: Moving Text

Moving a block of text from one place in a document to another requires you to (1) identify the beginning of the text to be moved, (2) identify the end of the block, (3) move the cursor to the new position, and (4) execute the move command itself.

By way of illustration, we will take the first paragraph in the document just created and place it at the end of the document. Follow these steps:

1. Indicate the beginng of the text to be moved by positioning the cursor at the first character of the first paragraph (the M in "Microprocessors"). Invoke the command to mark this position.

2. Position the cursor at the last character in the block to be moved (the period following the word "width"). Some word processors (for example, WordStar) require you to explictly enter another command to mark the end of the block, whereas others (for example, WordPerfect) implicitly assume that the cursor marks the end of the block. In any event, the first paragraph should be highlighted. (Should this not be true, try adjusting the brightness and/or contrast knobs on your monitor.)

3. Move the cursor to where the block (that is, the first paragraph) is supposed to go: after the second paragraph.

4. Execute the move command, after which the first paragraph should now be in its new position. Note, however, that depending on how you marked the block it may be necessary to add (or delete) blank lines before and/or after the paragraph that was moved.

Step 4: Other Block Operations

Once a block has been marked, that is, the beginning and ending positions have been indicated, any of a number of other block operations may also be accomplished. For example, you can move the cursor to the beginning of the document, execute the copy command, and observe that the paragraph beginning "Microprocessors are often" now appears in two places in the document. Experiment also with both the command to delete the highlighted block of text and the command to write it to an external file.

Step 5: Search-and-Replace Operations

If you copied the text exactly as it appeared in step 2, the acronym "mips" was entered in lowercase letters. Use the search-and-replace operation of your word processor to change "mips" to "MIPS."

This change could also have been accomplished with the insertion and/or replacement operations. The advantage of the search-and-replace function, however, is that it will locate the character string for you; the other approach requires you to search the document yourself. Most word processors provide several different means of accomplishing the same objective, and the technique you use depends entirely on your personal preference.

Step 6: Exit the Word Processor

Enter the save and quit command to return to the opening screen of your word processor, then complete the steps to return to the operating system.

Page Design

In order for output to appear properly on a printed page, the word processor must account for the size of the left and right margins, the distance from the top and bottom of a page to where text begins and ends, the physical dimensions of the page, the type size, and so on. Although all word processors build in **defaults** (preset values) for these parameters to free you from such concerns, an understanding of basic page layout is essential when you vary from the standard page and use other forms, for example, envelopes, odd-sized pages, or mailing labels.

Figure 4.4 shows a set of typical default values as they might exist in a word processor. The values assume the standard page size of $8\frac{1}{2} \times 11$ inches, and a printer which produces 6 lines per (vertical) inch and 10 characters per (horizontal) inch. It is easy to verify that the physical dimensions of the page correspond to the defaults established by the word processor.

The standard page length of 11 inches, in conjunction with the normal 6 lines of print per inch, provides a total of 66 lines to the page, all of which have to be accounted for by the word processor. As can be seen from Figure 4.4, 3 lines are allocated for the top margin and 8 for the bottom margin, leaving a total of 55 lines for text [66 − (3 + 8)].

In similar fashion, a page width of $8\frac{1}{2}$ inches together with horizontal spacing of 10 characters to the inch allows for 85 characters per line. Figure 4.4 implies that the word processor allocated 8 and 12 spaces for the left and right margin, respectively, leaving 65 positions for the text area [85 − (8 + 12)].

FIGURE 4.4
Typical page format.

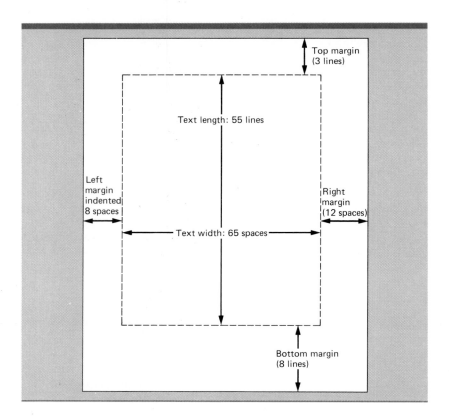

As already indicated, you will probably not need to alter the defaults of your word processor unless you are working with special (that is, nonstandard) forms. Should this occur, your word processor will either provide a page design menu which prompts you for information, or expect that you know the necessary commands to insert within a document.

Page Breaks

A word processor will break to a new page automatically when the last line of available text is reached (line 55 with standard defaults). This can prove awkward, as in the case of a table, when the entire table should appear on the same page. There are also times when a new page is desired, even if the previous page did not end on line 55. Even something as simple as automatic page numbering is not always desired, as in the case of a one-page letter.

To accommodate these and other problems, most word processors provide a series of pagination commands, such as those listed:

PAGE BREAK   Causes the next line to begin a new page.

CONDITIONAL PAGE ⟨nn⟩   Causes the next line to begin a new page if ⟨nn⟩ lines do not remain on the current page.

INCLUDE/OMIT PAGE NUMBERS   Include (or omit) page numbers, with the default varying from one word processor to the next. (Additional commands are usually available to control the location of the page numbers, for example, whether they should appear at the top or bottom of the page.)

PAGE NUMBER ⟨nn⟩   Page numbering is to begin on this page with the value ⟨nn⟩.

As you gain sophistication you will appreciate the utility of these and other page design commands. We suggest that you pause and review how these capabilities are implemented in the program you are using.

Sending Form Letters

You have undoubtedly been on the receiving end of more **form letters** than you care to remember. Now you will be able to use the technology of word processing to create form letters of your own. For example, when you look for a job upon graduation, you will send essentially the same letter to many different people. A word processor with a mail merge capability will simplify the task.

A **mail merge operation** takes the tedium out of sending form letters, as it creates the same letter many times, changing only the addressee's name and address (and other information, as appropriate) from letter to letter. The set of names and addresses is called a **file**, and the name and address of a particular individual constitute a **record**. There are many records but only one file; that is, there are as many records in the file as there are people who will receive the letter.

Each individual's record contains several pieces of data, or **fields**, for example, the person's name and address. Every record in the file contains the same fields in the same order, but the value of each field varies from record to record. The terms "field," "record," and "file" are depicted in Figure 4.5. In this example, there are two fields in each record, Name and Address, and there are three records in the file. It is of course possible to further subdivide name and/or

FIGURE 4.5   Field, record, file hierarchy.

	Name Field	Address Field
Record 1	Mr. Alan Moldof	2770 NW 115 Terrace Coral Springs FL 33065
Record 2	Mr. David Grand	1380 Veteran Avenue Los Angeles, CA 90024
Record 3	Ms. Marion Milgrom	63-38 77 Place Middle Village NY 11379

address into additional fields; for example, address could be sub-divided into four fields: street, city, state, and zip code. The precise form of the **record layout,** that is, the arrangement of fields within a record, depends on the requirements of the application.

The concept of a mail merge operation is illustrated in the context of the admissions process to a university. In our example, the chairperson of the Computer Information Systems Department wishes to send congratulatory letters to those students who have been accepted into the program. He drafts a single letter of acceptance and wants it mailed to every student.

In order for the process to work the chairperson must have access to the file of names and addresses of the admitted students. The mail merge operation will combine this file with the chairperson's form letter and produce a series of individual letters as shown in Figure 4.6. Figure 4.6*a* shows the form letter, Figure 4.6*b* shows the data file, and Figure 4.6*c* shows the merged letters.

The form letter of Figure 4.6*a* contains four embedded commands that relate specifically to the mail merge operation. Our example follows the convention of MicroPro's MailMerge, which uses a period (dot) in column 1 to indicate the special command. (Other programs avoid the use of embedded commands, prompting you instead for the primary file, which contains the form letter, and the secondary file, which contains the data.)

The first embedded command, .pa, causes each letter to begin on a new page; the second command ,.op, suppresses (omits) page numbers. Remember, it makes no sense for the second student to see "page 2" on the bottom of his or her letter. The third dot com-

FIGURE 4.6
Mail merge operation: (*a*) form letter, (*b*) data file, (*c*) merged letters.

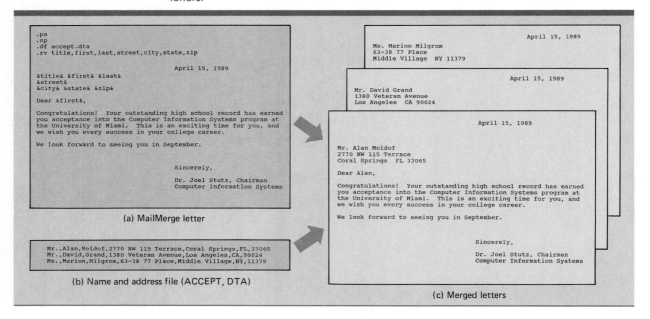

(a) MailMerge letter

(b) Name and address file (ACCEPT, DTA)

(c) Merged letters

TECHNOLOGY, McDONALD'S COLLIDE AS STUDENTS BEST BURGER BONANZA

McDonald's Restaurants, whose hamburgers have taken their place along with Mom and apple pie as a piece of Americana, was recently confronted by a computer and 26 students from the California Institute of Technology (Cal-Tech) following another American tradition—free enterprise.

It started when 187 McDonald's in five counties of Southern California held a sweepstakes during March. The $40,000 worth of prizes included a new sports car, a year's free groceries, a station wagon and free McDonald's coupons.

Entrants were required only to be a resident of one of the five counties and fill out either an entry blank or a three-by-five piece of paper with their name and address. No purchase was required and there was no limit to the number of times each person could enter.

The Cal Tech students, headed by senior John Denker, realized these rules presented them with an opportunity to turn their DP training to a money-making advantage.

The student's used the school's computer to print out 1.2 million entry blanks with their names on them. Denker said enough paper was used to cover "two and one half football fields or [reach] higher than a three-story building."

The program they wrote consisted of four simple lines of FORTRAN. Although Denker admitted it probably would have been more practical to have a regular printer do the entry blanks, the students had ready access to the computer and it was faster.

On the final day of the contest the students went to 90 McDonald's in the specified counties and started stuffing the entry boxes. Their computerized entries made up over one-third of the 3.4 million total number of entries.

McDonald's Not Pleased

McDonald's was not delighted with the student's high level of participation in the sweepstakes. Although Denker claimed their entries are legally valid, Ron Lopaty, president of the McDonald's Operator's Association of Southern California, said he feels "the students acted in complete contradiction to the American standards of fair play and sportsmanship."

The contest's purpose, he said, was "to give customers an opportunity, in a time of economic stress, to win free groceries and transportation. So you can understand our displeasure when their chances of winning were greatly reduced by the Cal Tech students using an unfair advantage of computerized entry blanks."

Part of the public agreed with him in letters and phone calls to both McDonald's and Cal Tech. The state's attorney general even received a petition signed by over two dozen Southern California residents which said "the use of equipment at a state or federally funded college, university or institution for the pursuit of personal interest, not to mention cheating American consumers, is an absolute outrage.

As for Cal Tech, it has taken no position on the issue, claiming it was the students' private endeavor.

Lopaty said McDonald's has agreed "to honor as 100% valid all the Cal Tech students' 1.2 million computerized entries" and, in fairness to the other entrants, will hold a second drawing in which all the computerized entries will be excluded and duplicate prizes of any won by the students will be awarded again.

For the students, the McDonald's caper, as they call the affair, has paid off. They have already been notified they've won a Datsun 710 station wagon, a year's free supply of groceries and innumerable $5 gift certificates.

"Part of the loot will be used to finance improvements in Page House, our residence here at Cal Tech," Denker said, "The rest will be donated to charity."

Denker was dismayed at the restaurant chain's reaction to the incident, saying he doesn't feel they violated American standards of fair play.

"Just because it is unexpected doesn't mean it's unfair," he explained. "We feel that by accepting the challenge to enter as often as you wish, we have acted in accordance with the best ideals of American sportsmanship."

There are those who agree with him, and Cal Tech garnered a prize of its own from one of them. The Burger King chain of restaurants, McDonald's arch rival, has awarded $3,000 to the school to set up a "John Denker Scholarship" in honor of the student who masterminded the scheme.

Source: Computerworld, June 4, 1975.

Authors' Comments:
Although the contest entries were not generated with the aid of a word processor, the Cal Tech prank illustrates the power of the computer as a letter writer. Hats off to Burger King for establishing the "John Denker Scholarship."

mand, .df, defines the file (ACCEPT.DTA in the example) that contains the set of names and addresses (Figure 4.6*b*). Finally, the .rv command is a variable definition statement that assigns names to the variables (fields) in the same order as they appear in the data file. This in turn allows the data in each field to be referenced by the assigned field name.

Observe carefully that each record in the data file of Figure 4.6*b* contains the student's title (Mr., Ms., and so on), first name, last name, street, city, state, and zip code, and that these fields are separated by commas. Observe also the correspondence between the data in Figure 4.6*b* and the variable definition in Figure 4.6*a*.

Now return to the letter itself, in Figure 4.6*a*, and note the ampersands which enclose several words. This is the mail merge program's way of indicating that a value is to be taken from a data file in lieu of printing the word as it appears. In other words, whenever the mail merge program encounters a variable name (a field beginning and ending with an ampersand), it will obtain the value for that variable from the data file.

Execution of the mail merge program will prepare the letters one at a time, with each letter containing a different name and address and beginning on a new page, until the file of names and addresses is exhausted.

The Electronic Dictionary

Only a few short years ago, the thought of using a computer to check everyday writing for spelling was the stuff of science fiction. Today, dictionaries are an integral part of any full-featured word processor, and there is absolutely no reason not to use one. (See the box entitled, "How Well Do You Spell?") To be practical, however, the use of a dictionary (and/or a companion thesaurus), requires the availability of a hard disk as well as memory beyond the 256Kb limit.

A **spelling checker** or **dictionary program** consists of a disk-based dictionary (containing the bulk of the words), an **auxiliary dictionary** (containing words not found in the regular dictionary and/or specialized terms, all of which are entered by the user), and a comparison program to process words in the user-supplied document against those in the dictionary. Any mismatches are considered misspellings and flagged on the screen. (Since the dictionary is not all-inclusive however, a flagged entry may not be an error at all.)

Dictionary programs may function in a variety of modes. Borland's Turbo Lightning (a stand-alone program which can be used with virtually any word processor) will catch mistakes immediately as they are entered at the keyboard. Although this capability appears absolutely fantastic the first time you see it, most individuals prefer to check spelling only after the entire document has been entered.

"YOU MENE I'VE BIN SPENDING THIS WHOL TERM WITH A DEFEKTIV REEDING MACHIN?"

HOW WELL DO YOU SPELL?

If you remain unconvinced about the benefit of a dictionary, take this simple test proposed by Steve Ditlea in the March 1987 issue of *Personal Computing*. Consider the following list of commonly misspelled words, and circle those spelled incorrectly.

Embarrass	Mediterranean
Accommodate	Recommend
Supersede	Omission
Precede	Perceive
Susceptible	

All nine words are spelled correctly, proving that the English language isn't easy. Note, too, that if you have a dictionary available with your word processor, you would be able to verify the spellings of all nine words in less than a minute.

Should you need further convincing about the relative worth of a dictionary program, remember that the human eye is generally uncritical and sees what it wants or expects to see. For example, read the sentence in the box, once and only once, counting the number of times the letter f appears in the sentence.

> Finished files are the result of years of scientific study combined with the experience of years.

There are six f's in the sentence, and if you got all six you are good. The average person spots only three, and you can feel reasonably proud if you got four or five. Our point in this seemingly trivial example is that our eyes are less discriminating than we would like to believe, allowing misspellings and simple typos to go unnoticed.

Authors' Comments:
What more can we say about the use of dictionary programs? Nothing detracts more from a term paper or business letter than a misspelling, a situation which is so easy to avoid.

Regardless of how you use the dictionary, any mismatch presents you with several choices, for example, to correct the word, to ignore the misspelling, or to add it to the auxiliary dictionary. Most programs will also supply you with a list of suggestions to simplify the correction process. Note, too, that any dictionary program is only as good as the dictionary on which it is based, and that programs vary widely in terms of implementation.

The Microlytics Word Finder program is illustrated in conjunction with Figures 4.7 and 4.8. Figure 4.8*a* brings up the first mistake "errrors," for which the program suggests three alternatives. You need only enter a "1" to select "errors," after which the substitution is made automatically in the existing document. Figure 4.8*b* flags "mispellings," but offers only one alternative.

Finally, Figure 4.8*c* flags "WordStar," which is spelled correctly, yet we cannot blame the dictionary for not knowing the specialized term. The appropriate choice is to add "WordStar" to the personal (auxiliary) dictionary so that it will not be flagged in future sessions. No correction is required.

One final point is that *no dictionary will flag properly spelled words which are used incorrectly.* In other words, a dictionary does not check for grammatical usage; for example, it cannot notice that "Two bee or knot too Bea" is not what it was meant to be.

FIGURE 4.7   Input to spelling checker program.

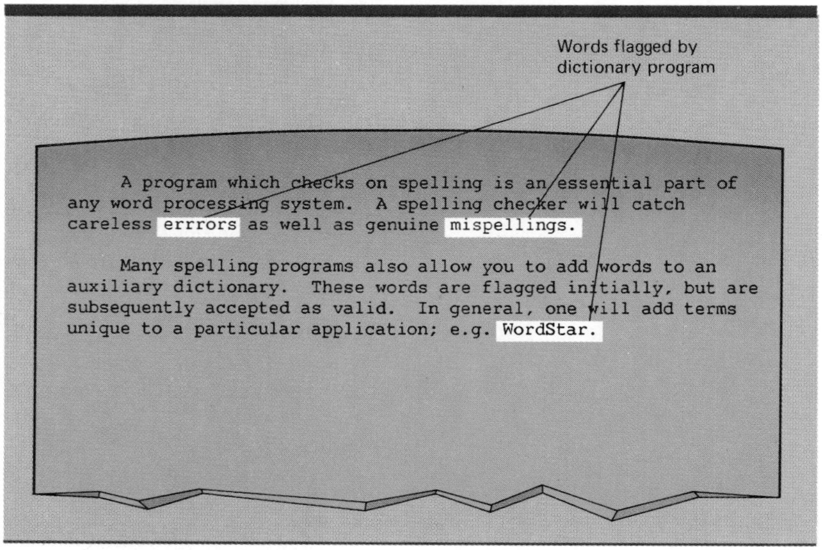

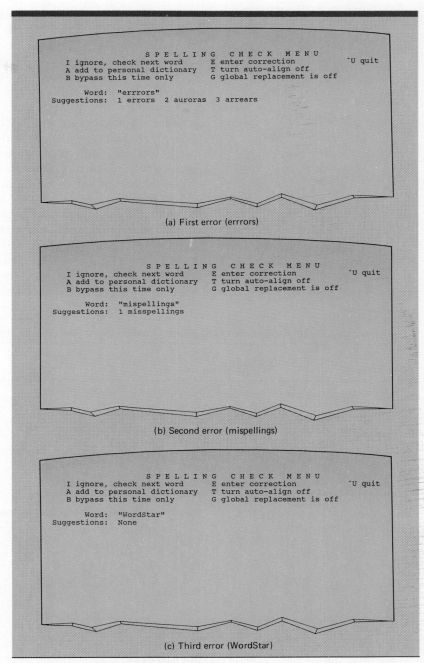

(a) First error (errrors)

(b) Second error (mispellings)

(c) Third error (WordStar)

FIGURE 4.8   Use of a dictionary. (a) First error (errrors). (b) Second error (mispellings). (c) Third error (WordStar).

The Electronic Thesaurus[1]

Mark Twain once said that the difference between the almost-right word and the right word is the difference between a lightning bug and lightning. The availability of several independent **thesaurus** programs within the last two years make it no longer a question of whether to use a thesaurus, but which one to pick. Even that decision is apt to be made for you, as today's full featured word processors will all include a thesaurus program (see Table 4.1). In any event the primary advantage of a thesaurus (manual or electronic) is that it helps you avoid repetition and polishes your writing accordingly. Use of a thesaurus program is both fun and educational and, to our way of thinking, is as essential as a dictionary.

A thesaurus program consists of an index file (containing root words), a dictionary file (with the synonym collection), and the program itself, which is **memory-resident;** that is, the thesaurus is loaded into memory before the word processor and remains there until it is called by a predefined keystroke combination. Invoking the the-

TABLE 4.1

Dictionary and Thesaurus Programs Used with Common Word Processing Programs

Word Processor	Dictionary Source	Dictionary Size	Thesaurus	Number of Synonyms
Multimate Advantage	*Webster's Ninth New Collegiate Dictionary*	110,000	*Miriam-Webster Thesaurus* (Proximity, Inc.)	470,000
Microsoft Word	Proprietary	80,000	Word Finder (Microlytics, Inc)	220,000
WordStar	*American Heritage Dictionary*	87,000	Word Finder (Microlytics, Inc)	220,000
WordPerfect	Proprietary	115,000+	Own	180,000

FIGURE 4.9
Input to thesaurus program.

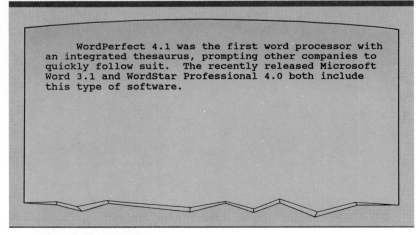

> WordPerfect 4.1 was the first word processor with an integrated thesaurus, prompting other companies to quickly follow suit. The recently released Microsoft Word 3.1 and WordStar Professional 4.0 both include this type of software.

[1]Steven Ditlea, "How Many Ways Can You Say Thesaurus," *Personal Computing*, May 1987; and Rubin Rabinovitz, "A Way with Words," *PC Magazine*, July 1987.

saurus causes it to search its dictionary and return a list of synonyms for the word at the current cursor position. Simply choose the word you want and the substitution is handled automatically.

Figures 4.9 and 4.10 illustrate the use of Microlytics' Word Finder program. Input to the thesauruas is shown in Figure 4.9, with three

FIGURE 4.10
Use of a thesaurus program.

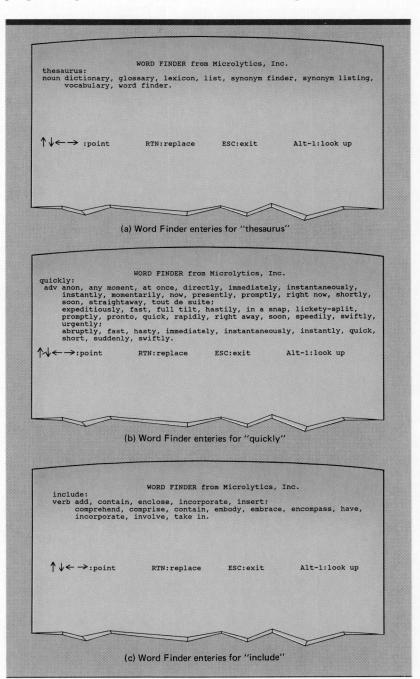

WORD FINDER from Microlytics, Inc.
thesaurus:
noun dictionary, glossary, lexicon, list, synonym finder, synonym listing,
     vocabulary, word finder.

↑↓←→ :point   RTN:replace   ESC:exit   Alt-1:look up

(a) Word Finder enteries for "thesaurus"

WORD FINDER from Microlytics, Inc.
quickly:
 adv anon, any moment, at once, directly, immediately, instantaneously,
     instantly, momentarily, now, presently, promptly, right now, shortly,
     soon, straightaway, tout de suite;
     expeditiously, fast, full tilt, hastily, in a snap, lickety-split,
     promptly, pronto, quick, rapidly, right away, soon, speedily, swiftly,
     urgently;
     abruptly, fast, hasty, immediately, instantaneously, instantly, quick,
     short, suddenly, swiftly.

↑↓←→:point   RTN:replace   ESC:exit   Alt-1:look up

(b) Word Finder enteries for "quickly"

WORD FINDER from Microlytics, Inc.
include:
 verb add, contain, enclose, incorporate, insert;
     comprehend, comprise, contain, embody, embrace, encompass, have,
     incorporate, involve, take in.

↑↓← →:point   RTN:replace   ESC:exit   Alt-1:look up

(c) Word Finder enteries for "include"

sets of synonyms listed in Figure 4.10. The number of choices is impressive in each instance, and as with a dictionary, you merely point to the desired word whereupon the substitution is automatically made in the document.

Syntax Checkers[2]

A PC-based **style analyzer** or **syntax checker** is designed to improve a document by finding errors in punctuation and/or by offering suggestions on writing style. These programs go beyond the function of a dictionary, for (as previously indicated) a dictionary cannot tell when a correctly spelled word is used incorrectly. Nor can it tell when upper- or lowercase letters are used inappropriately, when ending quotes are missing, when a word is inadvertently typed twice in a row, and so on.

In essence, a style analyzer or syntax checker program compares a document to a set of stored grammatical rules and phrases, but is

FIGURE 4.11
Example of a syntax checker.
(a) Text before syntax check.
(b) Messages produced by syntax checker.

A spelling checker may not be enough! These paragraphs contain several common errors that will be discovered by Grammatik that would not be caught by a spelling checker. FOr example, Grammatik checks for improper word usage as identified by a number of writing style manuals (such as "seldom ever"). it also checks for consistent punctuation, capitalizAtion, balanced quotation marks and parentheses, and and repeated words. In addition,it can produce a list of all unique words found in your document with the number of times each was used.

Grammatik comes with a dictionary of commonly misused phrases, and includes a complete set of utilities to build, sort, and merge phrase and jargon dictionaries of your own. It will check for the presence of certain words such as jargon or sexist terms. The phrase "all men are created equal may not make it.

Wordy phrase – suggest "Several, many, some."

Space missing

Capitalization error

Redundant phrase – suggest "seldom"

Capitalization error

Capitalization error

Doubled word

Unbalanced " – suggest " "

Gender-specific term – suggest "people"

[2]Robin Raskin, "The Quest for Style," *PC Magazine*, May 27, 1986; and Barbara and Robert Lewis, "Do Style Checkers Work?" *PC World*, June 1987.

severely limited in its ability to understand content or personal writing style. Nevertheless, such programs are very good at detecting errors in capitalization and/or punctuation, the kind of errors which prove most embarrassing.

Figure 4.11 contains one example of a paragraph which was run through the Grammatik program by Aspen Software. As you look at the figure, try covering up its bottom half and see how many errors you can find in the top portion. Then compare your results to those provided by the Grammatik program.

The stylistic suggestions are based upon a phrase dictionary included with the program. Grammatik objects to "a number of" as wordy, suggesting the use of "several," "many," or "some" in its place. It finds "seldom ever" redundant, and suggests "all men are created equal" is sexist. Unlike spelling, which is right or wrong, syntax (and thus the suggestions of a syntax checker) are subjective. Substitution of one phrase for another depends entirely on the viewpoint of the author, and there may well be valid reasons for rejecting the suggestions supplied by Grammatik or other like products.

The range of errors a syntax checker can spot is shown in Figure 4.11. The program captures errors in capitalization. It notices when

"IT SAYS, 'THREE PER CENT SPLIT INFINITIVES, 8 PER CENT PASSIVE VERBS, 16 PER CENT COMPOUND-COMPLEX SENTENCES, AVERAGE SENTENCE LENGTH 26 WORDS, PAPERBACK RIGHTS $3.2 MILLION, MOVIE SALES $8.3 MILLION, TOTAL TAKE $11.5 MILLION, LESS 15 PER CENT AGENT'S FEES.'"

a new sentence does not begin with an uppercase letter (for example, "it also" at the start of sentence 4). It will catch inconsistent use of uppercase letters ("FOr" in sentence 3, or "capitalizAtion" in sentence 4). Grammatik neatly flags double usage ("and and" in sentence 4), and catches unbalanced parentheses or quotation marks (as shown in the last sentence).

*Authors' Comments:
The results of an automated syntax checker do not always improve on the original, with the Gettysburg Address serving as a prime illustration. The example here is based on Workbench, a program similar in concept to Grammatik. Incidentally, the latter program was far more lenient than Workbench and provided only six suggestions. It objected to the use of "men" twice as gender-specific, and warned "that that nation might live" contained a doubled word. It found "altogether" in "altogether fitting and proper" a commonly misused word, suggesting "wholly" in its place. Finally, it flagged the use of "rather" twice as a weak adverb.*

REWRITING LINCOLN'S GETTYSBURG ADDRESS

Four score and seven years ago our fathers brought forth on this continent, a new nation, conceived in Liberty, and dedicated to the proposition that all men are created equal.

Now we are engaged in a great civil war, testing whether that nation or any nation so conceived and so dedicated can long endure. We are met on a great battlefield of that war. We have come to dedicate a portion of that field, as a final resting place for those who here gave their lives that that nation might live. It is altogether fitting and proper that we should do this.

But, in a larger sense, we cannot dedicate—we cannot consecrate—we cannot hallow—this ground. The brave men, living and dead, who struggled here, have consecrated it far above our poor power to add or detract. The world will little note nor long remember what we say here, but it can never forget what they did here. It is for us, the living, rather to be dedicated here to the unfinished work which they who fought here have thus far so nobly advanced. It is rather for us to be here dedicated to the great task remaining before us—that from these honored dead we take increased devotion to that cause for which they gave the last full measure of devotion; that we here highly resolve that these dead shall not have died in vain; that this nation, under God, shall have a new birth of freedom; and that government of the people, by the people, for the people, shall not perish from the earth.

Workbench Analysis

Readability (years of education required): 10.8
Average sentence length: 26.7 words
Your average is very high. A good average would be 15 to 20 words.
Sentence types: simple, 10 percent; complex, 40 percent. Your document contains many more complex sentences than is common for this type of text. One way to improve this text would be to rephrase the most important ideas in simple sentences.
Passive verb phrases: 13 percent

Revised Version

Eighty-seven years ago, our grandfathers created a free nation here. They based it on the idea that everybody is created equal. We are now fighting a civil war to see if this or any similar nation can survive. On this battlefield we are dedicating a cemetery to those who died for their country. It is only right. But in another sense, the task is impossible, because brave men, living and dead, dedicated this place better than we can.

Hardly anyone will notice or remember what we say here, but nobody can forget what those men did. We should continue the work they began, and make sure they did not die in vain. With God's help, we will have freedom again, so that the people's government will endure.

Source: Natalie Angier, "Bell's Lettres," *Discover Magazine,* July 1981, page 79. Reprinted by permission of Time, Inc.

Tips for Writing

If a blank screen and flashing cursor produce terror rather than inspiration, you are not alone, as evidenced by this quote from John Updike in *The New York Times*, "When I turn on the word processor, I feel I'm wasting electricity; with the pencil, I'm only wasting my own time." There is a definite art to writing, regardless of whether you use a yellow pad, typewriter, or word processor. What follows next is a collection of tips to get you up and running with a word processor. A few of the suggestions are our own, but much of the material was extracted from two excellent articles.[3]

Use outlines: In all likelihood you develop an outline prior to writing a term paper. When using a word processor, you should continue this process; namely, develop an outline before beginning the paper. This will help you organize your thoughts and produce a better-organized finished product. (Many word processors have an outlining feature to help you automate the process.)

Learn to type: The ultimate limitation of any word processor is the speed at which you enter data, hence the ability to type quickly is invaluable. Learning how to type (no matter what your age) is far from an insurmountable problem. One of the authors is self-taught and went from zero to 35 words per minute (wpm) in a month, practicing an hour a day. A month after that he was clocked at a steady 50 to 60 wpm, although he still has to look at the numbers. The availability of programs such as Typing Tutor III makes the task easier and more enjoyable. If you do any significant amount of writing at all, the investment will pay off many times.

Write now, edit later: A natural impulse is to use the skills of your word processor to continually edit the few paragraphs you've written. Resist, for if you edit constantly, chances are you will end a two-hour session having produced all of a page (sometimes less). Perfection doesn't exist and more often than not, overediting will drain the life out of what you are writing.

We suggest that you put down anything that pops into your head, as quickly as possible. One idea leads to another and your writer's block will be gone before you know it. Hemingway had his own method. He always left a writing session incomplete, with "one last thought remaining." This gave him a starting point for his next session, and he went on from there.

Delete with caution: You work too hard developing your thoughts to see them disappear in a flash. Hence, instead of deleting large blocks of text, try moving them to the end of your document or writing

[3]Terry Tinsley Datz, "Word Processing Tips", *PC World*, May 1985; and Jeremy Joan Hewes, "The Write Stuff," *PC World*, January 1984.

them to temporary files where they can be recalled later. A related practice is to remain in the insert mode (as opposed to the replacement mode) to prevent inadvertent deletion of text as new ideas are added.

Save often: A loss of power, whether its your fault or the power company's can destroy a creative masterpiece. The best insurance is to save your work constantly and, in addition, to save your work whenever you are interrupted.

You should also be aware of the space remaining on your disk. Don't, for example, begin a new document with less than adequate space available. Nothing is more frustrating than the message, "ERROR—Disk full, save terminated."

We also stress the importance of answering the date and time questions which are part of the booting procedure provided by DOS. The DIR command shows the time and date of a file's creation, the values of which are taken from the DOS initialization procedure, and which can help you recognize the most current version of a file. You may also find it useful to store a printed copy of the directory with the disk. (Pressing the Shift and PrtSc keys simultaneously provides hard copy of the screen.)

Customize your word processor: All word processors have a series of default settings that appear when the program is initially loaded. For example, the left and right margins may be set at columns 1 and 65, respectively; the word wrap, hyphen help, and justification toggles may be on; the line spacing single-spaced; and so on. Defaults are chosen to satisfy most of the people most of the time, and it would be difficult to criticize a program because of its settings.

Nevertheless, your style or application may be significantly different, to the point where it would be desirable to have an alternate set of default settings. Pay close attention to the *installation procedure*, which is described in the user manual, as some of these defaults may be changed by reinstalling the program.

Keep duplicate copies of all documents: Backup is mentioned many times throughout the book because it is so important. It is absolutely essential to maintain duplicate copies of your work, on a separate disk stored away from the computer. Sooner or later, you will lose a disk or accidentally erase a file or suffer a similar misfortune; better safe than sorry.

Also, be sure to print your document at the end of every session, saving it before printing it (power failures happen when least expected, for example, during the print operation). Hard copy is not as good as a duplicate disk, but it is better than nothing.

Use smaller files: Restrict your documents to 10 pages or less (merging the smaller documents into a completed work at the very end). Larger files can significantly slow the performance of most word processors, as evidenced by increased time to jump to the beginning (or end) of a document, slower scrolling, and so on. Smaller files also provide the advantage of safety in the event of error; that is, there is less to lose.

Develop your own conventions: It is important to establish your own set of procedures and use them consistently. This will enforce an organized approach, provide consistency between like documents, and avoid mistakes. Consider, for example, the choice of a file name. DOS permits up to eight characters, plus a three-character extension. Within these rules there is considerable flexibility.

Our students find it useful to use the course number as the beginning of a file name (for example, 621ASG.ONE, 621ASG.TWO). There are many workable schemes; simply design one which is suitable for your needs and stick to it. Realize, also, the subtleties inherent in your design. In the 621 scheme shown above, the backup file (assuming one is created by your word processor) for 621ASG.ONE (such as 621ASG.BAK in WordStar) will disappear as soon as a new version of 621ASG.TWO is created. This may or may not be desirable, depending on your point of view. Some individuals like to maintain a BAK file for each individual document as additional backup; others view this as a waste of space. As the saying goes, "pay your money and take your choice."

Another convention has to do with page layout, that is, margin settings, justification, hyphen help, and so on. In the best of all possible worlds, a word processor will allow you to store various style sheets (sometimes known as "boilerplates"), which can be used from session to session and which facilitate the production of consistent-looking documents. Hence, if this feature is available, you are well advised to make a separate version of each format that you use frequently (for example, one for letters, another for memos, a third for reports, and so on).

Be comfortable: Choose carefully the environment in which you will be working, paying close attention to a comfortable seat and the work surface itself. Do not be "penny wise and dollar foolish" by placing a $2000 system on a $20 bridge table. Nor should you use a conventional desk because its height (30 inches), is 4 inches greater than that of the computer table you should purchase. Indeed, individuals who type for long periods of time at a desk complain frequently of a stiff neck, tight shoulders, or aching back.

Be kind to your eyes: Eye strain can be reduced by periodically (every 15 or 20 minutes) looking up from the keyboard and focusing on an object at least 20 feet away. If you do wear eye glasses, review your prescription, making sure that it is appropriate for the relatively short distance between your eyes and the screen.

Reduce (if not eliminate) glare by adjusting the position of the monitor and/or the ambient light. Curtains or blinds can be used to diminish strong daylight, while overhead sources may also need to be reduced. It may also help to adjust the brightness and contrast settings on your monitor as lighting conditions change.

Take a break: The computer quickly becomes addictive, and we can almost guarantee that you will find yourself in front of the machine much longer than you expect. A "quick" five-minute change somehow stretches into ten minutes, then a half hour. Periodic breaks will keep you refreshed and help to sustain your creativity. You may even want to do some stretching, as shown in the insert below:

Neck relaxer (above, left): Let your head drop slowly to the left, then to the right. Slowly drop your chin to your chest. Turn your head all the way to the left, return it to the normal position and then turn your head all the way to the right. Return to normal position. Stimulates the neck muscles to alleviate a stiff neck.

Side stretch (above, right): Interlace your fingers. Lift your arms up over your head keeping your elbows straight. Press your arms backwards as far as you can. Then slowly lean first to the left and then to the right until you can feel the stretch along the sides of your body. Stretches the muscles along the side of your body from your arm to your hip.

Authors' Comments:
These are only 2 of 19 exercises developed by Denise Austin, an exercise physiology specialist. The program received the endorsement of the American College of Sports Medicine, and appeared in the booklet Tone Up at the Terminal, *sponsored by Verbatim Corporation.*

WordPerfect
CORPORATION

Year-end statistics for 1987:
Sales: $101.3 million
Net income: Not available
CEO: Bruce W. Bastian
Headquarters: 1555 North Technology Way
Orem, UT 84057
(801) 225-5000

Who would have thought it possible that an upstart company based in Utah with two employees and no venture capital could possibly succeed, let alone unseat the entrenched leaders of word processing? Yet it happened, and today WordPerfect Corporation is the undisputed leader in a highly competitive market, with 1987 sales of $100 million.

It all began at Brigham Young University, where in 1976 Bruce Bastian was a graduate student in music, director of the 120-piece Cougar Band, and eventually a victim of his own success. Bastian did all the arrangements for the band with the aid of a graphics program he had written, which could march the band around the screen and view it from every angle: the 50 yard line, both end zones, even the Goodyear blimp. Once he had selected a formation, the program would print out marching instructions for every member in the band.

Unfortunately for Bastian the band drew so much national attention that university officials felt it had outgrown its student director. Off they went in search of an individual with credentials, someone with a Ph.D. in music, and out went Bastian. Discouraged, he approached Alan Ashton, a Ph.D. in computer science on the BYU faculty and a fellow musician, who had worked his way through school giving trumpet lessons. Impressed with Bastian's program, Ashton convinced him to get a master's degree in computer science.

Upon graduation, Bastian turned down offers from IBM, Hewlett-Packard, Digital Equipment, and others to remain in Utah so that he could continue to work with Ashton. They managed to secure a contract to develop a word processor to run on a Data General minicomputer for the city of Orem, Utah, which allowed them to keep the rights to the program upon its completion. In May of 1979 they founded Satellite Software International (they saw the name on an abandoned boxcar) and were in business. A year later their program was ready to go, and by word of mouth they

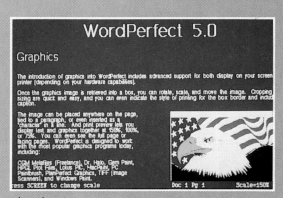

The roots of WordPerfect are traced to the BYU marching band

131

were able to sell it to many other Data General customers.

The announcement of the IBM PC in August 1981 gave them the opportunity of a lifetime. The converted version was ready in November 1982, renamed WordPerfect (the company name was changed later to WordPerfect Corporation), and sales have more than doubled every year. Today, InfoCorp estimates that WordPerfect has 30 percent of the market for full-featured IBM-compatible word processing software (compared to 15 percent each for MultiMate and Microsoft Word, 12 percent for WordStar, and 8 percent for IBM's Display Write). WordPerfect is available in Danish, Dutch, Finnish, French, German, Icelandic, Italian, Norwegian, Portuguese, Spanish, Swedish, and U.K. English. English-language versions also exist for the Apple II, Atari ST, Amiga, and Macintosh computers.

What sets WordPerfect apart from the competition is a remarkably simple user interface, consisting of a stripped-down screen, at the bottom of which is a single status line. There are no formatting codes to complicate the display, and no unrequested menus (although a complete help system is only a keystroke away).

As might be expected, the more than 750,000 end users of WordPerfect have provided the bulk of the corporate revenue. There are, however, a series of companion programs which can be purchased separately: PlanPerfect (a spreadsheet), DataPerfect (a database management program), WordPerfect Library (a utility program and desktop organizer), and WordPerfect Executive (an integrated program).

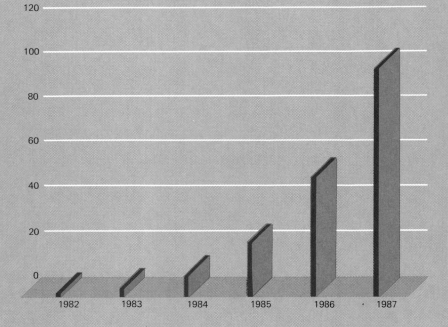

WORDPERFECT SALES
(millions of dollars)

Summary

The first half of the chapter covered several additional capabilities that are absolutely essential if you are to become a successful devotee of word processing. These included block operations (move, copy, delete, writing to an external file, and reading from an external file). We discussed the search-and-replace function with its associated options, including global, automatic and selective replacement, whole word replacement, forward and backward searches, and upper- versus lowercase searches. We also presented various types of save operations (save and resume editing, save and end editing, and quit without saving). Of greatest import was the Hands-On Exercise, which gave you a chance to practice this material on your own word processor.

The second half of the chapter focused on the more creative aspects of word processing. We began by considering page layout and design, showing how a document produced by a word processor is consistent with the physical page on which it will be printed. We covered the concept of a mail merge operation, which has application in almost every kind of business and which eliminates the tedium of producing form letters. We also presented the use of a dictionary, thesaurus, and syntax checker in conjunction with a word processor, and concluded with a series of writing tips designed to help you get the most out of word processing.

Key Words and Concepts

Automatic replacement
Auxiliary dictionary
Backward search
Block operations
Character string
Copy operation
Defaults
Dictionary program
Fields
File
Form letters
Global replacement
Ignore case
Mail merge operation
Memory-resident
Move operation

Page breaks
Read operation
Record
Record layout
Save operation
Search-and-replace function
Selective replacement
Spelling checker
Style analyzer
Syntax checker
Thesaurus program
Undo (or undelete) command
Whole word replacement
WordPerfect Corporation
Write operation

True/False

1. The two character strings in a search-and-replace operation must be the same length.

2. A search-and-replace operation will only work on one occurrence of the search string.

3. The strings "IBM" and "ibm" are considered to be different character strings.

4. The search-and-replace strings are limited to a single word.

5. A block move results in the designated text being in two places.

6. It is possible to designate an entire document as a single block of text.

7. It is possible to designate an individual word as a block of text.

8. It is not possible to change the default settings of a word processor.

9. A full-featured word processor, complete with dictionary and thesaurus, is not practical unless a hard disk is available.

10. All spelling checker programs are based on the same dictionary.

11. The auxiliary dictionary of a spelling checker is likely to be larger than the standard dictionary.

12. Answering the date and time prompts provided by DOS is a waste of time.

13. A file contains many records.

14. A record contains one or more fields.

15. The arrangement of fields within a record must be the same for every record in a file.

16. Undo and quit without saving are equivalent commands.

17. Undo and undelete are identical commands.

18. The speed of a word processor is unaffected by the size of the document it is editing.

19. All word processors are the same in terms of available features.

Multiple Choice

1. Which of the following is not a typical block operation?
   (a) Move
   (b) Delete

(c) Copy

(d) Hyphenate

2. Block operations can be performed on:
   (a) Sentences
   (b) Paragraphs
   (c) Entire documents
   (d) All of the above

3. In a mail merge operation, the recipients' names and addresses are contained in which files?
   (a) The form letter and data files
   (b) The form letter only
   (c) The data file only
   (d) The word processor program file

4. Which of the following are usually *not* found in an auxiliary dictionary?
   (a) Proper names
   (b) Words related to the user's particular application
   (c) Slang
   (d) Standard words of English usage

5. Which of the following would go undetected by a syntax checker?
   (a) Incorrect (poor) phraseology
   (b) Capitalization errors
   (c) Redundant (duplicated) words
   (d) Misspelled words

6. What is the most preferable way of backing up documents produced by a word processor?
   (a) On duplicate disks stored away from the computer
   (b) On duplicate disks kept with the computer
   (c) On the same disk as the original
   (d) As hard copy

7. Normal values for vertical and horizontal spacing, measured in lines per inch and characters per inch respectively, are:
   (a) 10 and 6
   (b) 6 and 10
   (c) 8 and 12
   (d) 12 and 8

8. Among the reasons cited for the success of WordPerfect are:
   (a) WordPerfect was the first word processor available for the PC
   (b) WordPerfect is currently the only word processor to supply a dictionary and a thesaurus
   (c) WordPerfect has an extremely simple user interface
   (d) All of the above

9. Execution of a block operation requires which of the following?
   (a) An indication of the beginning of the block
   (b) An indication of the end of the block
   (c) Specification of the particular operation, for example, move or copy
   (d) All of the above

10. The option that disregards whether lowercase or uppercase letters are found in a search string is:
    (a) Whole case
    (b) Ignore case
    (c) Replace case
    (d) Brief case

11. The option in a word processor that searches a document from the end to the beginning is referred to as a:
    (a) Inefficient search
    (b) Global search
    (c) Remaining search
    (d) Backward search

12. All of the following are options typically associated with a search and replace operation except:
    (a) Selective replacement
    (b) Automatic replacement
    (c) Whole word replacement
    (d) Defective replacement

13. The character strings in a search and replace operation must be:
    (a) The same length
    (b) The same case, either upper or lower
    (c) Both the same length and the same case
    (d) None of the above

14. Which single command would you use to negate all changes made to a document since the last save operation?
    (a) Undo
    (b) Ignore changes
    (c) Quit without saving
    (d) Save and quit editing

15. Which statement best describes the action of an electronic dictionary?
    (a) The detection and correction phases are both automatic
    (b) The detection and correction phases both require manual intervention
    (c) Only the detection phase is automatic
    (d) Only the correction phase is automatic

Exercises

1. A word processor can be used to prepare any kind of document, not only one which is limited to traditional text, for example, the set of dots below. Use your word processor to construct a set of dots as indicated. (To make life really interesting, you might try doing this with the *fewest* number of commands possible. Compare your solution to that of your neighbor.)

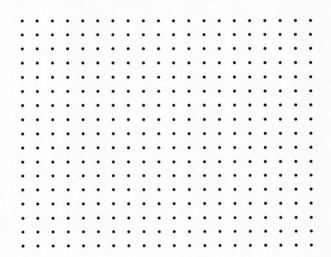

   The figure represents the children's games of "dots," in which the players take turns connecting two adjacent dots. Each player is allowed one line per turn, except in the event that the last line drawn completes a box. In that case, the player puts his or her initial in the box and goes again. The player with the most boxes at the end of the game wins. Most of the action takes place at the end of the game, at which time runs of 10, 20, or 30 boxes are possible. (The author has an 8-year-old daughter who loves the game, who constantly asked for blank forms, and who inspired this problem.)

2. As you become more proficient with word processors in particular, and computers in general, the few-second delay in response time which was previously acceptable becomes increasingly irritating.
   (a) Will conversion from a floppy-based system to a hard drive speed up the execution of your word processor? How?
   (b) Will the addition of extra memory speed execution?
   (c) Will changing computers help (for example, an XT to an AT, or an original PC to a low-end PS/2 model)?
   (d) Does the availability of a buffer for your printer speed things up?

FIGURE 4.12
Document for exercise 3 (*Source: Personal Computing*, March 1987, page 97.)

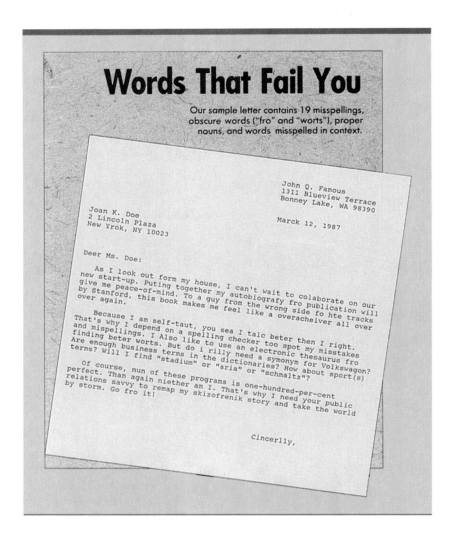

3. Figure 4.12 is reproduced from the article, "How Well Do You Spell?" by Steve Ditlea, which appeared in *Personal Computing*, March 1987, and was used to test various dictionary programs. Enter the document in Figure 4.12, *exactly as it appears*, to see how successful your word processor is in locating spelling errors.

4. Figure 4.13 is reproduced from the article, "How Many Ways Can You Say Thesaurus?" by Steve Ditlea, which appeared in *Personal Computing*, May 1987, and was used to test various thesaurus programs. Enter the document in Figure 4.13, *exactly as it appears*, to see how successful your word processor is in providing synonyms.

5. The concept of a mail merge operation, in which a file of names and addresses is combined with a form letter, greatly enhances

FIGURE 4.13
Document for exercise 4. (*Source: Personal Computing*, May 1987, page 108.)

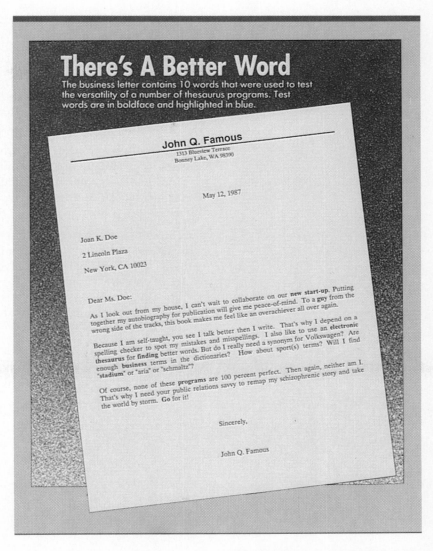

the power of a word processor. Assume that you are supporting a grass roots candidate for office in an upcoming election.

(a) Draft a form letter stating the qualifications of your candidate and requesting funds. Use ampersands in the draft of your letter to indicate the variables, which will be supplied from the file of names and addresses.

(b) How would you obtain the file of names and addresses? Do you think you would have to pay? How much?

(c) Assume that you obtain your file from an outside mailing list. Can it be obtained in "machine-readable" form? If not, describe the problems of data entry.

(d) Once the file has been made machine-readable, is it possible to easily obtain a subset of names and addresses (for example, for a list of people living in a designated zip code)? Do you see the necessity for a "database manager" in addition to a word processor?

(e) What additional commands are necessary to send the letters on a special-sized form that is 5 × 7 inches as opposed to the standard $8\frac{1}{2}$ × 11 inches? Indicate the commands to produce a $\frac{1}{2}$-inch border around the entire sheet so that the effective writing surface is 4 × 6 inches.

6. Consider the sentence, "They are proud of there county, the united states or Aremica," and explain why only one of the six existing errors will be caught by a dictionary program. What additional measures, besides a dictionary, are necessary to help ensure the accuracy of a document?

7. Assume that the letters in the example on page 116 are to go out on school stationery rather than computer paper, and investigate the cost and feasibility of the following solutions (feel free to add one of your own):

(a) "Friction feed" of individual letters, one at a time

(b) Mounting stationery on continuous-form paper

(c) Obtaining a device to feed individual stationery to the printer

What additional considerations are necessary to produce a set of envelopes corresponding to the acceptance letters?

CHAPTER 5

DESKTOP PUBLISHING

CHAPTER OBJECTIVES

After reading this chapter, you should be able to:

1. Define a type font; describe three characteristics that distinguish one font from another.

2. Distinguish between a serif and a sans serif typeface; give one example of each.

3. Define the units used to measure type size and line length; explain the relationship between these parameters.

4. Define leading; explain the relationship between type size and the amount of leading required.

5. Discuss the importance of a grid in the design of a document.

6. Describe three principles of graphic design.

Overview

Desktop publishing enables you to produce professional looking documents, without the need for external services such as those provided by a graphic designer, illustrator, or paste-up artist. A complete system fits compactly on your desk and provides you with total control over the form and content of the documents you produce. The term is attributed to Paul Brainerd, the president of Aldus Corporation (the subject of the corporate profile) and the originator of PageMaker, the program which ushered in the era of desktop publishing.

The effective use of desktop publishing requires proficiency in word processing, a sense of what constitutes acceptable layout and design, and a basic knowledge of *typography* (the process of type selection). Thus we differentiate between *serif* and *sans-serif* type faces, and describe the *point* system used to measure type sizes. We discuss *leading* (the measure of vertical spacing between lines) as well as horizontal *line length*, both of which are related to type size. The chapter also includes material on the *grid system of graphic design* and the basic design principles of *balance*, *unity*, and *emphasis*.

We begin with an overview of desktop publishing, discuss the components of a desktop system, and suggest what the concept can do for you.

Freedom of the press belongs to those who own one.

Paraphrased from a quote by A. J. Liebling

Desktop Publishing

Desktop publishing employs a combination of hardware and software to merge the output of a word processor, with graphics and/or external art, into a professional-looking document. In other words, you are no longer dependent on external services to prepare material for printing—these capabilities are now resident within the computer on your desk.

Potential applications of desktop publishing are everywhere and pertain to anyone with a need for effective written communication. Newsletters, promotional pieces, manuals, catalogs, proposals, reports, and so on are but a few examples. In addition, desktop publishing will save you time and money because you are doing tasks which used to be done by others, and further because you can see the results of your work immediately. For example:

- In traditional publishing you worked with a designer to create a layout, only to wait a week or more to see what it would look like. Now you create the layout on a computer screen.

- In traditional publishing you had to wait another week to see the effects of any proposed changes to the design. Now you see the changes as soon as they are made.

- In traditional publishing text was set by a professional typesetter who rekeyed the entire document (introducing errors and taking additional time in the process). Now you import your document from a word processor quickly, and without error.

- In traditional publishing you had to spend additional hours proofreading the typeset material. Now you do little proofreading because the document is printed exactly as it appeared in the word processor.

- In traditional publishing you were presented with sheets of text (called galleys) which gave no indication of how the finished document would look when it was broken into pages. Now you preview the finished piece immediately.

- In traditional publishing pictures were sent out for reduction to fit on a page. Now you scan images directly, reduce them, and bring them into the document.

- In traditional publishing a paste-up artist was used to cut up galleys and position the art. Now you do this yourself, and thus can experiment with many different layouts.

Here's What You
Desktop

Magazine by Tom Hamilton, Balloon Life Magazine, Inc.

Catalog by Judith Baldwin, Ceramic Supply of New York and New Jersey.

Brochure by Kristen Ransom, Communique, for the Duck Inn.

Letterhead, Business Card by Kristen Ransom, Communique, for Cooks Headquarters.

Tabloid by Bill Bosler, FDR Publications, for Thorek Hospital and Medical Center.

Small Business Communications by Lisa Menders for Frank's Nursery and Crafts, Inc.

Can Do With Publishing

A LAKEWOOD PUBLICATION

TRAINING DIRECTORS' FORUM

NEWSLETTER

A Forum for Leaders and Managers of Training

Volume 2, Number 4 *April, 1986*

Protecting a training budget when finances are tight requires timing, sales skills and corporate perspective

Is top management swinging the budget ax in your organization? If so, it's probably too late to prevent deep cuts in your department's spending unless you've already invested a large percentage of your time *selling* the importance of training.

Robert Schull, chief of operational air crew training at Scott Air Force Base, led a group discussion, How to Keep Training the #1 Priority, at Training Directors' Day at TRAINING '85 in New York. The main idea the group agreed upon, Schull says, is that training managers must keep alive the perception that vital organizations must continually nurture their people and therefore training must be unencumbered and the last entity to be cut when trimming budgets.

"The group had a variety of experiences. Basically what we came up with is that to make training a top priority chief trainers need to keep the impetus alive at staff meetings, through memos to CEOs, and through reports on the numbers and needs of people to be trained. Every department director in an organization has a view of what the department cannot afford to lose. But the only common thread throughout any organization has to be the training program. You must have commitment."

Schull presents a variety of data in statistical formats to make his case for the training he provides to all military airlift aircraft personnel: The percent of personnel totally qualified for particular jobs; lists of people who are not fully trained; projections about how many people must be trained in each of the next five years, based on attrition and promotions.

"If a training officer sits back and says nothing, training will be pushed aside. You have to understand how people get into power positions in organizations; it's the top sales people or the top production people who move up. And those people don't always have the management skills or the knowledge of what it takes to make the whole corporation work. Either a top manager has a brainchild of his own and will support a training program, or you have to put him through the program up

If management isn't sold on training you might as well stay home to bake cookies.

front to get the support. You have to get the support from the top down.

"If training is going to succeed we need to be vibrant, aggressive and action oriented. We've got to make people understand why these things are important and why anything less than the ideal might not have the desired impacts." Schull spends about 33 percent of his time selling the importance of training. "It's all the time I have. The majority of it is involved in protecting my budget."

An Alternative View

Often, Schull says, training directors say no to new concepts suggested for training due to a lack of funds. He suggests, however, that reevaluating how training dollars are spent can lead to restructuring that might satisfy the need for the new concept while retaining the integrity of existing training.

"The hardest thing for a training chief is to see what could be deleted, if necessary, to add something new. Often times it becomes a matter of restructuring a training system in order to in-

continued on page 2

INSIDE STORIES...

- The Editors' Forum...p.2
- Hiring Consultants...p.3
- How to Select a CBT Authoring Program...p.4
- Problem Column...p. 5
- Profile—Melinda Bickerstaff American Express...p.6
- Eye on Training—a column by Ron Zemke...p.7
- Directors' Notebbook...p.8

Contributors to this issue...p.5

Newsletter by Brian McDermott, Lakewood Publications.

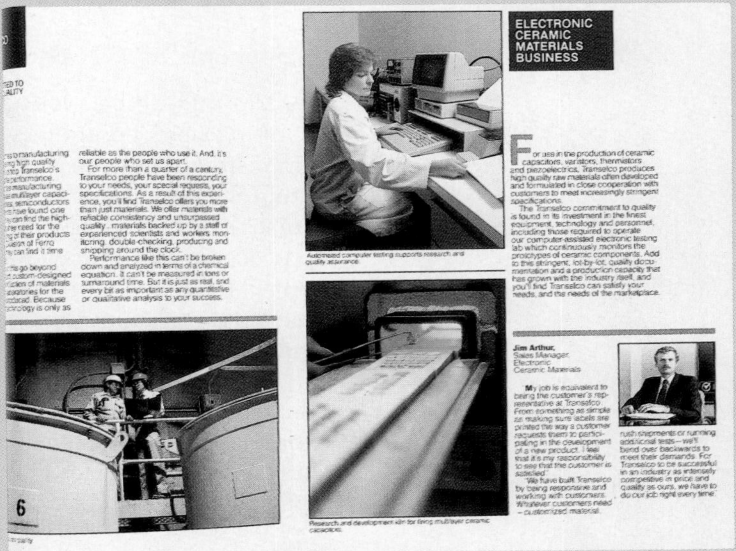

...TED TO ...ALITY

...s to manufacturing ...ng high quality ...s Transelco's ...performance ...s manufacturing ...multilayer capaci-...s, semiconductors ...s have found one ...can find the high-...need for the ...of their products ...ision of Ferro ...can find it time

...s go beyond ...custom-designed ...tion of materials ...ratories for the ...oduct. Because ...chnology is only as reliable as the people who use it. And, it's our people who set us apart.

For more than a quarter of a century, Transelco people have been responding to your needs, your special requests, your specifications. As a result of this experience, you'll find Transelco offers you more than just materials. We offer materials with reliable consistency and unsurpassed quality...materials backed up by a staff of experienced scientists and workers monitoring, double-checking, producing and shipping around the clock.

Performance like this can't be broken down and analyzed in terms of a chemical equation. It can't be measured in tons or turnaround time. But it is just as real, and every bit as important as any quantitative or qualitative analysis to your success.

6

Automated computer testing supports research and quality assurance.

ELECTRONIC CERAMIC MATERIALS BUSINESS

For use in the production of ceramic capacitors, varistors, thermistors and piezoelectrics, Transelco produces high quality raw materials often developed and formulated in close cooperation with customers to meet increasingly stringent specifications.

The Transelco commitment to quality is found in its investment in the finest equipment, technology and personnel, including those required to operate our computer-assisted electronic testing lab which continuously monitors the prototypes of ceramic components. Add to this stringent, lot-by-lot, quality documentation and a production capacity that has grown with the industry itself, and you'll find Transelco can satisfy your needs, and the needs of the marketplace.

Research and development kiln for firing multilayer ceramic capacitors.

Jim Arthur, Sales Manager, Electronic Ceramic Materials

My job is equivalent to being the customer's representative at Transelco. From something as simple as making sure labels are printed the way a customer requests them to participating in the development of a new product, I feel that it's my responsibility to see that the customer is satisfied."

"We have built Transelco by being responsive and working with customers. Whatever customers need —customized material, rush shipments or running additional tests—we'll bend over backwards to meet their demands. For Transelco to be successful in an industry as intensely competitive in price and quality as ours, we have to do our job right every time."

Brochure by Joanne and David Lenweaver, Lenweaver Design, for Transelco Division, Ferro Corporation.

Chapter 5
Fabrication

Various materials and techniques are available for making signs. In the following pages, a selection of sign fabrication methods for each type of sign making material are briefly described and commented on.

Wooden Signs

Painted or printed: Exterior grade plywood, made with waterproof glues, is a good inexpensive material for painted or printed exterior signs. Duraply or Permashield plywoods are covered with a fibreboard face, with a smooth surface for painting. In all cases, when plywood is used the edges should be protected and sealed from moisture.

Cut-out: Shaped letters or symbols can be sawn from wood, sanded and then finished by painting or with metallic finishes such as gold or aluminum leaf. Cut-out wooden letters painted with gold leaf are extremely durable and some have been known to survive over twenty years of exposure to the elements.

Carved: Redwood, cedar, cypress or special grades of pine can be used to produce carved wooden signs. The design to be reproduced is transferred at actual size to the solid wood block, and the craftsman will then carve the letter forms and image by hand. The elements in the sign are then painted by hand, often in a number of colours, and sometimes the finished sign is sealed with special protective sealant to guard it from the elements.

Routed: Routing machines (routers) can be used to inscribe letterforms into the face of wooden signs. These machines can be either hand held or controlled to follow the contours of a stencil guide. Painting and finishing is the same as for other wooden signs.

Sandblasted: Woods like redwood, with very even grain, can be sandblasted. The wooden sign block is covered with a rubber stencil from which the letterforms have been cut. A fine sand is then propelled against the exposed areas of the sign face, thereby etching a channel into the wood. A softer wood will provide a deeper cut. The sign can then be painted or sealed to protect it from the effects of the weather.

56

Metal Signs

Cut-out: Individual letters or symbols, as well as logotypes and other signatures can be cut in one piece from large sheets of metal. A pattern at full size is laid over a metal plate and a band saw is used to cut along the edges of the pattern. The rough edges are finished by filing or sanding. Most metals can be used to make this type of sign, including aluminum, stainless steel, bronze and brass and the result is a durable, prestige, low maintenance sign. To achieve alternate finishes, the metal can be plated, enamelled or anodized.

Routed: A pattern at full size is laid over a metal plate and the letterforms or image is cut and removed. The empty forms are then filled with acrylic letters which have been cut to match and fused to a sheet of acrylic of the same size as the metal plate. A light source placed behind the double layer sign will cause only the letters and symbols to become illuminated.

Fabricated sheet metal: Many separate pieces of sheet metal (stainless steel, copper or aluminum) are assembled by hand into large three-dimensional signs. The face and sides of the sign are fused together either by welding (aluminum), soldering (steel) or brazing (copper). Finishes include polishing, plating, anodizing or enamelling.

Cast: This process can be used to produce high quality, durable, prestige signs, either as individual letters or entire signs. It is often used to create plaques commemorating heritage or historic sites. The casting process involves making a pattern out of plastic, metal or wood; packing the pattern with molding sand to create a mold; and pouring molten metal into the mold. The cooled metal is removed from the mold and cleaned. It can be finished by machining, polishing, plating, anodizing, enamelling or painting.

Engraved: Metal signs made by this process have letters shallowly cut into the face of the sign. A metal or plastic pattern is made and a tracing device is used to transfer the pattern onto the metal plate using a rotating needle which engraves the plate. The engraved letters are sometimes filled with enamel (available in a variety of colours) to make them more prominent.

Etched: The lettering on this type of sign is in low relief. A precise artwork of the sign is photographed and used to create a film positive. A light sensitive gel when exposed through the film positive transfers the image to the plate. Areas not exposed to light remain unprotected and are etched when the plate is put into an acid bath. The etched letterforms are sometimes coloured or filled with enamels to make them more visible.

Wrought iron: Although this is not a common material for signs, it is possible to use wrought iron to make letterforms. Using a full size plan of the letters, a wrought iron craftsman can form the metal to the desired shape. Wrought iron needs to be painted to protect it for exterior use.

57

Book by Denise Saulnier, Communication Design Group Ltd., for the City of Halifax, Nova Scotia, Canada.

1986-87 SEASON
Pegasus PlayerS
Your Ticket to Magic and Excitement!

Program by Eda Warren, Eda Warren Design, for The Pegasus Players.

Yes, desktop publishing does give you total control of your documents throughout the entire process, as described above. Viewed another way, however, it shoulders you with additional responsibility, precisely because you are doing work that was formerly done by others. The process is described by Table 5.1, which lists 12 functions in the traditional publishing process that are now your obligation.

Components of a Desktop System

Desktop publishing evolved through a combination of technologies including faster computers, the laser printer, and sophisticated page composition software to manipulate text and graphics. Aldus Corporation's **PageMaker** was the first program to provide a true what-you-see-is-what-you-get environment, and thus eliminate the paste-up process of traditional publishing. The combination of PageMaker, Apple Macintosh, and LaserWriter printer was offered for the first time in July 1985, sold for about $10,000, and made desktop publishing a practical reality.

The selection of a desktop publishing system today is more complicated, in that the amount of available hardware and software has expanded greatly. You need to select the page composition software, computer, laser printer, and high-resolution monitor, and in addition, be sure that the individual items are compatible with one another.

TABLE 5.1

The Traditional Publishing Process

Person	Function
Publisher	Manages entire process
Author	Creates document and rough art
Editor	Controls quality and content
Copy editor	Controls grammar and consistency standards
Art Director	Sets direction of design and artwork
Designer	Sets format, font, and figure specifications
Artist	Creates illustrations and artwork
Production manager	Manages process from receipt of manuscript to camera-ready copy
Compositor	Sets document in type according to design specifications
Proofreader	Proofreads and corrects design and content errors
Paste-up artist	Pastes typeset copy and artwork onto paged boards to create camera-ready copy
Printer	Creates plates from camera-ready copy (boards) and prints and binds copies

Brout, Athanasopoulos, and Kutlin, *Desktop Publishing from A to Z*, McGraw-Hill, New York, 1986, page 10.

"WE LOVE YOUR 'WAR AND PEACE' MR. TOLSTOY, AND WE HOPE TO PUBLISH IT. BUT NO ONE HAS BEEN ABLE TO FINISH IT."

You may also want to include a scanning device which converts existing art and/or photographs into a form suitable for incorporation into a document. Each of these components is described in turn.

The most critical element is the **page composition software**, the program which pulls together text and graphics, and which produces the document on the screen according to your design specifications. **PageMaker** and Xerox Corporation's **Ventura Publisher** are two of the leading programs for the IBM environment. Both have the ability to import text files from a word processor and graphic images from other programs. Both will produce documents containing different type styles and sizes, multiple-column layouts, and other attributes of professional publications.

The **computer** may be either an Apple Macintosh or IBM-compatible, but it must be powerful. You should choose at least an "AT class machine," and we advise you to test the entire configuration before purchase.

The selection of a **laser printer** is one of the more difficult decisions, due to the large number of printers on the market. The

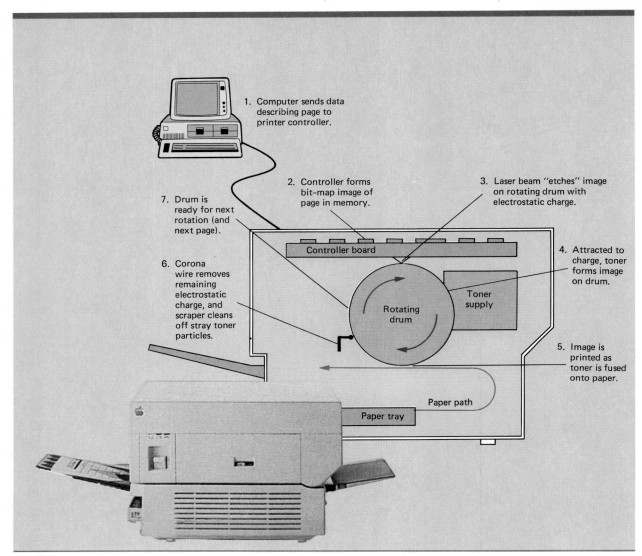

1. Computer sends data describing page to printer controller.

2. Controller forms bit-map image of page in memory.

3. Laser beam "etches" image on rotating drum with electrostatic charge.

7. Drum is ready for next rotation (and next page).

Controller board

4. Attracted to charge, toner forms image on drum.

6. Corona wire removes remaining electrostatic charge, and scraper cleans off stray toner particles.

Toner supply

Rotating drum

5. Image is printed as toner is fused onto paper.

Paper path

Paper tray

Side view of a laser printer. (*Source: Publish Magazine, May 1987, page 62.*)

decision often comes down to price and whether or not the printer supports PostScript (see the following box, entitled "PostScript"). The availability of PostScript generally increases the speed at which a document is produced. It also enables a laser printer to scale characters to any size, print in many different shades of gray, and create other special effects which make life easier for the desktop publisher. PostScript is not required, however, as page composition software runs on printers with or without PostScript).

The **monitor** should be of at least EGA (Enhanced Graphics Adapter) quality, otherwise you will not be able to view the finished

---

POSTSCRIPT

PostScript, a trademark of **Adobe System Inc.,** is a simple, yet highly sophisticated, interpretive programming language providing an exceptionally effective means of integrating all aspects of page composition: type, line graphics, photographs, and all other manner of graphic images. It provides a software interface between document-creation programs and output devices.

A page description written in PostScript is an executable program composed of various elements of the PostScript language. PostScript, like other computer languages, is made up of variables and constants, operators and operands, syntax and semantics, and a collection of rules of usage. PostScript is generally transparent to the user, with its source code generated by a word processing program or other document processing application.

Using the PostScript language to draw a straight line is one of the simplest activities to illustrate. The MOVETO operator is used to specify the starting point of the line segment, after which the LINETO operator draws the line from its origin to its ending coordinates. The program below draws a line 400 units long (each unit is 1/72 of an inch):

```
100 390 MOVETO
500 390 LINETO
STROKE
SHOWPAGE
```

The STROKE operator paints the line along the trajectory indicated by the current path. The SHOWPAGE operator initiates the output processing of the image.

To set a line of type it is necessary to select the typeface, scale it to size, indicate the word to set, and then give the instruction to set them. A single line of 12-point Times Roman type showing the words "PostScript is transparent" would be written as follows:

```
#Times-Roman FINDFONT 12 SCALEFONT
SETFONT
300 500 MOVETO
(PostScript is transparent) SHOW
SHOWPAGE
```

---

document. (The various IBM graphics standards are discussed in Chapter 9.

A **scanner** is optional but highly desirable because it converts any picture, photograph, or drawing into a form suitable for inclusion into a document. A scanner operates by passing a thin stream of light back and forth across the image, transforming the light or darkness at each point into binary values, which are stored in the computer's memory. Several scanners are available in today's environment (see the following box, entitled Scanners in Desktop Publishing).

The result of all these capabilities is a system in which you can write and edit text, create illustrations, incorporate photographs and other art, design and alter page layout, and produce a finished doc-

SCANNERS IN DESKTOP PUBLISHING

One of the fastest-growing applications for scanners may well be the desktop publishing market, which some observers have predicted will be a multi-billion-dollar industry by 1990. In its highest form, desktop publishing is the production of fully composed page layouts—including typeset text and graphic images—using a personal computer, page composition software, and a high-resolution output device like a typesetter or a laser printer. Ideally, you can merge text and scanned images on the same page, preview the page on-screen, and print it directly to a laser printer, camera-ready for reproduction.

Scanners have not played a major role in this process, but that's likely to change. For one thing, the price of the scanning hardware, like the price of high-resolution laser printers, is falling into the affordable range. This year, you can spend under $3,000 for a scanner that can perform some of the same feats as equipment that cost over $30,000 2 years ago. Scanning lets you incorporate more-complex graphics into your published pages. Users who already work with *PC Paint* or *PC Paintbrush* know that some images—complex logos or fine illustrations, for instance—take hours to re-create on-screen; these same images take only a few minutes to scan. In-house newsletter departments that now pay high prices for halftones of photographs of new and promoted employees will find that 300-dot-per-inch scanned images are an acceptable alternative. In either case, the low cost of the new scanners makes the purchase easy to justify.

Professional graphic artists, photographers, and printers consider scanned images inferior to traditional halftones, even when the images are printed on a 300-dpi laser printer. For many desktop publishing applications, however, the quality is adequate. Lots of people already use low-cost scanners with the Apple Macintosh, pulling scanned images onto page layouts, merging them with typeset text, and printing out camera-ready pages on laser printers at 300 dpi or typesetters at 1,200 or 2,400 dpi.

Desktop publishers who are willing to sacrifice true halftone quality in exchange for on-line image access and in-house control of production will happily invest in low-end scanning devices. These pioneers will be able to produce simple images for their newsletters and illustrated documents with little effort. Once software developers are convinced that this is a market worth supporting, we'll have access to all the software and printer drivers required for integrated desktop publishing on the PC.

Source: S. Venit, "Scanners in Desktop Publishing," *PC Magazine,* September 30, 1986.

ument ready for distribution. The system also allows you to play "what if" with your design by moving elements around the document, and to change type styles and sizes, all the while previewing the document as it will appear in print.

The end product can be a truly professional-looking document, but often falls short of expectations, because other basic skills are overlooked. In other words, the mere availability of these capabilities does not guarantee professional-looking documents, just as the use of a word processor will not turn you into a Shakespeare or a Hemingway. Other skills are necessary; hence, the remainder of the chapter introduces the basics of graphic design.

The Grid System of Design

Just as the building of a house begins with a blueprint, the production of a document begins with a design plan known as a **grid.** A grid consists of horizontal and vertical lines that do not appear in the final document, but which define the relationships among margins, columns, and the spaces between columns.

A grid may be simple or complex, but in any event is distinguished by the number of columns it contains, as illustrated by Figure 5.1. The one-column grid of Figure 5.1*a* is traditionally used for term papers, letters, and textbooks. Two- and three-column formats such

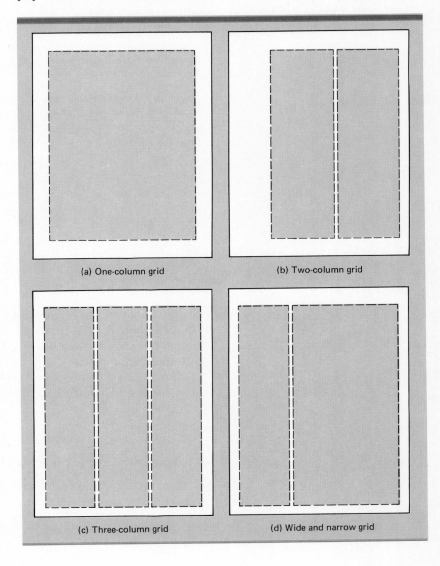

(a) One-column grid (b) Two-column grid

(c) Three-column grid (d) Wide and narrow grid

FIGURE 5.1
Various grid layouts.

as those shown in Figure 5.1*b* and 5.1*c* are more suitable for newspapers (newsletters) and magazines. The wide and narrow format of Figure 5.1*d* provides additional interest and is used in manuals and books. Other variations are also possible.

The conscious design of a grid will help you to organize your material, and will result in a more polished and successful publication. Adherence to the design will also help you to achieve consistency from page to page within a document (or from issue to issue of a newsletter).

WHERE TO GET HELP

Proficiency in desktop publishing requires an appreciation for graphic design as well as basic knowledge of publishing terminology. In preparing this chapter we have drawn heavily on these four excellent books, and we recommend them to you as well.

Jonathan Price and Carlene Schnabel, *Desktop Publishing, With Recipes for PageMaker*, Ballantine Books, New York, 1987.

Roger C. Parker, *The Aldus Guide to Basic Design*, Aldus Corporation, Seattle, Washington, 1987.

Judy E. Pickens, *The Copy-to-Press Handbook*, John Wiley & Sons, New York, 1985.

Michael L. Kleper, *The Illustrated Handbook of Desktop Publishing and Typesetting*, Graphic, Pittsford, New York, 1987.

Placing Art on the Grid

Art may be placed to fit within the grid, as shown in Figure 5.2, or to violate the grid, as in Figure 5.3. Staying within the grid is generally easier, whereas creatively straying from column boundaries produces more interesting pages.

Figure 5.2*a* and 5.2*b* shows how art is placed within a one- and two-column grid, respectively. Both examples follow several common guidelines:

- Place art after it is mentioned in the text.

- Allow a half-inch between art and text.

- Make art the same width as the text; box or center irregular art to make it the same width as the column.

- Position art at the top or bottom of a page, unless it is on a page by itself.

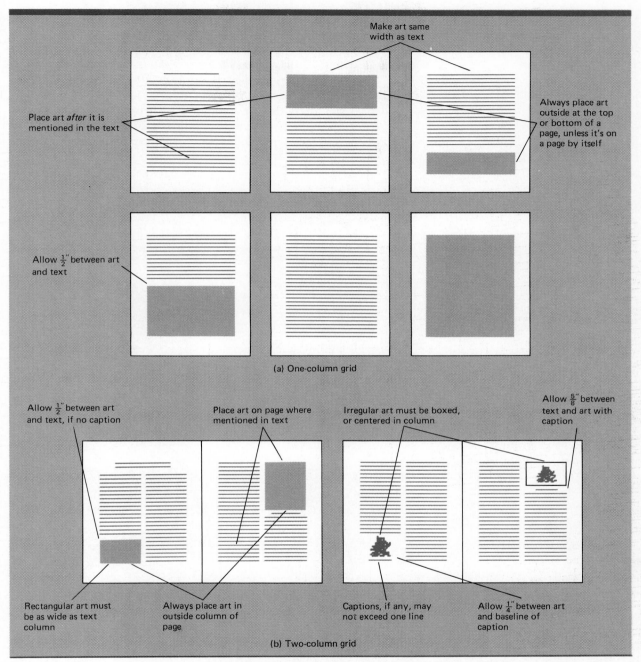

FIGURE 5.2   Placing art on the grid. (*Source:* Price and Schnabel, *Desktop Publishing,* Balantine Books, New York, 1987, pages 4–14.)

Figure 5.3 contains examples of art which violate the grid, but in ways that make sense and which enhance rather than detract from the overall design. Figure 5.3*a*, for example, extends the art over two columns, which in turn allows larger art than under the initial guidelines. Figure 5.3*b* wraps the text around the art and is more difficult to produce, but much more creative.

Figure 5.4 illustrates four completed pages, corresponding to the grids shown earlier in Figure 5.1. Notice how the underlying grid design is now obvious, and how you have become an instant expert on page composition.

FIGURE 5.3 Violating the grid. (*Source:* Price and Schnabel, *Desktop Publishing*, Balantine Books, New York, 1987, pages 4–15.)

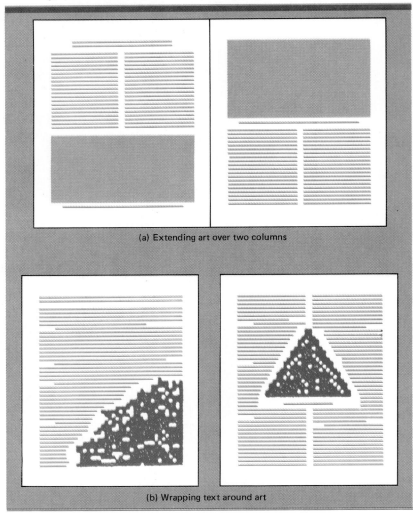

(a) Extending art over two columns

(b) Wrapping text around art

FIGURE 5.4
Various grid layouts. (*Source:* Parker, Roger C., *Aldus Guide to Basic Design,* Aldus Corporation, Seattle WA., 1987, pages 14, 16, 17, and 21.)

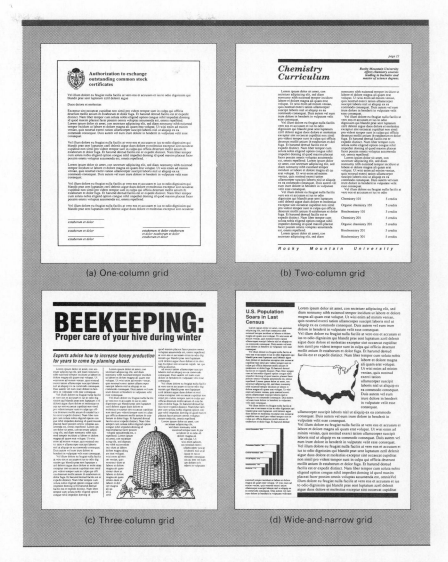

(a) One-column grid

(b) Two-column grid

(c) Three-column grid

(d) Wide-and-narrow grid

Typography

A second important aspect of graphic design is type selection, because how a document looks ultimately determines how successful it will be. The type you choose should always be consistent with the message you want to convey, neither too large nor too small, neither too bold nor too reserved. You wouldn't, for example, use the same type size and style to proclaim a year-end bonus as you would to announce a fourth-quarter loss and impending layoffs.

Typography is the process of selecting *type faces*, *type sizes*, and *spacing requirements* for a document. Each of these elements is discussed in turn.

Typefaces

A **typeface** is defined as a complete set of characters (upper- and lowercase letters, numbers, punctuation marks, and special symbols). Figure 5.5 contains only a few of the many typefaces available, the number of which can make the choice of a single typeface overwhelming to the novice desktop publisher. To further complicate matters, each typeface comes in a variety of sizes and styles.

The selection is made easier, however, by one major distinction: whether the typeface is **serif** or **sans serif**. A serif typeface has cross lines that end the main strokes of each letter; these lines are not present in a sans (from the French for "without") serif design. Serifs help the eye to connect one letter with the next and consequently are used most often with large amounts of text. By contrast, a sans serif typeface tends to be more effective with smaller portions of text and appears in headlines, corporate logos, airport signs, and so on.

FIGURE 5.5
Sample typefaces.

AVANT GARDE GOTHIC MEDIUM
ABCDEFGHIJKLMNOPQRSTUVWXYZ

BOOKMAN MEDIUM
ABCDEFGHIJKLMNOPQRSTUVWXYZ

COMMERCIAL SCRIPT
ABCDEFGHIJKLMNOPQRSTUVWXYZ

COMPUTER
ABCDEFGHIJKLMNOPQRSTUVWXYZ

GOUDY SANS MEDIUM
ABCDEFGHIJKLMNOPQRSTUVWXYZ

HELVETICA MEDIUM
ABCDEFGHIJKLMNOPQRSTUVWXYZ

OLD ENGLISH
ABCDEFGHIJKLMNOPQRSTUVWXYZ

TIMES ROMAN
ABCDEFGHIJKLMNOPQRSTUVWXYZ

American Indians made many products from the juice of the rubber tree, including bottles that bounced. In 1820, Englishman
Thomas Hancock cut the bottles into thin strips for use in garters.
Twenty five years later another Englishman, Stephen Perry, thought
of tying the strips into circles to produce the "elastic fastener", or
rubber band as we know it today.

(a) Times Roman (serif typeface)

**American Indians made many products from the juice of the
rubber tree, including bottles that bounced. In 1820,
Englishman Thomas Hancock cut the bottles into thin strips
for use in garters. Twenty five years later another Englishman,
Stephen Perry, thought of tying the strips into circles to produce the "elastic fastener", or rubber band as we know it
today.**

(b) Helvetica (sans serif typeface)

FIGURE 5.6   Times Roman versus Helvetica.

To appreciate the difference, consider Figure 5.6, which contains
the same passage set in both **Times Roman** (serif) and **Helvetica** (sans
serif). Times Roman and Helvetica were chosen for the example because they are two of the most widely used typefaces, and thus are
available on most laser printers. The Times Roman typeface in Figure
5.6a conveys a sense of authority; the Helvetica typeface in Figure
5.6b produces a more informal result.

Another example of the difference between these two typefaces
is found by comparing *Time* and *People* magazines, which are set in
Times Roman and Helvetica, respectively. Look through an issue of
each and notice immediately how two entirely different moods are
established merely by the choice of a particular typeface.

Type Size

Type size is measured in **points,** where one point is equal to 1/72 of
an inch; that is, there are 72 points to the inch. Technically speaking,
type size is measured from the baseline of one line of text to the
baseline of the next (when there is no additional space between lines).
More simply, it is measured from the top of the tallest letter in a
character set (for example, an uppercase T) to the bottom of the
lowest letter (for example, a lowercase y). Several examples of type
size are shown in Figure 5.7.

This is Times Roman 6 point

This is Times Roman 8 point

This Times Roman 10 point

This Times Roman 12 point

This Times Roman 18 point

This is Times Roman 24 point

FIGURE 5.7
Times Roman in varying type sizes.

Type Families

A **type family** consists of variations in **type style** or weight of the basic design. Figure 5.8 displays several members of the Helvetica family, including **boldface** and *italic* (two variations which are present in virtually every type family). A **type font** is a complete assortment of characters in one style and size of a particular family.

Vertical Spacing

The vertical space between lines of type is known as **leading** and is almost as important as the size of the type itself. (The term originates from the time when lead strips were inserted between the lines of

14 point Helvetica

14 point Helvetica Bold

14 point Helvetica Italic

14 point Helvetica Light

14 point Helvetica Light Italic

14 point Helvetica Bold Italic

14 point Helvetica Condensed

14 point Helvetica Condensed Italic

14 point Helvetica Black

FIGURE 5.8
Members of the Helvetica family.

set type.) Any specification of type size also includes the amount of leading; for example, a specification of 10 on 12 (10/12) means that 10-point type is used and that there are two points of leading between lines of type. In similar fashion, 12 on 15 (12/15) would imply 12-point type set with three points of leading.

Figure 5.9 illustrates various amounts of leading. Too much leading results in the lines being too far apart, whereas too little causes the lines to sit on top of one another. Either way, readability is impaired. A general guideline is that leading should constitute approximately 20 percent of the type size; for example, a type size of 10 points needs 2 points of leading.

Horizontal Measurement

Column width (line length) is measured in **picas** rather than inches, where 1 pica equals one-sixth of an inch; that is, there are 6 picas to the inch. Figure 5.10 contains the same passage set in varying column widths of 11, 22, and 30 picas, respectively.

Chester Carlson invented a dry means of copying, and patented the process of "xerography" [from the Greek *xeros* (dry) and *graphein* (to write)] in 1940. At least 20 companies rejected his proposal to market the device; until at last, the Haloid Company of Rochester, New York, was so excited about the possibility that it changed its name to Xerox.

(a) No leading (10/10)

Chester Carlson invented a dry means of copying, and patented the process of "xerography" [from the Greek *xeros* (dry) and *graphein* (to write)] in 1940. At least 20 companies rejected his proposal to market the device; until at last, the Haloid Company of Rochester, New York, was so excited about the possibility that it changed its name to Xerox.

(b) Two-point leading (10/12)

Chester Carlson invented a dry means of copying, and patented the process of "xerography" [from the Greek *xeros* (dry) and *graphein* (to write)] in 1940. At least 20 companies rejected his proposal to market the device; until at last, the Haloid Company of Rochester, New York, was so excited about the possibility that it changed its name to Xerox.

(c) Three-point leading (10/13)

FIGURE 5.9
Leading.

Various means of writing short-cuts have been recorded since Roman times, but it was not until 1837, when the Englishman Isaac Pitman published *Stenographic Soundhand*, that a uniform set of symbols was adopted. American Robert Gregg introduced an alternate method 50 years later.

(a) 11 picas (10/12 Times Roman)

Various means of writing shortcuts have been recorded since Roman times, but it was not until 1837, when the Englishman Isaac Pitman published *Stenographic Soundhand*, that a uniform set of symbols was adopted. American Robert Gregg introduced an alternate method 50 years later.

(b) 22 picas (10/12 Times Roman)

Various means of writing shortcuts have been recorded since Roman times, but it was not until 1837 when the Englishman Isaac Pitman published *Stenographic Soundhand*, that a uniform set of symbols was adopted. American Robert Gregg introduced an alternate method 50 years later.

(c) 30 picas (10/12 Times Roman)

FIGURE 5.10
Column widths.

Narrow columns (Figure 5.10*a*) are difficult to read because they are choppy; overly long columns (Figure 5.10*c*) can be just as bad because they seem to go on indefinitely. Obviously, then, there is a middle ground (Figure 5.10*b*) which makes a passage easiest to read.

One generally accepted guideline is that a column width of 45 to 65 characters is optimal. The type size therefore affects the column width: the larger the type, the longer the line. The actual determination of column width (in picas) is made with the aid of Table 5.2, which shows the average number of characters per pica in varying typefaces.

Assume, for example, that you have decided on 10 point Times Roman, and further that you want each column of text to contain the suggested maximum of 65 characters. You would require, therefore, a column width of 23 picas (65/2.86). The same 65 characters set in 8-point Times Roman would take only 18 picas (65/3.57).

TABLE 5.2

Characters per Pica

Typeface	Point Size										
	6	8	10	12	14	16	18	20	24	30	36
Times Roman	4.77	3.57	2.86	2.38	2.04	1.78	1.59	1.43	1.19	.95	.79
Times Roman Italic	4.90	3.68	2.94	2.45	2.10	1.84	1.63	1.47	1.22	.98	.81
Times Roman Bold	4.48	3.36	2.68	2.24	1.91	1.67	1.49	1.34	1.12	.89	.74
Times Roman Bold Italic	4.75	3.56	2.85	2.37	2.03	1.78	1.58	1.42	1.18	.95	.79
Helvetica	4.48	3.36	2.68	2.24	1.91	1.67	1.49	1.34	1.12	.89	.74
Helvetica Italic	4.34	3.26	2.60	2.17	1.86	1.62	1.44	1.30	1.08	.87	.72
Helvetica Bold	4.07	3.05	2.44	2.03	1.74	1.52	1.35	1.22	1.01	.81	.67
Helvetica Bold Italic	4.13	3.10	2.48	2.06	1.77	1.55	1.37	1.24	1.03	.82	.68

*These figures assume a combination of uppercase and lowercase letters.

Source: PC World Magazine, March 1987, page 180.

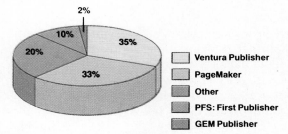

Ventura Publisher

PageMaker

Other

PFS: First Publisher

GEM Publisher

What desktop publishing program
do you use?

TRENDS IN DESKTOP PUBLISHING

A recent survey by *PC Magazine* confirmed the accuracy of two popular assumptions; namely, that PageMaker and Ventura Publisher are dividing the largest part of the market, and that standard office projects like newsletters and brochures are the main tasks.

The survey also indicated that most people who are not using desktop publishing intend to move in that direction. Of the 41 percent who said they don't currently use a desktop publishing program, 59 percent said they planned to get one.

Source: PC Magazine, August 1988; graphs, page 41.

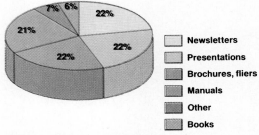

Newsletters

Presentations

Brochures, fliers

Manuals

Other

Books

What kinds of projects do you use
desktop publishing software for?

Additional Principles of Design

Thus far we have introduced the concept of desktop publishing, presented the grid system as the basis for overall document design, and covered the basics of typography. We continue now with a discussion of three additional design principles—*balance*, *unity*, and *emphasis*.

We suggest, however, that you view the ensuing discussion as general guidelines as opposed to hard-and-fast rules. You will find that your eye is the best judge of all. You should stick, therefore, to your own instincts, although you may not be able to quote the formal design principle. Much of what we say is subjective, and hence what works in one situation will not necessarily work in another. Above all, be willing to experiment and realize that successful design is often the result of trial and error.

Balance

The principle of **balance** means that equal visual weight falls on both sides of a page or on both pages of a two-page spread. Centering a column on a page produces balance, as will placing a short column with a headline next to a longer column without a heading.

Perfect balance, however, is often boring for the reader. Figure 5.11*a*, for example, is symmetrically balanced, yet it is dull in comparison to Figure 5.11*b*. The latter uses different-sized illustrations and wraps the text around the art for additional interest.

White space can also be used to balance a page, the theory being that a large area of white space has visual weight that offsets other

(a) Equal-sized art   (b) Unequal art

FIGURE 5.11
Avoiding static balance. (*Source: Aldus Guide to Basic Design*, page 6.)

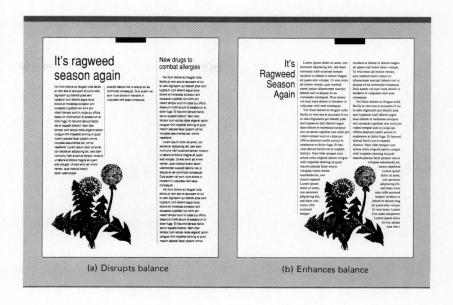

(a) Disrupts balance   (b) Enhances balance

elements. White space should, however, appear on the edges of a page as opposed to the middle. Thus the page in Figure 5.12*a* is somehow "off," whereas Figure 5.12*b* appears perfectly balanced.

Pages should also be balanced two at a time (a spread) as opposed to individually, because a reader generally views two (facing) pages together. This is well illustrated by Figure 5.13*a*, which shows individually balanced pages that do not look very well together. Figure 5.13*b*, on the other hand, rearranges the same material in a more appealing fashion.

Unity

The principle of **unity** states that all the elements on a page should look as if they belong together. Consider, for example, the mixture of typefaces in Figure 5.14*a* versus the uniform treatment afforded similar elements in Figure 5.14*b*. The page on the right clearly looks better.

Figure 5.14*a* is typical of what happens when someone uses too many typefaces (and too much clip art) simply because it is available. We are not advising that you restrict yourself to a single typeface, but rather that you use the same typeface for the same element. In other words, choose one typeface for headings and a different typeface for body copy. A combination of Helvetica and Times Roman for headings and body copy, respectively, is frequently chosen.

Unity is as important throughout a publication as it is on a single page; that is, the different types of pages should also have a consistent look, as evidenced by Figure 5.15. This type of unity can be achieved by using constant margins and by treating art in a uniform way.

FIGURE 5.13 Balance of facing pages. (*Source: Aldus Guide to Basic Design*, pages 10 and 11.)

Emphasis

The principle of **emphasis** (or contrast) calls for important ideas to attract more attention than supporting elements. There are many ways to achieve this effect, the easiest being variations in type size and style (albeit within the constraints of unity as mentioned above). Do *not*, however, set type in all capitals; a combination of upper- and lowercase letters is far more readable than text in which only uppercase letters are used.

FIGURE 5.14
Unity within a page. (*a*) Too many
type faces. (*b*) Unified page. (*Source:*
PC Magazine, October 13, 1987,
pages 174 and 175.)

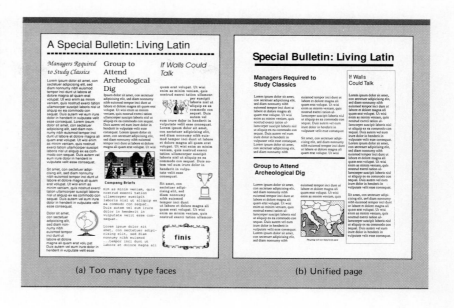

(a) Too many type faces   (b) Unified page

FIGURE 5.15   Unity within a publication. (*Source:* Price and Schnabel, *Desktop Publishing,* Balantine Books, New York, pages 4–13.)

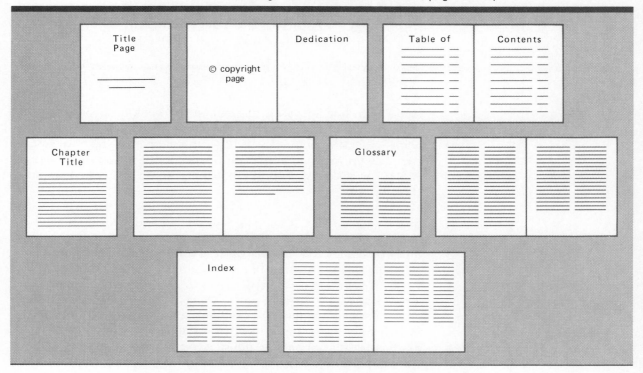

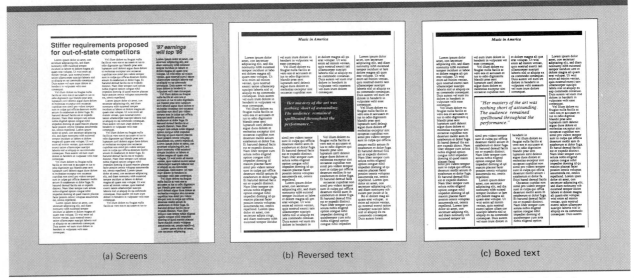

FIGURE 5.16   Achieving emphasis. (*Source: Aldus Guide to Basic Design*, pages 48 and 55.)

You can also take advantage of **screens** (shades of gray), **reverses** (white letters on a black background), or simple **boxes,** as shown in Figure 5.16. The **pull quotes** (short quotations from the text) in Figure 5.16*b* and 5.16*c* serve as graphic devices when no art is available.

A Word of Advice

It has been our approach throughout the book to incorporate the generic principles into Hands-On Exercises which require your participation at the computer. We hope, therefore, that you have a page composition program available (it need not be as sophisticated as PageMaker or Ventura Publisher), so that you will be able to do Hands-On Exercise 1.

Even if such a program is not available to you, we urge you to read through the exercise, especially steps 2 and 3, to appreciate the fact that *desktop publishing is not a carefree operation*. It is, in fact, time-consuming to learn as well as to implement, and requires considerable skill on the part of the operator.

The exercise takes you through the steps in developing a one- (or two-) page newsletter, ''Modern Office Trivia,'' based on the various figures in the chapter. The exercise is less structured than those elsewhere in the text, because that is the nature of desktop publishing. It is a flexible discipline, allowing you to make whatever decisions you wish, but that is precisely what makes it a complex procedure.

William Randolph Hearst

Joseph Pulitzer

Alfred A. Knopf

Now, your time has come.

YOU TOO CAN CREATE A PUBLISHING EMPIRE.

Authors' Comments:
Can you identify these publishing giants? William Randolph Hearst (1863–1951) received **The San Francisco Examiner** as a graduation present from his father, made it a financial success, and eventually owned papers in most major American cities. Joseph Pulitzer (1847–1911) became wealthy through **The St. Louis Post Dispatch** and **New York World** newspapers, but is better known for the prizes he endowed. Alfred A. Knopf (1893–1984) founded a publishing house which he later sold to Random House. The identity of the fourth gentleman is unknown.

(*Source:* Ad for "Scoop" Desktop Publishing Program, *Publish Magazine*, November 16, 1987, pages 14 and 15.)

You can, for example, choose any type size and any number of columns in a grid, but each combination accommodates a different amount of copy. How do you determine which parameters are best for you? Moreover, how do you adjust for the fact that no matter what parameters you select, the total amount of copy always seems to be longer or shorter than the amount of space you have allotted?

There are no easy answers, yet people continue to find satisfactory solutions, as evidenced by the explosion in the field. Do the exercise, experiment, and enjoy.

HANDS-ON EXERCISE 1: MODERN OFFICE TRIVIA

OBJECTIVE: To prepare a one- (or two-) page newsletter, "Modern Office Trivia," which incorporates the material on desktop publishing into a single exercise.

Step 1: Prepare the Copy

The copy for the newsletter will be drawn from the various illustrations throughout the chapter. (The factual information in all the features except "Liquid Paper" appeared in the article "Staples of the Modern Office," in the Living Today section of *The Miami Herald,* April 27, 1986.) Use your word processor to enter text as follows:

Figure 5.6	The rubber band
Figure 5.9	Xerography
Figure 5.10	Shorthand
Figure 5.17	Liquid paper
Figure 5.18a	The pencil and eraser
Figure 5.18b	The fountain pen
Figure 5.18c	The ball point pen

Step 2: Design the Grid

The number of columns in the grid is the single most important decision to make, and depends ultimately on how much copy (and art) you have to include. You want to begin, therefore, by estimating the total number of characters that were entered in step 1, and then choosing the appropriate column width and type size to accommodate that amount of copy.

Assume, for example, that you decide on a column width of 50 characters. (Remember our earlier guideline, which stated columns should contain from 45 to 65 characters.) You must then decide what size type you want, which in turn determines the number of columns you can fit on a page. Consider, for example, that 12- and 8-point Times Roman will yield two and three columns, respectively (on $8\frac{1}{2} \times 11$ paper), as follows:

12-point Times Roman:

$$\frac{50 \text{ characters/column}}{\boxed{2.38 \text{ characters/pica}}} = \frac{21 \text{ picas}}{\text{column}}$$
$$= \frac{3\frac{1}{2} \text{ inches}}{\text{column}} = \frac{2 \text{ columns}}{\text{page}}$$

See Table 5.2

8-point Times Roman:

$$\frac{50 \text{ characters/column}}{\boxed{3.57 \text{ characters/pica}}} = \frac{14 \text{ picas}}{\text{column}}$$
$$= \frac{2\frac{1}{3} \text{ inches}}{\text{column}} = \frac{3 \text{ columns}}{\text{page}}$$

See Table 5.2

Step 3: Complete the Type Specifications

The determination of type size goes hand in hand with the design of the grid, as depicted in step 2. Only two of a large number of potential options were explored, and many others are possible. You could, for example, reject 8-point type as too small and 12-point as too large, and opt instead for 10 point Times

Roman. (This would also allow two columns per page, but 60 rather than 50 characters per column.)

After deciding on the appropriate type size and resulting grid, you must then determine the amount of *leading* between lines. You will want at least one point of leading for the smaller type size (for example, 8 on 9) and two points for the larger sizes (10 on 12 or 12 on 14). Realize, too, that this specification also affects the amount of copy which fits on a page (for example, a specification of 10 on 11 permits more copy than 10 on 12 because there is *less* space between lines, and consequently more lines per page).

You also need to determine the type you will use in headings. It should be at least two points larger than the body type and could be set in a different style in the same family (for example, bold) or in a different family altogether. Ten-point Times Roman plain and 12-point Helvetica bold for the articles and headlines, respectively, is one combination that works well in almost all instances.

Step 4: Choose the Art
Try to find one or two pictures to include in your newsletter. The most likely source is a library of "clip art," which accompanies most page composition programs. You may also be fortunate enough to have a scanner available, in which case you are far less limited. Remember, too, that even if you have no art per se, you can still use pull quotes (screened or reversed) to add interest to your newsletter.

Step 5: Design the Masthead
A **masthead** announces the title of a newsletter and conveys something of its purpose. It is therefore the single most important design element and should be given special attention. Use the page composition program to design a suitable masthead (see exercise 3 at the end of the chapter), then place it at the top of the newsletter.

Step 6: Do a Rough Layout
Place your articles on the grid according to the design you have selected. Be sure to include the headline for each article, the art you selected, and captions (where appropriate).

Now check that your overall layout follows the design principles discussed in the chapter. It should be visually balanced without cramming too much information on a page. The different elements on the page should look as though they belong with one another, because you did not go overboard on variations in type, and because you didn't add art just for the sake of art. You should also have the appropriate amounts of emphasis to set off the headlines from body copy, and/or to highlight an important article.

Step 7: Apply the Finishing Touches
Although your newsletter is essentially finished, you can fine-tune it in several ways, depending on the sophistication of your page composition program (see the following box, entitled "Finer Points of Desktop Publishing"). Changing the column alignment (justifying it or not) is the easiest to implement, and the one with the most visual effect. Alignment, kerning, text wrap, and the elimination of widows and orphans are other features with which you might want to experiment.

"I'VE BEEN PUTTING OUT A NEWSLETTER DEALING WITH MY DAY'S ACTIVITIES, BUT RECENTLY ALL MY DAY'S ACTIVITIES CONSIST OF PUTTING OUT THE NEWSLETTER."

FINER POINTS OF DESKTOP PUBLISHING

Alignment describes how text lines up on a page or column. Text which is justified is aligned on both margins (that is, it is **flush right** and **flush left).** Text which is not justified is aligned on only one margin (for example, flush left, ragged right) or centered. Virtually all programs enable any of these choices.

Widows and orphans are single lines that look out of place. An orphan results when the first line of a new paragraph appears as the last line of the previous page; a widow occurs when the last line of a paragraph appears at the top of a new page. Some systems allow you to establish automatic controls for the minimum number of lines that can be separated by a page break, and thereby eliminate widows and orphans.

Text wrap is the ability to wrap text around graphic images. Some page composition programs will automatically shorten lines of text when a graphic is encountered. Other systems require you to make these changes manually.

Kerning is the subtraction of minute amounts of space between specific letter combinations so that the overall letter spacing is more consistent. Most page composition programs do kerning automatically.

GUIDELINES FOR TYPE SELECTION

- Select a typeface appropriate for its intended use. For example, do not use a light, flowing typeface in advertising copy for heavy machinery.

- Distinguish between headings, subheadings, and body copy with type of varying size. Choose a type size between 8 and 12 points for copy, and a size 2 points larger for headings.

- Use bold and/or italic type within the same family to emphasize text. Do not set type in all uppercase letters.

- Specify leading that is approximately 20 percent of the type size. For example, 10-point type should be set on 12-point lines (10 on 12).

- Choose a column width of appropriate length and in accordance with the type size; that is, larger type requires longer lines.

CORPORATE PROFILE:
ALDUS CORPORATION

Year-end statistics for 1987:
Sales: $39.5 million
Net income: $7.8 million
CEO: Paul Brainerd
Headquarters: 411 First Street
South Suite 200
Seattle, WA 98104
(206) 622-5500

"The dream of every commercial software engineer is to write a program that exploits the power of the microcomputer to solve a problem common to millions of people.... The result is more than making the dreamer rich.... The real result is to turn something that nobody thought was needed into an absolute necessity.... PageMaker, from Aldus Corp., may become the program that establishes desktop publishing as the new necessity." (Excerpted from a review of PageMaker in the September 16, 1985, issue of *Info World*.)

It is the typical Horatio Alger success story. Five unemployed computer types, who lost their jobs when their high-tech employer closed its local office, made a trip down the Oregon coast in January 1984. They rode in two cars, stayed in cheap motels, and talked about inventing something wonderful and getting rich. Along the way they stopped in the library at Oregon State, researched books on the history of printing, and stumbled on the name Aldus Manutius, who invented italic type in the sixteenth century. Thus was born the **Aldus Corporation.**

The five would eventually develop PageMaker, a program that allowed users of Apple's Macintosh to create high-quality

publications directly on the computer, without the tedious paste-up procedure necessary in traditional publishing. The motivator in the group was **Paul Brainerd,** who had worked for the *Minneapolis Star & Tribune* in the late 1970s and who had computerized the paper's editorial operations. Brainerd later left the newspaper to take a job with Atex Inc., the computer supplier for the newspaper. When Atex closed its Redmond, Washington, office,

Brainerd recruited four of his coworkers and invested $100,000 of his own money to fund the venture.

Brainerd's original idea was for a program to prepare newspaper ads on microcomputers. The trip down the Oregon coast was made to visit various papers and explore the concept, but the five soon realized that this highly specialized market was too small. They then rejected in succession several other proposals aimed at

ALDUS CORPORATION
SALES AND PROFITS
(millions of dollars)

publishers of one kind or another.

Finally they turned the concept around. Instead of bringing the microcomputer to publishing, they decided to bring publishing to the microcomputer and develop a software product that could be used by a broad audience. In hindsight it appears obvious, but at the time it did not seem possible that a mass market could exist for a publishing system aimed at people other than publishers.

The concept for PageMaker, however, was only the beginning. The link to the Apple Macintosh was crucial (it was the only computer then in existence with sufficient graphic capability), as was the tie to the LaserWriter, then in development. The key was to convince Apple. Brainerd coined the term **desktop publishing** to describe the new market he hoped to create, thinking PageMaker would sell Macs, much like VisiCalc had spurred demand for the original Apple II.

Brainerd was lucky, since Apple was looking for something to demonstrate the capabilities of its LaserWriter. The two companies agreed that Aldus would assist in the final testing of the LaserWriter in order to make it completely compatible with PageMaker. Moreover, every LaserWriter would be sold with a PageMaker demonstration program, and national advertising would further link the two. PageMaker would later be credited with boosting Apple sales by several million dollars, in that every $500 sale of PageMaker required $10,000 worth of Apple hardware. (PageMaker has since been adapted to run on IBM-compatible hardware.)

It remained, however, to convince the public. One of Brainerd's key decisions was to bypass the wholesale channel and sell only through qualified retail dealers. To that end he attended dealer training sessions in 21 cities in order to turn individual dealers

"We intend to maintain our leadership in desktop publishing through product innovation, joint efforts with other vendors, and an absolute commitment to customer service and support."

■ Paul Brainerd
President,
Aldus Corporation

into PageMaker specialists. The concept worked. PageMaker shipped its first product on July 15, 1985, and recorded sales of $13 million in the next year and a half. The initial public offering of Aldus stock in 1986 valued Brainerd's original stake in the company at $100 million.

Today, desktop publishing is a major segment of the computer industry, accounting for approximately $1 billion in annual revenue.

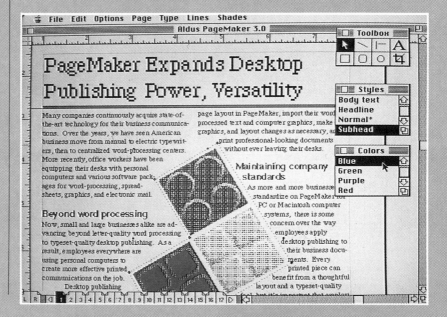

Summary

The chapter dealt entirely with desktop publishing, one of the most exciting and visible applications of microcomputers. The centerpiece of any desktop system is the page composition software, which enables you to express thoughts and ideas through text and graphics, and which provides immediate feedback on the appearance of your publication. A laser printer will then produce the document in finished form, ready for immediate distribution.

Bear in mind, however, that the mere availability of desktop publishing does not necessarily guarantee professional-looking work. Accordingly, we discussed the elements of typography, the grid system of design, and the principles of balance, unity, and emphasis to help you in the production of your documents.

Key Words and Concepts

Adobe Systems Inc.
Aldus Corporation
Alignment
Balance
Boldface
Boxes
Paul Brainerd
Desktop publishing
Emphasis
Flush left
Flush right
Grid
Helvetica
Italic
Kerning
Laser printer
Leading
Masthead
Page composition software
Page description language
PageMaker
Picas
Points
PostScript
Pull quotes
Reverses
Sans serif
Scanner
Screens
Serif
Text wrap
Times Roman
Type family
Type font
Type size
Type style
Typeface
Typography
Unity
Ventura Publisher
White space
Widows and orphans

True/False

1. Desktop publishing is a carefree operation.

2. Times Roman is an example of a sans serif typeface.

3. Helvetica 10-point bold and Helvetica 10-point italic are in the same family but represent distinct fonts.

4. The measurement "10 on 12" (10/12) relates to the spacing between lines.

5. There are 72 points to the inch.

6. There are 6 picas to the inch.

7. The length of a printed line is measured in points.

8. PageMaker will run on either a Macintosh or an IBM computer.

9. If pages within a publication are individually balanced, the entire publication will be balanced.

10. A well-balanced page should have exactly as much art as text.

11. The principle of variation suggests that many different typefaces should appear on the same page.

12. White space should never be used in a publication.

13. Desktop publishing requires the availability of a scanning device.

14. The grid system of design provides for publications of one, two, three, four, or more columns.

15. Art should never cross columns in a grid.

16. PostScript is an example of a page description language.

17. The selection of a page composition program requires the availability of PostScript.

18. Desktop publishing may be implemented on either the Apple Macintosh or IBM-compatible computers.

19. Smaller type sizes require longer column widths than do larger type sizes.

Multiple Choice

1. Desktop publishing:
   (a) Is only for professional publishers
   (b) Eliminates (or reduces) the need for external services
   (c) Increases the time and cost required to produce documents
   (d) Does not require proficiency in word processing or knowledge of graphic design

2. The first desktop publishing system was designed for the:
   (a) IBM PS/2 series
   (b) Apple Macintosh
   (c) Compaq Deskpro
   (d) Tandy 100

3. Times Roman and Helvetica
   (a) Are serif and sans serif type faces respectively
   (b) Are widely available

(c) Are used in *Time* and *People* magazines respectively

(d) All of the above

4. A type specification of 10 on 12 (10/12)
    (a) Indicates vertical spacing (leading)
    (b) Indicates column width (line length)
    (c) Indicates the left and right margins
    (d) Indicates the top and bottom margins

5. Widows and orphans refer to:
    (a) Single lines of text that look out of place
    (b) Art with no accompanying text
    (c) Text with no accompanying art
    (d) All of the above

6. Which type size is reasonable for columns of text, such as those appearing in a magazine?
    (a) 6 point
    (b) 10 point
    (c) 14 point
    (d) 18 point

7. Which column width is reasonable for columns of text such as those appearing in a magazine?
    (a) 6 picas or less
    (b) 12 to 18 picas
    (c) 18 to 36 picas
    (d) More than 36 picas

8. Typography is the process of:
    (a) Entering text and graphics into a computer terminal
    (b) Selecting typefaces, sizes, and spacing requirements
    (c) Merging text, graphics, and other art into a document
    (d) Converting a printed document into machine-readable form

9. Which guideline would you be least likely to follow when designing pages containing art?
    (a) Place art after it is mentioned in the text
    (b) Make art the same width as the text it accompanies
    (c) Position art at the top or bottom of the page
    (d) Leave no space at all between art and text

10. The grid system of design applies to publications with:
    (a) One column
    (b) Two columns
    (c) Three columns
    (d) All of the above

11. The use of screens, reverses, and/or pull quotes within a publication is intended for:
    (a) Emphasis
    (b) Balance
    (c) Unity
    (d) Variety

12. A balanced design:
    (a) Is best achieved by reviewing individual pages as opposed to facing pages
    (b) Will always be perfectly symmetrical, with equal amounts of text and art
    (c) Cannot be accomplished if white space remains on the page
    (d) All of the above
    (e) None of the above

13. Which combination of typefaces is most appropriate for reports and/or manuals?
    (a) Times Roman for body text and Helvetica for headlines
    (b) Helvetica for body text and Times Roman for headlines
    (c) Both are equally appropriate
    (d) Neither one is appropriate since different typefaces should never appear in the same document

14. 12 Point Times Roman and 12 Point Times Roman Bold are examples of:
    (a) Different typefaces
    (b) Different type families
    (c) Different type sizes
    (d) Different type fonts

15. The two most popular page composition programs are:
    (a) PageMaker and Ventura Publisher
    (b) Aldus and Adobe
    (c) PostScript and Scripsit
    (d) LaserWriter and LaserJet

Exercises

1. Use Figure 5.17 as the basis to experiment with type selection. Enter the text in a word processor, then use page composition software to implement the specifications below.
   (a) Times Roman, 10/12, flush left, ragged right, with a line length of 22 picas.
   (b) Times Roman, 10/12, flush left, flush right, with a line length of 22 picas.
   (c) Times Roman 8/9, flush left, ragged right, with a line length of 18 picas.
   (d) Times Roman 8/9, flush left, flush right, with a line length of 18 picas.
   (e) Repeat parts *a* through *d*, using Helvetica rather than Times Roman.

2. Figure 5.18 contains three proposed layouts for the opening of *Alice's Adventures in Wonderland*, all of which have been reduced from $8\frac{1}{2} \times 11''$ pages. Due to differences in type size, margin width,

Liquid paper was developed in 1951 by Bette Nesmith, an executive secretary working at the Texas Bank of Trust. Frustrated because an ordinary eraser would smear the carbon ink used in electric typewriters, she noticed that graphic artists corrected their mistakes by painting over them.

The next day she put some tempera waterbase paint in a bottle and took her watercolor brush to the office. Convinced she was on to something when other secretaries in the building began asking for correction fluid, she approached IBM about selling the product. (IBM wasn't interested, telling her to improve the product and then come back). Undaunted, Bette set up shop in her kitchen and talked her teenage son Michael into working as her first employee.

Michael Nesmith of the Monkees (bottom right), the first employee of Liquid Paper Corporation.

FIGURE 5.17 Text for exercise 1

FIGURE 5.18
Pages for exercise 2. (*Source: Publish Magazine*, May 1987, page 116.)

column width, and so on, each page contains a different amount of text. Can you arrange the pages in order, from the layout with the least text to the one with the most?

(a) Times Roman 10/12

Alice was beginning to get very tired of sitting by her sister on the bank, and of having nothing to do: once or twice she had peeped into the book her sister was reading, but it

(b) Times Roman 12/14

Alice was beginning to get very tired of sitting by her sister on the bank, and of having nothing to do: once or twice she had

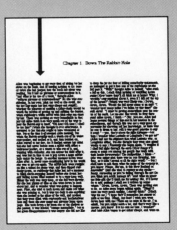

(c) Times Roman 12/12

Alice was beginning to get very tired of sitting by her sister on the bank, and of having nothing to do: once or twice she had peeped into the book

FIGURE 5.19
Type samples for exercise 3.

A pencil and an eraser had to be purchased separately until 1858 when Hyman Lipman thought of putting the two together. Lipman cut a groove in the top of a pencil, glued a small eraser onto the pencil, and sold his patent for $100,000!

Example 1

Catherine the Great first spoke of writing from "an endless quill," but it took another century until the first patent for a continuously flowing fountain pen was granted to D. Hyde of Reading, Pennsylvania, in 1830. It took another 50 years and more than 400 additional patents until Lewis Waterman solved the problem of keeping the ink flow constant.

Example 2

THE FIRST AMERICAN BALL POINT PENS WENT ON SALE AT GIMBELS IN NEW YORK IN 1945 AT $12.50 APIECE. BY 1949 BALL POINT SALES EXCEEDED THOSE OF THE FOUNTAIN PEN AND NEVER LOOKED BACK.

Example 3

3. Figure 5.19 contains three examples of text set in Times Roman, each of which contains a fundamental error in design. Identify the problem in each example and correct accordingly.

4. Figure 5.20 contains several potential mastheads for inclusion in the newsletter of Hands-On Exercise 1. Use your page composition software to replicate some or all of our designs, then develop your own.

5. Figure 5.21 contains a word puzzle in which you are to complete the 12 clues, then take the appropriate letter from each answer to decipher the secret message at the bottom of the figure. Most of the clues refer to a specific publishing term which was covered in the chapter. A few, however, refer to terms which were not

FIGURE 5.20
Creating a masthead.

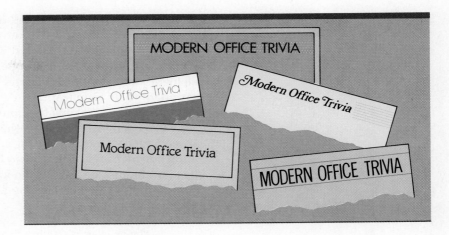

described, but which you may be able to get anyway, either through the publishing definition or the related clue (for example, the answer to number 12 is *signature*).

1. To add space between lines
   (British group Zeppelin). ___ ___ ___ ___
               10

2. Page for checking (potency of potables). ___ ___ ___ ___ ___ ___
             1

3. The matrix on which pages are planned
   (football field, minus Fe). ___ ___ ___ ___
           9

4. A typographic measurement
   (ballet position). ___ ___ ___ ___ ___
         4

5. Another typographic measurement (Yankee
   pronunciation of a kind of tightwad). ___ ___ ___ ___
         7

6. Putting the squeeze on a couple of characters
   ("coin" in Brooklyn). ___ ___ ___ ___ ___
         11

7. A long sheet of type (ship's kitchen). ___ ___ ___ ___ ___
         8

8. Planning the arrangement of a publication,
   by mechanical means or with software
   (congressional aide's floor plan). ___ ___ ___ ___ ___ ___ ___ ___ ___
         3

9. Dangling line of type (black arachnid). ___ ___ ___ ___ ___
         12

10. Label at top of page (soccer move). ___ ___ ___ ___ ___
          6

11. Heavy type (brave visage). ___ ___ ___ ___ ___
          5

12. A sheet of paper folded to form pages in
    multiples of four (a John Hancock). ___ ___ ___ ___ ___ ___ ___
          2

MESSAGE

___ ___ ___ ___ ___ ___ ___   ___ ___   ___ ___ ___ ___ ___ ___
7 3 5 10 12 2 6   4 11   1 8 9 12 2 6

FIGURE 5.21
Clues for exercise 5.
(*Source: Publish Magazine*)

6. Publishing puzzle: Composing a newspaper page or magazine spread is like solving a jigsaw puzzle. You have to fit together articles, photos, headlines, and other elements (like the newspaper's masthead) to form a coherent and readable whole. Each element should have a size and position on the page that's appropriate to its significance.

Figure 5.22 contains the components that make up the front page of a fictional newspaper, the *Midnight Express News*. They're spread out as they might be on a paste-up table. It's deadline time, and your managing editor (who has an unusual sense of humor) has left the instructions in the form of accompanying hints. Can you compose the page and be able to face your boss tomorrow morning?

1. The smallest photo is surrounded by four different stories.

2. The headline of the lead story, about the president, is to the right of the biggest picture.

3. The story about a natural disaster is illustrated by the biggest photo and is above the article on submarines.

4. The second lead story, which is about whales, is at the top of the far left column.

5. The biggest picture is directly under the masthead.

6. The paper's name is above the date of publication.

7. The second-largest photo is above the table of contents.

8. The motto goes on the masthead above the volume and issue numbers.

9. The story on cars and energy is below the second lead story.

10. The newspaper's price is above the lead story.

11. The table of contents is to the right and below the submarine story.

12. The composed page fits on a grid five columns wide and seven deep.

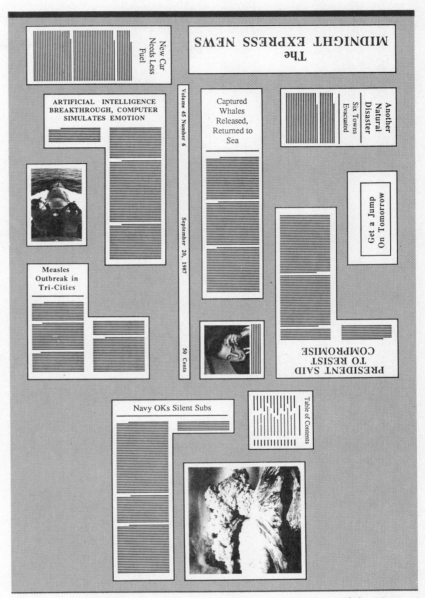

FIGURE 5.22   Publishing puzzle, exercise 6. (*Source*: "The Case of the Missing Dummy," *Publish Magazine*, September 1987, page 152.)

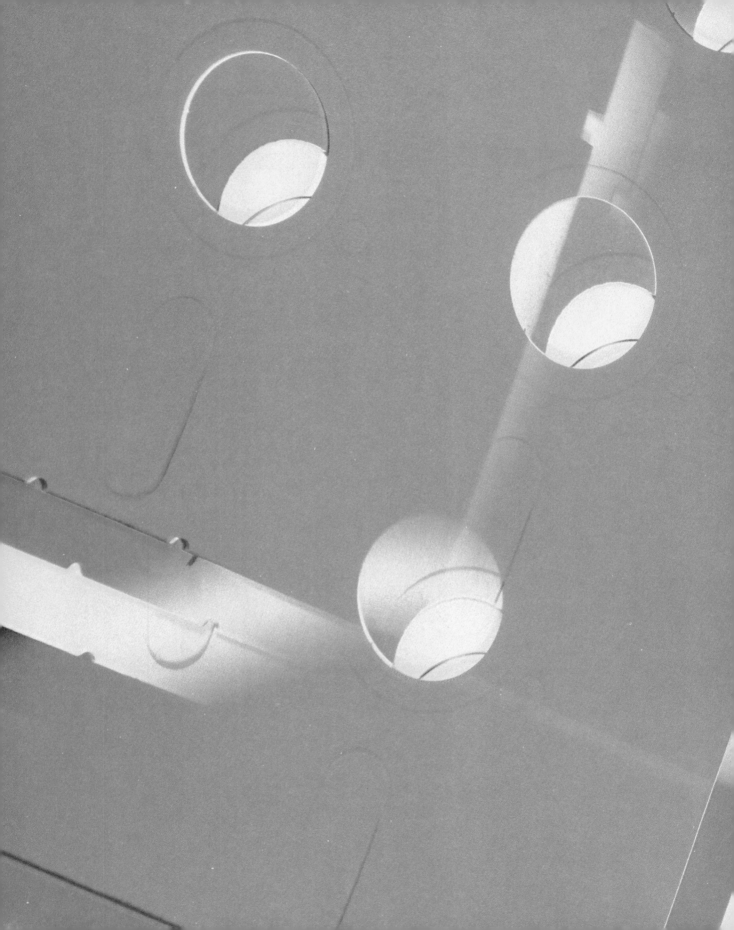

PART 3

SPREADSHEETS

CHAPTER 6

INTRODUCTION TO SPREADSHEETS

After reading this chapter, you should be able to:

1. Define an electronic spreadsheet.

2. Describe how the rows and columns of a spreadsheet are identified, and how its cells are labeled.

3. Name four types of cell entries and distinguish between them.

4. Define scrolling.

5. Distinguish between various modes of spreadsheet operation: entry, ready, and command.

6. Create and modify a simple spreadsheet, using whatever spreadsheet program is available to you.

7. Describe how to invoke common spreadsheet commands, including save, load (retrieve), insert, delete, and print.

Overview

This chapter introduces the electronic spreadsheet, perhaps the most widely used application of microcomputers by executives. Our intent is to show the wide diversity of business and other uses to which the spreadsheet model can be applied. We draw an analogy between the spreadsheet and the accountant's ledger, and derive a second example from an instructor's grade book. The chapter also covers fundamentals of spreadsheets, discussing how the rows and columns of a spreadsheet are labeled, how the cursor moves, and the concept of scrolling. We show that the contents of a cell may be a number, a label, a formula, or a special function.

The supplementary articles in the chapter are particularly relevant to the discussion of spreadsheet fundamentals. The piece on "The Discrete Charms of VisiCalc" discusses the power of spreadsheets in general and the unique role played by VisiCalc in their development. "Rank-and-File Thinking" alludes to the virtually unlimited number of applications of the spreadsheet model, and "The Great Spreadsheet Face-Off" aptly illustrates that there is no single best spreadsheet.

The Corporate Profile focuses on Apple Computer, the legendary company begun by Jobs and Wozniak. We selected Apple for this chapter because many people attribute at least a part of Apple's phenomenal early success to the availability of VisiCalc, the first spreadsheet program.

What Is an Electronic Spreadsheet?

An **electronic spreadsheet** is the computerized equivalent of an accountant's ledger. As with the ledger, it consists of a grid of rows and columns that enables you to organize information in a readily understandable format. Figure 6.1a and 6.1b shows the same information displayed in ledger and spreadsheet format, respectively.

FIGURE 6.1 Manual and electronic spreadsheets, example 1. (a) Typical account ledger sheet entries. (b) Spreadsheet with $20 unit price. (c) Spreadsheet with $22 unit price.

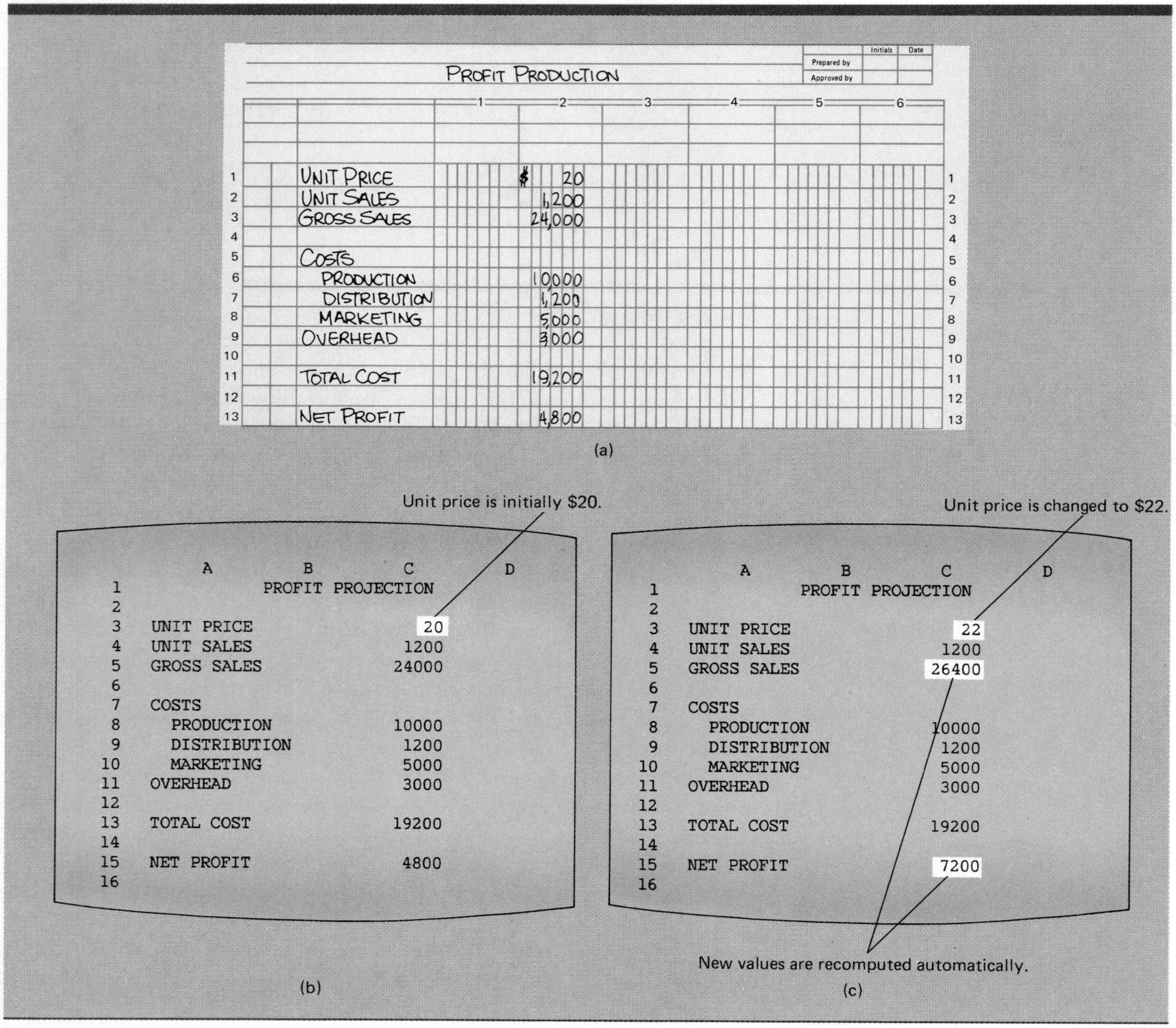

"What is the big deal?" you might ask. The big deal is that after you change an entry (or entries) the electronic spreadsheet will, automatically and almost instantly, recompute the entire spreadsheet. Consider, for example, the profit projection spreadsheet shown in Figure 6.1*b*. As the spreadsheet is presently constructed, the unit price is $20, producing gross sales of $24,000 and a net profit of $4800. If the unit price is increased to $22 per unit, the electronic spreadsheet recomputes every entry, adjusting the values of gross sales and net profit. The modified spreadsheet of Figure 6.1*c* appears automatically on your monitor.

With a bottle of white-out or a good eraser the same changes could also be made to the ledger. But imagine for a moment a ledger with hundreds of entries, many of which depend on the entry you wish to change. You can appreciate the time required to make all the necessary changes to the ledger by hand. However, the same spreadsheet, with hundreds of entries, will be recomputed automatically by the computer. And the computer will not make mistakes. Herein lies the big advantage of computer spreadsheets; the ability to make (or consider making) changes, and to have the computer carry out the recalculation faster and more accurately than could be accomplished manually.

A Second Example

A second example of a spreadsheet, with which you can easily identify, is that of a professor's grade book. The grades are typically recorded by hand in a notebook, which is nothing more than a different kind of accountant's ledger. Thus Figure 6.2 contains both manual and spreadsheet versions of a grade book.

Figure 6.2*a* depicts a handwritten grade book as it has been done since the days of the little red schoolhouse. For the sake of simplicity, only three students are shown, each with three grades. The professor has computed class averages for each of the three exams, as well as a semester average for every student in which the final counts *twice* as much as either test. For example, Adams's average is equal to: (100 + 90 + 81 + 81) / 4 = 88.

Figure 6.2*b* shows the same information as it might appear in an electronic spreadsheet, and is essentially unchanged from Figure 6.2*a*. Brown's grade on the final exam in Figure 6.2*b* is 78, giving him a semester average of 82 and producing a class average of 82 as well.

Now consider Figure 6.2*c*, in which the grade on Brown's final exam has been changed to 84. This in turn causes the class average on the final to go from 82 to 84, and Brown's semester average to change from 82 to 85. As with the accountant's ledger, a change to any entry within the grade book automatically updates all other val-

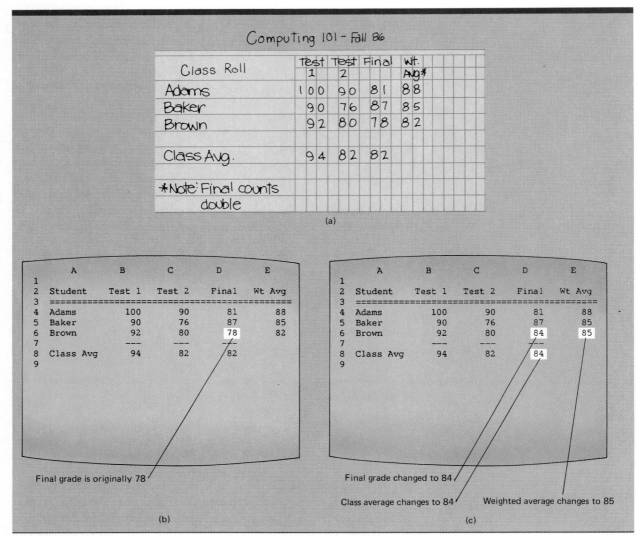

FIGURE 6.2 Manual and electronic spreadsheets, example 2. (a) An instructor's grade book. (b) Spreadsheet version. (c) Revised spreadsheet.

ues as well. Hence, when Brown's final exam was regraded, all dependent values (namely, the class average for the final as well as Brown's semester average) were changed.

As simple as the idea of an electronic spreadsheet may seem, it provided the first major reason for managers to have a personal computer on their desks. Essentially, anything that can be done with a pencil, a pad of paper, and a calculator can be done faster and far more accurately with an electronic spreadsheet.

"YOU NEVER GO TO YOUR COUNTING-HOUSE ANY MORE."

A Capsule History

The first computerized spreadsheet was developed by **Dan Bricklin** in 1979 while he was enrolled in a master's program in business administration at Harvard University. Much of the work he was required to do involved tedious calculations for complex business problems, which were often done on an accountant's ledger. With the help of **Robert Frankston,** a student who knew how to program, they developed the first electronic spreadsheet program and called it **VisiCalc** (for Visible Calculator).

VisiCalc went on to become one of the most successful software programs ever sold. It was initially written for the Apple II personal computer, but was soon converted to run on virtually any microcomputer. Indeed, many people credit Apple's early success to the availability of VisiCalc, which gave businesspeople a reason to buy a computer. Other spreadsheets soon appeared, each with its own particular improvement to the basic design suggested by VisiCalc.

A new generation of spreadsheets was born with the introduction of **Lotus 1-2-3** in 1982. Lotus was the first **integrated spreadsheet,** offering graphics and data management capabilities in conjunction with an enhanced version of the traditional spreadsheet. It was written expressly for the IBM PC, and it may have done for IBM what VisiCalc did for Apple. Lotus was an instant success, grossing $50 million in its first year and enabling Lotus Development Corporation (see the Corporate Profile in Chapter 7) to reign as the largest independent software company until 1987. (Microsoft is now number 1.)

The tremendous success of Lotus led naturally to the development of competing spreadsheets. Programs such as Paperback Software's **VP Planner** or Mosaic Software's **Twin** offer similar functions with the same "look and feel" of Lotus, yet at a significantly lower price. At the other end of the spectrum are more powerful programs such as Borland International's **Quattro** or Microsoft's **Excel**, which are designed for the increased capabilities of IBM's PS/2 series. Nor has Lotus Development Corporation stood still as it continues to enhance its products, most recently with the release of Version 3.0 in 1988.

THE DISCREET CHARMS OF VISICALC

One thing certain about the nascent age of personal computers is that a single useful program did more to give these machines respectability than all other major developments put together. The program was VisiCalc, the first good reason for business executives and managers to put personal computers on their office desks.

Now as ubiquitous as the three-piece suit, whether in its original form or as one of the dozens of sincerely flattering "visiclones" that rival it in sales, VisiCalc is no great shakes to look at. It presents you with a disarmingly simple screen, resembling a vast accountant's ledger made up of 254 rows and 63 columns (though it shows you only a small block of these at any one time). Each box, or "cell," can contain words, numbers, or (and herein lies its genius) formulas that operate on those numbers.

In one column, for example, the top cell might contain the label "Expenses." In the cells below there might be a variety of numbers, with the bottommost cell holding a formula instructing the computer to display the sum of all the numbers in the column. Then, no matter how many numbers are put in the cells in that column, the electronic spreadsheet program gives you a new running total of expenses each time you put it through its paces.

But VisiCalc can do far more than just add. Using a simple formula, you can program a cell to add the numbers in the first three rows, subtract the sum from a number held in the next row, multiply the result by a constant, divide by a number from another column, and write the number in a cell somewhere across the sheet. Then, after doing all that, VisiCalc can express the result as a percentage or in scientific notation rounded out to the nearest integer or to twelve decimals. Begin to get the picture?

In a trice, VisiCalc makes detailed calculations that would keep a platoon of accountants busy for hours. This is its tour de force, allowing you to get information you wouldn't dare ask for otherwise. It lets you crunch several alternate sets of numbers and compare the results. For the first time, the individual or small business can do what the big-leaguers have always been able to do with large, expensive computers: make several projections based on different assumptions and play them all out on paper.

Consider the possibilities. Say you own a widget factory. Here, on a disk, is the ability to reckon the unit cost for each individual widget, taking into account materials, labor, inflation, taxes, shipping and overhead. Should any one of these variables change, you just reenter that one value, press a button and—voila!—the projection's totals are all adapted to the new information. Or, if you're an investor in Consolidated Widget stock and your shares rise ten points while the prime drops a point, a few quick strokes can tell you if it makes sense to refinance the loan you got at 13 percent.

The speculative plugging in and recalculating of financial figures have charmingly been called "what-if games." These are the kinds of games that Masters of Business Administration spend two years in B-school playing so they can then creatively improve on a company's balance sheet. Unfortunately, there is a tendency on the part of MBAs and U.S. businessmen in general to rely on such games instead of common sense in running their affairs.

Is it worth noting that while electronic spreadsheets have been among the most successful personal computer programs in America, their importance overseas has generally been secondary to information filing and retrieval software; in Europe and Japan, it seems, facts are more important than projections. VisiCalc's success on these shores is indicative of America's business culture, including some of its disturbing flaws. Intended as an accurate planning tool, VisiCalc is often used instead to "fudge" financial figures in the eternal search for glowing projections.

With some of VisiCalc's results as fictitious as the budget estimates issued by federal agencies and yet just as vital to long-term planning (and waste), it's no wonder that administrators of all stripes have taken to using and abusing its powers. Don't think of it as software; think of it as realpolitik on a disk.

Source: David Nimmons, *Digital Deli.* ©1984 by Steve Ditlea. Workman Publishing, New York. Reprinted by permission.

Authors' Comments:
This delightful article provides a pleasant introduction to VisiCalc and, by extension, to spreadsheets in general. Of special interest is the cautionary note on the use of spreadsheets found in the last two paragraphs, a subject to which we frequently return in later chapters.

Spreadsheet Fundamentals

At this point you should have some appreciation of *what* spreadsheets can do. In this section, we move to a discussion of *how* they do it and begin by introducing various spreadsheet fundamentals. We describe how spreadsheets are labeled, discuss what kind of information you can store in a spreadsheet, tell you how to enter that information, and explain how you move from point to point within a spreadsheet.

Row and Column Labels

Figure 6.3 is a slightly modified version of the instructor's grade book. As you can see, the spreadsheet is divided into rows and columns, with each row and column assigned a label. Rows are given *numeric* labels ranging from 1 to the maximum row number available in a particular spreadsheet program. Columns are assigned *alphabetic* labels from column A to Z, then continue from AA to AZ and then from BA to BZ and so on, until the last column is reached.

The intersection of every row and column forms a **cell,** with the number of cells in a spreadsheet equal to the number of rows times the number of columns. The spreadsheet in Figure 6.3 has 5 columns labeled A through E, 9 rows numbered from 1 to 9, and a total of 45 cells. Each cell has its own unique **cell address;** for example, the cell at the intersection of column A and row 9 has the address A9.

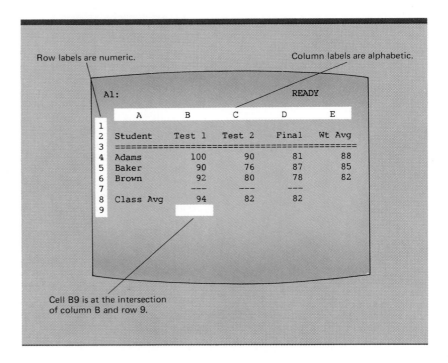

FIGURE 6.3
An instructor's grade book.

The maximum number of rows and columns depends on the spreadsheet program and the memory capacity of the computer being used. Commercial spreadsheets that allow you to develop very large models, in excess of 1 million cells, are commonly available. While this capacity greatly exceeds our present needs, it does provide an indication of the power of today's software.

Labels, Values, Formulas, and Functions

The spreadsheet in Figure 6.3 was developed one cell at a time by entering different types of information into the individual cells. Every entry in a spreadsheet falls into one of four classes: a *label*, a *numeric value*, a *formula*, or a *function*.

A **label** provides descriptive information about entries in the spreadsheet. It may consist of letters only (for example, Adams), letters and numbers, (for example, Test 1), or special characters (for example, – – –). Cells A4, B2, and C7 in Figure 6.3 contain the labels Adams, Test 1, and – – –, respectively.

A **numeric value** is simply a number, which in addition to being displayed on the spreadsheet, can be included in mathematical operations. Cells B4, C4, and D4 in Figure 6.3 contain the numbers 100, 90, and 81, respectively.

The contents of a cell may also call for the evaluation of a **formula** (or mathematical expression) such as the addition (multiplication, division, and so on) of the numeric values in other cell locations. It would be silly, for example, for you to enter the number 88 in cell E4, since the 88 represents the student's average and is in actuality the result of a computation. Instead you would enter the formula for calculating the average (B4 + C4 + 2 * D4) / 4, into cell E4 and trust in the spreadsheet to perform the arithmetic. In this way, should there be a change in any of the numbers on which the average is based (the test scores in cells B4, C4, or D4), the average would automatically be recalculated.

A cell can also contain a predefined mathematical calculation or **function,** such as @SUM(argument) or @AVG(argument). The entry enclosed in parentheses is called the **argument (range)** of the function. In Figure 6.3, for example, the entry in cell B8 can be expressed as: @AVG(B4..B6). The value for cell B8 will be computed as the average of the three cells in the *range of cells from B4 to B6, inclusive*. You can appreciate that special functions such as @AVG are often easier to use than the corresponding formulas, especially with larger spreadsheets (for example, classes with many students).

The means by which a spreadsheet distinguishes one type of entry from another is illustrated in Figure 6.4. This figure depicts the actual cell contents for every cell as they would be entered, in order to create the grade book of Figure 6.3.

Label entries in Figure 6.4 begin with either an apostrophe or quotation marks as shown in cells A2 and B2, respectively. (In Lotus,

FIGURE 6.4
Cell contents for creating Figure 6.3
(Lotus 1-2-3 implementation).

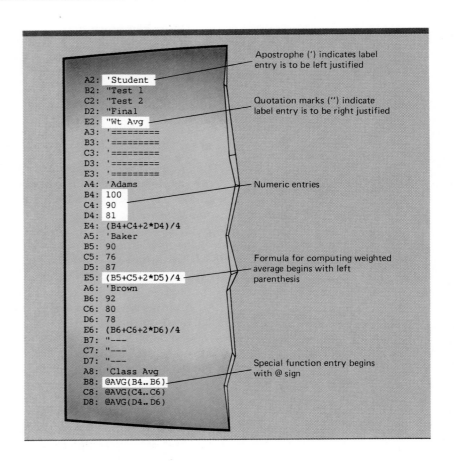

The figure shows the following cell contents with annotations:

```
A2:  'Student          ──── Apostrophe (') indicates label
B2:  "Test 1                 entry is to be left justified
C2:  "Test 2
D2:  "Final            ──── Quotation marks (") indicate
E2:  "Wt Avg                label entry is to be right justified
A3:  '=========
B3:  '=========
C3:  '=========
D3:  '=========
E3:  '=========
A4:  'Adams            ──── Numeric entries
B4:  100
C4:  90
D4:  81
E4:  (B4+C4+2*D4)/4
A5:  'Baker
B5:  90
C5:  76
D5:  87            ──── Formula for computing weighted
E5:  (B5+C5+2*D5)/4      average begins with left
A6:  'Brown              parenthesis
B6:  92
C6:  80
D6:  78
E6:  (B6+C6+2*D6)/4
B7:  "---
C7:  "---
D7:  "---            ──── Special function entry begins
A8:  'Class Avg           with @ sign
B8:  @AVG(B4..B6)
C8:  @AVG(C4..C6)
D8:  @AVG(D4..D6)
```

for example, preceding the label with ' or " aligns the label on the left or right side of the cell, respectively.) Numeric entries have a number as their first character (for example, 100, 90, and 81 in cells B4, C4, and D4, respectively). Formulas begin with a left parenthesis (or plus or minus sign) as shown for cell E4, and functions start with an @ sign as illustrated in cell B8.

The Active Cell and Screen Display

The **active cell** is defined as that cell within the spreadsheet where the cursor is presently located. The **cursor** is moved from cell to cell by pressing the **arrow keys** located on the number pad of the keyboard, and by using other keys whose meanings change depending on the program. Pressing the **home key,** however, almost invariably moves the cursor to the upper left corner of the spreadsheet, that is, to cell A1.

The concept of the active cell and its contents is illustrated in Figure 6.5 in which each screen is divided into two sections: the **control** (**summary**) **panel** and the **spreadsheet** itself. The actual format of the screen depends upon the specific spreadsheet you are using, but all programs are generally alike with respect to this division.

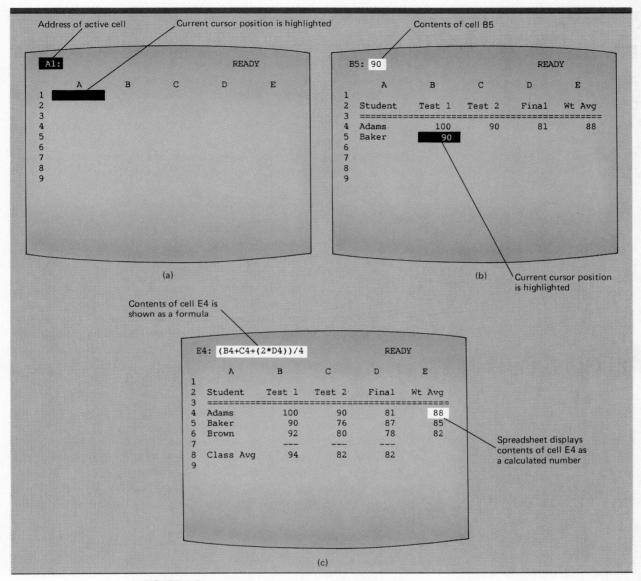

FIGURE 6.5
Displaying the active cell. (a) An empty spreadsheet. (b) Partially developed spreadsheet. (c) The control panel.

Figure 6.5*a* displays an empty spreadsheet. The control panel indicates the active cell (cell A1), and this cell in turn is highlighted in the spreadsheet itself. The upper right portion of the control panel displays READY, implying that entries may be made in the spreadsheet.

Figure 6.5*b* and 6.5*c* shows the spreadsheet at other stages of development. The cursor is positioned at cell B5 in Figure 6.5*b*, and this information is indicated in the control panel of that figure. The control panel also displays the contents of cell B5; that is, the number 90 corresponding to Baker's first test grade.

The cursor is positioned at cell E4 in Figure 6.5c. The control panel, however, displays the contents of cell E4 as a formula, (B4 + C4 + (2 * D4)) / 4, rather than the result of that formula. Virtually all spreadsheets use the symbols +, −, *, and / to indicate addition, subtraction, multiplication, and division. The precise rules for combining these symbols into arithmetic formulas are discussed in the next chapter.

Recall that entering formulas instead of numbers is preferable when results depend on values which may change. As Figure 6.5c shows, the control panel displays the formula or function on which a value is based, even though the active cell in the spreadsheet shows the numeric result.

Scrolling

A complete spreadsheet can rarely be displayed on the monitor in its entirety, meaning that only a portion of the spreadsheet is viewed at any one time. The section which is shown is usually limited to 8 columns and 20 rows, but again these numbers vary according to the spreadsheet in use and the monitor available.

Consider Figure 6.6. The specific rows and columns seen in the monitor are determined by an operation called **scrolling,** which displays different parts of the spreadsheet at different times. Scrolling is done automatically, as the location of the cursor changes.

Directing the cursor one column to the right, when it is already located in the rightmost column of the display screen, causes the entire screen to move one column to the right on the spreadsheet. Similarly, moving the cursor one row down, when it is currently in the bottom row of the display screen, causes the entire display screen to move one row down. Moving the cursor in this way enables you to display any section of the spreadsheet on the monitor. The row numbers and column letters corresponding to the section of the spreadsheet being viewed are displayed along the borders of the display screen.

THE ADVANTAGES OF SCROLLING

A spreadsheet in Version 2 of Lotus can contain up to 8196 rows and 256 columns, producing over 2 million available cells. Given that a monitor typically displays 20 rows and 8 columns at one time, it would require over 13,000 monitors to display the entire spreadsheet at one time. In other words, scrolling is an absolute necessity!

Modes of Operation

A spreadsheet has various modes of operation, the most important of which are: the ready mode, entry mode, and command mode. Operation always begins in the **ready mode,** where the arrow keys

FIGURE 6.6
Scrolling.

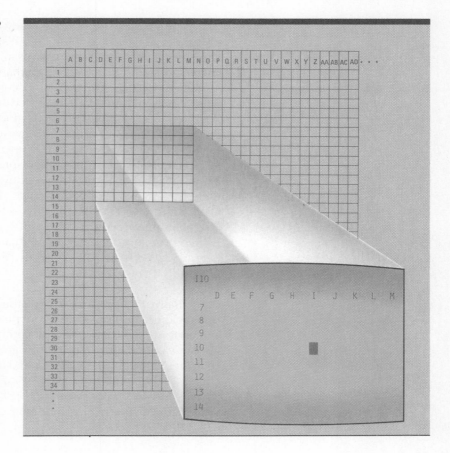

are used to move the cursor to the desired cell. When this has been accomplished, you switch to either the entry mode or the command mode.

As you start to enter data in a particular cell, for example, by typing the first letter of a student's name, you automatically leave the ready mode and begin the **entry mode.** Then, when you have completed the contents for this particular cell, you leave the entry mode (and return to the ready mode) simply by pressing any of the arrow keys. You can thus move to the next cell, where you begin anew in the entry mode. The process is repeated many times until the cell contents for all cells are completed.

As you can see, the entry mode focuses on individual cells. Sooner or later you will have to operate on a **range** (or group) of cells, and often the entire spreadsheet at one time. You will, for example, want to print the spreadsheet, save it, retrieve it, and so on. This is accomplished in the **command mode,** which manipulates a group of cells at one time and truly enhances the power of spreadsheet programs.

Typing a slash (/) from the ready mode is the most common way of entering the command mode. All spreadsheets allow you to select commands from a series of **menus** and **submenus** to accomplish the specific operation. Once the command mode has been entered, you remain there until the indicated command(s) have been executed, whereupon you are again returned to the ready mode.

Figure 6.7 depicts the three modes of operation. Figure 6.7a indicates that the ready mode is active and that the cursor is positioned in cell E5. You are free to enter (reenter) data in this cell or move to any other location in the spreadsheet. Note, too, that the contents of cell E5, as displayed in the control panel, consist of a *formula* to compute Baker's semester average. The computed value (85), however, is displayed in the spreadsheet.

Figure 6.7b captures the entry mode in the middle of entering Brown's name in cell A6. As you can see, the READY indicator has been replaced by LABEL to signify that the entry mode is active, and further that you are in the process of entering a label in the indicated cell.

Finally, Figure 6.7c displays the spreadsheet at the conclusion of development, and shows a hypothetical menu of commands in the control panel. Two rows of commands are shown. The first row contains commands to print, file, graph, or quit the worksheet. Note that the file option is highlighted, which implies that the submenu shown in the second row pertains to the file command. As you move the right or left arrow keys from print to file, graph, and so on, the submenus for the respective menu options are displayed.

Function Keys and Help Menus

As indicated in the chapters on word processing, the 10 (or 12) **function keys** are preset to execute common command sequences. Although the precise setting of the individual function keys varies from spreadsheet to spreadsheet, invariably there will be one established to invoke an **online help menu.** Learn the key that applies to your program (F1 is a typical setting), and use it whenever you need to retrieve the help menu.

Invoking the online help facility common to most spreadsheet programs allows you to pause at any time and clarify points of which you may be unsure. Control is transferred to a series of help screens which contain detailed information about most if not all spreadsheet features. The help screens lead you step by step through an online reference manual, after which you return to the point in your spreadsheet where you left off, that is, the point at which you first invoked the help facility. (We suggest that you use the PrtSc key in conjunction with the help screens to print out your own reference manual. Try it.)

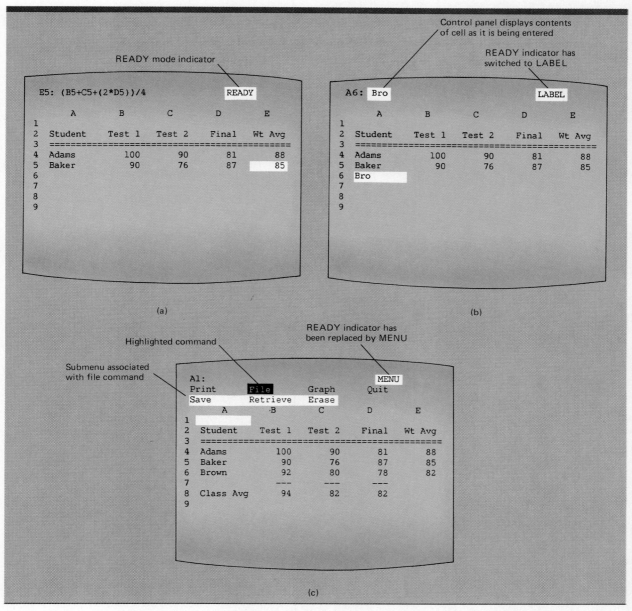

FIGURE 6.7 Modes of operation. (a) Ready mode. (b) Entry mode. (c) Command mode.

RANK-AND-FILE THINKING

You stride from cell to cell across a spreadsheet landscape, formatting A5, adjusting the formula in C26, then paging down to C100 for a peek at the bottom line. It is all done with a flick of the wrist or a tap of a mouse. You know where you are, where you want to go, and how to get there. The terrain is familiar; the navigation, second nature.

What makes it so easy? Why do we find the electronic spreadsheet so intuitive and straightforward? After all, a newcomer to such a program has much to master: the syntax of a macro command language, the distinction between a numeric label and a numerical value, the curious effects of circular dependencies among formulas, ranges, absolute and relative references, and more. The essential idea, however—the underlying scheme of cells organized into columns and rows—seems immediately and spontaneously comprehensible. The basic operating rules of a spreadsheet seem to be as obvious as those of a hammer or a shoe. Why?

In the case of the hammer and the shoe, anatomy explains all: They fit the hand and the foot. A similar, although more speculative, explanation of the spreadsheet's ready acceptance can also be proposed: Perhaps spreadsheets are peculiarly well fitted to the human mind. Such a hypothesis is unlikely ever to be proved or disproved, yet there is much circumstantial evidence in its favor. Gridlike patterns of intersecting columns and rows are exceedingly rare in nature, but they are quite common in human culture. Indeed, they turn up often enough, and in contexts unlikely enough, to suggest a human predisposition to organize the world in two-dimensional, tabular form.

Nature does not suggest grids: we impose them on the landscape for our convenience.

A good place to begin is with geography, with the lacework of parallels and meridians in which cartographers have enmeshed the globe. Strictly speaking, of course, lines of latitude and longitude do not form a grid, but they represent the closest approximation possible on a spherical surface. Furthermore, away from the poles and over small distances, lines of latitude and longitude do mark off the world into rectangles much like the cells of a spreadsheet. The resemblance is even clearer in the case of a road map, where positions are identified by the intersection of a lettered column and a numbered row. With latitude and longitude it is the line that is labeled. On the road map, it is the box or cell bounded by the lines that supplies the information.

Authors' Comments:
The article goes on to list several other applications of Cartesian models to physical systems and is a wonderful introduction to the widespread potential of the spreadsheet model.

Nature does not suggest these grids; we impose them on the landscape for our convenience. Where we physically shape the landscape, abstract grids often become concrete. Midtown Manhattan provides a well-known example: Numbered avenues go north and south and numbered streets go east and west. Without map or compass, visitors can readily find their way from First Avenue and 48th Street to Fifth Avenue and 59th, provided that they are not led astray by the intrusion of Lexington, Park, and Madison Avenues.

Source: Brian Hayes, *Lotus,* June 1985. Reprinted courtesy of Lotus Development Corporation.

CONCEPT SUMMARY

Spreadsheet Fundamentals

Spreadsheet: An electronic version of the accountant's ledger; makes recalculation fast, accurate, easy, and automatic

Cell: The intersection of a row and column establish a cell and establish the cell address; the number of cells in a spreadsheet is equal to the number of rows times the number of columns

Cell contents: May be entered in one of four ways—as a number, label, formula, or special function

Scrolling: Process by which different parts of a spreadsheet are visible in the monitor at any given time

Control panel: The portion of a screen display, showing the active cell and its contents

Modes of operation: Ready mode, entry mode, and command mode, with the latter two entered from the ready mode

VisiCalc: The first electronic spreadsheet

Lotus 1-2-3:   Today's dominant spreadsheet; however, programs such as Paperback Software's VP Planner, Microsoft's Excel, and Borland International's Quattro are giving Lotus a run for its money

---

Learning by Doing

Hands-On Exercise 1 develops the grade book of Figure 6.3, with emphasis on the entry mode of spreadsheet operation. It illustrates the ability of any spreadsheet to answer "what if" questions and also demonstrates the online help facility.

Our only assumption is that you have a spreadsheet program at your disposal. It doesn't matter which one, because the capabilities we demonstrate are so basic as to be available in any spreadsheet program. Should you have access to either Lotus or VP Planner, you will find the optional laboratory manuals useful. If not, *any* spreadsheet program will do. As with the other exercises in the text, our instructions are geared to a hardware configuration with two floppy disk drives. (If you are using a system with a hard drive, consult Chapter 13 for information on subdirectories.)

HANDS-ON EXERCISE 1:
CREATING A SIMPLE SPREADSHEET

OBJECTIVE: Create a spreadsheet corresponding to the professor's grade book of Figure 6.3, and the cell contents in Figure 6.4.

In this exercise you create a spreadsheet corresponding to the professor's grade book of Figure 6.3 by entering the cell contents of Figure 6.4, one cell at a time. (Keep this figure close at hand, as you will refer to it continually.) In so doing you will alternate between the ready and entry modes of spreadsheet operation, and distinguish between label, numeric, formula, and function entries.

Step 1: Boot the System and Load Your Spreadsheet Program
Boot the system, with either a DOS disk or the spreadsheet program disk if it contains DOS. Regardless of which method you use, you should wind up with the spreadsheet program disk in drive A and a formatted disk in drive B (to save the spreadsheet you will create in this exercise).

Enter the command to load the spreadsheet program. Respond to the program prompts until you see an empty spreadsheet with the cursor positioned in cell A1.

Step 2: Move the Cursor
Experiment with moving the cursor by pressing the four arrow keys on the numeric keypad. Note how the active cell is shown in the display panel at the top of the screen, and how the active cell is highlighted within the spreadsheet.

Move the cursor to any cell in column A and press the left arrow key. You should hear a beep, indicating that the cursor cannot move farther left. In similar fashion, pressing the up arrow key when the cursor is in row 1 will also produce a beep.

Starting from column 1, press the right arrow continually, until you observe a scrolling effect as the leftmost columns disappear from the screen. Position the cursor in row 1 and press the down arrow continually until scrolling is observed in this direction. Finally, press the Home key and watch the cursor jump to cell A1.

Step 3: Create the Spreadsheet
Refer to Figure 6.4 to create the grade book by entering one cell at a time. To complete row 4, for example, move the cursor to cell A4 and type Adams. (It is not necessary to type the apostrophe, as this is the default value in most spreadsheets for left justification.) Press the right arrow key after typing the s in Adams to move the cursor to cell B4, then enter the value 100. Press the right arrow key once again to move to cell C4, enter its value, then proceed to cell D4 in similar fashion. (It is usually *not* necessary to press the return key to terminate an entry; that is, the entry in cell B4 is completed as soon as you press an arrow key to move to another cell.)

When you reach cell E4, enter the *formula*, (B4 + C4 + (2 * D4)) / 4, to obtain the semester average. This instructs the spreadsheet to add the values in cell B4 (Adams's first test), plus the value in cell C4 (the second test), plus twice the value in cell D4 (the final), then to divide the sum by 4. (Remember the professor's grading scheme in which the final counts double.)

Don't forget to begin the formula with a left parenthesis to differentiate it from a label. Press the return key after you have entered the formula. The control panel points to cell E4 and displays the expression you just entered; however, the entry displayed in cell E4 is 88, the result of the expression.

Step 4: Complete the Spreadsheet
Enter rows 5 and 6 in similar fashion. Complete rows 2 and 3 by entering additional label information. Note the use of apostrophes (') and quotation marks ('') in Figure 6.4 to distinguish between left and right justification. Determine whether this convention applies to your spreadsheet as well, and if so, experiment with the two symbols to determine the difference.

Rows 7 and 8 are also straightforward, except that the latter uses the @AVG function to obtain the class average for each test. It is of course possible to use formulas for these cells, but we choose to illustrate the use of special functions.

A spreadsheet function typically begins with the @ sign and requires an argument, or range of cells. Hence, you enter @AVG(B4..B6) in cell B8 to calculate the class average on the first test. This command computes the average of the values contained in cells B4, B5, and B6. Similarly in cells C8 and D8 you would enter @AVG(C4..C6) and @AVG(D4..D6), respectively.

Check your spreadsheet, making sure it matches Figure 6.3. Fix any errors by first moving the cursor to the cell containing the error, and retyping the entry in that cell. (Most systems have an edit function, which enables you to make corrections quicker.)

Step 5: Experiment (What If?)
Now that the spreadsheet is finished, you can experiment with changes. Imagine that a grading error was made in Baker's second test, which is contained in cell C5. Move the cursor to cell C5 and enter the correct grade (say, 86 instead of the previous entry of 76).

The effects of this change ripple through the spreadsheet, automatically changing any cell whose formula and/or function depends on Baker's second test. Try making additional changes to the spreadsheet and note the speed with which these corrections are made.

Step 6: Use the Help Menu
Find out how to invoke the online help facility. Do this any time within the development process, and obtain information on specific spreadsheet capabilities.

Step 7: Save the Spreadsheet
Although the command mode has not been covered in detail, we ask that you save the spreadsheet just created. We think that the procedure should make intuitive sense now, and we assure you that everything will be explained following this exercise. Enter the command mode, then follow the menu to save the spreadsheet. Choose GRADES (or any other appropriate name) for the name of the file.

The Command Mode

Hands-On Exercise 1 ended by entering the command mode in order to save the spreadsheet for future use. Remember that while the entry mode is used to enter data in individual cells, the command mode is necessary to manipulate a range of cells. Hence all spreadsheet programs must provide certain basic commands which include:

Save command   To save a spreadsheet on a floppy or hard disk for future editing and printing.

Retrieve command   To retrieve (load) a spreadsheet which was previously saved on disk into memory. One word of caution, however: whenever a new spreadsheet is loaded into memory, any spreadsheet currently in memory will be lost.

Insert command   To insert a new row or column (or range of rows and columns) anywhere within the spreadsheet. Any cell addresses used in existing formulas are adjusted automatically to account for the new rows or columns. For example, if cell B6 contained the expression (B2 + B3) and a new row was inserted between rows 2 and 3, the expression in cell B6 (now B7) becomes (B2 + B4).

Delete command   To delete a row or column, or range of rows or columns, anywhere within the spreadsheet. Expressions will be adjusted automatically, as with the insert command. This command should be used judiciously because once a row or column has been deleted all entries in the deleted row or column are lost, and any other cells whose values depended on the deleted cells will now show error messages.

Print command To print the entire spreadsheet, or any range within a spreadsheet, directing the output to either a printer or an output file. In addition, the spreadsheet can be printed to display either the calculated values or the formulas which produced those values (that is, in the format of Figure 6.3 or Figure 6.7, respectively).

Because the typical spreadsheet program has many commands, each with many suboptions (the total number of possible combinations includes several hundred), most command menus have one or more submenus. By way of illustration consider Figure 6.8, containing the main menu for Version 2 of Lotus 1-2-3. Although your program may not follow this format exactly, our illustration is typical of what you will encounter.

The menu in Figure 6.8 displays 10 commands: worksheet, range, copy, move, file, print, graph, data, system, and quit, with the worksheet command highlighted. (Pressing the right and left arrow keys changes the position of the cursor, which in turn changes the highlighted command.)

Directly beneath the list of available commands is the submenu for the highlighted command. In this example, global, insert, delete, and so on, are the options available with the worksheet command;

FIGURE 6.8 The Lotus 1-2-3 (Version 2) main menu.

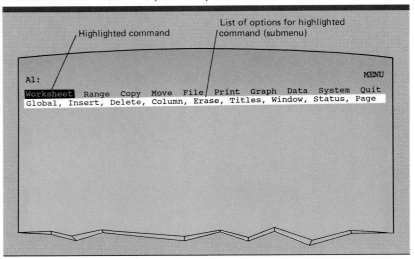

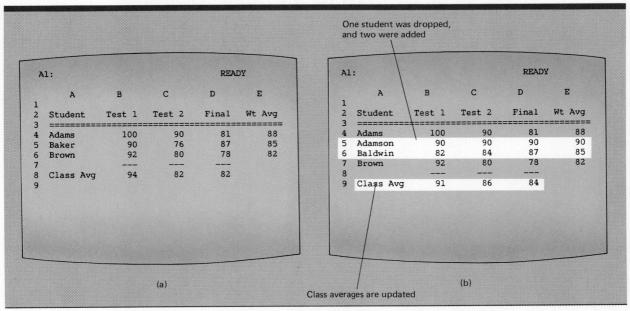

One student was dropped, and two were added

Class averages are updated

FIGURE 6.9 (a) Original and (b) modified grade books.

that is, global, insert, delete, and so on, constitute the *submenu* for the worksheet command.

In Lotus (and many other spreadsheets as well), a command is selected from a menu (or submenu) in one of two ways:

1. By moving the cursor, using the right and left arrow keys, to the desired command and pressing the enter key

2. By typing the first letter of the desired command (observe that every command in a given menu, for example, worksheet, range, copy, and so on, begins with a different letter)

We now extend the grade book example to further illustrate the command mode and command selection. Our example assumes that two new students have joined the class, and that one other has dropped the course. The original grade book is repeated in Figure 6.9*a*, with its modified counterpart shown in Figure 6.9*b*. As can be seen, Adamson and Baldwin have been added to the roll and Baker has disappeared. In addition, the class average for all three tests has been changed as a result of the altered enrollment.

Hands-On Exercise 2 stresses the command mode of operation and begins by retrieving the spreadsheet created in Hands-On Exercise 1. The exercise invokes the commands to add and delete students, print the spreadsheet in various formats, and finally to save and retrieve the spreadsheet from disk.

The Great Spreadsheet Face-Off

PC
NEWS:
AT&T 7300
AND COMPAQ TC

umber 11

THE GREAT SPREADSHEET FACE-OFF

In a unique and headline-grabbing contest the editors of *PC Magazine* staged "The Great Spreadsheet Face-off" during the weekend of February 29, 1985. They recruited 30 MBA candidates from the University of Pennsylvania's Wharton School, offering room and board at New York's Inter-Continental Hotel in exchange for their participation in the competition. The students were divided into 10 teams of 3 people each. Each team was assigned a popular spreadsheet package, with the competitors listed in alphabetical order: Enable, Framework, Lotus 1-2-3, Multiplan, PeachCalc, Pfs:plan, Smart Spreadsheet, SuperCalc3, Symphony, and VisiCalc.

The idea behind the competition was to test how quickly and how well a team of well-trained business minds could make each software package perform, given no previous experience with the package. The teams were asked to solve three business problems which grew progressively more difficult in terms of program skill and business knowledge.

Although Framework was declared the winner, the judges clearly stated that it was more the result of the team members' being able to use their program, rather than Framework itself. Indeed, *9 of the 10 packages were judged capable of solving all three problems*. While the results are perhaps anticlimactic to anyone looking for a clear winner, they did indicate that the key to software performance is the user's skill and judgment rather than any special features in the software itself.

Authors' Update

The players have changed considerably since this article first appeared three years ago. VisiCalc, for example, has come and gone, and powerful new entries such as Microsoft's Excel and Borland's Quattro must be given serious consideration. Nevertheless, the judges' conclusion is just as valid now as it was then, namely, that the key to spreadsheet performance often lies more with the user than with the software.

Wharton Students
Tackle Real-
World Problems
With 10 Top
Spreadsheets

22

355

HANDS-ON EXERCISE 2: BASIC SPREADSHEET COMMANDS

> **OBJECTIVE:** To illustrate the commands to insert or delete rows and columns in a spreadsheet; also, the commands to load, save, and print the spreadsheet.

This exercise takes up where Hands-On Exercise 1 left off. It begins by retrieving the existing spreadsheet, adds and deletes students, then subsequently saves and prints the modified spreadsheet.

Step 1: Enter the Command Mode

Load your spreadsheet program as you did in the previous Hands-On Exercise. You should see a blank spreadsheet, with the cursor positioned in cell A1 and the READY prompt in the upper right corner. Enter the command mode (perhaps by typing a slash as you do in Lotus).

STEP 2: Retrieve the Existing Spreadsheet

Experiment with your spreadsheet program to determine how different commands are chosen (in most programs the right and left arrow keys are used to go from one command to another). Select the necessary command(s) to retrieve your spreadsheet from the first exercise.

You will also be asked for the name of the spreadsheet to retrieve (GRADES, if you followed our suggestion in step 7 of the first exercise). The system pauses, then presto, the grade book is on the monitor.

Step 3: Delete a Row

Reenter the command mode, then execute the necessary command(s) to select the delete menu. You will be asked whether to delete a row or column and the range to delete. Specify row 5 to delete Baker, and observe that the entire row from column A to the last column in the spreadsheet is deleted.

Examine the revised spreadsheet after deleting Baker. Note especially how the class averages (now in row 7) have been changed to reflect the new class roster.

Step 4: Insert a Row

Reenter the command mode, then select the insert command. As with the delete command, you will be asked whether to insert a row or column and where the inserted row or column is to go. Indicate that you want to insert a new row 5, since Adamson is to go after Adams.

Enter the data for Adamson (as shown in Figure 6.9b) in the appropriate columns; that is, enter the test grades in columns B, C, and D, respectively, and enter the formula to compute a weighted average in cell E5. Note that as each test grade is entered, the class average for that test is updated automatically.

Step 5: Insert a Second Row

Insert another row, then enter data for Baldwin just as you did for Adamson, making sure you insert this row in its proper place. Observe again how class averages are automatically updated with the insertion (deletion) of new students.

Step 6: Save the Modified Spreadsheet

Spreadsheets should be saved periodically just as documents are with a word processor. Reenter the command mode and follow the procedure to save the spreadsheet under the name GRADES.

Your spreadsheet program will probably return a message indicating that GRADES already exists, asking whether the new version is to replace the previous version. An affirmative response here will result in the spreadsheet shown in Figure 6.9b replacing Figure 6.9a, with the latter gone forever. You can also save the revised spreadsheet under a new name (for example, NEWGRADE, in which case Figure 6.9a and 6.9b will exist on disk as GRADES and NEWGRADE, respectively).

Note, too, that the spreadsheet was saved before printing.

Step 7: Print the Spreadsheet

Once again enter the command mode, this time opting for the print command. A series of submenus will be displayed which present several options associated with the print command. Indicate that the output is to be directed to the printer (as opposed to a disk file). You will also have to specify the range to print, in this case cells A1..E9, which are the upper left and lower right corners of the entire spreadsheet. (It is also possible to specify a different range and print only a portion of the spreadsheet.)

Make sure the printer is turned on and that the paper is physically aligned in the printer. Finally, issue the command to initiate the actual printing.

Step 8: Print the Commands Generating the Spreadsheet

A spreadsheet may be printed in several formats; for example, Figures 6.3 and 6.4 contain the spreadsheet and cell entries which generated it. Although you are primarily interested in the values shown in Figure 6.3 (and printed in step 7), you may also want to print Figure 6.4 to view the cell contents that produced the spreadsheet.

To obtain a listing of cell formulas, follow the same procedure as in step 7, but this time include the additional commands to print *cell formulas* instead of *cell values*.

LOTUS ALTERNATIVES

Although Lotus 1-2-3 continues to be the dominant spreadsheet for the PC, the nearly one-year delay in delivering Version 3.0 gave competitors an unexpected opportunity. During this period, Microsoft Corporation introduced Excel while Borland International produced Quattro. Each of these spreadsheets maintains 1-2-3 compatibility, and, more significantly, each includes several capabilities not found in Lotus. The announcements were accompanied with heavy advertising, and each company quickly claimed to have sold in excess of 100,000 copies.

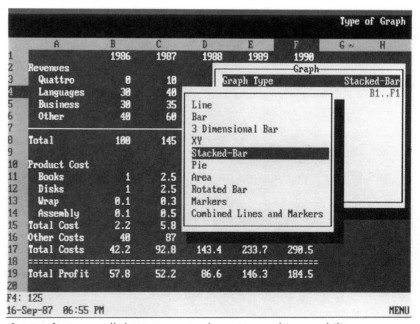

Quattro features pull down menus and greater graphics capability.

CORPORATE PROFILE:
APPLE COMPUTER

Year-end statistics for 1987:
Sales: $3.0 billion
Profits: $280 million
CEO: John Sculley
Headquarters: 20525 Mariani Avenue
             Cupertino, CA 95014
             (408) 973-2042

Sometime in early 1987 Apple Computer sold its 1-millionth Macintosh. What makes this event remarkable is not that it happened (although many predicted it never would), but that it took the company less time to reach this milestone with the Macintosh than with the Apple II. The Mac, the computer that was once relegated to students and hobbyists, has become respectable. An estimated 70,000 units are being shipped every month, with 70 percent of these destined for business.

This stunning success belies a rather shaky beginning, as Apple had twice before failed to attract business customers with the Apple III and Lisa computers. The original Macintosh, with its uninspiring 128Kb RAM, slow speed, lack of a hard disk, and scarcity of business software, was viewed by many as strike three. Critics suggested in no uncertain terms that the company stick to the education market instead of encroaching on IBM's territory. Introduced as "the computer for the rest of us," the Mac was supposed to revolutionize personal computing, but would instead lead to the the ouster of Steve Jobs, the charismatic cofounder of the company and original champion of the machine. Indeed, the Mac's initial inability to penetrate the corporate market led to speculation about Apple's ability to survive in the long run.

The outlook was grim in June 1985, when Apple announced its first-ever quarterly loss, laid off 20 percent of its work force, and saw the price of its stock sink to $15 (from an earlier high of $60). Shipments of the Mac, on which Apple had bet its future, were running at only 10,000 a month versus an 80,000-unit-a-month manufacturing capacity.

Enter John Sculley, who was recruited from Pepsico to salvage the corporate image. He cut expenses and moved to end the divisiveness within Apple by merging the Macintosh and Apple II groups into a single division, wresting control from Jobs in the process. Sculley then began an extensive marketing campaign for the Mac, and was successful in persuading leading software companies to write business software for the new machine. The availability of Microsoft's Excel, for example, finally enabled the Mac to go head to head with a PC running Lotus 1-2-3.

Most significant, however, was the fact that Sculley, unlike Jobs, would listen to what business wanted. The 512Kb "Fat Mac" and LaserWriter printer were announced in 1985, the 1-megabyte Macintosh Plus in 1986, and the Macintosh System Expansion (SE) and Macintosh II ("open" Mac) in 1987. The latter two machines can, with the proper accessories, run the full library of MS-DOS software, which marks a distinct departure from Apple's traditional position of "the other computer company."

Apple's dramatic turnaround was helped in no small measure by the fact that desktop publishing took off faster than anyone expected. Fancy charts, newsletters, and overhead transparencies began to appear by

209

Steven Jobs, John Sculley and Stephen Wozniak before the turmoil.

A scene from Apple's incredible Super Bowl commercial in which purchasers of IBM machines are depicted as lemmings.

Mac factory

Mac Print

The Mac II

the thousands, and suddenly the Mac and LaserWriter combination were the standard against which presentation materials were judged. Today the company continues to make new inroads into corporate America on the heels of desktop publishing. Its painful leadership change is history, the belt-tightening is over, and revenues and profits have once again reached record levels.

Although the Macintosh is clearly the future of the company, the Apple II was for years its flagship product, and any discussion of Apple Computer would be incomplete without it. In 1976 Steven P. Jobs, then 21, and Stephen G. Wozniak, aged 26 (both college dropouts), built a personal computer, not as a commercial product for an eventual billion-dollar company, but on a strictly for-fun basis. It came as almost a total surprise when a local store gave them their first order for 50 computers.

Needing capital, they raised $1350 by selling a used Volkswagen and set up shop in Jobs's garage, with Wozniak as engineer and Jobs as business manager. Shortly thereafter came the Apple II, which was the first computer to come fully assembled (as opposed to systems like the Heath kit), the first to offer color and music, and the first with 48Kb (other machines had 4Kb). The success of the Apple II was also due to the open design provided by the eight expansion slots, enabling companies everywhere to provide supporting hardware and software. Today there is an existing library of over 10,000 programs, and more than half the personal computers in America's classrooms are Apples.

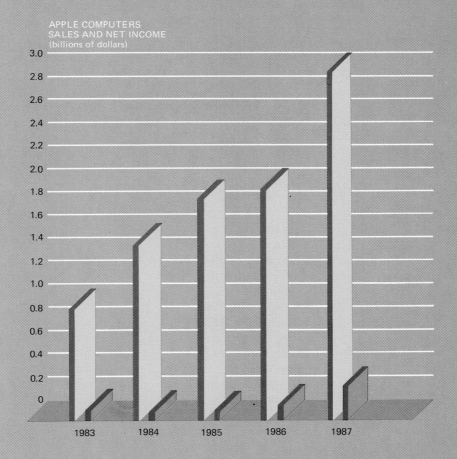

APPLE COMPUTERS
SALES AND NET INCOME
(billions of dollars)

Summary

Spreadsheets, more than any other application, have convinced businesspeople that the personal computer is an important tool in decision making. The chapter introduced you to the basics of these programs, enabling you to appreciate their power and flexibility and to understand why they have achieved such widespread acceptance. As we have indicated, all spreadsheet programs have similar capabilities and embrace similar concepts. Thus any spreadsheet allows you to enter numbers, labels, formulas, or functions into a particular cell. In similar fashion, all spreadsheet programs contain commands to print, save, and retrieve spreadsheets; insert and delete rows and columns; and so on.

The chapter also included two hands-on exercises consistent with our "learn by doing" approach, to provide you with a truer appreciation for the material. As we have continually stressed, however, the particular spreadsheet you acquire is not as important as your ability to actually use the program.

Key Words and Concepts

Active cell
Argument (range)
Arrow keys
Dan Bricklin
Cell
Cell address
Columns
Command mode
Control (summary) panel
Cursor
Delete command
Electronic spreadsheet
Entry mode
Excel
Formula
Robert Frankston
Function
Function keys
Home key
Insert command

Steven Jobs
Label
Lotus 1-2-3
Menus
Numeric value
Online help
Print command
Range
Ready mode
Retrieve command
Rows
Save command
Scrolling
Spreadsheet
Submenus
Value
VisiCalc
VP Planner
Stephen Wozniak

True/False

1. Lotus 1-2-3 was the first spreadsheet program.

2. The first spreadsheet program was developed by a computer systems engineer.

3. Lotus 1-2-3 was the first spreadsheet program to combine database management and graphics capabilities with a spreadsheet.

4. The size of the spreadsheet on all programs is the same.

5. Cells may contain values, labels, formulas, or functions.

6. The control panel displays the location of the active cell and its contents.

7. In general, the entire spreadsheet may be viewed at one time on a monitor.

8. There is no important difference between a value and a label entry in a spreadsheet, since they are both treated the same.

9. The argument of a function is the list of specifications enclosed within the parentheses.

10. Most spreadsheets contain commands to left- or right-justify a label.

11. Beginning an entry with a letter causes a spreadsheet to treat the entry as a label.

12. Beginning an entry with a $ causes a spreadsheet to treat the entry as a function.

13. The command mode is usually entered by pressing the backward slash (\).

14. The cursor may be moved to another cell from within the entry mode.

15. Inserting (or deleting) a row or column automatically adjusts cell references throughout a spreadsheet.

16. Scrolling is the operation that makes different parts of a spreadsheet visible at different times.

17. Lotus 1-2-3 is the only spreadsheet you should consider purchasing.

18. The entries 'Adams and "Adams are treated differently by most spreadsheet programs.

19. It is not possible to insert rows and/or columns after a spreadsheet has been developed.

Multiple Choice

1. The first spreadsheet was:
   (a) Lotus 1-2-3
   (b) VisiCalc
   (c) Symphony
   (d) Excel

2. In most spreadsheets, the command mode is entered by pressing the:
   (a) Backward slash key
   (b) Regular slash key
   (c) Esc key
   (d) F1 function key

3. A cell in a spreadsheet may contain a:
   (a) Function
   (b) Numeric value
   (c) Label
   (d) Mathematical expression
   (e) All the above

4. Once a spreadsheet has been created, you can easily:
   (a) Add additional rows and/or columns
   (b) Delete existing rows and/or columns
   (c) Both (a) and (b) above
   (d) Neither (a) nor (b) above

5. The "Great Spreadsheet Face-Off" demonstrated that:
   (a) Lotus 1-2-3 is clearly the best spreadsheet
   (b) Most spreadsheet programs will handle most applications
   (c) Spreadsheets are beyond all but the most sophisticated MBA student
   (d) Any business problem is amenable to solution by a spreadsheet

6. The maximum number of columns in a spreadsheet is:
   (a) Limited to 100
   (b) Limited to 26, as columns require alphabetic labels
   (c) Is dependent upon the spreadsheet program and available memory
   (d) None of the above

7. The entry @AVG(A4..A6):
   (a) Is invalid because the cells in the range are not contiguous
   (b) Computes the average of cells A4 and A6
   (c) Computes the average of cells A4, A5, and A6
   (d) None of the above

8. Which pair of individuals is most closely associated with the development of the spreadsheets?
   (a) Wozniak and Jobs
   (b) Bricklin and Frankston
   (c) Burns and Allen
   (d) Boole and Babbage

9. The spreadsheet entry F5 + F6 will be treated as a:
   (a) Mathematical formula (arithmetic expression)
   (b) Label
   (c) Special function
   (d) Numeric quantity

10. An electronic spreadsheet is superior to manual calculation because:
    (a) The spreadsheet computes its entries faster
    (b) The spreadsheet computes its results more accurately
    (c) The spreadsheet automatically recalculates its results whenever cell contents are changed
    (d) All the above

11. The cell address of the intersection of the second column with the second row would be:
    (a) B2
    (b) 2B
    (c) 22
    (d) Impossible to determine

12. The term "active cell" defines:
    (a) A cell whose contents will change if another cell in the row changes
    (b) The cell where the cursor is presently located
    (c) A cell whose contents can be moved elsewhere in the spreadsheet
    (d) None of the above

13. How many usable cells are there is a spreadsheet with 12 rows and 4 columns?
    (a) 16
    (b) 3
    (c) 48
    (d) Impossible to determine

14. Which of the following is generally the fastest way to get to cell A1 from cell G12?
    (a) The F5 (GOTO) function key
    (b) The PgUp or PgDn key
    (c) The Esc key
    (d) The Home key

15. Which of the following are modes of spreadsheet operation?
    (a) Ready, Set, Go
    (b) Retrieve, Load, and Erase
    (c) Entry, Command, and Ready
    (d) Exit, Quit, and Undo

Exercises

1. Design a spreadsheet which would be useful to you. You might want to consider applications such as an annual budget, the cost of a stereo or computer system, the number of calories you consume (burn) in a day, calculation of federal income tax, and so on. The applications are limited only by your imagination.

2. Answer the following conceptual questions with regard to spreadsheet fundamentals:
    (a) What are the various modes of operation? Describe the function of each mode.
    (b) What is a "what if"? Explain how the use of spreadsheets facilitates this type of analysis.
    (c) What is the address of the cell in row 20, column 10? In row 10, column 20? In row 40, column 40? How can you move quickly to the cell whose address is A1?
    (d) What are the four types of entries permitted in a cell? How does a spreadsheet distinguish between a label and a formula? between a label and a number?
    (e) What is the difference between printing cell values and cell formulas? Does the entire spreadsheet have to be printed every time?

3. Return to the grade book example of Figure 6.2 and implement the following changes:
    (a) The student's average is to weigh test 1, test 2, and the final equally, rather than counting the final as two exams.
    (b) A new student, Milgrom, must be entered on the roster with grades of 88, 80, 84, respectively.
    (c) Baker is to be dropped from the class roll.

    Treat each part (a, b, and c) independently; that is, return to the original spreadsheet before doing the manual calculation. Can you begin to appreciate the utility of having the computer recalculate automatically?

4. The insertion of Adamson and Baldwin in the extended grade book resulted in the automatic updating of the class average for all three tests to include the new students.
    (a) Would the automatic updating still take place if an additional student were inserted before Adams or after Brown? Why or why not?

(b) Would the automatic updating still have taken place if the entries in row 8 were expressed as formulas rather than functions, for example, (B4 + B5 + B6) / 3 in lieu of @AVG(B4..B6)? What exactly would happen?

(c) Can you make any general statements regarding the advantages (disadvantages) of using ranges and functions for computed values?

5. Indicate whether the following entries will be interpreted as numbers, labels, expressions, or functions. Answer with respect to how the entries will actually be interpreted as opposed to what the user probably intended.
   (a) E3 + E4 + E5
   (b) "@AVG(B1..B8)
   (c) 1989 sales
   (d) (B1 + B2 + B3) / 3
   (e) "2000
   (f) ^2000
   (g) '2000
   (h) 2,000
   (i) 2000
   (j) @200

FIGURE 6.10
Spreadsheet for exercise 7.

```
A3:  'Student
B3:  "Test 1
C3:  "Test 2
D3:  "Test 3
E3:  ' Average
A4:  '=========
B4:  '=========
C4:  '=========
D4:  '=========
E4:  '=========
A5:  'James
B5:  100
C5:  90
D5:  80
E5:  (B5+C5+D5)/3
A6:  'Milgrom
B6:  90
C6:  76
D6:  86
E6:  (B6+C6+D6)/3
A7:  'Jones
B7:  92
C7:  80
D7:  80
E7:  (B7+C7+D7)/3
B8:  "---
C8:  "---
D8:  "---
A9:  'Class Avg
B9:  @AVG(B5..B7)
C9:  @AVG(B5..B7)
D9:  @AVG(B5..B7)
```

6. Review the command mode associated with your spreadsheet and indicate the command sequence necessary to:
   (a) Insert a row
   (b) Retrieve an existing spreadsheet from disk
   (c) Save a spreadsheet on disk
   (d) Delete a column
   (e) Print the entire spreadsheet
   (f) Print the entire spreadsheet, showing cell formulas rather than values
   (g) Exit the spreadsheet program and return to DOS.

7. Figure 6.10 contains a list of cell formulas which will create a student grade book spreadsheet.
   (a) Reproduce the spreadsheet *exactly* as the commands are written. (There is an error in the formulas for cells C9 and D9.)
   (b) Assume the value in cell B7 changes from 97 to 83. What other cells will change? What are the new values? *Answer as the spreadsheet is presently constructed.*
   (c) Correct the formulas for cells C9 and D9. Reconstruct the spreadsheet with the correct formulas, using the original value of 92 for cell B7.
   (d) Again, assume that the value in cell B7 changes from 92 to 83. What other cells will change? What are the new values?

FIGURE 6.11
Spreadsheet for exercise 8.

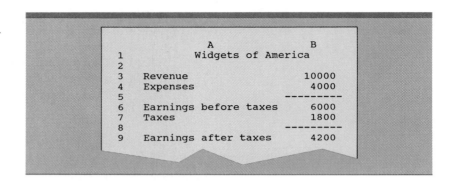

8. Figure 6.11 contains a simple spreadsheet showing the earnings for Widgets of America, before and after taxes. The cell values in cells B6, B7, and B9 in the figure may be produced in several ways, two of which are shown below. For example:

	Method 1	Method 2
Cell B6	10000 − 4000	+B3 − B4
Cell B7	.30 * 6000	.30 * B6
Cell B9	6000 − 1800	+B6 − B7

Which is the better method and why?

9. Figure 6.12 contains a simple profit projection in the form of a spreadsheet. Use whatever spreadsheet program is available to you and recreate Figure 6.12 on the computer. (Be sure, however, to enter formulas rather than numbers where appropriate, for example, in the cells containing gross income, total cost, and total profit.) After you have created the spreadsheet, consider the following modifications:

(a) Change the selling price in cell D4 to 6. Which number(s) changes in the spreadsheet?

(b) Add an overhead expense in cell D12 of $1000 (enter an appropriate label in cell A12). Which formula(s) has to be changed as a result of this additional expense? Which number(s) changes?

(c) Assume a tax rate of 30 percent. Enter the formula to compute the anticipated tax in row 16 and the after-tax profit in row 17.

(d) Assume the numbers in column D are for 1989. Create corresponding figures for 1990 in column E. Assume the number of units sold will be 10 percent higher, and that the selling price and all other costs increase by 8 percent.

(e) Add column F for 1991, using the same anticipated rates of change.

FIGURE 6.12
Spreadsheet for exercise 9.

```
                    A         B         C         D         E
        1
        2    Income
        3        Number of units              1500
        4        Selling price                   8
        5        Gross income                12000
        6
        7    Expenses:
        8        Material cost per unit          4
        9        Total material cost          6000
       10        Labor cost per unit             1
       11        Total labor cost             1500
       12
       13        Total cost                   7500
       14
       15    Gross profit                     4500
       16
       17
```

(f) After completing parts *a* through *e*, print the entire spread-sheet twice; once to show values and once to show the cell contents.

10. Figure 6.13 depicts a hypothetical stock portfolio, with prices (rounded to the nearest dollar) as of September 11, 1987. Look up current prices of these five companies and complete the spreadsheet. (Note that in order to be completely accurate, you may have to adjust for stock splits which have occurred since September 11, 1987.)

11. Replicate the hands-on exercises in the text (and lab manual) to produce the expanded gradebook of Figure 6.9*b* and the associated list of cell formulas. This time, however, *direct the spreadsheet output to a file rather than the printer*, then incorporate both outputs into a one page memo to your instructor *using a word processor*. The memo itself need not contain more than one or two sentences saying that this is your initial exposure to spreadsheets.

FIGURE 6.13
Spreadsheet for exercise 10.

```
                              Stock Portfolio

        Company      Number   Price    Value    Price    Value    Change in
                     Shares   9/11/87                              Value
        -----------------------------------------------------------------------
        IBM              25     158      3950
        Apple           100      54      5400
        MicroPro        200       6      1200
        MicroSoft        50      50      2500
        Lotus           100      30      3000
                                       =========
             Value of portfolio         16050
```

CHAPTER 7

GAINING PROFICIENCY

CHAPTER OBJECTIVES

After reading this chapter, you should be able to:

1. Describe at least four formats for numeric entries in a spreadsheet; discuss the various formats associated with label entries.

2. Explain the precedence of arithmetic operations within a spreadsheet.

3. Distinguish between protected and unprotected cells; explain how the protection feature is enabled or disabled.

4. Describe what is meant by a global setting; explain the use of a range command to change existing global settings.

5. Explain the use of pointing and how it is superior to explicit specification of ranges.

6. Describe the use of special functions within a spreadsheet; list the four types of functions which are generally available.

7. Move and copy ranges within a spreadsheet; distinguish between relative and absolute addresses.

8. Describe the edit mode.

Overview

This chapter continues the discussion of spreadsheets through the presentation of additional features designed to increase your proficiency with these programs. We cover the various formats available for both numeric and label entries, indicate how a cell (or group of cells) may be protected (or unprotected), how to edit the contents of individual cells, and how to alter column widths. Inherent in these discussions is the concept of global settings and how these settings may be overridden for specific cell ranges.

The chapter also includes material on arithmetic operations as well as the use of predefined special functions. Perhaps of greatest significance, however, is the section on the *copy* command, which enables the replication of a cell (or group of cells) from one portion of a spreadsheet to another, without having to individually reenter the contents of every cell.

All these capabilities are presented within the context of two new applications: dealing with the analysis of variable interest rates on a home mortgage and the preparation of sales invoices. As in previous chapters, all concepts are presented generically, after which they are implemented in Hands-On Exercises. The Corporate Profile on Lotus Development Corporation requires no further introduction.

221

Application: Mortgage Analysis

Figure 7.1 depicts a variable-rate mortgage analysis in which you enter the amount of a loan ($100,000) and the starting interest rate (7.00 percent), whereupon a table of monthly payments is produced. The spreadsheet is designed so that you can vary either or both of these values and view their effects on the resulting table. Implicit in this example are several new spreadsheet capabilities which include:

- *Formatting numeric entries:* The various numeric entries appear in different formats, for example, currency and percent. Note, too, that there are differences even within the currency format: the amount of the loan appears without cents, and the monthly payments include cents.

- *Formatting label entries:* Label entries within a cell may be left-justified, centered, or right-justified. In addition, a label entry may be made to fill a cell completely, as was done with the equal sign used to underline the column headings above the repayment amounts.

- *Changing column widths:* The columns in a spreadsheet can be of different widths (although the distinction is not readily apparent from Figure 7.1). Note, too, that while various columns can be of different widths, every cell within a given column must be of the same width.

- *Special functions:* The monthly payments in Figure 7.1 are computed with the aid of an @PMT function, one of many special functions available in spreadsheet programs.

- *Copying cells:* The development of a spreadsheet is eased considerably by copying formulas from one cell to another (or to several others), which spares you the trouble of repeatedly making the same entry in multiple cells. The formulas for the monthly payments, for example, are copied from one interest rate to the next, that is, from one row to the next.

```
            Variable Rate Mortgage Analysis

     Amount borrowed:           $100,000
     Starting interest:            7.00%

                          Monthly Payment
                      (15 Years)   (30 Years)
                      ==========================
           7.00%       $898.83      $665.30
           8.00%       $955.65      $733.76
           9.00%     $1,014.27      $804.62
          10.00%     $1,074.61      $877.57
          11.00%     $1,136.60      $952.32
          12.00%     $1,200.17    $1,028.61
```

FIGURE 7.1
Variable-rate mortgage analysis.

These concepts are discussed in detail, after which they will be applied in a Hands-On Exercise for the mortgage analysis. At that point you will once again be directed to the laboratory manual so that you can master the specific commands which apply to your spreadsheet program.

"THE MASKED MAN? HE'S THE LOAN ARRANGER."

THE RULE OF 72

An interesting side note associated with financial functions is the rule of 72, an estimating procedure that approximates the effect of compound interest. The rule states that "to find the time required for money to double, divide 72 by the interest rate"; for example, money doubles in six years at 12 percent (72/12 = 6). The rule is extremely accurate with interest rates ranging from 5 to 20 percent.

Formatting Numeric Entries

All spreadsheets allow considerable flexibility as to the form (format) in which numeric data are displayed. For example, you may display numbers with or without decimal places, dollar signs, commas, and

Format Specified	Number entered		
	12345	123.45	0.12345
General	12345	123.45	0.12345
Fixed Decimal (2 decimal places)	12345.00	123.45	0.12
(0 decimal places)	12345	123	0
Percentage (2 decimal places)	1234500.00%	12345.00%	12.35%
(0 decimal places)	1234500%	12345%	12%
Currency (2 decimal places)	$12,345.00	$123.45	$0.12
(0 decimal places)	$12,345	$123	$0
Comma (2 decimal places)	12,345.00	123.45	0.12
(0 decimal places)	12,345	123	0
Scientific (4 decimal places)	1.2345E+04	1.2345E+02	1.2345E-01
(2 decimal places)	1.23E+04	1.23E+02	1.23E-01

so on. Moreover, you can use several different formats within the same spreadsheet to further improve its appearance and readability.

The various formats are described below, in conjunction with the several examples in Figure 7.2.

General format: The entry is displayed exactly as it is entered, with the same number of digits to the right of the decimal; for example, 12345 is displayed as 12345, .12345 as .12345, and so on.

Fixed decimal format: The entry is displayed according to the number of user-specified decimal places; for example, if two decimal places are indicated, 12345 will be displayed as 12345.00, and .12345 will be shown as .12 (the last significant digit is automatically rounded up or down).

Percentage format: The entry is displayed as a percentage (according to the number of user-specified decimal places), with the percent sign appearing in the cell; for example, if no decimal places are indicated, .12 will appear as 12%, and 12 will be shown as 1200%.

Currency format: The entry is displayed with a dollar sign, commas where appropriate, and the number of user-specified decimal places. For example, 12345 would be displayed as $12,345 (with no decimal places) and $12,345.00 (with two decimal places).

Comma format: The entry is similar to that of the currency format in that commas and decimal places appear as appropriate, but it appears without the dollar sign. For example, 12345 would be displayed as 12,345 (with no decimal places) and 12,345.00 (with two decimal places).

Scientific format: The displayed entry consists of a multiplier (expressed as a decimal fraction, the precision of which is specified by the user, with a single digit to the left of the decimal point) and a whole number exponent of 10. For example, 12345 would appear as 1.2345E+04 if four decimal places were specified, but as 1.23E+04 with two decimals. The exponent, +04 in the example, corresponds to the number of places the decimal point is moved right or left. Very small numbers will have negative exponents; for example, the entry .0000012 would be displayed as 1.2E−06. Scientific notation is most useful with very large or very small numbers.

Formatting Label Entries

The format of label entries can also be specified, with the available options described below and illustrated in Figure 7.3:

Left justification: The first character in the label is displayed in the leftmost cell position. (In Lotus, left justification is the *default* format and is specified by beginning the label entry with an apostrophe.)

Right justification: The last character in the label is displayed in the rightmost cell position. (In Lotus, right justification is specified by beginning the label entry with quotation marks.)

Center: The label is centered in the cell. (In Lotus, centering is specified by beginning the label entry with a caret.)

Repeat: The character or string of characters is repeated within the cell as many times as possible, according to the width of the cell. (In Lotus, repetition is specified by beginning the label entry with a backward slash.)

Changing Column Widths

The appearance of a numeric entry is affected by the width of the column (cell) in which it is contained as well as its designated format. There is, for example, no problem displaying 12,345 (in comma format with no decimal places) in a cell that is 9 characters wide. You could not, however, show the same value in currency format (with two decimal places), because $12,345.00 takes 10 characters and exceeds the space allotted. A series of asterisks (*********) would appear, instead, to indicate that the cell width is insufficient. The problem is corrected either by changing the format or by increasing the column width.

The display of a label entry is treated differently and depends on whether the cell(s) immediately to the right of the label is empty. Assume, for example, that the label "Amount borrowed" is entered in cell A3, and further that cell A3 is 9 characters wide. If the adjacent cell (B3) is empty, the label in cell A3 ("Amount borrowed") will spill over and appear in its entirety on the spreadsheet. If, however, cell B3 is not empty, than the label in cell A3 will be truncated to 9 characters (appearing as "Amount bo"). The latter situation requires you to increase the width of column A to show the complete label.

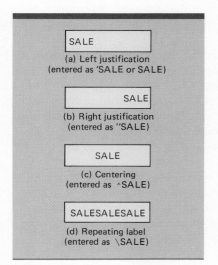

FIGURE 7.3 Formatting label entries (Lotus/VP Planner implementation).

FIGURE 7.4
Programmed functions
typically available.

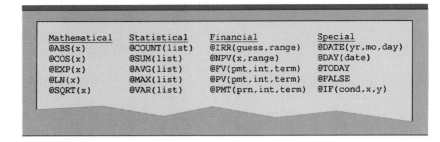

FIGURE 7.4
Programmed functions
typically available.

Mathematical	Statistical	Financial	Special
@ABS(x)	@COUNT(list)	@IRR(guess,range)	@DATE(yr,mo,day)
@COS(x)	@SUM(list)	@NPV(x,range)	@DAY(date)
@EXP(x)	@AVG(list)	@FV(pmt,int,term)	@TODAY
@LN(x)	@MAX(list)	@PV(pmt,int,term)	@FALSE
@SQRT(x)	@VAR(list)	@PMT(prn,int,term)	@IF(cond,x,y)

Special Functions

As indicated in Chapter 6, spreadsheet programs contain built-in formulas, known as **special functions.** One such function, @AVG, was introduced in the grade book example of the last chapter; another, @PMT, will be used in this chapter to compute the monthly payments in the mortgage analysis. Additional functions, @IF and @TODAY, are discussed with the sales invoice example later in this chapter. Still other functions are presented elsewhere in the text as appropriate.

Special functions fall naturally into several classes, for example, mathematical, statistical, or financial, as shown in Figure 7.4. Every function, however, begins with the @ sign and contains one or more **arguments;** that is, entries enclosed in parentheses. The precise nature of the argument(s) depends on the function itself.

Range Specification

A **range** is defined as a group of contiguous (adjacent) cells that form a rectangle. It can be as small as a single cell or as large as the entire spreadsheet. All ranges, however, fall into one of four general shapes: a single cell, a row or portion of a row, a column or portion of a column, or a rectangle consisting of multiple rows and columns. In each instance the range is specified by indicating *the address of the cells in the upper left and lower right corners of the rectangle*, as shown in Figure 7.5.

Many spreadsheet commands (for example, print, copy, move, insert, and delete) require that you indicate the range on which the command is to operate. In every instance you can specify the range in one of two ways: either explicitly or by pointing (see the following box, entitled "Specifying Ranges through Pointing").

Explicit specification requires that you manually enter the addresses of the beginning and ending cells (that is, the cells in the upper left and lower right of the rectangle) according to the convention associated with your spreadsheet, for example, A9..A14. **Pointing,** however, is generally easier and more accurate, as it makes use of the cursor keys to move directly to the beginning and ending cells, and consequently does not require precise knowledge of cell coordinates.

FIGURE 7.5
Spreadsheet ranges.

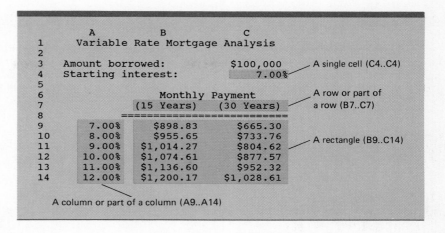

The use of a range in conjunction with other commands overrides the **default (initial) settings,** which exist in every spreadsheet program and which are established on a **global basis;** that is, they apply to every cell in the spreadsheet. Typical defaults are a cell width of nine characters, left justification for label entries, and general format for numeric entries.

Copy Command

The **copy command** enables you to replicate any cell (or range of cells) elsewhere in the spreadsheet without having to enter every cell individually. The command will be demonstrated in conjunction with Figure 7.6, which reproduces the mortgage spreadsheet described earlier. This time, however, the figure contains **cell formulas** (for the monthly payments) as opposed to **cell values.** (The dollar signs that appear in the various cell formulas are known as **absolute cell addresses,** and are discussed in the next section.)

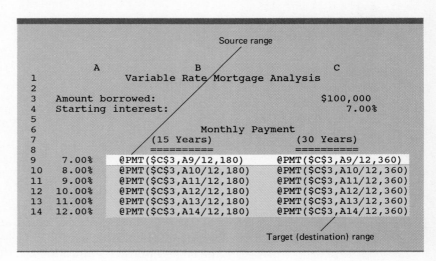

FIGURE 7.6
The copy command.

SPECIFYING RANGES THROUGH POINTING

Pointing is one of the more clever features of spreadsheet programs, enabling you to define ranges with the cursor keys rather than by specifying ranges explicitly. The technique not only saves time but also reduces errors; for example, you no longer need worry about entering A40 when you really mean A4. Consider the example below:

Step 1: Enter values in cells A1 through A4, then move the cursor to cell A5.
(Status indicator shows READY.)

```
A5:                          READY

              A
1             10
2             20
3             30
4             40
5
```

Step 2: Begin entering the @SUM function, stopping at the left parenthesis.
(Status indicator shows VALUE.)

```
A5:                          VALUE
@SUM(
              A
1             10
2             20
3             30
4             40
5
```

Step 3: Press the up arrow key to begin pointing operation, then move cursor to cell A1.
(Status indicator shows POINT.)

```
A1: 10                       POINT
@SUM(A1
              A
1             10
2             20
3             30
4             40
5
```

Step 4: Press the period to anchor the pointer, then use the down arrow to move to cell A4.
(Status indicator remains in POINT.)

```
A4: 40                       POINT
@SUM(A1..A4
              A
1             10
2             20
3             30
4             40
5
```

Step 5: Enter a right parenthesis when cursor is in cell A4 to end pointing operation.
(Status indicator shows EDIT.)

```
A5:                          EDIT
@SUM(A1..A4)
              A
1             10
2             20
3             30
4             40
5
```

Step 6: Press Return to end the edit operation, and the computed value of 100 appears in cell A5.
(Status indicator shows READY.)

```
A5: @SUM(A1..A4)             READY

              A
1             10
2             20
3             30
4             40
5             100
```

The @PMT functions which appear in row 9 of Figure 7.6 are very similar to those in the rest of the spreadsheet, and hence can be *copied* to rows 10 through 14. The @PMT function itself requires three arguments: the amount of the loan, the interest rate per period, and the number of periods (180 and 360 for 15- and 30-year mortgages, respectively). For example, the @PMT entry in cell B9 appears as shown below:

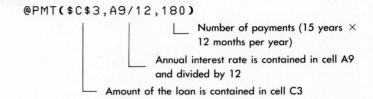

As we have indicated, the @PMT functions for cells B9 and C9 will be developed first, after which they will be copied to the remainder of the spreadsheet. We say therefore that cells B9 and C9 constitute the **source range** of the copy command, and cells B10 through C14 make up the **destination** (or target) **range.** Note too that the size and shape of the source and destination ranges may differ from one another.

Once again study the entries in cells B9 through B14, observing how similar they are to one another. Indeed, the only difference between the @PMT functions in cells B9 and B10 is in the interest rate per period, indicated as A9/12 and A10/12, respectively. The @PMT functions in column C for the 30-year mortgage show a similar pattern. These similarities enable you to use the copy command to replicate the @PMT functions in the source range consisting of cells B9 and C9, to the destination range made up of cells B10 through C14.

Relative versus Absolute Addresses

Every one of the @PMT functions in columns B and C of Figure 7.6 *reflect the associated interest rates in column A.* In other words, the @PMT functions in row 9 reflect the interest rate in row 9, the @PMT functions in row 10 reflect the interest rate in row 10, and so on. The adjustments occur during a copy operation because spreadsheets interpret these cell addresses as **relative** to the cell in which the formula (function) is contained. Consider again the @PMT function in cell B9:

```
@PMT($C$3,A9/12,180)
            └─ A9 is a relative address which will be adjusted
     └─ $C$3 is an absolute address which remains fixed
```

The entry A9/12 which appears in cell B9 is interpreted by the spreadsheet to mean "divide the contents of the cell one column to my left by 12." Thus when the @PMT function in cell B9 is "copied" to cell B10, it (the copied function) is adjusted to maintain this relationship. In other words, the spreadsheet does not copy the cell addresses exactly, but instead maintains the relative relationship.

A cell address can also be specified as **absolute,** meaning that it is *not* adjusted for its new position in the spreadsheet. Thus all the @PMT functions in Figure 7.6 are based on the *same* loan amount (that is, the entry in cell C3), and hence this address remains constant throughout the spreadsheet.

The dollar signs which appear before the row and column specification in Figure 7.6 (for example, $C$3) indicate absolute addresses, and follow the convention used by Lotus, VP Planner, and other spreadsheets. (A single dollar sign may be used to make the row address relative and the column absolute, or vice versa, but this is not discussed further.)

Move Command

Although the move command is not used explicitly in the mortgage example, its presentation is essential for the sake of completeness. The **move command** transfers any cell (or range of cells) within a spreadsheet from one place to another. After the move has taken place, the cells where the move originated (that is, the source range) are blank. (This is in contrast to the copy command, where the copied entries exist in two places.)

A simple move operation is depicted in Figure 7.7*a*, in which the contents of cells A1, A2, and A3 are moved to cells C1, C2, and C3. As can be seen, column A is empty after the move is completed. Moreover *the formula in cell C3 has been adjusted* to reflect the fact that it is adding the contents of cells C1 and C2 as opposed to cells A1 and A2 (before the move).

The adjustments in cell addresses are more subtle with a move command than with the corresponding copy operation. Consider, for example, Figure 7.7*b*, in which only the contents of cell A3 are moved (that is, cells A1 and A2 remain in place). This time, *the contents of cell C3 are unchanged* because the cells which it adds (cells A1 and A2) have not been moved.

Finally, consider Figure 7.7*c*, containing an additional cell formula in cell B1, which multiplies the contents of cell A3 by 4. As in the previous example, only the contents of cell A3 are moved, and

When things go wrong, where to look. . .

Look in the back.

Look at the ceiling.

Look at your shoes.

Look in your wallet.

FIGURE 7.7
The move command.

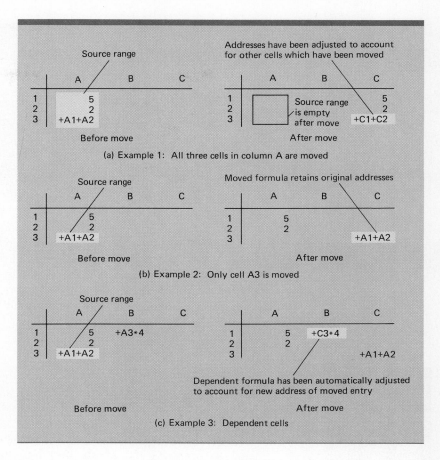

FIGURE 7.7
The move command.

(a) Example 1: All three cells in column A are moved

(b) Example 2: Only cell A3 is moved

(c) Example 3: Dependent cells

this formula (+A1+A2) remains unaffected. Note, however, that *the contents of cell B1 have been changed* even though cell B1 itself was not moved, because cell B1 refers to a cell affected by the move operation.

The move command provides a convenient way to implement a "cut and paste" operation, and so can be used to improve the appearance of a spreadsheet after it has been developed. We use the command, for example, to move labels from one place to another, but suggest you think twice about moving cell formulas because of the subtleties involved.

Editing

Editing enables you to change the contents of a cell, *without* having to retype its contents completely (if only a single character changes). Figure 7.8 depicts a partially completed spreadsheet in which the contents of cell A3 have been previously entered (and appear incorrectly as "Amount b_urrowed" rather than "Amount borrowed"). Thus instead of retyping the contents of cell A3 in its entirety, you can use the **edit mode** to change only the character(s) in error.

FIGURE 7.8
The edit mode.

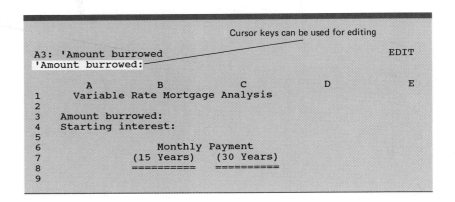

The edit mode causes the contents of the active cell to appear in the control panel. You can then use the right and left arrow keys, as well as the insert (Ins) and delete (Del) keys, to make corrections. Most spreadsheets also recognize the home and end keys to take you to the first and last characters, respectively.

The use of editing may simplify your work in the following Hands-On Exercise.

HANDS-ON EXERCISE 1: VARIABLE-RATE MORTGAGES

OBJECTIVE: Develop the mortgage analysis spreadsheet using Figure 7.9 as a guide. Figure 7.9a depicts the spreadsheet as it would appear on the screen (that is, with rows and columns appended); Figure 7.9b contains the various cell entries.

Step 1: Load Your Spreadsheet Program
Follow the steps in Hands-On Exercise 1 in Chapter 6. Be sure that the spreadsheet program is in drive A and that a formatted data disk is in drive B. End this step by viewing a blank spreadsheet on the screen, indicating that you are ready to build the mortgage template.

```
A1:  '   Variable Rate Mortgage
A3:  'Amount borrowed:
A4:  'Starting interest:
B6:  '        Monthly Payment
B7:  ''(15 Years)
C7:  ''(30 Years)
B8:  \=
C8:  \=
```

Step 2: Create the Mortgage Template
Enter the appropriate labels as shown below. The apostrophe and quotation marks preceding each label are the Lotus/VP Planner convention to indicate left and right justification, respectively. (Since most spreadsheets default to left justification, you needn't enter the apostrophe explicitly; you must, however, begin a label entry with quotation marks to affect right justification.)

A label may exceed the width of the cell in which it is entered, yet still appear in its entirety if the cell(s) to its immediate right is empty. The entry in cell A1, for example, is considerably longer than nine characters (the default width of column A), yet the entire label is displayed because the adjacent cells (B1 and C1) are empty.

This is also a good time to experiment with the *editing* capability of your spreadsheet to avoid retyp-

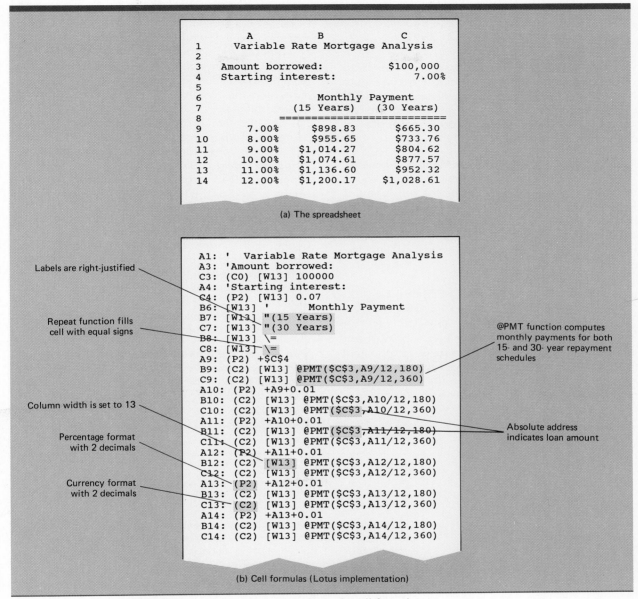

FIGURE 7.9   Variable-rate mortgage analysis: (a) spreadsheet, (b) cell formulas.

ing an entire label if only a single character is in error.

Step 3: Supply Initial Values

Enter the initial values for the amount borrowed and starting interest rate, in cells C3 and C4, respectively. *Be sure to enter these numbers as 100000 and .07.* In other words, do *not* enter a dollar sign, comma, or percent sign, as these are "illegal" characters; for-

matting will be accomplished in step 6 of the exercise.

Step 4: Compute Monthly Payments at the Starting Interest Rate

Supply the cell contents for the cells A9, B9, and C9. These entries correspond to the starting interest rate and monthly payments based on 15- and 30-year (180- and 360-month) loans as follows:

```
A9:  +$C$4
B9:  @PMT($C$3,A9/12,180)
C9:  @PMT($C$3,A9/12,360)
```

Your spreadsheet should now contain numerical values in cells B9 and C9 matching those in Figure 7.9a. However, the formatting will be different because the computations on your spreadsheet are carried out beyond two decimal places and, further, a dollar sign is not present.

Step 5: Compute the Remaining Monthly Payments

The similarities in rows 9 through 14 enable you to use a *copy* command to generate the cell formulas for the remaining monthly payments. You must, however, explicitly enter the formulas for row 10 because the entry in cell A10 is significantly different from that in cell A9. Accordingly, enter the following:

```
A10:  +A9+0.01
B10:  @PMT($C$3,A10/12,180)
C10:  @PMT($C$3,A10/12,360)
```

Invoke the copy command on your spreadsheet, which in turn will prompt for the range to copy *from* (cells A10 through C10), followed by the range to copy *to* (cells A11 through C14). The remaining interest rates and monthly payments should now appear in your spreadsheet.

Step 6: Format the Spreadsheet

Examine once again the entries in Figure 7.9b, noting that many cell formulas are preceded by a set of parentheses; for example, the cell contents for cells A9 and C9 begin with P2 and C2, respectively. The letters P and C denote *percentage* and *currency* formats, and the number 2 indicates the number of decimal places.

Use the *format* command to improve the appearance of your spreadsheet according to Figure 7.9. Use the *range* command to indicate the same format for contiguous cells in a single command; for example, cells A9 through A14 are all two-digit percentages, and cells B10 through C14 employ a currency format with two decimal places.

Step 7: Adjust Column Widths

Changing the format for cells B10 through C14 will most likely produce asterisks in some or all of these cells, to indicate that the cell(s) is *not wide enough* to display the computed value. Accordingly, you should increase the width of columns B and C as necessary. (The [W13] that appears in many entries of Figure 7.9b indicates a column width of 13.)

Step 8: Print the Spreadsheet

Save your spreadsheet. Now enter the necessary commands to print the spreadsheet in both cell value and cell formula formats, reproducing 7.9a and 7.9b, respectively.

CONCEPT SUMMARY

Formatting: The ability to alter the way in which a label or numeric entry is displayed.

Special function: A predefined formula, beginning with an @ sign and requiring one or more arguments. Special functions fall into various categories such as statistical, mathematical, or financial.

Range: A group of contiguous cells forming a rectangle. Ranges may consist of a single cell, a row (or part of a row), a column (or part of a column), or a group of rows and columns.

Pointing: A technique which uses the arrow keys to specify the beginning and ending cells in a range.

Copy command: Copies a cell or range of cells to another location(s).

Move command: Moves a cell or a range of cells to another location.

Relative address: A cell address in a formula which is in relation to the cell where it is contained, and which changes when copied.

Absolute address: A cell address in a formula which is fixed, and which does not change when copied. Absolute addresses are typically specified with a dollar sign.

Application: Sales Invoices

Figure 7.10 introduces a new application that will be used in the balance of the chapter to present additional concepts. The figure is divided in two parts: an empty spreadsheet or *template* in Figure 7.10*a*, and a completed sales invoice in Figure 7.10*b*.

The template is developed so that an individual untrained in the use of spreadsheets can retrieve the template and enter the particulars of a given order (that is, the customer's name, address, and items ordered). After the data has been entered, the invoice is gen-

FIGURE 7.10   Sales invoice: (a) empty template with (b) completed invoice.

```
03-Oct-88                              INVOICE

Customer: ┌─────────────────────┐
          │                     │
          │                     │
          └─────────────────────┘
          -----------------------------------------        Unprotected areas
Quantity          Item       Unit Price  Amount            allow data entry
          -----------------------------------------
          ┌─────────────────────────────────┐
          │                                 │
          │                                 │
          │                                 │
          └─────────────────────────────────┘
          -----------------------------------------
Subtotal
Discount
Tax
          -----------------------------------------
Total
```

(a) Invoice template

```
03-Oct-88                              INVOICE

Customer: Jessica Benjamin
          Main Street
          Anywhere, USA

          -----------------------------------------
Quantity          Item       Unit Price  Amount
          -----------------------------------------
        5 Gadgets              $5.50    $27.50
        1 Widget              $48.75    $48.75
        3 Gismos              $11.25    $33.75

          -----------------------------------------
Subtotal                               $110.00
Discount                                $11.00
Tax                                      $4.95
          -----------------------------------------
Total                                  $103.95
```

Current date appears automatically

10% discount applies only to orders over $100

(b) Completed invoice

erated. Preparation of a second invoice begins with retrieval of the template, followed by data entry, printing the invoice, and so on.

Implicit in the template and completed invoice of Figure 7.10 are several new spreadsheet concepts which are discussed in the remainder of the chapter. These include:

- *Cell protection:* Any cell (or group of cells) may be protected so that its contents cannot be accidentally altered. The template is designed so that data entry is permitted only in the cells that will contain the customer's name, address, and particulars of the order. In other words, access to the cells containing the various column headings and computational formulas is denied, so that the contents of these cells cannot be changed. This is a useful feature in instances when clerical (untrained) workers are entering the data.

- *Arithmetic operations:* All spreadsheet programs enable the use of standard arithmetic operations (addition, subtraction, multiplication, division, and exponentiation) in computing the contents of any cell. These operations are used throughout the invoice, for example, to compute the amount due for each item ordered, the subtotal, sales tax, discount, and final total.

- *Additional functions:* The date on which the invoice was prepared appears within the invoice and was obtained through the @TODAY function. A second function, @IF, is used to apply a conditional 10 percent discount to orders exceeding $100.

Cell Protection

A **template** is an "empty" spreadsheet containing all necessary formulas and column headings, but without any data. The invoice application develops a template, then retrieves it repeatedly to enter data for each new order, saving each completed spreadsheet under a new name.

It is quite likely, however, that the individual who enters the data is not trained in the mechanics of spreadsheets and so could unintentionally alter the contents of the wrong cells. There is, of course, no problem if new customer information is supplied (indeed, these values are meant to change), but difficulties would occur if formula entries were somehow changed or overwritten.

Cell protection can prevent this from happening. Until now, every cell (in all our examples) has been unprotected, meaning that the cell contents could be changed at will. You can, however, protect some (or all) cells within a spreadsheet to prohibit their (unintentional) alteration.

It would be logical, for example, to protect every cell in the sales invoice spreadsheet except those containing specific customer information, namely the customer's name, address, and items ordered. Once a cell (or cells) has been protected, it is no longer possible to enter, alter, or delete data in that cell. Any attempt to do so produces a "protected cell message" on the screen. It is also possible to **unprotect** cells should the developer of the spreadsheet wants to change a heading or cell formula.

Arithmetic Operations

A formula (or mathematical expression) is a combination of variables and arithmetic operations. Spreadsheet programs follow the same conventions as computer programming in general, in that the basic arithmetic operations are assigned special characters called operators, as follows:

^   Exponentiation

*   Multiplication

/   Division

+   Addition

—   Subtraction

A given formula may contain more than one of these operators, in which case a precedence of operations is established. Exponentiation is always performed first, followed by multiplication or division, followed by addition or subtraction. If two operations on the same level are present, for example, multiplication and division, then the operations are performed from left to right.

The normal order of mathematical operations can be changed by using parentheses, as all operations within a set of parentheses are performed first. Parentheses enclosed within other sets of parentheses are called **nested parentheses.** In all instances, however, the operation within the innermost set of parentheses is performed first.

Examination of the following examples will help you understand the importance of these precedence rules. The cell addresses in the examples refer to the following sample spreadsheet:

	A	B	C
1	3	5	2
2	3	12	1
3	4	7	6

Expression	Value	Explanation
+A1 + B1 * 3	18	Multiply the contents of cell B1 by 3, then add the result to the contents of cell A1. (Multiplication has a higher precedence than addition, and is performed first.)
+A2 − B3 + C2	−3	Subtract the contents of cell B3 from the contents of cell A2, then add the result to the contents of cell C2. (Addition and subtraction have the same precedence, so the operations are performed from left to right.)
+B2 / C1 * A2	18	Divide the contents of cell B2 by the contents of cell C1, then multiply the result by the contents of cell A2. (Multiplication and division have the same precedence, so the operations are performed from left to right.)
+B2 / (C1 * A2)	2	Multiply the contents of cell C1 by the contents of cell A2, then divide the contents of cell B2 by that product. (Any expression within parentheses is evaluated first; hence parentheses can be used to alter the normal sequence of operations.)
+B1 ^ C1 − B2 / A3	22	Raise the contents of cell B1 to the power in cell C1; divide the contents of cell B2 by the contents of cell A3, then subtract the quotient from the results of the exponentiation. (Exponentiation is performed first, followed by division and then subtraction.)
+A2 * (B1 + C3)	33	Add the contents of cell B1 to the contents of cell C3, then multiply that sum by the contents of cell A2. (The operation within parentheses is performed first.)

Additional Special Functions

Special functions were first presented in Chapter 6, and were illustrated further in conjunction with the mortgage analysis example. Two additional functions, @TODAY and @IF, are used in the spreadsheet for the invoice example.

@TODAY
The **@TODAY** function returns the current date (as obtained from the system date) in terms of the *number of days* between today's date

and December 31, 1899. For example, the value returned by the @TO-DAY function on October 7, 1988, would be 32,422. (You can convert the display to a more normal-looking 07-Oct-88 by changing the format for the cell containing @TODAY to a date format.)

Dates are stored internally in this same fashion (in date number form) to enable date arithmetic; that is, you can compute the number of days between two dates by subtracting the earlier date from the later one. You can then compute the number of weeks, months, quarters, or years simply by dividing. Be aware, however, that when an exact figure is needed, you must pay attention to fine points such as leap years and the exact number of days in a month.

@IF

The @IF function has three arguments, the first of which is a **logical relationship** containing an equal sign, a greater than sign, or a less than sign. If the relationship is true, the @IF function returns the second argument; if the relationship is false, the function returns the third argument.

The @IF function is used in the invoice template to compute a conditional 10 percent discount on orders over $100. Assume, for example, that the amount of the order is stored in cell D16, and that the @IF function is entered as follows:

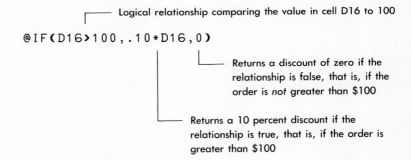

The @IF function compares the value in cell D16 (the amount of the order) to 100. If the relationship is true (that is, the order is *greater than 100*), the function returns the second argument corresponding to a discount of 10 percent. If, however, the relationship is false (that is, the order is *not* greater than 100), the function returns the third argument (a discount of zero).

Arithmetic Expressions versus Functions

The availability of programmed functions such as @IF or @TODAY within a spreadsheet offers capabilities which would not otherwise be possible. There are instances, however, when the same result could be obtained through an equivalent arithmetic expression, but even then the use of functions is preferable, as can be seen in Figure 7.11.

FIGURE 7.11
Arithmetic expressions
versus functions.

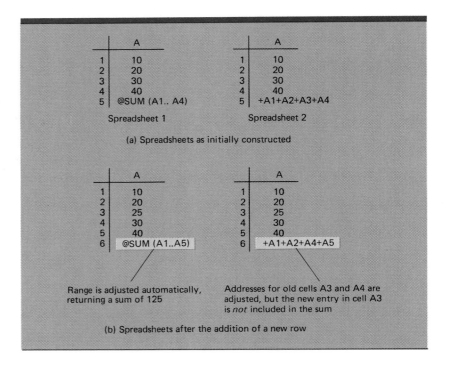

	A
1	10
2	20
3	30
4	40
5	@SUM (A1.. A4)

Spreadsheet 1

	A
1	10
2	20
3	30
4	40
5	+A1+A2+A3+A4

Spreadsheet 2

(a) Spreadsheets as initially constructed

	A
1	10
2	20
3	25
4	30
5	40
6	@SUM (A1..A5)

	A
1	10
2	20
3	25
4	30
5	40
6	+A1+A2+A4+A5

Range is adjusted automatically, returning a sum of 125

Addresses for old cells A3 and A4 are adjusted, but the new entry in cell A3 is *not* included in the sum

(b) Spreadsheets after the addition of a new row

The two spreadsheets in Figure 7.11*a* may appear equivalent, but the @SUM function in spreadsheet 1 is inherently superior to that of the arithmetic expression in spreadsheet 2. As the example is presently constructed, the entries in cell A5 of both spreadsheets return a value of 100.

"IF YOU ASK ME, THEY'RE NOTHING BUT DUST COLLECTORS."

INCLUDING NONNUMERIC VALUES IN ARITHMETIC RANGES

The use of the @SUM function can be further enhanced by including *non-numeric* values as the first and last entries within the range of numbers to be summed, for example, a blank cell and a row of equal signs, respectively. This enables any additional rows which are subsequently inserted above or below the original column of numbers (that is, above the 10 or below the 40) to be automatically included in the adjusted sum.

	A
1	
2	10
3	20
4	30
5	40
6	=====
7	@SUM(A1..A6)

Now consider what happens if a *new* row is inserted in both spreadsheets between existing rows 2 and 3, with the entry in the new cell equal to 25. Whereas the @SUM function is automatically adjusted to include the new value (returning a sum of 125), the arithmetic expression adjusts cell addresses but does *not* include the new value (returning the incorrect sum of 100).

The concept we have just illustrated is true of ranges in general; that is, they expand and contract to adjust for insertions and deletions, and consequently should be used wherever possible.

HANDS-ON EXERCISE 2: PREPARING A SALES INVOICE

OBJECTIVE: Develop the sales invoice template using Figure 7.12 as a guide. Figure 7.12a depicts the spreadsheet as it would appear on the screen (that is, with rows and columns appended); Figure 7.12b contains the various cell entries.

Step 1: Load Your Spreadsheet Program
Load your spreadsheet program as you have been doing throughout the chapter. Be sure to enter date and time correctly (when the system is booted), as the sales invoice will reflect the system date.

Step 2: Enter Row and Column Headings
Change the default widths of columns A, B, and C to 10, 21, and 10 characters respectively, then enter labels as shown below. Note the label formatting in effect.

```
D1:  ''INVOICE
A3:  'Customer
A8:  'Quantity
B8:  ^Item
C8:  'Unit Price
D8:  ''Amount
A16: 'Subtotal
A17: 'Discount
A18: 'Tax
A20: 'Total
```

```
              A                B              C           D
1    03-Oct-88                                        INVOICE
2
3    Customer:
4
5
6
7    ---------------------------------------------------------
8    Quantity            Item           Unit Price  Amount
9    ---------------------------------------------------------
10
11
12
13
14
15   ---------------------------------------------------------
16   Subtotal
17   Discount
18   Tax
19   ---------------------------------------------------------
20   Total
```

(a) The spreadsheet

```
A1:  (D1) PR [W10] @NOW
D1:  PR "INVOICE
A3:  PR [W10] 'Customer:
A7:  PR [W10] \-
B7:  PR [W21] \-
C7:  PR [W10] \-
D7:  PR \-
A8:  PR [W10] 'Quantity
B8:  PR [W21] 'Item
C8:  PR [W10] 'Unit Price
D8:  PR "Amount
A9:  PR [W10] \-
B9:  PR [W21] \-
C9:  PR [W10] \-
D9:  PR \-
D10: (C2) PR +A10*C10
D11: (C2) PR +A11*C11
D12: (C2) PR +A12*C12
D13: (C2) PR +A13*C13
D14: (C2) PR +A14*C14
A15: PR [W10] \-
B15: PR [W21] \-
C15: PR [W10] \-
D15: (C2) PR \-
A16: PR [W10] 'Subtotal
D16: (C2) PR @SUM(D10..D15)
A17: PR [W10] 'Discount
D17: (C2) PR @IF(D16>100,0.1*D16,0)
A18: PR [W10] 'Tax
D18: (C2) PR 0.05*(D16-D17)
A19: PR [W10] \-
B19: PR [W21] \-
C19: PR [W10] \-
D19: (C2) PR \-
A20: PR [W10] 'Total
D20: (C2) PR +D16-D17+D18
```

@TODAY function appears as @NOW

PR indicates protected cell

@IF function applies conditional discount

Colum widths have been changed

(b) Cell formulas (Lotus implementation)

FIGURE 7.12   Sales invoice: (a) spreadsheet and (b) cell formulas.

Step 3: Enter Rows of Dashed Lines

Move the cursor to cell A7, then enter the backward slash followed by a hyphen (\−) to fill cell A7 with hyphens. Use the copy command to duplicate this entry throughout row 7. Thus the source and destination ranges are A7..A7 and B7..D7, respectively. Now copy row 7 to row 9, then to row 15, and finally to row 19. (*Three distinct* copy commands are required.)

Step 4: Establish the Date

Move the cursor to cell A1 (press the Home key) and enter the function @TODAY. The cell contents will appear as @NOW, implying that the current value of the system date will be supplied as the value for this cell. The value returned by the @TODAY function is the *number of days* (approximately 32,000) between December 31, 1899, and the current date, and does not resemble the date as you would expect it. Now change the format of cell A1 to a date format (select DD-MMM-YY) and the more familiar date form (for example, 24-Nov-88) will be displayed.

Step 5: Enter Cell Formulas

Enter the necessary cell formulas to compute the amount due for each item ordered, the subtotal, discount, tax, and total order as follows:

```
D10:  +A10*C10
D11:  +A11*C11
D12:  +A12*C12
D13:  +A13*C13
D14:  +A14*C14
D16:  @SUM(D10..D15)
D17:  @IF(D16>100,.10*D16,0)
D18:  .05*(D16-D17)
D20:  +D16-D17+D18
```

Amount due is the quantity ordered times the unit price

Use the copy command to replicate entry in cell D10

Subtotal
Discount applies only to orders in excess of $100
Five percent sales tax on amount owed
Total equals the subtotal, less discount, plus tax

After you have entered the necessary formulas, change the format in cells D10 through D20 to currency (with two decimals). Change the format in cells C10 through C14 as well. (*Two* range format commands are necessary.)

Step 6: Suppress Superflous Zeros

Some spreadsheet programs (for example, Lotus version 2, but *not* VP Planner or Lotus version 1A) have a zero suppression command which prints blanks in lieu of computed zeros. The appearance of the template would be improved, for example, if the zeros which now appear in column D were suppressed.

Accordingly, enter the appropriate zero suppression command if it is available (/WGZY in Lotus version 2). Note, however, that zero suppression is *not* required to complete the exercise.

Step 7: Cell Protection

Invoke the command to *globally* protect every cell in the spreadsheet. Now use the range command to *unprotect* cells B3 through B6 (the customer name and address) and cells A10 through C14 (the specifics of the order).

   Save the invoice template under the name INVOICE.

Step 8: Create an Invoice

Create the sales invoice for Jessica Benjamin as presented earlier in Figure 7.10b by entering her name and address, as appropriate, together with her order. Observe how the computed values for subtotal, discount, tax, and total change automatically as each individual item is entered. Print the invoice after you have entered all three items. Save Jessica's invoice under the name JESSICA.

Step 9: Create a Second Invoice

Enter the appropriate command to retrieve the template saved in step 7. Enter data for a second customer, Joel Stutz, residing at Surryhill Place, Huntington, NY 11743. Joel has ordered six "widgets" and two "gismos," with the same unit prices in effect. Print his invoice as well, then save it under the name JOEL.

CONCEPT SUMMARY

Template: An "empty" spreadsheet containing cell formulas, and column and row labels, but no data.

Cell protection: The ability to prevent the accidental alteration of a cell's contents. Cells may be protected (unprotected) on a global basis or individually through a range command.

Arithmetic operations: Performed according to a predetermined hierarchy of operations; exponentiation first, then multiplication or division, then addition or subtraction, and from left to right if a tie.

@TODAY: A special function enabling the date of execution to be included within a spreadsheet; requires reformatting to convert the internally stored date into a more familiar format.

@IF(logical relation, exp 1, exp 2): A special function enabling a cell's value to be chosen from one of two other cells, depending on the result of a logical expression.

LOTUS

COMPUTING FOR MANAGERS AND PROFESSIONALS

Authors' Comments:
A computer magazine (of which there are over 100) is an excellent source for current information. These magazines dispense solid technical advice, describe and evaluate new products, and are well worth their subscription price.

COMPUTER MAGAZINES

A subscription to *Lotus Magazine* should be given serious consideration if spreadsheets are your primary application (even if you don't use Lotus 1-2-3). The magazine is much more than an extended commercial for Lotus and/or Symphony, although it does its share of proselytizing in that area. We like it for its articles describing spreadsheet applications, and for its Lotus-specific tips, tricks, and traps. Other magazines to consider:

● *PC Magazine,* published biweekly by PC Communications Corp., New York. The first IBM-specific magazine and a huge commercial success, *PC Magazine* is known for its in-depth technical reviews and its thorough coverage. Entire issues are usually devoted to specific topics: desktop publishing, spreadsheets, word processing, and so on.

● *PC World,* published monthly by PC World Communications, Inc., San Francisco. *PC World* was launched by the same people who began *PC Magazine* when they became disenchanted with a change in management. It is highly readable and contains ample technical information; there is little to differentiate the two magazines other than frequency of publication.

● *Personal Computing,* published monthly by Hayden Publishing Company, Hasbrouck Heights, NJ. We enjoy this magazine for its coverage of the industry as a whole, its upbeat writing, and its wide-ranging selection of articles. This is the magazine we would recommend buying second, after one of the PC publications.

● *The Database Adviser,* published monthly by Ashton-Tate, Torrance, CA. Required reading for anyone using the dBASE product line on a regular basis, as it contains technical information beyond what is in the manual as well numerous programming tips. The magazine also contains advertisements from the many companies which offer supporting products for dBASE.

COMPUTER BOOKS

While on the subject of supplementary reading, we could not resist the opportunity to play literary critic. The books on our list are neither textbooks nor reference manuals, and they are decidedly nontechnical in nature. We sought publications stressing the human side of computer use—books that were able to educate while simultaneously maintaining a sense of humor.

Our suggestions for recommended reading:

- *The Digital Deli,* written by The Lunch Group and Guests and edited by Steve Ditlea (Workman Publishing, New York, 1984). A delightful smorgasbord of articles, anecdotes, and pictures dealing with all aspects of the personal computer. Over 100 contributors wrote a page or two each. The book is fascinating reading and an absolute must.

- *The Compleat Computer,* by Dennie Van Tassel and Cynthia L. Van Tassel (SRA, Chicago, 1983). An outstanding series of selections from fiction, poetry, newspapers, cartoons, and advertising, depicting what non-computer specialists think about computers. The book also contains a series of thought-provoking exercises that make it suitable as a supplementary text for an introductory course on computers.

- *What's So Funny about Computers,* by Sidney Harris (William Kaufman, Los Altos, CA, 1982) and *A Much, Much Better World,* by Eldon Dedini (Microsoft Press, Bellevue, WA, 1985). A look at the lighter side of computers through the eyes of the cartoonist. Many of the over 200 cartoons in these books have appeared previously in other places, in sources as diverse as *Playboy* and *The Wall Street Journal.* The authors were kind enough to grant permission for us to reprint some of them in this text.

- *The Soul of a New Machine,* by Tracy Kidder (Little, Brown, Boston, 1981). This Pulitzer prizewinner tells the inside story about the design of a new computer at Data General Corporation. Remarkably, the author is able to maintain the interest of individuals with vastly different technical backgrounds; Kidder explains the basics for the novice, yet includes sufficient technical detail for the computer professional. The book conveys much information about the computer industry and the people who make it run.

- *On Wings of Eagles,* by Ken Follett (William Morrow, New York, 1983). This real-life adventure relates the story of two employees of Electronic Data Systems, who were taken hostage in Iran (a year prior to the seizure of the American Embassy) and subsequently freed in a dramatic rescue by their employer. The head of EDS, H. Ross Perot, actually walked in and out of an Iranian jail to tell his men that help was on the way. Suggested reading for your next plane ride.

CORPORATE PROFILE:
LOTUS DEVELOPMENT CORPORATION

Year-end statistics for 1987:
Sales: $396.0 million
Net income: $ 72.0 million
CEO: Jim Manzi
Headquarters: 161 First Street
Cambridge, MA 02142
(617) 577-8500

Lotus 1-2-3 made its debut at the fall 1982 Computer Dealers Exposition (COMDEX) where it sold a then astonishing $900,000 in three days. 1-2-3 went on to do $50 million in its first year, and triple that the next, and soon became the best-selling applications program in the world.

Why was Lotus so successful? It was not the first spreadsheet written, nor was it even the first to run on the PC. (Both VisiCalc and SuperCalc were available for MS-DOS machines two months before Lotus.) It was, however, the first spreadsheet written expressly for the 8088 microprocessor, and was better designed and better documented than its competition. 1-2-3 also came with its own programming language (macros), and took advantage of the PC's 10 function keys. The fact that Lotus had an unprecedented $4 million advertising budget at precisely the right time (when IBM was pushing its machines and businesses were buying them) no doubt assured its success. Whatever the reason, 1-2-3 is a phenomenon that may never be repeated.

Attempting to avoid the one-product syndrome epidemic in the software world, Lotus Development Corporation shipped the first copy of Symphony in June 1984. Television commercials billed Symphony as the encore to 1-2-3, touting its combined word processing, enhanced spreadsheet, communications, form-oriented database, graphics, and powerful command language, all of which were integrated into a single program. Yet despite Symphony, and the subsequent introduction of more than 20 other products, Lotus Development remains dependent on 1-2-3 for the bulk of its revenue (see the accompanying graph).

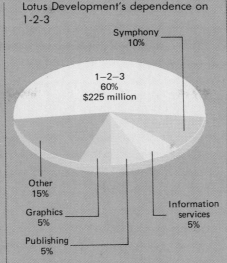

Lotus Development's dependence on 1-2-3

Symphony 10%

1–2–3 60% $225 million

Other 15%

Graphics 5%

Publishing 5%

Information services 5%

Even 1-2-3 itself may have no place to go but down, as it continues to face increased competition. Indeed, it may be only a matter of time before more powerful spreadsheets, such as Microsoft's Excel, eat into the 80 to 90 percent market share of IBM-compatible spreadsheets claimed by 1-2-3. On the other end of the scale, low-priced clones such as Paperback Software's VP Planner threaten 1-2-3 as well.

So what will the company do in return? For openers it introduced a totally revamped version of its flagship product, which includes three-dimensional spreadsheets among other features. It also adopted a strategy to reduce the risk of product development by acquiring new products through purchase of smaller companies rather than developing them internally.

Most significantly, perhaps, Lotus Development Corporation has completed the transformation from a startup phenomenon to industry heavyweight, with annual sales in the neighborhood of $400 million. Its founder Mitch Kapor has left the company to pursue other interests (after selling his Lotus stock for more than $50 million while still retaining 10 percent ownership). In his place sits Jim Manzi and a disciplined, market-oriented management team that appears to have the company headed for continued growth. Only time will tell whether they will be successful.

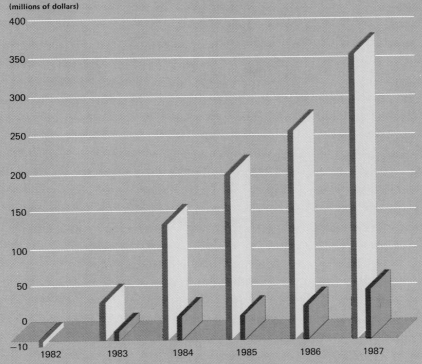

LOTUS DEVELOPMENT CORPORATION SALES AND NET INCOME
(millions of dollars)

Summary

The chapter revolved around presentation of two diverse applications, mortgage analysis and sales invoices, presented the necessary concepts for their development, and then directed you to parallel Hands-On Exercises so that you could implement the spreadsheets on the computer. Suffice it to say that on completion of the chapter, and especially the Hands-On Exercises, you will have achieved a degree of proficiency sufficient to develop your own spreadsheets in an almost limitless variety of application areas.

The generic concepts presented in the chapter included the various formats available for label and numeric entries, the concept of cell protection, and the hierarchy of arithmetic operations. We also covered the move and copy commands, and distinguished between relative and absolute addresses. The concept of a range (and its specification by pointing) is especially important, as it applies to almost every spreadsheet command. The chapter also included material on the @PMT, @TODAY, and @IF functions.

Key Words and Concepts

@IF	Global
@PMT	Left justification
@TODAY	Logical relationship
Absolute cell address	Move command
Argument	Nested parentheses
Cell formula	Percentage format
Cell protection	Pointing
Cell value	Protect command
Comma format	Range
Copy command	Relative cell address
Currency format	Right justification
Default (initial) setting	Scientific format
Destination range	Source range
Edit mode	Special function
Fixed decimal format	Template
General format	Unprotect command

True/False

1. A cell address which contains two dollar signs is an example of a relative address.

2. C1 + D1 will be interpreted as a label rather than a mathematical expression.

3. Every column in a spreadsheet must be the same width.

4. Cells within the same column can contain numerical entries in several different formats.

5. A spreadsheet may be printed in a variety of formats.

6. In the absence of parentheses, multiplication is always done before division.

7. In the absence of parentheses, multiplication is always done before addition.

8. A range may consist of a single cell.

9. The "from" and "to" ranges specified in a given copy command may be given as a column and rectangle, respectively.

10. Every cell in a spreadsheet should be protected when the spreadsheet is in the hands of an untrained individual, for example, a clerk entering data into a template.

11. Once a cell (or cells) has been protected, it can never be unprotected.

12. Global commands take precedence over range commands.

13. A total of eight cells are present in the range indicated by B1..C4.

14. Most spreadsheet commands apply only to individual cells as opposed to a range of cells.

Multiple Choice

1. The procedure which allows you to change the contents of a cell, *without* retyping the entire cell, is called:
   (a) Scrolling
   (b) Saving
   (c) Editing
   (d) Inserting

2. A spreadsheet containing only row and column labels, but no data, is called a:
   (a) Template
   (b) Fixed spreadsheet
   (c) Outline
   (d) Variable spreadsheet

3. Absolute cell addresses are typically specified with:
   (a) An ampersand
   (b) An asterisk
   (c) A dollar sign
   (d) A percent sign

4. Cells within a given column:
   (a) Must all be the same width
   (b) Must all be identically formatted
   (c) Must be the same width *and* identically formatted
   (d) All the above

5. A cell range may consist of:
   (a) A single cell
   (b) An entire row or part of a row
   (c) An entire column or part of a column
   (d) All the above

6. In the absence of parentheses, the order of operation is:
   (a) Exponentiation, addition or subtraction, multiplication or division
   (b) Addition or subtraction, multiplication or division, exponentiation
   (c) Multiplication or division, exponentiation, addition or subtraction
   (d) Exponentiation, multiplication or division, addition or subtraction

7. Which command will take a cell, or group of cells, and duplicate them elsewhere in the spreadsheet, *without* changing the original cell references?
   (a) Copy command, provided relative addresses were specified
   (b) Copy command, provided absolute addresses were specified
   (c) Move command, provided relative addresses were specified
   (d) Move command, provided absolute addresses were specified

8. The expression $+A2*(C3-C2)^A1$ will perform its operations in which order?
   (a) Multiplication, subtraction, exponentiation
   (b) Exponentiation, multiplication, subtraction
   (c) Subtraction, exponentiation, multiplication
   (d) Subtraction, multiplication, exponentiation

9. If a *label* entry contains more characters than the width of the cell in which it is found:
   (a) The extra characters are truncated under all circumstances
   (b) A series of asterisks is displayed
   (c) All the characters may still be displayed provided the cell to the right is empty
   (d) All the characters may still be displayed provided the cell to the left is empty

10. If a *numeric* entry contains more characters than the width of the cell in which it is found:
    (a) The extra characters are truncated under all circumstances
    (b) A series of asterisks is displayed
    (c) All the characters may still be displayed provided the cell to the right is empty

(d) All the characters may still be displayed provided the cell to the left is empty

11. To copy a cell or cells from one place in a spreadsheet to another:
    (a) The size and shape of the source and destination ranges must be the same
    (b) The source range must contain at least one absolute address
    (c) The destination range must contain at least one relative address
    (d) All the above
    (e) None of the above

12. Given that percentage format is in effect, and that the number .056 has been entered into the active cell, how will the contents of the cell appear?
    (a) .056
    (b) 5.6%
    (c) .056%
    (d) 56%

13. Given the following cell contents: A3 = 2, B3 = 10, and C2 = 2; what will be the results of the expression: +A3*B3/5 − 1*C2?
    (a) −2
    (b) 2
    (c) 20/3
    (d) None of the above

14. All the following are given as reasons for the success of Lotus *except*:
    (a) It was the first spreadsheet written expressly for the IBM PC (that is, the 8088 microprocessor)
    (b) It was the first spreadsheet to take advantage of function keys
    (c) It was heavily advertised prior to its distribution
    (d) Lotus Development bought Software Arts, the company which developed VisiCalc, and so eliminated the competition

15. In the entry, @SUM(B4..D4) the entry in parentheses is known as a(n):
    (a) Label
    (b) Argument or range
    (c) Formula
    (d) Function

Exercises

1. Discuss the following regarding the use of spreadsheets:
    (a) What would be the effect of mixing absolute and relative references in a cell address; for example, explain the difference between A4, $A$4, $A4, and A$4.

(b) Explain how it is possible for the source and target ranges in a copy command to be of different shapes, for example, a single cell and row of cells, respectively, or a column of cells and a rectangle. Are different-shaped ranges also possible in a move command?

(c) What advantage, if any, is to be gained by including a row of equal signs at the end of a range in an @SUM command?

(d) How can the Home, End, Ins, and Del keys be used in conjunction with the edit mode?

(e) Why is it necesary to print a spreadsheet in both cell value and cell formula format? Indicate the necessary commands to accomplish both operations.

(f) What advantage (other than convenience) is to be gained by using the repeat character in a cell; that is, why is \= superior to ========= (assuming a cell width of 9)?

2. Given the cell values A1 = 6, A3 = 3, A2 = 4, and A4 = 2, what value will be returned by the following expressions?

(a) (A1 + A2) ^ A4

(b) +A1 + A2/A3 ^ A4

(c) (A1 + A2) / A3 * A4

(d) (A1 + A2) / (A3 * A4)

(e) +A2 ^ A3 / A4

3. Consider the two spreadsheets shown in Figure 7.13 and the entries, @AVG(A1..A4) versus (A1 + A2 + A3 + A4)/4, both of which calculate the average of cells A1 through A4. Assume that a *new* row is inserted in the spreadsheet betwen existing rows 2 and 3, with the entry in the new cell equal to 100.

(a) What value will be returned by the @AVG function in spreadsheet 1 after the new row has been inserted?

(b) What value will be returned by the formula in spreadsheet 2 after the new row has been inserted?

(c) In which cell will the @AVG function itself be located after the new row has been inserted?

Return to the *original* problem, but this time delete row 2.

(d) What value will be returned by the @AVG function in spreadsheet 1 after the row has been deleted?

(e) What will be returned by the formula in spreadsheet 2 after the row has been deleted?

	A			A
1	10		1	10
2	20		2	20
3	30		3	30
4	40		4	40
5	@AVG (A1..A4)		5	(A1+A2+A3+A4) / 4
	Spreadsheet 1			Spreadsheet 2

FIGURE 7.13
Spreadsheets for exercise 3.

FIGURE 7.14
Spreadsheet for exercise 4.

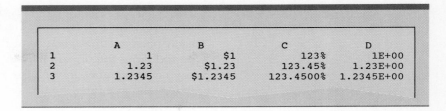

	A	B	C	D
1	1	$1	123%	1E+00
2	1.23	$1.23	123.45%	1.23E+00
3	1.2345	$1.2345	123.4500%	1.2345E+00

FIGURE 7.14
Spreadsheet for exercise 4.

4. Figure 7.14 contains a spreadsheet in which the same number (1.2345) has been entered in *every* cell. The differences in appearance between the various cell entries are produced by different formats in effect within the individual cells. Indicate the precise formatting for every cell.

5. Indicate whether the following are valid as cell ranges.
   (a) A3
   (b) A3..B3
   (c) A3..A10
   (d) A3..B10
   (e) A3..B4 *and* A7..B10

6. Use Figure 7.15 as a guide to answer the following questions regarding the copy command, and absolute versus relative addresses.
   (a) Given that the contents of cell B5 is (1 + A1) * A5, and that the contents of cell B5 are copied to the range of cells indicated by C5..E5. Indicate the cell formulas as they would appear in the copied cells.
   (b) Repeat part *a*, except with the destination range as B6..B8.
   (c) Now assume that the contents of cell B12 are (1 + $A$1) * A12, and that the contents of cell B12 are copied to the range of cells indicated by C12..E12. Indicate the cell formulas as they would appear in the copied cells.
   (d) Repeat part *c*, except with the destination range as B13..B15.

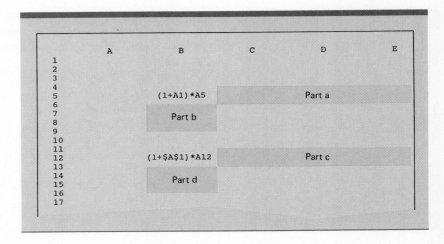

	A	B	C	D	E
1					
2					
3					
4					
5		(1+A1)*A5		Part a	
6					
7		Part b			
8					
9					
10					
11					
12		(1+$A$1)*A12		Part c	
13					
14		Part d			
15					
16					
17					

FIGURE 7.15
Spreadsheet for exercise 6.

7. The @PMT (P, I, T) function presented in the chapter can be used to prepare an amortization schedule for a loan. The amount of each payment that goes toward interest is the interest rate per period times the unpaid balance of the loan. The amount of each payment that goes toward the principal is the payment amount minus the amount which goes toward interest. Create an amortization schedule for a $5000 loan at 13 percent annual interest borrowed for a period of fifteen months. Use the template below as a guide in designing your spreadsheet.

```
                    Amortization Schedule

    Principal
    Interest
    Periods
    Payment


                    Toward      Toward       Loan
    Period         Interest   Principal    Balance

        0                                     5000
        1
        2
        3
```

8. Lotus (VP Planner) specific: What do the following command sequences do? (In some instances the command sequences are incomplete and would require additional information. Answer only to the extent of the command string.)
   (a) /WGC10   (f) /WIR
   (b) /WCS8   (g) /WDC
   (c) /RFC2   (h) /C
   (d) /RFF0   (i) /WGP
   (e) /WGFF0   (j) /RU

9. Figure 7.16 contains a new five-year sales and profit projection spreadsheet. Enter the necessary commands to reproduce the spreadsheet. The following sequence of operations is provided as a guide:
   (a) Step 1: Create the spreadsheet template consisting of the row and column headings (be sure to change the width of column A as necessary).
   (b) Step 2: Enter the formulas for the first year of the forecast (1988) together with the initial asumptions.
   (c) Step 3: Develop the necessary formulas for the second year of the forecast (1989).
   (d) Step 4: Copy the formulas for 1989 to the remaining years in the forecast.

	A	B 1988	C 1989	D 1990	E 1991	F 1992
1		1988	1989	1990	1991	1992
2						
3	Income:					
4	Projected unit sales	10,000	12,000	14,400	17,280	20,736
5	Unit price	$2.00	$2.10	$2.21	$2.32	$2.43
6	Gross revenue	$20,000	$25,200	$31,752	$40,008	$50,409
7						
8	Expenses:					
9	Variable cost per unit	$1.00	$1.08	$1.17	$1.26	$1.36
10	Total variable cost	$10,000	$12,960	$16,796	$21,768	$28,211
11	Overhead	$5,000	$5,500	$6,050	$6,655	$7,321
12	Total expenses	$15,000	$18,460	$22,846	$28,423	$35,532
13						
14	Net income:	$5,000	$6,740	$8,906	$11,585	$14,878
15						
16	Assumed rates of increase:					
17	Unit sales	20.00%				
18	Selling price	5.00%				
19	Variable cost	8.00%				
20	Overhead	10.00%				

FIGURE 7.16
Spreadsheet for exercise 9.

(e) Step 5: Alter formats as appropriate so that your spreadsheet matches Figure 7.16.

(f) Step 6: Print the spreadsheet as presently constructed in both cell value and cell formula format.

(g) Step 7: Change the initial assumptions to 20, 6, 9, and 12, respectively, and print the new set of cell values.

CHAPTER 8

ADVANCED CAPABILITIES

CHAPTER OBJECTIVES

After reading this chapter, you should be able to:

1. List several spreadsheet capabilities that are employed with large spreadsheets; describe what additional measures need to be taken in order to print large spreadsheets.

2. Differentiate between the commands for freezing titles and windowing, and between automatic and manual recalculation.

3. Use the @AVG, @MAX, and @MIN functions in a spreadsheet.

4. Explain the table lookup function and how it is used in a spreadsheet.

5. Combine values from individual spreadsheets into a single consolidated spreadsheet.

6. Explain what is meant by a spreadsheet macro; describe the procedure for implementing a macro within a spreadsheet.

Overview

This concluding spreadsheet chapter presents two additional applications, which in turn introduce several new capabilities. The first example shows how a spreadsheet may be used as a financial forecasting tool, and focuses on the development of large spreadsheets. It includes material on *freezing* row and column titles, dividing the screen into vertical and/or horizontal *windows*, and *manual* versus *automatic* recalculation.

The second application extends the earlier grade book example to include the use of a *table lookup* in addition to the *@MAX*, *@MIN*, and *@AVG* functions. The extended grade book also illustrates the *file combine command* to consolidate data from several spreadsheets into one. It also introduces the *macro* concept as both a convenient shortcut and a powerful programming tool.

The Corporate Profile focuses on the Compaq Computer Corporation, a leading manufacturer of IBM-compatible computers. Compaq has always offered advanced capabilities not found in IBM machines, and has grown faster than any corporation in American business.

Application: Financial Forecast

The area of financial planning and budgeting is one of the most common applications of spreadsheets in business. Figure 8.1 depicts one such illustration, in which the income and expenses of Get Rich Quick Enterprises are projected over an eight-year period.

GET RICH QUICK ENTERPRISES
Eight Year Forecast

	1988	1989	1990	1991	1992	1993	1994	1995
Income:								
Projected unit sales	10,000	11,800	13,924	16,430	19,388	22,878	26,996	31,855
Unit price	$2.00	$2.10	$2.21	$2.32	$2.43	$2.55	$2.68	$2.81
Gross revenue	$20,000	$24,780	$30,702	$38,040	$47,132	$58,396	$72,353	$89,646
Expenses:								
Variable cost per unit	$1.00	$1.08	$1.17	$1.26	$1.36	$1.47	$1.59	$1.71
Total variable cost	$10,000	$12,744	$16,241	$20,697	$26,377	$33,615	$42,839	$54,593
Overhead	$5,000	$5,500	$6,050	$6,655	$7,321	$8,053	$8,858	$9,744
Total expenses	$15,000	$18,244	$22,291	$27,352	$33,697	$41,667	$51,696	$64,337
Earnings before taxes:	$5,000	$6,536	$8,411	$10,688	$13,435	$16,729	$20,657	$25,309
Assumed rates of increase:								
Unit sales	18.00%							
Selling price	5.00%							
Variable cost	8.00%							
Overhead	10.00%							

FIGURE 8.1
Eight-year financial forecast.

Income in any given year is equal to the unit sales times the selling price per unit. In 1988, for example, 10,000 units are sold at a price of $2.00 per unit, to yield gross revenue of $20,000. The variable costs for the same year are $10,000 (10,000 units times $1.00 per unit);

"SAY, BROWN — TAKE 14 YEARS AND CHECK THIS ANSWER."

the fixed overhead is shown at $5000. Subtracting the total expenses from the estimated income yields earnings before taxes of $5000.

The estimated income and expenses for the other years in the spreadsheet are based on the series of assumptions shown in the lower left corner of Figure 8.1. A change in any one of these estimates necessitates an entirely new set of calculations, a tedious procedure if done manually. Use of a spreadsheet, however, allows you to vary these parameters and see the results immediately. It is strongly recommended that you *isolate assumptions* (away from the main body of the spreadsheet) so that they are clearly visible.

Consider, for example, what would happen if unit sales were to increase at 15 percent rather than the 18 percent shown originally. The 1989 sales estimate becomes 11,500 instead of 11,800, which requires corresponding adjustments in revenue, total variable cost, total expenses, and earnings before taxes. Because unit sales in each future year are based on the number of units in the previous year, these changes need to be reflected in all subsequent years as well. Spreadsheets, therefore, are a powerful tool in financial forecasting.

The next several pages develop the spreadsheet of Figure 8.1, and in so doing introduce new spreadsheet capabilities.

Freezing Titles

The financial forecast of Figure 8.1 is typical of many spreadsheets in that it is too large to be displayed on the monitor in its entirety, necessitating the scrolling operation described in Chapter 6. Recall, however, that while scrolling makes it possible to display different sections of the spreadsheet on the monitor, it can also result in the headings for existing rows and/or columns being lost from view as the cell pointer is moved to its new position. The problem is circumvented through the **titles command,** which is illustrated in Figure 8.2.

Consider first Figure 8.2*a*, which contains the entire spreadsheet with row and column labels included. Now assume that your monitor is large enough to display only 5 columns and 20 rows at one time (so that all of Figure 8.2*a* will not be visible at the same time). Assume further that you begin with columns A through E on the monitor, and then move the cell pointer to view column F. The resulting scrolling operation would cause column A (containing the row labels) to disappear from view.

In similar fashion, if you began with rows 1 through 20 on the monitor and then moved the cursor to include rows 21 through 23, the vertical scroll causes rows 1, 2, and 3 (containing the column headings) to disappear. Either way, once the headings have scrolled off the screen, interpretation of the numbers in the visible portion is difficult, if not impossible.

You can resolve the difficulty by freezing row and/or column headings through the titles command, as shown in Figure 8.2*b*, 8.2*c*, and 8.2*d*. Figure 8.2*b* depicts the use of *vertical* titles in which column

	A	B	C	D	E	F	G	H	I
1					GET RICH QUICK ENTERPRISES				
2					Eight Year Forecast				
3									
4		1988	1989	1990	1991	1992	1993	1994	1995
5									
6	Income:								
7	Projected unit sales	10,000	11,800	13,924	16,430	19,388	22,878	26,996	31,855
8	Unit price	$2.00	$2.10	$2.21	$2.32	$2.43	$2.55	$2.68	$2.81
9	Gross revenue	$20,000	$24,780	$30,702	$38,040	$47,132	$58,396	$72,353	$89,646
10									
11	Expenses:								
12	Variable cost per unit	$1.00	$1.08	$1.17	$1.26	$1.36	$1.47	$1.59	$1.71
13	Total variable cost	$10,000	$12,744	$16,241	$20,697	$26,377	$33,615	$42,839	$54,593
14	Overhead	$5,000	$5,500	$6,050	$6,655	$7,321	$8,053	$8,858	$9,744
15	Total expenses	$15,000	$18,244	$22,291	$27,352	$33,697	$41,667	$51,696	$64,337
16									
17	Earnings before taxes:	$5,000	$6,536	$8,411	$10,688	$13,435	$16,729	$20,657	$25,309
18									
19	Assumed rates of increase:								
20	Unit sales	18.00%							
21	Selling price	5.00%							
22	Variable cost	8.00%							
23	Overhead	10.00%							

(a) Spreadsheet with rows and columns

Column A is permanently visible

	A	F	G	H	I
1					
2					
3					
4		1992	1993	1994	1995
5					
6	Income:				
7	Projected unit sales	19,388	22,878	26,996	31,855
8	Unit price	$2.43	$2.55	$2.68	$2.81
9	Gross revenue	$47,132	$58,396	$72,353	$89,646
10					
11	Expenses:				
12	Variable cost per unit	$1.36	$1.47	$1.59	$1.71
13	Total variable cost	$26,377	$33,615	$42,839	$54,593
14	Overhead	$7,321	$8,053	$8,858	$9,744
15	Total expenses	$33,697	$41,667	$51,696	$64,337
16					
17	Earnings before taxes:	$13,435	$16,729	$20,657	$25,309
18					
19	Assumed rates of increase:				
20	Unit sales				
21	Selling price				
22	Variable cost				
23	Overhead				

(b) Spreadsheet with vertical titles

FIGURE 8.2
The titles command.

A (containing the row labels) remains permanently on the screen. Scrolling still takes place as you move beyond column E, but column A is frozen on the screen and the row labels are always visible. Note, too, that the columns displayed in Figure 8.2*b* are not consecutive; that is, column A is followed by column F (as columns B through E have disappeared as a result of scrolling).

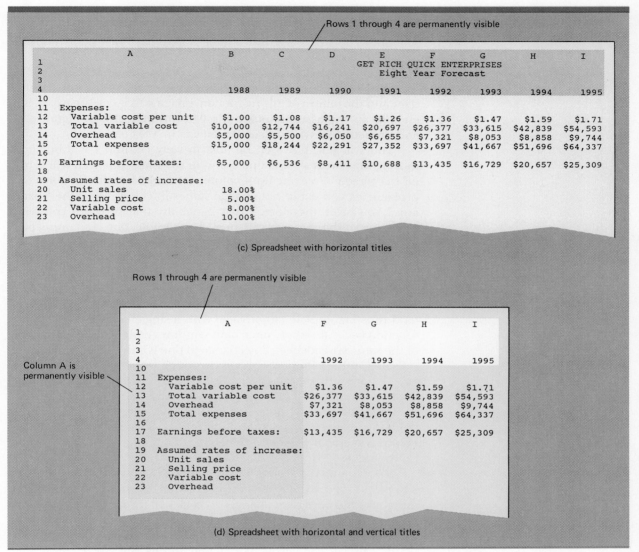

Rows 1 through 4 are permanently visible

	A	B	C	D	E	F	G	H	I
1					GET	RICH	QUICK	ENTERPRISES		
2						Eight Year Forecast			
3										
4		1988	1989	1990	1991	1992	1993	1994	1995
10									
11	Expenses:								
12	Variable cost per unit	$1.00	$1.08	$1.17	$1.26	$1.36	$1.47	$1.59	$1.71
13	Total variable cost	$10,000	$12,744	$16,241	$20,697	$26,377	$33,615	$42,839	$54,593
14	Overhead	$5,000	$5,500	$6,050	$6,655	$7,321	$8,053	$8,858	$9,744
15	Total expenses	$15,000	$18,244	$22,291	$27,352	$33,697	$41,667	$51,696	$64,337
16									
17	Earnings before taxes:	$5,000	$6,536	$8,411	$10,688	$13,435	$16,729	$20,657	$25,309
18									
19	Assumed rates of increase:								
20	Unit sales	18.00%							
21	Selling price	5.00%							
22	Variable cost	8.00%							
23	Overhead	10.00%							

(c) Spreadsheet with horizontal titles

Rows 1 through 4 are permanently visible

Column A is permanently visible

	A	F	G	H	I
1					
2					
3					
4		1992	1993	1994	1995
10					
11	Expenses:				
12	Variable cost per unit	$1.36	$1.47	$1.59	$1.71
13	Total variable cost	$26,377	$33,615	$42,839	$54,593
14	Overhead	$7,321	$8,053	$8,858	$9,744
15	Total expenses	$33,697	$41,667	$51,696	$64,337
16					
17	Earnings before taxes:	$13,435	$16,729	$20,657	$25,309
18					
19	Assumed rates of increase:				
20	Unit sales				
21	Selling price				
22	Variable cost				
23	Overhead				

(d) Spreadsheet with horizontal and vertical titles

FIGURE 8.2 *Continued*

Titles may also be frozen *horizontally*, as shown in Figure 8.2c. This time rows 1 through 4 (containing the column headings) are made permanent, and rows 1 through 4 and rows 10 through 23 are displayed. The visible rows are not consecutive, as rows 5 through 9 have disappeared through scrolling.

Titles may also be frozen in *both* directions simultaneously, as depicted in Figure 8.2d. Here you see rows 1 through 4 and rows 10 through 23, and columns A, and F through I. No matter what the subsequent scrolling operation, the cells displayed in the monitor will be labeled both horizontally and vertically.

Windows

The ability to freeze vertical and/or horizontal titles helps considerably in the manipulation of large spreadsheets. The technique is limited, however, because *you cannot work in the frozen area of the spreadsheet*, even though it is visible on the monitor. To better understand the nature of this restriction, imagine that you are exploring changes in the assumptions (cells B20 through B23) of Figure 8.2a and immediately want to see the effects in 1995 (column I).

You will not, however, be able to view column I without first moving the cursor several times, and in so doing column B will scroll off the screen. (Freezing both columns A and B would not solve the problem, as you could not change values in column B in the frozen area.) You need, therefore, a new capability that provides you with two views of the same spreadsheet, for example, one containing column B and one containing column I, and that *allows you to manipulate cells in either view*.

The **Window command** does precisely this by dividing the monitor in two, with the entire spreadsheet available (through scrolling) in both windows. You can go back and forth between the windows (and thus manipulate either view) with a single keystroke (usually a function key). Moreover, since both windows contain a different view of the *same* spreadsheet, any change in one window is automatically reflected in the other.

Windows may be implemented either vertically or horizontally, as shown in Figure 8.3a and 8.3b. For example, consider Figure 8.3a, in which the left and right vertical windows display two and three columns, respectively. Scrolling is in effect in both windows, with columns A and B visible on the left and columns G, H, and I visible on the right.

To explore the effects of a change in any of the model's assumptions, you would position yourself in the window on the left and make the necessary changes to cells B20 through B23. All values within the spreadsheet will be recalculated automatically, with the projected results for 1995 shown in the window on the right. In other words, you see the effects of a change in one cell (for example, cell B20) on other distant cells (for example, cell I17) without moving the cursor and losing its position.

Automatic versus Manual Recalculation

The ability of a spreadsheet to automatically recalculate the value of every cell, whenever a change is made to any other cell, is one of its primary attractions. The constant recalculation can, however, become annoying as spreadsheets grow in size and computations take longer. Accordingly most spreadsheets provide a capability to suppress *automatic* recalculation in favor of *manual* recalculation, which is done only at your request. Manual recalculation is practical when entering data into a large spreadsheet, and when it is unnecessary to see the calculated results until the final entries have been made.

	A	B	G	H	I
4		1988	1993	1994	1995
5					
6	Income:				
7	Projected unit sales	10,000	22,878	26,996	31,855
8	Unit price	$2.00	$2.55	$2.68	$2.81
9	Gross revenue	$20,000	$58,396	$72,353	$89,646
10					
11	Expenses:				
12	Variable cost per unit	$1.00	$1.47	$1.59	$1.71
13	Total variable cost	$10,000	$33,615	$42,839	$54,593
14	Overhead	$5,000	$8,053	$8,858	$9,744
15	Total expenses	$15,000	$41,667	$51,696	$64,337
16					
17	Earnings before taxes:	$5,000	$16,729	$20,657	$25,309
18					
19	Assumed rates of increase:				
20	Unit sales	18.00%			
21	Selling price	5.00%			
22	Variable cost	8.00%			
23	Overhead	10.00%			

Effects of changes are visible immediately in the alternate window

Changes are made when cell pointer is positioned here

(a) Vertical windows

	A	B	C	D	E	F
1					GET RICH	QUICK EN
2					Eight	Year Fo
3						
4		1988	1989	1990	1991	1992
5						
6	Income:					
7	Projected unit sales	10,000	11,800	13,924	16,430	19,388
8	Unit price	$2.00	$2.10	$2.21	$2.32	$2.43
9	Gross revenue	$20,000	$24,780	$30,702	$38,040	$47,132
	A	B	C	D	E	F
14	Overhead	$5,000	$5,500	$6,050	$6,655	$7,321
15	Total expenses	$15,000	$18,244	$22,291	$27,352	$33,697
16						
17	Earnings before taxes:	$5,000	$6,536	$8,411	$10,688	$13,435
18						
19	Assumed rates of increase:					
20	Unit sales	18.00%				
21	Selling price	5.00%				
22	Variable cost	8.00%				
23	Overhead	10.00%				

(b) Horizontal windows

FIGURE 8.3
Spreadsheet windows.

After manual recalculation is established, a CALC indicator will appear on the monitor whenever a cell is changed. The CALC indicator is intended to remind you that recalculation is required, because the spreadsheet does not reflect the value(s) just enterd in its computations. The CALC indicator will disappear when manual recalculation is applied, and it will reappear when (if) any additional changes are made.

Printing Large Spreadsheets

As you may have already realized, printing the spreadsheet for Get Rich Quick Enterprises poses still other problems in that the spreadsheet as presently constructed will *not* fit on standard $8\frac{1}{2} \times 11$ paper. One ingenious solution, which has since returned several million dollars to its author, is to print the spreadsheet sideways (see insert). As its name implies, **SIDEWAYS** facilitates the printing of large spreadsheets, by turning printed output 90 degrees so that the column headings occupy the 11-inch side of an $8\frac{1}{2}$-inch piece of paper.

Chances are, however, that such a program is not available to you, requiring an alternate technique to print spreadsheets extending beyond 80 columns. The easiest way is to print in **compressed mode** (at **17** characters per inch); this allows approximately 128 characters on an $8\frac{1}{2}$-inch page, with a half inch left over on either side.

You can switch to compressed mode by supplying the appro-

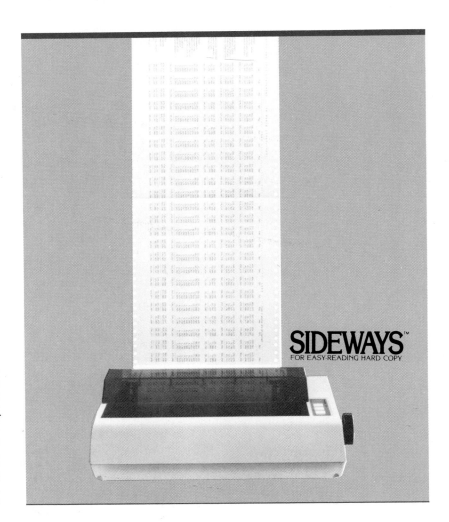

Authors' Comments:
Inspiration comes from the most unexpected places, as evidenced yet again by Frank Sinatra's "I Did It My Way." Paul Funk, the author of SIDEWAYS, was browsing in a computer store in 1983 as a VisiCalc spreadsheet was being printed in compressed mode. His friend, who liked to parody popular songs, was humming "I Did It Sideways," and the rest, as they say, is history.

priate *setup* string within the print command of your spreadsheet program. A simpler way is to locate the external switch on a dot matrix printer that accomplishes the same function. Either way, you will have to issue an extra command within the print sequence to *change the right margin* (normally set to 76) to increase the number of characters per line (for example, to 128).

A Guide to Spreadsheet Development

Spreadsheets such as the financial forecast for Get Rich Quick Enterprises are developed in stages, along the lines of Figure 8.4. You begin by entering the row and column headings, including the assumptions on which the model will be based. Next you enter the initial values and formulas for the first year of the forecast.

Figure 8.4*a* shows the spreadsheet at this stage of development. Cells B7 and B8 contain the *values* 10,000 and $2.00, respectively, corresponding to the unit sales and unit price for 1988. Cell B9, however, contains a *formula*, +B7 * B8, that computes the gross revenue for 1988 based on the values entered in cells B7 and B8. In similar fashion, the variable cost per unit (cell B12) and the overhead expense (cell B14) are entered as values, while total variable cost (cell B13), total expenses (cell B15), and earnings before taxes (cell B17) are entered as formulas.

Next you develop the formulas for 1989 (column C in Figure 8.4*b*), based on the results of 1988 and the set of assumptions that determine how these results will change. The sales in 1989, for example, are equal to the sales in 1988 times the appropriate increase; that is,

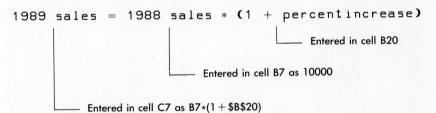

The formula to compute the sales for 1989 uses both absolute and relative addresses, so that it will be copied properly to the other columns in the spreadsheet for the remaining years in the forecast. Thus an *absolute address* is used to reference the cell containing the percent increase in sales (cell B20), because this number remains constant throughout the spreadsheet. A *relative address* is used to reference the sales from the previous year because this address changes from column to column. The remainder of column C is developed in similar fashion.

Finally, you copy the formulas for year 2 (column C) to the remaining years of the forecast (columns D through I) to obtain the finished model of Figure 8.4*c*. In so doing *columns D through I are produced for you by the copy command*, as opposed to your having to manually supply these entries.

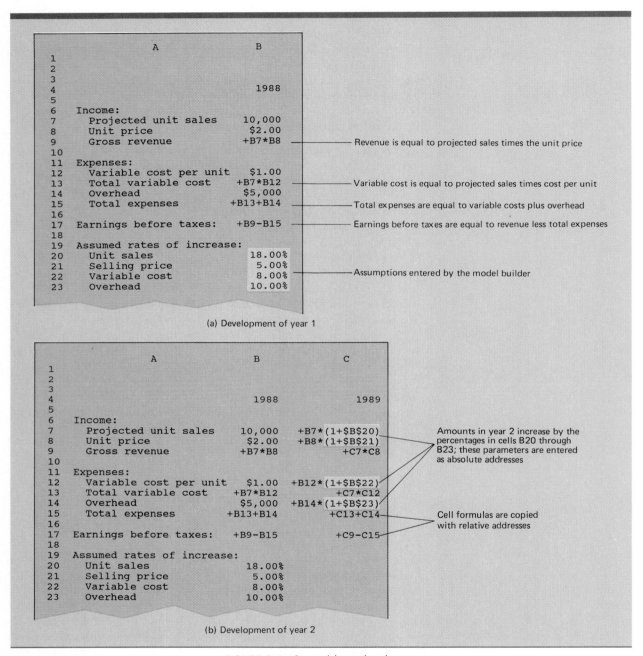

FIGURE 8.4   Spreadsheet development.

Formulas in 1989 are copied to years 1990 through 1995

	A	B	C	D	I
1					
2					
3					
4		1988	1989	1990	1995
5					
6	Income:				
7	Projected unit sales	10,000	+B7*(1+$B$20)	+C7*(1+$B$20)	+H7*(1+$B$20)
8	Unit price	$2.00	+B8*(1+$B$21)	+C8*(1+$B$21)	+H8*(1+$B$21)
9	Gross revenue	+B7*B8	+C7*C8	+D7*D8	+I7*I8
10					
11	Expenses:				
12	Variable cost per unit	$1.00	+B12*(1+$B$22)	+C12*(1+$B$22)	+H12*(1+$B$22)
13	Total variable cost	+B7*B12	+C7*C12	+D7*D12	+I7*I12
14	Overhead	$5,000	+B14*(1+$B$23)	+C14*(1+$B$23)	+H14*(1+$B$23)
15	Total expenses	+B13+B14	+C13+C14	+D13+D14	+I13+I14
16					
17	Earnings before taxes:	+B9-B15	+C9-C15	+D9-D15	+I9-I15
18					
19	Assumed rates of increase:				
20	Unit sales	18.00%			
21	Selling price	5.00%			
22	Variable cost	8.00%			
23	Overhead	10.00%			

(c) Completed spreadsheet

FIGURE 8.4 *Continued*

SPREADSHEET TIP

Data Fill Command

The **data fill command** (available in most spreadsheet programs) provides a convenient way to enter a sequence of numbers with a specified increment or decrement. In the financial forecast, for example, you could use the command to enter the column headings 1988 through 1995, rather than entering each value individually. The command string (as it appears in Lotus or VP Planner) is as follows:

```
/DF                      (Other prompts follow automatically)
Enter range: B4..I4      (Use pointing to indicate the range)
Start: 1988              (Indicate starting value)
Step: 1                  (Increment)
Stop:                    (No need to indicate ending value)
```

HANDS-ON EXERCISE 1:
A FINANCIAL FORECAST

OBJECTIVE: Develop the spreadsheet for Get Rich Quick Enterprises, using Figure 8.4 as a reference. Completion of this exercise requires the copy and formatting commands from Chapter 7, as well as the new material on large spreadsheets.

Step 1: Load Your Spreadsheet Program
Place the spreadsheet program in drive A and a formatted disk in drive B, then load your spreadsheet program as you have been doing throughout Chapters 6 and 7.

Step 2: Enter Row and Column Headings
Change the width of column A to 26 characters, then complete the necessary row labels in cells A6 through A23. Enter GET RICH QUICK ENTERPRISES as the title of the spreadsheet in cell E1, the subheading Eight Year Forecast in cell E2, and the years 1988 through 1995 as column headings in cells B4 through I4.

Step 3: Freeze Row and Column Titles
Move the cell pointer to cell B5, then invoke the command to freeze *both* horizontal and vertical titles. This in turn ensures that the title information in column A and rows 1 through 4 is always visible, regardless of where you are in the spreadsheet.

Step 4: Enter Formulas for Year 1 and Initial Assumptions
Complete the entries for 1988 in column B of the spreadsheet, using Figure 8.4a as a guide. Do *not* enter commas, dollar signs, or percent signs with the numeric values. Also, be sure to enter *formulas* as appropriate, rather than numeric values; for example, enter +B8 * B7 in cell B9 as opposed to 20000. The appearance of your numeric values will be different from ours, since formatting is not implemented until step 6.

Step 5: Complete the Spreadsheet
Complete the entries for 1989 in column C, using Figure 8.4b as a guide. Be sure you understand the distinction between relative and absolute addresses as indicated in the figure. When you have completed column C, use the copy command to replicate the formulas for 1989 (cells C7 through C17) to the remaining years of the forecast (columns D through I).

Check the accuracy of your work by moving the cell pointer to cell I17, verifying that it contains a projected net income of $25,309 in 1995. Note, too, that as you move the cell pointer, the row and column headings remain frozen on the monitor.

Step 6: Format the Spreadsheet
Format your spreadsheet so that its appearance matches the completed version in Figure 8.2a, in which several different formats are in effect for various cell ranges. Each format requires a separate command. In particular:

Currency with two decimals: Cells B8 through I8, and B12 through I12

Currency with no decimals: Cells B9 through I9, and B13 through I17

Comma with no decimals: Cells B7 through I7

Percentage with two decimals: Cells B20 through B23

Step 7: Establish Manual Recalculation
Change the recalculation mode to manual (from automatic), then alter the assumptions in cells B20 through B23 to .15, .04, .10, and .12, respectively. Do not be concerned when the word CALC appears in the lower right portion (or elsewhere) of the monitor, as this is a reminder that you must now explicitly (that is, manually) recalculate the spreadsheet to update your calculations.

Invoke the command to recalculate the spreadsheet, noting how new values appear and how the CALC indicator has disappeared. Move the cell pointer to cell I17 and note a projected income of $7118 for 1995 under the new set of assumptions.

Step 8: Divide the Spreadsheet into Windows
As you can gather from completing step 7, it would be much more convenient if cell I17 (containing the

final year's net income) were visible on the monitor simultaneously with cells B20 through B23. Accordingly, invoke the command to clear row and column titles, position the cell pointer anywhere in column C, then enter the command to divide the screen into *vertical windows*.

You should see two sets of row numbers, with the cell pointer positioned in the window on the left. Switch to the second window and position the cell pointer so that cell I17 is visible in this window, then switch back to the first (leftmost) window.

Change the assumptions back to their original values (.18, .05, .08, and .10, respectively) and re-calculate the spreadsheet. The net income for the final year (1995) will be visible in the right window without having to move the cell pointer.

Step 9: Print the Spreadsheet
Save the completed spreadsheet, then print it using the same procedure as in previous exercises. Realize, however, that in order for the entire spreadsheet to fit on a single piece of $8\frac{1}{2} \times 11$ paper, *you must use compressed print as well as increase the right margin.*

COMMAND SUMMARY

Supply the means by which your spreadsheet program accomplishes the following:

- Freezes horizontal and/or vertical titles

- Splits the screen into horizontal or vertical windows; moves the cell pointer from one window to the other

- Switches from automatic to manual recalculation; invokes manual recalculation when it's in effect

- Changes the right margin so that an increased number of characters (for example, 120) appear on one line.

THE MATRIX MENACE

Don't get me wrong, I'm a red-blooded, all-American boy: I like Mom and apple pie, I watch football on Sundays, and I couldn't do my job as well without spreadsheets. But spreadsheets are just tools, and like any other tools they can be dangerous if used without the proper caution and respect. A bulldozer is a useful tool, but think of how dangerous it could be in my hands—or in yours.

It's a little scary to consider how much depends on spreadsheets these days. Personal and corporate fortunes often hang in the balance. The scary part is how little auditing or examination is applied to the underlying model. Most people just look at the bottom line and try to make some sense of the results.

Yet it's not difficult to make a little mistake that can have a big impact. No matter how proficient you are with the software, your models are still vulnerable. If you're a spreadsheet novice, you are susceptible to errors of ignorance; as a sophisticated spreadsheet modeler, you're open to the more insidious errors of arrogance.

Although big mistakes are bad, smaller mistakes can be much worse. Most spreadsheet users have some expectations about the results of their analysis, or at least some reasonable feel for how the numbers should work. If the results are off by an order of magnitude, somebody is likely to question them strongly. But small errors can easily escape such common-sense scrutiny and live on to corrupt several generations of spreadsheets, as the output of one model is often used as input data for another.

Simple errors that live on the surface of spreadsheets are hard enough to detect, but more sophisticated models give errors the kind of safe hideout that Mad Dog Roy Earle would have given up Ida Lupino for. Keyboard macros, data tables ("what if" matrices), and graphics can automate a model so that you can conveniently evaluate multiple alternatives. Indeed, that ability is one of the greatest benefits of management by spreadsheet. But those same features make errors in logic or underlying algorithms harder to detect.

All right, enough complaining. Spreadsheets are too powerful not to use. There are a few common pitfalls to avoid, and some simple precautions that you can take, to keep the matrix mistake monster at bay.

It's easy and often tempting to copy a formula that shouldn't be replicated in full. For example, it's common practice to create a formula to sum the first column and then copy that formula across a row so that every column is totaled. If some of those columns have been designed to hold multiplier factors, the sum of those multipliers will be a meaningless number. The problem will be worse if the formula at the other end of the row sums all the column totals to arrive at a grand total. Since that grand total will include the meaningless sum of the multipliers, it will itself be meaningless. The beat goes on.

Or, when copying a formula, you might forget to make a cell reference absolute or you might make the wrong part of the reference absolute. (An absolute cell address is one that won't be adjusted for the new location to which it's copied. That is, the address is exactly the same in the copied formula as in the original formula.) If you make such a mistake, the formula adjustments will get you. If you're lucky, some cell reference will be adjusted to an empty cell, and you'll get an ERR label somewhere. But there's no guarantee of that.

Rounding errors commonly turn into Excedrin headache number 39. If, for example, you have a column of formulas that calculate portions of a whole amount and are expressed as percents, and if the range is formatted not to display any decimal places, you might have trouble getting the column to add up to 100 percent. The percent formula will create decimal (less than 1) values, and the rounding-off feature of the integer-only format will hide the effect of those values.

On the positive side, developing a few good habits can minimize the chances of catastrophe. Use a separate and clearly labeled area for data input and assumptions. That makes it easier to tell what the results are based on.

Date and number successive versions of the model so that you'll know you are incorporating the latest set of assumptions and data. You might also label the spreadsheet with the author's name and the file name under which the model is saved.

Print out all the formulas. A printed version enables anyone to audit the methodology as well as the mechanics of the model.

Incorporate cross-checks wherever possible. If there are several ways available to calculate an answer, use more than one and compare (or have the model compare) the results. Then you can track down the source of any discrepancies.

Test spreadsheet models using simple-to-follow and predictable data. If a model works correctly with simple data, it's more likely to give good results when it counts.

Name ranges or single cells as much as possible, and use those range names in formulas. You're much less likely to make an error in Total Sales − Total Expenses than in A20 − A40.

Once you've checked the accuracy and appropriateness of a formula, use the range- or cell-protection feature to avoid accidentally corrupting the validity you worked so hard to establish.

The power of the spreadsheet is at the same time its invitation to danger. We've heard of only a few cases in which spreadsheets have been at the root of real catastrophes. All it takes to avoid being such a statistic is to err on the side of caution.

So be careful, good luck, and a hearty "/QY" to one and . . . Oh no, I can't believe it—I forgot to save the final version.

Source: PC World, March 1985. Reprinted by permission.

Authors' Comments:
A superb article, and one the beginner should take to heart. Although this article first appeared more than three years ago, it is still right on the mark.

"The [spreadsheet] said we'd double in size, so Ed in Purchasing–remember Ed?–he got this great volume discount on office furniture."

Application: Grade Book Revisited

We come now to a second application in which we cover yet additional spreadsheet concepts. Figure 8.5 contains an expanded version of the earlier grade book illustration, which uses the @MAX, @MIN, and @AVG functions to compute statistics for the class as a whole. The use of these functions is more sophisticated than may appear initially; for example, the @MIN function is used to *drop the lowest grade* in calculating each student's semester average. (Carson's average, for example, is shown as 90 as opposed to 85, as it would be if all four grades were included in the average.)

The extended grade book in Figure 8.5 also implies that student averages can be converted to letter grades, by including the numerical ranges for each grade in a table within the spreadsheet. A table lookup function automatically converts one to the other, according to the professor's grading criteria as expressed in the table.

Finally, the application will illustrate the file combine command, in which data from multiple spreadsheets are consolidated into a single spreadsheet. Figure 8.6 shows how class averages from three sections of MAS120, each with its own spreadsheet, are combined into a fourth spreadsheet in which results from the three sections may be compared to one another.

FIGURE 8.5 Extended grade book.

@MIN function is used to drop lowest grade

	A	B	C	D	E	F	G	H
1		MAS 120 – SECTION 1						
2								
3	Student Name	Test 1	Test 2	Test 3	Test 4	Avg		Grade
4								
5	Adams	80	76	81	90	83.7		B
6	Brown	92	95	84	78	90.3		A
7	Carson	90	90	90	70	90.0		A
8	Coulter	45	45	30	89	59.7		F
9	Jones	88	94	98	76	93.3		A
10	Smith	60	50	60	87	69.0		D
11								
12	Class Average	75.8	75.0	73.8	81.7	Grading Criteria		
13								
14	High	92	95	98	90	0 – 59 F		
15	Low	45	45	30	70	60 – 69 D		
16	Range	47	50	68	20	70 – 79 C		
17						80 – 89 B		
18						90 – 100 A		

@AVG, @MAX, and @MIN functions used as appropriate

Table lookup function is used to assign grades

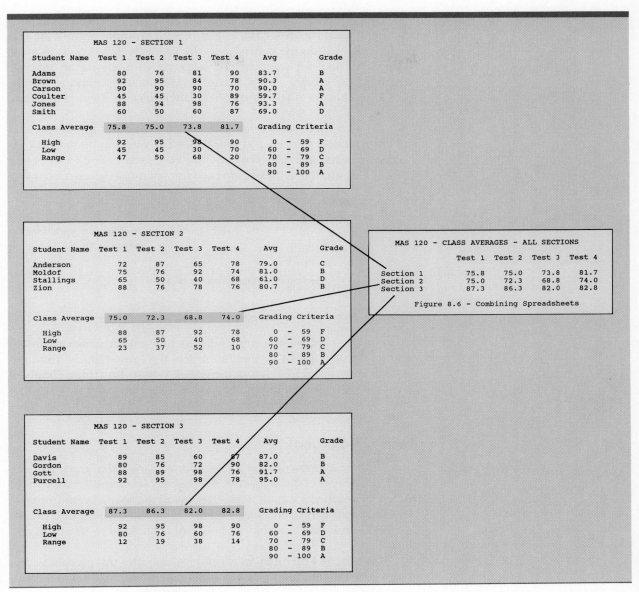

```
            MAS 120 - SECTION 1

Student Name   Test 1   Test 2   Test 3   Test 4      Avg          Grade

Adams             80       76       81       90       83.7           B
Brown             92       95       84       78       90.3           A
Carson            90       90       90       70       90.0           A
Coulter           45       45       30       89       59.7           F
Jones             88       94       98       76       93.3           A
Smith             60       50       60       87       69.0           D

Class Average   75.8     75.0     73.8     81.7      Grading Criteria

  High            92       95       98       90        0  -  59    F
  Low             45       45       30       70       60  -  69    D
  Range           47       50       68       20       70  -  79    C
                                                      80  -  89    B
                                                      90  - 100    A
```

```
            MAS 120 - SECTION 2

Student Name   Test 1   Test 2   Test 3   Test 4      Avg          Grade

Anderson          72       87       65       78       79.0           C
Moldof            75       76       92       74       81.0           B
Stallings         65       50       40       68       61.0           D
Zion              88       76       78       76       80.7           B


Class Average   75.0     72.3     68.8     74.0      Grading Criteria

  High            88       87       92       78        0  -  59    F
  Low             65       50       40       68       60  -  69    D
  Range           23       37       52       10       70  -  79    C
                                                      80  -  89    B
                                                      90  - 100    A
```

```
     MAS 120 - CLASS AVERAGES - ALL SECTIONS

                 Test 1   Test 2   Test 3   Test 4

Section 1          75.8     75.0     73.8     81.7
Section 2          75.0     72.3     68.8     74.0
Section 3          87.3     86.3     82.0     82.8

       Figure 8.6 - Combining Spreadsheets
```

```
            MAS 120 - SECTION 3

Student Name   Test 1   Test 2   Test 3   Test 4      Avg          Grade

Davis             89       85       60       87       87.0           B
Gordon            80       76       72       90       82.0           B
Gott              88       89       98       76       91.7           A
Purcell           92       95       98       78       95.0           A


Class Average   87.3     86.3     82.0     82.8      Grading Criteria

  High            92       95       98       90        0  -  59    F
  Low             80       76       60       76       60  -  69    D
  Range           12       19       38       14       70  -  79    C
                                                      80  -  89    B
                                                      90  - 100    A
```

FIGURE 8.6
Combining spreadsheets.

Additional Functions

The **@MAX, @MIN,** and **@AVG** functions return the highest, lowest, and average values, respectively, from an argument list. The list in turn may contain cell addresses, ranges, numeric values, functions, or mathematical expressions. The @MAX, @MIN, and @AVG functions are illustrated in conjunction with the simple spreadsheet in Figure 8.7.

	A	B	C	D
1	4	2	7	11
2	−2	4	5	−6
3	7	5	3	5

(a) The spreadsheet

Function	Value
@MAX (A1..D1)	11
@MAX (A1..A3)	7
@MAX (A1..D1, 16, 8)	16
@MIN (A1..D1)	2
@MIN (A1..A3)	−2
@MIN (A1..D1, 16, 8)	2
@AVG(A1..D1)	6
@AVG (A1..A3)	3
@AVG (A1..D1, 16, 8)	8

(b) Illustrative functions

FIGURE 8.7
The @MAX, @MIN, and
@AVG functions.

The first example, @MAX(A1..D1), returns the highest value in the range A1 through D1 (11 in Figure 8.7). Multiple arguments can be specified within the parentheses; for example, @MAX(A1..D1,16,8), returns the highest value in the range A1 through D1 *or* 16 *or* 8, whichever is greater (16 in Figure 8.7). Similar operations can be performed for the @MIN and @AVG functions as indicated in Figure 8.7.

The extended grade book uses a combination of the @MIN and @SUM function to drop a student's lowest grade in computing his or her semester average. The function was used in cell F5 of Figure 8.5 to compute the semester average for Adams, as shown below:

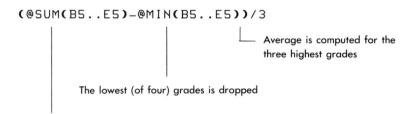

The above expression sums Adams's four grades, which are found in cells B5 through E5. It then subtracts the lowest grade (the minimum value found in cells B5 through E5) from this total. Finally, it divides the result of the subtraction by 3 (the number of grades remaining), to obtain an average of 83.7.

Table Lookup Functions

Consider for a moment how a professor assigns letter grades to students at the end of the semester. He or she first computes a semester average for each student (in which the lowest grade has been dropped). The professor then determines a letter grade according to a predetermined scale; for example, 90 or above is an A, 80 to 89 is a B, and so on.

The **table lookup function** effectively duplicates this process within a spreadsheet program by assigning a label value to a cell based on a numeric value contained in another cell. In other words, just as the professor "knows" where on the grading scale a student's numerical average will fall, the table lookup function determines where within a specified table a numeric value (for example, a student's average) can be found, and retrieves the corresponding label value (for example, the letter grade).

The table lookup function contains three arguments: the **numeric value** to look up in a table, the **range of cells** containing the table, and the **offset,** indicating where the corresponding label values are found. These concepts are illustrated in Figure 8.8, which was taken from the extended grade book in Figure 8.5.

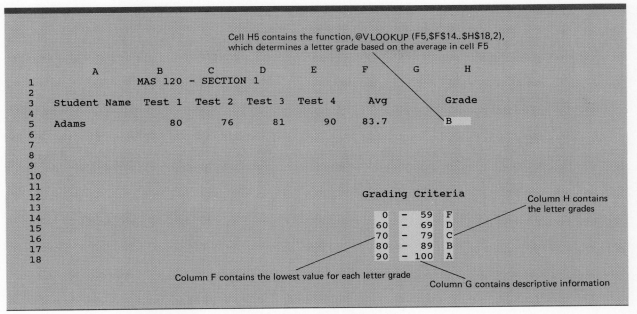

Cell H5 contains the function, @VLOOKUP (F5,$F$14..$H$18,2), which determines a letter grade based on the average in cell F5

	A	B	C	D	E	F	G	H
1		MAS 120 – SECTION 1						
2								
3	Student Name	Test 1	Test 2	Test 3	Test 4	Avg		Grade
4								
5	Adams	80	76	81	90	83.7		B
6								
7								
8								
9								
10								
11								
12					Grading Criteria			
13								
14					0	–	59	F
15					60	–	69	D
16					70	–	79	C
17					80	–	89	B
18					90	–	100	A

Column H contains the letter grades

Column F contains the lowest value for each letter grade

Column G contains descriptive information

FIGURE 8.8
Table of grade assignments.

The table in Figure 8.8 extends over three columns (F, G, and H), and five rows (14 through 18); that is, the table is located in the range F14 through H18. The **break points** (that is, the lowest value for each grade) are contained in column F, with the corresponding letter grades in column H. (Column G contains descriptive information and is not used in the lookup procedure per se.)

The table lookup function for Adams is contained in cell H5, and determines a letter grade based on the computed average in cell F5. Consider:

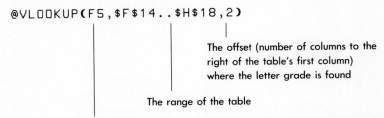

@VLOOKUP(F5,$F$14..$H$18,2)

The offset (number of columns to the right of the table's first column) where the letter grade is found

The range of the table

Value to look up (that is, cell containing student's numerical average)

The first argument in the **@VLOOKUP** function is the value to look up, which in this example is Adams's computed average, and is found in cell F5 of the spreadsheet.

The second argument is the range of the table, which is cells F14 through H18 as explained earlier. Absolute addresses are used to indicate the range so that the @VLOOKUP function may be copied to determine letter grades for other students. *The column in the table which contains the break points (column F) must be the first column in the table's range*, and the values in this column must be in increasing order.

The third argument is the offset, which indicates where the letter grades may be found. The offset is defined as *the number of columns to the right of the break point column* (two columns in the example) where the value to be returned by the function (that is, the letter grades) is found.

To determine the letter grade for Adams (whose computed average is 83.7), the table lookup function searches column F for the first value greater than 83.7 (the computed average found in cell F5). When that break point (90 in the example) is found, *the grade in the previous row two columns over (the offset value)*, is returned. In other words, to determine Adams's grade the table lookup function searches the column of break points for the first value greater than 83.7; this turns out to be 90 and is found in cell F18. The lookup function then retrieves the corresponding letter grade from cell H17, which is one row above this break point and two columns to the right.

Combining Spreadsheets

The **file combine command** is similar to retrieving an existing spreadsheet in that it retrieves a file from disk, but it has one important difference. The combine command places the spreadsheet being retrieved over the spreadsheet currently in use, combining values where they overlay one another. The retrieve command, on the other hand, erases the current spreadsheet before the new one comes into the work space.

The file combine command generally uses an additional spreadsheet (as shown in Figure 8.9a) to hold data from the other spreadsheets as they are retrieved one by one from the disk on which they are stored. The process is best explained by pretending that you have duplicated the row containing the class averages from the three individual spreadsheets onto plastic transparencies.

Now imagine placing the consolidated spreadsheet on your desk, then putting the transparency containing the class averages for section 1 on top of it. In so doing, you would have to align the section 1 transparency so that the class averages it contains coincide with cells B5 through E5 on the consolidated spreadsheet. The result, shown in Figure 8.9b, is precisely what happens when you invoke the file combine command of a spreadsheet program.

Now let's complicate things just a bit by laying the section 2 transparency over section 1. This time you have to align the overlaying transparency (section 2) so that it fits on top of cells B6 through E6 on the consolidated spreadsheet, as shown in Figure 8.9c. Finally, you would place the transparency for section 3 on top of the other two, aligning it over cells B7 through E7, as shown in Figure 8.9d.

```
               A            B        C        D        E
  1          MAS 120 - CLASS AVERAGES - ALL SECTIONS
  2
  3                      Test 1   Test 2   Test 3   Test 4
  4
  5      Section 1
  6      Section 2
  7      Section 3
```

(a) Empty consolidated spreadsheet

```
               A            B        C        D        E
  1          MAS 120 - CLASS AVERAGES - ALL SECTIONS
  2
  3                      Test 1   Test 2   Test 3   Test 4
  4
  5      Section 1        75.8     75.0     73.8     81.7
  6      Section 2
  7      Section 3
```

(b) Consolidated spreadsheet (with section 1)

```
               A            B        C        D        E
  1          MAS 120 - CLASS AVERAGES - ALL SECTIONS
  2
  3                      Test 1   Test 2   Test 3   Test 4
  4
  5      Section 1        75.8     75.0     73.8     81.7
  6      Section 2        75.0     72.3     68.8     74.0
  7      Section 3
```

(c) Consolidated spreadsheet (with sections 1 and 2)

```
               A            B        C        D        E
  1          MAS 120 - CLASS AVERAGES - ALL SECTIONS
  2
  3                      Test 1   Test 2   Test 3   Test 4
  4
  5      Section 1        75.8     75.0     73.8     81.7
  6      Section 2        75.0     72.3     68.8     74.0
  7      Section 3        87.3     86.3     82.0     82.8
```

(d) Completed consolidated spreadsheet

FIGURE 8.9   The file combine command.

THREE-DIMENSIONAL SPREADSHEETS

The next generation of spreadsheet programs promises the inclusion of a third dimension, in which similarly formatted spreadsheets (such as individual grade books) are kept together in a single file. The extra dimension requires the addition of a third coordinate to each cell address, for example 3A1, to indicate the cell in column A, row 1, of spreadsheet 3. As you can imagine, the capability will greatly simplify the consolidation process for the extended grade book.

HANDS-ON EXERCISE 2: EXTENDED GRADE BOOK

OBJECTIVE: Create three individual spreadsheets for sections 1, 2, and 3, then combine them into a single consolidated spreadsheet.

Step 1: Enter Student Data for Section 1
Load your spreadsheet program as you have done throughout the text. Set the width of column A to 13 characters, and the width of all other columns to 8. Enter column headings for rows 1, 2, and 3 as indicated in Figure 8.10, and row labels in cells A12 through A16. Supply the various test scores in cells A5 through E10 as shown earlier in Figure 8.5.

Step 2: Compute Student Averages
Move the cell pointer to cell F5, then enter the formula to compute the semester average for the first student, remembering the professor's policy of dropping the lowest test grade. Copy the entry in cell F5 to the cells in column F for the other students, then format column F so that the computed averages are displayed with one decimal place.

Move to cell B12 and enter the expression to compute the class average for test 1, @AVG(B5..B11). Enter similar expressions in cells B14 through B16 to compute the high, low, and range for the first exam as shown in Figure 8.10. Copy the entries in cells B12 through B16 to cells C12 through E16 so that these statistics are calculated for the other three exams.

Step 3: Enter the Table Lookup Function
Enter the table containing the numeric range for each letter grade in cells F14 through H18 as explained earlier. Note that column F contains numeric values (the grade break points), and that columns G and H contain label entries. Enter the appropriate @VLOOKUP function in cell H14 to obtain the letter grade for the first student, then copy this function to the remaining cells in column H for the other students.

The grade book for section 1 is now complete and should match Figure 8.5 exactly. Save the completed spreadsheet as SECTION1.

Step 4: Develop the Remaining Spreadsheets
Save the existing spreadsheet twice more as SECTION2 and SECTION3, then retrieve each of these spreadsheets in turn, changing student data as appropriate. You should wind up with three distinct spreadsheets, one for each section, as shown earlier in Figure 8.6.

Create a fourth spreadsheet to hold the consolidated results, and enter row and column headings as shown in Figure 8.9a.

Step 5: Combine the Individual Spreadsheets
Move the cell pointer to cell B5 in the consolidated spreadsheet, then execute the file combine command to retrieve the class averages for section 1. The command enables you to overlay the contents of cells B12 through E12 in the spreadsheet of SECTION1, on top of cells B5 through E5 in the consolidated grade book.

Position the cell pointer in cell B6 of the consolidated grade book and repeat the file combine command. This time you will combine (overlay) the contents of cells B12 through E12 in the spreadsheet of SECTION2 on top of cells B6 through E6 in the consolidated grade book. Finally move the cursor to cell B7 and repeat the file combine command a third time, bringing in the class averages for SECTION3.

STEP 6: EXPERIMENT
The extended grade book is finished, at least to the point of reproducing the consolidated spreadsheet of Figure 8.9. However, we suggest, that before leaving the example entirely, you experiment with the two spreadsheet tips which follow this exercise. You may also want to read the introduction on spreadsheet macros.

FIGURE 8.10
Cell entries for section 1 grade book.

```
B1:  [W8] 'MAS 120 - SECTION 1
A3:  [W13] 'Student Name
B3:  [W8] "Test 1
C3:  [W8] "Test 2
D3:  [W8] "Test 3
E3:  [W8] "Test 4
F3:  [W8] "Avg
H3:  [W8] 'Grade
A5:  [W13] 'Adams
B5:  [W8] 80
C5:  [W8] 76
D5:  [W8] 81
E5:  [W8] 90
F5:  (F1) [W8] (@SUM(B5..E5)-@MIN(B5..E5))/3
H5:  [W8] @VLOOKUP(F5,$F$14..$H$18,2)
              ROWS 6-11 contain data for different students

A12: [W13] 'Class Average
B12: (F1) [W8] @AVG(B5..B10)
C12: (F1) [W8] @AVG(C5..C10)
D12: (F1) [W8] @AVG(D5..D10)
E12: (F1) [W8] @AVG(E5..E10)
F12: [W8] '    Grading Criteria
A14: [W13] ' High
B14: [W8] @MAX(B5..B8)
C14: [W8] @MAX(C5..C8)
D14: [W8] @MAX(D5..D8)
E14: [W8] @MAX(E5..E8)
F14: [W8] 0
G14: [W8] ' -  59
H14: [W8] 'F
A15: [W13] ' Low
B15: [W8] @MIN(B5..B8)
C15: [W8] @MIN(C5..C8)
D15: [W8] @MIN(D5..D8)
E15: [W8] @MIN(E5..E8)
F15: [W8] 60
G15: [W8] ' -  69
H15: [W8] 'D
A16: [W13] ' Range
B16: [W8] +B14-B15
C16: [W8] +C14-C15
D16: [W8] +D14-D15
E16: [W8] +E14-E15
F16: [W8] 70
G16: [W8] ' -  79
H16: [W8] 'C
F17: [W8] 80
G17: [W8] ' -  89
H17: [W8] 'B
F18: [W8] 90
G18: [W8] ' - 100
H18: [W8] 'A
```

Macros

Assume for a moment that the professor changes an entry in one or more of the individual grade books. This in turn requires repetition of the entire file combination process (to recreate the consolidated

---

SPREADSHEET TIP

@RAND (Random Number Function)

The **@RAND** function returns a random number from 0 to 1, and is a convenient way to quickly generate test data for use within a spreadsheet. Consider, for example, how the function could be used to create a series of test grades within the grade book.

Since @RAND returns a number between 0 and 1, @RAND * 60 returns a value between 0 and 60, and @RAND * 60 + 40 returns a value between 40 and 100 (a reasonable range for exam grades). A series of test scores could be generated by entering the expression @RAND * 60 + 40 in cell B5 corresponding to Adams's grade on test 1), then *copying* that entry to cells C5, D5, and E5, to create Adams's three other test scores. You would then copy cells B5 through E5 to rows 6 through 10, to generate four test scores for each student.

Each of the 24 test grades will be based on a different random number. All 24 random numbers (and all 24 test grades) will change whenever the spreadsheet is recalculated. Note, too, that you will want to *format* the cell range containing the test grades to eliminate the decimal places.

SPREADSHEET TIP

Data Sort Command

The **data sort command** (available in most spreadsheet programs) provides a means to change the physical sequence in which the rows appear. In the grade book, for example, you could list students according to their computed average rather than alphabetically. The command sequence as it would appear in Lotus and/or VP Planner is as follows:

```
/DS                    (Other prompts follow automatically)
Data range: A5.H10     (Includes all data for each student)
Primary key: F5        (Field on which to sort)
Sort (A or D): D       (Highest average student listed first)
Go                     (Execute the sort)
```

---

spreadsheet), which as you can imagine is a tedious and error-prone procedure. Fortunately, however, there is a better way: The series of commands (contained within step 5 of the Hands-On Exercise) can be executed from a macro.

A **macro,** defined by Lotus as a "typing alternative," enables you to store multiple commands (in the form of the keystrokes they require) for future recall. Thus a macro saves time and effort, in that any series of spreadsheet commands can be recreated with only a keystroke or two once the macro has been established.

Creating a macro is similar to writing a program in any other computer language. You begin by defining the task the macro is to perform, for example, combining data from the individual grade books into the consolidated spreadsheet. You then execute the commands necessary to complete that task, writing down the precise keystrokes associated with every command.

Next you store the keystrokes you have recorded as labels within the spreadsheet itself. (A macro is best kept in the area below and to the right of the main body of the spreadsheet so that it is *unaffected* by later insertions or deletions of rows or columns.) Finally you give the macro a name, at which point it can be executed. In Lotus 1-2-3, macros are named with a single letter from A to Z or with the number zero, and they are activated by pressing the **Alt key.** For example, the keystroke combination Alt C would activate the series of keystrokes that had been previously associated with the macro named C.

Figure 8.11 contains a file combination macro (as it would be implemented in Lotus 1-2-3 or VP Planner) corresponding to the procedure followed in step 5 of the Hands-On Exercise. Every symbol in Figure 8.11 corresponds to a particular keystroke. The first line, for example, contains the command to erase the portion of the consolidated spreadsheet containing any class averages which were previously entered. Consider:

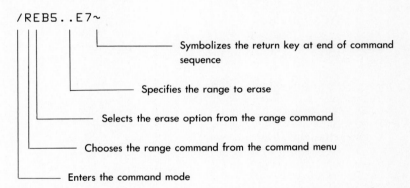

```
/REB5..E7~
```

Symbolizes the return key at end of command sequence

Specifies the range to erase

Selects the erase option from the range command

Chooses the range command from the command menu

Enters the command mode

The remaining keystroke sequences in Figure 8.11 correspond to the commands necessary to complete the file combination procedure. Detailed instructions for implementing this and other macros are provided in the optional laboratory manual which accompanies this text.

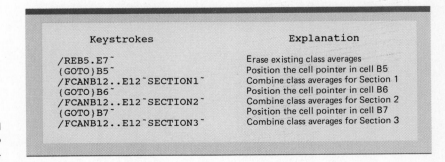

Keystrokes	Explanation
/REB5.E7˜	Erase existing class averages
{GOTO}B5˜	Position the cell pointer in cell B5
/FCANB12..E12˜SECTION1˜	Combine class averages for Section 1
{GOTO}B6˜	Position the cell pointer in cell B6
/FCANB12..E12˜SECTION2˜	Combine class averages for Section 2
{GOTO}B7˜	Position the cell pointer in cell B7
/FCANB12..E12˜SECTION3˜	Combine class averages for Section 3

FIGURE 8.11
The file combine macro
(Lotus/VP Planner implementation).

CORPORATE PROFILE:
COMPAQ COMPUTER CORPORATION

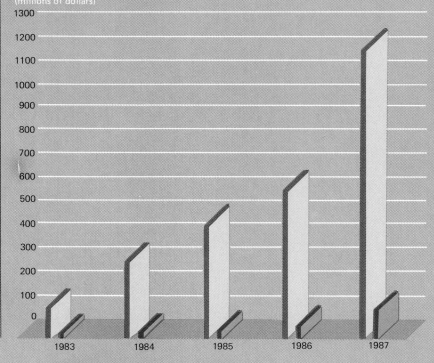

Year-end statistics for 1987:

Sales:	$1.224 billion
Profits:	$136 million
CEO:	Joseph R. Canion
Headquarters:	20333 FM 149
	Houston, TX 77070
	(713) 370-7040

"The odds of starting from scratch and getting where we are approach zero . . ." are the words used by Rod Canion, founder and CEO of **Compaq Computer Corporation**, to describe his company's meteoric rise from obscure startup to IBM's foremost rival in personal computers. Indeed, 1987 was yet another excellent year for Compaq Computer as it inched toward the billion-dollar mark in sales while continuing to remain extremely profitable. Demand for its products was so strong that the company was unable to fill all its spring orders until fall.

Compaq has always advocated strict adherence to the PC standard, and it has priced its machines at about the same level as their IBM counterparts. The key, however, has been to offer improved performance and/or something extra which was not available from IBM. Thus Compaq was the first to market a portable PC, the first to offer a portable PC with a hard disk, and the first to develop a PC equipped with internal tape backup.

Its most exciting innovation, however, was the September 1986 introduction of the Deskpro 386, the first PC-compatible computer to incorporate the Intel 80386 microprocessor. (IBM announced its own 386 machine, the PS/2 model 80, eight months later.) "Stepping ahead of IBM is a very tricky game . . . only history will tell if we're right," mused Canion at the time of the announcement. Canion was once again right on

the mark as 45,000 units worth $225 million, were sold six months after the announcement.

Compaq Computer would not have existed had Rod Canion found a topic for his Ph.D. dissertation in electrical engineering. Frustrated, he left the University of Houston and joined Texas Instruments (TI), climbing the ranks to a business manager. After 13 years he tired of TI's emphasis on technical excellence at the expense of marketing and left to go out on his own.

Ironically, his biggest complaint was that TI would not accept the importance of IBM products.

Canion's first idea was for circuit cards to expand the storage capacity of the PC. The idea for a portable PC compatible came later, on the fourth or fifth try. Initial sales began in January 1983 with the Compaq Portable (the suitcase-sized model inspired the company's name) and the Compaq Plus. These machines were the first full-function, 16-bit personal computers to run the business

COMPAQ COMPUTERS
SALES AND NET INCOME
(millions of dollars)

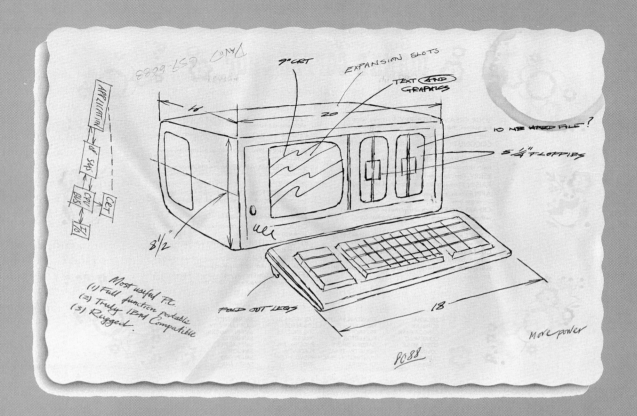

and professional software written for the IBM PC.

By the end of 1983, Compaq ranked second only to IBM in the sale of 16-bit personal computers in the United States. It had expanded manufacturing operations more than eightfold, raised $80 million in private venture capital, and achieved sales of $111 million, the greatest first-year performance in the history of American business. In 1984 Compaq introduced the Deskpro family of computers and tripled its sales to $329 million. In 1985 the company achieved another substantial increase to $503 million, enabling it to join the Fortune 500 only three years after it was founded (and faster than any other company).

Compaq Corporation seems well poised to achieve continued growth through sound management, coupled with the right blend of engineering and marketing. Employee morale is

---

A PICTURE WORTH $111,000,000

Not long ago, three businessmen met in a coffee shop to talk about an idea for a new personal computer. They made a rough design on the back of a place mat (see above). A lot of companies were already making personal computers, but they thought theirs just might work better.

The next year, they sold $111 million worth of their new computers, the Compaq Portable and the Compaq Plus. No company in America had ever grown that fast.

Source: Compaq Computer Corporation advertisement.

---

options, and everyone flies coach. Pinstripes are the norm, and Friday afternoon beer bashes are out. One final observation of Mr. Canion's is also worth noting:

"IBM? Yes, they set the standard. And thanks to them for doing that. But the standard is not in their hands anymore. More and more, there will be other alternatives.

Summary

The chapter introduced several advanced spreadsheet capabilities which, in combination with the two previous chapters, should provide you with reasonable proficiency in the use of these programs. We discussed features associated with large spreadsheets, namely the title and window commands, automatic and manual recalculation, as well as considerations for printing. The chapter also covered the table lookup function, presented the @MAX, @MIN, and @AVG functions, discussed the file combine command, and alluded to the use of spreadsheet macros. Recall also the box entitled "The Matrix Menace" and the cautionary advice on the use of spreadsheet programs in decision making.

The hands-on exercises within the chapter also included three "spreadsheet tips" (regarding use of the data fill and data sort commands, and the @RAND function). Helpful hints such as these are gleaned from columns which appear regularly in computer magazines, an excellent way to stay abreast of current developments. (See page 244 for our suggestions.)

Key Words and Concepts

@AVG	Data fill command
@MAX	Data sort command
@MIN	File combine command
@RAND	Isolating assumptions
@VLOOKUP	Macro
Alt key	Manual recalculation
Automatic recalculation	Offset
Break points	SIDEWAYS
Rod Canion	Table lookup function
Compaq Computer Corporation	Titles command
Compressed mode	Window command

True/False

1. Most spreadsheet programs require that a model's assumptions be isolated from the main body of the model.

2. The rows of a spreadsheet which are visible in the monitor at any one time must be numbered consecutively.

3. A spreadsheet may be printed in a variety of formats.

4. The titles command may freeze both row and column labels simultaneously.

5. Printing a spreadsheet in compressed mode guarantees that it will fit on a single sheet of $8\frac{1}{2} \times 11$ paper.

6. Spreadsheets should never be used in decision making.

7. The offset argument of a table lookup function specifies the column containing the values to be returned by the function.

8. The @MIN function in a spreadsheet program is restricted to two arguments.

9. Macros cannot be stored in the spreadsheet to which they refer.

10. A spreadsheet macro is limited to a single spreadsheet command and cannot extend beyond a single cell.

11. A spreadsheet will always recalculate the value of every cell whenever the contents of a single cell change.

12. It is not possible to combine values from different spreadsheets into a single consolidated spreadsheet.

13. Splitting a screen into vertical windows is synonymous with freezing titles vertically.

Multiple Choice

1. Which command combines data from two or more spreadsheets into a single spreadsheet?
   (a) File combine
   (b) Retrieve combine
   (c) Status combine
   (d) Worksheet combine

2. One danger inherent in the use of spreadsheets is:
   (a) Managers make assumptions about the future in order to make projections
   (b) Managers view the projected results as certainties
   (c) Managers are unable to understand the projected results
   (d) All the above

3. The @RAND function typically returns a value between:
   (a) 0 and 1
   (b) 1 and 10
   (c) 1 and 100
   (d) 1 and 1000

4. Given the cell contents A1 = 1, A2 = 2, A3 = 3, and A4 = 4, what is the value of @MAX(@RAND,@MIN(A2..A4))?
   (a) 2
   (b) 3
   (c) 4
   (d) None of the above

5. Which of the following is true regarding the placement of assumptions within a spreadsheet?
   (a) All the assumptions *must* appear together but can be placed anywhere within the spreadsheet
   (b) All the assumptions *must* appear together and, further, must be placed in the lower right-hand portion
   (c) The assumptions are not required to appear together and, further, can be placed anywhere within the spreadsheet
   (d) None of the above

6. How many arguments are present in the table lookup function @VLOOKUP?
   (a) 1
   (b) 2
   (c) 3
   (d) 4

7. The company which developed the first PC-compatible portable computer, and which achieved Fortune 500 status faster than any company in history, is:
   (a) Toshiba
   (b) Compaq
   (c) Apple
   (d) Tandy

8. The appearance of the word CALC at the (top or) bottom of a spreadsheet screen indicates that:
   (a) The results of the last cell formula must be computed manually with a calculator and entered by hand
   (b) The spreadsheet recalculates only when you tell it to do so
   (c) There is a calculation error within the spreadsheet
   (d) The spreadsheet has grown too large and recalculation is no longer possible

9. Which of the following is associated with the printing of large spreadsheets?
   (a) Printing in compressed mode
   (b) Companion programs such as Sideways
   (c) Printing with larger margins in effect
   (d) All the above

10. Which of the following may *not* be contained in the argument list of an @MAX or @MIN function?
    (a) Cell locations
    (b) Numeric values
    (c) Formulas
    (d) All of the above are valid as arguments

11. Which of the following is *not* appropriate to compute the average of the values in cells D2, D3, and D4?
    (a) The function @AVG(D2..D4)

(b) The function @SUM(D2..D4)/3

(c) The formula (D2 + D3 + D4)/3

(d) All of the above can be used

12. If the rows and/or columns displayed on the monitor are not consecutive:
    (a) An error has occurred
    (b) A circular reference exists within the spreadsheet
    (c) Row and/or column labels have been frozen
    (d) The situation is not possible

13. The use of windows within a spreadsheet implies that:
    (a) Changes in one window will not be reflected in the other
    (b) Rows and/or columns are also frozen
    (c) Relative and/or absolute addressing is no longer in effect
    (d) None of the above

14. A spreadsheet macro:
    (a) Is analogous to writing a computer program
    (b) Simplifies the execution of repetitive tasks within a spreadsheet
    (c) Should be stored in the area below and to the right of the main body of the spreadsheet
    (d) All the above

15. The recalculation mode of a spreadsheet is normally set to:
    (a) Automatic or manual
    (b) Automatic or standard
    (c) Functional or automatic
    (d) Functional or standard

Exercises

1. Modify the financial forecast for Get Rich Quick Enterprises to accommodate *all* the following:
   (a) Change the assumed rates of increase as follows:

Unit sales	15%
Selling price	6
Variable cost	10
Overhead	12

   (b) Change the initial conditions as follows:

Projected unit sales in 1988	$ 8,000
Overhead in 1988	10,000

   (c) Extend the forecast for an additional year to 1996.

2. Modify the extended grade book for section 1 (Figure 8.5) to accommodate each of the following changes (treat each change *independently*; that is, the solution to this problem consists of

three separate spreadsheets, for parts *a*, *b*, and *c*, respectively):

(a) Change the grading criteria so that *all* tests count equally; that is, you are no longer dropping the lowest grade.

(b) Assign different weights to the tests as follows: Tests 1, 2, and 3 each count 20 percent, and test 4 counts 40 percent (note the weights must sum to 100 percent). Display the weighting criteria in row 19.

(c) Change the grading scale as follows: A (94–100), B (86–93), C (76–85), D (65–75), F (below 65).

3. Differentiate between the following:
   (a) Splitting a spreadsheet into two vertical windows versus freezing vertical titles
   (b) Manual versus automatic recalculation
   (c) Printing cell values versus cell formulas
   (d) Printing a spreadsheet with a right margin of 76 versus 128

4. You are given the following cell entries:

   A1   50
   A2   40
   A3   30
   A4   20
   A5   10
   A6   0

   What value will be returned by the spreadsheet functions?
   (a) @IF(A1 = 0,A2,A3)
   (b) @SUM(A1..A6)
   (c) @MAX(A2..A4)
   (d) @MIN(A1..A3,5,A5)
   (e) @AVG(A1..A6)
   (f) @MIN(10,@MAX(A2..A4))
   (g) @MAX(10,@MIN(A2..A4))

5. The screen depicted in Figure 8.12 may look a bit strange on first viewing, in that neither the rows nor the columns are labeled consecutively.
   (a) What spreadsheet feature is in effect? Why is it being used?
   (b) Which columns are not shown from Figure 8.12? What do you think is contained in those columns?
   (c) Which rows are not shown in Figure 8.12? What is your best guess as to what those rows contain?

6. Figure 8.13 contains two versions of a spreadsheet in which sales, costs, and profits are to be projected over a five-year horizon. The spreadsheets are only partially completed, and the intent in both is to copy the entries from year 2 (cells C3 through C5) to the remainder of the spreadsheet. As you can see, the first spreadsheet uses only relative addresses and the second uses only absolute addresses. *Both spreadsheets are in error.*

FIGURE 8.12
Spreadsheet for exercise 5.

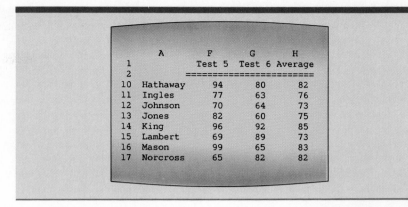

	A	F	G	H
1		Test 5	Test 6	Average
2		========================		
10	Hathaway	94	80	82
11	Ingles	77	63	76
12	Johnson	70	64	73
13	Jones	82	60	75
14	King	96	92	85
15	Lambert	69	89	73
16	Mason	99	65	83
17	Norcross	65	82	82

(a) Show the *erroneous* entries that will result when column C is copied to columns D, E, and F for both spreadsheets.

(b) What are the correct entries for column C so that the formulas will copy correctly?

7. Figure 8.14 depicts two common errors which often occur during printing operations. Identify the cause of each error, then indicate the necessary command(s) within the print sequence to correct the problem.

FIGURE 8.13
Spreadsheets for exercise 6.

	A	B	C	D	E	F
1		Year 1	Year 2	Year 3	Year 4	Year 5
2		==				
3	Sales	$1,000	(1+C8)*B3			
4	Cost	$800	(1+C9)*B4			
5	Profit	$200	+C3-C4			
6						
7	Assumptions:					
8	Annual sales increase:		10.00%			
9	Anual cost increase:		8.00%			

(a) Error 1: Relative addresses

	A	B	C	D	E	F
1		Year 1	Year 2	Year 3	Year 4	Year 5
2		==				
3	Sales	$1,000	(1+$C$8)*$B$3			
4	Cost	$800	(1+$C$9)*$B$4			
5	Profit	$200	+$C$3-$C$4			
6						
7	Assumptions:					
8	Annual sales increase:		10.00%			
9	Anual cost increase:		8.00%			

(b) Error 2: Absolute addresses

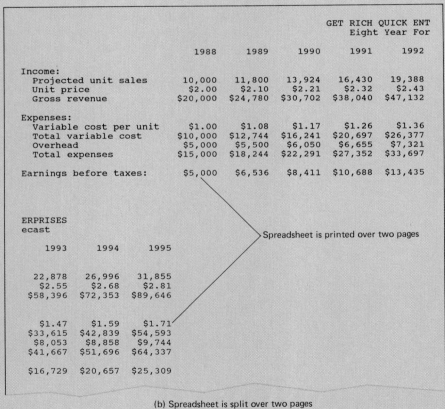

```
                                    GET RICH QUICK ENTERPRISES
                                         Eight Year Forecast

                     1988      1989      1990      1991      1992      1993      1994      1995

Income:
  Projected unit sales   10,000    11,800    13,924    16,430    19,388    22,878    26,996    31,855
  Unit price             $2.00     $2.10     $2.21     $2.32     $2.43     $2.55     $2.68     $2.81
  Gross revenue          $20,000   $24,780   $30,702   $38,040   $47,132   $58,396   $72,353   $89,646

Expenses:
  Variable cost per unit $1.00     $1.08     $1.17     $1.26     $1.36     $1.47     $1.59     $1.71
  Total variable cost    $10,000   $12,744   $16,241   $20,697   $26,377   $33,615   $42,839   $54,593
  Overhead               $5,000    $5,500    $6,050    $6,655    $7,321    $8,053    $8,858    $9,744
```
        Unintentional blank lines appear in the middle of the spreadsheet
```
Total expenses           $15,000   $18,244   $22,291   $27,352   $33,697   $41,667   $51,696   $64,337

Earnings before taxes:   $5,000    $6,536    $8,411    $10,688   $13,435   $16,729   $20,657   $25,309
```

(a) Unintentional blank lines in middle of spreadsheet

```
                                    GET  RICH QUICK ENT
                                        Eight Year For

                  1988      1989      1990      1991      1992

Income:
  Projected unit sales    10,000    11,800    13,924    16,430    19,388
  Unit price              $2.00     $2.10     $2.21     $2.32     $2.43
  Gross revenue           $20,000   $24,780   $30,702   $38,040   $47,132

Expenses:
  Variable cost per unit  $1.00     $1.08     $1.17     $1.26     $1.36
  Total variable cost     $10,000   $12,744   $16,241   $20,697   $26,377
  Overhead                $5,000    $5,500    $6,050    $6,655    $7,321
  Total expenses          $15,000   $18,244   $22,291   $27,352   $33,697

Earnings before taxes:    $5,000    $6,536    $8,411    $10,688   $13,435



ERPRISES
ecast

   1993      1994      1995


   22,878    26,996    31,855
   $2.55     $2.68     $2.81
   $58,396   $72,353   $89,646


   $1.47     $1.59     $1.71
   $33,615   $42,839   $54,593
   $8,053    $8,858    $9,744
   $41,667   $51,696   $64,337

   $16,729   $20,657   $25,309
```

Spreadsheet is printed over two pages

(b) Spreadsheet is split over two pages

FIGURE 8.14   Spreadsheets for exercise 7.

8. The problem of the "matrix menace" has been addressed in numerous articles, three of which are referenced below:

   - Steve Ditlea, "Spreadsheets Can Be Hazardous to Your Health," *Personal Computing*, January 1987, pages 60–69.

   - Marvin Bryan, "Swatting Spreadsheet Bugs," *Lotus Magazine*, January 1987, pages 107–108.

   - Jared Taylor, "Keeping Your Spreadsheet Honest," *PC Magazine*, May 13, 1986, pages 151–154.

   Research one or more of these articles to determine what additional measures you can take to validate the accuracy of spreadsheets you develop.

9. Examine carefully the numbers in the financial forecast of Figure 8.1. In particular, notice that the 1990 unit sales, unit price, and gross revenue are forecast as 13,924, $2.21, and $30,702, respectively. However, multiplication of 13,924 units times a unit price of $2.21 produces a gross revenue of $30,772 rather than the $30,702 which appeared in the spreadsheet. The numbers for total variable cost are off in a similar fashion, as are the corresponding numbers in all future years.

   Are there errors in Figure 8.1, or can these discrepancies be explained in some other way?

10. Answer the following with respect to modes of recalculation:
    (a) What is the default mode for recalculation, manual or automatic?
    (b) What is the command sequence (in your spreadsheet program) to implement manual recalculation?
    (c) What prompt appears on the screen after the command sequence in part *b* has been issued?
    (d) Why would you want to negate automatic recalculation?
    (e) How do you recalculate the spreadsheet within the manual recalculation mode?
    (f) Explain what is meant by *intelligent recalculation*, a feature introduced in the current generation of more powerful spreadsheet programs.

11. Where, within the consolidated spreadsheet of Figure 8.9, would you place the macro of Figure 8.11? What difficulties, if any, will be encountered in the macro as it stands, if additional students (for example, additional rows) are added to the individual spreadsheets? How can they be avoided?

12. The National Football League computes an efficiency rating for its quarterbacks according to statistics in four areas: percentage of completed passes, percentage of touchdown passes, percent-

AMERICAN CONFERENCE	ATTEMPTS	COMP	PERCENT COMP	YARDS GAINED	AVG YDS GAINED	TD PASS	PERCENT TD	INTCPT	PERCENT INTCPT	RATING
Kosar, Cleveland	389	241	61.95	3033	7.80	22	5.66	9	2.31	95.41
Marino, Miami	444	263		3245		26		13		
Krieg, Seattle	294	178		2131		23		15		
Kenney, Kansas City	273	154		2107		15		9		
Wilson, Los Angeles	266	152		2070		12		8		
Kelly, Buffalo	419	250		2798		19		11		
Elway, Denver	410	224		3198		19		12		
O'Brien, New York	393	234		2696		13		8		
Trudeau, Indianapolis	229	128		1587		6		6		
Moon, Houston	368	184		2806		21		18		
Esiason, Cincinatti	440	240		3321		16		19		
Fouts, San Diego	364	206		2517		10		15		
Malone, Pittsburgh	336	156		1896		6		19		

NATIONAL CONFERENCE	ATTEMPTS	COMP	PERCENT COMP	YARDS GAINED	AVG YDS GAINED	TD PASS	PERCENT TD	INTCPT	PERCENT INTCPT	RATING
Montana, San Francisco	398	266	66.83	3054	7.67	31	7.79	13	3.27	102.10
Simms, New York	282	163		2230		17		9		
Lomax, St. Louis	463	275		3387		24		12		
McMahon, Chicago	210	125		1639		12		8		
DeBerg, Tampa Bay	275	159		1891		14		7		
Cunningham, Philadelphia	406	223		2786		23		12		
Herbert, New Orleans	294	164		2119		15		9		
Wilson, Minnesota	264	140		2106		14		13		
White, Dallas,	362	215		2617		12		17		
Schroeder, Washington	267	129		1878		12		10		
Everett, Los Angeles	302	162		2064		10		13		
Campbell, Atlanta	260	136		1728		11		14		
Long, Detroit	417	232		2598		11		20		
Wright, Green Bay	247	132		1507		6		11		

FIGURE 8.15 Football data.

age of interceptions, and the average yards gained per attempted pass. These factors are combined into a formula in which an arbitrary weight is assigned to each factor as follows:

Efficiency rating = (completion percent + 4 * TD percent − 5 * interception percent + 5 * average yards per attempt + 2.5) * 5/6

Figure 8.15 contains data from the 1987 season. Enter these values into a spreadsheet, then compute the various percentages and efficiency ratings for all quarterbacks (You should be able to do the assignment even if you don't understand football.) As an aid in getting started, the correct results are included for Kosar and Montana.

CHAPTER 9

BUSINESS GRAPHICS

293

After reading this chapter, you should be able to:

1.   Distinguish between different types of graphs, stating the advantages and disadvantages of each type.

2.   Create a line graph, bar graph, pie chart, multiple bar graph, and stacked bar graph, in conjunction with a spreadsheet program.

3.   Differentiate between the X range, and the A, B, and C ranges as they relate to a spreadsheet program.

4.   Describe how a given spreadsheet can have several different graphs associated with it; differentiate between the command to save a spreadsheet versus the command to save a particular series of graph settings.

5.   Define "chart junk"; describe at least two other pitfalls to avoid in conjunction with business graphics.

6.   Distinguish between text and graphics mode; describe the various types of IBM graphics standards and the contribution of Hercules Corporation.

Overview

Business has always known that the graphic representation of data is an attractive, easy-to-understand way of conveying information. Until recently, however, a serious limitation to the use of such presentations was the necessity of having a graphic artist prepare the material. No more. Graphics today is one of the most exciting microcomputer applications, enabling professional-looking presentations to be produced in minutes, often with but a few simple keystrokes.

This chapter discusses the use of business graphics in conjunction with spreadsheet programs. You will be introduced to the various types of graphs available and see how easy it is to transform spreadsheet data into its graphic counterpart. The chapter also cautions you against several errors that commonly occur with computer graphics.

Although our emphasis throughout the text has been on software (as opposed to hardware), you will nevertheless find it useful to know something of the various graphic standards that exist for PC monitors and adapter cards. Accordingly, we explain the differences between IBM's CGA, EGA, and VGA implementations. The Corporate Profile focuses on the Hercules Corporation, the company that produced the first monochrome graphics card for the PC.

The Value of Graphics

The value of a graph to convey a message is aptly demonstrated by Figure 9.1, in which the same information is presented in both verbal and graphic form. Although identical facts are contained in Figure 9.1*a* and 9.1*b*, the information about the company is understood more quickly, and more easily, from the graphic presentation.

Of even greater significance is that the true picture of the company's growth is buried within a misleading report, yet the real pattern is immediately apparent from the graph. Shareholders should be concerned about the fact that profits have risen at a much slower

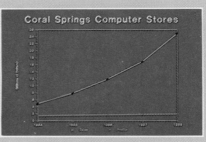

"Wow! What graphics!"

FIGURE 9.1
The value of graphics.

Report to shareholders:

    It gives me great pleasure to report that 1988 marked the fifth consecutive year in which new records were set for both sales and profits. Indeed I would like to take this opportunity to remind you once again of the impressive annual gains that have been achieved during the few short years of our existence.

    Sales have risen steadily during the time I have been chairman, from $5 million in 1984, to $8 million in 1985, $12 million in 1986, $17 million in 1987, and to $25 million for 1988. During that same period profits have grown by $100,000 each and every year, from $1.5 million in 1984 to $1.9 million in 1988.

    I am confident that we may look forward to similar growth in the years ahead.

                    David D. Distortion
                    President and CEO
                    Coral Springs Computer Stores

(a) Verbal description

Coral Springs Computer Stores

(b) Graphic description

rate than sales (that is, profit as a percentage of revenue has actually decreased), meaning that the company is less profitable as time goes on.

Thus in the case of Coral Springs Computers a picture is indeed worth 1000 words (and certainly more than the 125 in the chairperson's memo).

THE BEST STATISTICAL GRAPH EVER

A graph of Napoleon's abortive campaign into Russia (below) is not what you would expect in a chapter on business graphics. However, today's PC chartists would do well to emulate its concise yet eloquent presentation, which conveys a large amount of information with a minimum of effort.

The story begins at the left of the chart on the Polish–Russian border. The red band shows the course of the advancing army, with the width of the line representing the number of men at any point. The much narrower black band indicates the army's retreat from Moscow, vividly portraying its annihilation during the bitterly cold winter (the line at the bottom shows the temperature). Of the 422,000 troops that set out, only 10,000 returned.

Edward Tufte (see page 306) considers the 1869 drawing by Frenchman Charles Minard the best statistical graph ever done. He cites Minard's ingenious multivariate design which enables him to plot five variables for every point in the journey, all without taxing the reader. Thus at any point you see the position of the army in two dimensions, the direction of its advance, its size, and the weather.

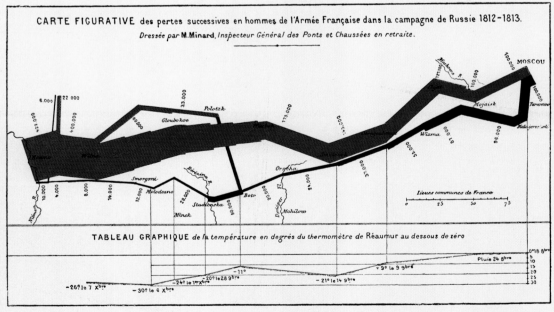

Business Graphics

The spreadsheet of Figure 9.2 will be used as the basis of our discussion on business graphics. As can be seen, the figure contains quarterly sales data for Ralph Cordell's Sporting Goods Establishment.

The numbers within the spreadsheet can be viewed in several ways: by quarter, by salesperson, or by a combination of the two. We see, for example, that the store achieved quarterly totals of $133,000, $147,500, $157,000, and $198,400 for the first, second, third, and fourth quarters, respectively. Each of these numbers can be further divided into the amounts achieved by the individual sales staff. Thus Friedel, Davis, and McGrath recorded sales of $50,000, $34,000, and $49,000, respectively, which collectively account for the store's total of $133,000 during the first quarter.

Figures 9.3 and 9.4 present this data in various graphic formats. The graphs in Figure 9.3 plot only a single variable (quarterly sales for the store as a whole); those in Figure 9.4 plot the quarterly sales for each individual salesperson. Collectively, Figures 9.3 and 9.4 represent the most common types of business graphs associated with spreadsheet programs, namely, a *bar graph*, *pie chart*, *multiple bar graph*, *stacked bar graph*, and *line graph*. Each of these is discussed in turn.

Bar Graphs

A simple bar graph is probably the easiest type of graph to understand. A **bar graph** plots the value of a numeric quantity or **quantitative variable** (such as sales) against a descriptive category or **qualitative variable** (such as quarter or salesperson).

Consider, for example, Figure 9.3*a*, in which the descriptive categories (1st quarter, 2nd quarter, and so on) are plotted on the *x* (horizontal) **axis**. The quantitative measure for each category (that is,

	A	B	C	D	E	F
1			Ralph Cordell Sporting Goods			
2			Quarterly Sales Figures			
3						
4	Sales Rep	1st	2nd	3rd	4th	Total
5	-------	-------	-------	-------	-------	-------
6	Friedel	$50,000	$55,000	$62,500	$95,400	$262,900
7						
8	Davis	$34,000	$48,500	$52,000	$62,000	$196,500
9						
10	McGrath	$49,000	$44,000	$42,500	$41,000	$176,500
11	-------	-------	-------	-------	-------	-------
12	Total	$133,000	$147,500	$157,000	$198,400	$635,900
13						

FIGURE 9.2
Ralph Cordell spreadsheet.

the quarterly sales) is plotted on the *y* (vertical) **axis** as a bar (or rectangle) whose height corresponds to the value of the quantitative variable.

Bar graphs are most appropriate when the number of categories is relatively small, say, seven or less; otherwise the bars run together and labeling becomes impossible.

Pie Charts

A **pie chart** is the most effective way to display proportional relationships. The "pie," or complete circle, denotes the total amount, with each slice of the pie corresponding to the appropriate share of the total. Accordingly, the pie chart in Figure 9.3*b* divides the "pie" representing yearly (total) sales into four sectors, one for each quarter, with the size of each sector proportional to the percentage of total sales in that quarter.

To develop a pie chart the graphics program must first compute total sales ($635,900 in our example), then calculate the percentage contributed by each quarter, and finally draw each slice of the pie in proportion to its computed percentage. In other words, the first-quarter sales of $133,000 account for 20.9 percent of the total, and so this slice of the pie is allotted 20.9 percent of the area of the circle. Some programs also offer the option of an *exploded* pie chart in which one or more pieces of the pie can be separated for emphasis.

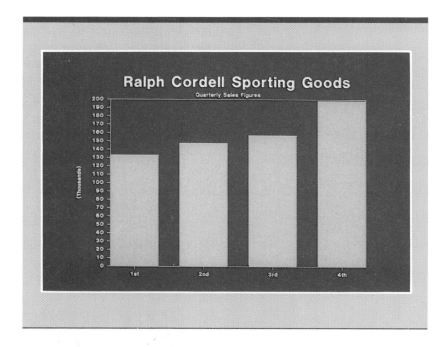

FIGURE 9.3*a*
Bar graph.

FIGURE 9.3*b*
Pie chart.

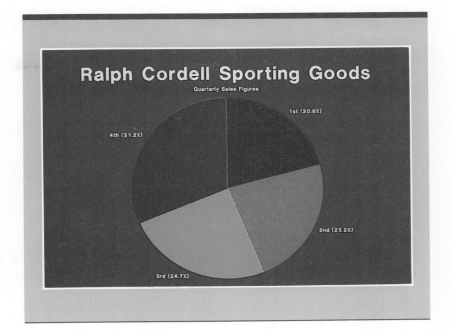

A pie chart is easiest to read when the number of slices is kept to a manageable number (not more than six or seven), and when small percentages (less than five) do not appear. The latter can sometimes be avoided by collectively grouping several separate, but small, categories into a single "other" category.

Multiple Bar Graphs

A **multiple bar graph** such as the one shown in Figure 9.4*a* is ideal for comparing several variables in the same graph. In this example each of the four quarterly sales totals is divided into separate amounts for Friedel, Davis, and McGrath (a total of 12 data points). Although it is possible to plot the quarterly sales for each person on individual bar graphs, the results are often more meaningful when shown together on a multiple bar graph as was done in Figure 9.4*a*.

Note, too, that a different shading (or color) is used for every salesperson so that they can be distinguished from one another, with the legends for the various sales staff appearing at the bottom of the graph. The number of variables (salespersons in our example) that can be plotted on a multiple bar graph depends on the specific program. Most programs (Lotus and VP Planner among them) accommodate six such **data ranges** (variables), which are designated A, B, C, D, E, and F, respectively.

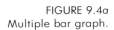

FIGURE 9.4a
Multiple bar graph.

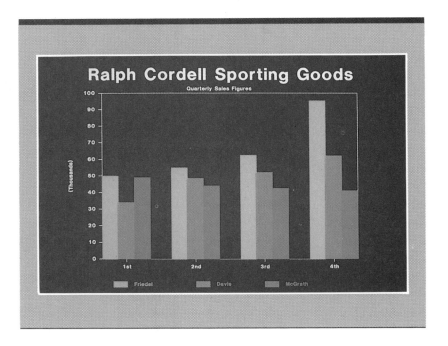

Stacked Bar Graphs

A **stacked bar graph** is similar to a multiple bar graph except that the bars are drawn on top of one another instead of side by side. Compare, for example, the stacked bar graph of Figure 9.4*b* to its immediate predecessor in Figure 9.4*a*. Although both graphs plot the identical 12 data points, there are in fact subtle differences in the way the data is presented.

The biggest difference is that the stacked bar explicitly totals the sales for each quarter while the multiple bar does not, which in turn produces entirely different **scales** on the *y* axis for each graph. The advantage of the stacked bar is that the quarterly totals are clearly shown and further that the relative contributions of each salesperson are apparent. The disadvantage is that the segments within each bar do not start at the same point, making it difficult to compare figures for the individual sales representatives.

Line Graphs

A **line graph** also plots a quantitative variable (such as sales) against a qualitative variable (such as quarter or salesperson). As with a bar graph, the quantitative values are plotted along the vertical scale (*y* axis) and the qualitative values along the horizontal scale (*x* axis). The individual data points are then connected by straight lines.

FIGURE 9.4*b*
Stacked bar graph.

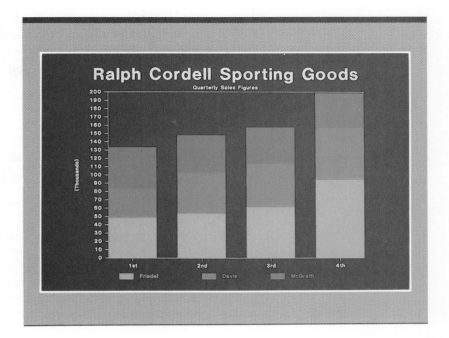

FIGURE 9.4*c*
Line graph.

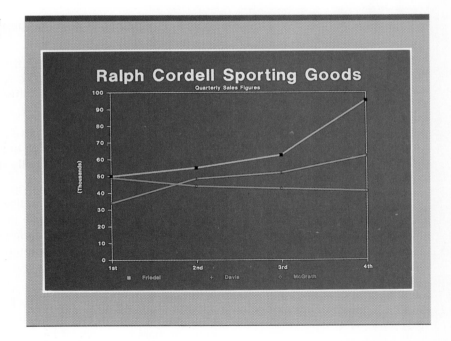

Line graphs are generally more meaningful when several quantitative variables are plotted against the same qualitative variable as shown in Figure 9.4*c*. The line graphs depict the same information as the multiple bar graph of Figure 9.4*a*, except that individual sales trends may be more apparent with the line graph. Note, too, that the lines for each salesperson are distinguished from one another with either a different color or a different symbol.

All the graph types just discussed are useful in their own right, with the decision on which to use depending on the nature of the data and the message to be presented.

Creating Graphs from a Spreadsheet

Hands-On Exercise 1, which follows shortly, directs you in the use of a spreadsheet program to re-create the graphs of Figures 9.3 and 9.4. We think you will be pleased at how easily programs such as Lotus and VP Planner convert spreadsheets into graphs. In essence, you call up a graph menu from the spreadsheet program, enter the appropriate selections, and the graphs will appear on your monitor or dot matrix printer. (Your system *must*, however, include graphics capability in order to do the exercise.)

It is helpful, however, to first explain some of the menu choices you will encounter in the exercise. Consider:

Type: The nature (type) of graph you want (for example, pie, line, bar, and so on).

X range: The cells containing the names of the descriptive categories or values of the qualitative variable. For example, the X range in Figure 9.2 consists of cells B4 through E4, which contain the labels "1st," "2nd," "3rd," and "4th.".

A Range: The cells containing values for the first (sometimes only) quantitative variable. The graphs in Figure 9.3, for example, designate the A range as consisting of cells B12 through E12, which in turn contain the quarterly sales data.

B, C, D, E, and F ranges: Up to five additional quantitative variables may generally be specified. The graphs in Figure 9.4, for example, each plot three quantitative variables (the quarterly sales for each salesperson) which are designated as the A, B, and C ranges, respectively.

Options: The place where you "dress up" your graph. Among the many choices available are a **title** for the graph (consisting of one or two lines), **labels** for the x and/or y axis, and **legends** to distinguish between bars in a stacked or multiple bar graph.

HANDS-ON EXERCISE 1:
BUSINESS GRAPHICS

OBJECTIVE: Use the graphics component of a spreadsheet program to produce the five types of business graphs. *This exercise requires that your computer have graphics capability.*

Step 1: Create the Spreadsheet
Create the spreadsheet for Ralph Cordell Sporting Goods, shown earlier in Figure 9.2. (Figure 9.5 contains the associated cell contents and will be useful in producing the spreadsheet.)

Save the spreadsheet when it is finished.

Step 2: Create a Bar Graph
Enter the graphics menu of your spreadsheet program. Specify the *type* of graph (a bar graph in this example), then indicate the data you want to plot. In this first example you are plotting quarterly sales, so that the *A range* extends from cells B12 through E12, which contain the sales data for each quarter.

Specify the command to *view* the graph, after which it should appear immediately on your monitor. The graph you see should resemble the bar graph shown earlier in Figure 9.3a, but it will not yet contain all the descriptive material which was present in our figure. In particular, your graph is missing the labels on the x axis as well as the two-line title at the top.

Return to the graphics menu and specify the X *range* as cells B4 through E4 (indicating the 1st, 2nd, 3rd, and 4th quarters), which in turn corresponds to the data points in cells B12 through E12. Now find the necessary menu option to enter the first and second line of the title as shown in Figure 9.3a.

View your graph again, and this time it should match ours.

Step 3: Save the Bar Graph
A single spreadsheet typically has multiple graphs associated with it, as evidenced by Figures 9.3 and 9.4, both of which were derived from the spreadsheet of Figure 9.2. Accordingly, you need to save *the settings of every graph individually as well as the spreadsheet as a whole.* In other words, you must execute a separate Graph Save command (for every graph) in addition to a File Save command (for the entire spreadsheet).

Save the settings of the bar graph just created, using the appropriate command from the graphics menu.

FIGURE 9.5   Cell contents for Ralph Cordell spreadsheet.

```
C1: 'Ralph Cordell Sporting Goods    C8: 48500
C2: '   Quarterly Sales Figures      D8: 52000
A4: 'Salesman                        E8: 62000
B4: ^1st                             F8: [W12] @SUM(B8..E8)
C4: ^2nd                             A10: 'McGrath
D4: ^3rd                             B10: 49000
E4: ^4th                             C10: 44000
F4: [W12] '     Total                D10: 42500
A5: \-                               E10: 41000
B5: \-                               F10: [W12] @SUM(B10..E10)
C5: \-                               A11: \-
D5: \-                               B11: \-
E5: \-                               C11: \-
F5: [W12] \-                         D11: \-
A6: 'Friedel                         E11: \-
B6: 50000                            F11: [W12] \-
C6: 55000                            A12: '   Total
D6: 62500                            B12: @SUM(B6..B11)
E6: 95400                            C12: @SUM(C6..C11)
F6: [W12] @SUM(B6..E6)               D12: @SUM(D6..D11)
A8: 'Davis                           E12: @SUM(E6..E11)
B8: 34000                            F12: [W12] @SUM(B12..E12)
```

Step 4: Create a Pie Chart

The best thing about computer-generated graphs is the ease with which they can be modified. You can, for example, go from a bar graph to a pie chart with a minimum of effort.

Return to the graphics menu, but this time designate a pie chart as the graph you want. Invoke the command to view the graph, and the pie chart of Figure 9.3b appears in place of the bar graph. The spreadsheet program automatically totals the individual data points in the existing A range (cells B12 through E12), then assigns an appropriate section of the pie to each category in accordance with its respective percentage of the total.

All the other information (the data to plot, the labels for the x axis, the two-line title, and so on) is retained until the graph settings are explicitly reset (cleared). In other words, the *settings* from the bar graph are automatically used for the pie chart unless you otherwise instruct the program.

Save the settings of the pie chart under a new name.

Step 5: Print the Bar Graph and Pie Chart

Individual graphs can be printed immediately as they are created or collectively in a single step. The choice is immaterial and entirely up to you.

Execute the necessary commands to print the bar graph and pie chart, consulting the optional laboratory manual for additional details.

Step 6: Reset the Graph

The two graphs just created are based on the same data (the quarterly totals in cells B12 through E12), and consequently used common labels for the x axis as well as similar title information. Accordingly, all that was necessary to go from one graph to the next was to change the graph type as was done in step 4.

The graphs in Figure 9.4, however, plot different data (the individual salesperson totals in rows 6, 8, and 10) and thus new settings are necessary. Execute the command to *reset* the current settings.

Step 7: Create a Multiple Bar Graph

A multiple bar graph consists of several individual bar graphs. Unlike step 3, however, you are plotting three sets of numbers for each quarter, corresponding to the quarterly sales figures for each of the three salespeople. Thus you should indicate three distinct data ranges, one each for Friedel, Davis, and McGrath, respectively.

Specify the A range (for Friedel) as cells B6 through E6, the B range (for Davis) as cells B8 through E8, and the C range (for McGrath) as cells B10 through E10. View the graph; it will closely resemble Figure 9.4a, but it will not yet contain a *legend* to identify the different shadings (which are produced automatically by the spreadsheet program).

Find the legends option in the graphics menu, then indicate cells A6 (Friedel), A8 (Davis), and A10 (McGrath) as the legends for the A, B, and C ranges, respectively. Your graph should now match Figure 9.4a.

Save and/or print this graph as you see fit.

Step 8: Create a Stacked Bar Graph

Once again, you can move easily from one graph type to another, in this case from a multiple bar graph to a stacked bar graph, simply by changing the type parameter. Create the stacked bar graph of Figure 9.4b, then save and/or print it as you see fit.

Step 9: Create a Line Graph

Change the type of graph from stacked bar to line, and a graph resembling Figure 9.4c will come into view. (Your graph may be different from ours, however, because line graphs, unlike bar graphs, do not automatically begin the vertical scale at zero. If this is true of your spreadsheet program, you should invoke the *manual scaling* option to start your scale at zero, so that your graph will match ours exactly.) Save and/or print this graph as appropriate.

Step 10: Save the Spreadsheet

Return to the opening spreadsheet menu, save the spreadsheet, then exit the program and return to DOS.

POLAROID PALETTE

"Let us in no way minimize the opportunity, or the danger, involved. The 30 minutes an executive spends on his feet formally presenting his latest project to corporate superiors are simply and absolutely the most important 30 minutes of that or any other managerial session."

Walter Kiechel III, *Fortune Magazine*

(*Left*) Polaroid palette. (*Right*) Graphics created using the Polaroid palette.

Polaroid has long dominated the instant camera market since its 1948 introduction of the 60-second Land camera (named for Dr. Edwin H. Land, its inventor). Now Polaroid has introduced instant gratification to the computer field with the Polaroid Palette, which shoots color screens and produces slides and/or prints in 60 seconds.

The Palette retails for approximately $1500 and includes the necessary components (cameras and film) for shooting, developing, and mounting color slides, plus the necessary cables to tie everything together. The associated software makes it possible for you to edit your graphics and change colors.

Polaroid is not alone in the field, and many other sources should be considered. (See "Putting it all on Film," *PC World*, May 13, 1986; and "Slide Production Services," *Lotus Magazine*, July 1987.)

Authors' Comments:
Business graphics is one of the most exciting, fastest growing, and fastest changing areas of personal computers. However, generating the graph is only half the battle, as the colorful computer presentation must still be transferred to another medium in order to be shared with a wider audience.

Use and Abuse of Graphics

The Hands-On Exercise just completed demonstrates how easily numbers in a spreadsheet may be converted to their graphic equivalent. Unfortunately, the numbers can just as easily be converted into erroneous or misleading graphs. According to Edward Tufte:

> Lying graphics cheapen the graphical art everywhere. . . . When a chart on television lies, it lies millions of times over; when a *New York Times* chart lies, it lies 900,000 times over to a great many important and influential readers. The lies are told about the major issues of public policy—the government budget, medical care, prices, and fuel economy standards, for example. The lies are systematic and quite predictable, nearly always exaggerating the rate of recent change.

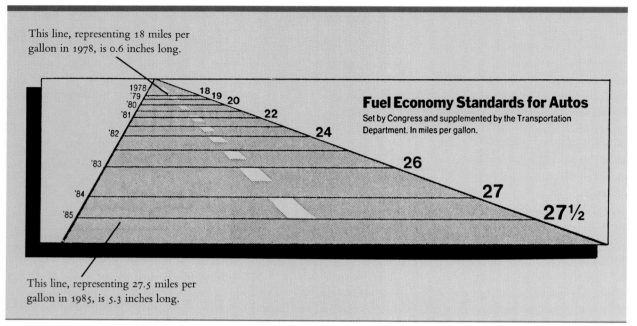

This line, representing 18 miles per gallon in 1978, is 0.6 inches long.

1978
'79
'80
'81
'82
'83
'84
'85

18 19 20

22

24

Fuel Economy Standards for Autos
Set by Congress and supplemented by the Transportation Department. In miles per gallon.

26

27

27½

This line, representing 27.5 miles per gallon in 1985, is 5.3 inches long.

FIGURE 9.6
Use and abuse of graphics (example 1). (*Source: The New York Times*, August 9, 1978, page D-2.)

Consider, for example, Figures 9.6 and 9.7 (the examples are from Tufte), both of which misleadingly exaggerate the point they are trying to make. Figure 9.6 depicts the improvement in fuel economy mandated by Congress, from 18 miles per gallon (mpg) in 1978 to 27.5 in 1985.

The problem with Figure 9.6 is that the graphic effect is far more pronounced than the corresponding change in the data. In other words, while the required fuel economy increased by 53 percent (from 18 to 27.5 miles per gallon), the length of the lines representing these numbers increased by more than 15 times that amount, or a staggering 783 percent!

Figure 9.7 shows a similar exaggeration, but for a different reason. The problem here is that the data (the purchasing power of one

---

THE VISUAL DISPLAY OF QUANTITATIVE INFORMATION

Any contest for a book title least likely to attract the reader would surely consider *The Visual Display of Quantitative Information*, by **Edward Tufte.** Yet according to every review we have read, the dry-as-a-thesis title is the only bad thing about a book described as an "accurate, funny, and downright rude course in the history and practice of graphics" (Stephen Manes, *PC Magazine*, May 26, 1987, page 107). Tufte's work is a superb exposition on how to design informative charts without boring, confusing, or misleading the reader, and appeals therefore to both statisticians and personal computer chartists.

The Visual Display of Quantitative Information is available only through its publisher, Graphics Press, POB 430, Cheshire, CT 06410.

FIGURE 9.7
Use and abuse of graphics
(example 2.) (*Source: Washington
Post*, October 25, 1978, page 1.)

dollar) is one-dimensional, yet the graphic reflects the size (area) of a dollar bill and is two-dimensional. Hence if the 1978 dollar is to accurately reflect its purchasing power compared to the dollar in 1958, it should be approximately twice as large as shown in the figure.

The preceding examples are interesting and provocative illustrations because they were extracted from real sources and involve

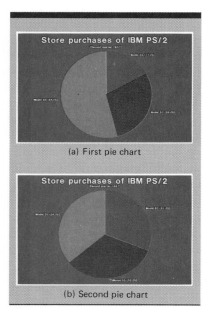

FIGURE 9.8
Sales data for the PS/2. (*Note:* Model 80 was not shipping during the second quarter.)

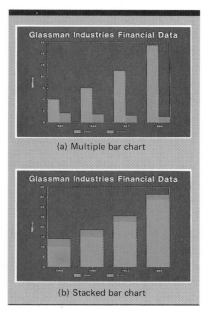

FIGURE 9.9
Adding dissimilar quantities.

real data. Although the graphics in these figures go beyond the capabilities of a simple spreadsheet program, graphs constructed with programs like Lotus or VP Planner are also replete with errors of which you should be aware. Accordingly, we have collected several examples from student assignments for your consideration.

Improper (Omitted) Labels

The difference between *unit sales* and *dollar sales* is a concept of great importance, yet one which is consistently missed by students and professionals alike. Consider, for example, the two pie charts in Figure 9.8a and 9.8b, which indicate the sales activity for the PS/2 series in the second quarter of 1987, immediately after the initial announcement. (Only three models were being shipped during this period, models 30, 50, and 60; see Table 1.1 on page 21 for details of the individual machines.)

The two pie charts reflect very different percentages and would appear therefore to contradict one another. In actuality, both sets of numbers are correct because the percentages depend on whether they are measured in units or dollars. The model 30 was the cheapest model, and accounted for 54 percent of the units shipped (Figure 9.8a). However, because the model 30 was priced significantly below the other two, it accounted for only 38 percent of the sales volume as measured in dollars (Figure 9.8b). *Neither chart is properly labeled* (there is no indication of whether units or dollars are plotted), which in turn may lead to erroneous conclusions on the part of the reader.

Adding Dissimilar Quantities

The conversion of a multiple bar to a stacked bar graph is a simple matter, requiring only a few keystrokes. Unfortunately, however, because the procedure is so easy, it is often done without thought and in situations where the stacked bar graph is inappropriate.

Consider, for example, Figure 9.9a and 9.9b, containing a multiple and stacked bar graph, respectively. The multiple bar graphs of Figure 9.9a show steadily increasing sales for the period 1985 through 1988 in conjunction with steadily decreasing profits. The situation is a pessimistic (yet realistic) picture of the company's financial position.

The stacked bar graphs in Figure 9.9b plot the exact same numbers yet portray a deceptively optimistic trend, because the yearly totals are based on the *addition of dissimilar quantities*. In other words, sales and profits represent entirely different concepts and cannot be added together in any meaningful fashion.

Chart Junk

The temptation to use **chart junk** (too many colors, too many type sizes or styles, too much clip art, or other exotic features) is often

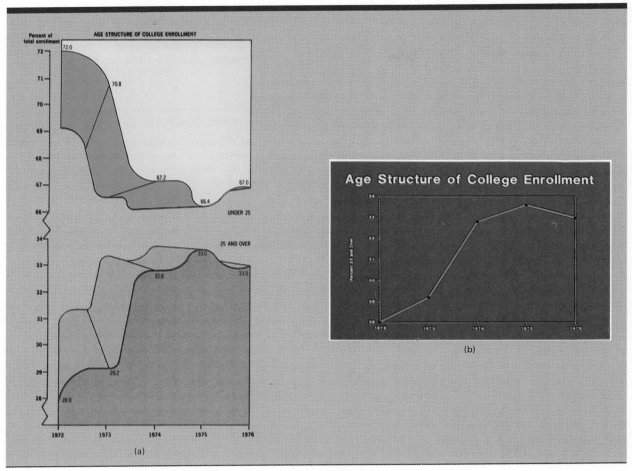

FIGURE 9.10   Chart junk. [*Source* (panel a): *Forbes*, May 18, 1987.]

more than the computer enthusiast can resist. With this in mind, consider Figure 9.10*a*, Tufte's choice for possibly the worst graph ever to find its way into print. (Although the figure was obviously not done with the graphics capability of a spreadsheet program, these programs do in fact offer plenty of opportunity for similar treatment. Tufte's example simply takes it to the extreme.)

Figure 9.10*a* appears at first to say a great deal; but on closer examination it says relatively little. The chartist apparently wanted to convey the percentage of college enrollment for two groups: those under 25, and those 25 and over. However, since the total percentage in any given year adds to 100, the same amount of information can be communicated with only half the chart (top or bottom). Moreover, the peculiar three-dimensional effect totally confuses the presentation, as does the use of five colors to portray what are in reality only five data points.

The ordinary line graph of Figure 9.10*b* imparts the identical information but in a far clearer presentation. The point is simply that any graph must ultimately succeed on the basis of its content alone, and seldom, if ever, is made more effective through the addition of superfluous effects.

P. T. BARNUM WOULD HAVE LOVED COMPUTER GRAPHICS

According to a recent study by the Management Information Systems Research Center at the University of Minnesota, business presentations using graphs, slides, clip art, and other visual aids were 43% more persuasive than plain vanilla presentations using mere facts and ideas.

This piece of information will no doubt be seized on by graphics groupies—all those folks who would love to sell you ever more exploding pie charts, blinking icons, VCR-computer interfaces, monitors as big as the Radio City Music Hall screen, and so on. In fact, a columnist for a major computer publication not long ago hailed the dawn of graphics as "thinking tools" and urged all us verbal and numerical types to develop something called graphics literacy—a quality, according to the columnist, scandalously lacking among sophisticated computer users.

As a person whose livelihood depends on words, I may be prejudiced, but I honestly don't think a picture (much less a pie chart) is worth a thousand of them. Notice that I used the word *worth*. I don't question the finding that visually enhanced presentations are 43% more *popular*. I suspect that a poll of high school freshmen would reveal that the Classics Comics version of *Moby Dick* is at least 43% more popular than Melville's original prose. But the book is still worth more by any intellectual standard. Using graphics to sell ideas may be good business, but it's not the leap into some wondrous high-tech future that some would have us believe.

The real problem with flashy visuals is that they can easily become a geewhiz end in themselves. Listen to psychiatrist Elliot N. Wineburg, assistant clinical professor at the Mount Sinai School of Medicine in New York, who uses biofeedback to help victims of Raynaud's Disease (painful contraction of the blood vessels of the fingertips), stress, and other conditions. A patient's fingers are hooked to an electronic sensor, which is in turn connected to an Apple II and a printer. As the patient practices biofeedback techniques, the computer generates what Dr. Wineburg describes as "beautiful color graphs that people have confidence and trust in." The only problem, Wineburg adds, is that computer graphics are by no means the only or the best way to gauge the effectiveness of biofeedback. "You could just as easily have a light going on and off or a musical tone ringing. But many people—especially business people—prefer the computer because it implies that they're on the cutting edge of medicine."

In some ways, the romance with graphics is part of a larger problem: the "If It Comes Out of a Computer, It Must Be Smart" syndrome. We've all heard of editors and professors who find reports more impressive when they have justified margins, and board members and clients who put blind faith in any figures printed in dot-matrix typeface on fanfold paper. This is an old story and not surprising in a corporate culture that frequently mistakes good tailoring for brains. But it also says something about the awe in which the computer is still held by nonusers. I include in that category numerous executives who have an XT on the desk and not a clue as to how to use it effectively.

People don't like to be reminded that they're ignorant. (One fascinating sidelight to the Minnesota study, in fact, was the discovery that "the better the presenter one is, the more one needs to use high-quality visual support."

Phineas Taylor Barnum (1810–1891)

In other words, if you're a great speaker, people will hold it against you unless you throw in some clip art. Lousy speakers don't have this problem.) Everybody can grasp a picture, even one based on faulty information or one that provides only partial details. Computer graphics especially occupy an amazing niche. They come out of a dazzling and frequently intimidating technology, but at the same time, they appeal to the lowest common denominator.

I think we have a new syndrome here, one that moves way beyond the notion that if it comes out of a computer, it must be smart: the "If It Comes Out of a Computer and I Understand It, I Must Be Smart" syndrome.

P. T. Barnum would have loved it.

Source: Lindsy Van Gelder, *Lotus Magazine,* June 1987, page 170.

Authors' Comments:
A superb essay, and one we should all take to heart. Computer graphics are certainly a powerful tool, but like all tools they should be used with caution and discretion.

Graphics Standards

Any discussion of graphics leads inevitably to the selection of a monitor and the associated graphics adapter (graphics board). We think it important, therefore, that you understand the many options available in today's environment and so we include this section on graphics standards.

In the early days of the IBM PC, you had to choose between a **monochrome monitor** capable of displaying high-resolution (sharply defined) text but *not* graphics, and a **color monitor** that could display graphics but produced text of inferior quality. Thus if you required high-resolution text, you had to sacrifice the additional impact of color and graphics, yet color stuck you with fuzzier screens unsuitable for business use.

If this sounds unreasonable, remember that the PC was designed primarily for word processing, spreadsheet, and data management applications. Graphics were *not* seen as an important business use, and color was hardly considered. Indeed, the computers of the day that supported color (the Apple II, the Commodore 64, and the Radio Shack Color Computer) were perceived as "home" computers used for video games, an image IBM sought to avoid.

Graphics Mode versus Text Mode

The difference in resolution between monochrome and color is explained by considering the two modes in which output is displayed. Color monitors use the **graphics mode,** which produces images as a combination of individual picture elements, or **pixels,** with every pixel mapped separately on the screen.

The number of lines and pixels per line, into which a monitor is divided, determines the number of picture elements it can display. The more pixels a screen has, the sharper (clearer) the resultant picture, and the higher its **resolution.** The original IBM **Color Graphics Adapter** (CGA), for example, divided the monitor into 200 lines, with 320 pixels per line, or 64,000 pixels in all.

Monochrome monitors, on the other hand, display output in the **text** (character) **mode,** and divide the screen into only 25 rows and 80 columns (2000 cells in all). Images are formed by selecting one of 256 predefined characters for each of the 2000 cells. The 256 characters in turn consist of the alphabet (upper- and lowercase), the digits 0 through 9, punctuation marks (comma, period, semicolon, and so on), special characters (asterisk, slash, brace) as well as a host of **graphics characters** (⊤, ⊤, ⊥, ⊥, ⊢, ⊣, and so on).

The **character mode** used in the monochrome monitor produces an effective resolution of 720 × 350 pixels (as opposed to the CGA resolution of only 320 × 200), because each of the 2000 characters displayed on the screen itself consists of a 9 × 14 character matrix. The numbers 720 × 350 are obtained by multiplying 9 by 80 (the number of dots across the matrix times the number of columns in the screen), and 14 × 25 (the number of dots down the matrix times the number of rows on the scrren).

The advantage to the text mode is that it is faster than the graphics mode (you are filling only 2000 cells as opposed to 64,000 or more pixels). It also requires significantly less memory, again because you have to indicate values for fewer elements. The disadvantage is that programmers cannot create their own characters, because they are limited to the 256 available. Moreover, characters must be displayed in a fixed position on the screen; that is, they must go into one of the 2000 cells and cannot be offset by half a line or half a column.

CGA, EGA, and VGA

Advances in technology over the last several years have eliminated the need to choose between high-resolution monochrome text versus low-resolution color graphics. The first significant improvement was the Hercules Graphics Card (see the Corporate Profile), which provided graphics capability in the monochrome mode. IBM's original **Color Grahics Adapter (CGA)** has been replaced by the **Enhanced Graphics Adapter (EGA),** and more recently by the **Video Graphics Array (VGA),** each with greater resolution than its predecessor. A summary of the major IBM standards appears in Table 9.1.

TABLE 9.1

IBM Graphics Standards

	Year Introduced	Resolution*	Color Selection	Character Matrix
MDA	1981	720 × 350	N/A	9 × 14
CGA	1981	320 × 200	4 (2 palettes)	8 × 8
EGA	1984	640 × 350	16 of 64	8 × 14
VGA	1987	640 × 480	256 of 256K	9 × 16

*An inverse relationship exists within any given standard between *resolution* and the *number of colors* displayed simultaneously. VGA, for example, achieves its resolution of 640 × 480 with a maximum of 16 colors; the resolution drops to 320 × 200 if 256 colors are displayed simultaneously.

CGA (left) produces readable text and graphs, but note the difference in clarity when compared with EGA (right). The EGA characters are more distinct and the patterns within the pie chart crisper. The differences become more noticeable in the close-up detail (insets). (*Source: Personal Computing*, December 1987, page 121.)

The differences between EGA and VGA are harder to notice than those between EGA and CGA, but the characters and patterns are sharper in VGA. The real distinction lies in the number of colors you can display simultaneously. With EGA, that's 16 colors; in VGA, it's 256. (*Source: Personal Computing*, December 1987, pages 121 and 123.)

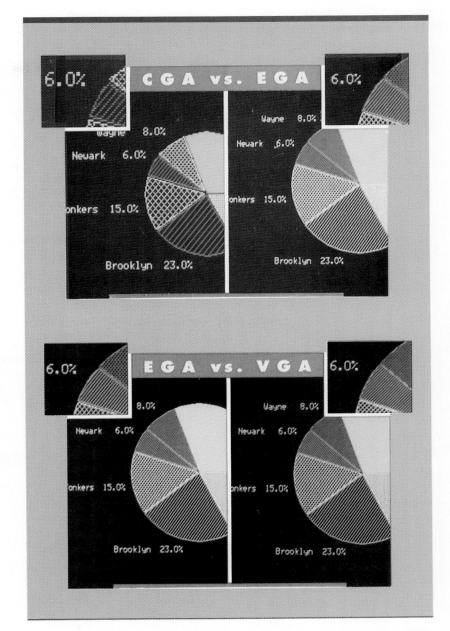

Note also, that the *graphics adapter* (the monochrome, CGA, EGA, or VGA graphics card) and *graphics display* (the monitor) must be compatible with one another. The software also has to support the graphics standard, or else the additional capability is wasted. Virtually all MS-DOS applications support EGA, yet because VGA is newer, there are far fewer applications to take advantage of its high resolution and increased color. In other words, just because you purchase a PS/2 system with VGA capability does not mean that your software will utilize the VGA parameters.

"It's called chess. It's like a video game without a screen."

Authors' Comments:
It seems that almost as soon as one
graphics standard is announced, a new
one looms on the horizon. The
popularity of applications such as
computer aided design (CAD) and
desktop publishing has spurred demand
for ultrahigh resolution monitors. The
Amdek 1280, for example, provides a
resolution of 1280 × 800, a significant
improvement over VGA.

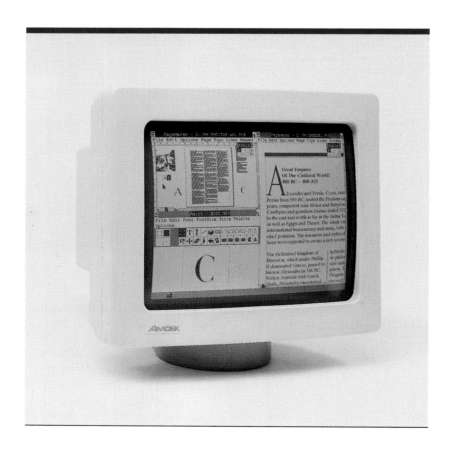

Hercules.

Year-end statistics for 1987:

Sales: $45 million (estimated)
CEO: Jim Harris
Headquarters: 2550 Ninth Street #210
Berkeley, CA 94710
(415) 540-6000

How often have you heard the adage, "Necessity is the mother of invention", which in the case of the **Hercules Corporation** led to the creation of an expansion board to integrate graphics capability into the IBM monochrome display. Kevin Jenkins and Van Suwannukul, the two partners who began the company, were pursuing vastly different interests in 1981 when IBM first announced the PC. Van Suwannukul was a Ph.D. student in engineering at Berkeley, and Jenkins was the publisher of an art magazine.

To write a dissertation in his native Thai language, Van Suwannukul developed his own word processor, but he was surprised to learn that IBM did not provide the high-resolution graphics necessary to process the complex letters of that alphabet. Undaunted, he developed the now ubiquitous **Hercules Graphics Card**, which incorporates graphics into the high-resolution monochrome display.

Shortly thereafter, Van Suwannukul was introduced to Kevin Jenkins by a mutual friend who knew that the two shared a common interest in computers. Jenkins convinced his new acquaintance to forget about the word processor, sure that the graphics board would be a commercial success. They set up shop in a garage in Hercules, California, and the rest, as they say, is history.

The two partners sold the first several hundred (of the more than 250,000 original Hercules cards that would eventually be produced) by personally going from store to store. The demand for their product grew exponentially when a then tiny company named Lotus announced support for the Hercules card, after which other major software developers followed suit. During the first several months of its existence it was the only product of its kind, enabling Hercules to emerge as the unquestioned market leader. Today, however, there are more than 100 vendors of low-, medium-, and high-resolution graphics cards, in both monochrome and color, a sure sign that "imitation is the sincerest form of flattery."

Hercules maintains its dominant position in a market expected to reach $750 million by 1990,

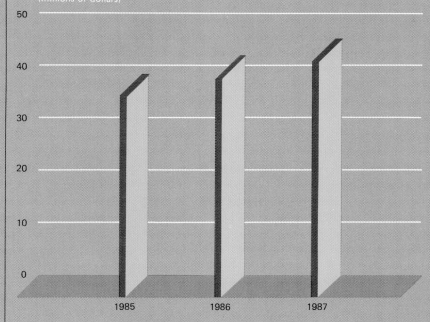

HERCULES COMPUTER TECHNOLOGY
ESTIMATED SALES INCOME
(millions of dollars)

through continued technical innovation. July 1986 marked the introduction of the Hercules Graphics Card Plus, featuring **Ramfont,** an innovative proprietary design combining the best of both text and graphics modes. RamFont enables users to create custom character sets of up to 3072 characters (as opposed to the 256 in the standard text mode) while operating significantly faster than ordinary graphic displays.

The InColor card (color version of the Hercules Graphics Card Plus) was announced in early 1987 and maintained full compatibility with all of Hercules's previous offerings. It displays 16 colors from a 64-color palette in 720×348 pixel resolution (numbers which match the original monochrome standard of the PC).

Most popular application programs support the various Hercules cards which in turn increases their own capability. Microsoft Word, for example, takes advantage of RamFont to nearly quadruple the speed of scrolling, while Lotus 1-2-3 uses it to almost double the on-screen display of data. WordPerfect, WordStar, Multimate, and other word processors take advantage of RamFont to display characters not available in standard text mode.

Approximately 1 million Hercules cards of all types have been sold through 1987, in more than 35 foreign countries.

Hercules links its advertising to application programs.

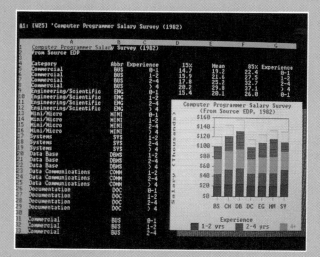

RamFont increases the amount of on-screen data displayed. (Count the number of rows in the spreadsheet.)

Summary

Information depicted in a chart or graph is more quickly understood than a written exposition of the same material. This basic premise, in conjunction with the rapid growth of computer technology, has accounted for the explosion in computer-generated graphics over the past several years. Indeed, what was only recently the province of a graphics department and professional artists is today within the reach of anyone possessing a personal computer.

The chapter began with a presentation of the basic types of business graphs: line graphs, bar graphs, pie charts, multiple bar graphs, and stacked bar graphs. It then moved to a Hands-On Exercise in which various graphs were created through use of a spreadsheet program. The chapter continued with several examples of improperly drawn and misleading graphs, and stressed the need for accurate data representation. The chapter also described the various IBM graphics standards currently in effect: CGA, EGA, and VGA.

Key Words and Concepts

A (B, C, D, E, and F) ranges	Multiple bar graph
Bar graph	Pie chart
Character mode	Pixels
Chart junk	Polaroid palette
Color Graphics Adapter (CGA)	Qualitative variable
Color monitor	Quantitative variable
Data ranges	RamFont
Enhanced Graphics Adapter (EGA)	Resolution
Graphics characters	Scale
Graphics mode	Stacked bar graph
Hercules Corporation	Text mode
Hercules Graphics Card	Title
Legends	Edward Tufte
Line graph	Video Graphics Array (VGA)
Monochrome monitor	X range

True/False

1. A pie chart is the graph type best suited to display time-related data.

2. A spreadsheet program typically has graphing capabilities.

3. Graphics are not possible with portable computers.

4. Pie charts and multiple bar charts can be used with the same data ranges.

5. Stacked bar charts and multiple bar charts can be used with the same data ranges.

6. A bar chart plots one quantitative and one qualitative variable.

7. A single File Save command will save the settings of every graph associated with a particular spreadsheet.

8. Screen images may be easily transferred to color slides and/or prints for effective presentations.

9. Increasing the number of pixels increases the resolution.

10. The original IBM monochrome monitor included graphics capability.

11. CGA, EGA, and VGA list the various IBM color graphic standards in order of increasing resolution.

12. VGA is likely to be supported by the majority of existing MS-DOS applications.

13. A monochrome monitor typically has a resolution of 720 × 350.

14. In general, the more colors and the more special effects, the better the graph.

Multiple Choice

1. Common business graphs include:
   (a) Bar graphs, pie charts, and line graphs
   (b) Solid, dotted, and color graphs
   (c) One-, two-, and three-dimensional graphs
   (d) Linear, algebraic, and geometric graphs

2. Which items are required to produce a graphic result of spreadsheet data?
   (a) The Polaroid Palette
   (b) A stand-alone (extra) graphics program
   (c) At least 640Kb
   (d) All the above
   (e) None of the above

3. Which sequence lists IBM graphic standards in the order they were introduced (and in order of increasing resolution)?
   (a) CGA, EGA, VGA
   (b) EGA, VGA, CGA
   (c) VGA, CGA, EGA
   (d) CGA, VGA, EGA

4. Business graphics are typically used in conjunction with a:
   (a) Word processing program
   (b) Spreadsheet program
   (c) Data management program
   (d) Communications program

5. Computer-generated business graphs:
   (a) Cannot portray accurate representations of spreadsheet data
   (b) Are not possible with PC-compatible computers
   (c) Can change from one graph type to another with minimum effort
   (d) Prevent the misrepresentation of data

6. In order to represent three different variables on the same graph, you would:
   (a) Define three ranges, designated as X, Y, and Z, respectively
   (b) Define three ranges, designated as A, B, and C, respectively
   (c) Define three ranges, designated as 1, 2, and 3, respectively
   (d) Conclude the situation is not possible

7. Multiple sets of data can be represented on all the following, *except*:
   (a) Line graphs
   (b) Pie charts
   (c) Multiple bar graphs
   (d) Stacked bar graphs

8. The original Hercules card made it possible to:
   (a) Display graphics on a monochrome monitor
   (b) Use a color monitor
   (c) Increase the resolution of text on a color monitor
   (d) All the above

9. Which of the following graph types best portrays proportions?
   (a) Pie charts
   (b) Line charts
   (c) Stacked bar charts
   (d) Multiple bar charts

10. Which of the following would best be used to display additive information about different quantitative variables?
    (a) Pie charts
    (b) Stacked bar charts
    (c) Bar charts
    (d) Line charts

11. The Polaroid Palette is used to:
    (a) Display multiple graphs at the same time
    (b) Plot 7-color graphs on paper
    (c) Allow monochrome monitors to display in color
    (d) Produce color slides and/or prints from screen displays

12. Information presented in a stacked bar graph can be easily converted to a:
    (a) Pie chart
    (b) Multiple bar graph
    (c) Single bar graph
    (d) Single line graph

13. Which of the following graph types is best suited for depicting time-related data?
    (a) Bar graph
    (b) Pie chart
    (c) Line graph
    (d) Stacked bar graph

14. Computer graphics is one of the fastest-growing application areas for all the following reasons *except*:
    (a) There is a shortage of artists to do business graphics
    (b) Graphics programs allow the rapid creation of graphs directly from spreadsheets
    (c) Businesspeople are finding graphs to be very effective in the presentation of data
    (d) Computer-generated graphs are easy to modify

15. A monochrome monitor that is divided into 25 rows and 80 columns:
    (a) Has a total of 2000 pixels
    (b) Displays images in graphics mode
    (c) Can under certain circumstances display color output
    (d) None of the above

Exercises

1. The graphs depicted in Figure 9.3 all convey essentially the same information, albeit in different formats. Is one kind of graph more effective than the other? Why or why not? In similar fashion, the graphs in Figure 9.4 also display the same information, again in different formats. Is there a preference here as well?

2. The value of a graph is aptly demonstrated by writing a verbal equivalent to a graphic analysis. Accordingly, write the corresponding written description of the information contained in Figure 9.4a. Can you better appreciate the effectiveness of the graphic presentation?

3. The spreadsheet of Figure 9.11 is the basis for the three graphs of Figure 9.12. Although the graphs may at first glance appear to be satisfactory, each reflects a fundamental error. Discuss the problems associated with each.

4. Redo the graphs for Ralph Cordell Sporting Goods so that salesperson (rather than quarter) is the independent variable. In other

words, construct graphs which correspond to those in Figures 9.3 and 9.4 as follows:

(a) A bar graph with the same data

(b) A pie chart with the same data

(c) A multiple bar graph (three sets of four graphs each) showing the quarterly totals for each salesperson

(d) A stacked bar graph corresponding to part *c*

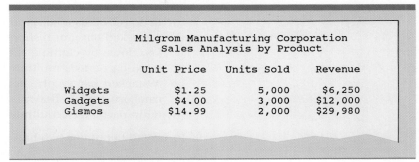

		Milgrom Manufacturing Corporation	
		Sales Analysis by Product	
	Unit Price	Units Sold	Revenue
Widgets	$1.25	5,000	$6,250
Gadgets	$4.00	3,000	$12,000
Gismos	$14.99	2,000	$29,980

FIGURE 9.11   Spreadsheet for exercise 3.

FIGURE 9.12   Graphs for exercise 3.

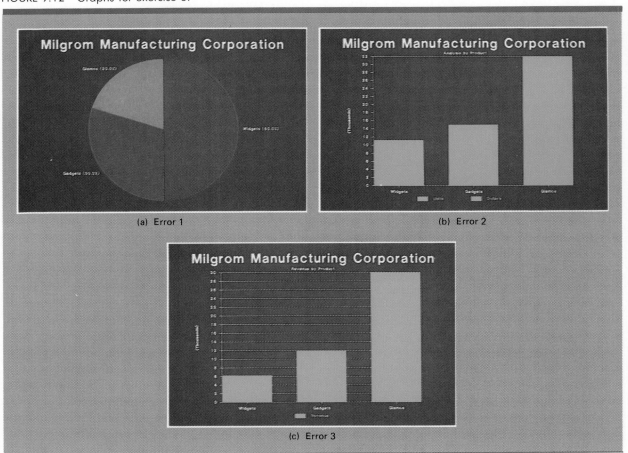

5. Figure 9.13 contains a spreadsheet with sales data for the chain of four Michael Moldof clothing boutiques. Use the spreadsheet to develop the following graphs:
   (a) A pie chart showing the percentage of total sales attributed to each store
   (b) Redo part *a* as a bar graph
   (c) A pie chart showing the percentage of total sales attributed to each type of clothing
   (d) Redo part *c* as a bar graph
   (e) A stacked bar graph showing total dollars for each store, broken down by clothing category
   (f) Redo part *e* as a multiple bar graph
   (g) A stacked bar graph showing total dollars for each clothing category, broken down by store
   (h) Redo part *g* as a multiple bar graph

6. Figure 9.14 contains two line graphs, both of which plot the *exact same data*. Figure 9.14a, however, makes it appear that inflation will soar during the next few years, while Figure 9.14b shows a far slower rate of increase. What is the difference between the two graphs? Which graph is more honest?

7. Develop a multiple bar graph to convey the following data concerning the distribution of personal computers in the United States for the years 1986 and 1991. Could this data be expressed equally well in a pair of pie charts?

> According to data supplied by International Data Corporation, IBM's market share (in terms of units shipped) is expected to remain fairly constant, going from 22 percent in 1986 to an estimated 24 percent in 1991. The share of PC compatibles will increase significantly, however, rising from 28 to 44 percent, as will the share of Motorola 68000–based PCs (such as Apple's Macintosh), which is estimated to rise from 8 to 22 percent. The growth in these areas comes at the expense of machines that fall in neither category (other machines) whose share will drop from 42 to 10 percent.

FIGURE 9.13
Michael Moldof spreadsheet
(for use in exercise 5).

Michael Moldof Men's Boutique - January Sales					
	Store 1	Store 2	Store 3	Store 4	Total
Pants	$25,000	$28,750	$21,500	$9,400	$84,650
Shirts	$43,000	$49,450	$36,900	$46,000	$175,350
Underwear	$18,000	$20,700	$15,500	$21,000	$75,200
Accessories	$7,000	$8,050	$8,000	$4,000	$27,050
Total	$93,000	$106,950	$81,900	$80,400	$362,250

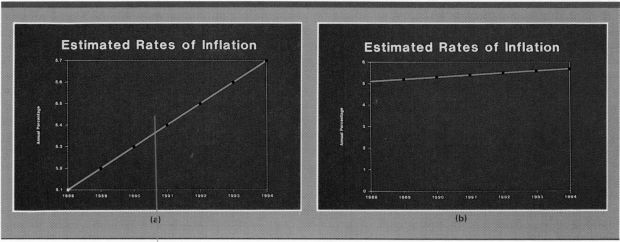

FIGURE 9.14 Graphs for exercise 6.

8. Develop the graph(s) you feel is most appropriate to convey the following data about the distribution of small system office equipment. (The data was obtained in response to the question, "What type of small systems equipment is most likely to be emphasized by your organization for its new office/MIS applications?")

> According to a recent survey reported in the November 15, 1987, issue of *Datamation*, the percentage of offices emphasizing minicomputers is decreasing substantially, from 44.4 percent in 1985, to 39.7 percent in 1986, to 26.8 percent in 1987. This compares to an increase in the emphasis of the PC from 52.3 percent, to 58.7 percent, to 61.5 percent over the same period. The corresponding numbers for independent workstations (including dedicated word processors) were reported as 3.3, 1.6, and 11.7 percent, respectively.

9. Find examples in the chapter which demonstrate (or violate) the following graphic principles from Tufte:
   (a) Graphic excellence is that which gives to the viewer the greatest number of ideas in the shortest time with the least ink in the smallest space.
   (b) The representation of numbers, as physically measured on the surface of the graphic itself, should be directly proportional to the numeric quantities represented.
   (c) Clear, detailed, and thorough labeling should be used to defeat graphic distortion and ambiguity.
   (d) In time-series displays of money, deflated and standardized units of monetary measurement are nearly always better than nominal units.
   (e) The number of information-carrying (variable) dimensions depicted should not exceed the number of dimensions in the data.

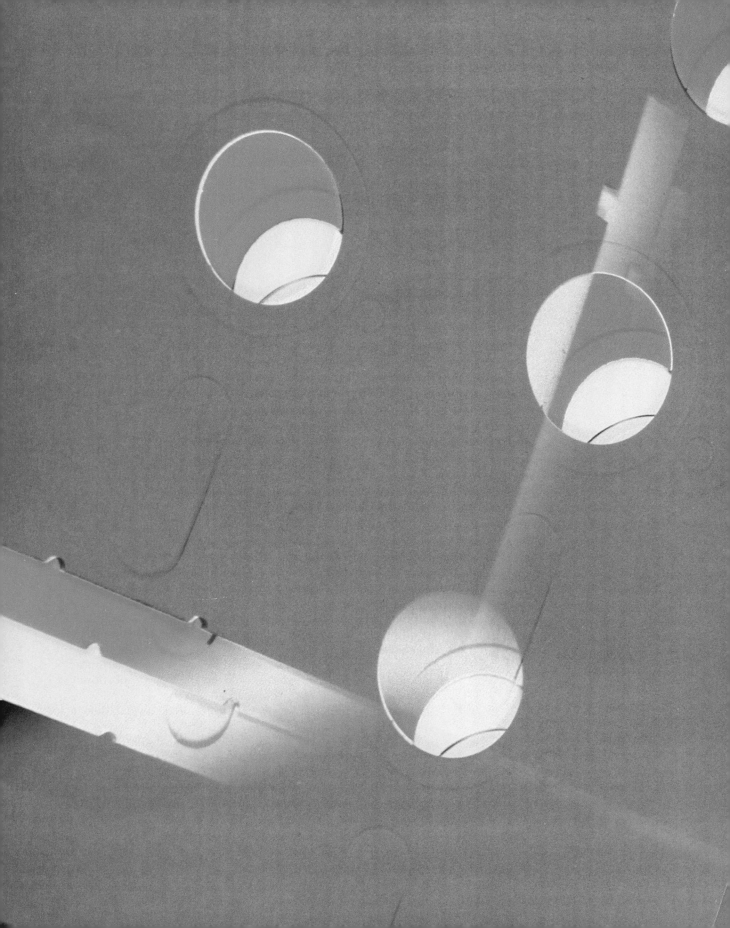

PART 4

DATA MANAGEMENT

CHAPTER 10

INTRODUCTION TO DATA MANAGEMENT

After reading this chapter, you should be able to:

1.   Define the terms field, record, and file; describe what is meant by the term file structure.

2.   Differentiate between character, numeric, date, and logical fields.

3.   Distinguish between an ascending and a descending sequence, and between a major and a minor key.

4.   Describe what is meant by file maintenance; list its three basic operations.

5.   Distinguish between data and information; describe the techniques used to convert data to information.

6.   Define GIGO; state its relevance to data management.

7.   Describe indexing; explain how the availability of indexes makes it possible to list a given file in multiple sequences.

8.   Describe what is meant by a relational database and the advantages of this type of file organization.

Overview

This chapter introduces the subject of data management. We begin with the presentation of a manual record keeping system, emphasizing that the principles under which it operates are similar to those of computerized data management. We define basic data management terms such as *field, record, file*, and *database*, then cover the *file maintenance* functions that enable new records to be *added* and existing records to be *modified* or *deleted*.

The major objective of any data management system is the analysis of data, a process discussed in the second half of the chapter. We stress the distinction between *data* and *information*, and show how one is converted to the other. We also include two Hands-On Exercises that apply the generic concepts to specific data management software, through use of the laboratory manuals that accompany the text.

The Corporate Profile focuses on Ashton-Tate Corporation, the developer of the dBASE series, the dominant data management software for the PC.

Vocabulary

All businesses maintain data of one kind or another. Companies store data for their employees; magazines and newspapers keep data on their subscribers; political candidates monitor voter lists, and so on. While each of these examples maintains different types of data, they all operate under the same principles of record keeping, regardless of whether they use manual or computer-based systems. Our study of data management is made easier, therefore, if we approach the subject from the viewpoint of a manual system, then extend those concepts to implementation on a computer.

Imagine, if you will, that you are the personnel director of a medium-sized company with offices in several cities, and that you *manually* maintain employee data for the company. Accordingly, you have recorded the specifics of every individual's employment (for example, their name, salary, work site, title, hire date, and so on) in a manila folder, and you have stored the entire set of folders in a file cabinet. You have also written the name of each employee on the label of his or her folder and have arranged the folders alphabetically in the filing cabinet.

The manual system just described illustrates the basics of data management terminology. The manila folders of the manual system are known as **records** in a data management system. The complete set of manila folders, that is, the collection of employee records, is called a **file**. Every manila folder contains the same categories of data for each employee such as his or her name and salary. In a computerized data management system, these categories are called **fields.** The order of fields within a record is the same for every record in the file, and is called the **file structure.**

The manila folders are arranged alphabetically in the file cabinet (according to the employee name on the label of each folder) to simplify the retrieval of any given folder. The records in a data management system are also kept in sequence, according to a particular field in every record (for example, social security number or last name), which is known as a **key.**

Figure 10.1 illustrates this terminology in the context of an employee file with 16 records. There are six fields in every record, and the arrangement of fields within a record (the file structure) is constant from record to record, that is, social security number, name, salary, hire date, title, and location. In the example, social security number has been chosen as the key field, so that the records are shown in sequence according to social security number.

Normal business operations will require you to make repeated trips to the filing cabinet, because the contents of the manila folders should always reflect the current state of the business. Thus whenever a new employee is hired, you will have to add a manila folder. In similar fashion, you will need to delete the folder of any employee who resigns from the company, as well as modify the folder of any employee who receives a raise, changes location, and so on. Changes of this nature (additions, deletions, and modifications) are known as **file maintenance operations,** and are necessary in both manual and computerized systems.

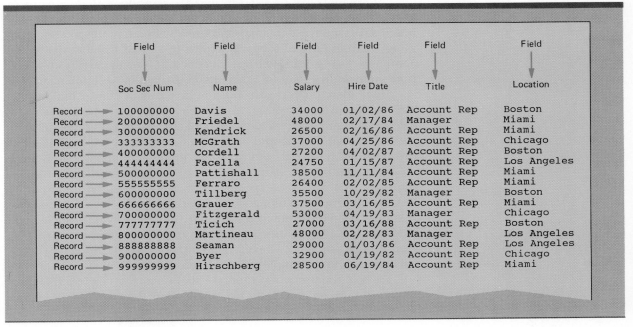

	Field	Field	Field	Field	Field	Field
	Soc Sec Num	Name	Salary	Hire Date	Title	Location
Record →	100000000	Davis	34000	01/02/86	Account Rep	Boston
Record →	200000000	Friedel	48000	02/17/84	Manager	Miami
Record →	300000000	Kendrick	26500	02/16/86	Account Rep	Miami
Record →	333333333	McGrath	37000	04/25/86	Account Rep	Chicago
Record →	400000000	Cordell	27200	04/02/87	Account Rep	Boston
Record →	444444444	Facella	24750	01/15/87	Account Rep	Los Angeles
Record →	500000000	Pattishall	38500	11/11/84	Account Rep	Miami
Record →	555555555	Ferraro	26400	02/02/85	Account Rep	Miami
Record →	600000000	Tillberg	35500	10/29/82	Manager	Boston
Record →	666666666	Grauer	37500	03/16/85	Account Rep	Miami
Record →	700000000	Fitzgerald	53000	04/19/83	Manager	Chicago
Record →	777777777	Ticich	27000	03/16/88	Account Rep	Boston
Record →	800000000	Martineau	48000	02/28/83	Manager	Los Angeles
Record →	888888888	Seaman	29000	01/03/86	Account Rep	Los Angeles
Record →	900000000	Byer	32900	01/19/82	Account Rep	Chicago
Record →	999999999	Hirschberg	28500	06/19/84	Account Rep	Miami

FIGURE 10.1
Data management terminology.

Data versus Information

Putting data into the computer is relatively easy. Retrieving it quickly in a meaningful form is quite another matter. As you shall see, a data management system not only lets you enter *data* into the computer, but it also makes possible the conversion of that data into *information*. It is important, therefore, that you understand the difference between these terms.

Data refers to a fact or facts about a person, place, or thing. In our example, it includes such items as an employee's name, title, and salary. **Information,** on the other hand, is data that has been rearranged into a form perceived as useful by the recipient, for example, a list of employees earning more than $35,000 or a total of all employee salaries. Put another way, data is the raw material and information is the finished product.

Information can be used to make a decision, raw data cannot. For example, in assessing the effects of a contemplated across-the-board salary increase, management needs to know the total payroll rather than individual salary amounts. In similar fashion, decisions about next year's hiring will be influenced, at least in part, by knowing how many individuals are currently employed in each job category.

How, then, do you go about the business of converting data to information? The answer is through a combination of *selection* and *calculation*, and then presentation of the results in a meaningful *sequence*. Figures 10.2 and 10.3 depict several reports which were produced from the data in Figure 10.1 to illustrate these techniques.

Selection implies that only some of the records in a file, that is, those records meeting a specified criterion, should be included in the resulting report. A report produced through the selection process is known as an **exception report,** three examples of which are shown in Figure 10.2. Figure 10.2*a* lists just the employees who are managers, Figure 10.2*b* lists those who earn more than $35,000, and Figure 10.2*c* lists those who are employed in Miami.

Each of the exception reports lists the employees in a different *sequence*, consistent with the overall nature of the report. Thus Figure

Name	Salary	Hire Date	Location
Fitzgerald	53000	04/19/83	Chicago
Friedel	48000	02/17/84	Miami
Martineau	48000	02/28/83	Los Angeles
Tillberg	35500	10/29/82	Boston

(a) Employees who are managers

Name	Salary	Hire Date	Title	Location
Fitzgerald	53000	04/19/83	Manager	Chicago
Friedel	48000	02/17/84	Manager	Miami
Martineau	48000	02/28/83	Manager	Los Angeles
Pattishall	38500	11/11/84	Account Rep	Miami
Grauer	37500	03/16/85	Account Rep	Miami
McGrath	37000	04/25/86	Account Rep	Chicago
Tillberg	35500	10/29/82	Manager	Boston

(b) Employees earning more than $35,000

Name	Salary	Hire Date	Title
Friedel	48000	02/17/84	Manager
Hirschberg	28500	06/19/84	Account Rep
Pattishall	38500	11/11/84	Account Rep
Ferraro	26400	02/02/85	Account Rep
Grauer	37500	03/16/85	Account Rep
Kendrick	26500	02/16/86	Account Rep

(c) Miami employees by seniority

FIGURE 10.2
Exception reports.

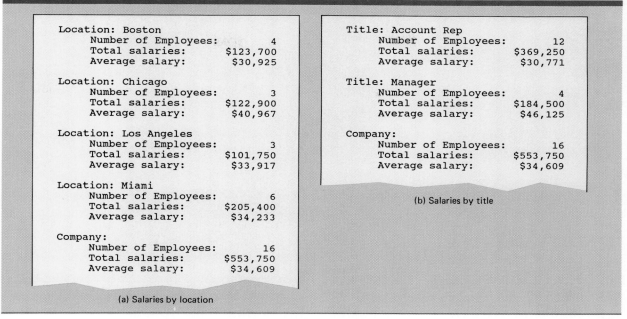

```
Location: Boston
        Number of Employees:        4
        Total salaries:         $123,700
        Average salary:          $30,925

Location: Chicago
        Number of Employees:        3
        Total salaries:         $122,900
        Average salary:          $40,967

Location: Los Angeles
        Number of Employees:        3
        Total salaries:         $101,750
        Average salary:          $33,917

Location: Miami
        Number of Employees:        6
        Total salaries:         $205,400
        Average salary:          $34,233

Company:
        Number of Employees:       16
        Total salaries:         $553,750
        Average salary:          $34,609
```

(a) Salaries by location

```
Title: Account Rep
        Number of Employees:       12
        Total salaries:         $369,250
        Average salary:          $30,771

Title: Manager
        Number of Employees:        4
        Total salaries:         $184,500
        Average salary:          $46,125

Company:
        Number of Employees:       16
        Total salaries:         $553,750
        Average salary:          $34,609
```

(b) Salaries by title

FIGURE 10.3
Summary reports.

10.2*a* lists employees alphabetically, Figures 10.2*b* shows them in decreasing order of salary, and Figure 10.2*c* displays them in chronological order according to the date on which they were hired. Sequencing is done independently from selection, and further enhances the utility of a particular report.

Calculation takes advantage of what the computer does best, that is, "number crunching," and is often used to produce **summary reports** such as those in Figure 10.3. Reports of this nature omit the salaries of individual employees (known as detail lines), showing summary totals instead, and are used by management to present an aggregate view of an organization. Figure 10.3*a* displays the salary totals for each location, as well as for the company as a whole. Figure 10.3*b* depicts similar information, but for employee titles rather than locations. Note, too, the sequences in which the results are presented: alphabetically by location in Figure 10.3*a* and alphabetically by title in Figure 10.3*b*

Sequencing can also be used independently, without selection or calculation, to produce information. Figure 10.4, for example, contains an employee census by location, listing employees alphabetically by last name within each location. Selection was not used, (all employees are listed) nor were any calculations performed, yet the report of Figure 10.4 is inherently more useful than the original data of Figure 10.1. The sequence in this example is based on two keys, location and name. Location is the more important, **major key;** name is the less important, **minor key.** (Other, equally correct terminology refers to location as the "primary key" and name as the "secondary key.")

Soc Sec Num	Name	Salary	Hire Date	Title	Location
400000000	Cordell	27200	04/02/87	Account Rep	Boston
100000000	Davis	34000	01/02/86	Account Rep	Boston
777777777	Ticich	27000	03/16/88	Account Rep	Boston
600000000	Tillberg	35500	10/29/82	Manager	Boston
900000000	Byer	32900	01/19/82	Account Rep	Chicago
700000000	Fitzgerald	53000	04/19/83	Manager	Chicago
333333333	McGrath	37000	04/25/86	Account Rep	Chicago
444444444	Facella	24750	01/15/87	Account Rep	Los Angeles
800000000	Martineau	48000	02/28/83	Manager	Los Angeles
888888888	Seaman	29000	01/03/86	Account Rep	Los Angeles
555555555	Ferraro	26400	02/02/85	Account Rep	Miami
200000000	Friedel	48000	02/17/84	Manager	Miami
666666666	Grauer	37500	03/16/85	Account Rep	Miami
999999999	Hirschberg	28500	06/19/84	Account Rep	Miami
300000000	Kendrick	26500	02/16/86	Account Rep	Miami
500000000	Pattishall	38500	11/11/84	Account Rep	Miami

FIGURE 10.4
Employees listed alphabetically within location.

The utility of the reports in Figure 10.2, 10.3, and 10.4 is dependent on the accuracy of the data as it is entered in the file; consequently, it is only as good as the data itself. It should be emphasized, therefore, that not even the most sophisticated data management system can compensate for inaccurate or incomplete data, a principle aptly stated by the acronym **GIGO** (**garbage in, garbage out**) (see the following box, entitled "GIGO").

GIGO

GIGO means if you give the computer incorrect information it will give back incorrect output—Garbage *In*, Garbage *Out*. When astronauts L. Gordon Cooper and Charles Conrad splashed down 103 miles off target, it was no fault of theirs or of their computer. The re-entry was computer guided. In determining the exact time for firing retro rockets, the programmer had assumed that the earth revolved exactly once every 24 hours, whereas in fact—as we know from having to squeeze in a whole extra day every fourth year—it makes slightly more than one revolution in that time. But if you're orbiting the earth many times and someone fires the retros exactly at 1:51 P.M., after figuring on a day of precisely 24 hours, you can wind up off target by a significant number of miles—which is just what happened to astronauts Cooper and Conrad. GIGO

Source: Dennie L. Van Tassel and Cynthia L. Van Tassel, *The Compleat Computer*, copyright Science Research Associates, 1983, 1976, Dennie Van Tassel. Reprinted by permission of the publisher.

File Design

Implicit in the process of data management is the creation of the file itself and with that the all-important determination of what data is needed. *You must first decide exactly what information the system is*

CONCEPT SUMMARY

Data Management Vocabulary

Field: A basic category of data

Record: One or more fields that describe a logical entity

File: A set of records

File structure: The arrangement of fields within a record; every record in a file contains the same fields in the same order

File maintenance   The process of entering, modifying, or deleting data

Information: Data which has been processed into a form perceived as useful by the recipient; accomplished through selection, sequencing, and calculation

GIGO: An acronym for "garbage in, garbage out," which says in essence that a data management system is only as good as the data on which it is based

Exception report: A report showing only those records meeting a specified selection criterion

Summary report: A report showing totals only, rather than data from individual records

---

to provide, then determine the fields the system requires to accomplish its objectives. You can then design a file structure which indicates to the data management system the fields in each record, their order, their length, and the type of data in each. These decisions are subjective in nature, and consequently there can be multiple solutions for a given system.

The decision(s) on data type, however, is less flexible than the other parameters. In other words, once you have decided to include a particular field, its data type follows automatically from the purpose of the field. Four distinct data types are commonly used, as follows:

- **Numeric fields** store values that can be used in a calculation such as an employee's salary. The contents of a numeric field are restricted to numbers, a decimal point, and a plus or a minus sign. No other characters (a comma, dollar sign, and so on) may be entered in a numeric field.

- **Character fields** store character or text data such as an employee's name, location, or title. Any character at all including letters, numbers, and special characters may be entered into a character field. Even fields containing all numbers, such as a social security number or zip code, should be described as character fields because no calculations are required for these fields.

- **Date fields** enable you to enter dates in formatted fashion (that is, with slashes), and further allow these dates to be used in date arithmetic (for example, calculating an individual's age from his or her birth date).

- **Logical fields** (which did not appear in Figure 10.1) are assigned to fields that can assume only one of two values, and are entered as true or false (or yes or no); for example, an employee is vested (or not) in a pension plan. Logical fields are preferable to one-position character fields because they are more efficient.

After you have defined the file structure, data is entered into the system on a record-by-record basis. Should you make a mistake during data entry, you can correct errors in one of two ways: by *editing* or by *browsing*. The editing mode of a data management system displays only one record at a time, but in a more descriptive way than does browsing, which shows several records at once. Either or both techniques can be used, depending on individual preference.

All data management systems provide the ability to delete records as well as add them. Most systems, however, distinguish between **physical deletion** and **logical deletion**: A logically deleted record is still in the file except that it is "hidden" from view, making it possible to restore that record at a later time; a physically deleted record has been permanently removed without possibility of recall.

We continue now with Hands-On Exercise 1 to implement the concepts of file maintenance.

HANDS-ON EXERCISE 1: FILE MAINTENANCE

OBJECTIVE: Define a file structure; add, modify, and delete records for the file in Figure 10.1.

Step 1: Load the Data Management Software
Boot the system, entering the proper date and time information. Place a program disk containing your data management system in drive A, and a formatted disk in drive B.

Execute the command to load your data management program.

Step 2: Create the File Structure
Invoke the command(s) to create a file structure as typified by Figure 10.5. Most systems prompt you for the characteristics of each field, one field at a time. As you can see, every field requires a field name (for example, SOCSECNUM), data type (for example, character or numeric), length, and (if numeric) number of decimal places.

Step 3: Verify that the File Structure Is Correct
Review the completed file structure to make sure that it has been entered correctly. Verify that the char-

Field	Field Name	Type	Width	Dec
1	SOCSECNUM	Character	9	
2	NAME	Character	16	
3	SALARY	Numeric	6	
4	HIREDATE	Date	8	
5	TITLE	Character	16	
6	LOCATION	Character	12	

FIGURE 10.5 The file structure.

acteristics of each field are what you intend them to be. Should you discover an error (for example, an omitted field or invalid data type) modify the file structure according to the commands available.

Step 4: Enter Data for the First Three Records
Execute the command to add (append) records to the data file. Most systems provide a screen similar to

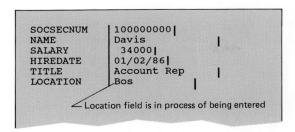

```
SOCSECNUM   │100000000│
NAME        │Davis
SALARY      │   34000│              │
HIREDATE    │01/02/86│
TITLE       │Account Rep           │
LOCATION    │Bos
                                │
```
└─ Location field is in process of being entered

FIGURE 10.6   Screen for data entry.

the one in Figure 10.6, which reflects the file structure. Note how the field names and lengths displayed in Figure 10.6 correspond to the field definitions of Figure 10.5

Enter the data shown in Figure 10.1 for the first record in the file (Davis). When you are satisfied that it is correct, press the appropriate key to move to the next (that is, the second) record. Enter data one field at a time for Friedel, as you did previously for Davis. Enter data for the third record as well (Kendrick), then save the file and exit from the data entry mode.

Step 5: Enter the Remaining Records

Retrieve the file from step 4 and check that it contains all three records. In this way you are sure that you can in fact save and retrieve a file, and can proceed to enter the remaining records with confidence.

Return to Figure 10.1 and enter data for the remaining 13 records. Check carefully that the data is entered correctly. Note, too, that should you need to make a correction, you have only to change the field(s) in error rather than retype the entire record.

Save the completed file.

Step 6: Deleting Records

If you have done the exercise correctly, there will be no need to delete any records. Chances are, however, that you may have inadvertently appended a blank record somewhere in the file, in which case it should be deleted. If this is not the case, experiment with the delete command (logical as well as physical) by positioning yourself at the third record in the file (Kendrick), and delete that record. (Be sure to reenter Kendrick's record so that the file is complete when you save it for the final time.)

Step 7: Exit the Data Management System

Save the completed file, exit the data management system, and return to DOS.

WHEN THE COMPUTER IS DOWN

The most frightening words in the English language are, "Our computer is down." You hear it more and more as you go about trying to conduct your business.

The other day I was at the airport attempting to buy a ticket to Washington and the attendant said, "I'm sorry, I can't sell you a ticket. Our computer is down."

"What do you mean your computer is down? Is it depressed?"

"No it can't be depressed, That's why it's down."

"So if your computer is down, just write me out a ticket."

"I can't write you out a ticket. The computer is the only one allowed to issue tickets on the plane." I looked down the counter and every passenger agent was just standing there drinking coffee and staring into a blank screen.

"What do all you people do?"

"We give the computer the information about your trip, and then it tells us whether you can fly with us or not."

"So when it goes down, you go down with it."

"That's very good sir, I haven't heard it put that way before."

"How long will the computer be down?" I wanted to know.

"I have no idea. Sometimes it's down for 10 minutes, sometimes for two hours. There is no way we can find out without asking the computer, and since it's down it won't answer us."

"Don't you have a backup computer, when the main computer goes down?"

"I doubt it. Do you know what one of these things costs?"

FOUR LITTLE WORDS THAT STRIKE FEAR IN THE HEART IN THE 1980'S.

"The computer is down."

"Let's forget the computer. What about your planes? They're still flying, aren't they?"

"I couldn't tell without asking the computer, and as I told you. . . ."

"I know, it's down. Maybe I could just go to the gate and ask the pilot if he's flying to Washington," I suggested.

"I wouldn't know what gate to send you to."

"I'll try them all," I said.

"Even if the pilot was going to Washington, he couldn't take you if you didn't have a ticket."

"Why don't I give you the money and you could give me a receipt and I could show that to the pilot as proof that I paid?"

"We wouldn't know what to charge you. The computer is the only one who keeps track of air fares because they change every hour."

"How about my credit card?"

"That's even worse. When our computer is down it can't notify the credit card computer to charge the fare to your account."

"Is there any other airline flying to Washington within the next few hours?"

"I wouldn't know," he said, pointing at the dark screen. "Only 'IT' knows."

"And at the moment 'IT' don't know nothing."

"'IT' knows it," he said defensively, "'IT' just can't tell me."

By this time there were quite a few people standing in lines. The word soon spread to other travelers that "the computer was down." Nobody knew exactly what this meant, but some people went white, some people started to cry, and still others kicked their luggage.

A man in a red blazer came out. "Please don't get excited. Wichita has been notified."

"What's Wichita got to do with it? I asked.

"That's where our main computer went down. But as soon as it gets over its glitch, it's going to buy everyone who missed his plane a free drink."

Source: Art Buchwald, "When the Computer Is Down," *Los Angeles Times*, 1984. Reprinted by permission of the author.

Authors' Comments:
As computerization continues to permeate every phase of our society, the importance of reliability increases. Art Buchwald has a unique gift for satire, and his piece on our dependence on the computer is a classic.

Indexing

The records in Figure 10.1 are stored in order by social security number, corresponding to the *physical* sequence in which they were entered in the hands-on exercise. The reports in Figures 10.2 through 10.4, however, display the records in different *logical* sequences, for example, by name, salary, and date of hire. The ability to store records in one sequence and list them in another (or several others) is made possible through **indexing**.

Consider, for example, Figure 10.7a, which contains five records from the original employee file, and assume that you have been asked to list these records alphabetically by last name. In other words, rather than displaying the records in the *physical* order in which they are stored (that is, records 1, 2, 3, 4, and 5), they will be retrieved and listed in the *logical* sequence shown in Figure 10.7b. Thus record 4 (Cordell) will appear first, then record 1 (Davis), then records 2, 3, and 5 (Friedel, Kendrick, and Pattishall, respectively). The logical sequence (that is, records 4, 1, 2, 3, and 5) is stored in a separate file known as **index**.

FIGURE 10.7   A file and its indexes.

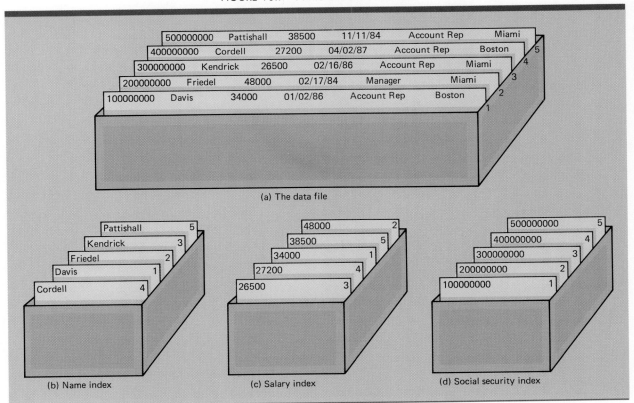

(a) The data file

(b) Name index

(c) Salary index

(d) Social security index

Several different indexes may be associated with the same file as implied by Figures 10.7*b*, 10.7*c*, and 10.7*d*, all of which reflect different logical sequences for the data of Figure 10.7*a*. Records can be listed alphabetically in accordance with the index of Figure 10.7*b*, they can be listed in increasing order of salary in conjunction with the salary index of Figure 10.7*c*, and they can be listed by social security number in accordance with the index of Figure 10.7*d*.

An index does not contain any data per se, but instead provides the sequence in which records are to be retrieved from the associated data file. The salary index in Figure 10.7*c*, for example, directs the data management system to begin with record 3 (containing a salary of 26500), then record 4 (with a salary 27200), then records 1, 5, and 2 (with salaries of 34000, 38500, and and 48000, respectively).

An index in data management is analogous to the index found in any book. Both indexes are arranged according to a *key* phrase or field, and both indicate where the corresponding information may be located, by providing the page number in the book or record number in the file. In addition, an index is stored separately from the data to which it refers; that is, it is kept in a separate section at the back of a book, or as a separate file in a data management system.

FIGURE 10.8
Adding records to an indexed file.

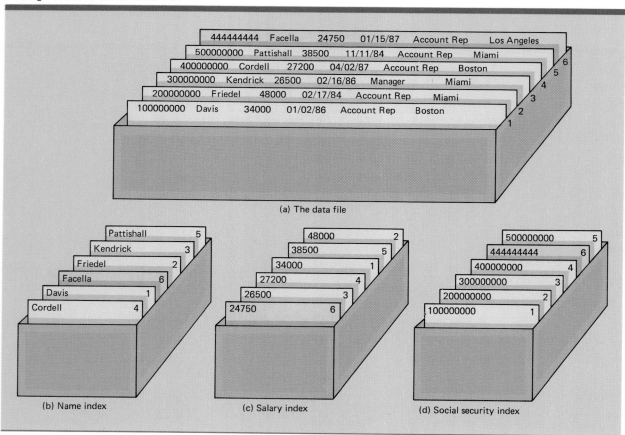

(a) The data file

(b) Name index

(c) Salary index

(d) Social security index

Adding Records

The contents of any file will change continually during business operations. New records will be added, existing records will be modified, while still other records will be deleted. Suffice it to say that the indexes associated with a file must change in parallel with the file itself.

Figure 10.8 continues the earlier example of a single data file with three indexes (name, salary, and social security number). A sixth record (Facella) has been appended to Figure 10.8*a*, which in turn produces changes in the indexes of Figures 10.8*b*, 10.8*c*, and 10.8*d*.

As you can see, Facella is *physically* the sixth (last) record in the data file (Figure 10.8*a*), yet it is *logically* the third record in the alphabetic index (Figure 10.8*b*), the first record in the salary index (Figure 10.8*c*), and the fifth record in the social security sequence (Figure 10.8*d*). In other words, the indexes have been updated to reflect the addition of the new record and *thus* maintain the various sequences *in which records are retrieved*.

The further addition (or deletion) of any record to the file of Figure 10.8*a* will require corresponding adjustments to the various indexes. Fortunately, however, a data management system provides the necessary commands to adjust these indexes automatically, and hence frees you from the need for manual changes.

Data Manipulation

We come now to Hands-On Exercise 2, in which you will be asked to create the reports of Figures 10.2, 10.3, and 10.4. In so doing, you will use several additional commands in your data management sys-

"FOR OPENERS, YOUR CREDIT IS LOUSY."

tem to index a file, select records, and perform calculations. As with all other hands-on exercises, it will be necessary to consult the optional laboratory manual for the precise commands in your particular data management system.

HANDS-ON EXERCISE 2: DATA ANALYSIS

OBJECTIVE: Use the employee file created in the first hands-on exercise to produce the reports of Figures 10.2, 10.3, and 10.4.

Step 1: Load the Data Management System
Load the data management system as you did in the previous hands-on exercise, with the program disk in drive A and the formatted data disk in drive B.

Step 2: Retrieve the Employee Data File
Invoke the command to establish drive B as the **default drive** (that is, the drive the system will use in all future file operations unless instructed otherwise). Execute the command to retrieve the employee file of Figure 10.1.

Step 3: Generate the Exception Reports
Each of the exception reports of Figure 10.2 lists employees in a different sequence, requiring that a different index be used prior to the generation of each report. Note, too, that some type of selection command is required for each report, so that only those records meeting the specified criterion are displayed. Execute the appropriate commands in your system to create Figure 10.2.

Step 4: Create the Summary Reports
The summary report in Figure 10.3a requires the number of employees in each location, the total salaries for all employees in each location, and the average salary of all employees in each location. The statistics for this report require a total of 12 commands (three commands for each of four locations). Execute the appropriate commands in your system to produce Figure 10.3.

Step 5: List Employees Alphabetically by Location
The report in Figure 10.4 uses an index derived from two fields, name and location, as employees are listed alphabetically within each location; that is, location is the major key and last name is the minor key. Execute the appropriate commands in your system to produce Figure 10.4.

Step 6: Experiment
The possibilities for additional reports based on the employee file of Figure 10.1 are virtually endless. We suggest, therefore, that you use the capabilities presented in this exercise to experiment with your system and that you create several additional reports of your own design.

Exit the data management system when you are finished.

COMMAND SUMMARY

Data Management

Supply the command(s) in your data management system to:

Create (modify) a file structure

Move from field to field within a record

Move from record to record within a file

Add (append) a new record

Modify (change) an existing record

Delete an existing record

List records in different sequences

Select records meeting a specified criterion

Change the default drive

Direct output to the printer

EYEBALLING A SOLUTION

What is the population of Denver, Colorado? An impossible question you say. On the other hand, if we asked it this way, "Is the population of Denver (a) 4,913,960; (b) 491, 396; or (c) 49,139?" you'd have a good chance of picking (b), the correct answer.

You would probably realize that 4 million is too many and that 49,000 is too few. In other words, you would be able to "eyeball" a solution and discard obviously incorrect answers without having a previous idea of the correct answer. In much the same way you can use your intuition to validate, to at least some degree, most computer-generated output.

Try your hand at the following questions, taken from *Games* magazine, to refine your numerical common sense:

What Is:

1. The population of Denver, Colorado?
   (a) 4,913,960
   (b) 491,396
   (c) 49,139

2. The total number of passenger cars sold in the U.S. in 1980?
   (a) 64,000,300
   (b) 6,400,030
   (c) 640,003

3. The estimated number of divorces granted in the U.S. in 1981?
   (a) 1,193,000
   (b) 119,300
   (c) 11,930

4. The elevation of Mt. Everest in feet?
   (a) 29,000
   (b) 2,900
   (c) 290,000

5. The total number of Viet Nam war veterans in the U.S.?
   (a) 9,061,000
   (b) 906,100
   (c) 90,610

6. The weight of a Boeing 747 jumbo jet in pounds
   (a) 77,500
   (b) 775,000
   (c) 7,750,000

7. The number of people in the world whose principal language is English (as of mid-1981)?
- (a) 39,100,000
- (b) 391,000,000
- (c) 3,910,000,000

8. The height of Chicago's Sears Tower in inches?
- (a) 17,448
- (b) 174,480
- (c) 1,744,800

Source: Material complied from various issues of *Games* magazine, Answers: (1) b; (2) b; (3) a; (4) a; (5) a; (6) b; (7) b; (8) a

Authors' Comments:
Garbarge In, Gospel Out, is another interpretation of the GIGO acronym, and refers to the fact that computer output is too often accepted without further consideration as to its validity. The adjacent piece shows how, with a little thought, you can apply common sense to computer generated output to be sure the results are at least reasonable.

What Is a Database?

The term **database** is one of the most misused terms associated with the study of computers. Strictly speaking, a database consists of *two or more related files*, and should *not* be used in conjunction with systems built around a single file. In other words, the material thus far has dealt with a single employee *file*, and *not* an employee *database*.

The necessity for a more sophisticated organization (that is, a database rather than a single file) can best be appreciated by continuing the personnel example we have used throughout. Assume, for example, that you are asked to maintain data about locations and job titles, in addition to the earlier employee data. You are now required to record the street address for each location, and whether the office at that location is in a building that is owned or rented by the company. In similar fashion, you are to keep track of the salary range and minimum education requirement associated with every employee title.

One (inefficient) way to store the additional title and location data is to append it to the individual employee records as shown in Figure 10.9. The difficulty with this approach is that of **redundancy**, because the identical data is stored in several records. Thus the Miami street address is found three times (in the records for Friedel, Kendrick, and Pattishall), while the "Account Rep" title data is repeated four times. A move by the Miami office to a different location would necessitate searching through the entire employee file to find *all* occurrences of the Miami data, so that the *identical* change could be made in every instance. This is, to say the least, a time-consuming and error-prone procedure.

A second problem occurs with the *addition of a new title or location* which, as Figure 10.9 now stands, cannot be created unless an employee already exists with these characteristics. This is counter to what happens in the real world where management first decides on the new title or location and then assigns the employee, rather than the other way around.

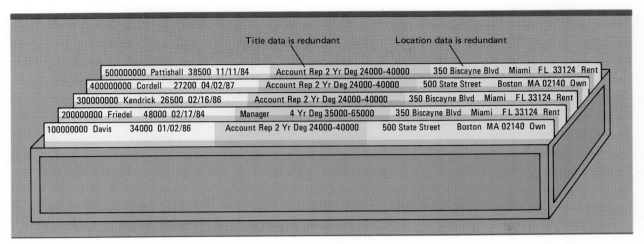

Title data is redundant   Location data is redundant

500000000 Pattishall 38500 11/11/84	Account Rep 2 Yr Deg 24000-40000	350 Biscayne Blvd Miami FL 33124 Rent
400000000 Cordell 27200 04/02/87	Account Rep 2 Yr Deg 24000-40000	500 State Street Boston MA 02140 Own
300000000 Kendrick 26500 02/16/86	Account Rep 2 Yr Deg 24000-40000	350 Biscayne Blvd Miami FL 33124 Rent
200000000 Friedel 48000 02/17/84	Manager 4 Yr Deg 35000-65000	350 Biscayne Blvd Miami FL 33124 Rent
100000000 Davis 34000 01/02/86	Account Rep 2 Yr Deg 24000-40000	500 State Street Boston MA 02140 Own

FIGURE 10.9
Conventional file structure.

The *deletion of a record* in Figure 10.9 poses a third problem of yet a different nature. What happens, for example, if Friedel were to leave? Friedel's record would be deleted from the employee file, which in turn would remove all data for the "Manager" title as well, because Friedel is the only employee with that title.

All three problems can be eliminated through a database organization consisting of three independent files, one for employees, one for titles, and one for locations, as shown in Figure 10.10. The

"Miss Elliot, it's inevitable every company will need a relational data base to compete. Can you please find out what a relational data base is?"

employee and title files are related to one another by a common title field which appears in both files. In similar fashion, the employee and location files are associated through a common location field. Although this approach may seem more complicated, it greatly simplifies all types of file maintenance operations.

Consider, for example, how easy it is to change the location of the Miami office. The modification would be made only once, that is, in the Miami record of the location file in Figure 10.10c. Nothing would be done to the employee records (Friedel, Kendrick, and Pattishall) of Figure 10.10a. In other words, the employee records do not contain location data per se, but only a pointer (relation) to the corresponding location record in Figure 10.10c. These pointers do *not* change; only the Miami data changes. Hence the change in data for the Miami office is made only once (in the location file), yet it will be automatically reflected for every employee in Miami.

The addition of a new title or location is done directly in the appropriate file (Figure 10.10b or 10.10c), without concern for whether an employee with this location or title actually exists. In similar fashion, deleting an employee from Figure 10.10a would not affect the titles or locations in the other files.

FIGURE 10.10
Relational database.

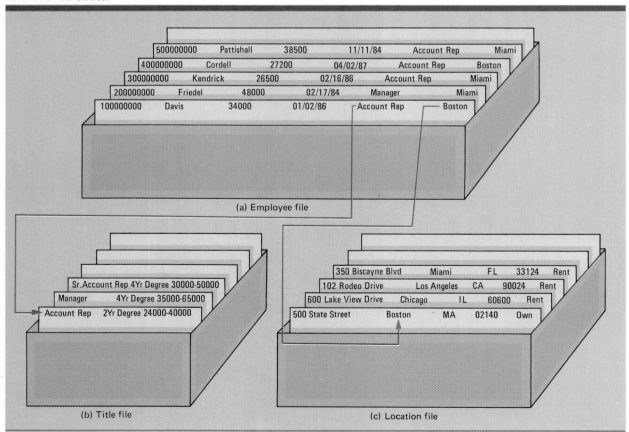

(a) Employee file

(b) Title file

(c) Location file

CORPORATE PROFILE:
ASHTON-TATE

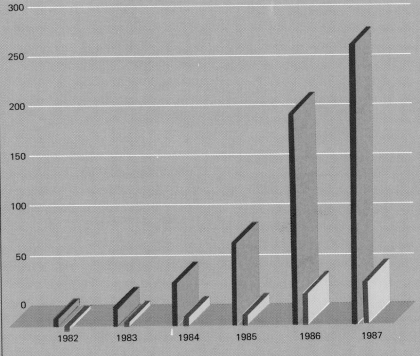

ASHTON·TATE

Year-end statistics for 1987:
Sales: $267 million
Profits: $43 million
CEO: Edward M. Esber, Jr.
Headquarters: 20101 Hamilton Avenue
Torrence, CA 90502
(213) 329-8000

A December 1984 article in *PC World* termed the success of Ashton-Tate's dBASE II, one of the great enigmas in software history. The article went on to say that the program was difficult to learn and plagued with bugs, and that it often required the services of a professional programmer. Yet for years it far outclassed the competition in power and flexibility, and the fact remains that dBASE II was extremely successful.

The program was developed initially in 1977 by Wayne Ratliff, a systems designer at the Jet Propulsion Laboratory (JPL) near Pasadena, California. Ratliff had been using a FORTRAN-oriented database manager written for mainframes to retrieve and analyze space-gathered information. Over a period of two years, and working on his own time, Ratliff converted the system to run on a microcomputer, improving it to the point where his version was more powerful than the original. He named his effort Vulcan (after the home planet of *Star Trek*'s Mr. Spock), and tried to market the program through ads in BYTE Magazine. Unsuccessful (less than 50 copies were sold), and failing to recoup even his advertising budget, he considered selling out for $3000.

Enter George Tate and Hal Lashlee, whose Discount Software Group had been founded in 1980 on an initial investment of $7500,

and which was then grossing $1 million a year. Tate and Lashlee had guessed correctly that a mail-order software company offering low prices, prompt delivery, and after-sale support would be highly profitable in the emerging microcomputer industry. Looking for additional products, they contacted Ratliff and negotiated

exclusive marketing rights to Vulcan in return for a generous royalty and a commitment to improve the program. Tate and Lashlee promptly changed the name to dBASE II, a flashier name that also implied an improvement over dBASE I (a product that never existed). Two years later they would change their company's

ASHTON-TATE
SALES AND NET INCOME
(millions of dollars)

345

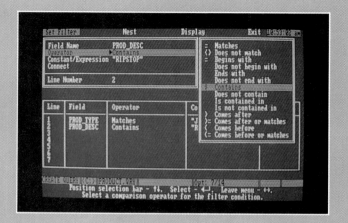

name to **Ashton-Tate,** because it had a better ring then "Tate-Lashlee" or "Lashlee-Tate." (Mr. or Ms. Ashton is a figment of the imagination.)

dBASE III followed in 1984, dBASE III Plus in 1986, and dBASE IV in 1988, with each new version more powerful than its predecessor. The dBASE series has been translated into at least nine languages (French, German, Italian, Spanish, Portuguese, Danish, Dutch, Swedish, and Norwegian) and has collectively sold in excess of two million copies.

Ashton-Tate itself has grown to a $250 million company which is currently number three in the industry (behind Microsoft and Lotus). More important, perhaps, it has managed to diversify to the extent that approximately 40 percent of its revenues are derived from other products. Foremost among these are MultiMate (a word processor), the Master Graphics series, and Framework II (an integrated package combining multiple applications into a single program with a common user interface).

Summary

The first of two chapters on data management described a manual system for employee record keeping, and maintained this as a running example throughout. We began with definitions of basic terms (field, record, and file), distinguished between data and information, and discussed how one is converted to the other. We also differentiated between exception and summary reporting, and showed how both types of reports provide useful information to a decision maker. Finally, we defined a database and described the advantages offered by this type of file organization.

The essence of the chapter, however, is in the two Hands-On Exercises, which directed you in the implementation of these concepts on the computer. The first exercise focused on data entry and the means by which records are added, modified, or deleted. The second exercise produced several reports through the processes of selection, calculation, and sequence.

Key Words and Concepts

Additions	Index
Ashton-Tate	Information
Calculation	Key
Character field	Logical deletion
Data	Logical field
Database	Major key
Date field	Minor key
dBASE	Numeric field
Default drive	Physical deletion
Deletions	Primary key
Editing	Record
Exception report	Redundancy
Field	Secondary key
File	Selection
File maintenance operations	Sequencing
File structure	Summary report
GIGO (garbage in, garbage out)	

True/False

1. Data and information are synonymous.

2. Exception reporting means that only a limited subset of records appears in a given report.

3. Summary reporting and exception reporting are synonymous.

4. Exception reports are due only under "exceptional" circumstances (for example, leap year).

5. A sophisticated data management system will produce correct reports from invalid data.

6. Records appearing in an exception report are obtained through the process of selection.

7. The order in which records appear in a given report is most likely immaterial.

8. It is preferable to store an individual's years of service rather than his or her hire date, since the latter requires a calculation to determine years of service.

9. Upper-level management is likely to be more interested in detail reports rather than in summary reports.

10. Upper-level management is likely to be more interested in raw data rather than in information.

11. Social security number and zip code must be defined as numeric fields in a file structure.

12. Most data management systems include the capability to perform date arithmetic.

13. All file management systems are database management systems.

14. The dBASE series is the only data management software available for the IBM PC.

15. It is possible for a given file to have several indexes associated with it.

16. A file contains one or more records.

17. Every record in a file has the same number of fields.

18. A file may not be indexed on a field which is not present in its file structure.

19. A file may not be indexed on more than one key.

20. Major key and primary key are synonymous.

Multiple Choice

1. A file structure describes:
   (a) The fields contained within a record
   (b) The order of appearance of every field within a record
   (c) The length and type of data in every field in a record
   (d) All the above

2. File maintenance consists of:
   (a) Any operation performed by the computer
   (b) Summary and exception reporting
   (c) Additions, modifications, and deletions
   (d) All the above

3. Data is converted to information through:
   (a) Additions, modifications, and deletions
   (b) Editing and browsing
   (c) Sequence, selection, and iteration
   (d) Sequence, selection, and calculation

4. Four valid data types are:
   (a) Alphanumeric, numeric, alphabetic, and special
   (b) Decimal, integer, real, and ordinal
   (c) Field, record, file, and database
   (d) Character, numeric, date, and logical

5. What is the appropriate hierarchy of terms (from smallest to largest)?
   (a) Character, file, record, field, database
   (b) Character, field, record, file, database
   (c) Database, file, record, field, character
   (d) Field, record, character, database, file

6. Categories of information within a record are known as:
   (a) Fields
   (b) Files
   (c) Parameters
   (d) Keys

7. A field that has a value of true or false is a:
   (a) Data field
   (b) Logical field
   (c) Physical field
   (d) Key field

8. A character field can contain:
   (a) Letters
   (b) Numbers
   (c) Special characters
   (d) All the above

9. An exception report:
   (a) Is produced only under exceptional circumstances
   (b) Is likely to print every record in the file
   (c) Is produced through the process of calculation
   (d) Is produced through the process of selection

10. Records listed according to an index are said to be:
    (a) In logical, but not necessarily physical, order
    (b) In physical, but not necessarily logical, order

    (c) In both logical and physical order

    (d) In neither logical nor physical order

11. Data which has been processed into a form perceived as useful by the recipient is known as:

    (a) Artificial intelligence

    (b) Information

    (c) Processed data

    (d) A relational database

12. A record which has been logically, but not physically, deleted:

    (a) Must contain at least one logical field in its file structure

    (b) Must contain all logical fields in its file structure

    (c) Can be recalled at a future time

    (d) Is not possible

13. GIGO stands for:

    (a) Gee, I goofed, ok

    (b) Grand illusions, go on

    (c) Garbage in, garbage out

    (d) Global indexing, global order

14. The listing of records from high to low according to a given key is called a:

    (a) Primary sequence

    (b) Secondary sequence

    (c) Descending sequence

    (d) Ascending sequence

15. Which company developed and currently markets the dBASE series?

    (a) IBM

    (b) Microsoft

    (c) Ashton-Tate

    (d) MicroPro

Name	Location	Depart-ment
Milgrom	New York	1000
Samuel	Boston	2000
Isaac	Boston	2000
Chandler	Chicago	2000
Lavor	Los Angeles	1000
Elsinor	Chicago	1000
Tater	New York	2000
Craig	New York	2000
Borow	Boston	2000
Kenneth	Boston	2000
Renaldi	Boston	1000
Gulfman	Chicago	1000

Exercises

1. Rearrange the data in the adjacent table according to the specified sequences:

    (a) Major field: department (descending); minor field: name

    (b) Primary field: department; secondary field: location; tertiary field: name (all are ascending)

2. Every data management system has predetermined limits built into it. With respect to the program available to you, what is:

    (a) The maximum number of fields per record?

    (b) The maximum number of records per file?

    (c) The maximum number of characters per record?

3. Careful attention must be given to designing a file structure, or else the resulting system will not perform as desired. Consider the following:

   (a) An individual's age may be calculated from his or her birth date, which in turn can be stored as a field within a record. An alternate technique would be to store age directly in the record and thereby avoid the calculation. Which field, that is, age or birth date, would you use? Why?

   (b) Social security number is typically chosen as a record key in lieu of a person's name. What attribute does the social security number possess which makes it the superior choice?

   (c) An individual's name is normally divided into two (or three) fields corresponding to the last name and first name (and middle initial). Why is this done (that is, what would be wrong with using a single field which consisted of the first name, middle initial, and last name, in that order)?

4. Figure 10.11 contains an additional field, old salary, which is to be appended to the original file of Figure 10.1. Use the data management system available to you to do the following:

   (a) Modify the original file structure to include the old salary as a six-position numeric field.

   (b) Modify all the records in the file to include the new data.

   (c) Prepare a report, listing all employees in alphabetic order, which shows each employee's name, present salary, previous salary, and percent salary increase.

   (d) Generate an exception report listing employees with salary increases of 10 percent or more (with employees listed in descending order of salary increase).

   (e) Create a second exception report listing employees with salary increases of 5 percent or less (with employees listed in ascending order of salary increase).

Soc Sec Num	Name	Old Salary
100000000	Davis	32500
200000000	Friedel	44000
300000000	Kendrick	24000
333333333	McGrath	30000
400000000	Cordell	25000
444444444	Facella	23000
500000000	Pattishall	36500
555555555	Ferraro	25000
600000000	Tillberg	34500
666666666	Grauer	33000
700000000	Fitzgerald	51000
800000000	Martineau	41200
777777777	Ticich	24000
888888888	Seaman	24500
900000000	Byer	31000
999999999	Hirschberg	26500

FIGURE 10.11
Data for exercise 4.

5. Use your data management system to produce the following exception reports, based on Figure 10.1. Note, however, that some of the reports are *not* possible, in which case you should indicate why they can't be developed.
   (a) Employees earning less than $30,000 (in ascending order of salary)
   (b) Employees whose last salary increase was at least 10 percent
   (c) Employees with at least five years of service (with the most senior employee appearing first)
   (d) Employees older than 30 (with the youngest employee listed first)
   (e) Account reps earning more than $35,000 (in alphabetic order)
   (f) An alphabetic list of the employees in Miami and Chicago
   (g) Employees in Boston who were hired before 1/1/84.

6. Figure 10.12 contains statistical data for 30 (arbitrarily chosen) countries.
   (a) List the 5 largest countries (in terms of area).
   (b) List the 10 largest countries (in terms of population).
   (c) List the 5 countries with the highest population density.

FIGURE 10.12   Statistical data for 30 countries.

Country	Year Admtd to UN	Population (1984)	Area (sq miles)
Algeria	1962	21300000	918497
Argentina	1945	29627000	1065189
Bangladesh	1974	96539000	55598
Brazil	1945	131305000	3286470
Burma	1948	35480000	261288
Canada	1945	25142000	3851809
China	1945	1022054000	3691521
Congo	1960	1694000	132046
Egypt	1945	45809000	385201
Finland	1955	4850000	130119
France	1945	54872000	210040
Germany, East	1973	16724000	41825
Germany, West	1973	61493000	96011
Ghana	1957	13367000	92098
Hungary	1955	10691000	35919
India	1945	730572000	1269420
Israel	1949	3958000	8219
Japan	1945	119896000	147470
Kenya	1963	18580000	224081
Mexico	1945	75702000	761604
Portugal	1955	10008000	36390
Spain	1955	38234000	195988
Sweden	1946	8331000	179896
Switzerland	1945	6500000	15941
Togo	1960	2838000	21853
USSR	1945	272500000	8649490
United Kingdom	1945	56023000	94222
United States	1945	234249000	3615123
Vietnam	1977	57612000	127207
Zaire	1960	31250000	905063

7. As the chapter implied, the need for data management is almost endless. Accordingly, describe at least two physical systems which are potential applications for a data management system. For each application,
   (a) List several fields required for the file structure. For each field listed, suggest a suitable length and data type.
   (b) Specify at least three reports which could be produced by your system.

8. Research the Fortune 500 (or a similar list) to obtain the gross revenue and net income, for the present and previous year, for the 20 largest corporations. Use your data management system to create a file containing these data, then prepare the following reports:
   (a) An alphabetical list of all 20 companies, showing every field for every company.
   (b) A list of the 10 companies with the highest revenue in the current year, in ascending order of revenue. List the company name and revenue for the current year.
   (c) A list of all companies with a net income of at least $1 billion, in descending order of income. List the company name and net income for the current year.
   (d) A list of those companies with an increase in net income over the previous year of at least 10 percent, in ascending order of the percentage increase. List the company name, net income for both years, and rate of increase in net income.

CHAPTER 11

PROGRAMMING FOR DATA MANAGEMENT

After reading this chapter, you should be able to:

1. Define structured programming; explain how the concept of one entry point and one exit point applies to each of the basic building blocks.

2. Distinguish between flowcharts and pseudocode; describe two conventions to follow in writing pseudocode.

3. Discuss the requirements of a menu-driven program; develop the logic for such a program according to the discipline of structured programming.

4. Implement a menu-driven program on the computer.

Overview

Although we were pleased with the reports from Chapter 10 and said nothing to the contrary, the methodology in that chapter was in reality quite primitive. Repeatedly having to enter commands one at a time via the keyboard is a time-consuming and error-prone procedure. It would be far better if the commands could be stored permanently into a file, with the entire file recalled as necessary. In other words, we need to develop a set of commands, or *program*, capable of manipulating data and creating the reports.

The major objective of this chapter, therefore, is to develop a *menu-driven* program capable of producing reports similar to those in Chapter 10. You will see that a primary characteristic of this program is its ease of use by a non-computer-literate individual. A second characteristic is its inherent flexibility, enabling the program to generate a variety of reports based entirely on the user's request(s) for information.

The chapter begins with the requirements of the menu-driven program. We develop the logic necessary to write the program and in so doing, we discuss both *structured programming* and *pseudocode*. This material may seem a bit removed from data management (and it is), but we believe it is essential for you to have some knowledge of proper programming procedure. The Hands-On Exercise at the end of the chapter returns to the menu-driven program and neatly links all the material.

> To understand computers is to know about programming. . . . Everyone should write at least a few programs—not to make a career of it, but just to know what it's about. . . . If you've never written a program, it's like never having driven a car. You may get the general idea, but you may have little clear sense of the options, dangers, constraints, possibilities, difficulties, limitations, and complications.
>
> **Ted Nelson**
> *Computer Lib/Dream Machines*, Microsoft Press, 1987

The Corporate Profile features Borland International, currently the fifth largest independent software company and a vendor of several programming languages.

A Menu-Driven Program

Figure 11.1 contains data for the United States which will be the basis of our example. All 50 states are listed, with the area, population, and year of admission to the Union shown for each. Let us assume that this data has been entered into a file, and consider but a few of the several hundred reports that could be produced:

1. The 5 smallest states (in terms of area)

2. The 10 largest states (in terms of population)

3. The first 13 states admitted to the Union

4. The 12 states with the highest population density

Reports of this nature require that the data in Figure 11.1 be manipulated to produce four basic report types (area, population, year of admission, and density), and further that each report can list any number of states in either ascending or descending sequence. Imagine, however, the tedious nature of producing such reports using the methodology of the previous chapter, which requires you to enter a series of (dBASE) commands for each report (assuming, of course, that you know the necessary command syntax). Wouldn't it be simpler if you could execute a program that asks in English which report(s) you want?

Figure 11.2 demonstrates exactly that capability. Figure 11.2*a*, *b*, and *c* shows how specifics might be obtained on the type of report (area, population, date of admission, or density), the order in which to list the states (ascending or descending), and the number of states to include. The program collects all three responses and then produces the resulting report as shown in Figure 11.2*d*. Consider how much easier such a *menu-driven program* is to use than the method from the previous chapter.

Implicit in Figure 11.2 is a **data validation** capability, which enables the program to reject invalid responses. In other words, the program is expecting a response of A, B, C, or D to indicate the type of report, and it must be smart enough to reject any invalid response (that is, a response other than A, B, C, or D). In similar fashion, the program should validate the desired sequence (either ascending or descending) and the number of states to include in the report (from 1 to 50). Only after valid responses have been obtained can the report be generated.

FIGURE 11.1
Data for the menu-driven program.

State	Entered Union	Population (1980)	Area (sq miles)
Alabama	1819	3,893,888	51,609
Alaska	1959	401,851	589,757
Arizona	1912	2,718,215	113,909
Arkansas	1836	2,286,435	53,104
California	1850	23,667,902	158,693
Colorado	1876	2,889,964	104,247
Connecticut	1788	3,107,576	5,009
Delaware	1787	594,338	2,057
Florida	1845	9,746,324	58,560
Georgia	1788	5,463,105	58,876
Hawaii	1959	964,691	6,450
Idaho	1890	943,935	83,557
Illinois	1818	11,426,518	56,400
Indiana	1816	5,490,224	36,291
Iowa	1846	2,913,808	56,290
Kansas	1861	2,363,679	82,264
Kentucky	1792	3,660,777	40,395
Louisiana	1812	4,205,900	48,523
Maine	1820	1,124,660	33,215
Maryland	1788	4,216,975	10,577
Massachusetts	1788	5,737,037	8,257
Michigan	1837	9,262,078	58,216
Minnesota	1858	4,075,970	84,068
Mississippi	1817	2,520,638	47,716
Missouri	1821	4,916,686	69,686
Montana	1889	786,690	147,138
Nebraska	1867	1,569,825	77,227
Nevada	1864	800,493	110,540
New Hampshire	1788	920,610	9,304
New Jersey	1787	7,364,823	7,836
New Mexico	1912	1,302,894	121,666
New York	1788	17,558,072	49,576
North Carolina	1789	5,881,766	52,586
North Dakota	1889	652,717	70,665
Ohio	1803	10,797,630	41,222
Oklahoma	1907	3,025,290	69,919
Oregon	1859	2,633,105	96,981
Pennsylvania	1787	11,863,895	45,333
Rhode Island	1790	947,154	1,214
South Carolina	1788	3,121,820	31,055
South Dakota	1889	690,768	77,047
Tennessee	1796	4,591,120	42,244
Texas	1845	14,229,191	267,338
Utah	1896	1,461,037	84,916
Vermont	1791	511,456	9,609
Virginia	1788	5,346,818	40,817
Washington	1889	4,132,156	68,192
West Virginia	1863	1,949,644	24,181
Wisconsin	1848	4,705,767	56,154
Wyoming	1890	469,557	97,914

It is important also for you to recognize the *generality* implied by the input screens of Figure 11.2*a*, *b*, and *c*. You could just as easily have asked for a report listing the states in ascending order of population, descending order of area, and so on. Hence the menu-driven program is not only easy to use but flexible as well in terms of its ability to generate a large number of reports.

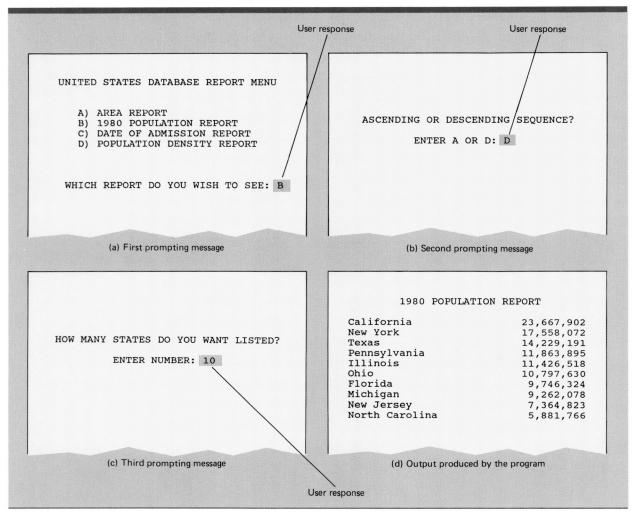

FIGURE 11.2 Output of the menu-driven program.

Thus Figure 11.2 effectively establishes the requirements of a menu-driven program, namely, that it must:

1. Accomplish a variety of tasks, for example, produce four different report types (area, population, density, and year of admission). Further, it should be able to list a variable number of states for each report, in either ascending or descending sequence.

2. Validate user inputs, for example, ensure that the user has asked for an appropriate report, sequence, and number of states

3. Be easy to use and not require any knowledge of programming languages or data management systems.

The remainder of the chapter is aimed at developing a program with these capabilities. First, however, comes a discussion of programming methodology, a discipline known as *structured programming*.

MAP-MASTER

Map-Master, by Ashton-Tate, is a sophisticated graphics program that combines data analysis with mapping capabilities. This figure, for example, shows the 10 most populous states on the map and produces a much more vivid picture than the report of Figure 11.2d. Map-Master includes the United States map (boundary file) as well statistical data for every state. Many additional maps (boundary files) are also available, for example, Manhattan zip codes or counties in the United States.

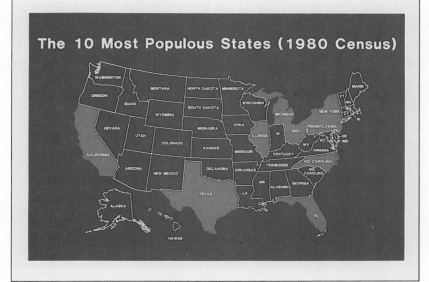

Structured Programming

Much time and effort has been devoted to finding the best way to write computer programs. The outcome of that research has given rise to a discipline known as **structured programming**, which applies to any language, be it dBASE, BASIC, Pascal, COBOL, and so on. The discipline seeks to produce programs that are logically correct and that can be easily read and maintained by someone other than the original author.

A structured program is one which uses only three types of elementary building blocks to solve a problem. These are *sequence*, *selection*, and *iteration*, and they are depicted in Figure 11.3. (A fourth building block, *case*, is sometimes included in an extended definition and is also shown.) The fact that these structures are sufficient to express any desired logic was first postulated in a now-classic paper by Bohm and Jacopini.[1]

In Figure 11.3, each building block (or structure) is drawn as a **flowchart,** or pictorial representation of programming logic. Flowcharts use special symbols to communicate information. A rectangle indicates a processing statement, a diamond indicates a decision, and a small circle connects portions of the flowchart. All of the elementary building blocks have one key feature in common, namely, a **single entry point** and a **single exit point.**

The **sequence structure** in Figure 11.3a implies that program statements are executed sequentially, that is, one after another. In other words, block A is executed first, and then block B.

The **selection structure** of Figure 11.3b shows a conditional statement, which provides a choice between two actions. If the condition is true, block A is executed; if it is false, block B is executed. The

FIGURE 11.3
The building blocks of structured programming. (*Note:* The case statement is an extension to the fundamental definition.)

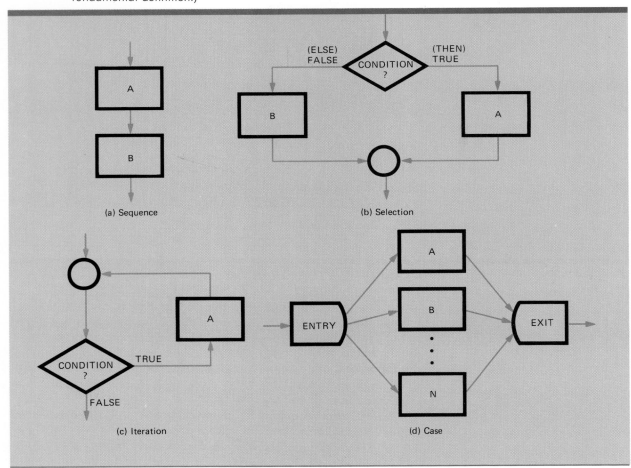

(a) Sequence

(b) Selection

(c) Iteration

(d) Case

[1]Bohm and Jacopini, "Flow Diagrams, Turing Machines and Languages with Only Two Formation Rules," *Communications of the ACM*, May 1966.

" AM I FAMILIAR WITH FORTRAN? I MAY BE—
WHAT'S HIS FIRST NAME?"

condition is a single entry point to the structure and both paths meet in a single exit point.

The **iteration** (or looping) **structure** in Figure 11.3c calls for the repeated execution of one or more statements. A condition is tested and, if it is true, block A is executed. If, however, the condition is false, control passes to the next sequential statement after the iteration structure. Again, there is exactly one entry point and one exit point from the structure.

The **case** (or multibranch) **structure** in Figure 11.3d is an extension of selection, as it presents a choice between *more* than two statements, only one of which can be true. A condition is evaluated and a branch to one of several paths is taken, depending on the value of the condition. As with the other fundamental building blocks, there is one entry point and one exit point.

Sufficiency of the Basic Structures

The theory of structured programming says simply that an appropriate combination of building blocks may be derived to solve any problem. Combinations are built through a series of substitutions in which a complete elementary structure (sequence, selection, iteration, or case) replaces either block A or block B anywhere it appears in Figure 11.3.

The point is illustrated in Figure 11.4, which is essentially a selection structure. However, instead of specifying a single statement for the true and false branches (as was done in Figure 11.3b), an elementary building block is used. Thus if condition 1 is true, an iteration structure is entered; if it is false, a sequence structure is

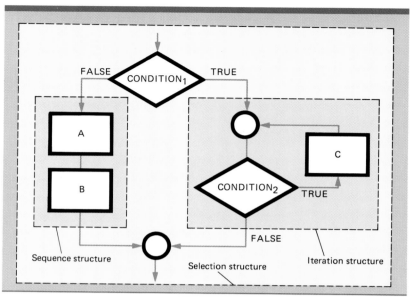

FIGURE 11.4 Sufficiency of the basic structures.

executed instead. Both the iteration and sequence structures meet at a single point, which in turn becomes the exit point for the initial selection structure.

ADA LOVELACE: THE FIRST COMPUTER PROGRAMMER

Today's computer programmers are clever indeed, but few could hold a light emitting diode to Augusta Ada Lovelace in terms of creativity. She saw the art as well as the science in programming, and she wrote eloquently about it. She was also an opium addict and a compulsive gambler.

As the only legitimate offspring of Lord Byron, Ada would have been a footnote to history even if she hadn't been a mathematical prodigy. Though Byron later wrote poignantly about his daughter, he left the family when she was a month old and she never saw him again. Biographers tend to be rather hard on Ada's mother, blaming her for many of her daughter's ills. A vain and overbearing Victorian figure, she considered a healthy daily dose of laudanum-laced "tonic" the perfect cure for Ada's nonconforming behavior.

Ada was well tutored by those around her (British logician Augustus De Morgan was a close family friend), but she hungered for more knowledge than they could provide. She was actively seeking a mentor when Charles Babbage came to the house to demonstrate his Difference Engine for her mother's friends. Then and there, Ada resolved to help him realize his grandest dream: the long planned but never constructed Analytical Engine. Present on that historic evening was Mrs. De Morgan, who wrote in her memoirs:

While the rest of the party gazed at this beautiful instrument with the same sort of expression and feeling that some savages are said to have shown on first seeing a looking glass or hearing a gun, Miss Byron, young as she was, understood its workings and saw the great beauty of the invention.

If Babbage was the force behind the hardware of the first computer, Ada was the creator of its software. As a mathematician, she saw that the Analytical Engine's possibilities extended far beyond its original purpose of calculating mathematical and navigational tables. When Babbage returned from a speaking tour on the Continent, Ada translated the extensive notes taken by one Count Manabrea in Italy and composed an addendum nearly three times as long as the original text. Her published notes are particularly poignant to programmers, who can see how truly ahead of her time she was. Prof. B. H. Newman wrote in the *Mathematical Gazette* that her observations "show her to have fully understood the principles of a programmed computer a century before its time." Among her programming innovations for a machine that would never be realized in her lifetime were the subroutine (a set of reusable instructions), looping (running a useful set of instructions over and over), and the conditional jump (branching to specified instructions if a particular condition is satisfied).

Ada also noted that machines might someday be built with capabilities far beyond the technology of her day and speculated about whether such machines could ever achieve intelligence. Her argument against artificial intelligence in "Observations on the Analytical Engine" was immortalized almost a hundred years later by Alan M. Turing, who referred to this line of thinking as "Lady Lovelace's Objection." It is an objection often heard in debates about machine intelligence. "The Analytical Engine," Ada wrote, "has no pretensions whatever to originate anything. It can do whatever we know how to order it to perform."

It is not known how or when Ada became involved in her clandestine and disastrous gambling ventures. Unquestionably, she was an accomplice in more than one of Babbage's schemes to raise money for his Analytical Engine. Together they considered the profitability of building a tic-tac-toe machine and even a mechanical chess player. And it was their attempt to develop a mathematically infallible system for betting on the ponies that brought Ada to the sorry pass of twice pawning her husband's family jewels to pay off blackmailing bookies.

Ada died when she was only thirty-six years old, but she is present today in her father's poetry and as the namesake of our government's newest computer language. In the late 1970s the Pentagon selected for its own use, a specially constructed "superlanguage," known only as the "green language" (three competitors were assigned the names "red," "blue" and "yellow") until it was officially named after Ada Lovelace. Ada is now a registered trademark of the United States Department of Defense.

Source: Digital Deli, © 1984 by Steve Ditlea. Workman Publishing, New York. Reprinted with permission of the publisher.

Authors' Comments:
Our book is dedicated to the incredible foresight and pioneering genius of Charles Babbage and Ada Lovelace. Although Ada herself recognized that a machine with capabilities far beyond the technology of her day would someday be built, even she would be utterly dumbfounded by the power of today's computers.

Pseudocode

Although small flowcharts of the type drawn in Figures 11.3 and 11.4 are useful, their popularity has dropped significantly in recent years. The decline may be attributed to many factors. Flowcharts are time-consuming to draw, difficult to follow and maintain, and stretch over several pages for realistic problems. More important, perhaps, is the fact that flowcharts were rarely used for their intended purpose,

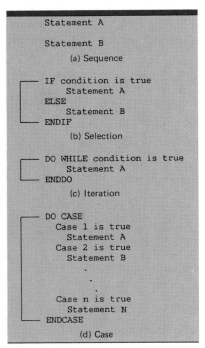

```
        Statement A

        Statement B

            (a) Sequence

 ┌─  IF condition is true
 │         Statement A
 │      ELSE
 │         Statement B
 └─  ENDIF

            (b) Selection

 ┌─  DO WHILE condition is true
 │         Statement A
 └─  ENDDO

            (c) Iteration

 ┌─  DO CASE
 │      Case 1 is true
 │          Statement A
 │      Case 2 is true
 │          Statement B
 │             .

 │             .

 │             .
 │      Case n is true
 │          Statement N
 └─  ENDCASE

            (d) Case
```

FIGURE 11.5
Structured programming
in pseudocode.

which was as a development aid in writing programs. In theory, a programmer was supposed to draw a flowchart *before* writing a program; in practice, however, it was often drawn *after* the fact.

Programmers did, however, willingly and often write notes to themselves prior to coding a program. The formalization of this technique of "neat notes to oneself" came to be known as **pseudocode**. The technique has a distinct block structure that is conducive to structured programming.

An example of pseudocode, corresponding to the flowcharts of Figure 11.3, is shown in Figure 11.5. As you can see, pseudocode uses English-like statements similar to computer instructions to describe logic. It is not, however, bound by formal syntactical rules as is a programming language.

Nevertheless, there are certain conventions that make pseudocode easier to read. For example, we like to indent as shown in Figure 11.5, and to use vertical lines to indicate the extent of the selection, iteration, and case structures. We also use ENDIF, ENDDO, and END-CASE to further highlight the range of the elementary building blocks.

With practice, pseudocode can be written quickly and easily. The only real limitation is a restriction to the elementary building blocks (sequence, selection, iteration, and case) that in turn causes pseudocode to flow easily from the top down. Good pseudocode should be sufficiently precise to serve as a real aid in writing a program, and sufficiently informal to be intelligible to nonprogrammers.

Developing the Menu-Driven Program

Thus far we have presented the elementary building blocks of structured programming and discussed how that logic may be expressed in pseudocode. In this section we apply those concepts to develop the logic for the menu-driven program. Accordingly, pause for a moment to review the program requirements that were postulated earlier, realizing that the completed program will consist of two major sections, *user input* and *report generation*. The user input portion accepts and validates input parameters, after which the report generation segment creates a report based on the inputs provided.

User Input

The **user input** portion of the program is developed first and, in very general terms, contains statements to:

1. Obtain the report type (area, population, date of admission, or density)

2. Obtain the report sequence (ascending or descending)

3. Obtain the number of states (from 1 to 50) to include in the report

There is, of course, considerable detail implied in each of these steps. In step 1, for example, the user is asked to input a response indicating the type of report desired, and enters either A, B, C, or D (corresponding to the area, population, admission, and density reports, respectively). The program then checks the validity of that response, and if invalid, asks the user to again enter the type of report desired. The new response is also validated, and the process is repeated until a proper answer is obtained. Similar statements are then executed to obtain responses for the report sequence and number of states. Perhaps you can already see how combinations of the basic building blocks will implement this procedure.

The logic for steps 1, 2, and 3 is expressed in the pseudocode in Figure 11.6. The figure contains parallel instructions for each of three responses; that is, report type (area, population, year of admission, or density), report sequence (ascending or descending), and number of states (1 to 50).

Consider first the logic to obtain the report type shown in Figure 11.6a. A loop is established in which the user is asked continually for a response, until a valid response is obtained. The execution of that loop is controlled by a **switch**, or temporary storage location

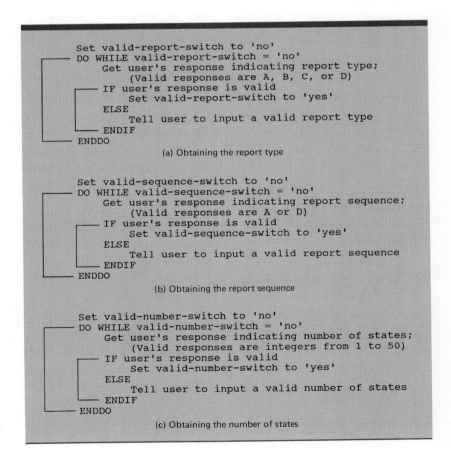

```
Set valid-report-switch to 'no'
DO WHILE valid-report-switch = 'no'
     Get user's response indicating report type;
          (Valid responses are A, B, C, or D)
     IF user's response is valid
          Set valid-report-switch to 'yes'
     ELSE
          Tell user to input a valid report type
     ENDIF
ENDDO
```
(a) Obtaining the report type

```
Set valid-sequence-switch to 'no'
DO WHILE valid-sequence-switch = 'no'
     Get user's response indicating report sequence;
          (Valid responses are A or D)
     IF user's response is valid
          Set valid-sequence-switch to 'yes'
     ELSE
          Tell user to input a valid report sequence
     ENDIF
ENDDO
```
(b) Obtaining the report sequence

```
Set valid-number-switch to 'no'
DO WHILE valid-number-switch = 'no'
     Get user's response indicating number of states;
          (Valid responses are integers from 1 to 50)
     IF user's response is valid
          Set valid-number-switch to 'yes'
     ELSE
          Tell user to input a valid number of states
     ENDIF
ENDDO
```
(c) Obtaining the number of states

FIGURE 11.6
Pseudocode for data entry portion.

which can assume one of two values (yes or no). The switch is set initially to "no" (that is, a valid response has not yet been obtained) and the loop is entered. A response is obtained, and if the response is valid the switch is set to "yes," and the loop is terminated.

If on the other hand an invalid response is supplied, the switch remains set to "no" and the loop is repeated; that is, you are again asked for a response, and that response is checked. The process continues an indeterminate number of times until finally a valid response is obtained, at which point the loop is terminated and the program continues with the next block of statements. Figure 11.6*b* and 11.6*c* contains similar logic to obtain the remaining parameters.

Report Generation

The **report generation** portion of the completed program also consists of three segments, each of which is based on a particular user input. Thus in order to create a particular report, the program will

1. Write an appropriate heading line, then open the file in corresponding logical sequence (by area, population, admission, or density) based on the report type requested

2. Process records in ascending or descending order according to the sequence requested by the user

3. Write the correct number of detail lines according to the number of states requested

The logic for the three steps of the report generation segment is expressed in the pseudocode of Figure 11.7. The case structure of Figure 11.7*a* evaluates the report type, and based on this value, it writes an appropriate heading and opens the file in proper logical sequence. (Implicit in these statements is the assumption that four distinct indexes, on area, population, year of admission, and density, have been previously created so that individual states can be accessed in the appropriate logical order.)

The selection structure in Figure 11.7*b* determines whether states are to be listed in ascending or descending sequence. They are listed in ascending sequence by starting at the beginning of the appropriate index and moving forward. Conversely, states are listed in descending sequence by starting at the end of the index and moving backward. (Implicit in this logic is the assumption that the indexes were established in ascending order; for example, the index on area begins with Rhode Island and continues to Alaska.) Thus if you requested states to be listed in descending order (the largest state first), the program begins at the end of the index (that is, Alaska) and moves backward.

The iteration structure in Figure 11.7*c* produces the actual report, writing one detail line for each pass through the loop. The loop itself is controlled by a **variable** (or temporary storage location) that serves as a **counter.** The counter is initialized to zero *outside* the

FIGURE 11.7
Pseudocode for report generation
portion.

```
DO CASE
    CASE 1: Write report heading for Area report
            Open file and use area index
    CASE 2: Write report heading for Population report
            Open file and use population index
    CASE 3: Write report heading for Admission report
            Open file and use admission index
    CASE 4: Write report heading for Density report
            Open file and use density index
END CASE
```
(a) Write the appropriate heading

```
IF report sequence is ascending
    Start with first state in index (and move forward)
ELSE
    Start with last state in index (and move backward)
ENDIF
```
(b) Open the file in correct logical sequence

```
Set counter to zero
DO WHILE counter < number of states
    DO CASE
        CASE 1: Write detail line for Area report
        CASE 2: Write detail line for Population report
        CASE 3: Write detail line for Admission report
        CASE 4: Write detail line for Density report
    END CASE

    IF report sequence is ascending
        Go to next state
    ELSE
        Go to previous state
    ENDIF

    Increment counter by 1
ENDDO
```
(c) Write the proper number of detail lines

loop and incremented by one *inside* the loop, until it eventually equals the number of states requested. When this occurs (and the proper number of detail lines have been written), the loop is terminated and the program ends.

Since each report type requires a different type of detail line (for example, the area report contains the state name and area, the population report contains the state name and population), the case structure within the loop assures that the appropriate detail line is written. Also, observe the presence of an IF statement to determine whether to move forward in the file to the next state (ascending sequence) or backward in the file (descending sequence) to the previous state.

> Design long, program short. Don't be in a rush to write code. Think about the problem from every angle, figure out in detail how different strategies affect each other. When you're sure the design is right, code it. Impatience is the enemy. Design is productive work.
>
> **Ted Nelson**
> *Computer Lib/Dream Machines*, Microsoft Press, 1987

Implementing the Menu-Driven Program

You should be satisfied that the pseudocode in Figures 11.6 and 11.7 will accomplish the objectives of the menu-driven program. As previously indicated, however, pseudocode depicts logic only and does not correspond to any programming language. Hence in order for the program to actually run on the computer, it has to be converted to the programming language (command mode) associated with your data management system.

The hands-on exercise which follows takes you through the procedure for implementing the program on the computer. Although the exercise is structured generically, it is (of course) necessary to learn the syntax of a particular language. Thus you need the optional laboratory manual which accompanies this text in order to complete the exercise.

HANDS-ON EXERCISE 1: MENU-DRIVEN PROGRAMS

OBJECTIVE: To demonstrate the command mode of a data management system through the development of a menu-driven program.

Step 1: Convert the Pseudocode to a Programming Language
Select a programming language, for example, dBASE, then convert the pseudocode of Figures 11.6 and 11.7 into that language. Enter the program you have just written into the computer, using either a word processor or the editor in your data management system.

Step 2: Load the Data Management System and Supporting Files
Load the data management system in drive A and the disk containing your program in drive B. (The disk in drive B should already contain the United States data file as well as the indexes needed to list states in alternate sequences.)

Step 3: Execute the Menu-Driven Program
Everything is set. Your program is on the disk in drive B, together with the necessary data and index files. Invoke the command to execute the program, and the prompting messages (shown earlier in Figure 11.2) should appear on the screen. Enter appropriate responses, relax, and enjoy the results.

Step 4: Debugging
The menu-driven program is long and essentially unfamiliar, and thus offers many opportunities for you to make mistakes. When errors occur (and they will), the data management system will try its best to help you in the form of diagnostic messages.

In all likelihood you will omit apostrophes, spell words incorrectly, or make other similar errors that violate the syntax of your data management system. dBASE, for example, responds by indicating a **syntax error** and asks you for a course of action. Assume, for illustration, that you omitted the closing apostrophe in a print message; that is, you *erroneously* entered:

Ending quote missing

```
@7,28 SAY 'A) AREA REPORT □
```

as one of the first lines in your program. (The entry beginning, "@7,28 SAY," is a dBASE statement to position the first character of the entry enclosed in quotes in row 7, column 28 of the monitor.) The following messages would appear when you tried to execute the program:

```
Unterminated string.
```
Nature of the error

```
@7,28 SAY 'A) AREA REPORT
called from   B:menu.prg
```
File name containing the program being executed

```
Cancel, Suspend, or Ignore
```
dBASE request for corrective action

dBASE is asking whether you want to cancel execution completely, suspend it temporarily (so that you can fix the problem immediately), or ignore the error and attempt to continue execution. You should correct the error, then try to reexecute the program.

Step 5: Generate the Required Reports

Once your program has been "debugged" you can use it to generate as many reports as you like. You might, for example, create the following reports first discussed at the beginning of the chapter, namely:

1. The 5 smallest states (in terms of area)
2. The 10 largest states (in terms of population)
3. The first 13 states admitted to the Union
4. The 12 states with the highest population density

From DARTEK Computer, Fall/Winter 1987 catalog.

There it is! The man in your program that caused all of those problems!

Rear Admiral Grace Hopper, the oldest officer in active duty in the Navy, retired in 1986 at the age of 79.

THE FIRST "BUG"

The first recorded bug was an unlucky moth that was crushed to death in one of the relays of the electromechanical Mark II computer, bringing the machine's operation to a screeching halt. The cause of the failure was discovered by Grace Hopper, who promptly taped the moth to her logbook, noting, "First actual case of bug being found."

The word **bug** has come to mean a mistake in a computer program; **debugging** refers to the process of correcting program errors.

The glossary of Ashton-Tate's *Advanced Programmer's Guide* for dBASE III Plus contains the following definitions:

Endless loop—See Loop, endless

Loop, endless—See Endless loop

We don't know whether these entries were deliberate or not, but the point is made either way. Endless loops are an especially frustrating bug, and are often caused by failing to properly reset a switch.

CORPORATE PROFILE:
BORLAND INTERNATIONAL

Year-end statistics for 1987:
Sales: $56 million (estimated)
Net income: $11 million (estimated)
CEO: Philippe Kahn
Headquarters: 4858 Scotts Valley Drive
Scotts Valley, CA 95066
(408) 438-8400

Borland International was started without the benefit of venture capital, because no one would invest in a then unknown Frenchman, who preferred Hawaiian shirts and pastel pants to the conventional business suit. His philosophy was also very different from that of the typical software company. Programs were priced under $100, shipped without copy protection, sold exclusively through the mail, and accompanied by an unconditional 60-day money-back guarantee.

Today **Borland International** is the fifth largest independent software publisher (behind Microsoft, Lotus, Ashton-Tate, and WordPerfect), with annual sales in excess of $50 million. The company is extremely profitable, and with the exception of Microsoft, it has the most diversified product line in the industry.

Philippe Kahn arrived in the United States in 1982 with a wife, two daughters, and $2000. Unable to obtain work because he lacked the necessary green card, he began his own company and showed an uncanny knack for finding the right product and bringing it to market. His first offering was neither a word processor nor a spreadsheet, but a programming language, Turbo Pascal. The response to a single advertisement in *BYTE Magazine* for the $49.95 program was so overwhelming that sales reached $150,000 the first month. Turbo Pascal has since sold over 500,000 copies, and has become the official language for the scholastic programming contests sponsored by The Association for Computing Machinery (ACM).

BORLAND INTERNATIONAL
ESTIMATED SALES AND PROFITS
(millions of dollars)

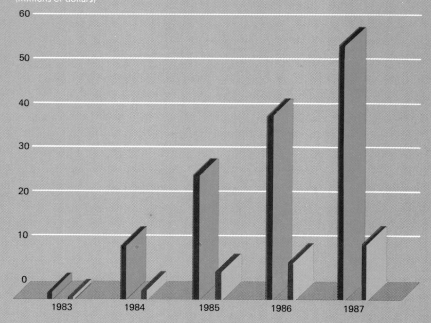

SideKick came next and was even more sensational. It was aimed at a broader audience than was Turbo Pascal and popularized the concept of memory-resident software. SideKick was the first program that allowed you to interrupt what you were doing and access common desktop accessories. Thus you could stop in the middle of any application to use a calculator, check your calendar, dial a phone number, or write notes on a memo pad, then drop the accessory and return to where you were previously. SideKick eventually sold over a million copies, and still accounts for approximately 20 percent of Borland's gross revenue.

Other innovative products followed. Turbo Lightning was the first RAM-resident spelling checker and thesaurus. Turbo Prolog offered graphics and other interactive capabilities, and sold well to corporations working in the area of artificial intelligence and expert systems. Seeking yet additional diversification, Borland acquired Analytica Corporation, primarily for the rights to Reflex, a powerful, easy-to-use data management program. Originally priced at $495, Reflex had sold only 1200 copies in nine months. Kahn, however, promptly slashed the price to $99.95 and sold 100,000 copies in the next nine months!

In 1987 Borland spent $2 million to launch Quattro, a powerful spreadsheet program aimed at the corporate market and positioned to compete directly with Lotus. Quattro offers full 1-2-3 compatibility, is not copy protected, and at $195 is less than half the $495 price of its competitor. Best of all, it includes many features not found in Lotus version 2.01: a macro-recorder, three-dimensional spreadsheets, and an intelligent recalculation feature that recomputes only the cells affected by changes.

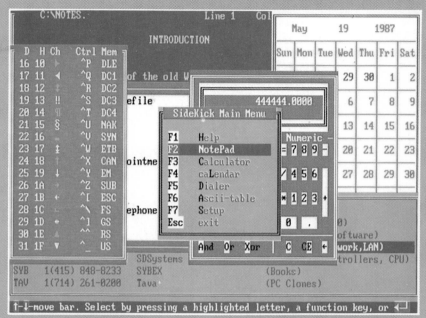

SideKick lets you stack all of its utilities, one on top of the next. You can move forward and backward through them with the Esc key and an appropriate Alt key combination. You can also return to a previously displayed SideKick application without exiting subsequent programs.

Quattro: The Natural Evolution

1970
HAND-HELD CALCULATOR

1979
VISICALC®

1982
LOTUS 1-2-3®

1987
QUATTRO™

The introduction of Quattro was accompanied by a $2 million advertising campaign.

Turbo Pascal premiered in November 1983, and became the first of many successes for Philippe Kahn. Today it is the official language for scholastic programming contests sponsored by the Association for Computing Machinery (ACM).

Summary

Implementation of a data management application generally requires programming skills. An unsophisticated individual may of course *use* a data management system, but a programmer is often needed to *develop* the application. It seems reasonable, therefore, to study programming theory in conjunction with data management, and both topics were presented.

The chapter revolved around a menu-driven program capable of generating multiple reports about the United States. The requirements of the program were for ease of use, flexibility, and data validation. The chapter also covered the theory of structured programming, and discussed how logic for the menu-driven program can be expressed in pseudocode. All these concepts were tied together in the concluding hands-on exercise, which implemented the menu-driven program on the computer.

Key Words and Concepts

Bohm and Jacopini
Borland International
Bug
Case structure
Counter
Data validation
Debugging
Flowchart
Iteration structure
Philippe Kahn
Ada Lovelace
Menu-driven program

Pseudocode
Report generation
Selection structure
Sequence structure
SideKick
Single entry point
Single exit point
Structured programming
Switch
Syntax error
User input
Variable

True/False

1. A structured program is guaranteed not to contain logical errors.

2. Structured programming can be implemented in a variety of languages.

3. The logic of any program can be expressed as a combination of only three types of logic structures.

4. The "one entry/one exit" philosophy is essential to structured programming.

5. The case structure is one of the three basic logic structures.

6. A flowchart is probably the most popular way of communicating program logic.

7. Pseudocode has precise syntactical rules.

8. A person using a menu-driven program needs a detailed knowledge of computer programming.

9. Pseudocode makes no provision for an unconditional branch.

10. Pseudocode is restricted to the basic building blocks of structured programming.

11. Pseudocode is usually more succinct than the equivalent flowchart.

Multiple Choice

1. The woman recognized as history's first programmer was:
   (a) Ada Lovelace
   (b) Grace Hopper
   (c) Susan B. Sperry
   (d) Anna Burroughs

2. Which of the following is an extension to the original definition of structured programming?
   (a) Sequence
   (b) Selection
   (c) Iteration
   (d) Case

3. What do the building blocks of structured programming have in common?
   (a) They each have a condition statement
   (b) They each comprise a complete program
   (c) They each have one entry point and one exit point
   (d) All the above

4. Which of the following expresses a multibranch situation?
   (a) Sequence
   (b) Selection
   (c) Iteration
   (d) Case

5. Which of the following is associated with the iteration structure?
   (a) DO BEFORE
   (b) DO AFTER
   (c) DO WHILE
   (d) DO NEXT

6. Why is the use of traditional flowcharts declining?
   (a) They are incapable of representing the building blocks of structured programming
   (b) They are often drawn after a program is developed, and hence are not used for their intended purpose
   (c) Programmers are not familiar with their use
   (d) All the above

7. Which of the following is true of pseudocode?
   (a) It can be input directly into a compiler
   (b) It may be characterized as "neat notes to oneself"
   (c) It embodies a formal syntax just like a true computer language
   (d) It may not be used with a language other than dBASE

8. Which of the following is the most convenient way to represent a user's selection from one of five possible menu choices?
   (a) Sequence
   (b) Selection
   (c) Iteration
   (d) Case

9. Which of the following is a requirement of the menu-driven program developed in the text?
   (a) Ease of use
   (b) The ability to validate user input
   (c) Flexibility
   (d) All the above

10. The term "bug," referring to a programming error, was first used by:
    (a) Ada Lovelace
    (b) Grace Hopper
    (c) Susan Sperry
    (d) Anna Burroughs

11. The program known as "SideKick":
    (a) Was developed as a desktop organizer
    (b) Is a product of Borland International
    (c) Is an example of a memory resident program
    (d) All the above

12. According to its most basic definition, a structured program:
    (a) Consists of only three types of logic structures
    (b) Is a program without GOTO statements

(c) Is limited to 500 statements

(d) Is a program written initially without mistakes

13. A loop in a program may be controlled by:
(a) A switch
(b) A counter
(c) Both (a) and (b)
(d) Neither (a) nor (b)

14. An IF/ELSE statement in a programming language implements which building block of structured programming?
(a) Sequence
(b) Selection
(c) Iteration
(d) Case

15. Which of the following does *not* evaluate a condition?
(a) Sequence
(b) Selection
(c) Iteration
(d) Case

Exercises

1. The following problem pertains neither to a data management system nor to a common business application. It is a problem with which you are totally unfamiliar, and consequently one for which you have no preexisting bias toward a solution. Nevertheless, it serves to demonstrate the applicability of both structured programming and pseudocode to virtually any physical setting.

    A robot is sitting on a chair, facing a wall a short distance away. The objective is to (a) develop the necessary logic (restricted to the basic building blocks of structured programming) to have the robot walk to the wall and return to its initial position, and (b) express that logic in pseudocode. The robot understands the following commands, which are to be used in your solution:

    STAND

    SIT

    TURN (turn right 90 degrees)

    STEP

    STOP

    In addition, the robot can raise its arms and sense the wall with its fingertips. (However, it cannot sense the chair on its return trip, since the chair is below arm level.) Thus the robot must count the number of steps to the wall or chair (assume the wall is an *integer* number of steps away) using the following commands:

ADD (increments counter by 1)

SUBTRACT (decrements counter by 1)

ZERO COUNTER (sets counter to zero)

ARMS UP

ARMS DOWN

We strongly recommend that various solutions be presented in class. Select a volunteer to act as the robot, and see whether the submitted solutions actually accomplish the objective.

2. This exercise is also unrelated to data management for the same rationale as in the previous problem. The objective here is to provide a series of commands to the robot so that it can move through a maze to reach a goal. It is a simple maze in that the robot doesn't have to backtrack; that is, once it enters the maze, it makes steady progress to reach its objective. Although the robot understands all the commands in exercise 1, *you are to use only the STEP, TURN, and STOP commands* in this exercise.

Note, too, that every time the robot takes a step, it returns a condition code: AT WALL or NOT AT WALL. If AT WALL is returned, the robot is standing directly in front of a wall and cannot proceed further. If NOT AT WALL is given, the robot can take at least one step directly ahead.

A typical maze is shown in Figure 11.8. The robot has reached the goal when it is confronted by a wall on three sides. The problem is to develop the necessary logic to get the robot through *any* maze of the type shown (that is, a maze in which you never have to backtrack). In doing the exercise, you should *assume that the robot is facing into the maze to start*. Your logic must be structured and must consist entirely of sequence, selection, iteration, and/or case building blocks.

FIGURE 11.8
Maze for exercise 2.

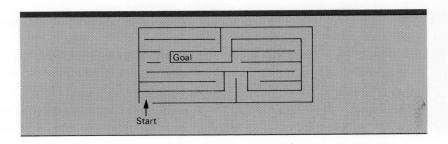

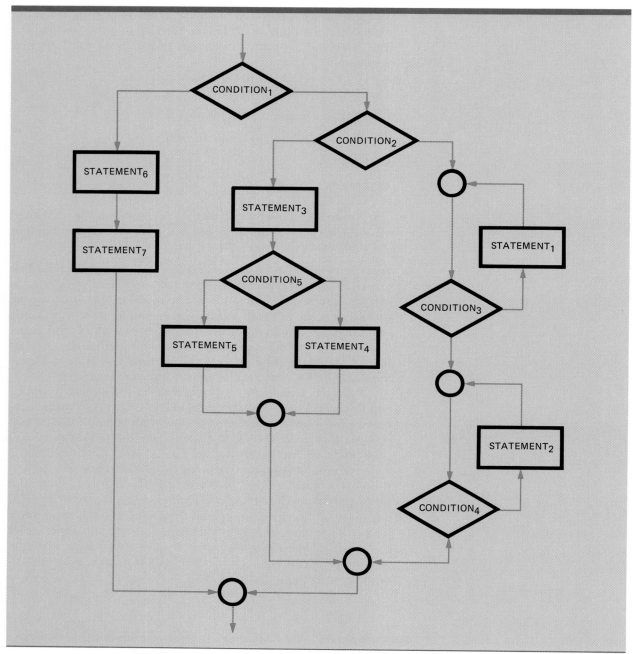

FIGURE 11.9
Flowchart for exercise 3.

3. Identify the elementary building blocks (there are eight in all) of Figure 11.9. Express the equivalent logic in pseudocode as well.

4. Figure 11.10 contains three reports, each purporting to list the 10 states with the highest density, but each containing a serious error *which you are to identify*. The reports were produced, not by our

FIGURE 11.10
Reports for exercise 4.

FIGURE 11.10
Reports for exercise 4.

State	Population (1980)	Area (sq mi)	Density (pers/mi)
New Jersey	7364823	7836	940
Rhode Island	947154	1214	780
Massachusetts	5737037	8257	695
Connecticut	3107576	5009	620
Maryland	4216975	10577	399
New York	17558072	49576	354
Delaware	594338	2057	289
Ohio	10797630	41222	262
Pennsylvania	11863895	45333	262
Texas	14229191	67338	211

(a) First erroneous report

State	Population (1980)	Area (sq mi)	Density (pers/mi)
Alaska	401851	589757	1
Wyoming	469557	97914	5
Montana	786690	147138	5
Nevada	800493	110540	7
South Dakota	690768	77047	9
North Dakota	652717	70665	9
New Mexico	1302894	121666	11
Idaho	943935	83557	11
Utah	1461037	84916	17
Nebraska	1569825	77227	20

(b) Second erroneous report

State	Population (1980)	Area (sq mi)	Density (pers/mi)
New Jersey	7364823	7836	939.870
Rhode Island	947154	1214	780.193
Massachusetts	5737037	8257	694.809
Connecticut	3107576	5009	620.398
Maryland	4216975	10577	398.693
New York	17558072	49576	354.165
Delaware	594338	2057	288.934
Ohio	10797630	41222	261.939
Pennsylvania	11863895	45333	261.705
Illinois	11426518	56400	202.598
*** Total ***			4803.304

(c) Third erroneous report

menu-driven program, but by students in our classes who entered commands interactively (from the dot prompt in dBASE). The point of this problem is that most individuals do not question the accuracy of computer-generated output.

5. Modify the pseudocode for the menu-driven program to include a fifth permissible report type, per capita income. Is this change difficult to make? What additional steps are necessary to implement this change in the actual program?

6. Select one or more programming languages which are available for the PC. For each language chosen:
   (a) For which class of problems is the language intended?
   (b) What are some distinguishing features of the language?
   (c) Who developed the language? When?
   (d) How many versions of the language are available for the PC? Can you obtain pricing and other information about a particular version(s) from the vendor? Does the language have an approved standard which the different versions follow?

7. Figure 11.11 contains data for quarterbacks in the National Football League at the end of the 1987 season. Develop a menu-driven program that will enable the user to specify:
   (a) One of four report types: touchdown passes, interceptions, overall quarterback rating, or total passing yardage.

FIGURE 11.11   Date for exercise 7.

Quarterback	Yds Gained	TD Passes	Interception	Rating
Campbell, Atlanta	1728	11	14	65.03
Cunningham, Philadelphia	2786	23	12	83.02
DeBerg, Tampa Bay	1891	14	7	85.28
Elway, Denver	3198	19	12	83.36
Esiason, Cincinatti	3321	16	19	73.12
Everett, Los Angeles	2064	10	13	68.36
Fouts, San Diego	2517	10	15	70.04
Herbert, New Orleans	2119	15	9	82.85
Kelly, Buffalo	2798	19	11	83.81
Kenney, Kansas City	2107	15	9	85.83
Kosar, Cleveland	3033	22	9	95.41
Krieg, Seattle	2131	23	15	87.56
Lomax, St. Louis	3387	24	12	88.54
Long, Detroit	2598	11	20	63.21
Malone, Pittsburgh	1896	6	19	46.68
Marino, Miami	3245	26	13	89.22
McMahon, Chicago	1639	12	8	87.38
Montana, San Francisco	3054	31	13	102.10
Moon, Houston	2806	21	18	74.16
O'Brien, New York	2696	13	8	82.83
Schroeder, Washington	1878	12	10	71.03
Simms, New York	2230	17	9	90.00
Trudeau, Indianapolis	1587	6	6	75.35
White, Dallas,	2617	12	17	73.18
Wilson, Los Angeles	2070	12	8	84.63
Wilson, Minnesota	2106	14	13	76.67
Wright, Green Bay	1507	6	11	61.58

(b) The number of quarterbacks to include in the report (from 1 to 28).

(c) Whether the quarterbacks are to appear in ascending or descending sequence of the statistic requested.

8. The flowchart in Figure 11.12 expresses a series of decisions and their associated actions. State whether the following are true or false on the basis of the flowchart.

(a) If X > Y and W > Z, then *always* add 1 to B.

(b) If X < Y, then *always* add 1 to D.

(c) If Q > T, then *always* add 1 to B.

(d) If X < Y and W < Z, then *always* add 1 to D.

(e) There are no conditions under which 1 will be added to both A and B simultaneously.

(f) If W > Z and Q < T, then *always* add 1 to C.

FIGURE 11.12
Flowchart for exercise 8.

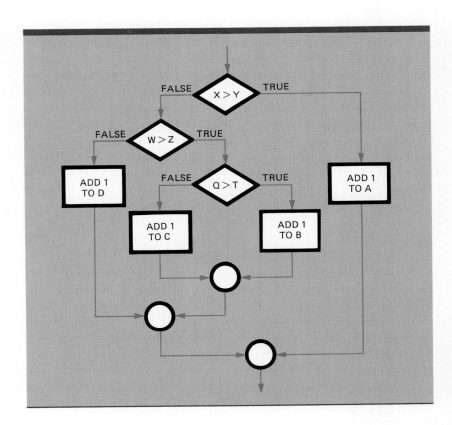

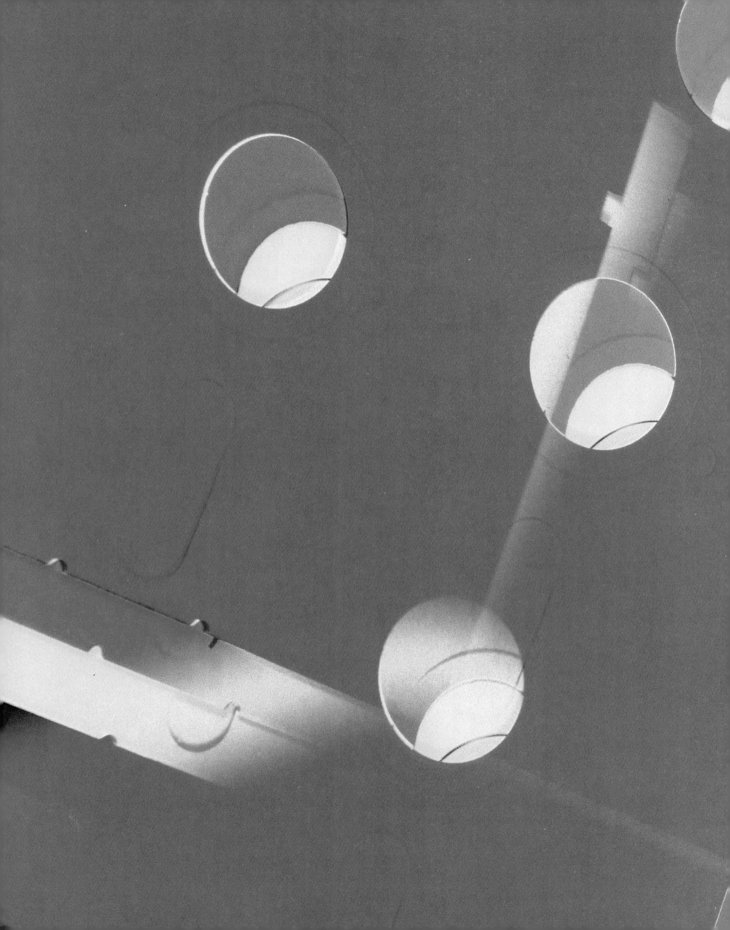

PART 5

ADVANCED
TOPICS

CHAPTER 12

COMMUNICATIONS

CHAPTER OBJECTIVES

CHAPTER OBJECTIVES

After reading this chapter, you should be able to:

1. List several milestones in the history of communications.

2. State the purpose of a serial port and a modem.

3. List three types of services provided by an information utility.

4. List four functions performed by a general-purpose communications package.

5. Describe conceptually how one signs onto an information utility.

6. Describe the rationale for local area networks.

7. Define topology; distinguish between star, ring, and bus network configurations.

Overview

Approximately 50 years ago, H. G. Wells suggested the possibility of a "world encyclopedia," a living body of knowledge that would be alive and grow, and that would contain the mental background of every intelligent being in the world. H. G. Wells never owned a personal computer, yet he accurately foresaw the incredible amount of knowledge that is available through today's online information services. Data processing and communications were once viewed as separate industries, yet it is increasingly difficult, if not altogether impossible, to distinguish between the two.

Suffice it to say that any study of computers would be incomplete without some discussion of communications, which is presented in this chapter within the context of the microcomputer. We cover the basics of communications theory, networking, and the types of online information services available. The chapter begins with a historical perspective on the development of modern communications.

Milestones in Communications

The capabilities of modern communications would utterly astound our ancestors. Did you ever stop to think that it took five months for Queen Isabella to hear of Columbus's discovery of America, or that it took two weeks for Europe to learn of Lincoln's assassination?

We take for granted immediate news of everything that is going on in the world, but it was not always so. Modern technology and future predictions are easier to comprehend when we view them in terms of our past. What follows next is a list of what the authors consider some of the more significant events in the annals of communications. Our list is arbitrary and includes items chosen not only for technological innovation, but also for creativity and human interest.

Pheidippides's Run

For centuries, the speed of communication was in essence the speed of transportation. Perhaps no event so dramatizes this limitation as Pheidippides's run following the battle of Marathon in 490 B.C.

As told in the history books, a badly outnumbered Greek force defeated an invading Persian army on the plains of Marathon, 20 miles from Athens. Fearing that the defeated Persians would regroup and attack Athens, and that the city would surrender without knowing of the victory, the Greek general dispatched his swiftest runner, Pheidippides, to convey the news. As he reached the city, he stumbled, delivered his message, and fell dead of exhaustion.

Paul Revere's Ride

"One if by land and two if by sea" refers to lanterns hung from the North Church in Boston to indicate the route the British were taking. The lanterns were the signal for Paul Revere to begin his famous ride, immortalized forever by Longfellow's poem describing the midnight ride of Paul Revere, perhaps the most famous communication in American history.

In actuality, Revere made two rides, on April 16 (to warn the patriots to move their military supplies) and again on April 18 (to tell the people to take up arms). Few people know that Revere was accompanied on the second ride by two other patriots, William Dawes and Samuel Prescott, and that he was captured by a British patrol and subsequently released. Dawes and Prescott escaped.

Reuters News Service

Reuters today is a worldwide news gathering agency owned by the British Press Association. It was founded in 1849 by Paul Julius von Reuter, and the creativity of its founder merits Reuter's inclusion in our list of communication milestones. The original service used *carrier pigeons* to bring closing market prices on the stock exchange in Brussels, Belgium, to Aix-la-Chapelle (now Aachen), Germany.

Pony Express

All of us have complained about the cost of a first-class stamp and the few days it may take for the mail to go across the country. Our complaints would sound silly, however, to someone spending $5 to send a half-ounce letter to California that took 10 days to get there. That was the rate charged by the Pony Express, which in its day provided the fastest possible delivery to the west coast.

The route of the Pony Express stretched 1966 miles from St. Joseph, Missouri, to Sacramento, California. Relay stations were set up every 10 to 15 miles along the way where lonely keepers took care of the horses. Young riders rode at top speed from one station to the next for wages of $100 to $150 per month. In all, there were about 190 stations, 400 station keepers and assistants, 400 horses, and 80 riders. Despite the hardships of riding in all kinds of weather, and the constant attacks by Indians and outlaws, the mail was lost only once in the more than 650,000 miles logged by the riders.

The Pony Express existed for barely a year and a half (from April 3, 1860, to October 24, 1861), when telegraph connections were completed between the east and west coasts. Unable to compete, the promoters of the Pony Express were ruined financially.

Telegraph

Samuel B. Morse, an artist turned inventor, is credited with building the first commercially practical telegraph. Morse's line stretched from Washington to Baltimore, and was soon extended to New Jersey. Some enterprising individuals used the telegraph to communicate lottery results to New York, where hefty sums were won before people caught on to this new form of "instantaneous" communication. Less than 10 years later, the entire country east of the Mississippi was connected with over 18,000 miles of telegraph wire.

Western Union was formed in 1856 and completed the first telegraph line to the west in 1861 (causing the demise of the Pony Express). It made a fortune for its backers, building the line in less than three months for $500,000, then selling $6 million worth of public stock. Profits continued to pour in, with the going rate of $1 per word.

Transatlantic Cable

The first transatlantic message was sent in 1858 via an undersea cable stretching from Newfoundland to Ireland. Unfortunately, the cable functioned for only four weeks. Cyrus Field, the businessman behind the project, saw his firm go bankrupt, causing the cable to be temporarily abandoned.

Eight years later, on July 27, 1866, a new and successful cable was completed, also under the auspices of Field. He was awarded a gold medal by Congress and eventually helped to promote New York City's elevated railroad.

Telephone

Although Alexander Graham Bell receives universal credit for the telephone, he narrowly beat his rival, Elisha Gray, to the patent office. Bell eventually withstood over 100 legal challenges brought by Gray and his supporters concerning Bell's right to the key patents.

The original telephone patent.

Interestingly enough, Bell's financial backer and father-in-law, Gardiner Hubbard, initially dismissed the telephone as a curiosity, offering to sell the rights to the telephone to Western Union for $100,000. (Western Union wasn't interested.) Perhaps Hubbard was influenced by a quotation attributed to Rutherford B. Hayes, nineteenth president of the United States, who said of the telephone, "That's an amazing invention, but why would anyone ever want to use one?"

Radio

The development of radio is attributable to many individuals of different nationalities. It begins with the research of James Clerk Maxwell, a British physicist of the nineteenth century who showed that electricity and light both travel in the form of waves, and predicted that electromagnetic waves could be transmitted through space from electric discharges. Heinrich Hertz, a German scientist, became the first person to actually create these waves, and he further showed that waves could be measured as to length and frequency.

It was an Italian, however, Guglielmo Marconi, who was the first to send and receive wireless communications over a distance, successfully transmitting such signals across the English Channel in 1898, and across the Atlantic in 1901. Marconi, himself, became the world's first sportscaster when he reported the progress of the 1899 America's Cup races in New York Harbor to two newspapers over the wireless transmitter he invented.

Sputnik

In 1957 the Soviet Union shocked the world (and jolted the United States into accelerating its own space program) when it launched Sputnik, the first manufactured object to orbit the earth. From this dramatic beginning modern statellite communications enable us to know all that is going on in the world almost at the instant it happens; whether it is the death of a national leader, the outcome of a battle, or the results of the Super Bowl. Indeed, satellites transmit the human voice around the world faster than it can be shouted from one end of a football field to the other.

First moon walk.

QUOTATIONS IN THE HISTORY OF COMMUNICATION

490 B.C.   ''Rejoice, we conquer.''
—Pheidippides, bringing word of the Greek victory at Marathon

May 24, 1844   ''What hath God wrought?''
—Samuel B. Morse on the telegraph

August 16, 1858   ''Europe and America are united by telegraphy.''
—Queen Victoria to President James Buchanan as she sent the first transatlantic telegram

Summer 1876   ''Mr. Watson, come here. I want you.''
—Alexander Graham Bell's first words on the telephone

December 12, 1901   ''S S S S . . .''
—Guglielmo Marconi, sending the letter S, in the first wireless signal across the Atlantic

July 20, 1969   ''One small step for man, one giant leap for mankind.''
—Neil Armstrong, landing on the moon

The Basics of Communications

We have certainly come a long way from Pheidippides's run and are now ready to discuss the main subject of the chapter. **Data communication** is the transmission of data from one computer to another; be it communication from mainframe to mainframe, from PC to PC, or from mainframe to PC. The term **telecommunications** is used to describe data communications at a distance, and **teleprocessing** describes the combination of long-distance communication and data processing.

Our discussion will focus on PC communications, either to another PC or to a remote mainframe computer. Four elements are always present in any communication: a sender, a message, the transmission line over which the message is sent, and the receiver. Each of these will be covered in turn.

In order to communicate with another computer, your PC first has to be physically connected to the telephone line. This requires a hardware interface, known as a *modem*. Next, you dial the number of the receiving computer to establish a *communications channel* (link) over which data will be transmitted. Finally, you need *communications software* to coordinate the data transfer between the two computers.

"NOW THAT IT CAN COMMUNICATE WITH OTHER COMPUTERS, IT SAYS IT DOESN'T WANT TO COMMUNICATE WITH US."

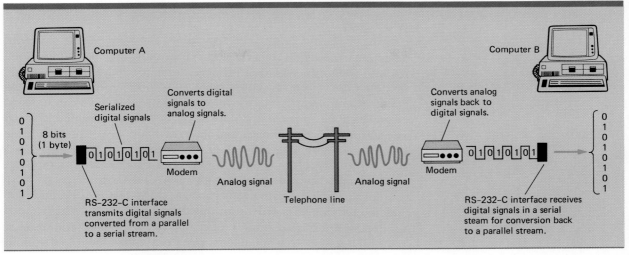

FIGURE 12.1
The essence of communications.

We begin with an overview of the communications process as depicted by Figure 12.1. The first step toward understanding communications is to look at data in its most basic form: a series of electronic pulses in two varieties. These values are represented numerically as **bits** (*binary digits*). Every character (for example, a letter or a number) consists of eight bits, or one **byte,** according to a commonly accepted coding scheme known as **ASCII.** (ASCII is an acronym for American Standard Code for Information Interchange and is described further in Appendix B.)

Every message transmitted by a computer, be it words, numbers, or even pictures, is broken down into bytes, which are further broken into bits. A computer processes one byte at a time, yet the message is carried over telephone lines one bit at a time. Accordingly, a device known as an **RS-232C interface** is used to convert the parallel stream of eight bits (one byte) to a serial stream for transmission, and then back again on the receiving end.

The process does not end there. The telephone was built for voice transmission and uses an **analog signal,** which represents information in a continuous, smoothly varying signal. A computer, on the other hand, is a digital device with discrete signals and represents data as the presence or absence of an electronic voltage.

Modulation is the process of converting a digital signal to an analog one; **demodultation** is the reverse process. A **modem** (derived from *mo*dulate and *dem*odulate) is a device that performs both functions. Modems are used to connect personal computers to the telephone system, and are necessary because of the need to convert between analog and digital signals.

On the transmitting end, a modem converts binary signals (1s and 0s) produced by a computer or peripheral device to analog signals which can be sent over the public phone system. On the receiving end, the modem converts the analog signal back to a digital signal, which is forwarded to the computer or associated device.

Modems

Selecting a modem is the first step in beginning telecommunications. As with every other kind of PC peripheral, there are many modems commercially available which differ as to price and capability. The speed of a modem, that is, the maximum rate at which it can transmit or receive data, is one of its more important characteristics. The rate is measured in **bits per second (bps)** or **baud,** with the two terms often used interchangeably. (Technically, however, the bits per second and the baud rates need not be the same. These situations are not common, however, and are not discussed further.)

A data transfer rate of 600 bps or slower is considered a low speed; 1200 to 9600 is a medium speed; and over 9600 is a high speed. (High-speed modems require specially installed data communications lines and are not suitable for personal computers.) As the transfer rate of a modem increases, so too does its price, although the cost of all modems has dropped significantly. For many years 300 bps was the choice of most personal computer owners. Today, however, modems with 1200 bps are increasingly popular and even 2400 bps is not uncommon.

Although higher-speed modems do cost more, they return some savings in the form of reduced communications costs. Most information services charge according to the amount of "connect time"; hence the faster the modem, the less time spent transmitting data, and the lower the communication cost. It takes approximately one minute to fill a 24 × 80 screen at 300 baud, but only 16 seconds at 1200 baud, and 8 seconds at 2400 baud.

FIGURE 12.2   (a) External modem. (b) Internal modem.

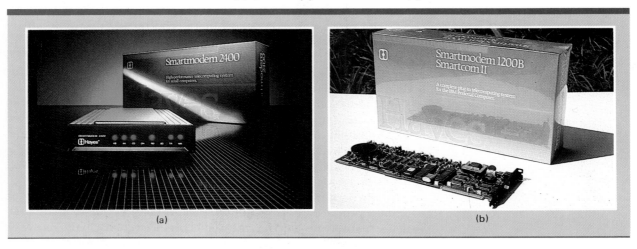

(a)   (b)

"This year, Christmas is easy for me. I'm sending all my gifts through my modem."

Modems are also differentiated according to their physical design, that is, whether they are intended to fit into an expansion slot *inside* the PC's system unit or to stand alone on the desktop as shown in Figure 12.2. (An older type of modem, the **acoustic coupler** is rarely seen today. This device was distinguished by its rubber cups which fit directly over a telephone head set.)

An internal modem is generally cheaper than an external modem. It requires neither its own external power supply nor attendant cable, and reduces clutter. In addition, if security is an issue, internal modems are harder to steal given that the system unit is adequately bolted down.

External modems, also called stand-alone or freestanding modems, work with a variety of personal computers. This is important only if you expect to change computers, for example, if you go from an Apple to an IBM. They make it easier to set switches and control volume, and generally have flashing lights on the front allowing you to monitor the progress of a telephone call. External modems take additional desk space and require their own electrical outlet.

Authors' Comments: Computer viruses are a growing problem which come into play as you employ the communications capability of your machine. Be careful.

A COMPUTER VIRUS
What It Is and How It Spreads

Creation: A programmer writes a tiny bit of computer code, which can attach itself to other programs and alter them or destroy data kept on a computer disk. The virus also can reproduce by copying itself to other programs stored on the same disk.

Distribution: Most often, the virus is attached to a piece of normal software, which becomes its Trojan horse. The virus spreads as the owner of the Trojan horse exchanges software with other computer enthusiasts via electronic bulletin boards or by trading floppy disks.

Infection: The more its host program is swapped, the more the virus replicates itself, until it becomes pervasive. But no one is aware of the infection, because the virus has been designed to remain dormant—perhaps for months.

Attack: At a predetermined time, the virus activates itself. It takes its cue from the internal clock/calendar that computers use to time-stamp their work. The virus seizes control of the computer and works its mischief.

Prevention: Do your utmost to protect the security of your system, especially when exchanging software or otherwise communicating with the outside world. Consider the use of an antivirus program (or vaccine) which attempts to foil viruses by keeping them out of your system, preventing them from replicating if they do get in, and otherwise blocking their malicious tricks.

Source: Business Week, August 1, 1988, page 70; and PC Magazine, June 28, 1988, page 35.

1200
BPS*

Modem Cost:
$250–$600

■ These modems are the most commonly used in business today. As a class, they are not particularly sensitive to noise on the telephone line; but if they encounter noisy conditions, they will try to step back to 300 bps or quit to retransmit—either way, the result will be higher transmission costs.

$12,222

2400
BPS*

Modem Cost:
$400–$900

■ These modems are becoming much more popular in business. They are somewhat more sensitive to noise than the 1200-bps modems, so there may be more dropped connections and, therefore, higher costs. Also, you won't benefit from their speed if they connect to 1200-bps systems.

$ 6,930

9600
BPS*

Modem Cost:
$1,500–$2,000

■ As a class, these modems have the potential for being the most sensitive to noise. How sensitive depends on the choice of components and error-correction scheme. Also, many of these modems can't step back to 1200 bps and so won't connect to remote modems that run at that speed.

$ 2,696

18,000
BPS*

Modem Cost:
$2,000–$2,400

■ Because of sophisticated error correction schemes and a lot of on-board computing power, these modems are the least sensitive to noisy telephone lines. They are also capable of stepping back only slightly on the bps rate to offset line problems—and thus run fairly true to the bps rate.

$ 1,638

*A throughput rate of 80 percent was used, so that at 1200 bps, for example, the actual transmission rate was 960 bps; the throughput rate may vary according to telephone line quality.

Communications Channel

A modem transmits data along a path known as a **communications channel,** or communications link. The flow of data along this path is characterized according to its direction, speed, and sequencing, each of which is discussed in detail.

Direction of Data Flow

Communications channels fall into one of three categories: *simplex, half-duplex,* or *full-duplex,* depending on the direction of data flow. In simplex transmission, data travels in one direction only, whereas in half- or full-duplex it moves in both directions. The difference between the latter two is that full-duplex permits data to flow in both directions simultaneously, while in half-duplex data flows in one direction at a time.

A **simplex channel** is analogous to a one-way street; that is, data can be transmitted in one direction only. Simplex transmission is used by devices which either send or receive data, but not both. For example, point-of-sale (POS) terminals in department stores may transmit data to a host computer over a simplex line, as the terminals serve only for data entry and do not receive information. Conversely, a high-speed printer might receive data over a simplex channel but does not send any. Simplex transmission is *not* used to connect two personal computers, as both devices must be able to transmit and receive.

A **half-duplex channel** transmits data in both directions, but only in one direction at a time. It is analogous to a two-way street undergoing construction, where traffic is halted at one end and allowed to pass in one direction, then halted at the other end and permitted to pass in the opposite direction. Half-duplex transmission requires devices which can both send and receive, and it is often used with personal computers. However, when the computer on one end of the line is transmitting, the computer on the other end cannot respond until the message is completed.

A **full-duplex channel** transmits data in both directions simultaneously and is analogous to a two-way street with traffic passing in both directions. Each end of a full-duplex line is assigned a different frequency so that messages don't interfere with one another. Transmission of data is faster than with half-duplex, as the system is not burdened with overhead created by continually reversing direction. Full-duplex transmission is the mode used most often by personal computers.

Figure 12.3 depicts simplex, half-duplex, and full-duplex transmissions.

FIGURE 12.3
Simplex, half-duplex, and full-duplex transmission.

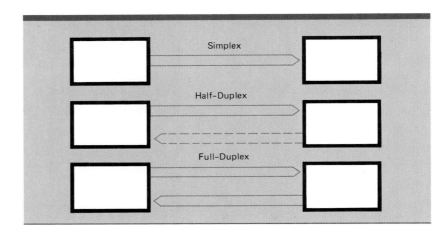

Speed of Transmission

A modem and the communications channel work in harmony with one another. Accordingly, it does you absolutely no good to spend the extra money for a modem capable of transmitting data at 1200 baud if the line over which the data flows is rated at only 300. Realize, also, that the number of bits per second is different from the number of **characters per second (CPS);** for example, a 1200-baud line (1200 bps) generally transmits at 120 cps.

Recall that any transmitted message takes the form of bits, which in turn are grouped into bytes, then words, and then sentences. Given 8 bits to a byte (character), and a 1200-bps line, why then are only 120 characters transmitted per second, rather than 150 (1200/8)? The answer has to do with still another parameter of data transmission, known as sequencing.

Sequencing

The bits in a message travel in groups. In **asynchronous transmission,** data is sent and received one character at a time, with each character preceded by a "start bit" and ending with a "stop bit." Hence 10 bits are required to transmit each character: 8 for the character itself, plus 1 on either end. The presence of start and stop bits explains why a 1200-bps line transmits at 120 cps.

In the asynchronous scheme, the receiving device knows that whenever it gets a start bit, the next 8 bits will constitute a character. Thus, the time interval between characters in asynchronous transmission may vary. Asynchronous transmission is used with a human-machine interface as when data is entered from a keyboard. The advantage of asynchronous transmission is that data can be transmitted whenever it is convenient for the sender.

In **synchronous transmission,** data is sent without the intervening start and stop bits. Data is sent at fixed times, with blocks of characters sent in a single transmission in a timed sequence. This

FIGURE 12.4
Synchronous versus asynchronous
transmission.

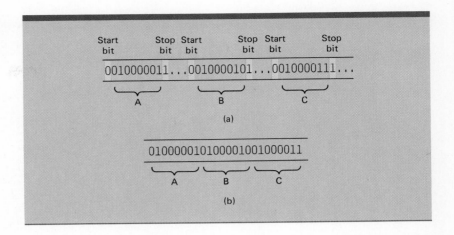

contrasts with asynchronous transmission which sends a single character at random intervals.

Synchronous transmission is more complex to implement than asynchronous transmission, as both sender and receiver must be synchronized according to a carefully controlled clock. It requires more expensive equipment, but it offers the advantage of higher-speed transmission, as fewer bits are transmitted by virtue of eliminating the start and stop bits associated with asynchronous transmission. Synchronous transmission is generally used in mainframe-to-mainframe communications.

Figure 12.4 depicts both synchronous and asynchronous transmissions.

Parity Checking

All data communications are subject to noise (distortion) in the line, which can alter the value of transmitted data, in turn producing garbled messages. **Parity checking** is a technique designed to detect these types of errors. A **parity bit** is an extra bit that is added to every byte, to check whether the other bits in that byte have been altered in transmission. Parity can be specified as odd or even.

The value of the parity bit depends on the other bits in the byte. If parity is specified as even, then in each byte the total number of bits set to 1, including the parity bit, must be even. The situation is depicted in Figure 12.5.

Appendix B discusses the bit representation of various characters; for example, according to Table B.1, the bit configuration for the letter T is 01010100. Note that three of the eight bits are set to 1. Now if even parity is used, the parity bit will also be set to 1, bringing to four the total number of bits set to 1. The letter U, on the other hand, already has four 1s, as its ASCII representation is 01010101; hence its parity bit will be set to 0 to retain the even number of 1s.

When parity checking is used, the sending and receiving com-

FIGURE 12.5
Parity checking.

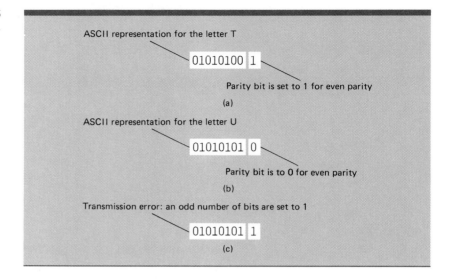

ASCII representation for the letter T

01010100 1

Parity bit is set to 1 for even parity

(a)

ASCII representation for the letter U

01010101 0

Parity bit is to 0 for even parity

(b)

Transmission error: an odd number of bits are set to 1

01010101 1

(c)

puters automatically add the number of 1s in each transmitted character. Assume, for example, that the character shown in Figure 12.5*c* is received and that even parity is specified. The receiving computer would not know whether the intended transmission was for the letter T, the letter U, or for that matter an entirely different character. It would, however, be able to indicate that the message was received incorrectly because an odd number of bits were set to 1.

Communications Software

The previous discussion provides some idea of the many parameters needed to establish a link between the sending and receiving computer; in other words, you and the person with whom you wish to communicate must agree to use the same type of signals. The settings which constitute this agreement are known as a **communications protocol**, and are implemented with **communications software.**

To establish a protocol first hook up your computer, modem, and telephone. Load your communications package and when prompted, supply instructions about the service you will be calling. You will need to find out what rules are used by the receiving computer and to instruct your system to follow the same rules. Then, depending on the instructions you supply, the communications package will direct your computer as to how fast data are transmitted, whether half-duplex or full-duplex is used, whether transmission is asynchronous or synchronous, and so forth. **Handshaking** refers to the initial contact between two computers in which the settings are determined; most communications software will store these values in a file to facilitate reconnection.

As with other areas of personal computer software, the number of products to choose from is staggering. Be sure that the program you select fulfills basic communications requirements such as:

- Accessing information utilities such as The Source or Compu-Serve.

- Connecting your computer to electronic mail services.

- Accessing computer bulletin boards and/or allowing remote access to your PC by other computers.

- Exchanging files between your PC and other computers.

- Turning your PC into a terminal for direct hookup with remote mainframe computers. **Emulation** is the process of one device (for example, a PC) assuming the appearance of another (for example, a terminal with which the mainframe is familiar).

Information Utilities

A multipurpose **information utility** provides services in three general areas: *communications*, *transactions*, and *information access*. Communications services allow you to send and receive electronic mail, engage in online conferencing, or view and post news on computer bulletin boards. Transaction services include electronic shopping, banking, and brokerage services. But it is the information services function which is the most exciting, as it supplies access to an almost unlimited supply of online information. Consider:

> Your broker calls, pitching a stock you've never neard of. You hear phrases like "unique opportunity" and "hold it until it doubles." Meanwhile, you're wondering if this is the firm's special of the day or if the broker is late on his Ferrari payments. But instead of listening passively to your broker's polished spiel, you turn to your personal computer and tap through to your favorite database. "I don't feel very good about that one, Joe," you say. "The stock's already trading near its 52 week high, and earnings estimates were revised downward last week. The price/earnings ratio is skyhigh, compared with other companies in the same industry. Besides, I see that the entire board of directors has the same last name. It just doesn't sound like something I'm interested in."[1]

> Mark Carlton, an attorney for Mobil Oil in Chicago, is faced with a tricky legal problem that must be solved in a few short hours. Instead of going to a law library and spending precious time paging through casebooks, statutes, and law reviews, he sits down at his PC, dials into a legal database, and within minutes has located most, if not all, of the relevant cases and commentaries. With a few additional searches he finds where the cases have been cited, searches federal statutes, and examines the complete texts of relevant law review articles going back many years. He then prints several full articles and parts of others and scans them,

[1]*Forbes*, May 6, 1985.

pen in hand. Within a short time, without leaving his desk, Mark has tapped into a larger body of legal knowledge than is contained in even the largest law libraries.[2]

Nick Tarlson, vice president of finance for Braw Electric in San Francisco, has just received a call from the president of a large energy production company, who has proposed a merger of the two companies. "I'd like your decision as soon as possible on whether we should proceed with discussions," the president says. Nick hangs up and turns on his PC. He loads an integrated communications/spreadsheet package and dials an on-line database filled with detailed financial information on thousands of companies. Within minutes he finds the data he needs on the potential partner and downloads it into a spreadsheet. By the end of the morning, Nick has analyzed the company's financial reports and has determined that the other company has several weaknesses. "Based on your financial condition, your offering price is much too low," he tells the company president later that same day. Both parties know Nick is right. He has done his homework, and his company has the negotiating edge.[3]

CompuServe screens.

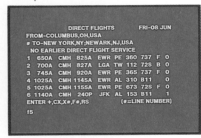

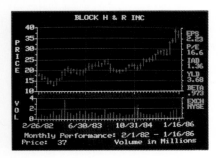

What's apparent from these and other examples is that all sorts of people are dialing into all kinds of online information services. The only problem (if there is one) is that there is too much information available, and one is almost overwhelmed by an abundance of riches. (The *Directory of On-line Databases*, edited by Kenneth R. Duzy, lists 2764 remote data banks.) With so many possibilities, the choice of where to go and what kind of service to obtain is truly a mind-numbing affair.

In attempting to bring order to the chaos, realize that there are basically two types of data banks: the narrow, well-defined systems serving the needs of a particular group (which constitute the vast majority) and a lesser number of multipurpose information utilities (for example, The Source or CompuServe, discussed below) which are less specific. The former provide access to the thousands (hundreds of thousands) of bibliographic references to the professional literature in a particular field. The latter are broader in scope and generally have something for everyone. Remember, too, that each online system has its own special services and flavor, and that no single service can be all things to all people.

Chances are, however, that as a beginner you would be most likely to dial into a general-purpose information utility such as *CompuServe* or *The Source*, two of the more widely used and better known services. The two systems are almost identical in the kind and quantity of information available, and you will not go wrong with either one.

[2]Eric Brown, "Encyclopedia Electronica," *PC Word*, May 1985.
[3]*Ibid*.

CompuServe

CompuServe is the nation's largest system, with 200,000 plus subscribers. It was acquired by H&R Block in 1980 and operates as a wholly owned subsidiary. CompuServe is available 24 hours a day from anywhere in the world.

CompuServe caters to both the consumer and the businessperson through its Consumer Services and its Executive Information Services, respectively. Consumers may take advantage of EasyPlex **electronic mail,** shop via the Electronic Mall, make travel arrangements through TWA's reservation system, and talk to each other via a national bulletin board.

Subscribers to the Executive Information Service can do all the above, and in addition have access to a spectrum of financial, demographic, and editorial information. Stock quotes and commodity prices are available, as is historical market information, market and industry indexes, and national and international news wire services.

The Source

The Source (based in McLean, Virginia) was founded by Source Telecomputing Corporation (STC) in 1979, and acquired by The Reader's Digest Association in 1980. Its transmissions are carried by Telenet and other networks, allowing members to reach The Source with a local telephone call. Members in outlying regions may access The Source via WATS lines at a surcharge.

The Source has specifically courted the business user; its average member is in his or her late thirties and most have a college education. Seventy-five percent are business leaders and professionals, and over half the subscribers use the service for business purposes. The Source offers news, weather, and sports information; business and investing data (including online stock trading); and electronic shopping.

Authors' Comments:
Busy signals are annoying anytime,
whether you are trying to dial a
computer or obtain Springsteen tickets.
As far as the computer is concerned,
you generally have better luck dialing at
off hours, for example, early in the
morning or late at night.

COMMUNICATIONS SNAFU

Amazed AT&T employees are still calling it Boss Monday, but to rock fans it was simply the day Bruce Springsteen tickets went on sale in Washington. Lines were jammed by hundreds of thousands of attempted phone calls, an estimated 130 percent above normal. The added callers were trying to buy 30,000 tickets (at $18.50 each) for Springsteen's concert the next Monday at Robert F. Kennedy Stadium. Back home after a triumphant tour of Europe, Springsteen was resting and rehearsing for his new 25-city, 9-week American tour. The scramble for tickets to the concerts also caused communications snafus in Maryland, Virginia, New York City, New Jersey and Delaware. Asked if Government communications were affected, the White House's Larry Speakes replied, "We've got ways to get around it." That's a comfort. Otherwise, Kremlin strategists planning a missile strike might be deciding, "First thing we do is announce free Springsteen tickets to the next 1000 callers in every U.S. city."

Source: Time, August 5, 1985. Copyright 1985, Time, Inc. All rights reserved.

Bulletin Boards

A **bulletin board service (BBS)** is similar in many ways to bulletin boards found in college dorms, offices, supermarkets, and other public places. They contain the equivalent of want ads, graffiti, jokes, personal messages, and so on. Anyone who dials a computer bulletin board can sift through its contents, read messages left by other callers, and leave his or her own messages for future callers.

You can even establish your own bulletin board provided you are willing to devote a computer to its operation. You will also have to install an extra telephone line, plug the computer into that line, and leave it turned on 24 hours a day. Then you obtain the appropriate software, so that the bulletin board computer automatically answers telephone calls from other computers, accepts and stores messages from outside users, and allows those people access to the information stored in its files. Issuing passwords to restrict access to the system is common, as is a nominal initiation fee. That's essentially all there is to it.

HANDS-ON EXERCISE 1: TELECOMMUNICATIONS SOFTWARE

OBJECTIVE: Use telecommunications software to communicate with a remote computing facility.

Step 1: Obtain an Account Number
Begin by deciding with whom you will communicate (for example, the computing center on campus), so that you can obtain an account number or user name that will allow you access to the system. You will also need other information, such as the phone number to dial and which communications parameters are in effect for the host computer.

Step 2: Load the Telecommunications Program
Boot the system with a DOS disk, or with the program disk of your telecommunications program if it contains DOS. Supply the necessary date and time responses required by DOS.

Enter the command to execute the telecommunications program, for example, SCOM for Smartcom, or PROCOMM for Procomm. Follow the prompts supplied by the communications program to reach its dial-up menu, which will resemble Figure 12.6.

Step 3: Establish a Protocol
Figure 12.6 contains a hypothetical **dial-up menu** that is typical of many communications packages. In essence, the menu enables you to store a different set of communications parameters, that is, a different protocol, for every computer with which you communicate.

Follow the prompts produced by your program to add a new phone number (for the computer you will access) to the dial-up menu. Note that in order to complete this step you will have had to obtain (in step 1) the following information:

Phone number
Duplex   Half or full
Parity   Even, odd, or null
Data bits   7 or 8
Stop bits   Usually 1
Baud rate   300, 1200, or 2400

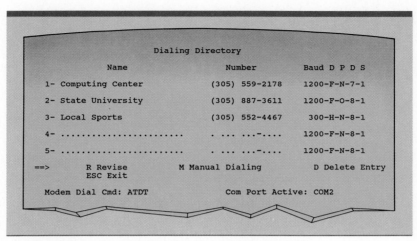

```
                    Dialing Directory

          Name                 Number         Baud D P D S

   1- Computing Center      (305) 559-2178    1200-F-N-7-1

   2- State University      (305) 887-3611    1200-F-O-8-1

   3- Local Sports          (305) 552-4467     300-H-N-8-1

   4- .....................   . ... ...-....   1200-F-N-8-1

   5- .....................   . ... ...-....   1200-F-N-8-1

   ==>      R Revise        M Manual Dialing        D Delete Entry
            ESC Exit

      Modem Dial Cmd: ATDT           Com Port Active: COM2
```

FIGURE 12.6   The dial-up menu.

A typical protocol in effect at many installations is 1200 baud, full-duplex, null parity, 8 data bits, and 1 stop bit.

Step 4: Originate a Call
Issue the command to dial the phone number, at which point you should hear an audible touch-tone sequence as the modem does the dialing. If you are successful, that is, the host computer answers your call, you will hear a high-pitched signal and see a CONNECT message on the monitor. Press the return key several times until the host system provides you with a welcome message.

Step 5: Log On
Follow the log-on procedure of the host computer, which normally prompts you for your account number (user name) and password. The account number uniquely identifies you to the host computer, and your password protects your account from unauthor-ized access by other people. You may also consider periodically changing your password to further protect your account.

Step 6: Conduct Your Business
Now that you are connected, you can accomplish what you set out to do. If you are a regular user of this particular system, you may want to check your "mailbox" for messages from other users, or check the system's bulletin board for general announcements. You may also want to **download** a file from the host computer to your system, or **upload** from your system to the host.

Step 7: Log Off
Be sure to terminate the session properly. Failure to log off in the prescribed manner can make it difficult for you to subsequently log on and/or result in additional communications charges.

TROUBLESHOOTING

Telecommunications requires a synchronized link between two computers miles apart, and hence it is not unusual for problems to develop. Fortunately, however, the problems which do occur are generally easy to correct.

● *If you do not hear the modem dial. . .* it may be because the modem is not connected to the proper communications port. For example, most *external* modems, attach to communications port number COM1, whereas most *internal* modems are configured for communications port number COM2. Thus if you improperly connected an internal modem to COM1, nothing is likely to happen.

Note too that if you have a touch-tone line, the modem must receive the dialing prefix ATDT (*attention dialing touch-tone*) before it receives the phone number. The dialing prefix is supplied automatically by some, but not all, communications software. Thus if your package does not enter the prefix, you must type ATDT followed by the phone number, and further *you must press the shift key while typing ATDT*, as Caps Lock does not produce the same signal.

● *If you hear the modem dial but have problems connecting. . .* it is usually because one or more of the communications parameters are improperly set. Return to the dial-up menu and verify that the correct parameters have been entered.

There may also be a problem in the way the phone number was entered in the dial-up directory. The necessity to obtain an outside line, for example, requires you to precede the phone number (of the computer) with a 9 and a comma. The former reaches the outside line, while the latter instructs the modem to pause until it receives the dial tone of the outside line. Thus if you are calling 123-4555, you would list it in the directory as 9,123-4555.

● *If you are dropped suddenly in the middle of a session. . .* it is probably due to either call waiting (a problem you can handle) or a noisy phone line (which you can't). Most phone companies provide a means to temporarily disable the call waiting service which you should invoke every time you use a modem. Unfortunately, however, the phone company is not likely to be sympathetic to complaints of a noisy line, since they do not generally guarantee phone lines for data communications.

Local Area Networks

Perhaps the computer laboratory in your school makes use of a manual switch to connect two or more computers and one printer, enabling several students to share a common printer. By virtue of the switch you can rearrange connections without plugging and un-plugging cables, and more importantly reduce the cost required to equip the PC laboratory. The concept is easily extended to more than two computers and/or multiple printers.

Since a manual switch requires human intervention to change connections, the situation just described is not technically a network. Nevertheless, it provides a good illustration of a primary motivation for establishing a network, namely, the desire to reduce hardware costs by sharing peripheral devices. The ultimate motivation, how-ever, is to share data and/or programs in addition to hardware de-vices.

A **local area network (LAN)** connects multiple PCs with this ob-jective. It spans a limited geographical distance (typically only a few hundred feet) and is often limited to a single building or a single department within a building (for example a computer laboratory).

The devices in a local area network transmit signals through cables or, in some cases, ordinary telephone wire. Modems are not used.

Figure 12.7 is a conceptual view of a local area network in which several computers share two printers and a hard disk. The figure also contains a **gateway,** which is a device that permits one network to communicate with an external network.

An individual at any computer in the network can create a spreadsheet or letter and send it to any other computer in the network. The person on the receiving end can review and/or edit the document and return it to the sender. Either individual can print the document on the dot matrix or laser printer.

Access to shared data in a network is controlled by a **file server** (which may be either software or hardware), which decides who gets access to which files and when. Thus if you and your computer are in the process of updating a file, the file server will deny access to that file to anyone else during the update. A file server can also prevent designated users from viewing specified files or it may let others read certain files but not change them.

Some networks provide every user with a private area of the hard disk known as a *volume*. Thus a **volume server** is analogous to a file server except that it pertains to all files on a specific area of the disk (volume). The file server, on the other hand, applies to all files without regard to their location.

FIGURE 12.7
A local area network.

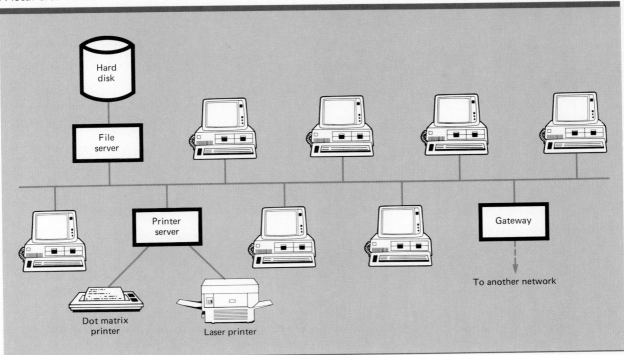

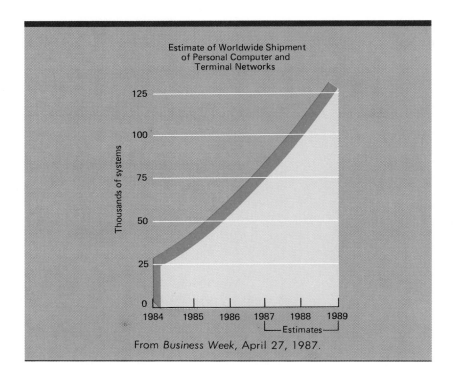

Estimate of Worldwide Shipment
of Personal Computer and
Terminal Networks

From *Business Week*, April 27, 1987.

198?: THE YEAR OF THE NETWORK

Every year since 1982 industry forecasters have proclaimed "the year of the network," and every year they have been wrong. Beset by technical shortcomings and customer skepticism, networks simply didn't sell as quickly as they were supposed to. Indeed, only 6 percent of the 13 million personal computers installed in U.S. corporate offices were connected to a local area network according to a 1987 estimate by market researcher Dataquest, Inc.

Finally, however, the problems are being solved and the idea is catching on. Analysts at International Data Corp. expect the number of networks installed worldwide to reach 220,000 in 1987, up from 52,000 in 1984 (see graph). Industry giants such as Digital Equipment, AT&T, Hewlett-Packard, Apple, and IBM have introduced new products to go after a market which until now has been dominated by smaller companies such as Ungermann-Bass, Novell, 3Com, and Fox Research. The entry of these large companies is expected to add credibility to technology that has had only limited acceptance, with the end result that worldwide sales of computer networks could hit $3.5 billion by 1990.

Perhaps the 1990s will be the "Decade of the Network."

Source: Adapted from "Suddenly the Heavyweights Smell Money in Computer Networks," *Business Week*, April 27, 1987, pages 110–113.

Network Topology

The **topology** of a network describes the way computers in the network connect to one another. Three common types of network connections, star, bus, and ring, are shown in Figure 12.8.

THAT REMINDS ME OF THE NETWORK YOU PUT IN.....!

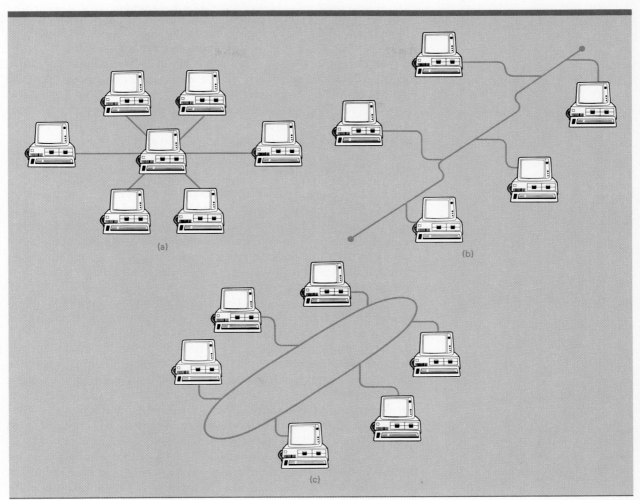

FIGURE 12.8
(a) Star, (b) bus, and (c) ring
networks.

Figure 12.8*a* shows a **star network,** consisting of a central computer and several satellites. All requests for communication go through the central computer. The network is simple to establish but not very reliable, as it is entirely dependent on the central computer. In other words, if the central unit goes down, the entire system is disabled. Star networks are typically used where a large mainframe computer is accessed by remote terminals.

Figure 12.8*b* shows a **bus network,** in which a single communications channel (cable) connects the devices to one another. (The beginning and end of the network do not connect to one another.) In a bus network, information is passed between any two devices, one pair at a time. The communicating devices seize control of the common cable (bus), transmit the message, and then release the bus. Bus topology is used in local area networks when the computers and supporting devices are spread throughout a building, because it is an easy matter to run a single communications channel through the building. (Figure 12.7 is another example of a bus network.)

Figure 12.8*c* shows a **ring network,** in which a single communications channel runs through the entire system and connects the beginning and ending devices. Unlike the star network, the ring network has no central computer; thus failure of one computer will not prevent the remaining devices from interacting. Devices connected in a ring topology communicate more efficiently than those in a bus.

IBM's Token Ring Network

The IBM token ring network is only one of several LAN systems on the market, but given the dominant position of IBM it is a system which merits consideration. The **token ring network** runs over ordinary telephone wire and does *not* require special cabling to be installed. (IBM did not invent the token concept or the idea of a ring configuration, and it is reputed to have paid a $5 million fee to clear a patent filed by Olof Soderblom of the Netherlands.)

Figure 12.9 depicts the operation of a network in which a **token,** or electronic signal, passes each device in the network thousands of times a second. Any device wishing to transmit data to another device within the network must first get hold of the token. Access to the network will be granted automatically if the token is free, otherwise the device wishing to transmit must wait until the token becomes available. Once the free token is secured, the sending device attaches its message and the now busy token races to the recipient, who copies the message and sends a confirmation. The token is then released and becomes available for other messages.

The token ring network ensures reliable transfer of data because only one device at a time can possess the token and thereby access the network. The speed of the process makes it appear that the network is instantly responding to requests for service; in reality, however, only one user at a time is using the facility. The token ring scheme runs into difficulty only when too many computers are attached to the network.

FIGURE 12.9
IBM's token-passing ring network.
(Courtesy of *The New York Times*.)

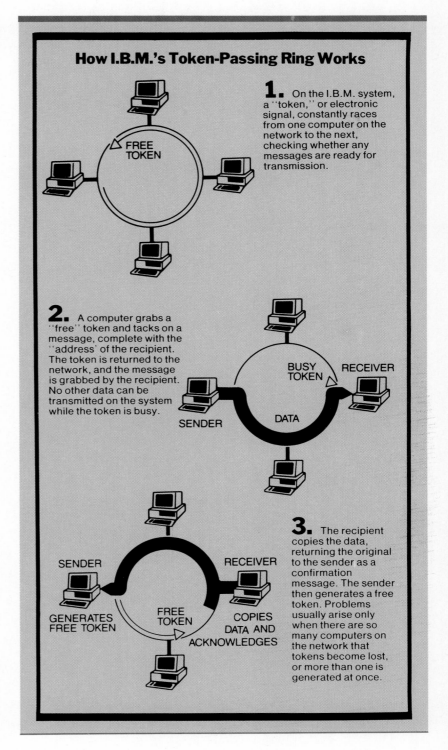

How I.B.M.'s Token-Passing Ring Works

1. On the I.B.M. system, a "token," or electronic signal, constantly races from one computer on the network to the next, checking whether any messages are ready for transmission.

FREE TOKEN

2. A computer grabs a "free" token and tacks on a message, complete with the "address" of the recipient. The token is returned to the network, and the message is grabbed by the recipient. No other data can be transmitted on the system while the token is busy.

BUSY TOKEN   RECEIVER

SENDER   DATA

3. The recipient copies the data, returning the original to the sender as a confirmation message. The sender then generates a free token. Problems usually arise only when there are so many computers on the network that tokens become lost, or more than one is generated at once.

SENDER   RECEIVER

GENERATES FREE TOKEN   FREE TOKEN   COPIES DATA AND ACKNOWLEDGES

Year-end statistics for 1987:
Sales: $33.6 billion
Profits: $2.0 billion
CEO: Robert E. Allen
Headquarters: 550 Madison Avenue
           New York, NY 10022
           (212) 605-5500

The divestiture has been painful. Then again, any action aimed at one of the world's largest companies, which took 10 years and $400 million in legal fees, could not by definition be easy.

The now well-known reorganization of AT&T began during 1974 when the Justice Department filed an antitrust suit against the Bell system, charging that it had monopolized communications markets. When it was finally over on January 1, 1984, the company that Alexander Graham Bell had begun over 100 years earlier ceased to exist. In its place was a much smaller AT&T and seven regional companies, each of which was still among the nation's largest businesses.

The new companies, or "Baby Bells," now provide all local calling and access to long-distance lines, as well as directory assistance and/or customer equipment. The residual AT&T (which includes Bell Laboratories and Western Electric) retained its long-distance service as well as responsibility for the customer equipment in place. In addition it could compete openly in both the communications and computer industries. In essence, the settlement saddled the now much smaller AT&T with extraordinary losses in communications services, while at the same time eliminating restrictions that had prohibited

the sale of its computer technologies.

Things began reasonably well with first-year revenues and net income of approximately $34

billion and $1.6 billion, respectively; not bad for a "new" company. Two years later, however, the business outlook was much less optimistic. Although

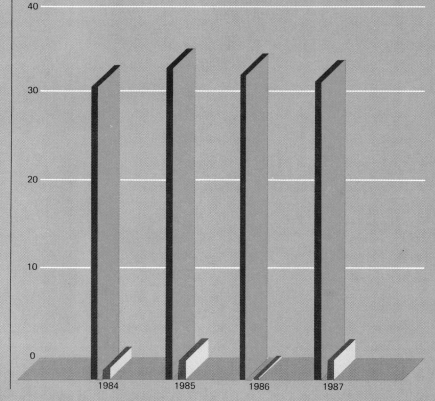

AT&T
SALES AND NET INCOME
(billions of dollars)

Telephone workers (1890s).

Alexander Graham Bell (1867).

long-distance operations remained extremely profitable, business and residential customers returned huge amounts of equipment, which in turn reduced rental income by some $2 billion. AT&T lost nearly $1 billion more on its 1986 computer operations, effectively wiping out earnings for the entire year and prompting the elimination of 27,000 jobs, a revolutionary development for a company that once offered lifetime security.

Painful as this has been, the much slimmer AT&T now competes more effectively in the global marketplace. More than 40 new computer products were

From *Personal Computing*, November 1987, page 36.

announced in 1987 alone, among them the AT&T 6312 and 6386 personal computers, both of which are based on the Intel 80386 microprocessor. The 6312 is designed for single users, is expandable to 13Mb RAM, and comes in a 20Mb, 40Mb, or 68Mb configuration. The 6386 services a network of up to 32 users, is expandable to 48Mb RAM, comes with a 40Mb, 68Mb, or 135Mb hard disk, and retails for just over $10,000 in its maximum configuration. The company also announced its DOS supervisor, which enables users to run up to eight MS-DOS applications simultaneously.

411

Summary

The once separate fields of computing and communications are fast merging, making it essential that any introductory book on computers include material on communications as well. Accordingly, this brief introductory chapter provided material directed at two basic issues: who to talk to, and how to establish the necessary connection.

Our first suggestion was that you begin with a general-purpose information utility such as CompuServe or The Source, which provide three types of services: communications (for example, electronic mail or conferencing), transactions (for example, banking at home), and information access (consulting online databases of which there are several hundred). We also included an introduction to local area networks.

The bulk of the chapter, however, dealt with the second question and discussed in detail the parameters needed to establish a communications protocol. We said that data could be transmitted in simplex, half-duplex, or full-duplex modes, that transmission could be synchronous or asynchronous, that parity checking may or may not be involved, and finally that the rate of transmission varies considerably, with 300, 1200, and 2400 bps common for personal computers. All this material was effectively summarized in a hands-on exercise directing you in the use of a telecommunications package.

Key Words and Concepts

Acoustic coupler	Emulation
Analog signal	File server
ASCII	Full-duplex channel
Asynchronous transmission	Gateway
AT&T	Half-duplex channel
Baud	Information utility
Bits per second (bps)	Local area network (LAN)
Bulletin board service (BBS)	Modem
Bus network	Modulation
Byte	Parity bit
Characters per second (cps)	Parity checking
Communications channel	Ring network
Communications protocol	RS-232C interface
Communications software	Serial port
CompuServe	Simplex channel
Data communication	The Source
Demodulation	Star network
Dial-up menu	Start bit
Download	Stop bit

Synchronous transmission
Telecommunications
Teleprocessing
Token

Token ring network
Topology
Uploading
Volume server

True/False

1. Personal computers have to be the same brand to communicate with each other.

2. A modem for the IBM PC can be contained entirely within its system unit.

3. The Hayes 1200 modem transmits data at 1200 cps (characters per second).

4. Synchronous, rather than asynchronous transmission, is most likely used for high-speed machine-to-machine communication.

5. Odd and even parity can be used simultaneously.

6. Simplex transmission is likely to be employed when data is transmitted between two personal computers.

7. CompuServe and The Source are examples of general-purpose information utilities.

8. The RS-232C device is an example of a modem.

9. A modem is all that is required to establish communication with another computer.

10. Every computer in a local area network (LAN) requires a modem.

11. A computer bulletin board is likely to let you upload a file with very few security precautions.

12. Local area networks are intended to share peripheral devices rather than data or software.

13. A local area network cannot have more than eight participating computers.

14. The IBM token ring network works over ordinary telephone wire.

15. There are eight bits in a byte.

Multiple Choice

1. In which year was the telephone invented?
   (a) 1851
   (b) 1876
   (c) 1901
   (d) 1926

2. Which of the following converts a parallel stream of 8 bits to a serial stream, and vice versa?
   (a) An RS-232C interface
   (b) A modem
   (c) An asynchronous terminal
   (d) A parity transmitter

3. Which device converts a digital signal to an analog signal, and vice versa?
   (a) An RS-232C interface
   (b) A modem
   (c) An asynchronous terminal
   (d) A parity transmitter

4. Which of the following is *not* a valid description of data flow direction?
   (a) Simplex
   (b) Full-simplex
   (c) Half-duplex
   (d) Full-duplex

5. Which of the following is a true statement about parity checking?
   (a) It *must* be used on all data transmissions
   (b) It will detect *and* correct errors in data transmission
   (c) It is specified as either even or odd
   (d) All the above

6. The presence of start and stop bits is characteristic of:
   (a) Asynchronous transmission
   (b) Synchronous transmission
   (c) Parity transmission
   (d) Communication problems

7. A communications protocol:
   (a) Is a standard that sets rules for communication between computers
   (b) Is a military officer specializing in data communications
   (c) Determines the type of local area network in effect
   (d) All the above

8. The process of copying a file from a computer bulletin board to your system is known as:
   (a) Uploading the file
   (b) Downloading the file
   (c) Crossloading the file
   (d) Transmitting the file

9. Which of the following is *not* a type of network topology?
   (a) Star network
   (b) Constellation network
   (c) Ring network
   (d) Bus network

10. Local area networks are intended to:
    (a) Share data among connected computers
    (b) Share peripheral devices among connected computers
    (c) Share programs among connected computers
    (d) All the above

11. What is a reasonable guess as to the number of online databases currently available?
    (a) Less than 10
    (b) From 10 to 100
    (c) From 100 to 1000
    (d) More than 1000

12. "Handshaking" is a term to describe:
    (a) The sign-on procedure for a bulletin board service
    (b) The initial contact between two communicating computers
    (c) The break in contact at the end of a session
    (d) None of the above

13. Given that the ASCII representation for the letter B is 01000010, and that even parity is in effect:
    (a) The bit string 01000010 0 will be transmitted
    (b) The bit string 01000010 1 will be transmitted
    (c) A total of 8 parity bits will be transmitted
    (d) A total of 9 data bits will be transmitted

14. Which of the following does *not* require communications software?
    (a) Accessing CompuServe and/or The Source
    (b) Exchanging files between your PC and other computers over the telephone
    (c) Accessing computer bulletin boards
    (d) Linking files between spreadsheets and graphics programs

15. Given a 2400-baud line and that asynchronous transmission is in effect, how many characters per second are transmitted?
    (a) 24,000
    (b) 2,400
    (c) 300
    (d) 240

Exercises

1. Try to locate a local area network on campus so that you can answer the following:
   (a) Who is allowed access to the network? What kind of security procedures are in effect?
   (b) What kind of devices, and how many of each, are on the network?

(c) Which company provided the network software? Have there been any problems during the installation of the network?

(d) What software is available to individuals on the network?

(e) Does the purchase of one copy of a program, for example, Lotus or dBASE, legally entitle every user access to that program? How is the situation handled on your network?

(f) Which data files are available to users of the network? Is every user allowed access to all these files? What happens if two users want to access the same file simultaneously?

2. To the extent that it's possible, repeat Hands-On Exercise 1 at your school or university.

(a) What problems (if any) did you have in doing the exercise?

(b) Is the response time on the mainframe as fast as it is on a PC? Does the response time vary according to the time of day you log on? Why should this be so?

(c) What advantages does the mainframe provide over a stand-alone PC? Over a networked PC?

(d) What advantages does a PC provide over a mainframe?

3. Communications costs associated with online information services such as The Source or CompuServe are greatly affected by the transmission rate of the communications channel.

(a) Approximately how long does it take to transfer a 20Kb file at 300 bps?

(b) Repeat part a for 1200 and 2400 baud, respectively. Can you see how a higher initial outlay may significantly reduce communications cost?

(c) Studies have shown that a switch from a 1200-baud line to 2400 baud reduces communications costs by approximately one-third rather than one-half. Can you account for the apparent discrepancy?

4. Contrary to what the ads of Federal Express and its competitors may tell us, there may be faster and cheaper ways of transmitting information.

(a) What is the cost of a 2-ounce letter sent by Federal Express or one of its competitors? How long does it take to deliver the letter?

(b) How long (and at what cost) does it take to transmit the same letter by computer (assume a three-page letter, double-spaced). What parameters are necessary for you to accurately determine the cost of transmission?

(c) How long does it take to transmit the contents of a floppy disk (360Kb)? Answer for 300 and 1200 baud, respectively.

(d) What is the approximate cost of this transmission if you do not have access to a WATS line (assume telephone charges of $1.00 per minute)?

(e) What is the cost of mailing a disk? Answer for both first-class and overnight service.

FIGURE 12.10
Data transmissions for exercise 5.

5. Figure 12.10 contains the result of two data transmissions, each one byte long.
   (a) Which of the two is *valid under even parity*? What character does it represent? What would be the corresponding odd parity transmission?
   (b) Which of the two is *invalid under even parity*? Can you tell with any degree of certainty which character was transmitted? Explain why parity checking is an *error detection* technique rather than one for *error correction*.

6. Assume that you intend to use a PC as an aid in investing, and consequently you want to obtain financial data for all the stocks listed on the New York Stock Exchange. Find at least two information services that will provide the data you require. For each service:
   (a) Determine the initiation fee (if any) and the monthly subscription rate.
   (b) What communication software is necessary for you to access the service? What is the associated cost?
   (c) Does the service let you trade stocks? If so, compare its commission charges with that of a full-service brokerage.

CHAPTER 13

THE POWER USER

CHAPTER OBJECTIVES

After reading this chapter, you should be able to:

1. Discuss the importance of subdirectories; explain the function of the MD, CD, RD, TREE, PATH, and PROMPT commands.

2. Define the terms track, cluster, and sector; describe how to calculate the storage capacity of a disk.

3. Describe the relationship between the File Directory and File Allocation Table; discuss how it is possible to unerase a file.

4. Explain the use of the SORT, MORE, and FIND filters; discuss how the < and > symbols are used to alter the source and destination associated with various commands.

5. Explain the use of the F1 and F3 function keys, and how they can simplify the repetition and/or editing of DOS commands.

6. Describe what is meant by a batch file and the special role of the AUTOEXEC.BAT file.

7. Describe the BACKUP and RESTORE commands; discuss additional backup procedures.

8. Discuss the role of utility programs such as SideKick and the Norton Utilities.

Overview

In just a few short years three generations of microprocessors have drastically changed the performance characteristics of the personal computer. We have witnessed equally dramatic increases in the amount of memory available, and in the capacity, speed, and reliability of secondary storage devices. In much the same way we have become more sophisticated users who continually expect and demand more of the systems we purchase.

Consider, for example, that it has been only a few months since the semester began, and you were first exposed to the rudiments of DOS and word processing. Initially, you may have been thrilled with the mere availability of a word processor, yet you have probably progressed to where you perceive 256Kb RAM as inadequate and a floppy disk drive as too slow. The point we are making is that it is time to expand your knowledge of the PC and its operating system so that you can evolve from novice to "power" user.

Note, too, that despite the tremendous promise implied by OS/2, there are still some *10 million MS-DOS machines* in existence (with thousands more being added every month). In 1987 alone, 3 million 8086/8088 machines were shipped, none of which were capable of running OS/2. Another 3 million such machines are forecast for ship-

"Oh, do you sell data? I'll probably need some of that too."

ment as late as 1990! In other words, MS-DOS will be with us for many years, and it behooves you to learn as much about that operating system as possible.

Accordingly, the present chapter focuses entirely on MS-DOS, effectively continuing the discussion begun earlier in Chapter 2. It begins with material on *subdirectories*, and includes information on disk capacity and file allocation, the BACKUP and RESTORE commands, and the SORT, FIND, and MORE filters. The chapter also shows you how to establish a *virtual disk* (RAM drive) in a CONFIG.SYS file, indicates how it is possible to "unerase" a file, and concludes with a discussion of *batch* files and the special role of AUTOEXEC.BAT.

The Corporate Profile focuses on Intel Corporation, the developers of the 8086/8088, 80286, and 80386 microporcessors, without which the PC would not exist as we know it.

Subdirectories

The acquisition of a hard disk is by far the single most important step you can take to improve your overall capability. Mastery of a hard disk, however, requires that you learn how to organize the files on the disk in an efficient manner, which in turn leads to a discussion of subdirectories.

As you shall see, **subdirectories** are nothing more than a way of logically subdividing a disk into separate areas, much as a book is divided into chapters. In other words, you can establish one subdirectory to hold your word processing program and a different sub-directory to hold the documents it creates. You can also create different directories (the terms directory and subdirectory are used interchangeably) for each type of document, for example, one for each course you are taking, one for your personal correspondence, and so on. In similar fashion, you can establish still other directories for your spreadsheet, data management, and other applications.

To better appreciate the importance of subdirectories, consider that by the time you have completed all the Hands-On Exercises on word processing, spreadsheets, and data management, your data disk is likely to contain 50 or more files. Displaying the contents of that disk as a single directory would require several screens and, further, would mix all the different types of files together. Imagine how much more complicated the situation becomes when a hard disk, capable of storing hundreds (or thousands) of files, is used instead of a floppy. Subdirectories provide a way out of this dilemma.

Figure 13.1 depicts a series of subdirectories as they might appear on a disk. The arrangement in the figure is often described as a **tree structure**, because the various entries "branch" downward from the **root directory** at the top of the figure. In our example the root directory contains five subdirectories: SIDEKICK, WORDSTAR, DOS, DBASE, and LOTUS, with the last of these (LOTUS) containing two additional subdirectories of its own (BOBDATA and PAULDATA). Note, too, that any or all of the other subdirectories in the figure could in turn have their own subdirectories.

Another way to view Figure 13.1 is to regard the root directory as the *parent*, and the SIDEKICK, WORDSTAR, DOS, DBASE, and LOTUS subdirectories as its *children*. The LOTUS directory in turn is viewed as the parent of the PAULDATA and BOBDATA subdirectories. The family tree can go down as many generations as desired (although too many generations will become confusing and inefficient).

FIGURE 13.1
The use of subdirectories.

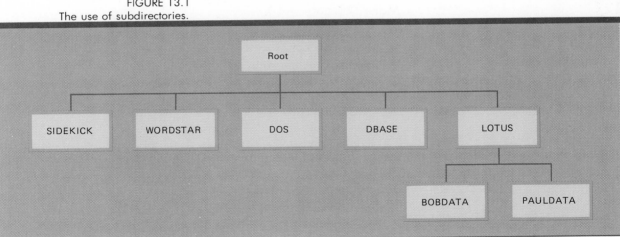

FIGURE 13.2
Listing of the root directory.

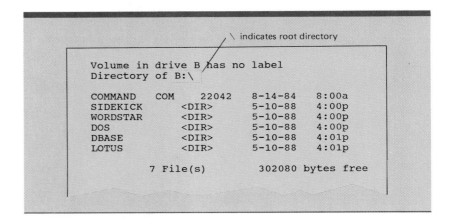

```
                                           \ indicates root directory

        Volume in drive B has no label
        Directory of B:\

        COMMAND    COM    22042    8-14-84    8:00a
        SIDEKICK          <DIR>    5-10-88    4:00p
        WORDSTAR          <DIR>    5-10-88    4:00p
        DOS               <DIR>    5-10-88    4:00p
        DBASE             <DIR>    5-10-88    4:01p
        LOTUS             <DIR>    5-10-88    4:01p

             7 File(s)           302080 bytes free
```

The root directory, as well as every subdirectory, can contain a combination of files and/or other subdirectories. The essential point, however, is that the contents of *each subdirectory are independent of all other subdirectories*. In other words, execution of a DIR command shows only those files and/or subdirectories that belong to the directory you are in.

Consider, for example, Figure 13.2, which shows the contents of the root directory as they would appear in response to a DIR command. The root directory contains the file COMMAND.COM, as well as the five subdirectories corresponding to the tree structure of Figure 13.1. However, the subdirectories BOBDATA and PAULDATA do *not* appear as these are children of the LOTUS subdirectory.

Six DOS commands, make directory (MD), change directory (CD), remove directory (RD), TREE, PATH, and PROMPT, will be discussed in conjunction with subdirectories.

Make Directory (MD)

The **make directory (MD, or MKDIR)** command creates a new subdirectory, and requires that the proper **path** (the means to travel to the directory in question) be in effect at the time the command is issued. With respect to Figure 13.1, you couldn't, for example, create the BOBDATA subdirectory in isolation; rather, you would have to indicate that BOBDATA is a child of LOTUS subdirectory, which in turn is the child of the root directory.

The backslash (\) is used in conjunction with the MD (and other) command(s) to separate the name of one subdirectory from another, and thus indicate the path DOS takes to reach a given subdirectory. For example, the commands below would create the LOTUS and BOBDATA subdirectories as they appeared in Figure 13.1.

MD\LOTUS   (Initial backslash implies that the path
                            begins at the root directory)

`MD\LOTUS\BOBDATA`   (Multiple slashes separate one sub-
                      directory name from another)

The initial backslash in each command begins the path at the root directory. In addition, if more than one backslash appears within a given path specification (as in the second example), then each successive backward slash represents a further downward level in the tree.

However, you need not always specify the complete path from the root to a subdirectory, but only that portion that extends from the directory where you are currently located. Thus if you wanted to create the LOTUS subdirectory and *were already in the root directory*, you would not have to include the initial backslash (to indicate the root directory). In similar fashion, given that you wanted to create the BOBDATA subdirectory *and were already in the LOTUS subdirectory*, you wouldn't have to respecify that information. Thus the commands:

`MD LOTUS`   (Assumes you are in the root directory)

`MD BOBDATA`   (Assumes you are in LOTUS subdirectory)

are equivalent to the previous commands, provided that you were positioned in the proper subdirectory when the commands were issued. However, the command MD \BOBDATA is *not* appropriate under any circumstances, as it would create BOBDATA directly under the root directory rather than the LOTUS subdirectory. DOS does not place a limit on the maximum number of subdirectories which can be created, although the maximum length of any path specification is 63 characters.

MD is an internal command.

Change Directory (CD)

The **change directory (CD, or CHDIR)** command changes the current directory and works in a fashion similar to the MD command with respect to specification of a path. Thus the commands:

`CD \LOTUS`

`CD \LOTUS\BOBDATA`

will move you to the LOTUS and BOBDATA subdirectories, respectively, regardless of where you were located when the commands were issued. This is because *each command contained the complete path specification beginning at the root directory, as dictated by the initial backslash.*

As previously indicated, however, the complete path specification may not be necessary depending on which subdirectory you are in when the commands are issued. The following commands are therefore equivalent to the two previously issued, provided you are in the proper subdirectory.

```
CD LOTUS          (Assumes you are in the root directory)

CD BOBDATA        (Assumes you are in LOTUS subdirectory)
```

Note also that *DOS always goes to the root directory when the computer is turned on (or whenever the system is rebooted).*

The change directory command is one of the most frequently used DOS commands, and as such has several variations to consider. In particular, issuing the command with no parameters will display the name of the current subdirectory, whereas CD followed by two periods moves you to the parent of the current subdirectory. You can also move directly to the root directory by specifying a simple backslash. In other words,

```
CD          (Displays the name of the current subdirectory)

CD ..       (Moves to the parent of the current subdirectory)

CD \        (Moves immediately to the root directory)
```

CD is an internal command.

Remove Directory (RD)

The **remove directory (RD or RMDIR)** command removes a subdirectory. Under no circumstances, however, can it remove the root directory or current subdirectory; that is, you cannot be in the subdirectory you intend to remove. In addition, the command requires that all the files in the subdirectory to be removed have been erased.

The following commands will remove the BOBDATA subdirectory from Figure 13.1:

```
CD \LOTUS\BOBDATA    (Changes to the BOBDATA subdi-
                      rectory)

ERASE *.*            (Erases all files in the BOBDATA
                      subdirectory)

CD ..                (Returns to the LOTUS subdirec-
                      tory, that is, the parent of BOB-
                      DATA)
```

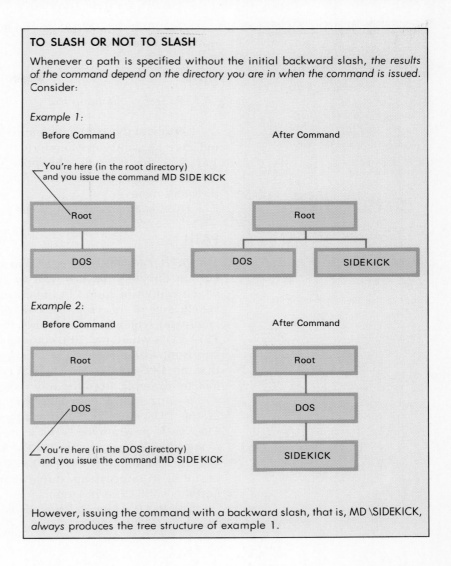

TO SLASH OR NOT TO SLASH

Whenever a path is specified without the initial backward slash, *the results of the command depend on the directory you are in when the command is issued.* Consider:

Example 1:

Before Command | After Command

You're here (in the root directory) and you issue the command MD SIDE KICK

Root | Root

DOS | DOS | SIDEKICK

Example 2:

Before Command | After Command

Root | Root

DOS | DOS

You're here (in the DOS directory) and you issue the command MD SIDE KICK

SIDEKICK

However, issuing the command with a backward slash, that is, MD \SIDEKICK, *always* produces the tree structure of example 1.

RD BOBDATA   (Removes BOBDATA subdirectory)

RD is an internal command.

TREE

Not being able to "see the forest" for the trees is a problem which besets all users, particularly beginners. Accordingly, DOS provides the **TREE** command, which displays the "forest," that is, all subdirectories (and optionally the files within each directory) that currently exist on a disk.

```
Path: \SIDEKICK
Sub-directories: None

Path: \WORDSTAR
Sub-directories: None

Path: \DOS
Sub-directories: None

Path: \DBASE
Sub-directories: None

Path: \LOTUS
Sub-directories:    PAULDATA
                    BOBDATA

Path: \LOTUS\PAULDATA
Sub-directories: None

Path: \LOTUS\BOBDATA
Sub-directories: None
```

FIGURE 13.3
Output of the TREE command.

The TREE command may be issued with or without a file (/F) option as follows:

```
TREE

TREE/F     (File option)
```

Output of the TREE command (without the file option) is shown in Figure 13.3, and corresponds to the original tree structure of Figure 13.1. Note that if the file (/F) option had been included, then all the files in each subdirectory would be shown immediately under the directory name.

TREE is an external command.

PATH

The **PATH** command causes DOS to search directories other than the current directory for files with an extension of COM, EXE, or BAT, which cannot be found in the current directory. To appreciate the significance of this command, recall that TREE is an *external* DOS command, which in turn requires the availability of the program file TREE.COM when the TREE command is issued. Assume further that you want to issue the TREE command when in a directory other than the DOS subdirectory (which contains the TREE.COM program file), for example, from the root directory.

Issuing a TREE command from the root directory would result in the DOS message, "Bad command or filename" because the TREE.COM program file is not in the root directory. Thus if you are to successfully execute the TREE command from the root directory, you must either copy the TREE.COM program file to this directory (resulting in unnecessary duplication of files), or tell DOS where to find the TREE.COM program.

The PATH command accomplishes the latter objective through the command:

```
PATH C:\DOS
```

which tells the operating system to look in the DOS subdirectory of drive C for any program files it cannot find in the current directory. (You should always indicate the *complete* path specification, including the drive and root directory.)

More than one subdirectory may be searched by specifying multiple paths in a single PATH command, and separating the paths by semicolons. For example, the command:

```
PATH C:\DOS;C:\LOTUS;C:\WORDSTAR
```

searches the subdirectories DOS, LOTUS, and WORDSTAR in that order after first searching the current subdirectory.

A PATH command remains in effect until the next PATH command is issued. You can, however, cancel an existing path specification by issuing the command with just a semicolon. Specification of the command by itself (that is, PATH with no parameters) will display the current path. In other words:

PATH C:\DOS;C:\UTILITY   (Changes the current path)

PATH   (Displays the current path)

PATH;   (Cancels the current path)

PATH is an internal command.

PROMPT

The appearance of the DOS prompt, typically A> (or C>), indicates that DOS is waiting for a command, and further that the default drive is drive A (or drive C). It is possible, however, to change the prompting message to include the current directory and/or additional information.

The format of the **PROMPT** command is simply PROMPT $c, where $c denotes one (or more) of the following:

t	The time
d	The date
p	The current directory of the default drive
v	The version number
n	The default drive
g	The ">" character
l	The "<" character
=	The "=" character
Blank	The " " character

Examples of the PROMPT command are shown in Table 13.1. The first example displays the current drive and directory and is, in our opinion, the most useful alternate specification of the prompt. The extra information takes some getting used to, but the constant reminder of where you are (which directory you are in) saves mistakes in the long run.

The last example, PROMPT ng, restores the prompt to its default value, as does PROMPT with no parameter.

PROMPT is an external command.

TABLE 13.1

Examples of the PROMPT Command

Command	Result
PROMPT pg	C:\LOTUS\BOBDATA
PROMPT $	(No prompt displayed)
PROMPT $d	Sat 1-21-1989
PROMPT ng	C>

The following Hands-On Exercise provides you with the opportunity to implement the various commands associated with subdirectories. Although subdirectories are of greatest benefit in systems with a hard disk, they may also be used with floppy disks, and the exercise is in fact written for a two-drive floppy system. This is because:

1. You may not have a hard disk available on which to practice.

2. If you make a mistake, you have not affected the hard disk, and so the consequences of an error are minimized.

SAVING KEYSTROKES WITH THE FUNCTION KEYS

Commands entered at the keyboard are stored in a keyboard buffer, the contents of which can be recalled through the **F1 and/or F3 function keys.** The F1 key returns the last command issued one character at a time; the F3 key returns the buffer contents in their entirety.

The function keys are useful when successive commands are similar in nature as in the case of creating and then changing to a subdirectory, for example,

```
C> MD \LOTUS\PAULDATA
C> CD \LOTUS\PAULDATA
```

Instead of typing the CD command in its entirety, you could simply type C (the character which changes from the previous command), then press the F3 function key to retrieve the remainder of the previous (MD) command from the keyboard buffer, then press Return to execute the CD command. Try it.

HANDS-ON EXERCISE 1: SUBDIRECTORIES

OBJECTIVE: Use the DOS commands associated with subdirectories, namely, MD, CD, RD, TREE, PATH, and PROMPT.

Step 1: Boot the System

Place a DOS system disk in drive A and a newly formatted disk in drive B, then turn on the computer. The disk in drive B should also be bootable and include the system files; that is, it should have been formatted with the command FORMAT B:/S.

Step 2: The PROMPT Command

Given that the entire exercise deals with subdirectories, it will be useful to always know the directory you are in. Accordingly, enter the command

```
PROMPT $P$G
```

whereupon the next prompt which appears should be A:\>. The presence of the backslash indicates that you are currently in the root directory of drive A.

Step 3: List the Initial Directory

Type B: to change the default drive to drive B, then enter the DIR command to obtain a directory of the disk in drive B. The only file you should see is COMMAND.COM (taking 22,042 bytes in DOS 3.0 or less in DOS 2.10). *Make sure the system indicates drive B as the default.*

Step 4: The MD Command

Create the top half of the tree structure of Figure 13.1 by entering the following commands in succession:

```
MD SIDEKICK

MD WORDSTAR

MD DOS

MD DBASE

MD LOTUS
```

When you have finished, execute the DIR command once again. You should see the presence of the five subdirectories in the root directory; that is, your directory should resemble Figure 13.2 from the previous discussion. (Since each of the preceding subdirectories belongs directly to the root, a backslash could have been included in each MD command, for example, MD \SIDEKICK.)

Step 5: Create Additional Subdirectories

Create two subdirectories in the LOTUS directory with the commands:

```
MD \LOTUS\PAULDATA

MD \LOTUS\BOBDATA
```

The backslashes show the path of the subdirectories; for example, PAULDATA belongs to LOTUS, which in turn belongs to the root directory. Issuing a DIR command at this point would display the same directory as in step 4, as the system is still in the root directory. (Neither PAULDATA nor BOBDATA would appear in the root directory, as they both belong to LOTUS.)

Step 6: The CD Command

Type the command CD \LOTUS (or equivalently, CD LOTUS *without the backslash*, since you are still in the root directory) to enter the LOTUS subdirectory. Now issue a DIR command to obtain the directory listing of Figure 13.4.

Observe that the display of a subdirectory always contains two special entries, a single period and a double period, which appear in lieu of file names in the directory listing. The single period identifies this "file" as a subdirectory; the double period is used by DOS to represent the higher-level directory (that is, the parent) which contains this subdirectory. The use of subdirectories also requires a certain amount of overhead, as evidenced by the fact that the remaining disk capacity of 294,912 bytes is approximately 7000 bytes less than what existed at the beginning of the exercise.

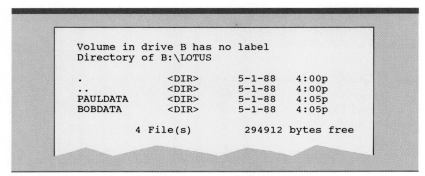

```
Volume in drive B has no label
Directory of B:\LOTUS

.               <DIR>        5-1-88      4:00p
..              <DIR>        5-1-88      4:00p
PAULDATA        <DIR>        5-1-88      4:05p
BOBDATA         <DIR>        5-1-88      4:05p

        4 File(s)           294912 bytes free
```

FIGURE 13.4   Directory listing for Lotus subdirectory.

Step 7: Copying Files to a Subdirectory

This step shows how files may be copied to a subdirectory, and copies all files from the DOS system disk in drive A to the newly created DOS subdirectory in drive B. Enter the commands:

```
CD \DOS

COPY A:*.* B:
```

Since you already have a copy of COMMAND.COM in the root directory, it is unnecessary to keep a second copy in the DOS subdirectory. Hence enter the command ERASE B:COMMAND.COM after the files have been copied. [Under DOS 3.20 (or higher) the system will return a message indicating "Insufficient disk space" when it attempts to copy all the files from the system disk. In this instance you need to erase COMMAND.COM, after which you can copy the one remaining file with the command, COPY A:XCOPY.COM B:]

STEP 8: The PATH Command

Issue the commands below to return to the root directory and execute the CHKDSK program.

```
CD \        (Change to the root directory)

CHKDSK      (DOS will indicate, "Bad com-
            mand or file name")
```

You did not make an error; the system is simply saying it can't find the program file CHKDSK.COM in the current directory. (Recall that CHKDSK is an *external* command and requires the availability of CHKDSK.COM.) Remain in the root directory and issue the commands:

```
PATH B:\DOS      (Supply a path to the sub-
                 directory    containing
                 CHKDSK.COM)

CHKDSK           (CHKDSK will execute suc-
                 cessfully)
```

Step 9: The TREE Command

Type the command TREE (with no parameters) to display the subdirectories on your disk as shown previously in Figure 13.3. Now enter the TREE command with the file option TREE/F to obtain a listing of the files in each subdirectory.

Step 10: The RD Command

Make sure you are still in the root directory, then enter the command RD SIDEKICK to remove the SIDEKICK subdirectory. (The system will execute the command without an additional message, then display the DOS prompt.) You can verify the success of the RD command by entering another TREE command (omit the file option) to show that the SIDEKICK subdirectory has been removed.

COMMAND SUMMARY

Subdirectories

Root directory   The main directory, from which all subdirectories originate; DOS always boots to the root directory

MD, or MKDIR   The command to make (create) a directory; must be issued before a directory can be used

CD, or CHDIR   The command to change directories; CD by itself will indicate the current directory, CD . . will return to the parent directory, and CD \ returns to the root directory

RD, or RMDIR   The command to remove (delete) a directory; a directory must be empty before it can be removed

TREE   An external command which displays all subdirectories (and optionally all files within each subdirectory)

PATH   The command which indicates where else to search if the specified program cannot be found in the current directory; PATH by itself displays the current path

PROMPT   External command to change the default DOS prompt of A> or C> to a more informative entry

SIDEKICK—THE FIRST DESKTOP ORGANIZER

Pop-up, **RAM-resident,** or more officially, TSR (terminate and stay resident) utilities enable you to temporarily leave the application on which you are working, enter the utility, then return to the application at the point where you left off. SideKick was the first and, today, four years and nearly a million copies later, is the standard against which competitors are judged. The concept behind the program was to provide immediate access to the same accessories that an individual has at a desk, namely, a calculator, calendar, notepad, and telephone dialer (a convenient ASCII character table is also included).

The *notepad* allows you to edit (and/or create) files of up to 45Kb anywhere on your disk. Regardless of which word processor you use, the ability to access a capable editor from within an application is invaluable (and something the authors do all the time). You can, for example, write notes to yourself in the middle of a spreadsheet session, or temporarily suspend execution of a dBASE program to edit dBASE program files. The notepad also includes a clipboard feature in which you can capture screens of application programs for subsequent inclusion into other documents.

The *calculator* works in binary, hexadecimal, or decimal, and it mimics the operation of a standard calculator. The *telephone dialer* includes a directory feature which can pick numbers off the screen or search a designated file (by name, company, or mnemonic code). The calendar moves forward or backward, allows you to enter appointments for the day in question, then prints the calendar as directed.

Authors' Comments:
To our way of thinking a desktop organizer is a major convenience, and one you shouldn't do without. Needless to say, the success of SideKick has spawned many competitors, some of which go well beyond the program they copied. (See "TSR Desktop Organizers: More Features, Fewer Conflicts," PC Magazine, August 1987, for a review of 14 such programs.)

Disk Fundamentals

Whether you use a hard or a floppy disk, and if the latter, irrespective of whether you choose the older $5\frac{1}{4}$-inch or new $3\frac{1}{2}$-inch model, data is stored essentially the same way. It is recorded on concentric circles known as **tracks,** with each track divided into an equal number of **sectors** (see Figure 13.5a). In addition, every sector on every track, from the innermost (smallest track) to the outermost (largest track), holds the same amount of data.

The amount of data contained on a disk depends on several factors:

1. The number of *recording surfaces* (for example, whether data are written on one or two sides) and/or the number of platters (on a hard disk) as shown in Figure 13.5b

2. The number of *tracks* per recording surface

3. The number of *sectors* per track

4. The number of *bytes* per sector

By way of illustration, let us calculate the storage capacity of the ubiquitous double-sided, double-density, $5\frac{1}{4}$-inch disk which has the following parameters: 40 tracks per surface, 9 sectors per track, and 512 bytes per sector. Consider:

$$= \frac{40 \text{ tracks}}{\text{surface}} \times \frac{9 \text{ sectors}}{\text{track}} \times \frac{2 \text{ surfaces}}{\text{disk}} \times \frac{512 \text{ bytes}}{\text{sector}}$$

$$= \frac{360 \times 1024 \text{ bytes}}{\text{disk}}$$

$$= \frac{360\text{Kb}}{\text{disk}}$$

Advances in technology continue to pack increasing amounts of data onto all types of storage media; for example, the capacity of the $5\frac{1}{4}$-inch floppy disk has increased from 160Kb in the original PC, to 360Kb as shown above, to 1.2Mb for the quad density floppy in the AT. The actual numbers are unimportant; what is significant is the concept of how data is stored on disk and what factors influence a disk's capacity (namely, the number of recording surfaces, the number of bytes per sector, the number of sectors per track, and the number of tracks per surface).

Given an awareness of disk capacity, we next consider how individual files are stored and retrieved. DOS allocates space to every file in terms of logical units called *clusters* rather than sectors, and allocates *a minimum of one cluster* to every file.

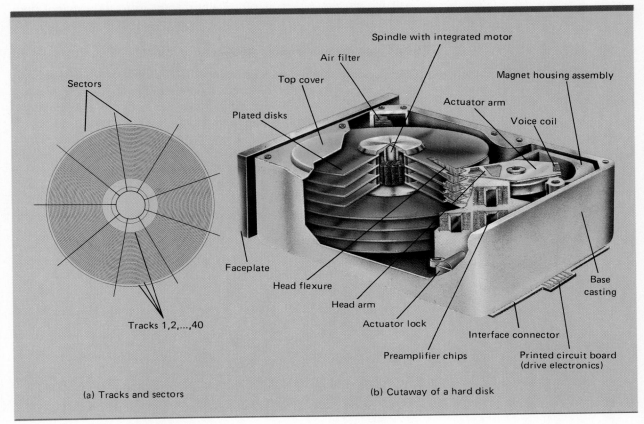

Sectors

Plated disks

Faceplate

Head flexure

Head arm

Actuator lock

Preamplifier chips

Tracks 1,2,...,40

Top cover

Air filter

Spindle with integrated motor

Actuator arm

Magnet housing assembly

Voice coil

Base casting

Interface connector

Printed circuit board (drive electronics)

(a) Tracks and sectors

(b) Cutaway of a hard disk

FIGURE 13.5 Disk capacity.

A **cluster** consists of a predetermined number of sectors, with the actual number of sectors depending on the storage medium and formatting program. A floppy disk, for example, has two sectors per cluster, whereas clusters on a hard disk contain anywhere from 4 to 16 sectors, each with 512 bytes. This in turn translates to minimum file sizes of 2048 to 8192 bytes, respectively, which means that indiscriminately filling a hard disk with numerous "small" files consumes significantly more space than you may have thought previously. (In similar fashion, every file on a floppy disk requires at least 1024 bytes regardless of its size.)

To further complicate the situation, the clusters assigned to a given file need not be contiguous. In other words clusters for the same file can be found on different tracks and even different recording surfaces. Assume, for example, that a word processor creates documents A and B in sequence, then is used to edit document A. DOS does not store the new (edited portion) of document A next to the original document, because that space is already taken by document B. Instead, the edited portion of document A is assigned the next available cluster, which is physically distant from the original document.

The File Directory and File Allocation Table

DOS uses a combination of the cluster concept, File Directory, and File Allocation Table for disk management. The **File Directory** has a separate entry for each file, containing (among other items) the name of the file, its size, and the date and time the file was last modified. The directory also contains a pointer to the **File Allocation Table (FAT)**, which indicates the first cluster assigned to the file. The situation is explained with the aid of Figure 13.6.

The File Directory in Figure 13.6 has entries for three files: FILE.ONE, FILE.TWO, and FILE.THR. In order to retrieve a particular file, DOS determines the first cluster used by that file from the File Directory, then goes to the FAT to retrieve the additional clusters. For example, FILE.ONE begins in cluster 1, which in turn points to cluster 2, which in turn points to cluster 3, at which point the end of file (EOF) is reached. In similar fashion, FILE.TWO is contained in clusters 4 and 5, and FILE.THR in cluster 6.

FIGURE 13.6   Conceptual view of file allocation on disk.

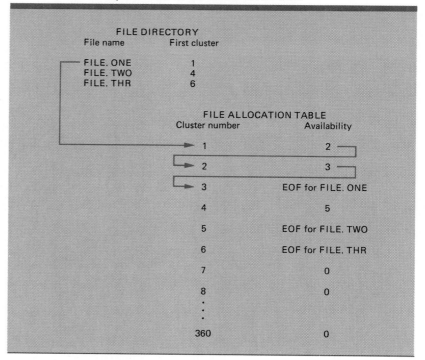

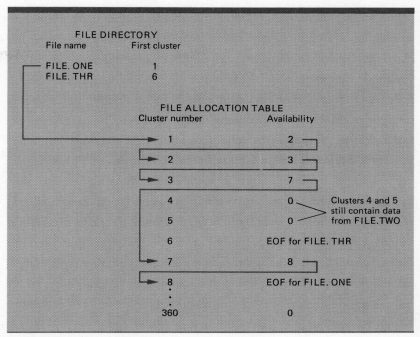

FIGURE 13.7   Conceptual view of file allocation on disk/II.

As implied by Figure 13.6, the FAT is a listing of all the clusters on the disk, with a unique identifying number assigned to each cluster. The availability entry associated with each cluster contains a pointer (that is, the number of the next cluster used by that file), an end-of-file (EOF) marker, or a zero indicating that the cluster is not presently in use and hence is available to store new data.

Now consider what happens if FILE.ONE gets larger, after which FILE.TWO is deleted, as depicted in Figure 13.7. As indicated, FILE.ONE requires additional space and so is assigned the first available cluster(s), which in our example are clusters 7 and 8; that is, FILE.ONE is now spread over clusters 1, 2, 3, 7, and 8. (This process is repeated whenever a file is saved, so that eventually the file becomes *fragmented* as other files are scattered in similar fashion.)

The deletion of FILE.TWO results in a different action, as the operating system marks the clusters formerly used by the file as being available; that is, the pointers are changed to zeros to indicate that data from other files may be subsequently written in the clusters previously assigned to FILE.TWO. Realize, however, that as Figure 13.7 now stands, FILE.TWO could be "unerased" by restoring the pointers to what they were in Figure 13.6 (see the box on the Norton Utilities).

PETER NORTON: COMPUTER GURU

Building a Booming Business around Utility Programs

Peter Norton has made a name for himself in software, not with flashy applications or entertaining games, but with utilities. Utilities are handy programs that simplify working with your files. If it's hard to imagine a booming software business centered around utilities, try to recall the last time your computer mysteriously lost a file. What would you have given for a program that could find and restore the information on your disk?

"I just want to publish useful and profitable stuff."

The Norton Utilities have made believers out of thousands of personal-computer owners. They have also turned this 43-year-old California native into an extremely wealthy man.

Norton didn't set out to make millions. In fact, he began developing his utilities as a hobby. While working as a data-processing consultant for an insurance firm, he began programming the personal computer for fun. "Snooping programs," he calls his first efforts, "programs that would show me the intimate structure of the disk. I'd blow a few files, but I knew that the data was on the disk. I just couldn't get to it."

As he developed his utilities and became familiar with the IBM PC, Norton realized that other people could profit from his knowledge. He printed a series of tip sheets, and on the back he advertised his utilities. He sent the flyers to computer stores and user groups, and slowly gained a reputation as something of a PC savant. Word spread as he visited user groups and began writing articles for IBM PC–oriented magazines. A book publisher invited him to write about IBM's new microcomputer. *Inside the IBM PC*, published by Robert J. Brady Co. in 1983, has since become one of the classic texts about the IBM Personal Computer.

Norton has also recently developed a new program, *The Norton Commander*, which is a command shell for DOS. Although many firms have tried to sell DOS shells—programs that simplify the command structure of DOS—few have had wide commercial success. Norton attributes this to the time it takes to learn them. He hopes to overtake competitors by offering such features as simple scrolling through directories, optional use of a mouse, and disk maintenance.

Norton seems to be as proud of his industry-maven status as he is of his business success. He continues to write computer books and magazine articles because he believes they are invaluable in "helping the populace cope with computers without getting indigestion." And, yes, they also help make the Norton name a household word.

Adapted from Paul Freiberger, *Lotus Magazine*, September 1986, page 24.

Filters, Piping, and Redirection

A DOS **filter** is a program that reads data from an input device (usually the keyboard), modifies (or filters) the data, then writes it to an output device (usually the monitor). Three filters are provided by DOS:

SORT   Rearranges data in ascending (descending) sequence

MORE   Displays the output one screenful at a time, pausing at the end of each screen and requiring the user to press any key to continue

FIND   Searches the input data for all lines containing a designated character string (enclosed in quotes)

Each of these filters may be used in conjunction with the **piping** feature, indicated by a vertical bar (**¦**), which allows output from one program (or command) to be used as input to another. In other words, piping involves the chaining of one program or command to another.

One common use of piping is to combine the TYPE command with the MORE filter, for example, TYPE ¦ FILEONE ¦ MORE (where FILEONE is the name of the file). Recall that the TYPE command displays the contents of a file on the screen, without pausing from screen to screen when large files are displayed. Inclusion of the MORE filter, however, pauses the display at the end of every screen, which greatly enhances the utility of the TYPE command.

The following list contains several other examples of the DIR command in combination with piping and the various DOS filters:

DIR ¦ SORT   Produces a directory in alphabetical order

DIR ¦ MORE   Pauses the display of the directory

DIR ¦ SORT ¦ MORE   Produces a directory in alphabetical order, pausing the display at the end of a screen

DIR ¦ FIND "<DIR>"   Includes only subdirectories in the listing of the current directory

DIR ¦ FIND "<DIR>" ¦ SORT   Includes only subdirectories in the listing of the directory, showing them in alphabetic order

In addition to filters and piping, DOS also provides a *redirection* feature in which input to a program can come from other than the standard input device (keyboard) and/or output can go to other than the standard output device (monitor). (Piping is in fact a form of redirection.) The less than and greater than signs designate the input and output devices, respectively. For example, DIR > LPT1 directs output of the DIR command to the printer instead of the monitor, and the command SORT < DATA.TST indicates that the SORT filter is to receive its input from the file DATA.TST.

The SORT, MORE, and FIND filters are all *external* commands. (Filters, piping, and redirection are further illustrated in Hands-On Exercise 2).

Batch Files

As you learn more about DOS and continue to use the computer, you will find yourself repeatedly executing the same set of commands. For example, you may begin every session by establishing the same series of alternate paths, changing to the same default prompt, and loading one or more of the same utility programs. However, rather than having to continually retype the same sequence of commands, it would be far more convenient to store the commands in a file and then invoke the file (with only a few keystrokes). This is precisely what is done in a **batch file,** which consists entirely of individual DOS commands.

In essence, then, a batch file may be viewed as a program whose instructions consist of individual DOS commands which are executed in succession. You can choose any name for a batch file (so long as it is in accordance with the rules for naming other DOS files), but you must specify the extension BAT. The batch file is executed by typing the name of the file; for example, type HOMEWORK to execute the commands in the batch file HOMEWORK.BAT.

There is also a special batch file named **AUTOEXEC.BAT,** which if it is present *in the root directory of the default drive* will be executed automatically whenever the system is booted. In other words, you can store the commands to accomplish normal housekeeping in an AUTOEXEC file, and have them executed whenever you turn on the computer. Figure 13.8, for example, contains a typical AUTOEXEC.BAT file for the owner of a hard drive who has acquired some common utility programs.

The PATH command appears first, and directs the system to other subdirectories if the designated program(s) cannot be found in the current subdirectory. Three alternate paths are specified and are separated with semicolons. The DOS subdirectory is included to provide access to external DOS commands. A UTILITY subdirectory (containing programs such as the Norton Utilities) is also specified, as is a SIDEKICK subdirectory for the SideKick program.

```
PATH C:\DOS;C:\UTILITY;C:\SIDEKICK
PF 2
QUADCLOK
SK
PROMPT $P$G
DIR
```

FIGURE 13.8 A typical AUTOEXEC.BAT file.

Next, three programs are executed in succession. The command PF 2 executes a *screen saver* program (known as Phosphor Friend) to blank out the monitor if no commands are entered in a period of two minutes. QUADCLOK is another utility program (associated with a multifunction board by QUADRAM), which supplies DOS with the date and time as extracted from a battery-operated clock. (The PF and QUADCLOK programs are found in the UTILITY subdirectory.) Finally, the command SK loads SideKick.

The PROMPT command expands the normal DOS prompt to include the current subdirectory, and the concluding DIR command presents us with the files on the root directory.

The Question of Backup

It's bound to happen: Sooner or later you will be unable to recover an erased file, or worse yet, you will suffer hardware problems in which your disk is damaged and your files are gone. Take our word for it, nothing is more unpleasant than searching for a file which isn't there and/or discovering that the file you do retrieve is missing 50Kb worth of data. *Now*, when you are first becoming a serious user, is the time to develop good habits rgarding the protection of your data.

The only difficult aspect about backing up a floppy system is to remember to do it. Lack of time is not an excuse, as execution of the DISKCOPY command takes but a minute or two. We suggest that you keep at least two backup copies, and further that you keep the copies in different locations, for example, at home and in the office.

The procedure is obviously more complex when a hard disk is involved, because a 20Mb device contains the equivalent of approximately 55 floppies, each with 360Kb of data. You can still, however, provide effective backup with floppy disks by copying specific files at the end of every session. In other words, even though a disk contains up to 20 (or more) megabytes, only a few files are likely to change in each session, and those are the only files which need to be copied. Note, too, that it is generally more important to back up data files rather than commercial software, as the vendor can always supply another copy of the program. Replacing the spreadsheet containing the departmental budget for the next five years or duplicating your version of the great American novel is far more difficult.

DOS also provides the **BACKUP** (and corresponding **RESTORE**) command to transfer all the files on a hard disk to floppies, but the process is time-consuming and borders on the impractical. It is possible (and more productive) to back up selectively; for example, back up only those files which have been modified since the last backup (/M parameter), or only those files which have been modified since a specified date (/D parameter).

Backed-up files *cannot*, however, be used as data files until they have been restored to the hard disk. BACKUP, unlike COPY, does not produce an exact duplicate of a file, as it inserts additional control data which is subsequently used by the RESTORE command. The advantage of the BACKUP command over COPY is that when the file or files to be backed up exceed the capacity of a single floppy, you are automatically prompted for additional disks as necessary.

One alternative to consider is the purchase of a **tape backup** system, in which the contents of a 20Mb, 30Mb, or even 60Mb disk are reliably copied onto a single cassette. Best of all, the operation is accomplished in a matter of minutes, without you having to sit and patiently swap disks in and out of the machine. Yes, these units

The Galaxy 3220T features both under-3-minute hard disk image backup and restore and flexible file-by-file operations. The menu-driven software also offers a toggle into DOS, online help, and the ability to restore selected files from a disk image into any directory. Tapes can hold up to 20Mb of data and require no preformatting. (From *PC Magazine*, February 11, 1986.)

are expensive ($1000 is not uncommon), but prices are coming down all the time. Moreover, ask youself, "What is the cost of going *without* backup, when (not if) disaster strikes?" In other words, pay now or pay later.

CATALANO'S TUNNEL

Storing Computer Data under the Hudson River

Rodents, muggers, and harried commuters aren't the only inhabitants lurking undergound in New York City. If you know where to look, you can also find floppy disks and other types of magnetic media.

To discover why, you have to begin at the beginning. In 1874 a fellow named D. C. Haskin got the bright idea of connecting New York and New Jersey by an underground train. Haskin hired an engineering company and blasted away at a tunnel that would connect the two states beneath the murky depths of the Hudson River.

But like many other ambitious entrepreneurs of the last century, Haskin eventually found himself short of cash. In 1882 he went bankrupt, leaving behind a bunch of unpaid bills, angry creditors, and a tunnel that stretches from the site of today's World Trade Center complex to within 2,000 feet of the Jersey shore.

Switch to the present. Manhattan is bursting with floppy disks, disk packs, magnetic tapes, and other effluvia of the computer age. Safe storage locations within the island city are at a premium. Enter Paul Catalano.

Catalano is chairman and president of Dataport, a company that specializes in finding safe storage places for important business records. "I first became aware of this enormous facility during a survey we made in 1978. At the time, I tried to obtain it from the Port Authority [of New York and New Jersey, the site's owner]. They wouldn't do it." In 1984, after months of secret negotiations, Catalano obtained a 40-year lease from the Port Authority.

At one time the underground facility was also the old Hudson-Manhattan Terminal and Power Station. Catalano says that the three-square-block area tunnel has 30-foot-thick cement on bedrock sidewalls and a 9-foot-thick, 35-foot-high ceiling. It is set deeper into the earth than New York's present subway system. He points out that the structure is fireproof, theftproof, and highly secure even against nuclear blasts. "Best of all," he says, "it's within walking distance of Wall Street."

Dataport is sinking some $3 million worth of improvements into the tunnel. When sophisticated fiber optics are available, companies will be able to ship data to the site either electronically through a fiber-optic network or by truck.

The tunnel stored its first records on January 1, 1986.

Source: John Edwards, "Catalano's Tunnel," *Lotus Magazine,* February 1986, page 12.

Authors' Comments: Catalano's Tunnel provides the ultimate in backup, and certainly more protection than what the average PC user will require. Nevertheless, we hope you take the spirit of the article to heart, and we urge you to keep copies of your data in two different locations.

BEYOND DOS 2.00

Every command discussed up to this point is available in DOS 2.00. Thus, despite the fact that DOS 3.00 was announced as far back as 1984, millions of users have never felt the need to upgrade. However, the 1988 announcement of DOS 4.00 may well be the convincing factor due to the following:

- *A new DOSSHELL command* which creates an AUTOEXEC.BAT file, that substitutes a graphical interface instead of the cryptic C (or A) prompt. The interface in turn displays a menu to facilitate switching from one directory to the next, and further simplifies the execution of application programs.

- *Elimination of the 32Mb limit on hard disks* which made it necessary for owners of large disks (40Mb and up) to logically divide their disks into multiple volumes. Thus a 120Mb (available with the PS/2 model 70) can now be recognized as a single drive, as opposed to having to previously create four partitions (drive C, D, E, and F).

As you would expect, DOS 4.00 also supports the many new commands introduced in the previous release. Among them:

- *Inclusion of a virtual disk progrm (VDISK.SYS)* to create a **RAM disk** (virtual disk) in which a portion of memory (RAM) is used to simulate the operation of an ordinary disk. Operation of the virtual disk is very fast, but its contents are lost whenever the system is restarted or when power is lost. The RAM drive is implemented by including the necessary reference in the CONFIG.SYS file as shown:

```
DEVICE=C:\DOS\VDISK.SYS 200
```

The DEVICE command indicates the path to the VDISK.SYS program (on the DOS subdirectory in drive C), as well as the intended size of the virtual disk (200Kb).

- *A new ATTRIB command* that enables a file to be made "read only," which in turn prevents accidental deletion of that file.

- *A different space allocation scheme* to improve the likelihood of recovering lost files. Under 2.10, files were saved in the space most *recently surrendered* (which contains the clusters you would most likely want to "unerase"). DOS 3.00, on the other hand, allocates the space that was erased the longest time ago, thereby increasing the chances for successful data recovery.

- *Minor modifications in the FORMAT command*, making it more difficult to accidentally reformat a disk. The command now produces a warning message if you attempt to format drive C. It also requires you to specifically press the return key to initiate the formating operation, whereas the previous version accepted any key.

- *The addition of five keyboard programs*, KEYBUK (United Kingdom), KEYBGR (German), KEYBRF (French), KEYBIT (Italian), KEYBSP (Spanish), any of which can replace the keyboard program resident in ROM. The particular keyboards contain characters unique to the specific language (for example, accent marks) and also alter the position of special characters.

• *A new XCOPY command* (in DOS 3.20 and higher), combining fetures of the COPY and BACKUP commands, which is the easiest way to back up portions of a hard disk onto floppies.

THE DUMPTY DICTIONARY

Beginner: A person who believes more than one-sixteenth of a computer salesperson's spiel.

Advanced user: A person who has managed to remove a computer from its packing materials.

Power user: A person who has mastered the brightness and contrast controls on any computer's monitor.

Sales manager: Last week's new sales associate.

Consultant: A former sales manager who has mastered at least one-tenth of the dBASE III Plus manual.

Warranty: Disclaimer.

Service: Cursory examination, followed by utterance of the phrase "It can't be ours" and either of the words "hardware" or "software."

Support: The mailing of advertising literature to customers who have returned a registration card.

Videotex: A moribund electronic service offering people the privilege of paying to read the weather on their TV screens.

Artificial intelligence: The amazing, humanlike ability of a computer program to understand that the letter y means "yes" and the letter n means "no."

Electronic mail: A communications system with built-in delays and errors designed to emulate those of the United States Postal Service.

DOS shell: An educational tool forcing computer users to learn new methods of doing what they already can.

Turbo card: A device that increases an older-model computer's speed almost enough to compensate for the time wasted in getting it to work.

Clone: One of the many advanced-technology computers IBM is beginning to wish it had built.

IBM Product Centers: Historical land marks forever memorializing the concept of "list price only."

American-made: Assembled in the United States from parts made abroad.

CD-ROM: An optical device with storage sufficient to hold the billions of predictions claiming it will revolutionize the information industry.

Enhanced: Less awful in some ways than the previous model, and less likely to work as expected; e.g., "Enhanced Graphics Adapter," "Enhanced Keyboard," "Enhanced Extended Memory Specification."

Convertible: Transformable from a second-rate computer into a first-rate doorstop or paperweight. (Lexicological note: replaces the term "junior.")

Upgraded: Didn't work the first time.

Upgraded and improved: Didn't work the second time.

Memory-resident: Ready at the press of a key to disable any currently running program.

Multitasking: A clever method of simultaneously slowing down the multitude of computer programs that insist on running too fast.

Encryption: A powerful algorithmic encoding technique employed in the creation of computer manuals.

Desktop publishing: A system of software and hardware enabling users to create documents with a cornucopia of typefaces and graphics and the intellectual content of a Formica slab; often used in conjunction with encryption.

High resolution: Having nothing to do with graphics on IBM-compatible microcomputers.

Source: Stephen Manes, "The Dumpty Dictionary, Version 2.0," *PC Magazine*, October 28, 1986, page 111.

Authors' Comments:
Once again, Stephen Manes has come up with a set of tongue-in-cheek definitions. We hope you enjoy them and think about them as well. (You will find Version 1.0 in Chapter 2.)

HANDS-ON EXERCISE 2:
ADVANCED DOS COMMANDS

OBJECTIVE: Demonstrate the FIND, SORT, and MORE filters; use the ATTRIB and VDISK capabilities of DOS 3.00; implement an AUTOEXEC.BAT file.

Step 1: Boot the system
Place the disk created in the previous Hands-On Exercise in drive A and boot the system. Enter a DIR command to refresh your memory, but this time direct output of the command to the printer; that is, enter the command:

```
DIR > LPT1
```

Step 2: Create a RAM Disk (Requires DOS 3.00)
The creation of a RAM disk requires the establishment of a CONFIG.SYS file, a file used by DOS to establish a flexible environment. (CONFIG.SYS must be present on the root directory of the disk used to boot the system.) Enter the commands:

```
COPY CON: CONFIG.SYS
DEVICE=\DOS\VDISK.SYS 100
Press the F6 key followed by the return key
```

The COPY command copies a *source* file [in this case commands typed from the CONsole (or keyboard)] to a *destination* file, CONFIG.SYS. The latter consists of a single DEVICE command which specifies where the VDISK.SYS file is found. The 100 indicates the size (in kilobytes) of the virtual disk. Pressing the F6

key signifies the end of the source file (that is, no more commands will be entered from the console).

After entering a DIR command to verify that the CONFIG.SYS file is indeed present, reboot the system (Ctrl, Alt, and Del). You should see the following messages on the screen as the system comes up:

```
VDISK Version 1.0 virtual disk D:
     Sector size adjusted
     Directory entries adjusted
     Buffer size:          100 KB
     Sector size:          128
     Directory entries      64
```

You can also enter the command DIR D: to view the contents of the RAM drive (which is empty at this time).

Step 3: The ATTRIB Command (Requires DOS 3.00)
Enter the command PATH \DOS so that the system will be directed to the DOS subdirectory in this and future steps, should it be unable to find the command in the current subdirectory. Now enter the command:

```
ATTRIB +R CONFIG.SYS
```

to change the attribute of the newly created CONFIG.SYS file to read only, meaning that the file cannot be accidentally erased. Now try the command ERASE CONFIG.SYS, to which the system should respond "ACCESS DENIED". (The command ATTRIB −R CONFIG.SYS will remove the protection.)

Step 4: The MORE Filter

Make sure you are in the DOS subdirectory (the CD command, with no parameters, will indicate the current subdirectory), then issue a simple DIR command. The files in the directory will scroll off the screen, as there are too many to fit on one screen. Now reissue the DIR command, but couple it with a filter; that is,

```
DIR¦MORE
```

This time you will see one screen of data, with the message ——More——appearing at the bottom. Press any key to continue and the next screen appears.

Step 5: Create an AUTOEXEC.BAT File

Create a simple AUTOEXEC.BAT file to accept the date and time, establish a path to the DOS subdirectory, and change the prompt character to include the current subdirectory. The file itself may be established with a word processor or with the COPY CON command as follows:

```
CD \              (AUTOEXEC.BAT is in root directory)
COPY CON: AUTOEXEC.BAT
DATE
TIME
PATH A:\DOS       —— (The AUTOEXEC.BAT file)
PROMPT $P$G
```
Press the F6 key followed by the enter key

The COPY CON command copies subsequent entries from the console (keyboard) to the file specified; in this case, AUTOEXEC.BAT. The file consists of four DOS commands: DATE, TIME, PATH, and PROMPT, as indicated. When the last command (PROMPT) has been entered, press the F6 key (to indicate the end of the file to be copied) followed by the enter key, as indicated.

Boot the system, that is, press Ctrl, Alt, and Del simultaneously and observe what happens. (Creation of the RAM disk will occur independently of the AUTOEXEC file as a consequence of the CONFIG.SYS file established in step 2.)

Step 6: The Cluster Concept

Figure 13.9a shows the root directory at the start of the exercise, and 13.9b at the end. The latter figure

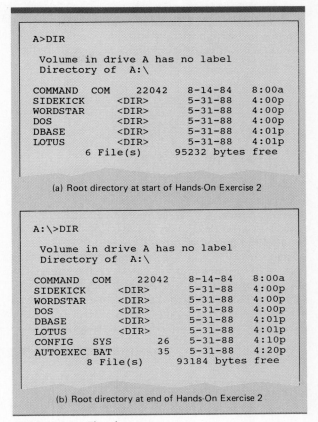

```
A>DIR

 Volume in drive A has no label
 Directory of  A:\

COMMAND   COM    22042    8-14-84    8:00a
SIDEKICK       <DIR>      5-31-88    4:00p
WORDSTAR       <DIR>      5-31-88    4:00p
DOS            <DIR>      5-31-88    4:00p
DBASE          <DIR>      5-31-88    4:01p
LOTUS          <DIR>      5-31-88    4:01p
        6 File(s)       95232 bytes free
```

(a) Root directory at start of Hands-On Exercise 2

```
A:\>DIR

 Volume in drive A has no label
 Directory of  A:\

COMMAND   COM    22042    8-14-84    8:00a
SIDEKICK       <DIR>      5-31-88    4:00p
WORDSTAR       <DIR>      5-31-88    4:00p
DOS            <DIR>      5-31-88    4:00p
DBASE          <DIR>      5-31-88    4:01p
LOTUS          <DIR>      5-31-88    4:01p
CONFIG    SYS      26     5-31-88    4:10p
AUTOEXEC  BAT      35     5-31-88    4:20p
        8 File(s)       93184 bytes free
```

(b) Root directory at end of Hands-On Exercise 2

FIGURE 13.9   The cluster concept.

contains only three files (COMMAND.COM, CONFIG.SYS, and AUTOEXEC.BAT), in addition to the various subdirectories, and we urge you to set up your hard drive in a similar uncluttered fashion. In other words, you should make efficient use of subdirectories, leaving as few files as possible on the root directory.

Note, too, the difference in available disk space between the two figures (95,232 bytes in Figure 13.9a versus 93,184 bytes in Figure 13.9b). The latter figure contained two additional files (CONFIG.SYS and AUTOEXEC.BAT), which collectively are 61 bytes in length; yet they decreased the available space on the disk by 2048 bytes (95,232 − 93,184). The apparent discrepancy is attributed to the fact that every file is assigned a minimum of one cluster regardless of its size, as was explained previously in the section on disk capacity.

Step 7: The DIR Command (with SORT and FIND)

The directory in Figure 13.9b lists the files and subdirectories contained in the root directory in no particular order. You can obtain an alphabetic directory and/or restrict the display to contain only subdirectories (or only files) through the SORT and FIND filters. Consider:

```
DIR ¦ SORT

DIR ¦ FIND "<DIR>"

DIR ¦ FIND/V "<DIR>"
```

Do not be surprised to see one or two additional files (whose names you do not recognize) displayed with the directories. Execution of DIR ¦ SORT, for example, causes the output of the DIR command to be sent to a *temporary* file, which is then input to the SORT filter, which in turn displays the output on the screen. (The temporary file is then deleted.) The output of any of the above commands can be sent to the printer through redirection, for example, DIR ¦ SORT>LPT1.

Step 8: The SORT Filter
The SORT filter may be used to sort the lines of data in any ASCII file as shown in Figure 13.10. Use the COPY CON command as shown in Figure 13.10a to create a test file, then sort the file as shown in Figure 13.10b and 13.10c. The less than sign in Figure 13.10b indicates that input is to be taken from the file TEST.DAT (as opposed to the standard input device); the greater than sign in Figure 13.10c redirects the sorted output to the printer.

Step 9: The FIND Filter
The FIND filter may also be applied to any file(s) as indicated by Figure 13.11. Figure 13.11a contains two sample files (which can be created with the COPY CON command), and Figure 13.11b, c, and d depicts variations in the FIND command. As indicated, the filter can be used with multiple files simultaneously, and hence has an advantage over the comparable command in a word processor; that is, FIND is useful when you are not sure which of several documents contains a particular character string.

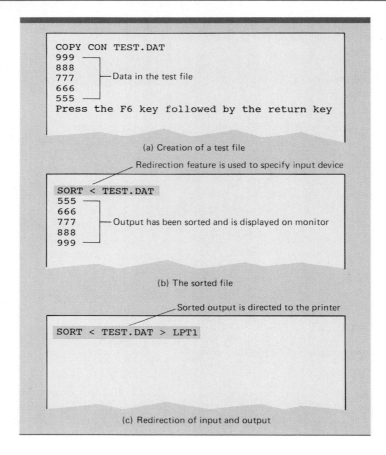

```
COPY CON TEST.DAT
999 ┐
888 │
777 ├─── Data in the test file
666 │
555 ┘
Press the F6 key followed by the return key
```

(a) Creation of a test file

Redirection feature is used to specify input device

```
SORT < TEST.DAT
555 ┐
666 │
777 ├─── Output has been sorted and is displayed on monitor
888 │
999 ┘
```

(b) The sorted file

Sorted output is directed to the printer

```
SORT < TEST.DAT > LPT1
```

(c) Redirection of input and output

FIGURE 13.10
The SORT filter.

```
         FILE.ONE          FILE.TWO
         AAA111            AAA
         BBB222            BBB
         CCC333            CCC
```

(a) The sample files

The line containing the character string is displayed

```
FIND "111" FILE.ONE

---------- FILE.ONE
AAA111
```

(b) Applying the filter to one file
(character string is found)

```
FIND "AAA" FILE.ONE FILE.TWO

---------- FILE.ONE
AAA111

---------- FILE.TWO
AAA
```

(c) Applying the filter to two files
(character string is found in both files)

```
FIND "aaa" FILE.TWO

---------- FILE.TWO
```

(d) Applying the filter to one file
(character string is not found)

FIGURE 13.11
The FIND filter.

COMMAND SUMMARY

Advanced DOS Concepts

CONFIG.SYS   The configuration file used by the operating system to recognize additional devices; for example, a virtual disk

VDISK   A DOS file that enables you to create a virtual (RAM) disk; requires DOS 3.00 or higher

< >   Symbols used to change the standard input (keyboard) and output (screen) devices, respectively

SORT   External DOS filter used to list data in ascending or descending sequence; used in conjunction with the < and > symbols or with other DOS commands

MORE   External DOS filter which sends one screen of data at a time, then pauses until the user presses another key

FIND   External DOS filter used to locate designated character strings

F1 and F3   DOS function keys to save keystrokes in repeating (or altering) the last executed DOS command

ATTRIB   External command to set (remove) the "read only" byte associated with every file; available in DOS 3.00 and higher

BACKUP   The primary (and cumbersome) means provided by DOS for backing up a hard disk onto multiple floppy disks; requires that copied files be *restored* (via the RESTORE command) before they can be used as data

XCOPY   A superior command to BACKUP for copying files on a hard drive to floppies; available in DOS 3.20 and higher

AUTOEXEC.BAT   The batch file that is executed automatically whenever the system is booted

DOSSHELL   A new command in DOS 4.00 that replaces the C prompt with a graphical user interface

"WE'RE SPONSORED BY A LOCAL COMPUTER COMPANY."

It executes 4,000,000 instructions a second, has an addressable memory of 4 billion bytes, and is the equivalent of 275,000 transistors, yet it sells for only a few hundred dollars and is smaller than your fingernail. These impressive statistics describe the Intel 80386 microprocessor, the latest addition to a family of products that power the IBM PC, PS/2, and PC-compatible microcomputers.

The microprocessor was invented in 1969 when a Japanese company asked the then fledgling Intel Corporation to design a set of five custom chips for an electronic calculator. Ted Hoff, the engineer in charge of the project, had a better idea, and proposed a single general-purpose chip that could be used for a variety of applications. "Instead of making the device act like a calculator," he said, "I wanted to make it function as a general-purpose computer programmed to be a calculator."

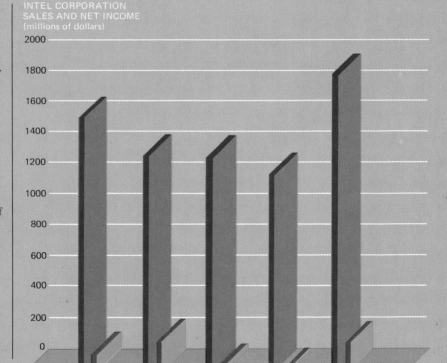

INTEL CORPORATION
SALES AND NET INCOME
(millions of dollars)

The Intel Family of Microprocessors

Processor	Date	Bit Size	Addressable Memory (Bytes)	Instructions per Second	Equivalent Transistors
4004	1971	4	640	60,000	2,300
8080	1974	8	64,000	290,000	5,000
8086	1977	16	1,000,000	333,000	5,500
8088	1978	8/16	1,000,000	333,000	20,000
80286	1982	16	16,000,000	2,000,00	134,000
80386	1985	32	4,000,000,000	4,000,000	275,000

Thus was born the 4004 microprocessor, the world's "first computer on a chip," measuring one-eighth of an inch wide by one-sixth of an inch long, and capable of 60,000 operations a second. Primitive by today's standards, the 4004 was nevertheless equal in computing power to the ENIAC, an early mainframe computer that contained 18,000 vacuum tubes and occupied 3000 cubic feet of space.

Interestingly enough, Intel initially saw the microprocessor as a way to sell more memory chips, the business it was in at the time of Hoff's invention. The company had been founded a year earlier in 1968 by Robert Noyce, one of the individuals credited with the invention of the integrated circuit. Robert Noyce is hardly a household word, yet some say he changed the course of human events every bit as much as Edison, Bell, and Ford had before him. (His story is told remarkably well in *The Chip*, by T. R. Reid, published by Simon and Shuster.) In retrospect Noyce's idea seems obvious, namely "to combine multiple devices on a single piece of silicon, in order to make interconnections part of the manufacturing process, and thus reduce [the] size, weight, and cost per active element" (from the laboratory notebook of Robert Noyce).

The Intel Corporation began officially as N M Electronics (for Noyce Moore Electronics, Gordon Moore being Noyce's partner). The name was not especially creative but it was better than Moore Noyce (pronounced "more noise") Electronics. Eventually, Noyce decided on using the first syllables of the words "integrated electronics," hence the name Intel. Gross revenues during the first year of operation totaled $2672.

The Intel Corporation today is a billion-dollar enterprise, employing thousands of workers in factories all over the world. It, together with Microsoft and IBM, has effectively established the standard for microcomputers.

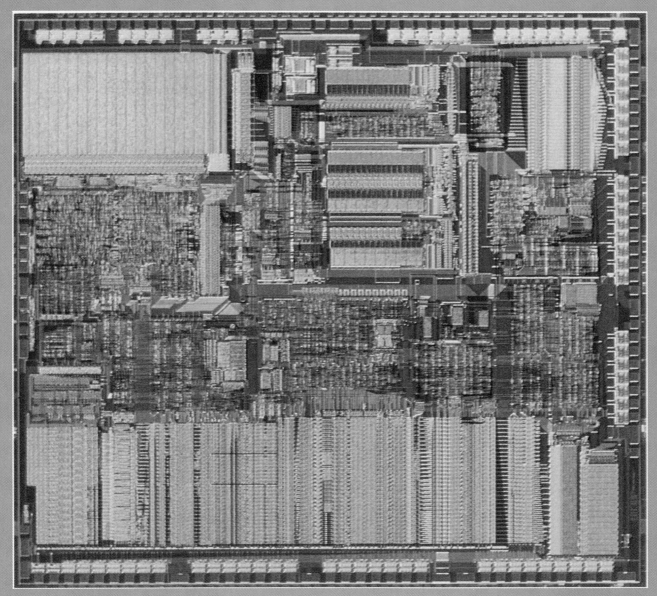

The Intel 80386

Summary

The material in this chapter is absolutely essential if you are to use a personal computer with any degree of proficiency. First and foremost came the information on subdirectories, and the associated MD, CD, RD, TREE, PATH, and PROMPT commands, which enable efficient organization of files on a hard disk. The chapter also suggested that you investigate utility programs from independent vendors (for example, SideKick and/or the Norton Utilities).

Additional DOS commands were covered, including the SORT, MORE, and FIND filters, as was the use of batch files. The importance of proper backup procedures was discussed, the BACKUP and RESTORE commands were introduced, and the availability of tape backup was also mentioned. Several new features of DOS 3.00 were also introduced. These included the availability of a virtual disk device, the ATTRIB and XCOPY commands, foreign keyboards, changes to the FORMAT command, and space allocation procedures.

Key Words and Concepts

ATTRIB	PATH
AUTOEXEC.BAT	Piping
BACKUP	PROMPT
Batch file	RAM disk
Change directory (CD or CHDIR)	RAM-resident program
Cluster	Remove directory (RD or RMDIR)
CONFIG.SYS	RESTORE
DOSSHELL	Root directory
F1 and/or F3 function keys	Sectors
File Allocation Table (FAT)	SideKick
File Directory	SORT filter
FIND filter	Subdirectories
Intel Corporation	Tape backup
Make directory (MD or MKDIR)	Tracks
MORE filter	TREE
Norton Utilities	VDISK
Robert Noyce	XCOPY

True/False

1. A given PATH command may specify more than one subdirectory.

2. Every disk *must* contain an AUTOEXEC.BAT file.

3. The DIR command lists *every* file contained on a disk.

4. The CD command creates a directory.

5. Tree structures are *not* permitted on floppy disks.

6. The commands MD NEWDIR and MD \NEWDIR are equivalent so long as they are issued from the root directory.

7. Output of various DOS commands can be directed to the printer in lieu of the screen.

8. The DOS BACKUP and RESTORE commands are the only way to back up a hard disk.

9. The DOS prompt can be changed to include the current directory of the default drive.

10. The size of a cluster is the same, regardless of whether a file is stored on a floppy or a hard disk.

11. TREE and PATH are both external DOS commands.

12. FIND, MORE, and SORT are external DOS commands (filters).

13. The RENAME command applies to directory names as well as to file names.

14. DOS 3.00 does not contain any commands not found in DOS 2.10.

15. The capacity of a $5\frac{1}{4}$-inch floppy disk is always 360Kb.

16. A $3\frac{1}{2}$-inch floppy holds approximately one-half as much information as the larger $5\frac{1}{4}$-inch floppy.

17. It is possible to "unerase" files with the UNERASE command, available in DOS 3.00 (and higher).

18. CD .. will always return to the root directory.

19. Specification of the TREE command with the file option will list every file contained on a disk.

20. Specification of a RAM disk requires installation of a QUADRAM or AST multifunction board.

Multiple Choice

1. Assume you are currently in the root directory. Which of the following will create a subdirectory named STOCK under a subdirectory named DBASE?
   (a) MD \DBASE, followed by MD STOCK
   (b) MD \DBASE, followed by CD \DBASE, followed by CD \STOCK
   (c) MD \DBASE\STOCK
   (d) None of the above

2. Which of the following commands will list *every* file on a disk?
   (a) DIR
   (b) DIR *.*
   (c) TREE/F
   (d) All the above

3. The F1 and F3 function keys are used by DOS to:
   (a) Save and delete files
   (b) Copy files to and from a hard disk
   (c) Recall the previously issued command from a buffer
   (d) Store DOS commands in a keyboard buffer

4. Assume that the PATH command PATH \DOS;\WORDSTAR is active, that you issued the command WS, and that the system returned the message "Bad command or filename":
   (a) The program (or batch file) WS may exist on the disk but is not in the current directory or in the DOS or WORDSTAR subdirectories
   (b) The program (or batch file) WS cannot possibly exist anywhere on the disk
   (c) An incorrect version of DOS is in use
   (d) None of the above

5. The DOS PROMPT command:
   (a) Sends a message to another computer
   (b) Erases what is currently on the screen
   (c) Changes the character indicating DOS is waiting for a command
   (d) Enables you to edit batch files

6. Establishment of a RAM disk:
   (a) Requires the availability of a hard drive
   (b) Requires an appropriate command in the AUTOEXEC.BAT file
   (c) Requires an appropriate PATH entry to the VDISK.SYS file
   (d) All the above

7. The DOS command TYPE MESSAGE.TXT ¦ MORE:
   (a) Is equivalent to the command TYPE MESSAGE.TXT ¦ SCREENS
   (b) Will work in the absence of a PATH command, and regardless of the subdirectory from where it is issued
   (c) Displays the contents of the file MESSAGE.TXT one screen at a time (prompting the user to press any key to continue from one screen to the next)
   (d) All the above

8. Assume you create the following one-sentence file using a word processor: "I like working with microcomputers." The actual amount of space required to store this file on disk is:
   (a) 34 bytes (since the file contains 34 characters)
   (b) 1024 bytes (assuming the file is stored on a $5\frac{1}{4}$-inch floppy disk)

(c) Impossible to determine from the information given; the file will, however, take the same amount of space regardless of what type of disk it is stored on

(d) None of the above

9. The PATH command:
   (a) Searches other directories for program and/or batch files not found in the current directory
   (b) Searches every subdirectory on the disk, whether it is specified or not
   (c) Changes to a new subdirectory
   (d) None of the above

10. The AUTOEXEC.BAT file:
    (a) Must be present on every disk used to boot the system
    (b) Must be in the root directory if it is to have any effect
    (c) Must be used in conjunction with a CONFIG.SYS file
    (d) All the above

11. The commands MD\LOTUS and MD LOTUS:
    (a) Can never, under any circumstances, produce the same result
    (b) Are equivalent if issued from the root directory
    (c) Require that the LOTUS subdirectory be empty
    (d) None of the above

12. Which of the following is *not* a valid form of the CD command?
    (a) CD
    (b) CD . .
    (c) CD \
    (d) CD *.*

13. Which of the following is an *external* filter?
    (a) SORT
    (b) MORE
    (c) FIND
    (d) All the above

14. Which of the following will *not* necessarily increase the capacity of a floppy disk?
    (a) Increasing the number of bytes per sector
    (b) Increasing the number of sectors per track
    (c) Increasing the number of sectors per cluster
    (d) Increasing the number of tracks per recording surface

15. Which of the following displays the output of the DIR command on the printer?
    (a) DIR TO PRINT
    (b) DIR>LPT1
    (c) TYPE ¦ DIR
    (d) PrtSc DIR

Exercises

1. (a) Calculate the storage capacity (in kilobytes) of a single-sided disk with the following parameters: 40 tracks per side, 8 sectors per track, and 512 bytes per sector. (These are the parameters that existed for the initial IBM announcement in August 1981.)

   (b) Repeat part a using the parameters for the quad density drive in the AT (80 tracks per side, 15 sectors per track, 512 bytes per sector, and two recording surfaces).

   (c) Explain the significance of formatting a floppy drive with and without the system files (that is, FORMAT B: versus FORMAT B:/S) in terms of the amount of space available for data. Answer with specific requirements for DOS 3.00.

2. Given the File Directory and File Allocation Table entries shown in Figure 13.12:

   (a) Calculate the space allotted to each file (assume that one cluster is equal to two sectors, and that each sector contains 512 bytes).

   (b) Assume that FILE.B is expanded and requires two additional clusters. Indicate the associated changes to the FAT (assume that the first two available clusters are assigned to the file).

   (c) Assume that FILE.C is expanded and requires one additional cluster. Indicate the associated changes to the FAT (assume that the first available cluster is assigned to the file).

   (d) Assume that FILE.A is erased. Indicate the associated changes to the FAT.

   (e) Explain how it is possible to "unerase" FILE.A.

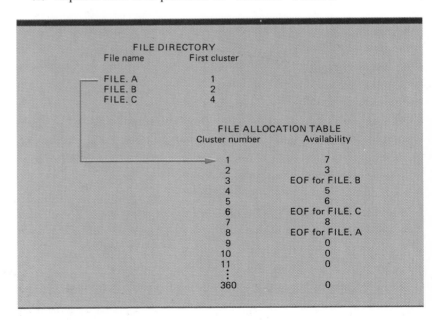

FIGURE 13.12
File Directory and File Allocation Table (exercise 2).

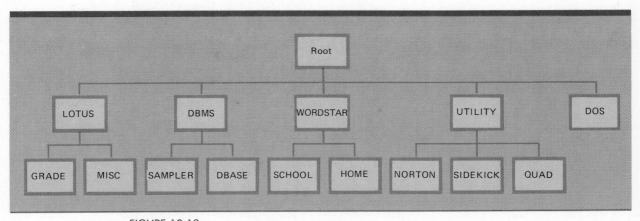

FIGURE 13.13
Tree structure for exercises 3 and 4.

3. Given the tree structure of Figure 13.13, supply the command(s) to accomplish the following, *being sure you're in the proper subdirectory* (where necessary) for your commands to take effect.
   (a) Create a subdirectory, SOLEIL, under the existing SAMPLER subdirectory.
   (b) Copy all files from the disk in drive A to the newly created SOLEIL subdirectory.
   (c) Remove the existing dBASE subdirectory.
   (d) Display the current subdirectory.
   (e) Obtain a directory of all files on the DOS subdirectory.
   (f) Show the directory structure of the disk, directing output of the command you issue to the printer.
   (g) Repeat part *f*, but this time list the associated files in each subdirectory.

4. Create an AUTOEXEC.BAT file which will accomplish the items listed below. (Use the tree structure of Figure 13.13 as a guide.)
   (a) Change the prompt to show both the current directory and the default drive.
   (b) Establish drive D as a RAM drive of 200Kb (indicate the necessary supporting files which must be present at the time the AUTOEXEC.BAT file is executed).
   (c) Update the system date and time with the QUADCLOK command (which is found in the QUAD subdirectory).
   (d) Load SideKick (accomplished by the command SK).
   (e) Enable the programs contained in the SIDEKICK, DOS, and NORTON subdirectories to be run from anywhere on the disk.
   (f) Return to the root subdirectory.

5. Create a self-booting disk that will request date and time information, then take the user into a "DOS Shell" similar to Figure 13.14. The menu you create should ask the user which application program he or she wants to run, whereupon your batch file(s) should contain the necessary commands to enter the appropriate

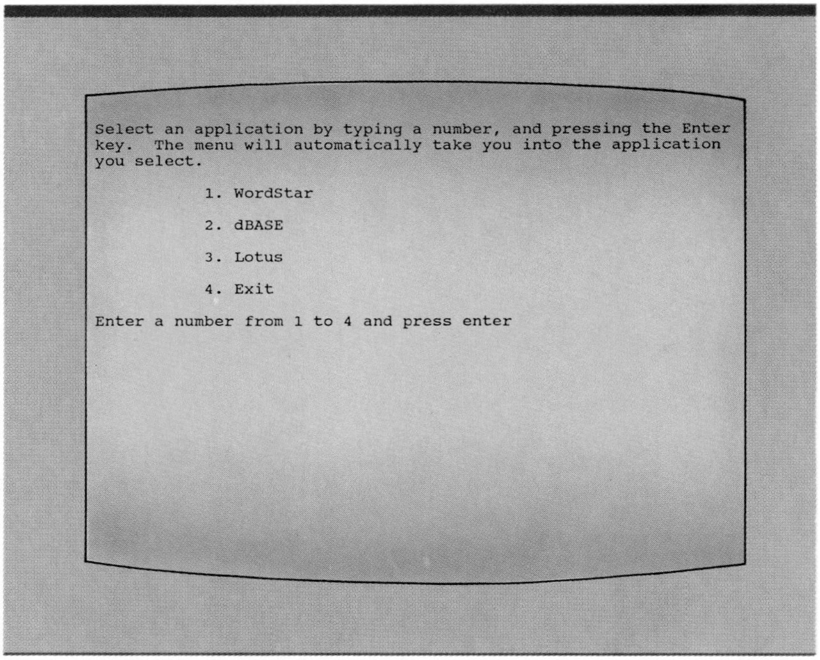

```
Select an application by typing a number, and pressing the Enter
key.  The menu will automatically take you into the application
you select.

               1. WordStar

               2. dBASE

               3. Lotus

               4. Exit

Enter a number from 1 to 4 and press enter
```

FIGURE 13.14   DOS shell for exercise 5.

subdirectory to "execute" the program. The menu should also contain an "exit" option in which the user is returned to the DOS prompt.

The problem is not difficult once you realize that the user's response of 1, 2, 3, or 4 can in turn execute a batch file named 1.BAT, 2.BAT, 3.BAT, or 4.BAT, respectively. Each of these batch files in turn will contain the necessary commands to execute the appropriate application. For example, the file 1.BAT might contain these commands:

CD\WORDSTAR	(To change directories)
WS	(To load WordStar)
CD \	(To return to the root directory)
MENU	(To reexecute MENU.BAT, which displays the menu)

Realize that for the purpose of the exercise the command to load WordStar (WS) can be replaced by a message stating that WordStar would be loaded. Other commands that you might want to include in your batch files are CLS, to clear the screen, and/or ECHO ON/OFF, to suppress the DOS commands from echoing on the screen (and confusing the user).

6. Show the tree structure that would be created by issuing the following commands in succession:

```
CD\
MD  SUB1
MD  SUB2
MD  SUB3
CD  SUB1
MD  SUB4
MD  SUB5
MD  SUB6
CD  SUB6
MD  SUB7
MD  SUB8
```

Assume now that *you are in the SUB1 directory* and that the following commands are issued from this directory. Indicate whether there is a problem, and if so, state the nature of the problem. Answer with respect to the tree structure just created.

(a) CD SUB2

(b) RD SUB6

(c) MD SUB5

(d) MD SUB9\SUB10

APPENDIXES

APPENDIX A

NUMBER SYSTEMS

A number system is a set of symbols controlled by a well-defined set of rules for measuring quantities. The value of every digit is determined by its position; as you move from right to left (that is, away from the decimal point), each succeeding digit is multiplied by a higher power of the base in which you are working. For example, the number 1976 in base 10 is equal to:

$$1000 \quad + \quad 900 \quad + \quad 70 \quad + \quad 6$$

$$1 \times 10^3 \quad + \quad 9 \times 10^2 \quad + \quad 7 \times 10^1 \quad + \quad 6 \times 10^0$$

We use the decimal number system (base 10), but the choice is arbitrary. The ancient Babylonians, for example, had 12 symbols for numbers and thus developed a base 12 (duodecimal) number system. (Base 12 has carried to modern usage in telling time, and in purchasing certain commodities, for example, a dozen eggs.) Had we been given 2, 8, or 16 fingers, we might have adopted the binary, octal, or hexadecimal system, respectively.

Number systems are easily understood if you approach the subject from existing knowledge, that is, base 10. Everything about any other base can be related back to base 10. *All concepts are identical.* Thus the decimal system has 10 digits, 0 through 9, the octal (base 8) system has 8 digits, 0 through 7; the binary (base 2) system has 2 digits, 0 and 1; and so on. Base 10 expresses a number in terms of powers of 10; base 8 in powers of 8; base 2 in powers of 2; and so on.

Hexadecimal, or base 16, is another number system which appears frequently in computer applications. It uses 16 digits (0 through 9, and the letters A, B, C, D, E, and F to represent the numbers 10 through 15 as a single character). Numbers are expressed as powers of 16. Hexadecimal takes some getting used to, but it too follows the rules common to all number systems.

Table A.1 illustrates four common number systems. What is obvious from Table A.1 is that the more symbols available, the more concise is the representation of a particular quantity. The number 1024, for example, requires 11 binary digits and only 3 hex digits.

TABLE A.1

Four Common Numbers Systems

Decimal	Binary	Octal	Hexadecimal
1	1	1	1
2	10	2	2
8	1000	10	8
10	1010	12	A
16	10000	20	10
100	01100100	144	64
1000	1111101000	1750	3E8
1024 (1Kb)	10000000000	2000	400
65355	1111111111111111	177777	FFFF

The decimal number system served humankind adequately for thousands of years, until the advent of digital computers. It is much easier to build a binary computer requiring only two values, as opposed to a "base 10" machine that needs 10 values. Binary calculations can be performed by flipping switches back and forth or changing the direction of a magnetic field from right to left. Accordingly, all computers are built as binary machines, and for this reason we begin our study of number systems with base 2. To indicate which base we are talking about, we shall surround the number by ( )'s and use a subscript to indicate the base. If the parentheses are omitted, base 10 is assumed.

Binary Numbers

Base 2 has two digits, 0 and 1. The value of a digit is determined by its position, which represents a specific power of 2; for example, the binary number $(10110)_2$ is equal to the decimal number 22. The decimal value is obtained by expanding digits in the binary number by increasing powers of 2 as you move away from the decimal point. Thus:

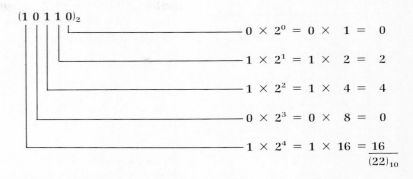

$$(1\ 0\ 1\ 1\ 0)_2$$

$$0 \times 2^0 = 0 \times 1 = 0$$
$$1 \times 2^1 = 1 \times 2 = 2$$
$$1 \times 2^2 = 1 \times 4 = 4$$
$$0 \times 2^3 = 0 \times 8 = 0$$
$$1 \times 2^4 = 1 \times 16 = \underline{16}$$
$$(22)_{10}$$

Easy enough? Try the following examples as practice:

$$(11011)_2 = (27)_{10} \quad \text{and} \quad (100101)_2 = (37)_{10}$$

Addition

Just as you can add in decimal, you can add in binary. Binary addition is much less complicated than decimal addition; it just takes a little practice. The principles of addition in either base are identical, and if you truly understand decimal arithmetic, you should not find it difficult to work in binary or, for that matter, in any other base. Consider, first, the following addition in base 10:

$$\begin{array}{r} 38 \\ + \underline{46} \\ 84 \end{array}$$

If you add like most people, your thoughts begin with "8 + 6 = 14; write down 4 and carry 1." Now analyze that statement. You are working in base 10 with valid digits 0 to 9. "14" cannot be written as a single digit; thus, you write down 4 and carry 1. In actuality, you are exchanging 10 units for one "10," and thus have a carry of 1. Involved? Yes, but that is precisely the process you follow. Addition in base 10 has become so ingrained over the years that you do all that automatically. Now let's translate that thought process to the binary system.

$$\begin{array}{r} (\ \ 10)_2 \\ + \underline{(\ \ 11)_2} \\ = (\ \ \ \ )_2 \end{array}$$

Begin the addition, one column at a time, starting in the right-most (units) column. Zero plus 1 equals 1. Move one column to the

TABLE A.2

Binary and Decimal Equivalents

Decimal		Binary
1	⟷	1
	+	1
2	⟷	10
	+	1
3	⟷	11
	+	1
4	⟷	100
	+	1
5	⟷	101
	+	1
6	⟷	110
	+	1
7	⟷	111
	+	1
8	⟷	1000
	+	1
9	⟷	1001
	+	1
10	⟷	1010

left, and add 1 and 1 to get 2, except that you can't write "2" as a single binary digit. Accordingly, you write down zero and carry one because you exchange two units for one "2." The process seems involved but it is analogous to base 10, in which you exchange 10 units for one "10"; now you exchange two units for one "2." Returning to the original example,

$$\text{Carry} = 1$$
$$(\ 10)_2$$
$$+\ (\ 11)_2$$
$$=\ (101)_2$$

In other words, two $(10)_2$ plus three $(11)_2$ equals five $(101)_2$. It takes a little getting used to, but it makes more sense with practice. After all, it took quite a while to learn how to add in base 10. To check your understanding, and to gain a little practice, consider Table A.2, which contains the binary equivalents of the decimal numbers from 1 to 10.

HOW A COMPUTER ADDS

A computer does all of its work using the binary number system. To understand completely how this is done requires knowledge of electrical engineering, which is obviously way beyond the scope of the text. Nevertheless, an explanation of how a computer adds may be of interest.

All computer arithmetic is derived from three logical operations: AND, OR, and NOT, which manipulate the binary numbers 0 and 1. The properties of a logical function are explicitly stated in a *truth table*, a systematic representation of all possible binary outcomes. A truth table uses a 1 to present true, a 0 to indicate false. Consider:

OR				AND				NOT	
A	B	Output		A	B	Output		A	Output
0	0	0		0	0	0		0	1
0	1	1		0	1	0		1	0
1	0	1		1	0	0			
1	1	1		1	1	1			

Four combinations are possible for two input variables, A and B, each of which has two possible values, 0 and 1. In order for the OR operation to be considered true (that is, to achieve a value of 1), either A or B or both have to be true (equal to 1).

The AND operation also has four possible inputs. However, for the result of an AND operation to be true (to achieve the value 1), both A and B must be true (equal to 1).

The NOT operation is the simplest, as it has only a single input. NOT reverses the value of the input; hence if the input is initially true (a value of 1), the output is false (a value of 0), and vice versa.

Let us consider a very simple application of these gates, the *half-adder*, which adds two digits and produces a sum. Half-adders may be combined to add two binary numbers consisting of several digits each.

A half-adder to add 1 and 1 is shown in Figure A.1. The figure uses the commonly accepted engineering symbols for the AND, OR, and NOT gates. (We have inserted the words AND, OR, and NOT within the symbols for ease of understanding.)

Two binary inputs are delivered simultaneously to the OR gate at the top and the AND gate at the bottom. The output of the OR gate is routed to a second AND gate. Simultaneously, the output of the first AND gate is sent to a NOT gate, and this result is also sent to the second AND gate.

The output of the top AND gate becomes the right-hand digit of the sum, and the output of the bottom AND gate becomes the left-hand digit. Four combinations of inputs are possible, with four different outputs. You may verify that the half-adder correctly produces the following binary sums:

$$0 + 0 = 00 \qquad 0 + 1 = 01$$
$$1 + 0 = 01 \qquad 1 + 1 = 10$$

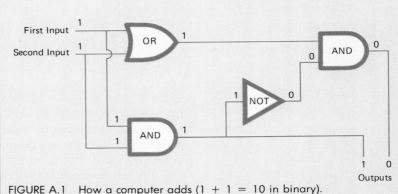

FIGURE A.1   How a computer adds (1 + 1 = 10 in binary).

Authors' Comments:
An absolutely delightful exposition of AND, OR, and NOT (in addition to other material) is given by Srully Blotnick in a series of three articles in Forbes Magazine (of all places), beginning October 11, 1982. Mr. Blotnick presents the material with the aid of analogies to French and Chinese restaurants and a New York disco. His material is worthwhile reading.

Hexadecimal Numbers

In practice you never see the internal contents of a computer's memory displayed in binary, because binary is too cumbersome. Nor do you see memory displayed in decimal, because binary to decimal conversion is time-consuming and inexact with fractional numbers. The hexadecimal (base 16) number system solves both problems. It is much more concise than binary and provides direct and exact conversion to and from binary; that is, four binary digits are exactly equal to one hex digit ($2^4 = 16$). (Octal, base 8, would also serve as a satisfactory shorthand, since 8 is an even power of 2; indeed, several computers have been built as "octal," or base 8, machines.)

Just as base 10 has 10 digits, 0 to 9, base 16 has 16 digits, 0 to 9 and A to F. The numbers 0 through 9 are used as before, and the letters A through F are chosen for the numbers 10 through 15; that is, the letter A stands for 10, B represents 11, C is 12, D is 13, E is 14, and F is 15. In a decimal number each digit represents a power of 10; in a hex number each digit represents a power of 16. Consider the hex number $(12AB)_{16}$ and obtain its decimal equivalent:

$(1\ 2\ A\ B)_{16}$

$$B \times 16^0 = 11 \times \quad 1 = \quad 11$$
$$A \times 16^1 = 10 \times \quad 16 = \quad 160$$
$$2 \times 16^2 = \ 2 \times \ 256 = \quad 512$$
$$1 \times 16^3 = \ 1 \times 4096 = \underline{4096}$$
$$(4779)_{10}$$

Addition

Hexadecimal addition is made simple if you again use the thought processes of decimal arithmetic. Consider

$$\begin{aligned}
\text{Carry} &= \ 1 \\
&\ (39)_{16} \\
+ \ &\ \underline{(59)_{16}} \\
&\ (92)_{16}
\end{aligned}$$

Thus 9 plus 9 equals 18; hex cannot express 18 as a single-digit number; so you write down 2 and carry 1 (that is, $18 = 16 + 2$). It seems complicated only because you are so used to decimal arithmetic. The concepts of addition are identical in both bases, and it is only a matter of time and practice to be comfortable in both.

Since hexadecimal includes some "strange-looking" digits (that is, A, B, C, D, E, and F), another example will be helpful. Consider

$$\begin{aligned}
\text{Carry} &= \ 1 \\
&\ (AB)_{16} \\
+ \ &\ \underline{(38)_{16}} \\
&\ (E3)_{16}
\end{aligned}$$

B plus 8 equals 19 (remember, B denotes 11). Hex cannot express 19 as a single digit, so you write down 3 and carry 1 (that is, $19 = 16 + 3$). Now A, 3, and 1 (the carry) equal 14, which is represented by E in hex. Although you are working in hex, you still think in decimal. After a while, however, these actions will become automatic, and you will find yourself bypassing decimal altogether.

Conversion to Binary

A computer functions internally as a binary machine, but its contents are often displayed as hexadecimal numbers. How does the conversion from binary to hex take place? Consider, for example,

$$(10110100)_2 = (\ ?\ )_{16}$$

One way is to convert the binary number to a decimal number

"It was bound to happen — they're beginning to think like binary computers."

by expanding powers of 2 and then convert the decimal number to its hex equivalent by repeated division by 16. Thus

$$(10110100)_2 = (180)_{10} = (B4)_{16}$$

There is, however, a shortcut. Since $2^4 = 16$, there are exactly four binary digits to one hex digit. Simply take the binary number and divide it into groups of four digits; begin at the decimal point and work right to left, that is, 1011 0100. Then take each group of four digits and mentally convert to hex. Thus

$$(0100)_2 = (4)_{10} = (4)_{16}$$

and

$$(1011)_2 = (11)_{10} = (B)_{16}$$

Hence,

$$(1011\ 0100)_2 = (B4)_{16}$$

The process works in reverse as well. The hex number ABC can be immediately converted to the binary number 101010111100. As verification, convert ABC to decimal and then go from decimal to binary.

The advantages of hex notation should now be apparent. It is a more concise representation of the internal workings of a machine than is binary, yet unlike decimal conversion, it is immediate and exact. As stated earlier, octal (base 8) would also be suitable as a shorthand, and several computers have used octal notation in lieu of hex.

APPENDIX B

BITS AND BYTES

Bits and Bytes

A **byte** is the smallest addressable unit of computer storage. It consists of eight bits (*binary digits*), where each bit is stored internally as either a 0 or a 1, corresponding to the "off" and "on" states in electric circuits. A single bit, however, cannot be referenced because an isolated zero or one is essentially meaningless. It is only a group of bits, for example, a byte, that conveys useful information.

ASCII

A total of 256 bit combinations are possible within a byte. We arrive at the number 256 because each of the eight bits within a byte can assume one of two possible values (0 or 1); hence there are 2^8, or 256, combinations in all.

    The arrangement of bits within a byte on the PC follows the American Standard Code for Information Interchange (ASCII, pronounced "as-key") coding scheme. The most obvious set of ASCII

TABLE B.1

ASCII Codes *

Character	Binary	Hex	Decimal	Character	Binary	Hex	Decimal	Character	Binary	Hex	Decimal
A	01000001	41	65	a	01100001	61	97	0	00110000	30	48
B	01000010	42	66	b	01100010	62	98	1	00110001	31	49
C	01000011	43	67	c	01100011	63	99	2	00110010	32	50
D	01000100	44	68	d	01100100	64	100	3	00110011	33	51
E	01000101	45	69	e	01100101	65	101	4	00110100	34	52
F	01000110	46	70	f	01100110	66	102	5	00110101	35	53
G	01000111	47	71	g	01100111	67	103	6	00110110	36	54
H	01001000	48	72	h	01101000	68	104	7	00110111	37	55
I	01001001	49	73	i	01101001	69	105	8	00111000	38	56
J	01001010	4A	74	j	01101010	6A	106	9	00111001	39	57
K	01001011	4B	75	k	01101011	6B	107				
L	01001100	4C	76	l	01101100	6C	108				
M	01001101	4D	77	m	01101101	6D	109				
N	01001110	4E	78	n	01101110	6E	110				
O	01001111	4F	79	o	01101111	6F	111				
P	01010000	50	80	p	01110000	70	112				
Q	01010001	51	81	q	01110001	71	113				
R	01010010	52	82	r	01110010	72	114				
S	01010011	53	83	s	01110011	73	115				
T	01010100	54	84	t	01110100	74	116				
U	01010101	55	85	u	01110101	75	117				
V	01010110	56	86	v	01110110	76	118				
W	01010111	57	87	w	01110111	77	119				
X	01011000	58	88	x	01111000	78	120				
Y	01011001	59	89	y	01111001	79	121				
Z	01011010	5A	90	z	01111010	7A	122				

* In actuality, ASCII is a 7-bit code (defining 128 characters), with the eighth (leftmost) bit set to zero. Many vendors, including IBM, have appropriated the "extra" bit to define an additional 128 characters. The eighth bit can also be used as a parity bit if only 128 characters are specified.

characters are those used to represent letters, numbers, and punctuation. However, there are also bit combinations assigned to every key on the keyboard, including backspace, return, cursor movement keys, and so on. The complete set of ASCII characters may be found in Appendix G of the IBM BASIC manual; a subset is presented in Table B.1.

In Table B.1 each character is followed by its bit sequence, the corresponding hexadecimal representation, and its decimal equivalent. The binary representation is included in the table to remind you that the computer is, after all, a binary machine. Hexadecimal is shown because it is a convenient shorthand for binary, while decimal is included because of your familiarity with base 10.

ASCII codes are not as arbitrary as they may seem initially. A closer look at Table B.1, for example, shows that the bit representations for the alphabet are in sequence beginning with a hexadecimal 41 for the letter A, 42 for B, and so on up to 5A for the letter Z. Similar patterns can be found for the numbers and the lowercase letters as well.

Program Patchwork

Bits and bytes, binary and hex, what's it all for? Most, if not all, of the time you will be able to use application software exactly as you purchase it. Occasionally, however, it may be necessary for you to fix, or *patch*, a software package that doesn't perform exactly the way you would like it to, and then you will need to use this material.

By way of illustration we will develop a simple exercise to change the opening message produced by DOS. Recall, for example, that DOS requests the date and time, followed by the message "The IBM Personal Computer DOS," whenever the system is booted. Our exercise will modify this message to read "The ABC Personal Computer DOS."

To accomplish the change it is necessary to:

1. Locate the character string "The IBM Personal Computer DOS" within the COMMAND.COM program.

2. Change the message to "The ABC Personal Computer DOS."

3. Record the changes on disk.

TABLE B.2

Commonly Used DEBUG Commands

Command	Purpose
Display	Displays the contents of a file
Enter	Overwrites (changes) bytes in a file
Search	Finds a particular character string
Write	Records any changes on disk
Quit	Ends the DEBUG session and returns to DOS

Microsoft provides a program called DEBUG.COM, which enables you to do all these tasks. The particular DEBUG.COM commands that will be needed in the exercise are shown in Table B.2:

Memory Dump

DEBUG.COM operates on machine language, which in actuality is stored in binary, but which is expressed in hexadecimal for convenience. Hence the DEBUG.COM program displays the contents of memory as shown in Figure B.1, a format known as a *memory dump*.

A memory dump is divided into three parts. The left-hand third of the figure gives the address of the first byte in each line (0FE0 in the first line of Figure B.1). The middle portion contains the contents of the 16 bytes in that line; that is, 50 is the contents of location 0FE0, 65 is the contents of location 0FE1, and so on. The final third gives the ASCII interpretation for the hex contents; for example, "*P*" corresponds to 50, as indicated in the table of ASCII codes in Table B.1.

The following hands-on exercise illustrates the use of the DEBUG.COM program. As previously indicated, the exercise will change the message "The IBM Personal Computer DOS" that appears when the system boots, to read "The ABC Personal Computer DOS". A printout of the results is shown in Figure B.2.

```
0FE0   50 65 72 73 6F 6E 61 6C-20 43 6F 6D 70 75 74 65   Personal Compute
0FF0   72 20 44 4F 53 0D 0A 56-65 72 73 69 6F 6E 20 32   r DOS..Version 2
1000   2E 31 30 20 28 43 29 43-6F 70 79 72 69 67 68 74   .10 (C)Copyright
1010   20 49 42 4D 20 43 6F 72-70 20 31 39 38 31 2C 20    IBM Corp 1981,
1020   31 39 38 32 2C 20 31 39-38 33 0D 0A 24 4C 69 63   1982, 1983..$Lic
1030   65 6E 73 65 64 20 4D 61-74 65 72 69 61 6C 20 2D   ensed Material -
1040   20 50 72 6F 67 72 61 6D-20 50 72 6F 70 65 72 74    Program Propert
1050   79 20 6F 66 20 49 42 4D                           y of IBM
```

FIGURE B.1
A memory dump.

```
A>DEBUG COMMAND.COM                              ──── STEP 2 - Invoke DEBUG. COM.

-S 0100 FFFF "The IBM Personal Computer" ──── STEP 3 - Find character string to be changed.
71F8:0FD8
71F8:882B
71F8:B2A5

                                                ──── STEP 4 - Display the message.
-D 0FD8
71F8:0FD8  54 68 65 20 49 42 4D 20                        The IBM
71F8:0FE0  50 65 72 73 6F 6E 61 6C-20 43 6F 6D 70 75 74 65  Personal Compute
71F8:0FF0  72 20 44 4F 53 0D 0A 56-65 72 73 69 6F 6E 20 32  r DOS..Version 2
71F8:1000  2E 31 30 20 28 43 29 43-6F 70 79 72 69 67 68 74  .10 (C)Copyright
71F8:1010  20 49 42 4D 20 43 6F 72-70 20 31 39 38 31 2C 20   IBM Corp 1981,
71F8:1020  31 39 38 32 2C 20 31 39-38 33 0D 0A 24 4C 69 63  1982, 1983..$Lic
71F8:1030  65 6E 73 65 64 20 4D 61-74 65 72 69 61 6C 20 2D  ensed Material -
71F8:1040  20 50 72 6F 67 72 61 6D-20 50 72 6F 70 65 72 74   Program Propert
71F8:1050  79 20 6F 66 20 49 42 4D                          y of IBM

-E 0FD8 "The ABC Personal"                      ──── STEP 5 - Enter the new character string.

                                                ──── STEP 6 - Display the modification.
-D 0FD8
71F8:0FD8  54 68 65 20 41 42 43 20                        The ABC
71F8:0FE0  50 65 72 73 6F 6E 61 6C-20 43 6F 6D 70 75 74 65  Personal Compute
71F8:0FF0  72 20 44 4F 53 0D 0A 56-65 72 73 69 6F 6E 20 32  r DOS..Version 2
71F8:1000  2E 31 30 20 28 43 29 43-6F 70 79 72 69 67 68 74  .10 (C)Copyright
71F8:1010  20 49 42 4D 20 43 6F 72-70 20 31 39 38 31 2C 20   IBM Corp 1981,
71F8:1020  31 39 38 32 2C 20 31 39-38 33 0D 0A 24 4C 69 63  1982, 1983..$Lic
71F8:1030  65 6E 73 65 64 20 4D 61-74 65 72 69 61 6C 20 2D  ensed Material -
71F8:1040  20 50 72 6F 67 72 61 6D-20 50 72 6F 70 65 72 74   Program Propert
71F8:1050  79 20 6F 66 20 49 42 4D                          y of IBM
                                                ──── STEP 7 - Write change to the disk.
-W
Writing 4580 bytes

                                                ──── STEP 8 - Exit DEBUG.
-Q


Current date is Tue  1-01-1980
Enter new date: 11-14-1986
Current time is  0:00:12.57
Enter new time: 10:11

The ABC Personal Computer DOS ──── STEP 9 - Boot the system with new message.
Version 2.10 (C)Copyright IBM Corp 1981, 1982, 1983
```

FIGURE B.2   Results of hands-on exercise (Step 1 not shown).

HANDS-ON EXERCISE 1: PATCHING A PROGRAM

OBJECTIVE: Use DEBUG.COM to patch a machine language program.

Step 1: Create a Bootable Disk
Place a DOS system disk in drive A and a blank disk in drive B. Boot the system, then format the disk in drive B with the command FORMAT B:/S. The disk in drive B is now bootable (and contains a copy of COMMAND.COM which will be patched in the exercise).

The DEBUG.COM program is found on the diagnostics disk (found in the IBM *Guide to Operations*). Place this disk in drive A, then copy DEBUG.COM to the newly formatted disk in drive B.

Put the diagnostics disk away and place the newly formatted disk in drive A. Type DIR, checking that the disk in drive A contains COMMAND.COM and DEBUG.COM.

Step 2: Invoke DEBUG.COM
Type the command DEBUG COMMAND.COM in response to the system prompt (A>). DEBUG.COM will load the contents of the file COMMAND.COM into the computer's memory. When you see the DEBUG prompt (a hyphen), the program is ready to accept your commands.

Step 3: Locate the Character String to Be Changed
The *search* (locate) command is used to find a character string within a file. Enter the command: S 0100 FFFF "The IBM Personal Computer." This instructs DEBUG.COM to search for the character string "The IBM Personal Computer," beginning at offset (location) 0100 (the lowest possible address) and continuing to location FFFF (the highest possible). Both addresses are in hex.

Step 4: Display (Dump) the Character String
The T in "The IBM Personal" begins at offset 0FD8

as returned by the search command from step 3. (The actual address may, however, be different, depending on the version of DOS you are using.)

The contents of any location can be verified by "displaying" the contents of memory. Type the command D 0FD8 (or whatever location was returned in step 3) to display the contents of memory beginning at this location.

Step 5: Enter the New Replacement Character String
The *enter* command changes the program in memory. Type the command E 0FD8 "The ABC," which will enter this character string beginning at location 0FD8 in lieu of "The IBM."

Step 6: Display the Modification
Use the *display* command to verify the effects of step 5. Type the command D 0FD8 and observe that the change was made.

Step 7: Write the Modification
The enter command alters memory but does not change the file as it exists on disk; the *write* command permanently records the change. Type the command W (for write).

Step 8: Exit DEBUG.COM
Type Q (for quit) to exit DEBUG.COM.

Step 9: Try It
Boot the system by pressing Ctrl, Alt, and Del simultaneously. Answer the date and time prompts, then observe the message "The **ABC** Personal Computer DOS."

APPENDIX C

BUSINESS CASE STUDIES

Overview

One objective of this book is to teach you to use application software such as spreadsheets or data management. A broader objective, however, is to develop an appreciation for the microcomputer as a business tool. In other words, programs such as Lotus or dBASE are really means to an end (that of problem solving), rather than an end unto themselves.

Accordingly, this appendix contains four case studies, each consisting of several pages of facts and figures (some of them extraneous to the central issue). The presentation is, however, typical of what to expect in a business setting. The intent is for you to read through each case, determine the relevant information, and then use the appropriate software to solve the problem. An abbreviated (and generic) solution follows the case presentation, with *complete* solutions (as implemented in VP Planner and/or dBASE) found in the optional laboratory manual.

Table C.1 summarizes the nature of the case studies and the associated concepts. Note, too, that each case is followed by a *case assignment*, which parallels the case description, and which is intended to provide additional practice.

TABLE C.1

Business Case Studies and Assignments

Case Study	Objectives	Case Assignment
International Mining Resources	Emphasis on model building and isolation of assumptions within a spreadsheet; uses all basic spreadsheet commands with attention to cell ranges, formatting, copying, relative and absolute addresses, and financial functions.	Locke Pharmaceuticals
Porter Realty	Focus on the combination of multiple spreadsheets into one; includes commands for file extraction, file combination, cell protection, and macros. Integrates graphic presentation with spreadsheet capabilities.	Washburn Publishing
Carolton Furniture	Development of a simulation model for production scheduling, an application not normally associated with spreadsheets; includes the @RAND, @IF, @VLOOKUP, @MAX, and @MIN functions.	Europa Tile
Dade County Metro Zoo	Design of a file management system to include both file maintenance and data retrieval, and the incorporation of these functions into a mail-merge application. Emphasis is on the definition of the file structure with respect to which fields should be included, as well as field type and field length.	Michael Essman

CASE STUDY:
INTERNATIONAL MINING RESOURCES

Preview

The central issue in the International Mining Resources (Intercorp) case is to forecast the capital that will be returned to the company over an eight-year horizon. All cash investments have been made, and it remains only for Intercorp to reap the benefits of its earlier investment. As you read the case, try to identify the projected revenues and associated costs of production. Terms such as "depreciation" and "depletion allowance" creep into the discussion and affect the solution.

Presentation

Earl Peters, president of International Mining Resources Corporation (Intercorp), was sitting in his office in Lima, Peru. In his mind he was going over possible questions he might be expected to answer the following week. Next Monday he would be meeting with a group of high-ranking executives of Intercorp's parent corporation, National Oil Corporation, including the president of National Oil, at National Oil's headquarters for Latin American operations in Miami.

Mr. Peters had just returned from the Moquegua coal mine where he watched the first train loaded with coal from the mine leave for Puerto de Coles. This seemingly inconsequential event marked the culmination of three years of work and the investment of $200 million by his company in the mine. Now that the mine was operational, Mr. Peters realized that a whole new realm of potential problems had descended upon him. The first problem was this meeting in Miami, the purpose of which was to discuss the opening of the mine and the anticipated capital transfers back to the parent company.

Background

The International Mining Resources Corporation (Intercorp) was founded on September 1, 1985, as a wholly owned subsidiary of the National Oil Corporation. The founding of this corporation was the result of a joint venture between National Oil Corporation and Cabones de Peru S. A. (Carperu), a government-owned and -operated company headquartered in Lima, Peru. The joint venture involved the building and the operation of the world's second largest coal mine in the Moquegua region of southern Peru.

The agreement called for the equal sharing by both parties of all costs associated with the development of a coal mine, and the construction of a rail line linking the mine with a port located 40 miles away. As of August 1, 1988, the total cost had reached $400 million. The agreement also called for the equal sharing, for the first eight years of operation, of all coal extracted from the mine. At the beginning of the ninth year Car-

peru would become the sole owner and operator of the mine.

The entire facility was designed for an annual capacity of 8 million tons, although this maximum capacity would not be realized for the first few years of operation (see Exhibit 1). Any expansion of this capacity would have to be agreed upon by both parties, and the associated costs of expansion would be shared equally.

The coal extracted from the mine would be marketed independently by the two parties. Intercorp would be required to pay a 20 percent royalty to the government of Peru on all coal which it sold from the mine. The 20 percent royalty would be based upon the gross revenue received by In-

tercorp for all coal sold from the mine.

The Miami Meeting

The main issue, which Mr. Peters knew he would be expected to dis-

EXHIBIT 1

Output Capacity of Moquegua Mine*

Year	Anticipated Output (Tons)
1988	4,000,000
1989	6,500,000
1990	7,200,000
1991	8,000,000
1992	8,000,000
1993	8,000,000
1994	8,000,000
1995	8,000,000

*Production is shared equally between Intercorp and Carperu.

EXHIBIT 2

International Mining Resources Corporation Balance Sheet April 30, 1988

Current assets:	
Cash	$ 1,756,900
Accounts receivable	0
Inventories:	
Mined coal	5,678,000
Fuel	1,220,400
General supplies	2,348,600
Total current assets	$11,003,900
Long-term assets:	
Land and mines	0
Buildings	22,743,200
Machinery	78,452,980
Equipment	33,534,720
Total long-term assets	$134,730,900
Total assets	$145,734,800
Current liabilities:	
Accounts payable	2,168,563
Accrued expenses	4,231,877
Total current liabiities	$ 6,400,440
Stockholders' equity:	
Common stock	139,334,360
Retained earnings	0
Total liabilities	$145,734,800

cuss, was the forecast of cash flows to be generated from the Peruvian operation to the parent, National Oil. All of Intercorp's net income would be transferred to National Oil as common stock dividends (National Oil owned 100 percent of Intercorp's common stock). To date, National Oil had invested $200 million dollars in the project, of which $134,730,900 was on buildings, equipment, and machinery. Intercorp's balance sheet as of April 30, 1988, is shown in Exhibit 2. All buildings, equipment, and machinery would be depreciated over the eight-year life of the project using the sum-of-the-years'-digits method of accelerated depreciation. No depreciation had been charged prior to 1988. For income tax purposes Intercorp was eligible to apply a depletion allowance of 10 percent of the total sales as a cost of the coal extracted from the mine. Inter-

corp's fiscal year ran from May 1 to April 30.

Mr. Peters anticipated that the selling and administrative expenses would total approximately $1.3 million per year in 1988 and would increase at the rate of 5 percent per year for the life of the project. Mr. Peters estimated that the cost of mining a ton of coal would be $5.65. Coal would be sold F.O.B. Puerto de Coles, so that the only transportation cost involved was the cost from the mine to the port, which was estimated to be 85 cents per ton. The costs of mining and of transporting coal to the port were both principally labor. Mr. Peters felt that he should allow for a 7 percent annual increase in these costs over the life of the project.

Mr. Peters felt certain that Intercorp would have no problem in selling their entire share of the production from the mine in for-

eign markets, principally in Europe. The main competition in this market, besides Carperu, would be Poland and Australia. The current price for coal in this market was approximately $32 per ton. If conditions in the world market for coal remained stable, as had been the case over the preceding 10-year period, then Mr. Peters saw little change in this price over the life of the contract, perhaps a 3 percent annual increase. If, however, competition in this market were to become more fierce, Mr. Peters anticipated that the price could drop to as low as $25 per ton. On the other hand, another oil embargo or similar upheaval in the world crude oil market could result in a significant increase in the price of coal; in this case, Mr. Peters estimated that the price could rise to perhaps $50 per ton within the eight-year life of the project.

Solution

Mr. Peters's problem is the projection of cash flow accruing to the parent company as a result of the Peruvian operation. It is necessary, therefore, to sift carefully through the case to determine projected revenues and costs, and to relate these numbers in meaningful fashion. Complete analysis requires knowledge of accounting conventions to indicate the impact of depreciation and depletion allowances on cash flow.

A cash projection (for the initial set of assumptions) is shown in Figure C.1. As you can see, the numbers for each year are grouped into three sections. The top three lines contain the projected sales, price, and revenue. The middle portion itemizes all expenses, and the bottom rows compute the resulting cash flow. The very bottom of the spreadsheet lists the assumptions and initial conditions.

```
=================================================================================================
                                International Mining Resources, Inc.
                                  Cash Flow Projections  1988-1995
=================================================================================================
                             1988       1989       1990       1991       1992       1993       1994       1995
Sales
  Tons                    2000000    3250000    3600000    4000000    4000000    4000000    4000000    4000000
  Price                     32.00      32.96      33.95      34.97      36.02      37.10      38.21      39.36
  Revenue                64000000  107120000  122215680  139869056  144065127  148387081  152838693  157423854

Costs
  Manufacturing
    Cost per ton             5.65       6.05       6.47       6.92       7.41       7.92       8.48       9.07
    Total mfg cost       11300000   19647875   23287266   27685972   29623990   31697669   33916506   36290661
  Sales & Admin           1300000    1365000    1433250    1504913    1580158    1659166    1742124    1829231
  Royalties              12800000   21424000   24443136   27973811   28813026   29677416   30567739   31484771
  Depletion               6400000   10712000   12221568   13986906   14406513   14838708   15283869   15742385
  Depreciation           29940200   26197675   22455150   18712625   14970100   11227575    7485050    3742525
  Transportation
    Cost per ton             0.85       0.91       0.97       1.04       1.11       1.19       1.28       1.36
    Total trans cost      1700000    2955875    3503394    4165146    4456706    4768676    5102483    5459657
Total costs:             63440200   82302425   87343764   94029372   93850493   93869210   94097772   94549230

Earnings before taxes      559800   24817575   34871916   45839684   50214635   54517871   58740922   62874624
Taxes (48% rate)           268704   11912436   16738520   22003048   24103025   26168578   28195643   30179820
After tax earnings         291096   12905139   18133396   23836636   26111610   28349293   30545280   32694805
Add back non cash items
  Depreciation           29940200   26197675   22455150   18712625   14970100   11227575    7485050    3742525
  Depletion               6400000   10712000   12221568   13986906   14406513   14838708   15283869   15742385
Cash flow             -200000000   36631296   49814814   52810114   56536166   55488223   54415576   53314199   52179715

Assumptions                  Initial conditions:                    Financial summary:

% increase in mfg cost     7%  Initial investment       200000000   Net present value @15%             24781933
% increase in coal price   3%  Depreciable assets       134730900   Internal rate of return               18.48%
% increase in trans cost   7%
% increase in sls & admin  5%
```

FIGURE C.1
Eight-year cash flow.

The revenue for each year is the number of tons sold times the price per ton. The latter number is projected to increase at a constant rate (3 percent in Figure C.1), so that the 1989 price is equal to 1.03 times the price in 1988 and so on. (Careful reading of the case shows that *International Mining receives only one-half the annual production, with the other portion going to the Peruvian government.*)

Expenses are broken into several categories. Manufacturing, transportation, and administrative costs are assumed to increase at independent rates, with the stated percentage indicated at the bottom of the spreadsheet. Royalties and depletion are 20 and 10 percent of revenue, respectively.

Depreciation is figured according to the *sum-of-the-years'-digits* method, which allows the greatest write-off in the earlier years. In order to compute the fraction of the total depreciable assets allowed in the first year, the sum of the digits for the eight-year depreciable life is computed to be 36 (that is, $1 + 2 + 3 + 4 + 5 + 6 + 7 + 8 = 36$). Hence 8/36's of the asset can be depreciated in the first year, 7/36's in the second year, and so forth until the last 1/36 is depreciated in the eighth year.

The earnings before taxes are equal to the revenue minus the total expenses. The corporate tax rate is assumed to be 48 percent, so that the after-tax earnings can be computed. The noncash expenses of depreciation and depletion allowance are then added to the after-tax earnings in order to determine the actual cash flow. Finally, the lower right-hand portion of the spreadsheet displays the internal rate of return and net present value, both of which are computed from built-in spreadsheet functions.

The completed spreadsheet can be used as a model in answering "what if" questions about the project; for example, what is the impact on the internal rate of return if the price of coal were to increase at 5 percent rather than 3? All that is necessary to answer these and similar questions is to go to the section in the spreadsheet where the assumptions are stored, make the appropriate change, and recalculate.

The laboratory manual develops the spreadsheet of Figure C.1 in four separate phases, as highlighted by Figure C.2, and summarized below:

Phase 1: Development of spreadsheet template, consisting of all row and column headings. Commands include: column widths, formatting of numeric and label entries, the titles command, and editing.

Phase 2: Development of year 1 and the initial assumptions; generic concepts include formula entry, arithmetic operations, and the hierarchy (precedence) of those operations.

FIGURE C.2
Phased implementation for intercorp spreadsheet.

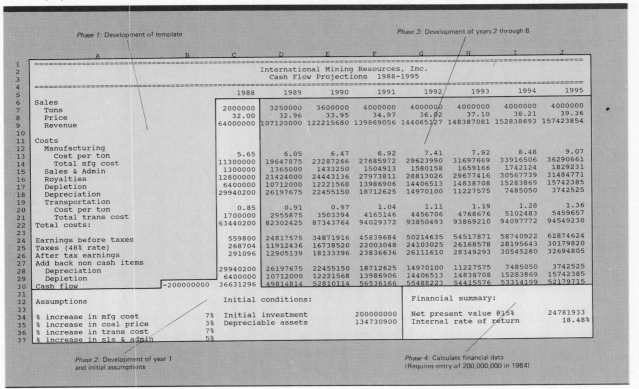

Phase 3: Development of years 2 through 8; generic concepts include the copy operation, with distinction between relative and absolute copying.

Phase 4: Financial analysis; generic concepts include predefined spreadsheet functions, IRR, and NPV.

**Locke Pharmaceuticals Company
Balance Sheet, December 31, 1987
(Dollar Figures in Millions)**

Assets	
Current assets:	
Cash	$ 21.0
Marketable securities	46.0
Accounts receivable	132.0
Inventories	164.6
Total current assets	363.6
Fixed assets:	
Net plant and equipment	332.0
Patents and other intangibles	113.0
Miscellaneous other assets	67.4
Total fixed assets	512.4
Total assets	876.0

Liabilities and Stockholders' Equity	
Current liabilities:	
Accounts payable	87.0
Notes payable	112.0
Accrued expenses	109.0
Accrued taxes	12.4
Total current liabilities	320.4
Long-term debt	223.0
Common stock	200.0
Retained earnings	132.6
Total liabilities	876.0

**Locke Pharmaceuticals Company
Statement of Income, 1987
(Dollar Figures in Millions)**

Net sales	$736.1
Cost of sales	506.0
Sales and administration	22.4
Interest	42.8
Income before taxes	164.9
Income taxes	79.2
Net income	85.7

Case Assignment: Locke Pharmaceuticals

On June 10, 1988, John Locke, the president of Locke Pharmaceuticals, was contemplating his company's investment of $13 million in a new venture. The venture involved building a new plastic molding plant on a piece of property adjoining their headquarters building. The new plant had been in the planning stages since December. An architect had been engaged to draw plans for the new plant, a marketing analysis on the new product line to be produced at the plant had been conducted, and bank financing had been arranged. The option which had been acquired on a piece of property adjoining the plant would expire at midnight on June 30. Mr. Locke felt some trepidation about the impending commitment, not concerning the thoroughness of the plan, but rather the validity of the assumptions on which the plans were being made. He wished that he had a little more time to assess the impact of changes in these critical assumptions.

Background

Locke Pharmaceuticals was founded in 1962 as a manufacturer of quality chemicals, which it sold for medicinal, nutritional, industrial, and laboratory purposes. In the years since its founding, the company had grown to be a major supplier of chemicals and prescription drugs. Approximately 30 percent of its sales were made directly to other pharmaceutical companies and industrial users. The remaining 70 percent were made directly to wholesale and retail distributors. A balance sheet and income statement for 1987 are shown in Exhibit 1.

In January 1987 Locke Pharmaceuticals had purchased a small hospital supply company headquartered in Jackson, Mississippi. The primary reason for the acquisition was to obtain the patent rights to a new over-the-counter pain reliever for which the company had just received FDA approval. In evaluating the company's other products, Locke was intrigued by another patent for a plastic trachea tube which had been received in 1984. The company had never invested in equipment to produce the trachea tubes, but had licensed two other companies to manufacture the tubes.

Future Sales of Plastic Trachea Tubes *

Year	Units
1989	1,600,000
1990	1,750,000
1991	1,960,000
1992	2,160,000
1993	2,279,000
1994	2,460,000
1995	2,670,000
1996	2,980,000
1997	3,361,000
1998	3,765,000

* Market research firm's predictions of future sales of plastic trachea tubes by Locke within their existing channels of distribution. The market research firm suggested an initial retail price of $3.00 per tube with an annual price increase of 5 percent.

The New Plant

Locke hired a market research firm to study the feasibility of building a plant to produce the trachea tubes, which would then be sold under the Locke name. The results of the study are summarized in Exhibit 2.

After receiving these sales figures, John Locke hired an industrial engineering consultant to make recommendations on the type of automated extrusion equipment to purchase, and to estimate the manufacturing costs associated with the production quantities predicted by the marketing research firm. The results of the industrial engineers report are summarized in Exhibit 3.

Locke then hired an architect to draw plans for the new plant and to estimate construction and equipment costs. These cost estimates are shown in Exhibit 4. The plant and equipment would be depreciated over a 10-year life using the straight-line method of depreciation. Taxes were estimated to be 48 percent of earnings for the new division.

After all the preliminary information gathering steps had been performed, John Locke sat at his desk staring at the option agreement on the purchase of a piece of property adjoining their plant. The purchase price on the land was $400,000 and the agreement would expire in less than three weeks. As he stared at the option agreement, he went over in his mind all the critical assumptions and forecasts upon which he had to base his decision on the new plant.

On the far side of his desk sat the IBM PC which he had recently purchased but had not yet had a chance to use. He recalled an article which he had read in a business magazine about the application of spreadsheet programs such as Lotus or VP Planner in financial analysis. He wondered if in three weeks' time he could learn to use Lotus to get a handle on the information on the new plant. Use your spreadsheet program to develop a financial forecast for Mr. Locke.

EXHIBIT 3

Manufacturing Costs for Plastic Trachea Tubes *

Manufacturing cost per unit	$ 0.64
General and administrative cost of plant operation per year	840,000.00

* Summary of industrial engineer's report. Manufacturing costs are assumed to increase at 4.5 percent annually; sales and administrative costs are budgeted for a 3 percent annual increase.

EXHIBIT 4

Summary of Architect's Cost Estimates for New Plant

Building cost	$ 4,231,800
Plant equipment	6,545,300
Furnishings	1,250,000
Plans	200,000
Parking lot	500,000
Fences and landscaping	460,000
Total cost	$13,187,100

CASE STUDY:
PORTER REALTY COMPANY

Preview

The Porter Realty case involves the management of three independent sales offices in the greater Boston area. It describes the real estate industry, indicating how both the company and individual agents earn money by listing and/or selling property. The manager in the case is confronted with preparing reports for individual offices that detail the various sales and listing combinations. She must then combine the multiple reports from the different offices into a summary report which totals data from all three offices.

As you read the case, put yourself in the position of the operating manager. Imagine how you would go about combining data from the separate offices, and what types of graphic output would be most helpful.

Presentation

In 1987 Laura Evans accepted an offer of $3.2 million from the Walker and Rose Corporation in return for 51 percent of the stock in her own company, Porter Realty. Ms. Evans had founded Porter in Boston, in 1971. Through hard work, ability, and a knack for selecting and training real estate salespeople, she had built the company to Boston's ninth largest, with annual sales of $28 million.

The Operation of a Realty Company Porter Realty has three sales offices located in different residential areas north of Boston. Although the sales in each office generally consist of property within the respective sales district, agents quite often list and sell property within the other districts. Each of-fice employs approximately 20 sales agents who work directly under an office manager. The three office managers report to Ms. Evans, who works out of an administrative office located in Cambridge.

The sales commission on residential real estate is 6 percent, with the commission divided equally between the listing and selling agencies. (The Multiple Listing Service makes it possible for agencies to earn money by listing properties without necessarily selling them.) In other words, it is possible for Porter to sell property listed by other agencies and, in turn, for other agencies to sell property listed by Porter. This produces three possible sales situations:

1. A property can be listed by an agent in one Porter office and sold by an agent in that office or another Porter office. In either event, Porter is both the listing and the selling agency.

2. A property can be sold by a Porter agent which was listed by an outside agency.

3. An agent in a non-Porter office can sell a Porter-listed property.

Porter earns the most money in the first situation, that is, by selling its own listed property. The agent who lists the property receives 25 percent of the total (6 percent) commission. The remaining 75 percent of the commission is divided equally (50 percent each) between the agent who sells the property and Porter Realty.

The situation is more complex in cases 2 and 3: There is a split between the listing and selling agency, as well as between the agency and the agent making the sale. In the second case, both Porter and the Porter agent receive a sales commission but no listing commission. A Porter agent who sells a property listed by another agency receives 70 percent of the sales commission due to Porter. (The commission due to the selling agency, that is, to Porter, is 3 percent of the sales price, or one-half the total 6 percent commission.) Porter retains the remaining 30 percent of the 3 percent commission to the selling agency.

The third scenario is exactly the reverse; both Porter and the Porter agent receive a listing commission but no sales commission. The listing agency receives 50 percent of the sales commission (3 percent of the total price), which is split equally between Porter and the listing agent.

Operating under a New Owner In the sales agreement Ms. Evans was retained as the manager of Porter Realty for a period of 10 years. When she first thought of staying on as the manager of Porter, she had expected that things would remain pretty much the same. In terms of the day-to-day operation of the company, this had proven to be true. However, the accountability to Walker and Rose, in the form of reporting requirements, was more difficult than she had ever imagined. It was not unusual, for example, for someone at Walker and Rose to call and ask for a summary of all sales activity over a recent period, and to want the report within 24 hours.

OFFICE	PRICE	SPECIFICS	DATE
Cambridge	189,000	Office sale - Outside listing	1/ 3/89
Watertown	44,500	Outside sale - Company listing	1/ 4/89
Arlington	77,900	Office sale - Company listing	1/ 5/89
Arlington	88,700	Outside sale - Company listing	1/ 5/89
Cambridge	235,000	Office sale - Company listing	1/ 5/89
Watertown	66,200	Office sale - Outside listing	1/ 5/89
Cambridge	120,000	New listing	1/ 6/89
Arlington	65,400	Outside sale - Company listing	1/ 6/89
Cambridge	234,000	Outside sale - Company listing	1/ 7/89
Arlington	125,000	New listing	1/ 8/89
Cambridge	178,900	Office sale - Company listing	1/ 8/89
Watertown	44,500	Office sale - Company listing	1/ 9/89
Arlington	88,000	Office sale - Outside listing	1/ 9/89
Arlington	110,000	New listing	1/10/89
Cambridge	218,900	Office sale - Outside listing	1/10/89
Cambridge	189,600	Office sale - Outside listing	1/11/89
Watertown	99,000	New listing	1/11/89
Cambridge	326,000	Office sale - Outside listing	1/11/89
Cambridge	210,000	Office sale - Company listing	1/11/89
Watertown	94,500	Office sale - Company listing	1/11/89
Arlington	64,000	New listing	1/12/89
Cambridge	176,900	Office sale - Company listing	1/12/89
Watertown	86,700	Office sale - Outside listing	1/13/89
Cambridge	310,000	New listing	1/13/89
Watertown	91,500	Office sale - Outside listing	1/13/89
Arlington	134,900	New listing	1/14/89
Watertown	67,000	Outside sale - Company listing	1/14/89
Cambridge	459,000	Office sale - Outside listing	1/14/89
Cambridge	198,000	New listing	1/15/89
Arlington	112,600	Outside sale - Company listing	1/15/89
Cambridge	125,000	Outside sale - Company listing	1/16/89
Watertown	178,900	New listing	1/17/89
Arlington	62,500	Office sale - Company listing	1/19/89
Cambridge	148,000	Office sale - Outside listing	1/19/89
Watertown	62,800	Office sale - Outside listing	1/20/89
Watertown	137,900	Office sale - Company listing	1/22/89
Arlington	55,900	Outside sale - Company listing	1/22/89
Cambridge	150,000	Office sale - Company listing	1/22/89
Arlington	52,500	Office sale - Outside listing	1/24/89
Cambridge	245,000	New listing	1/24/89
Watertown	73,500	Outside sale - Company listing	1/24/89
Arlington	178,500	Outside sale - Company listing	1/25/89
Cambridge	237,000	Office sale - Company listing	1/26/89
Watertown	210,000	New listing	1/27/89
Arlington	112,000	Office sale - Company listing	1/28/89
Watertown	216,800	Office sale - Outside listing	1/28/89
Arlington	66,800	Outside sale - Company listing	1/28/89
Cambridge	278,000	Outside sale - Company listing	1/29/89
Watertown	98,000	New listing	1/30/89
Watertown	121,900	Outside sale - Company listing	1/31/89

FIGURE C.3   January 1989 sales data.

Ms. Evans was also required to produce a monthly report summarizing the sales activity in each office. This report had to include a statement, by office, of all property listed, listed property sold, nonlisted property sold, and listed property sold by other agencies. In addition, the report had to show how much was paid in commissions and what the net contribution was to the company.

Ms. Evans found that the time she was devoting to compiling reports was seriously limiting the time she had to operate the business. To remedy the situation she hired an assistant who was a graduate of the MBA program at Boston University. The new assistant had taken courses in computer information systems, and thought that the administrative burden could be relieved by utilizing a microcomputer to analyze sales data. As a starting point, she had compiled raw sales figures for the three offices for January 1989, as shown in Figure C.3.

Solution

Ms. Evans's problem is typical of many business situations in which routine reports are submitted on a periodic basis. The solution begins with the design of a uniform reporting format for each sales office. Our solution (for the Cambridge office) is shown in Figure C.4, which divides data into four categories:

1. New listings

2. Property sold and listed by a Porter office

3. Property sold by the Porter office and listed by an outside agency

4. Property sold by an outside agency and listed by Porter

```
                    PORTER REALTY COMPANY - CAMBRIDGE OFFICE

                      Monthly Sales Report - January 1989

                                  PROPERTY          PROPERTY         OUTSIDE
                                    SOLD/             SOLD/            SALE/
                                   COMPANY           OUTSIDE         COMPANY
                        NEW        LISTING           LISTING         LISTING
                      LISTING
                     ----------   ----------       ----------      ----------
                      120000        235000           189000          234000
                      310000        178900           218900          125000
                      198000        210000           189600          278000
                      245000        176900           326000
                                    150000           459000
                                    237000           148000
                     ----------   ----------       ----------      ----------
Total Sale            873000       1187800          1530500          637000
Gross to Porter                      71268            45915           19110
Commissions Paid                     44543            32141            9555
Net to Porter                        26726            13775            9555

Monthly Summary
  New Listings        873000
  Total Sales         136293
  Commissions Paid     86238
  Net to Porter        50055
```

FIGURE C.4
January sales data: Cambridge office.

The top half of the report lists each of the individual transactions in one of four columns, as described above. The total activity in each category is tabulated, after which the commissions are calculated. No commissions are due for the new listings shown in the first column, as none of the properties have as yet been sold.

The most profitable situation occurs in the second column, which displays the properties both sold and listed by the Cambridge office, and results in the entire 6 percent commission being paid to the office. The gross to Porter is therefore .06 × $1,187,800, or $71,268. Porter is obligated to pay 25 percent of that to the agents who listed the property and splits the remaining 75 percent with the agents who sold the property. Hence the commission Porter pays is .25 * $71,268 to the listing agents, plus (.50 * .75) * $71,268 to the selling agents, for a total of $44,253. The net to Porter is its gross minus the commissions paid, or $26,726.

The third column contains property sold by the Cambridge office which was listed elsewhere. Porter is entitled to a sales commission (50 percent of the total commission or 3 percent of the selling price), but not to a listing commission. The gross to Porter is .03 * $1,530,500, or $45,915. Porter, in turn, is obligated to pay 70 percent of its commissions to the agents who sold the properties, resulting in a net to Porter of $13,775.

Finally, the fourth column is the reverse of the third; that is, it contains property sold by outside offices that were listed by agents in Cambridge. Porter receives 50 percent of the 6 percent total commission as the listing agency, resulting in a gross of $19,110. It splits this equally with the agents who originally listed the properties, resulting in commissions paid of $9555 and a net of the same amount.

The bottom portion of the report contains the monthly summary for the Cambridge office. We see that both the office and its sales personnel had a good month, with individual commissions and net to Porter of $86,238 and $50,055, respectively.

Figure C.4 does not, however, summarize information for the company as a whole, which is comprised of three individual offices. Thus in order to comply with reporting requirements imposed by the parent corporation, Ms. Evans needs to extract data from the Cambridge report and combine it with similar data for the other two offices. The parent organization is not likely to be interested in the details of each transaction, but only in the totals. Accordingly, Ms. Evans needs to combine information from the three reports into one, as depicted in Figure C.5.

Note, too, that Ms. Evans's primary objective is to relay information about the sales activity for the month of January. This can be done in either tabular or graphic form, with the latter often having greater impact. Accordingly, she plans to accompany her report with graphic output, as shown in Figure C.6.

Panels C.6a and C.6b display the same information: a breakdown of January's new listings by office, albeit in different form. Figure C.6a

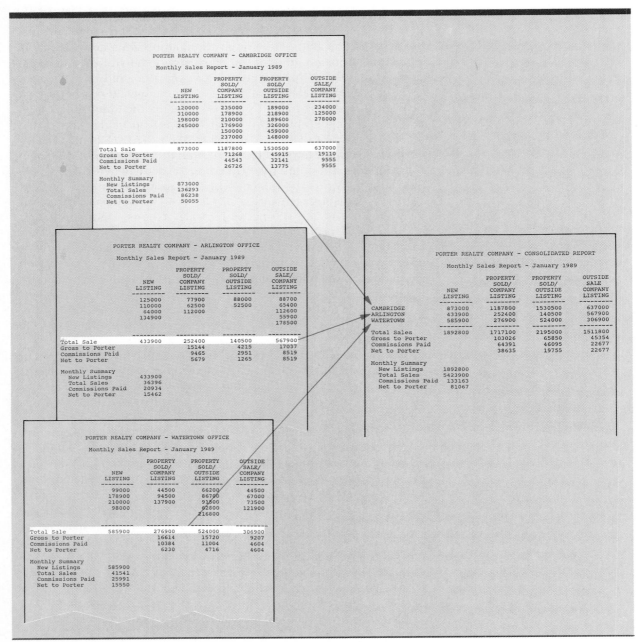

FIGURE C.5
Combined report for the three offices.

presents the information in a simple bar chart; Figure C.6*b* uses a pie chart. In similar fashion, Panel C.6*c* and C.6*d* also conveys identical information, again in different form. Figure C.6*c* breaks down January sales by office and by type of sale, presenting the data in multiple bar charts. Figure C.6*d* displays the sales information in the form of stacked bar charts.

FIGURE C.6
Graphical output using Lotus.
January listing by office, by type: (a)
bar graph, (b) pie chart.

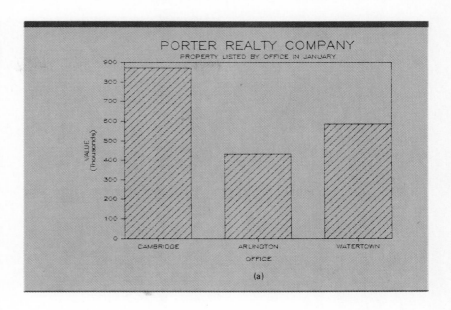

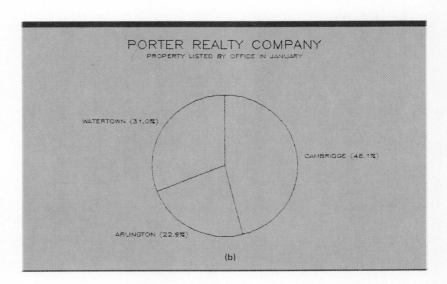

The laboratory manual develops the complete solution in five phases as described below:

Phase 1: Development of the individual office reports which list every transaction in each office

Phase 2: Extraction of data from the individual spreadsheets for later inclusion into a consolidated spreadsheet

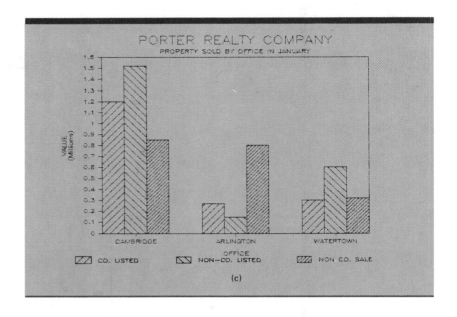

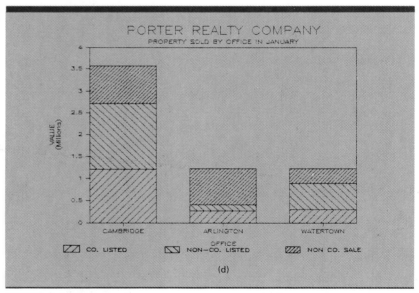

FIGURE C.6 Graphical output using Lotus. January listing by office, by type: (c) multiple bar graph, (d) stacked bar graph.

Phase 3: Combination of the extracted spreadsheets into a single consolidated spreadsheet

Phase 4: Graphic presentation which produces line, pie, bar, and stacked bar output

Phase 5: Macros and user-defined menus

Case Assignment: Washburn Publishing

The Washburn Publishing Company was founded in 1987 in Springfield, Illinois, by Robert Washburn. Mr. Washburn had spent the first 15 years of his career working in the publishing industry for Richard D. Irwin, Inc., in Homewood, Illinois. In 1986 an elderly aunt of Mr. Washburn had passed away and bequeathed him an inheritance of $500,000. He and his wife both felt that the best thing to do with the inheritance was to invest it in their own business. Since publishing was the business which Mr. Washburn knew best, it was his first and only choice for a business venture.

The segment of the publishing market which Washburn concentrated on was college textbooks. Mr. Washburn had spent six years working as an acquisition editor for Irwin, and he felt confident in his ability to obtain contracts on potentially successful books. Within the first year Washburn had signed contracts on 12 texts, all in the area of business administration. By the end of 1987, nine of the original texts were in production and Mr. Washburn had directed his attention to hiring a sales force. In January 1988, Mr. Washburn had hired four salespersons and had assigned them to four geographic areas of the country:

NE   (south to Virginia, west to Illinois)—Randall Scott

SE   (north to North Carolina, west to Louisiana)—Barbara Wendell

SW   (east to Texas, north to Colorado)—Anna Hernandez

NW   (east to Iowa, south to Idaho)—Peter Jeffreys

From February through December of 1988 the sales force worked in selling the company's line of nine business textbooks and in contacting potential authors of new books of the Washburn line.

Commissions

Textbooks are sold at wholesale prices to university and college bookstores. Authors are paid a 15 percent royalty based upon the wholesale price. The sales force is paid on a straight 2 percent commission basis. For example, if a salesperson sold 12,500 copies of a text with a wholesale price of $15.50, the commission would be:

$$(.02 \times 12,500 \times \$15.50) = \$3,875.00$$

The four members of the Washburn sales force are paid an annual salary in addition to their commissions, which are paid quarterly. The computation of the quarterly commission is based upon the number of texts actually shipped during the preceding quarter.

Figure C.7 shows the number of books of each title that were sold during 1988.

FIGURE C.7
Washburn case sales data.

	Scott	Wendell	Hernandez	Jeffereys
Macroeconomics by Smith ($21.80)	2480	9800	6250	8200
Business Statistics by Thomas ($22.90)	8445	300	9590	1200
Quantitative Methods by Galvin ($18.90)	7458	7190	1360	3789
Marketing Management by Nelson ($16.75)	8400	2690	8954	5790
Organizational Behavior by Campbell ($15.50)	4878	8667	6676	1670
Business Law by Sullivan ($12.60)	2600	980	1270	2488
Management by Lawson ($17.60)	8776	2789	6470	6008
Managerial Accounting by Powell ($19.75)	6800	2459	6225	7299
Corporate Finance by Randall ($16.95)	6540	1470	2806	4880

The January Sales Meeting

In early January of 1989, Mr. Washburn was preparing for the company's first annual sales meeting, which was scheduled for the end of the month. The purpose of the meeting was to introduce the four members of the sales force to five new salespersons who had just been hired, to discuss the company's first year of operation, and to acquaint the sales force with the 1989 line of textbooks, which included additional titles.

In addition to the sales data of Figure C.7, Mr. Washburn also wanted to create individual reports for each of his sales staff, presenting sales both in units and in dollars, as well as commissions earned. He also wanted an overall report that would summarize sales, royalties, and commissions on each textbook. Use your spreadsheet program to develop the necessary reports.

CASE STUDY: CAROLTON FURNITURE COMPANY

Preview

The Carolton Furniture Company case extends the use of spreadsheets to the development of a simulation model. The Caroltons must determine how to increase production capacity in order to satisfy an increase in demand for a desk they manufacture. On the one hand, if they underexpand they will be unable to meet demand on time and suffer shortage penalties. Conversely, if they overexpand, their inventory will increase unnecessarily, resulting in higher storage costs. Embedded within the case are the dollar amounts you will need to calculate the shortage penalties and inventory costs.

The Caroltons must also decide

whether their increased capacity should come from overtime or from additional workers they would hire. The case description contains the data to assign dollar amounts to each alternative.

Presentation

The Carolton Furniture company was founded in 1977 in Hickory, North Carolina, by two brothers, Joseph and Richard Carolton. Their father Emile had spent 20 years as a shop supervisor for one of the area's largest furniture companies. He had always longed to open his own factory but was never quite able to do it. The dream was left to his two sons, Joseph and Richard, who under the tutelage of the elder Carolton began manufacturing office desks in the garage of the family home.

The Carolton desk was designed by the elder Carolton and was made from solid walnut and walnut veneer. The desk was ideally suited for banks, doctors' offices, law offices, and other businesses. The desk was distributed through an office furniture store located in downtown Raleigh. The store kept one of the Carolton desks on its showroom floor and special-ordered the desks from Carolton as it received customer orders.

Working in their garage, the brothers were able to manufacture a maximum of four desks per week. Demand for the desks at the office furniture store was uneven; in some weeks none were ordered, and then in one week a local bank ordered 12. In 1986 the orders from the store had averaged five per week, and in December of 1986 the brothers had a backlog of 34 desks. The office furniture store informed Carolton that a nine-week delay in receiving an order was unacceptable to its customers, and that it was going

to discontinue carrying their desk if the delays persisted.

In January of 1987 the brothers applied for and received a $100,000 loan from a local bank to expand their operation. The brothers leased space in an industrial plaza and purchased several pieces of used woodworking machinery from a local furniture manufacturer. In the new plant they initially employed 20 workers and had the capacity to manufacture 32 desks per week. By March the new plant was fully operational, and by June the backlog had been reduced to only four desks.

The New Delivery Agreement In July of 1988 Joseph Carolton, the brother responsible for marketing, was approached by the furniture retailer regarding the retailer's opening of two new office furniture showrooms in the cities of Charlotte and Chapel Hill. Since the Caroltons had expanded their operation and reduced the delivery time to only one week, the Carolton desk had become one of the retailer's best-selling items, with orders averaging 10 per week. The retailer was sure that the desk would be as popular in the two new showrooms which he was planning to open in January.

The assurance which the retailer wanted from Joseph Carolton was that the Caroltons would be able to continue to satisfy the retailer's increased demand for the desk. The retailer also stressed the fact that the one-week delivery time was crucial, since the retailer did not keep a large inventory of desks, and since sales would be lost if customers had to wait long periods.

The retailer estimated that January demand for the three showrooms would average about 40

desks per week. The demand pattern would again be uneven, but the retailer thought that the following distribution was a fairly good estimation of the demand pattern that would occur:

Demand	Probability
10	.03
20	.12
30	.24
40	.28
50	.17
60	.11
70	.05

In order to assure the retailer that the one-week delivery schedule could be met, Joseph agreed that for each one-week delay in the delivery of a desk there would be a 5 percent reduction in the cost of the desk to the retailer. The cost of the desk to the retailer was $310.

The Current Plant Operation The Carolton plant is divided into four functional areas: cutting, lamination, assembly, and finishing, with each desk requiring all four operations. In the cutting department the separate pieces for the desk are cut on power saws from rough lumber stock. In the lamination department a $\frac{1}{8}$-inch sheet of walnut veneer is applied, by gluing, to the desktop. In the same operation a $\frac{1}{4}$-inch veneer is applied to the edges of the desktop. In the assembly department the entire desk is assembled from the parts and tops, which were delivered from the cutting and lamination departments on dollies. In the finishing department, four coats of a lacquer finish are applied to the desktops and two coats applied to all other exposed surfaces.

The Caroltons employ multiple crews of four workers (one worker for each department). Currently there are four complete crews, each with four workers. In addition to these production crews, there is a shop supervisor, a stock worker who is responsible for the delivery of wood to the cutting department, a dolly operator who transports the parts and semifinished desks between departments, and a forklift operator who transports the finished desks to a storage area where he also loads the desks onto the company's delivery truck.

With the current staffing of 4 workers in each department, the company can produce 20 desks per week on its regular shift. Existing labor agreements limit paid overtime to 25 percent of the regular production. The Caroltons estimate that by adding a worker in each department they could increase the weekly output during the regular shift by 8 desks. Workers within each department are paid $6.30 per hour and receive time and a half ($9.45) for each hour of overtime worked.

The Conflicting Strategies Upon Joseph's return from his meeting with the retailer, he and Richard met to discuss their strategy in increasing their plant's output. It was Richard's feeling that the new demand could be met entirely by overtime with the existing labor force. He reasoned that with 25 percent overtime, the brothers could produce 40 desks a week, which was the average projected weekly demand. Richard was very uneasy about hiring additional workers, remembering the layoffs in the last recession and the adverse effect on company morale.

Joseph felt that the cost of Richard's strategy would be high. He was particularly concerned about overtime, and further about not being able to meet demand in peak weeks when overtime could not keep up. It was Joseph's feeling that by increasing the work force by four, eight, or even twelve workers they could build up sufficient inventories to not only reduce the necessity of overtime but also reduce the chances of not being able to deliver within one week. (Both brothers agreed that workers would be hired in crews of four, one for each production department.)

Richard countered that Joseph's strategy would result in excessive inventory. He reasoned that each desk had a cost to the company of $250, and that to carry an inventory of desks, they would need additional financing from their bank. The bank was currently charging 12.5 percent interest. It would therefore cost $31.25 in capital costs alone to keep a desk in inventory for one year. By the time insurance was added in he felt that the cost would be about $1.80 per week. In addition, since space was limited at the factory, they would have to store desks at a warehouse located directly across the street in the same plaza at a cost of $2.40 per week per desk. They would be charged for one week's storage for any portion of the week which a desk was stored at the warehouse.

The brothers wished that there were some way in which they could bring all these facts together in order to get a better feel for which strategy they should pursue. They knew that the cost of an error could be considerable, and they wondered if their new PC could be of any assistance in analyzing their options.

Solution

The issue in the Carolton case is simply the size of the work force needed. Essentially, they can utilize overtime as required, or hire additional workers (increasing the size of the permanent work force) and build compensating inventories during slower periods. They may also employ some combination of the two strategies.

Richard felt that liberal utilization of overtime would be the best strategy. His brother Joseph wanted to avoid excessive overtime and rely more on inventory buildups by increasing the work force size to at least five crews. What the Caroltons really need is a crystal ball which will tell them what the demand will actually be. Since this is impossible, the next best thing would be for them to have a model of the system on which they could experiment and try their alternate policies.

The Caroltons can create a mathematic model of their system through the technique of *simulation*. Let us assume for the time being that a simulation model has been developed, that various policies have been tested (four, five, and six crews), and that summary statistics have been collected from the model. Our objective, therefore, is to analyze the output from the simulation and select an optimal strategy for the problem.

Figure C.8 contains the results of three simulation experiments for four, five, and six crews, respectively, with each experiment representing the operation of the factory for 25 weeks. As can be seen from parts *a*, *b*, and *c* in the figure, the total cost for four crews is $140,847, for five crews $135,240, and for six crews $162,288.

Judging from Figure C.8, five crews is the best solution, but more information is required before a firm conclusion can be reached. The demand for desks is *random*, which means that you cannot expect to obtain the exact costs of Figure C.8 for every simulation of 25 weeks. The number in Figure C.8 are representative of what the costs will be, but additional simulation runs should be performed before reaching a firm decision on the optimal strategy.

FIGURE C.8
Results with four, five, and six crews.

```
SUMMARY OF SIMULATION RESULTS - 4 CREWS
=========================================
SIMULATED WEEKS                        25
WAGES                            $100,800
AVG ORDERS PROD'D                   38.56
AVERAGE BACKLOG                     23.12
COST OF BACKLOG                    $8,959
OVERTIME
     HOURS                           3280
     COST                         $30,996
AVERAGE INVENTORY HELD              0.88
INVENTORY CARRYING COST              $92
PRODUCTION COST                  $140,847
```
(a)

```
SUMMARY OF SIMULATION RESULTS - 5 CREWS
=========================================
SIMULATED WEEKS                        25
WAGES                            $126,000
AVG ORDERS PROD'D                    41.6
AVERAGE BACKLOG                         0
COST OF BACKLOG                        $0
OVERTIME
     HOURS                            800
     COST                          $7,560
AVERAGE INVENTORY HELD                 16
INVENTORY CARRYING COST            $1,680
PRODUCTION COST                  $135,240
```
(b)

```
SUMMARY OF SIMULATION RESULTS - 6 CREWS
=========================================
SIMULATED WEEKS                        25
WAGES                            $151,200
AVG ORDERS PROD'D                      48
AVERAGE BACKLOG                         0
COST OF BACKLOG                        $0
OVERTIME
     HOURS                             0
     COST                             $0
AVERAGE INVENTORY HELD             105.6
INVENTORY CARRYING COST          $11,088
PRODUCTION COST                  $162,288
```
(c)

FIGURE C.9
Tabular output
of 10 simulation runs.

RUN	4 crews	5 crews	6 crews
1	$140,847	$135,240	$162,288
2	$128,427	$130,284	$165,984
3	$117,852	$133,728	$169,428
4	$141,812	$131,111	$161,574
5	$117,729	$133,098	$168,798
6	$145,249	$132,846	$160,876
7	$132,130	$129,318	$165,018
8	$145,437	$139,876	$161,154
9	$160,455	$144,919	$161,994
10	$142,305	$135,529	$162,432
Average	$137,224	$134,595	$163,955
Std dev	$12,610	$4,476	$3,010

Figure C.9 shows the results of ten simulations for four, five, and six crews; Figure C.10 displays the same information graphically. The total cost for each system varies considerably (as expected), but not so much as to preclude a decision. The *average* cost for a 25-week period over the ten runs for four, five, and six crews is $137,224, $134,595, and $163,955, respectively. We conclude, therefore, that the strategy of operating with five crews is the best, because it results in a lower average cost of production.

Also of interest is the *variability* (standard deviation) in cost from run to run, which is far higher for the four-crew system than for

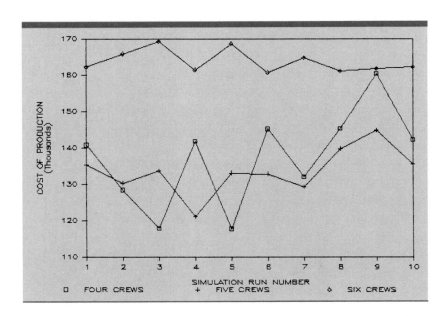

FIGURE C.10
Graphical output
of 10 simulation runs.

either of the other two. Any business prefers to operate in as stable an environment as possible, and the five-crew system meets this criterion. Operating with only four crews would put the Caroltons in a much more volatile situation, with costs ranging from a low of approximately $117,000 to a high of $160,000. In conclusion, the Caroltons can hire one additional crew, confident that they have analyzed the situation as fully as possible with the available data.

Figure C.11 contains the output of one simulation for four crews. The upper left-hand portion of the spreadsheet contains relevant input data for the simulation, including the number of crews, wage rates, inventory carrying costs, back order costs, and the number of weeks to be simulated. The numbers were obtained from information provided in the case description. This section contains all the factors under the control of the decision maker.

Directly under the simulation inputs is the probability distribution of the demand for desks. This table contains specific demand levels, the probability of that demand level, and the cumulative probability of that demand level (the probability of observing less than that demand). The exact form of this table is dictated by the specific spreadsheet program being used; in this case it is in the format required by Lotus (which is different from the usual definition of cumulative probability).

The actual simulation run occupies the bottom half of the spreadsheet. In each of the 25 weeks of the simulation a number of orders is received, and based upon the regular time and overtime capacities, a number of desks is produced. The difference between what was to be produced and what was actually produced results in a change either in the level of inventory or in the number of back orders (or if there is a perfect match, there will be no changes in either).

Consider, for example, week 1. An order for 20 desks is generated, according to the demand distribution for desks and a generated random number. The factory produces 32 desks (its regular capacity with four crews), resulting in an ending inventory of 12 desks. The ending inventory for week 1, that is, the 12 desks, is equal to the beginning inventory for week 2.

In week 2, an order for 40 desks is received. However, only 28 new desks need to be produced, due to the existing inventory of 12 left over from the previous week. Since the factory always operates at its full capacity of 32 desks, there will be an ending inventory of 4 desks, which carries over into the next week.

Week 3 sees an incoming order for 50 desks, which, given the existing inventory of 4, means that 46 new desks are required. This time, the regular capacity of 32 plus the overtime capacity of 8 is unable to meet the demand, so there is a backlog of 6 desks.

The system continues in similar fashion for 25 weeks. The totals of the 25-week operation combined with the cost data at the top of the spreadsheet produce the overall summary of results in the middle of the spreadsheet (which was examined earlier in Figure C.8a). The

```
=================================================================================
        STOCHASTIC INVENTORY SIMULATION
=================================================================================
```

```
SIMULATION INPUTS  .
==================================
# OF 4 PERSON WORK CREWS        4
PROD'N RATE DESKS/CREW/WEEK      8
HOURLY WAGE RATE/WORKER       6.30
OVERTIME WAGE RATE/WORKER     9.45
BACKLOG COST/DESK/WEEK       15.50
INV CARRY COST/DESK/WEEK      4.20
OVERTIME/WORKER(hours/week)     10
NUMBER OF WEEKS IN SIMULATION   25
```

Inputs to simulation
(controlled by decision maker)

```
      DEMAND DISTRIBUTION
      ==================
            CUM    AVERAGE
     PROB   PROB   DEMAND
     ----------------------
     0.03    0       10
     0.12   0.03     20
     0.24   0.15     30
     0.28   0.39     40
     0.17   0.67     50
     0.11   0.84     60
     0.05   0.95     70
```

Probability distribution
of demand

```
SUMMARY OF SIMULATION RESULTS
=====================================
SIMULATED WEEKS                      25
WAGES                          $100,800
AVG ORDERS PROD'D                 38.56
AVERAGE BACKLOG                   23.12
COST OF BACKLOG                  $8,959
OVERTIME
   HOURS                          3280
   COST                        $30,996
AVERAGE INVENTORY HELD             0.88
INVENTORY CARRYING COST            $92
PRODUCTION COST               $140,847
```

Total cost of one 25-week
simulation for four crews

```
===================================================================================
                          NO. OF NO. OF
             NO. OF  DESKS  REG      DESKS  DESKS  NO. OF  # DESKS
       RAND  ORDERS  TO BE  TIME  OT PROD'D PROD'D DESKS     IN     BEG   END   AVG    OT
WEEK   NUMB  REC'D  PROD'D  CAP  CAP REG TIM ON OT PROD'D  BACKLOG  INV   INV   INV   USAGE
-----------------------------------------------------------------------------------
 1  0.14     20      20     32   8    32     0     32       0       0    12     6     0
 2  0.41     40      28     32   8    32     0     32       0      12     4     8     0
 3  0.69     50      46     32   8    32     8     40       6       4     0     2    160
 4  0.89     60      66     32   8    32     8     40      26       0     0     0    160
 5  0.00     10      36     32   8    32     4     36       0       0     0     0     80
 6  0.45     40      40     32   8    32     8     40       0       0     0     0    160
 7  0.74     50      50     32   8    32     8     40      10       0     0     0    160
 8  0.65     40      50     32   8    32     8     40      10       0     0     0    160
 9  0.86     60      70     32   8    32     8     40      30       0     0     0    160
10  0.13     20      50     32   8    32     8     40      10       0     0     0    160
  .
  .
  .
25  0.74     50     116     32   8    32     8     40      76       0     0     0    160
```

Ending
inventory
for week 1
is starting
inventory
for week 2

FIGURE C.11
Simulation model for Carolton
Furniture Company.

production cost is the sum of the regular time wages, overtime wages, back order costs, and inventory carrying costs. The summary portion of the spreadsheet is the basis for the analysis of the production decision.

The laboratory manual develops the spreadsheet of Figure C.11 in four phases, as highlighted by Figure C.12 and described below:

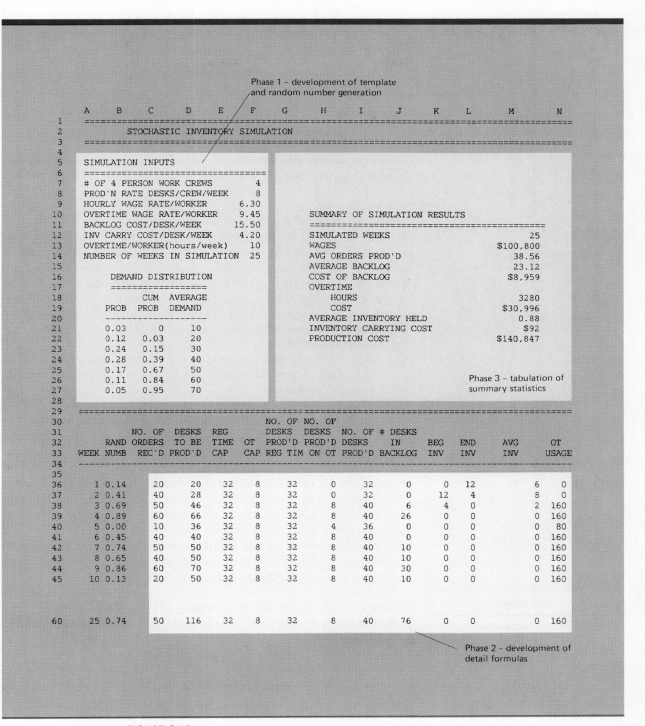

Phase 1 – development of template and random number generation

Phase 3 – tabulation of summary statistics

Phase 2 – development of detail formulas

FIGURE C.12
Phased development of simulation model.

Phase 1: Development of the spreadsheet template, the probability distribution of demand, and generation of random demands. Generic concepts include random number generators and table lookups.

Phase 2: Development of the formulas to monitor inventory and back order levels during the simulation. Generic concepts include the @MAX, @MIN, and @IF functions.

Phase 3: Development of the simulation summary section, and graphic display of simulation run results.

Case Assignment: Europa Tile Company

The Europa Tile Company was founded in 1981 in Los Angeles, California, by Richard Sanders. Prior to moving to California, Richard Sanders had been the manager of a chain of flooring stores in New Jersey. With the aid of a loan from the Small Business Administration, he opened his first store in 1981 and since then has added one store almost every year. He currently owns and operates eight retail stores in the greater Los Angeles area. The stores carry a complete line of flooring products, including carpeting and linoleum, but their principle product line is imported ceramic tile. Nearly all the tile they sell is imported from either Mexico or Italy.

All the Mexican tile is purchased from a distributor in San Diego, California. The Italian tile is obtained from a distributor in Newark, New Jersey. The Mexican tile distributor is able to make deliveries within two days. On the other hand, the Italian tile distributor makes deliveries out of his main warehouse in New Jersey, and deliveries to California take 10 days. Because of the two-week delivery and the fact that customers are generally unwilling to wait that length of time, Sanders routinely maintains a large inventory of the best-selling Italian tile pattern, called the Milano tile. In almost every instance, when tile on hand was insufficient for immediate delivery, the sale was lost. Sanders insists, therefore, on an inventory policy in which he will never run short of the Milano tile.

Weekly demand for the Milano pattern varies. Sanders reviewed his records of demand for the product over the past seven years, and compiled the following distribution of demand in square feet:

He believes that this distribution is representative of future demand for the Milano tile. The Milano tile is a one-square-foot tile retailing for $3.25. The cost per tile from the distributor to Europa is $2.15. The transporation cost from the New Jersey warehouse is 12 cents per tile. In addition, there is a $660 charge for each order processed at the New Jersey warehouse. This cost covers the extra preparation which Europa requires to eliminate tile breakage during shipping.

Sanders estimates that Europa's cost of processing an order is $340. This cost includes the administrative paperwork associated with processing an order and, more significantly, the cost at his warehouse of unpacking an order and placing it in inventory.

Demand	Probability
1000	.12
2000	.23
3000	.35
4000	.18
5000	.08
6000	.04

Sanders recently requested that his company's accounting firm estimate Europa's cost of carrying inventory. After an analysis of Europa's cost of borrowed funds, insurance, and warehouse operating costs, the accounting firm estimated that the cost was approximately 32 percent of the dollar value of the inventory held. When Sanders learned of this carrying cost, he thought immediately about the stock of the Milano tile which he had been maintaining in his warehouse. The day he received the report from the accounting firm, he called the manager of his warehouse and found that there were 65,000 Milano tiles in inventory. The warehouse manager told him that this is the inventory level which he maintains in order to avoid any chance of not being able to fill a customer order. He said that his policy is to order 50,000 tiles whenever the number on hand drops below 50,000. The manager always placed his order at the end of the week, receiving the delivery exactly two weeks later.

A quick calculation told Sanders that he had $147,550 invested in the Milano inventory, which at the 32 percent carrying cost resulted in $47,216 per year to carry this level of inventory. He looked over at his IBM PC and wondered if he could use a spreadsheet program to develop a less expensive inventory policy. He specifically wondered what the cost would be if they ordered 50,000 tiles whenever the level on hand dropped below 12,000, which would be at least a two-week supply. Then he realized that he would do a lot better if he ordered in quantities of less than 50,000.

Develop a simulation model of the Europa Tile Company in order to suggest an optimal inventory policy.

CASE STUDY: DADE COUNTY METRO ZOO

Preview

The Dade County Metro Zoo case is centered on the development of a fund-raising system. Karen Jackson, the recently appointed director of special programs at the zoo, is given the task of building a mailing list, soliciting donations, and monitoring contributions as they are received.

As you read the case try to determine precisely what informa- tion is required from the system, and what data inputs are neces- sary to generate that information. Think carefully about which fields to include, and what the field length and data type should be for each field included in the file structure.

Presentation[1]

Karen Jackson was happy in her new position as director of special programs for the Dade County Metro Zoo. Already she had won- derful plans for week-long sum- mer camps for elementary and ju- nior high students, picnic dinners under the stars, special seminars, and so on. She realized, however, that those functions would have to wait until there were sufficient funds to finance them. The open- ing of the last exhibits had re- sulted in a cost overrun, and there

[1]The case study is a simplification of the Adopt an Animal campaign in use by the zoo. Ms. Jackson and Mr. Marder, however, are products of the authors' imagination. A complete solution to this case, including an extension to mailing labels, is found in chapter 5 of R. Grauer and M. Barber, *Data Management through dBASE*, McGraw-Hill, New York, 1989.

was little money left for new programs.

Karen settled quickly into one of her primary functions, the grim reality of fund raising, and was determined to make her first project a very successful one. She knew she needed a clever basis for the appeal, and was stuck until the idea of "adopt an animal" campaign popped into her mind. She would solicit contributions on three levels: $25 for a reptile, $50 for a bird, and $100 for a mammal. Adopting "parents" would receive a personalized adoption certificate, a picture of their animal, and educational information about the zoo. Karen also thought of using the guest book maintained at the zoo entrance as the source for a mailing list. She hoped that those persons who had already visited the zoo would be as excited as she about the zoo's potential.

Feeling good about her proposal, she approached Mr. Marder, the zoo director. He gave her an enthusiastic approval, but cautioned her about the need to maintain strict records. Luckily, Karen had been exposed to application software as an undergraduate business major. The zoo provided access to a PC, and she knew that it, along with the data management software, would be an invaluable tool in organizing and producing the information she needed.

Karen had already determined that her first task would be to generate a series of form letters for use in the appeal. She also recognized the need to update her records to reflect contributions as they were received, and to prepare reports reflecting the source and amount of the donations. Karen also wanted the system to

be capable of future mailings, and hence wanted to record the date on which a donation was received. She took out a yellow legal pad, and in organized fashion she began to list the reports she wanted:

1. A set of personalized letters to potential donors soliciting donations

2. A set of personalized thank you notes to individuals who contributed to the campaign; a list of people who contributed but who had not yet been sent thank you notes

3. A master list (in alphabetic order) or people who contributed to the campaign; also summary information on the total amount of money raised, the number of people who contributed, and the amount of the average contribution

Solution

The first consideration is to develop an appropriate file structure which in turn requires reconciliation of the available *input* and the desired *output*. You must be absolutely certain that the data you collect will be sufficient to produce all the necessary reports, or else the system will not be successful.

Unfortunately, however, the design of a file structure tends to be taken for granted and consequently is too often poorly done. We have seen many instances of clients requesting additional reports only to be told that extensive (and expensive) programming changes would be necessary or, worse, that the system contained insufficient data to enable the modifications they request. Accordingly, the importance of carefully designing the file structure cannot be overemphasized.

Figure C.13 contains our suggested file structure, which may or may not correspond to what you envisioned as you read the case. Indeed, whether or not our solutions are the same is not really im-

FIGURE C.13
Suggested file structure.

Field	Field Name	Type	Width
1	LASTNAME	Character	16
2	FIRSTNAME	Character	12
3	PREFIX	Character	3
4	STREET	Character	24
5	CITY	Character	18
6	STATE	Character	2
7	ZIPCODE	Character	5
8	DONATION	Numeric	3
9	DONOR DATE	Date	8
10	ADOPT	Character	1
11	THANK YOU	Logical	1

portant, as there are many satisfactory answers. What is essential, however, is that the structure which is chosen contain all necessary data so that the required reports can be generated. The figure may seem obvious upon presentation, but it does reflect the results of many decisions as indicated:

1. The fields to be included

2. The size of each field

3. The data type of each field

4. The order of the fields within a record

Consider, for example, how these questions affect the most "obvious" of fields: a person's name. No one will contest that a "name" field is necessary, and further that the system should include an individual's first and last name, and a prefix (for example, Mr. or Ms.) for that name. It is less obvious what the size of the name field should be and/or that the name should be divided into three separate fields.

What would be wrong, for example, if the name were treated as a single field (31 positions in all), consisting of the prefix, first name, and last name, in that order? Consider the consequences of a single field (instead of the three in the figure) in light of the following names:

Dr. Joel Stutz

Mr. Philip Glassman

Ms. Helen Rumsch

Whether you realize it or not, the names are listed in alphabetic order according to the design criterion of a single name field, and therein lies the problem. In other words, when the system indexes records by name, it does so beginning with the *leftmost position* (that is, prefix) and hence the rather unusable "alphabetic" sequence. It should be apparent, therefore, that last name requires its own field if the system is to list records alphabetically.

Given the necessity of separating out the last name, is anything further to be gained by treating the prefix as a separate field as opposed to its being part of the first name? The answer is yes, because the case description alludes to the need for both solicitation letters and thank you notes. Perhaps you will eventually choose salutations in the form of "Dear Joel" as opposed to the more formal "Dr. Joel Stutz," which would require that the prefix be separate from the first name. This may or may not be the case, but it costs nothing at this point to opt for the separate fields.

Several other decisions are also implied by the file structure of Figure C.13. Two lines were used for the address (consisting of street on line 1, and city, state, and zip code on line 2) instead of three lines (omitting a line for company name). The shorter address requires less storage, and also simplifies programming for both report forms and mailing labels. It does, however, preclude the use of a business affiliation. Two lines were chosen in this instance only after examining the potential data base and finding that residential addresses appeared almost exclusively.

Regardless of whether you go with two- or three-line addresses, zip code must be stored as a separate field in order to be able to index on this field and thereby take advantage of bulk mail (which requires presorting by zip code). The *length* of zip code should not, however, be automatically set to five positions in every application, as some systems may require the newer "zip + 4" designation. Five positions was deemed suitable in this system given the preponderance of residential addresses.

The size of the first and last name fields is more arbitrary. Sixteen positions were specified for the last name, but 15 or 17 would have sufficed equally well. Does that mean that lengths of 12 or 24 positions are also acceptable? Probably not. Our experience has been that 12 is generally too small, and 24 too large; that is, the allotted space should be large enough to contain the names in the file, but not so large as to continually waste space when shorter names are present.

Even with the specification of *field type*, things are not always as they seem. Zip code is designated as a character rather than a numeric field, because characters are processed more efficiently than numbers (and arithmetic is never performed on zip code). In other words, the numeric data type is reserved for fields that will be used in calculations, rather than for any field composed of digits.

The case description intimated that future (or repeated) mailings might be possible, and hence a *date field* is included within the file structure. Knowledge of the date on which a donation is received will ensure that individuals who contribute will not be solicited too often (for example, more than once a year).

The adoption field illustrates the use of a one-position *code* to designate the type of animal (for example, R, B, and M for reptile, bird, and mammal, respectively). Use of codes rather than expanded values in a file structure results in considerable savings of storage space on a disk, and in more efficient (and less error-prone) processing.

The final field in the file structure is an example of a *logical field*, that is, a field with two possible values, true or false (which may be entered as T, F, t, f, Y, N, y, or n). The purpose of the "thank you" field in our example is to indicate whether or not a thank you note has been sent. Although a one-position character field would appear to satisfy this requirement equally well, logical fields are processed more efficiently and are preferred for that reason.

The end result of these deliberations has produced the file structure shown earlier in Figure C.13. As can be inferred from the discussion, there are no hard-and-fast rules for designing a file structure. The decisions which are made as to the fields needed, their sizes and types, reflect the needs of the present (and future) system, and are often subjective in nature.

After the file structure has been designed, you can proceed to the production of mailing labels and associated reports. As in all previous cases, the laboratory manual implements the complete solution in phases, as indicated:

Phase 1:   Design of the file structure as discussed

Phase 2:   Creation of test data for use in subsequent steps; review of commands needed to add, modify, and delete records

Phase 3:   Report generation consistent with the requirements of the case study

Phase 4:   Generation of form letters and associated mailing labels

Case Assignment: Michael Essman, Stockbroker[2]

As the 747 taxied to the end of the runway, Mike Essman turned to his wife, smiled, then settled back into his seat for the long ride home. The two weeks in Australia had been wonderful, and the fact that his brokerage house had picked up the tab for the truly deluxe accommodations made it even better. Indeed, he was one of only 180 brokers out of the firm's 11,000 to have achieved sufficient sales production to merit the trip. The realization that he had accomplished this in less than five years made it all the more gratifying.

Last year's success was in the past, however; and as the plane took off, Mike's thoughts turned to increasing his sales level in the coming year. He was motivated now more by ego than by money, although the money certainly helped, especially as his income had

[2]A complete solution to the case, including an extension to the dBASE screen generator and file maintenance, is found in chapters 9 and 10 of R. Grauer and M. Barber, *Data Management through dBASE*, McGraw-Hill, New York, 1989.

grown from almost nothing to well into six figures. Moreover, the client assets he had under management virtually guaranteed a very comfortable income as long as he maintained his existing accounts. Yes, he had what he wanted materially, but he still craved recognition within the industry as being among the very best. His problem was that of any salesperson, namely, how to increase sales production.

Mike knew he was lucky to have entered the business just as the unprecedented bull market of the early 1980s was getting under way, yet he also knew that his success was due to more than luck. He thought of the approximately 10,000 "cold" calls he had made over the last year alone (40 calls a day, 5 days a week, 50 weeks a year), and of the 9500 rejections those calls had produced. Still and all, they had yielded some 500 new accounts, which is how he got to Australia in the first place. He thought fondly of his first manager, Norm MacGregor, who effectively reduced selling to a numbers game; namely that if the number of contacts was sufficiently large, the accounts would follow. MacGregor's advice to him was simply that "selling is like shaving, do it every day or you're a bum." The recent October crash only meant that he would have to work harder during the coming year to maintain his current level of production.

The problem was that there were only so many hours in a day, and that it simply wasn't possible to increase the amount of time on the phone. He had gotten to the point where he could tell within the first minute of a conversation whether the contact was worth pursuing, and it took him only another two minutes to determine the prospect's investment objective (growth or income) and the amount of money he or she had to invest. He realized for the first time that the system he maintained on 3×5 inch index cards was not efficient for following up on those contacts who expressed an interest for additional information. Clearly, he needed a better way to manage repeat phone calls and/or follow up mailings, especially when a prospect responded, "Call me in two weeks" or "Send me the next annual report." Perhaps a computer might help, but how?

The major brokerage he worked for provided adequate computer support for existing clients but did little in the way of data mangement for prospective clients. Then it hit him: His goal for the coming year would be to use the PC sitting on his desk to solicit new accounts.

Develop the necessary file structure around which Mike's new system can be built.

GLOSSARY

A> prompt The signal that drive A is the default drive and that the operating system is waiting for a response.

Absolute cell address A cell address which does not change when moved or copied, for example, $B$3.

Access time A mechanical delay, measured in thousandths of a second, required by a disk drive to locate data.

ALU (See arithmetic-logic unit.)

Application programs Programs written in a computer language which accomplish useful work.

Argument A value passed to a function.

Arithmetic-logic unit One of two parts of the CPU. The ALU performs arithmetic and logical operations.

Ascending order A sorting sequence from smallest to largest value, for example, A to Z or 1 to 1000.

ASCII American Standard Code for Information Interchange. ASCII assigns specific numeric values to all printable and nonprintable characters.

Asynchronous transmission Transmission occurring at random intervals, which uses start and stop bits to mark the beginning and ending of a byte.

AUTOEXEC.BAT A batch file, which if present in the root directory is executed automatically by DOS after booting.

Automatic recalculation The recalculation of cell entries in a spreadsheet without a specific request from the user for doing so.

Automatic replacement The replacement of one string with another without asking the user for confirmation; opposite of selective replacement.

Auxiliary dictionary A dictionary separate from the main dictionary which contains words added by the user.

Auxiliary storage (See external storage.)

Backup procedures Guidelines to determine the frequency and manner in which valuable data will be copied to other storage media.

Batch file A file which contains multiple DOS commands to be executed in sequence.

Baud A measure of data transmission speed, approximately equal to the number of bits per second.

Binary numbers Numbers represented in base 2, consisting of the digits 0 and 1. Computers store data internally as binary numbers.

Bit A *bi*nary dig*it* consisting of a 0 or 1.

Block operations Any word processing command affecting more than one character; for example, a block may consist of a word, sentence, paragraph, or even the entire document.

Boldface A darker version of the current typeface.

Boot To start up the computer and load DOS.

Bug An unanticipated logical error which occurs during program execution.

Bulletin board A remotely accessed filing system which allows users to exchange information and programs.

Bus network A network in which different computers share a common communication channel (the bus).

Byte The smallest addressable unit of memory; a byte normally consists of 8 bits.

C> prompt The signal that drive C is the default drive and that the operating system is waiting for a response.

Camera-ready copy High-resolution output that can be submitted to a printer without further modification.

Case structure A structured programming construct to express a multibranch situation.

Cell An area where data can be entered into a spreadsheet; occurs at the intersection of a row and column.

Cell address The location of a cell within a spreadsheet; for example cell A3 is found at the intersection of column A and row 3.

Central processing unit The "brain" of the computer; the CPU consists of the control unit and the arithmetic-logic unit.

CGA Color Graphics Adapter—an IBM graphics standard announced in 1981 with resolution of 320×200.

Character field A field which can contain anything at all; that is, letters, numbers, or special characters.

Cluster Two or more sectors on a disk drive which are treated as a single logical entity; a cluster is the minimum amount of space allocated to a file, regardless of the file size.

Cold start Booting the computer by turning on the power.

Command mode The means by which commands are entered in a spreadsheet; the command mode is typically entered with a /.

505

Command processor The part of DOS known as COM-MAND.COM, which interprets commands entered from the keyboard or other input devices.

Communication channel A data path which establishes a link between two computers.

Communications protocol A predefined set of prompts and responses, which two computers follow when communicating.

Communications software Programs which allow a computer to emulate a remote terminal.

Compressed-mode printing Printing at 17 characters per inch.

Conditional page break The start of a new page when less than *n* lines remain on the current page.

CONFIG.SYS A file (on the root directory) which is consulted by DOS when the system is booted, and which contains logical device assignments.

Copy command A DOS, word processing, or spreadsheet command to duplicate files, text, or cells, respectively.

Correspondence quality A print quality just shy of letter quality, and nearly indistinguishable from that produced by a typewriter. Correspondence quality is usually the best quality offered by a dot matrix printer.

CPS Characters per second—a measure of speed.

CPU (See central processing unit.)

Ctrl, Alt, and Del keys Three keys which when pressed simultaneously, will cause a warm boot.

Cursor A blinking marker which signals where the next typed character will appear on the screen.

Daisy wheel printer A letter-quality impact printer.

Data The input to a program.

Data validation Checking to see that incoming data is consistent with the program's specifications.

Database A collection of related files.

DEBUG.COM A program supplied with DOS which allows the user to patch programs.

Debugging The process of detecting and correcting execution errors within a program.

Default drive The drive on which external files are assumed to reside, and the drive to which files will be saved, unless otherwise specified.

Default setting The options a program assumes to be in effect when it first starts up.

Delete command A DOS, word processing, or spreadsheet command to delete files, text, or cells, respectively.

Demodulation Conversion of an analog signal to a digital signal.

Desktop publishing The combination of hardware and software to combine text and graphics into a form suitable for publication.

Destination range The cell or cells within a spreadsheet which are the object of a copy or move command.

DO-WHILE (See iteration structure.)

DOS Disk operating system—the operating system produced by Microsoft for PC and PC-compatible computers. (See operating system.)

Dot matrix printer A printer which creates characters by imprinting with a matrix of pins. Industry standards call for matrixes of 9 and 24 pins.

Downloading a file Sending a file from the host computer to a remote computer.

Dvorak keyboard A keyboard arrangement in which the most frequently used keys are positioned for the easiest access. Notwithstanding this advantage, the industry standard is still the QWERTY keyboard.

Editing Changing the contents of a document or spreadsheet.

EGA Enhanced Graphics Adapter—an IBM graphics standard announced in 1984, with resolution of 640×350.

Enter key The key which when pressed instructs the computer to execute the last command entered; also known as the return key.

Exception report A report listing all records which meet a specified condition.

Extension (See file specification.)

External command A DOS command which is not memory-resident, for example, FORMAT, TREE, and DISKCOPY.

External storage Permanent storage of data on magnetic or optical media.

FAT (See File Allocation Table.)

Field One or more data categories which together comprise a logical record.

File A set of related records.

File Allocation Table A table maintained by DOS which stores information on the size and location of every file on a disk.

File combine command A command which combines one spreadsheet with another.

File directory A listing of all files on a disk containing for each file, the filename and extension, together with the date and time it was created.

File server The node in a computer network which stores the users' remotely accessed files.

File specification The complete description of a file, consisting of its name and an optional extension.

Filter A DOS program which modifies the output of another program, for example, MORE, FIND, and SORT.

Floppy disk A flexible plastic disk coated with a magnetic solution and used for external storage.

Flowchart A symbolic representation of program flow using lines and geometric symbols.

Font A given typeface and style displayed in a particular point size, for example, 10-point Times Roman bold.

Footer Text or numbers which are automatically printed at the bottom of each page in a document.

Format The process of preparing a disk to hold data by dividing it into tracks and sectors.

Formatted disk A disk which is capable of storing data.

Full-duplex transmission Simultaneous transmission in two directions across a common data path.

Function key A key (designated as F1, F2, and so on) which can be assigned one or more commands by an applications program.

Gateway A data path which connects two otherwise incompatible systems so that they may communicate.

GIGO Garbage in, garbage out—the dictum stating that a good program given bad data will produce bad results.

Global replacement The substitution of one character string with another in every occurrence in a document.

Global setting A default setting affecting every subsequent entry in a document or spreadsheet.

Graphics mode A display mode which individually maps every pixel on the screen.

Grid The specification in desktop publishing of the margins, column settings, headers, footers, and graphics which carry over to every page of the publication.

Half-duplex transmission Transmission in either direction across a common data path, although only one computer can transmit at a time.

Handshaking The establishment of a communications protocol in the initial contact between two computers.

Hard carriage return The code embedded into a document whenever the return key is pressed; it forces a line feed at the point that the code is inserted.

Hard copy A paper printout.

Hard disk A hard metal disk used to store relatively large amounts of data.

Hardware The physical components of the computer.

Header Text or numbers which are automatically printed at the top of each page of a document.

Hexadecimal numbers Numbers represented in base 16, consisting of the digits 0–9, and the letters A–F.

Home key The key which returns the cursor to the beginning of a line or screen in a document, or to cell A1 of a spreadsheet.

Hyphen-help Suggestions provided by a word processor on where to hyphenate a word.

Indexing The process by which records in a file are arranged in a logical sequence, which is typically different from the physical order in which they were stored.

Information Data which has been processed into a form perceived as useful by the recipient.

Insert command The means to insert a row or column into a spreadsheet.

Insert mode The mode in a word processor in which newly entered text repositions existing text; the opposite of replacement (or typeover) mode.

Internal command DOS commands which remain memory-resident after booting, for example, DIR, COPY, and ERASE.

Internal memory The random-access memory (RAM) or volatile memory of the computer.

Iteration structure A structured programming construct which repeats a procedure until a condition is satisfied. Also known as a loop.

Justification The alignment of text flush with the left, right, or both margins of a document.

Kerning Subtle adjustment of the distance between adjacent letters in a document.

Key A field within a record upon which records can be indexed.

Kilobyte (Kb) 2 to the 10th power, or 1028 bytes.

Label An alphanumeric cell entry in a spreadsheet.

Laser printer A printer which creates a high-resolution image by focusing a rapidly moving laser beam on a photostatic drum.

Leading The vertical distance between lines of text as measured in points.

Left-justified Text aligned flush with the left-hand margin of a document.

Letter-quality printer A printer which produces output equivalent in quality to that of a typewriter.

Load command A command which retrieves a file from secondary storage and places it into memory.

Local area network (LAN) Computers linked together over short distances, sharing files and/or peripheral devices.

Logging on The process of identifying yourself to a multiuser computer in order to gain access to the system.

Logical deletion The marking of a record for subsequent deletion from a file.

Logical field A field which can store only the values true or false.

Macro The ability to store and recall multiple keystrokes which aid in customizing an applications program.

Mail merge   A feature available with many word processors to combine a form letter with a secondary data file to produce personalized letters.

Mainframe computer   A large multiuser computer system.

Major key   The first (primary) key upon which a sort or search operation will take place.

Management information system   A combination of hardware, software, people, and procedures intended to satisfy the informational needs of an organization.

Manual recalculation   The recalculation of cell entries in a spreadsheet only upon explicit request.

Megabyte (Mb)   2 to the 20th power, or 1,048,576 bytes.

Memory   (See internal memory.)

Menu   The displayed options available to a user at a particular point in a program.

Microcomputer   A desktop computer, typically designed for a single user.

Microprocessor   A single chip of silicon containing the CPU or brain of a computer; the Intel series of microprocessors is used by IBM in the PC and PS/2 computers.

Minicomputer   A multiuser computer smaller than a mainframe.

Minor key   The secondary (less important) key used for sort or search operations.

Modem   Modulator-demodulator—a device to convert the digital signal produced by a computer to an analog signal for transmission over phone lines, and vice versa.

Modulation   Conversion of a digital signal to an analog signal.

Monochrome monitor   A monitor which displays only one color, for example, green on black.

Mouse   A pointing device used to select menu options and/or otherwise enter data.

Move command   A command to move blocks of text in a document or cell ranges in a spreadsheet.

MS-DOS   (See DOS.)

Multitasking   The concurrent execution of multiple programs on one computer, by allowing the CPU to rapidly switch between the programs.

Near-letter quality   (See correspondence quality.)

Networks   Interconnected computers which communicate with one another and share files and/or peripheral devices.

Norton Utilities   A series of highly useful programs to analyze storage allocation on disk, and/or retrieve lost files.

Number systems   Numbers represented in different bases, the two most well known being base 2 (binary) and base 10 (decimal).

Numeric field   A field which can hold only numeric values.

Octal numbers   Numbers represented in base 8, consisting of the digits 0 through 7.

Offscreen formatting   An older mode of word processing in which the text displayed on the screen contained control characters to indicate underlining or boldface, and hence differed from what emerged on paper.

Online help   Onscreen explanations displayed by a program to provide assistance for the user.

Onscreen formatting   The current mode in word processing whereby "what you see is what you get"; that is, text is displayed on the monitor in the same form as it will appear in hard copy.

Operating system   Software which allows the user to interact with the hardware of the computer.

OS/2   An operating system designed to run on more powerful microcomputers based on the Intel 80286 and 80386 microprocessors. Chief among its enhancements is the ability to multitask and directly address more than 640Kb of memory.

Page break   The start of a new page.

Page description language   A special-purpose computer language used in conjunction with laser printers for page composition.

Parity bit   An extra bit in a byte used to check the validity of data transmission. Parity is designated as odd or even.

Patching a program   Modifying an object (machine language) program through use of the DEBUG.COM utility.

Path   One or more subdirectories which are checked by the operating system when searching for a file.

PC-compatible   Hardware which is plug-compatible (interchangeable) with the IBM PC standard.

PC-DOS   (See DOS.)

PC keyboard   The keyboard of a personal computer.

Peripheral   Any stand-alone device, such as a printer, that is connected to a computer through cables.

Physical deletion   The permanent removal of records in a file or database, which have been previously marked for deletion.

Pica   A unit of horizontal measurement equal to $\frac{1}{6}$ of an inch; that is, there are 6 picas in 1 inch.

Piping   Redirecting the output of one program so that it becomes the immediate input of another program.

Pixel   A dot (picture element) on a computer screen which is illuminated to create an image; the more pixels on a screen, the greater its resolution.

Point size   A unit of vertical measurement used in specifying type size; there are 72 points to the inch.

Pointing (in spreadsheets)   Selecting a cell or range of cells by highlighting them with the cursor keys or a mouse.

Port   A multipin connector, into which a cable may be plugged to connect a peripheral device to the computer.

PostScript   A page description language developed by Adobe Systems.

Print spooler   Hardware and/or software which prints output previously produced by one program, while the computer executes another program.

Program   Instructions written in a computer language to accomplish a specific task.

Prompt character   A character which indicates that the computer is awaiting further instructions.

Proportional spacing   A method in which different letters are assigned different amounts of space depending on their width; for example, "m" requires more space than "i."

Protected cell   A cell in a spreadsheet whose contents cannot be altered.

Pseudocode   Neat notes to oneself which specify program logic.

QWERTY keyboard   The standard keyboard layout used by almost all typewriters in the English-speaking world, named for the first six letters in the second row.

Ragged margin   Text which is not aligned (justified).

RAM   Random Access Memory—Temporary or transient memory into which DOS and all other programs are loaded before execution.

RAM disk   A portion of memory which temporarily functions as a disk drive, in order to facilitate very rapid input and output operations.

RAM-resident program   A program remaining in RAM until the end of the session, and which can be called from within the currently running application. SideKick, by Borland International, pioneered the use of such programs.

Range   Contiguous cells in a spreadsheet in the shape of a rectangle; a range may consist of a single cell, a row, a column, or a group of rows and columns.

Record   A set of related fields which are often represented as a single line in a file.

Reformatting   The procedure by which a word processor changes the appearance of a document in accordance with newly established options (line spacing, margin settings, and so on).

Relational database   A collection of related files in which every file shares at least one key field with at least one other file.

Relative cell address   A cell address which changes when copied to another cell, for example, B3.

Replacement mode   The mode in a word processor in which newly entered text types over (replaces) existing text; the opposite of insert mode.

Report generation   The creation of meaningful and well-organized output.

Resolution   The clarity with which onscreen or printed output is displayed.

Retrieve command   (See load.)

Return key   (See enter key.)

Right-justified   Text aligned flush with the right-hand margin of a dcoument.

Ring network   A local area network in which the computers are linked together by a single wire in a loop.

ROM   Read Only Memory—memory whose contents can be read but not modified.

Root directory   The topmost point in a hierarchical or tree structure; the one directory which must be present on every disk.

RS-232C interface   A device to convert a parallel stream of 8 bits (that is, a byte) to a serial stream for data transmission, then back again.

Ruler line   A line in a word processor which displays current margin and tab settings.

Sans serif typeface   A typeface which omits the connecting lines at the end of each character so that the letters are more distinct from one another, for example, Helvetica.

Save command   A command which writes the current contents of RAM to disk, and in so doing creates a permanent copy of the file.

Scanner   An optical device which can read text or graphics into memory.

Scrolling   A process by which different portions of a word processing document, or spreadsheet, are made visible on the screen.

Search-and-replace   A word processing command that looks for a given character string in order to substitute another character string.

Sector   A portion of a track on a floppy or hard disk; one sector typically stores 512 bytes of data.

Selection structure   A structured programming construct which conditionally executes a block of code; selection is implemented in a computer language with an IF statement.

Selective replacement   An option which asks the user for confirmation prior to completing the replacement operation; opposite of automatic replacement.

Sequence structure   A structured programming construct which executes blocks of code in the order in which they appear.

Serial communication   Transmission which proceeds one bit at a time.

Serif typeface A typeface with lines at the end of each character to visually connect one letter to the next, for example, Times Roman.

Simplex transmission Transmission in only one direction along a data path.

Soft carriage return An implied carriage return inserted by a word processor as text wraps from one line to the next.

Software A computer program; a set of instructions to accomplish a specific task.

Source disk The disk from which individual files (or the entire disk) are copied to the target (destination) disk.

Source range The range from which cell entries are copied or moved.

Spreadsheet An arrangement of rows and columns in which data is entered for analysis.

Star network A local area network in which the remote computers are hung radially off a central server, like spokes on a wheel.

Status line A line in a word processor appearing at the bottom or top of the screen, which indicates the document being edited, the location of the cursor, and the major options currently in effect.

Structured programming The use of sequence, selection, iteration, (and) case constructs to create programs.

Subdirectories Directories which branch from the parent or root directory in a hierarchical or treelike fashion.

Submenu A menu which itself was an option on the menu from which it was called.

Summary report A report which omits detail lines in order to concentrate on the totals.

Synchronous transmission Transmission between two computers at predefined time intervals.

Syntax checker A companion program to a word processor, which analyzes a document for grammatical errors and/or stylistic inconsistencies.

Tape backup The procedure by which the contents of a hard drive are copied to magnetic tape.

Target disk The disk to which the contents of the source disk will be copied.

Telecommunications The transfer of data over long distances, usually via phone line.

Teleprocessing Telecommunications which incorporates data processing.

Template A spreadsheet containing labels and/or formulas but no data.

Terminal emulation Use of a personal computer as a computer terminal.

Toggle switch A key which switches back and forth between two modes of operation; for example, con-

tinually pressing the Caps Lock key causes the computer to alternate between upper- and lowercase.

Token ring network A local area network in which the linked computers take turns sharing an electronic token. The computer with the token is allowed to communicate while the others must wait their turn.

Topology The physical layout of computers in a network.

Track A concentric circle on a disk onto which data may be written.

Type family A group of related typefaces in different sizes or styles; for example, Times Roman or Helvetica.

Type size The vertical height of a given typeface as measured in points from the top of the tallest letter to the bottom of the lowest; for example, from the top of an uppercase A to the bottom of a lowercase y.

Type style An attribute of a typeface, for example, boldface or italic.

Typography The process of selecting type for a publication.

Undo command A command which reverses the action of the most recently executed command.

Unprotected cell A cell in a spreadsheet whose contents can be changed.

Uploading a file Electronically transferring a file from a remote computer to the host computer.

VGA Video Graphics Adapter—An IBM graphics standard announced in 1987, with resolution of 640 × 480.

VisiCalc The first spreadsheet program.

Volume server The hub of a network, which contains the files of each user stored in separate volumes.

Warm boot Restarting an already running computer by pressing Ctrl, Alt, and Del, to clear memory and reload DOS.

Whole word replacement Replacement of a character string, only if it appears as a separate word, rather than as part of a word.

Wild card A DOS character (? or *) which is used to match any single character or set of characters in an operation.

Windows The division of a screen into two or more views of the same spreadsheet, each of which can be manipulated independently.

Word processing The use of a computer and appropriate software to create, edit, save, and print text and other documents.

Word wrap A word processing feature which causes lines of text that would otherwise extend beyond the right margin to continue onto the following line.

Write-protected disk A disk whose notch has been covered to prevent accidental modification or erasure of its contents.

ACKNOWLEDGMENTS

Page 5, cartoon: Sidney Harris.

Page 7, box: "Why Is a Computer Like an Elephant?" Ken Uston, Digital Deli. Copyright © 1984 by Steve Ditlea, Workman Publishing, New York. Reprinted with permission of the publisher.

Page 7, photo: Leonard Lee Rue III, NAS-Photo Researchers.

Page 8, photos: Courtesy of IBM Corporation.

Page 9, cartoon: Bob Schochet.

Page 9, box: From "11 Influential Computers and/or Their Programs—Past to Present," *The Book of Lists, 2.* Copyright © 1980 by Irving Wallace, David Walleckinsky, Amy Wallace, and Sylvia Wallace. By permission of William Morrow and Company.

Page 15, photos: courtesy of IBM Corporation.

Page 16, photos: Daisy wheel, courtesy of Qume Corporation; Laserwriter, courtesy of Apple Computer Corporation; and Proprinter, courtesy of IBM Corporation.

Page 17, photo: Courtesy of IBM Corporation.

Page 19, photos: Courtesy of IBM Corporation.

Page 21, box: "Softening a Starchy Image," Copyright © 1983 by Time Inc. All rights reserved. Reprinted with permission.

Page 22, both photos: Courtesy of IBM Corporation.

Page 23: Wide World Photos.

Page 24: Courtesy of IBM Corporation.

Page 28, cartoon: David Quintanar.

Page 28, photo: Courtesy of IBM Corporation.

Page 30, cover of *Scientific American:* The Science Museum, London.

Page 30: Courtesy of IBM Corporation.

Page 40, cartoon: From *A Much, Much Better World* by Eldon Dedini. Reprinted by permission of Microsoft Press. Copyright © 1985 by Eldon Dedini. All rights reserved.

Page 40, photos: AT&T 6312 WGS, courtesy of AT&T; Compaq Deskpro 386/20, courtesy of Compaq Computer Corporation; Zenith Z-150, courtesy of Zenith Corporation; Leading Edge Model D, courtesy of Leading Edge; Tandy 1000, courtesy of Radio Shack.

Page 52, photos: Courtesy of BASF Corporation.

Page 59, all photos: Courtesy of Microsoft Computer Corporation.

Page 74; cartoon: Sidney Harris.

Page 75, photo: Arthur Grace/Sygma.

Page 88, cartoon: Sidney Harris.

Page 94, photo: Ken Regan/Camera Five.

Page 96, photos: Wordstar ad and Wordstar 5.0, MicroPro Corporation.

Page 129, photo: Bettmann Newsphotos.

Page 129, cartoon: From *A Much Much Better World*, by Eldon Dedini. Reprinted by permission of Microsoft Press. Copyright © 1985 by Eldon Dedini. All rights reserved.

Page 117, photo: Rip Griffith/Photo Researchers, Inc.

Page 119, cartoon: Sidney Harris.

Page 125, cartoon: Sidney Harris.

Page 130, photos: From *Tone Up at the Terminals* by Denise Austin, 60 West Ninth Street, New York, NY, 10011.

Page 131, logo: Courtesy of Wordperfect Corporation.

Page 131, photos: (bottom left) courtesy of Brigham Young University; (bottom right) courtesy of Wordperfect Corporation.

Pages 144–145: "Here's What You Can Do with Desktop Publishing," courtesy of Aldus Corporation.

Page 147, cartoon: Sidney Harris.

Page 150, photo: Dennis Kitchen.

Page 161, cartoon: From *A Much, Much Better World* by Eldon Dedini. Reprinted by permission of Microsoft Press. Copyright © 1985 by Eldon Dedini. All rights reserved.

Page 169, cartoon: Sidney Harris.

Page 171, logo: Courtesy of Aldus Corporation.

Page 172, photos: Courtesy of Aldus Corporation.

Page 177, photo: Wide World Photos.

Page 189, cartoon: Sidney Harris.

Page 190, photo: The New York Public Library—Picture Collection.

Page 200, photo: Tomas DuFriedmann/Photo Researchers, Inc.

Page 206, photo: Reprinted from *PC Magazine*, May 28, 1985. Copyright © 1985 by Ziff Davis Publishing Company.

Page 209, logo: Courtesy of Apple Computer Corporation.

Page 210, photos: Top, Rick Brown/The Picture Group; bottom, courtesy of Apple Computer Corp.

Page 223, cartoon: Sidney Harris.

Page 230, cartoon: From *A Much, Much Better World* by Eldon Dedini. Reprinted by permission of Microsoft Press. Copyright © 1985 by Eldon Dedini. All rights reserved.

Page 240, cartoon: Teresa McCracken.

Page 244: Lotus Publishing Company, May 1987.

Page 245, logo and photos: Courtesy of Lotus Development Corporation.

Page 258, cartoon: Sidney Harris.

Page 264: Courtesy of Funk Software Corporation.

Page 271, cartoon: Educational Assistance Ltd., Glen Ellyn, IL.

Page 282, logo: Compaq Computer Corporation.

Page 283, photos: Compaq Computer Corporation.

Page 295, cartoon: Copyright © 1984 by Aaron Bacall.

Page 296, photo: Courtesy of Edward Tufte.

Page 296, graph: *Forbes Magazine*, May 1987.

Page 310, photo: The Bettmann Archive.

Page 314, cartoon: With permission of Jo Linkert and *TV Guide* magazine.

Page 315, logo: Courtesy of Hercules Computer Corporation.

Page 316, photos: Courtesy of Hercules Computer Corporation.

Page 329, cartoon: Sidney Harris.

Page 336, photo: Stratus-John Pearson, Inc.

Page 339, cartoon: Sidney Harris.

Page 343, cartoon: Reprinted courtesy of Applied Data Research, Inc.

Page 345, logo: Courtesy of Ashton-Tate.

Page 345, photos: Courtesy of Ashton-Tate.

Page 359, map: Courtesy of Ashton-Tate.

Page 362, photo: Culver Pictures.

Page 369: Photo, Courtesy of Sperry Corporation; cartoon, G. McCory.

Page 370, logo: Courtesy of Borland International.

Pages 371–372, photos: Courtesy of Borland International.

Page 388, photo: AT&T Corporate Archives.

Page 389: Courtesy of NASA.

Page 390, cartoon: Sidney Harris.

Page 392, photos: Courtesy of Hayes Microcomputer Products, Inc.

Page 393, cartoon: Sidney Harris.

Page 400, photos: Compuserve.

Page 401, photo: Neal Preston/Camera Five.

Page 406, cartoon: Jack Schmidt.

Page 410, logo: Courtesy of AT&T.

Page 411, photos: Top, courtesy of AT&T Corporate Archives.

Page 420, cartoon: From *A Much, Much Better World* by Eldon Dedini. Reprinted by permission of Microsoft Press. Copyright © 1985 by Eldon Dedini. All rights reserved.

Page 433, photo: From *PC Magazine*, June 9, 1987.

Page 448, cartoon: Sidney Harris.

Page 449, logo: Intel Corporation.

Page 450, cartoon: Sidney Harris.

Page 451, photo: Intel Corp.

Page 467, cartoon: Sidney Harris.

Page 470, cartoon: Sidney Harris.